# California Real Estate *Principles*

## 13ᵀᴴ EDITION
## 2nd Printing

# Walt Huber
## Glendale Community College

COPYRIGHT 1976, 1977, 1978, 1979, 1985, 1989, 1994, 1995, 2003, 2004, 2005, 2006, 2008, 2011, 13th Edition - **2nd Printing**
Educational Textbook Company, Inc.
P. O. Box 3597
Covina, California 91722
(626)339-7733
(626)332-4744 (Fax)
www.etctextbooks.com

Library of Congress Cataloging-in-Publication Data

California Real Estate Principles - Walt Huber

Summary: Covers all material in Real Estate Principles classes with special emphasis on California real estate laws. Very clear and simple language, easy-to-read format with photographs, charts, and graphs. Includes glossary and index. Suitable for consumers, students, and teachers wishing information about personal real estate transactions. This textbook is designed to fulfill the course requirement necessary to take the California Real Estate Salespersons and Broker's Exams.

ISBN   (10-digit) 0-916772-09-8
       (13-digit) 978-0-916772-09-3

Printed in the United States of America

This publication is designed to provide accurate and authoritative information in regard to the subject matter covered. It is sold with the understanding that the publisher is not engaged in rendering legal or other professional services. If legal or other expert assistance is required, the services of a competent professional person should be sought. All advice is given as purely anecdotal, and reflects the opinions and experiences of the authors, but is not held out as standard operating procedure. Practice varies throughout the state and brokerage by brokerage.

Forms reprinted with permission, CALIFORNIA ASSOCIATION OF REALTORS®. Endorsement not implied.

# Preface

"Sassy," our Social Networking Butterfly™, is a reminder that social media is becoming and ever more present entitity in the real estate realm.

This is the era of Social Media. No longer just a personal social tool, social networking sites like Facebook, Twitter, LinkedIn, and other social sites are changing the face of the real estate business. To be effective and therefore profitable in this brave new world, a knowledge of this online technology is a must for any real estate salesperson or broker, and mastering it may be the key to leaping ahead of the competition who are stuck practicing the rapidly diminishing "old school" methods of doing business. With over 750 million subscribers spending time on the most popular social networking sites, it's in your best interest to go where your customers are... and increasingly, that's online.

Real estate is a social business – so social networking is a perfect fit in this digital generation! As a broker, or as a salesperson working for a broker, questions like whether to utilize a Facebook Group or Facebook Business Page are **Customer Relationship Management (CRM)** decisions that more and more real estate professionals have to make. Are you prepared to meet the challenges of this new and formidable technology?

I want to express my appreciation to the many people who helped to make this text possible. I received advice and helpful suggestions from the **California Department of Real Estate** (dre.ca.gov) and advice and forms from the **California Association of REALTORS®** (car.org).

We would also like to thank Levin P. Messick, IFAC, President, AC Appraisals, Inc. and instructor at Mt. San Antonio College; Arlette Lyons, CRS, GRI, President and owner of Lyons and Associates, Inc. REALTOR® and instructor at Mt. San Antonio College; and Chris Hamilton, instructor at Golden West College. We would also like to thank the late Fred Martinez, former instructor at City College of San Francisco.

Special thanks for the valuable assistance given by the people who helped design and produce this book: Philip Dockter, art director; Troy Monroe Stacey, cover design; Colleen Taber, executive editor; Linda Serra and Andrea Adkins, editors; and Rick Lee, pre-press editor and layout.

 *Meet our charming trademark character "Hubie, the Internet Mouse." But don't let his quirky good looks fool you—he's one heck of a businessman! Let this little "mouse about town" guide you to all the best websites on the Internet, and maybe help make the learning experience a little more fun in the process.*

# Acknowledgments

This book contains the input of many prominent educators and real estate professionals. Their involvement as contributing advisors has made it possible for us to cover a wide range of material in detail and, at the same time, offer practical perspectives based upon their extensive classroom and industry experience. Their contributions were invaluable and merit our most sincere thanks.

Hal Madson
Allan Hancock College

Alfred J. Guetling
American River College

Steve Sodergren
Antelope Valley College

Joe Newton
Bakersfield College

Thurza B. Andrew
Butte College

Donald T. Brown
Butte College

Joseph F. Belohlavek
Cabrillo College

Robin Sherman
Cabrillo College

Melvin Brady
Cerritos College

John T. Martinez
Chabot College

Richard McCartney
Chabot College

John A. Culver
Chabot College

Robert Andersen
Chabot College

Earl H. Bond
Chaffey College

J. O. Wright
Chaffey College

Keith H. Kerr
City College San Francisco

Carol A. Jensen
City College San Francisco

Hal Bouley
Coastline College

Allen C. Shute
College of The Canyons

Ken Determan
College of The Canyons

Stan Reyburn
College of The Desert

Jeff Eddy
College of The Sequoias

John A. Miller
Contra Costa College

Ronald G. Rueb
Contra Costa College

Corina D. Rollins
Contra Costa College

D. Blazej
Cuesta College

Fred C. Hoey
Cuesta College

Gregory Daunoras
Cuyamaca College

Rick Chehab
De Anza College

John R. Morrissey
Diablo Valley College

Tim Murphy
Diablo Valley College

Leo Saunders, GRI, CRB
Diablo Valley College

Dr. Elliott J. Dixon
East Los Angeles College

Olivia Vasquez Anderson
East Los Angeles College

Michael Botello
El Camino College

Dr. Donna Grogan, GRI, CPM
El Camino College

Bud Zeller
Folsom Lake College

Charles Krackeler
Foothill College

Gary Carter
Fresno City College

Dr. Robert J. Bowers
Fullerton College

Peter Kirianoff
Fullerton College

Chris Hamilton
Golden West College

Karen Obuljen
Golden West College

Dino Vlachos
Golden West College

Frank Pangborn
Irvine Valley College

Bob Anderson
Los Angeles City College

Alex Yguado
Los Angeles Mission College

John J. Meichtry
Los Angeles Mission College

Thomas Morehouse
Los Angeles Pierce College

Harold Lerner
Los Angeles Pierce College

Robert R. Enger
Los Angeles Pierce College

Bernard Grabois
Los Angeles Valley College

Jerry Fish
Los Medanos College

Frank Coon
Los Medanos College

Patricia Moore
Los Medanos College

R. Joseph Banuat, CRS, CRB
Los Medanos College

Ignacio Gonzalez
Mendocino College

Harvey Rafel
Merced College

Tom Gee
Merritt College

Edward L. Culbertson
MiraCosta College

Frank Diaz
Mission College

Gerald A. W. Haight
Modesto Junior College

Joseph G. Ansel
Monterey Peninsula College

Mary Ann Zamel
Mt. San Antonio College

Arlette A. Lyons
Mt. San Antonio College

Paul Guess
Mt. San Jacinto College

Charles C. Van Zee
Mt. San Jacinto College

Heli Sairanen
Napa Valley College

Bruce Gold
Orange Coast College

David Kemp
Palomar College

June Ann Reese
Rio Hondo College

Gilbert Mosqueda
Rio Hondo College

Michael Bernston
Riverside Comm. College

Pat Hogarty
Sacramento City College

William A. Mcgrath
Sacramento City College

Nick Zoumbos
San Bernardino Valley College

Paul Grutsis
San Bernardino Valley College

Michael Durrett
San Bernardino Valley College

Dr. Shad Jefferies
San Diego Mesa College

John Wallace
San Diego Mesa College

Norma F. Hurley
San Joaquin Delta College

Raymond O' Connor
Santa Barbara City College

Steve Herndon
Santa Rosa Junior College

Jim Michaelson
Santa Rosa Junior College

Dr. Evelyn D. Winkel
Santiago Canyon College

William Rawlings
Santiago Canyon College

Kim Tyler
Shasta College

Marty Carrick
Shasta College

M. Wurschmidt
Shasta College

Mike Walker
Sierra College

Joseph A. McNeill, Jr.
Solano Community College

Robert C. Cass
Southwestern College

Chris Grover
Victor Valley College

Carl W. Hefke
West Hills College

Jerome L. Fox
West Los Angeles College

Abraham H. Farkas
West Los Angeles College

Faz Elahi
West Los Angeles College

Don Holman
West Los Angeles College

George H. Miller
West Valley College

Lance Shoemaker, J.D.
West Valley College

James R. Overton
Yuba College

**Real Estate Specialists**

Charles Ellis

Robynn L. Allveri, Esq.
San Diego State University

James Short
San Diego State University

Reginald Woolfolk
West Valley Occupational Cntr.

Evan Morris
North Valley Occupational Cntr.

Claudia Wagner
North Valley Occupational Cntr.

Lorraine Abrams
West Valley Occupational Cntr.

Stan Hechinger
CAL-LAND International

Hugh C. Damon
TMH Home Mortgage Co.

# Table of Contents

## Chapter 3:    Encumbrances                              49

## Chapter 4:   Agency and Its Responsibilities   71

## Chapter 5:   Contracts       *113*

# *Chapter 6:* *Landlord and Tenant*                    155

# Chapter 7:  Escrows and Title Insurance  185

# *Chapter 8:   Real Estate Finance*                217

# TABLE OF CONTENTS

## Chapter 9:   *Financial Institutions*      263

## TABLE OF CONTENTS

## *Chapter 10: Appraisal Basics*       *303*

## *Chapter 11: Appraisal Methods*      *333*

## *Chapter 13: Taxation of Real Estate*     *399*

## *Chapter 14: Licensing, Education, and Associations*　　*431*

## *Chapter 15: Real Estate Math*      *473*

# TABLE OF CONTENTS

# SUNSET BROKERS

## Scott Chapin

http://www.bankhomes.com

493-4357

# CHAPTER 1
# *Introduction to Real Estate*

## I. California's Real Estate Market

### A. CALIFORNIA DEPARTMENT OF REAL ESTATE (DRE)

In California, real estate licensing laws are regulated by the Department of Real Estate (DRE), which is headed by the Real Estate Commissioner. The California DRE is widely recognized as a progressive organization whose example is followed by other states.

Sassy, the Social Networking Butterfly™, indicates a social network-friendly website at **dre.ca.gov**. You can follow the DRE through Twitter, YouTube, or you can subscribe to the California Department of Real Estate "News Flash" **RSS (Really Simple Syndication)** feed to get news delivered directly to your email or desktop! See page 435 for DRE details.

### B. HIGH COST OF REAL ESTATE

Real estate values throughout California were reduced unevenly due to the "Financial Crisis" and the "Great Recession." Even though job opportunities have temporarily decreased, California's population growth rate is expected to equal or surpass that of the national average in the next decade. The "Great Recession" has slowed down the construction of houses, apartments, and condominiums. As a result, housing demand is sluggish.

With the state's abundance of 112 community colleges and many universities generating so many educated professionals, is it any wonder that the average personal income of a college graduate in California is so high?

California's remarkable economy is due no doubt to our dominance in:

1. design, innovation, and technology,
2. public investments in a variety of technology areas,
3. private venture capital attracting opportunities in energy efficiency, applying technology to the health care system, Internet, telecommunications, and
4. market opportunities for California's exports of goods and services.

A home is an expensive venture that includes a home loan payment. This payment usually equals 25 percent to 28 percent of the wages earned monthly by the homeowner,

## CHAPTER OUTLINE

*The popularity of "Social Media" has dramatically changed how real estate brokerages market their services. Social networks are online communities that "by invitation" reveal personal and/or business information in "profiles" and share "connections" to other users with whom they share something in common.*

although this percentage may be higher in California. The monthly payment is only part of owning a home. Property taxes, fire insurance, repairs, and furnishings are expenses that will further increase the monthly cost of maintaining a home.

*California real estate market values are continually adjusting in the aftermath of the Financial Crisis.*

---

# eLicensing
# California Department of Real Estate (DRE) Online

The California Department of Real Estate (DRE) website at **dre.ca.gov** provides a wealth of information about real estate subjects, as well as licensing services. The DRE "eLicensing" online system offers (among others) the following services:

1. Scheduling/rescheduling exam dates
2. Viewing exam results
3. Confirming license issuance
4. Renewing salesperson and broker licenses
5. Filing changes in mailing address
6. Changing employing broker of salesperson

## The DRE Social Networking Connection

The DRE website includes several links to social networking sites to which the DRE subscribes. **YouTube** videos offer helpful advice, such as warnings concerning loan modification scams. **Twitter** (and **Twitter en Español**) allows you to stay updated on an incredibly wide variety of topics directly related to the DRE. You can join and follow its *TWEETS, which are text-based posts of up to 140 characters* @DRE_RealEstate.

*DRE news and information is available through RSS feeds, which deliver headlines and summaries to your desktop or Web browser.*

A RSS feed is a regularly updated summary of web content, along with links to full versions of that content. Instead of remembering to visit a favorite Web site, the news comes directly into your computer daily or at whatever interval you want.

What's more, most RSS feeds contain just links, headlines, or brief synopsis of new information only. That means the small amount of Web data can be sent to any cell phone, pager, or handheld computer without a lengthy download. More importantly, RSS gives you control over receiving information you want without revealing information about yourself. Unlike subscribing to an e-mail newsletter, you never have to give out your e-mail address with an RSS feed. That avoids the possibility of receiving spam or unwanted junk e-mail from the Web site.

---

## C. REAL ESTATE: A PROFITABLE PROFESSION

With the high cost of real estate comes the potential for high profits in the selling of real estate. A purchase as important as a home requires a great deal of knowledge and usually entails the services of a real estate professional. Because brokers and real estate salespeople are paid by commission, the higher the cost of housing, the higher the price of their services. A *COMMISSION is an amount paid, usually as a percentage of the selling price, to a broker for services.* The broker is responsible for paying his or her salespeople their part of any commissions.

*The maximum commission that can be charged by a real estate broker in the sale of residential 1-to-4 unit property is negotiable between the principal and broker.*

### 1. Increasing Profits By Using Social Networks – The Facebook Phenomenon

Of the 750 million social network members, 500 million subscribe to Facebook alone. Facebook is becoming an integral component to the success of any real estate brokerage that hopes to remain relevant, competitive, and therefore profitable. The real estate business has always been based on personal relationships, so the shift from anonymous online interactions to the more personal relationship aspect of social networking sites is a natural transition.

# II. Historical Influence

**www.ca.gov**
Welcome To California
**www.calhist.org**
California History

## A. CALIFORNIA'S COLORFUL HISTORY

California's colorful history gives a unique flavor to its customs and lifestyles. The first Europeans to actively settle in California were Spaniards. In 1769, they began the famous mission system along El Camino Real, now known as U.S. Highway 101 and California 1. They established *fortified trading posts, called* **PRESIDIOS**, at San Diego, San Francisco and Monterey.

The *first cities, called* **PUEBLOS**, were Los Angeles and San Jose. Spain's king granted vast ranchos to favored civil and military officers. Many streets, towns and landmarks in California still bear their names. The state's distinct architectural style, the rambling, cool, thick-walled adobe structure with red tile roof, dates from the Spanish period.

In the early 1800s, California became a self-governing province of newly independent Mexico. The ruling government attempted land reform, breaking up the huge Spanish ranchos and giving ownership to Mexican citizens. This disturbed the large American population in California and led to war with Mexico.

The United States' war with Mexico ended on February 2, 1848, with the **Treaty of Guadalupe Hidalgo**. As part of the settlement, the United States purchased from Mexico more than 500,000 square miles of land, including the present states of Nevada, Utah, New Mexico, Arizona, and California. In an extraordinary example of political-economic timing,

Mexico deeded over all rights to this province within weeks of John Sutter's explosive discovery of gold near Sacramento.

The **Gold Rush** brought thousands of new citizens swarming to the west coast. Many settled permanently, founding towns and businesses, and expanding the already well-established orchards, vineyards and cattle ranches. Foreign trade crowded the coastal cities with goods and increased immigration. **California achieved full statehood on September 9, 1850**, and from that time on the state's population increased until it could boast of having the largest population in the nation (over 12.5%). The newly established legislature adopted a land ownership recording system that recognized and protected the early land grants. This recording system provides an interesting and complete history of the ownership of California lands and their subsequent division and subdivision.

*38 million Californians now make up 12.5% of the U.S. population.*

In 1917, California passed the first real estate licensing law in the nation. Although this first law was declared unconstitutional, the Real Estate Act of 1919 was upheld by the State Supreme Court. Licensing laws are a reasonable exercise by the state to regulate the conduct of its citizens in the interest of the public good.

# III. Real and Personal Property

## A. OWNERSHIP IS A BUNDLE OF RIGHTS

*"Property" is defined as the "rights and interests that a person has in the thing owned."*

Commonly referred to as a "bundle of rights," some of these rights include possession, enjoyment, control, and disposition (see **Figure 1-1** for more details). There are two types of property: **Real Property** (immovable) and **Personal Property** (movable), formerly called "chattel" or "chattel real."

*Real property is "immovable" by law.*

**Figure 1-1**  OWNERSHIP IS A "BUNDLE OF RIGHTS"

### Bundle of Rights Theory

The bundle of rights theory views property ownership rights as a large bundle of sticks, where each "stick" is a property right. Individually, these rights represent various, specific forms of ownership; the more of these you hold, the more completely you own the property. So if you lease the property to someone, you give up one of your "sticks" (the right of possession). The basic rights of ownership include the rights of:

1. **Possession** – the right to occupy, rent, or keep others out.
2. **Enjoyment** – the right to "peace and quiet" without interference from past owners and others.
3. **Control** – the right to physically change or keep the property the way you like it.
4. **Disposition** – the right to transfer all or part of your property to others as you see fit.

## B. REAL PROPERTY

**REAL PROPERTY** *is the right or interest that a person has in the land or anything attached to the land.*

*Real property is legally defined as:*

1. *Land*
2. *Anything permanently attached or affixed to the land*
3. *Anything incidental or appurtenant to the land*
4. *Immovable by law*

### 1. Land

*LAND OWNERSHIP is commonly thought of as owning the surface of the earth; in other words, the ground we walk and build upon. But ownership also gives us rights to the space that is above our land and extends below our feet to the center of the earth, as* **Figure 1-2** *illustrates.*

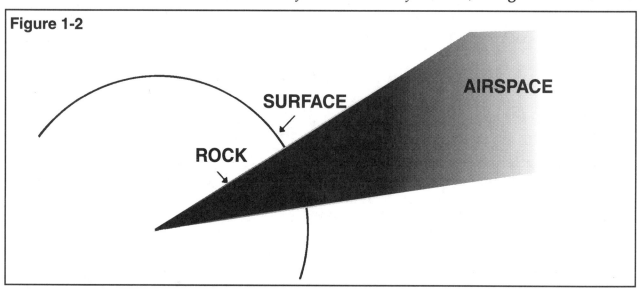

**Figure 1-2**

AIRSPACE

SURFACE

ROCK

An **AIRSPACE RIGHT** *is the right to the use of the airspace above the surface of the earth.* It is real property. In reality, the courts have restricted, to a reasonable height, the right of the property owner to use this space. An example for allowing only reasonable use of airspace is the need for airlines to have public "air highways" to provide us with transportation.

This airspace above the ground can be leased or sold in the same manner that mineral rights can be leased or sold. Airspace is an effective way to fully utilize the prime construction sites in many of our larger cities by building "up" instead of "out." An example of effective airspace use is storage space leased under our freeway overpasses by Caltrans, our state highway maintenance division.

Condominiums are another good example of airspace use. Inside a condominium, one only owns the airspace (area within the finished walls). The owner also owns a fractional share of the entire project (common area). Each owner may use the airspace within his or her unit in any manner he or she wishes, unless it violates the bylaws of the homeowner's group.

Generally, all that is beneath the surface of the earth belongs to the owner as real property. *MINERAL RIGHTS are the rights to unmined minerals (solids), such as gold, silver, and borax, that are part of the real property, but can be removed.* However, there are some exceptions: oil and other minerals can be claimed by the owner as personal property when removed from the ground. This is because they are considered, by law, to be "fugitive (meaning moving) substances." As an owner, you may sell your mineral rights below 500 feet; or you may exercise your "right of surface entry" above the 500-foot level.

A *RIPARIAN RIGHT is the right of a landowner to the reasonable use of moving, free flowing water on, under, and adjacent to his/her land (like a river or stream within the watershed), provided that its use does not infringe on the rights of any neighboring landowners.*

*Riparian rights can be severed by condemnation or prescription.*

A *LITTORAL RIGHT is the right of a landowner to the reasonable usage of a nonflowing body of water (with a shoreline) abutting his/her land.*

*Riparian rights refer to moving water (rivers and streams), and littoral rights refer to bodies of water with a shoreline (oceans and lakes). Remember "R" for rivers and "L" for lakes.*

*APPROPRIATION OF WATER (Doctrine of Appropriation) is the private taking and use of water flowing on the public domain from its natural course.*

*Riparian rights include the right to reasonably "appropriate" water as needed.*

*PERCOLATING WATER refers to underground water not found in a defined channel (natural water course).* A spring that originates underground and seeps up through the soil is an example of percolating water. A landowner has the right, in common with others, to take his/her share of underground (percolating) waters for beneficial use. The *ALLOCATION (taking) by the state (not city or county) of surplus underground water for beneficial use of non-owners is also referred to as APPROPRIATION.*

*POTABLE WATER refers to water that is suitable for human consumption.*

*SURFACE WATER RIGHTS prohibit the diversion of runoff from rain unless confined to a channel (river or stream) to the property of another.* An owner can use reasonable means to protect against floodwater, but not at the expense of his/her neighbor.

### 2. Attached to the Land ("Improvements")

*Anything attached to the land, such as buildings, fences, walls, walks and shrubs, are called* IMPROVEMENTS, and become **real property** when they are permanently incorporated, integrated in, affixed or attached to the land. Buildings that rest on the land or anything attached by cement, nails, screws, and plaster are examples of real property, as is a **bearing wall** that supports the upper part of a structure.

*Real property is the land and anything attached to the land (called "improvements").*

### 3. Incidental or Appurtenant to the Land

Anything that is incidental or appurtenant to the land is real property. *APPURTENANT means ownership transfers with the land automatically without the need of a separate conveyance (runs with the land)*. Certain things that are a part of the land must be sold with the land or else the usefulness of the land is reduced.

For example, **MUTUAL WATER COMPANIES** *are organized by water users in a given district to supply ample water at a reasonable rate.* They are usually corporations in which the owners of each parcel of land are given a share of stock. The stock is appurtenant to the land; that is, each share of stock is attached to the land and cannot be sold separately.

**Easements** that allow the use of someone else's land, such as a driveway to enter your land, also go with the land being sold if it is the only way to access the land.

*Stock in a mutual water company is real property and appurtenant (runs with the land) and thus automatically transfers to the buyer.*

### 4. Immovable by Law

**That which by law is considered immovable is real property.** Under California law, established crops and trees are a part of the land. The only exception is when a contract of sale for these items is made before the land is sold. If you have such a contract, it is a good idea to record it at the appropriate county recorder's office to assure that everyone has notice of the sale.

*Natural growth (vegetation attached by roots) is real property as are cultivated crops (like unpicked fruit or corn) until they are severed, mortgaged, or sold.*

## C. PERSONAL PROPERTY

**PERSONAL PROPERTY** *is any property that is movable and cannot be properly classified under the definition of real property.* Items such as clothes, furniture, and automobiles are tangible and easily movable. Personal property can also be documents that represent value, such as stocks, bonds, or leases.

*Minerals, oil, and gas, when extracted, are also considered personal property.*

**EMBLEMENTS** *are planted growing crops that are cultivated annually by a tenant farmer on leased land.* Unlike landscaping, these crops belong to the tenant even after the expiration of the lease.

*If previously contracted for sale, the "fruit" of a commercial orchard may be personal property, but the trees upon which it grows are real property.*

When buying personal property, your receipt is called a "**Bill of Sale.**" The Bill of Sale states that the goods have been paid for and that no outstanding loans exist on the personal property. It is always considered good practice to obtain a Bill of Sale. **Figure 1-3** is an example of a Bill of Sale.

*The ownership of personal property is transferred with a "bill of sale." An instrument used to secure a loan on personal property is called a "security agreement."*

## D. FIXTURES

**FIXTURES** *are items of personal property that are attached to, or incorporated into, the land in such a manner as to become real property.* The courts use these five tests to determine if an item is a fixture:

**Figure 1-3**   ### TRANSFERS TITLE OF PERSONAL PROPERTY

# BILL OF SALE

In consideration for the sum of _Three hundred fifty and .......... no/100_

_____$350.00_____ as payment in full is hereby acknowledged from

(Mr John Q. Smart       for the purchase of       (a Maytag washer

and dryer, serial numbers #H02257 and #D376240).

Executed on _April 19, 20XX_
in the county of                     California.
_Sacramento_

_Robert Seller_

Signature of Seller

M **1. Method of attachment**
A **2. Adaptability**
R **3. Relationship of the parties**
I **4. Intention**
A **5. Agreement**

We sometimes use an acronym (in this case, **MARIA**) to help you remember!

### 1. Method of Attachment

If an item can be removed by simply being unplugged, it is probably personal property. On the other hand, if it is attached by cement, plaster, screws, nails or plumbing, it is probably real property. If removal of an item would leave permanent damage or an unusable area, it is surely real property. A rug lying in a living room would be considered personal property; carpet affixed to the floor would be considered real property.

_Cost, size, and time installed are NOT tests in determining if something is a fixture (real property)._

### 2. Adaptability

The adaptability of personal property refers to ordinary use in connection with the land. If property is well adapted for the land or building, it is probably a fixture.

### 3. Relationship of the Parties

If a fixture is not mentioned in a contract, and is affixed to the property, most courts will give the seller the benefit of the doubt. A refrigerator that is just plugged in would be considered personal property and would remain with the seller. To protect yourself, any questionable fixtures should be mentioned in the purchase agreement. **Real estate salespeople remember: your client should secure a bill of sale for any questionable items.** In the case of a tenant and landlord, the court usually rules in favor of the tenant. There are, however, no set rules. A court decision is dependent upon the facts of each individual case.

### 4. Intention

If you plan to remove an item of personal property, you may not permanently attach it to the land.

### 5. Agreement

Disputes between buyers and sellers often arise regarding what items remain with the property. It is advisable to secure, in writing, any personal property that you want to remain as personal property. If you are buying a house, list all items you want to accompany the house, such as light fixtures, drapes or a fireplace screen. If you are selling, list only the items that will remain with the house. Remember: if in doubt, put it in writing!

*Any item can be specifically identified as being included or excluded as part of the sale. It is advisable to identify, in writing, any personal property that is to be included as part of the sale.*

### E. TRADE FIXTURES (Always Personal Property) (Removable – Exception to the Rule)

***TRADE FIXTURES** are personal property used in the normal course of business,* such as shelving or refrigeration units. A tenant may remove any trade fixture he or she installed provided the real property is left in the same condition as he or she found it. In this sense, trade fixtures are an exception to the rules of personal property.

*A "bill of sale" transfers trade fixtures because they are personal property.*

# IV. Methods of Land Description

In California, every parcel of land must be properly described or identified. If the property is to be sold, financed or leased, a recognized legal description is required. The following three methods are accepted as means of property identification.

A. Metes and Bounds (Surveyor's Maps – Irregular Parcels)
B. Sections and Townships (U.S. Government Survey – Rural)
C. Lots, Blocks, and Tracts (Recorded Subdivision – Cities)

*The legal description of a property is the minimum legal description of real property that appears in a listing on rural property.*

### A. METES AND BOUNDS (Surveyor's Maps)

***METES AND BOUNDS** (measuring boundaries) is the method of identifying (describing) property by its boundaries, distances, and angles from a given starting point.* In the past, surveyors often used natural objects as a starting point in their descriptions. A ***MONUMENT** is a fixed*

---

## Digital Maps (Useful to Clients)

Real estate salespeople and brokers may incorporate digital maps to show the location of their properties to clients. Two helpful applications are: (1) *GOOGLE EARTH, which offers maps and satellite images for searches.* Its best feature is the ability to see actual streets and building from several different views, and (2) *MAPQUEST.COM, the best feature of which is it gives the driver precise step by step directions to get their destination with maps.*

---

**Figure 1-10**

### Doing the Math – Acres and Area

An **ACRE** *is an area of land that contains 43,560 square feet.* So, if the area of a lot has more than 43,560 square feet, there is more than an acre of land. On the other hand, if there is less than 43,560 square feet in a lot, it is smaller than an acre.

    **AREA** *is a definite amount of space within a shape.* In America, area is usually measured in square feet, but may also be measured in square yards or square meters in other parts of the world. Most test questions about area refer to a rectangular or square shape. The area of a rectangular or square shape is obtained by multiplying length x (times) width. The answer is in square feet. The area of a square lot 100 feet x 100 feet is 10,000 square feet.

*Example (1):* How many acres is a parcel of land that measures 330 feet by 660 feet?

*Answer:*

Area     = Length x Width
217,800  = 330 feet x 660 feet

*Note: 1 acre = 43,560 square feet*

$\dfrac{217,800}{43,560}$ = **5 ACRES** (Round if necessary)

*Example (2):* If an acre is divided into four equal lots, with each lot placed parallel to the other and having a depth of 240 feet, what is the width of each lot?

*Answer:*

Area     = Length x Width
43,560  = 240 feet (x 4 lots)   x ? feet
43,560  = 960 feet            x ? feet

$\dfrac{43,560}{960}$ = **45.375 feet wide (Round to 45.4 feet wide)**

See Chapter 15 (Real Estate Math) for more problems.

**Figure 1-11**

## Reference Table

One **ACRE** is 43,560 square feet; 4,840 square yards.

One **SQUARE ACRE** is 208.71 feet on each side, but this number is generally rounded off to 209 feet.

One **MILE** is 5,280 feet long.

One **SQUARE MILE** contains 640 acres.

One **SECTION** is one mile square, containing 640 acres.

One **TOWNSHIP** (standard) is six miles square (36 square miles).

One **COMMERCIAL ACRE** is an acre minus any required public dedications.

One **ROD** is 16.5 feet long (5.5 yards). There are four rods, or 66 feet, to one chain, and 320 rods to a mile.

## V. CHAPTER SUMMARY

In California, real estate licensing laws are regulated by the **Department of Real Estate (DRE)**. You can follow the DRE through Twitter, YouTube, or you can subscribe to the California Department of Real Estate "News Flash" **RSS (Really Simple Syndication)** feed to get news delivered directly to your email or desktop.

Commission rates are fully negotiable between broker and buyer/seller, with the broker responsible for paying his or her salespeople their part of any commission.

California was purchased by the United States from Mexico as part of the **Treaty of Guadalupe Hidalgo** in 1848, just weeks before the discovery of gold by John Sutter, and became a state on **September 9, 1850**. California's Legislature passed the nation's first real estate licensing law in 1917.

**Real property** is generally immovable, passed by deed, and includes the right or interests in: 1) the land; 2) anything permanently attached or affixed to the land; and 3) anything incidental or appurtenant to the land. Anything attached to the land, like fences, walls, etc., become real property when they are permanently incorporated or integrated in, affixed, or attached to the land (called **improvements**). Land ownership is not only the surface of the earth but the **airspace** above it and that which is below, like mineral rights. Real property can be thought of as a **bundle of rights**, which includes the rights of possession, enjoyment, control, and disposition.

**Personal property** is movable, like a refrigerator or washing machine, but can include **emblements** (annually harvested crops) and some substances beneath the land, like oil and minerals when they have been removed from the land.

Anything that is **appurtenant** to the land means it is transferred with the land (runs with the land). An example is stock in a mutual water company. (Water suitable for drinking is referred to as **potable water**.) **Title** to real property is passed with a **deed**, while title to personal property is passed with a **bill of sale**.

A **fixture** is an item of personal property that is attached to or incorporated into the land in such a way as to become real property. The courts use the **MARIA** method to determine if an item is a fixture: **Method of attachment**, **Adaptability**, **Relationship of the parties**, **Intention**, and **Agreement**. **Trade fixtures** are personal property used in the normal course of business, such as shelving or refrigeration units which can be removed by tenants, who are responsible for any damage caused by their removal.

In California, every parcel of land must be properly described and identified. The three methods of identification include the **Metes and Bounds method**, the **Section and Township method**, and the **lots, blocks, and tracts method**. Metes and Bounds is the method of identifying property in relationship to its boundaries, distances, and angles from a given **starting point**.

**Sections and Townships** are used in a government survey system used to identify public and private lands. This system uses **base lines** (running east and west) and **meridian lines** (running north and south), as well as defining **townships** (36 square mile sections of land, where each section is 640 acres). **Lots, blocks, and tracts** make up subdivisions, which are approved by the Department of Real Estate and the city, and then recorded on a **Subdivision Map** in the County Recorder's Office.

## VI. TERMINOLOGY

**A.** Acre
**B.** Admission Date
**C.** Airspace
**D.** Base Lines
**E.** Bill of Sale
**F.** Bundle of Rights
**G.** Chattel or Chattel Real
**H.** Commission

**I.** Condominium
**J.** Emblements
**K.** Fixtures
**L.** Meridian Lines
**M.** Metes and Bounds
**N.** Personal Property
**O.** Potable Water
**P.** Range

**Q.** Real Property
**R.** Riparian Rights
**S.** Rod
**T.** Section
**U.** Township
**V.** Trade Fixtures

1. **P** A column of land six miles wide, determined by a government survey, running in a north-south direction, lying east or west of a principal meridian.
2. **K** Personal property that has become permanently attached to the land or improvements that are legally treated as real property; examples: plumbing fixtures, or built-in range, etc.
3. **V** Personal property used in a business, attached to the property, but removable by the tenant.
4. **I** A structure of two or more units where the interior airspace of each unit is individually owned; the balance of land and improvements is owned in common by all the owners.
5. **L** Imaginary north-south lines used in U.S. government surveys.
6. **N** Property that is movable and not real property.
7. **E** A written instrument that passes title of personal property from vendor (seller) to the vendee (buyer).

20/22

8. __H__ An amount, usually a percentage, paid to a broker as compensation for his or her services.

9. __M__ A legal description of land, setting forth all the boundary lines with their terminal points and angles.

10. __F__ All of the legal rights relevant to ownership of property including rights of use, possession, encumbering and disposition.

11. __U__ In the survey of public lands, a territorial subdivision six miles long, six miles wide and containing 36 sections, each one square mile.

12. __Q__ Land, improvements, items permanently attached to the land, appurtenances and that which is immovable by law.

13. __G__ A personal property interest in real property; an old term meaning personal property.

14. __A__ An area of land equaling 43,560 square feet, or a tract about 208.71 feet square.

15. __R__ The right of a landowner, whose land borders a stream or waterway, to use and enjoy the water, provided such use does not injure the rights of other owners.

16. __T__ A square of land (U.S. government survey) that contains 640 acres and is one square mile.

17. __S__ This old unit of measurement is 16 1/2 feet long (5.5 yards).

18. __C__ The reasonable space above a parcel; or in a condominium, the cubic area of a space within the walls.

19. __P__ Imaginary east-west lines that intersect meridian lines to form a starting point for the measurement of land.

20. __O__ Water that is suitable for human consumption.

21. __J__ Crops (produced on leased land by a tenant farmer) from an annual cultivation considered personal property.

22. __B__ September 9, 1850.

## Answers to the matching terminology are found on page 550.

## VII. CHAPTER QUIZ

1. Property is defined as:

    a. the rights or interests that a person has in the thing owned.
    b. freehold estates.
    c. only personal property.
    d. things that buyers and sellers own.

2. The initials RSS refer to:

    a. Really Specific Systems.
    b. Really Simple Syndication.
    c. Reference Section Specifics.
    d. none of the above.

3. "Potable water" refers to:

    a. well water on the property.
    b. water suitable for irrigation.
    c. water suitable for drinking.
    d. water suitable for cooking.

4. Which of the following would normally be considered real property?

    a. Trade fixtures
    b. Chattel reals
    c. Vegetation
    d. Deeds of trust

5. The ownership of personal property is transferred by using a:

    a. grant deed.
    b. financing statement.
    c. trust deed.
    d. bill of sale.

6. A loan secured by personal property usually consists of:

    a. a financing statement and trust deed.
    b. a promissory note and a trust deed.
    c. FHA or VA insurance.
    d. a security agreement.

7. Which of the following is NOT a test for a fixture?

    a. Adaptability
    b. Agreement
    c. Cost and size of the item
    d. Intention

8. California has how many principal intersections of base lines and meridian lines?

    a. One
    b. Two
    c. Three
    d. Five

9. A township contains:

    a. one square mile only.
    b. a six-mile by six-mile square of land.
    c. 36 square miles.
    d. both b and c.

10. A commercial acre is:

    a. an acre of land used only for agricultural purposes.
    b. an acre of land where an industrial building is situated.
    c. an acre of land where retail buildings are situated.
    d. an acre less the amount of land dedicated for public improvements (sidewalks, alleys, etc.).

ANSWERS: 1. a; 2. b; 3. c; 4. c; 5. d; 6. d; 7. c; 8. c; 9. d; 10. d

# CHAPTER 2
## *Estates, Transfers, and Titles*

In the previous chapter, we explained the differences between real and personal property. In this chapter, we will illustrate the types of estates (ownership) that you may have, the ways in which you can hold title and the methods of transferring real property.

# I. Estate Ownership

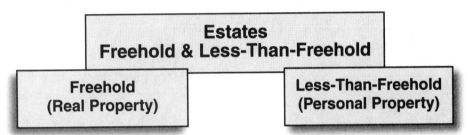

## A. ESTATES (Ownership Interest in Land)

An **ESTATE** *is an interest, share, right or equity in real estate that varies from the minimal right of a renter to the maximum right of a full owner.*

*An estate is an ownership interest in land.*

Estates are either **(1) freehold** or **(2) less-than-freehold**, depending upon the degree of ownership and the duration of interest. Freehold estates are real property and less-than-freehold estates are personal property. Less-than-freehold estates come with certain rights for the use of real property (see **Figure 2-1**).

## B. FREEHOLD ESTATES (Real Property)

*The two major types of freehold estates are: 1) fee simple estates and 2) life estates.*

The two types of freehold estates are the greatest degree of ownership you can have under the law.

### 1. Estates in Fee

A fee simple estate is the most complete form of ownership and the most common in California. This can be referred to as fee, fee ownership, or fee simple. *FEE SIMPLE*

23

# CHAPTER 2

## CHAPTER OUTLINE

**Figure 2-1**

*means an owner has transferred all rights of a property to a new owner for an indefinite duration of time (perpetual).* All transfers are assumed to be fee simple unless the grant part of the deed limits, by the use of conditions, the property's use.

*An estate in fee (also called "fee simple" or "fee") is the greatest interest a person can hold; it is of "indefinite duration" (perpetual), "freely transferable," and "inheritable" (referred to as an estate of inheritance). An estate in fee is a freehold estate.*

### a. Conditions That Restrict a Fee Estate (Fee Simple Defeasible Estate)

A *FEE SIMPLE DEFEASIBLE ESTATE (or qualified fee estate) is a fee estate that is subject to particular limitations imposed by the grantor of the estate.* **Breaking any condition of the transfer may be grounds for terminating or revoking the property transfer.**

**Example:** Duke sold his property to Jane with the condition that Jane must never use it for any purpose other than as a private residence. However, after owning the property for several years, Jane decided to start a board and care facility for handicapped adults. The estate may revert to Duke because it is a fee simple defeasible estate.

**Example:** A buyer agrees not to sell alcoholic beverages on a property. This condition is included in the deed. The buyer has taken fee simple defeasible title to the property. If a person takes title subject to a condition (subsequent) that liquor not be sold on the premises, and then turns around and breaks this promise, the previous title holder has grounds to reclaim title through a court action.

In this chapter we have briefly discussed conditions, as in CC&Rs (Covenants, Conditions, & Restrictions). For a more complete discussion of other types of private restrictions, please see Chapter 3.

## CHAPTER 2

### 2. Life Estate (Indefinite Period)

*A life estate is an example of a freehold estate.*

A **LIFE ESTATE** is an ownership interest in real property that only exists for the life of any designated person or persons (often the grantee). The usual intent of this type of estate is to provide a lifetime residence for an individual. A life estate can be created by either a will or a deed. When that designated person dies, the estate reverts back to the original owner. A person holding a life estate is free to lease the property to someone else, but this lease is also subject to the lifetime limitation.

*A life estate holder may lease the property to someone else, but if the designated person dies, the estate ends and all rights, including any tenant rights, revert back to the original owner/grantor.*

**Example:** John owns a life estate based upon his own life. He leases the property to a tenant on a five-year lease. John, the life tenant, dies two years later. The lease is terminated.

The life tenant usually has certain interests and obligations as long as the life estate is in effect. The life tenant:

1. has the right of physical possession of the property;
2. has the right to all rents and profits, but this terminates when the life estate holder dies;
3. can usually lease the property, but not beyond the time frame of the life estate;
4. is obligated to keep the property in good repair, although he or she is not required to make improvements;
5. may not damage or destroy any permanent part of the property to the detriment of succeeding interests, and
6. is usually responsible for all annual costs and expenses.

*The party (grantor) granting a life estate is said to hold an **ESTATE IN REVERSION**.*

*If I give you a life estate, you hold "possession" for as long as you live. You can lease it out. However, if you lease it out, when you die, possession reverts back to me, or any specified person (estate in remainder).*

If an owner granting a life estate names another person to receive title upon the death of the current life estate holder, that other person claims an **ESTATE IN REMAINDER**. The holder of an estate in remainder or estate in reversion has no right to the use and enjoyment of the property until the current life tenant dies.

## C. LESS-THAN-FREEHOLD ESTATES (No Title to Real Property)
### (A Leasehold is Personal Property)

*A less-than-freehold estate is also called a leasehold estate, and is considered personal property.*

*LESS-THAN-FREEHOLD ESTATES are personal rights to the use of real property for a period of time.* They are more commonly referred to as **leases** or rental agreements, which give tenants various rights to use real property for a specified period.

*A similarity between owning a condominium and renting an apartment is the occupier of each unit has an estate in real property.*

The tenant (renting the apartment), however, only has possession of the property (see **Figure 2-2**).

**Figure 2-2**

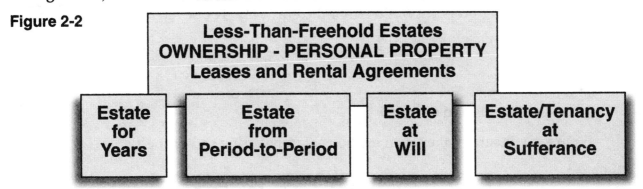

### 1. Estate For Years (Tenancy for a Fixed Term)

An *ESTATE FOR YEARS is a lease for a fixed period of time, agreed to in advance.* This period can be from a few days up to 99 years. No notice to terminate is necessary.

*Whether a lease is for two months or seven years, it is considered an "estate for years," personal property, and chattel real.*

### 2. Estate From Period-To-Period (Periodic Tenancy)

An *ESTATE FROM PERIOD-TO-PERIOD is a renewable agreement to rent or lease a property for a period of time, where the rental or lease amount is fixed at an agreed to sum per week, month, or year.* A notice to terminate must be given (usually 30 days).

### 3. Estate At Will

An *ESTATE AT WILL is a rental agreement that can be terminated by either party (lessor or lessee) at any time,* although by California law, there must be at least a 30-day notice to vacate (so there is no true "estate at will" in California).

*An estate at will can be terminated by either the lessor or the lessee.*

### 4. Estate At Sufferance/Tenancy At Sufferance

An *ESTATE AT SUFFERANCE occurs when the person renting or leasing a particular property remains after the expiration of the stated term without the landlord's consent.*

A *TENANCY AT SUFFERANCE occurs when a tenant remains in the property after expiration of a lease without the owner's consent.*

The four main types of less-than-freehold estates are explained in further detail in Chapter 6, "Landlord and Tenant."

# II. Acquisitions and Transfers

*Alienation is the opposite of acquisition. "Acquisition" means to acquire, buy, or pull in, whereas "alienation" means to transfer, sell, or push away.*

## A. TRANSFERS

A sale is the means by which real estate is usually transferred. A sale is the most familiar way of transferring property, but it is not the only way. The seven basic ways to transfer real property are:

1. **Deed**                          5. **Accession**
2. **Will**                          6. **Occupancy**
3. **Probate**                       7. **Dedication**
4. **Intestate Succession (no will)**

**Figure 2-3** illustrates the seven methods of transferring real property.

**Figure 2-3**

### 1. Transfer by Deed

*The deed is NOT the title, but is "evidence" of the title.*

The most common method of acquiring title to a property is by deed transfer. In California, **CONVEYANCE** *is the document used to effect the transfer of title to property from one person to another.* This is usually accomplished by a simple written document known as a deed. A **DEED** *is a written instrument that conveys and evidences title.*

The **GRANTOR** *is the person who grants property or property rights (seller).* The **GRANTEE** *is the person to whom the grant is made (buyer).* A grantee cannot be a fictitious person (i.e., Batman or Catwoman), but it can be a person with a fictitious name (i.e., Microsoft, Inc.).

*Grant deeds must have a "granting" type clause (action clause). The grantor is the person transferring real property. Both grant deeds and quitclaim deeds are signed only by the grantor, at which time they are considered to be "executed."*

There are two basic types of deeds: (1) grant deed and (2) quitclaim deed. All other deeds are versions of these two deeds.

A *GRANT DEED is a document that transfers title (evidence of property ownership), with the key word being "grant"* (see **Figure 2-4**). The grant (or warranty) aspect of the deed is a promise that:

a. The owner (grantor) has not conveyed title to the property to any other person (grantee).

b. The property is free of any encumbrances (liens or other restrictions) other than those already disclosed to the grantee. A grant deed also transfers any **after-acquired title**, meaning that rights obtained after the sale has been completed are also conveyed.

These warranties are part of the grant deed, although they are not written into the deed. They are called *IMPLIED WARRANTIES because they are not expressed in writing, but are present.*

*Grant deeds contain "implied warranties" that are NOT expressed in writing.*

It should be noted that the grant deed does not necessarily give one all the rights to a property. Easements, rights of way, mineral rights, building restrictions and other types of restrictions may still restrict the use of the property.

*A person who transfers title to real property is the grantor; therefore anyone who signs a grant deed or a quitclaim deed is a "grantor." The person receiving property is the "grantee."*

A *QUITCLAIM DEED is a deed that conveys all the present rights or interest that a person may have in a property, without any warranty, title, or interest.*

*Quitclaim deeds make NO "covenants" (promises); they guarantee nothing. They only convey any rights the grantor may have.*

A quitclaim deed can give absolute ownership or only such title as one may hold. If there is no ownership interest, then nothing can be acquired. Read the quitclaim deed in **Figure 2-5**. Note that there are no warranties; just the clause, "do hereby remise, release, and forever quitclaim to…" This deed is used primarily to clear a cloud on title from the records. A *CLOUD ON TITLE is a claim, encumbrance or condition that impairs the title to real property until disproved or eliminated, as, for example, through a quitclaim deed or a quiet title legal action.*

A *QUIET TITLE ACTION is a court proceeding to remove a cloud on title to real property.* It is usually a minor defect that requires a quitclaim deed before a title insurance company will clear the transfer. A quitclaim deed is often used in divorce actions, so that one party may have clear title.

*The ownership of real property may best be determined by a quiet title action.*

**Example:** For three generations the Mendez family has owned the mining rights to mine gold on Diego's land. Last month, Diego sold his land to a developer who promptly enclosed the land with a large chain-link fence that had only one access, a locked gate. The Mendez family should institute a quiet title action.

*If a buyer purchases a property on an installment plan and abandons that property after a few payments, then there will likely be a "cloud on the title" if the contract was recorded.*

## Figure 2-4

RECORDING REQUESTED BY

AND WHEN RECORDED MAIL DOCUMENT AND
TAX STATEMENT TO:

NAME

STREET
ADDRESS

CITY, STATE &
ZIP CODE

TITLE ORDER NO. _____

ESCROW NO. _____

| S | R | U | PAGE | SIZE | DA | MISC | LONG | RFD | COPY |
|---|---|---|------|------|------|------|------|------|------|
|   |   |   |      |      |      |      |      |      |      |
| M | A | L | 465 | 426 | PCOR | NCOR | SMF | NCHG | EXAM |
|   |   |   |     |     | T: |  | CTY | UNI |  |

SPACE ABOVE THIS LINE FOR RECORDER'S USE ONLY

# GRANT DEED

TRA: _____

APN: _____

**The undersigned grantor(s) declare(s)**
DOCUMENTARY TRANSFER TAX    $ _____
☐ computed on full value of property conveyed, or
☐ computed on full value less liens and encumbrances remaining at time of sale.
☐ Unincorporated Area        City of _____

FOR VALUABLE CONSIDERATION, receipt of which is hereby acknowledged, I (We) _____

_____
(NAME OF GRANTOR(S))

hereby remise, release and grant to _____

_____
(NAME OF GRANTEE(S))

the following described real property in the City of _____ ,County of _____ ,

State of _____ .

(Insert Legal Description)

DATED: _____        _____

_____

STATE OF CALIFORNIA                    }
COUNTY OF _____            }

On_____ before me, _____ personally appeared
(here insert name and title of the officer)

_____

who proved to me on the basis of satisfactory evidence to be the person(s) whose name(s) is/are subscribed to the within instrument and acknowledged to me that he/she/they executed the same in his/her/their authorized capacity(ies), and that by his/her/their signature(s) on the instrument the person(s), or the entity upon behalf of which the person(s) acted, executed the instrument.

I certify under PENALTY OF PERJURY under the laws of the State of California that the foregoing paragraph is true and correct.

WITNESS my hand and official seal.

Signature _____ (SEAL)

MAIL TAX STATEMENT AS DIRECTED ABOVE

## Figure 2-5

RECORDING REQUESTED BY

AND WHEN RECORDED MAIL DOCUMENT AND
TAX STATEMENT TO:

NAME

STREET
ADDRESS

CITY, STATE &
ZIP CODE

TITLE ORDER NO. _____
ESCROW NO. _____

| S | R | U | PAGE | SIZE | DA | MISC | LONG | RFD | COPY |
|---|---|---|------|------|------|------|------|------|------|
| M | A | L | 465 | 426 | PCOR | NCOR | SMF | NCHG | EXAM |
|   |   |   |   |   | T: | | CTY | UNI | |

SPACE ABOVE THIS LINE FOR RECORDER'S USE ONLY

# QUITCLAIM DEED

TRA: _____

APN: _____

**The undersigned grantor(s) declare(s)**
DOCUMENTARY TRANSFER TAX   $ _____
☐ computed on full value of property conveyed, or
☐ computed on full value less liens and encumbrances remaining at time of sale.
☐ Unincorporated Area        City of _____

FOR VALUABLE CONSIDERATION, receipt of which is hereby acknowledged, I (We) _____

_____
(NAME OF GRANTOR(S))

hereby remise, release and quitclaim to _____

_____
(NAME OF GRANTEE(S))

the following described real property in the City of _____ ,County of _____ ,

State of _____ .

(Insert Legal Description)

DATED: _____          _____

_____

STATE OF CALIFORNIA
COUNTY OF _____

On _____ before me, _____ , personally appeared
(here insert name and title of the officer)

_____ ,

who proved to me on the basis of satisfactory evidence to be the person(s) whose name(s) is/are subscribed to the within instrument
and acknowledged to me that he/she/they executed the same in his/her/their authorized capacity(ies), and that by his/her/their
signature(s) on the instrument the person(s), or the entity upon behalf of which the person(s) acted, executed the instrument.

I certify under PENALTY OF PERJURY under the laws of the State of California that the foregoing paragraph is true and correct.

WITNESS my hand and official seal.

Signature _____ (SEAL)

MAIL TAX STATEMENT AS DIRECTED ABOVE

A **VALID DEED** has all the following essential elements:

    a. It must be in writing.
    b. The parties (grantee and grantor) must be properly named and have legal capacity.
    c. The property must be adequately described (need not be legal description).
    d. There must be a granting clause (action clause).
    e. It must be signed by the granting party (grantor).

*A valid deed passes title when the deed is recorded (which is a form of delivery), thereby giving constructive notice.*

A deed does not take effect until it is delivered and accepted. In order for title to be transferred, the grantor must sign the deed and deliver it with the intention of passing title immediately.

---

Some subtypes of grant or quitclaim deeds used in California are:

**GIFT DEED** – *Granted as a gift of love and affection.* No other consideration is necessary, but is void if given to defraud creditors.

**TAX DEED** – *Given if property is sold as payment of past-due property taxes.*

**ADMINISTRATOR'S DEED or EXECUTOR'S DEED** – *Given to the purchaser of the deceased person's real property.*

**SHERIFF'S DEED** – *Granted to the purchaser at a court-ordered sale.*

**TRUSTEE'S DEED** – *Given to the purchaser of property at a trust deed foreclosure sale.*

**GUARDIAN'S DEED** – *Used by a guardian to transfer the real property of minors or incompetents.*

**LAND PATENT** – *Used by the government to grant public land to an individual.*

---

*A deed does NOT have to be acknowledged to be valid. Delivery and acceptance of the deed is presumed with recording.*

The following are the three basic methods of delivery:

    **1.** *MANUAL DELIVERY is a direct transfer of the deed from the grantor to the grantee.*

    **2.** *DELIVERY THROUGH RECORDING is the act of putting the title of record in the grantee's name at the county recorder's office. The grantee must have agreed to the recording.*

    **3.** *CONDITIONAL DELIVERY requires that a specific event take place before title can be passed, and must be handled by a disinterested third party. The deed is then delivered manually.*

*A "trust deed" is NOT a deed, but rather a conveyance; it gives bare (or naked) legal title to a trustee with the power to sell.*

### 2. Transfer by Will (Testate)

A **WILL** *is a document, created by a person, stating how that person's property is to be conveyed or distributed upon his or her death.* It also leaves instructions as to the disposition of the body upon death. This is known as dying *TESTATE, which means having made and left a valid will. A* **TESTATOR** *or* **TESTATRIX** *is one who makes a will. To* **BEQUEATH** *is to transfer personal property by will; to* **DEVISE** *is to transfer real property by will.* There are two types of wills that can legally dispose of real and personal property:

    a. Witnessed will (typed)
    b. Holographic will (handwritten)

A **WITNESSED WILL** *is a typed document usually prepared by an attorney, dated, signed by the property owners and declared to be a will by at least two witnesses (***three signatures total***).*

A **HOLOGRAPHIC WILL** *is entirely handwritten by the owner, dated, and signed.* Since it is in the owner's own handwriting, no other formalities and no witnesses are required, unless the will is signed with an "X," in which case it must be witnessed.

*A holographic will is NOT a printed form.*

A **CODICIL** *is a change in a will before the maker's death.*

**Note:** A **REVOCABLE LIVING TRUST** *is a trust that is effective during the life of the owner, rather than upon his or her death.* It can eliminate probate (to prove a will) cost and serve the same function as a will. The property is placed in a trust created for the heirs and may consist of both real and personal property. It is revocable at the discretion of the benefactor (owner), but becomes fully enforceable upon that person's death. There can be a considerable estate tax savings under this arrangement, depending on the size of the estate. At the very least, a revocable living trust protects the interests of everyone involved while avoiding the time and expense of probate. This type of trust is, however, rather complicated to set up, so an attorney specializing in this field should be consulted.

### 3. Transfer by Probate (Superior Court Approval)

**PROBATE** *is a Superior Court procedure to determine a will's validity, any creditors' claims, and establish the identity of the beneficiaries.* There are charges for the court probate action and fees for any related attorney costs.

*The real estate commission for a property that is in probate is set by court order.*

After a person dies, an **administrator (male)** or **administratrix (female)** is appointed by the court to temporarily take possession of the property until probate is finalized. An **executrix** is a female person appointed by will to administer the estate of the deceased person (**executor** is a male).

*The minimum length of time for probate is six months. A party has four months to file a claim for probate.*

**Note:** Wills and living trusts are legal devices for transferring property at death. To protect yourself, have an attorney draw up a will or living trust that reflects your desires, or leave your own handwritten (holographic) will.

*Customarily, the court confirms a probate sale and sets the broker's commission.*

### 4. Transfer by Intestate Succession (No Will)

*If there is no will, the procedure used for transferring the deceased's property to his or her heirs is called* **INTESTATE SUCCESSION.** The law of intestate succession provides for the disposition of the property. The rules for dividing the property are complex and dependent upon the relationship of the kin.

*Separate property: If the decedent has no will and leaves a spouse and one child, property is divided equally, 50-50. If there is a surviving spouse and two or more children, 1/3 goes to the spouse and 2/3 to the children. If there is no surviving spouse, property is divided equally among the children.*

**ESCHEAT** *is the term used if there is no will and there are no heirs; the property will go to the state of California.* This is not automatic. There is a **five-year period** during which heirs can make claims to the state for the property.

*If a person dies intestate and leaves no heirs, his/her estate will go to the state of California if no heirs are found during a five-year period. Individuals do NOT acquire property by escheat.*

### 5. Transfer by Accession (Natural Causes)

**ACCESSION** *occurs when an owner acquires title to additional land by natural causes, that is, additions to the property by natural growth. The addition to land from natural causes, such as earthquakes, volcanoes, or the action of moving water is known as* **ACCRETION.** *For example, a river, over time, may slowly deposit soil on one of its banks. These deposits of earth made through the natural action of water, called* **ALLUVIUM,** become the real property of the landowner who holds title to the river bank. **AVULSION** *is the sudden, violent tearing away of land by, for example, a river.* Title to that land is lost by the property owner.

*The owner of property adjacent to the water flow can acquire title to additional land by accession or accretion.*

Permanent fixtures attached to the land or buildings by residential tenants must be left with the building. Any improvements that are mistakenly placed on the property must also remain. *Placement of improvements and permanent fixtures on property that do not legally belong to the person who placed them is called* **ENCROACHMENT.**

*A fence built over the property line onto a neighbor's lot is a form of encroachment. The neighboring landowner has three years from discovery to take action for its removal.*

### 6. Transfer by Occupancy

Ownership of real property, or the use of real property, can be gained through three types of occupancy:

    a. Abandonment
    b. Adverse Possession
    c. Prescription (by use)

## a. Abandonment

*ABANDONMENT is the relinquishing of a right or interest with the intention of never again reclaiming it.* One cannot acquire title to abandoned real property without court action, but a landlord can acquire possession of a property that is left (abandoned) by a tenant simply by gaining full control of the property. In the case of a lease, a financially troubled tenant might negotiate a release or abandon the property, thereby forfeiting part of the deposit.

*When a tenant voluntarily moves out of an apartment and never returns, this is called abandonment or vacating.*

## b. Adverse Possession

*ADVERSE POSSESSION is acquiring title to another's property through continuous and notorious occupancy for five years under a claim of title.* It is the legal way to acquire title without a deed. Title may be obtained through adverse possession only if certain conditions are met:

1. **Open and notorious occupancy** – The adverse possessor must live on, or openly use, the property in such a way that the titled owners might easily detect his or her presence.

2. **Hostile and adverse** – The adverse possessor must possess the property hostile to the legal owner, without his or her permission or any rental payment (consideration).

3. **Uninterrupted use for five years** – The adverse possessor must use the property continuously for at least five consecutive years.

4. **Right or color of title** – The adverse possessor must have some reasonable claim of right or color of title (perhaps a defective written instrument) as a basis for his or her assertion. For example, a person could claim that his uncle gave the property to him before he died, but the deed is missing.

5. **Property taxes** – The adverse possessor must have paid all taxes levied and assessed on the property for five consecutive years.

The courts will require substantial proof before ruling there is an adverse possession. To obtain marketable title, or before a title insurance company can insure a property, clear title must be obtained by a court decree. This essentially means that a "quiet title" action is brought in court to prove that all requirements have been fulfilled. In the peoples' interest, adverse possession is not possible against public or government lands, but only against privately owned lands.

## c. Easement by Prescription

*PRESCRIPTION is an easement, or the right to use another's land, which can be obtained through five years of continuous use.* Its requirements are similar to those of adverse possession, the differences being that by prescription: 1) only the use of the property has been obtained, and 2) taxes are still paid by the property owner (paying the property taxes is not a requirement for an easement by prescription).

*Unlike "adverse possession," "prescription" is the "use" of a property, NOT the transfer of the title.*

### 7. Transfer by Dedication

*DEDICATION is the gift (appropriation) of land, by its owner, for some public use.* To be fully dedicated, the land must be accepted for such use by authorized public officials. Dedication may be either (1) voluntary or (2) mandated by statute.

# III. Title (Forms of Ownership)

## A. TITLE

*TITLE is the right to ownership of land and the evidence of that ownership.* There are six distinct methods of holding title. **Figure 2-6** displays the six ways a person, or persons, may hold title to real property and whether a single title holder has the right to will or sell his or her share independent of the other owners. *VESTING is the placing of a person's (or persons') name on the deed and the description of the method by which that person will hold title.*

| Figure 2-6 — Methods of Holding Title (Vesting) Concurrently or in Severalty | | |
|---|---|---|
| **A SINGLE TITLE HOLDER** | **WILL** | **SELL** |
| SEVERALTY ("Sole Ownership") | YES | YES |
| TENANCY IN COMMON | YES | YES |
| JOINT TENANCY | NO | YES |
| TENANCY IN PARTNERSHIP | NO | NO |
| COMMUNITY PROPERTY | YES | NO |
| COMMUNITY PROPERTY (w/Right of Survivorship) | NO | NO |

*Vesting is the method by which one holds title. A deed to a fictitious name is valid; a deed to a fictitious person is void.*

### 1. Severalty (Sole Ownership)

*SEVERALTY is the sole and separate ownership of property by one individual or by a corporation.* The word "severed" means to sever, to cut off or separate. The name severalty is misleading; it means single.

*Severalty means "sole ownership."*

Property held by corporations is owned in severalty, as if by a single individual. A *CORPORATION is a body of persons treated by law as a single "legal person," having a personality and existence distinct from that of its shareholders.* A corporation can go on forever; it does not die.

Examples to show ownership by severalty are:

as a natural person, a real person

"Mary Smith, a single woman"
**or**
"Mary Smith, an unmarried woman"

or as a legal person; charter granted by the state

"Urban Analysis Inc., a corporation"

Sometimes married people wish to keep ownership to certain properties as separate property (in severalty). They may then use the phrase:

"Mary Smith, a married women, as her sole and separate property"
**or**
"Jim Smith, a married man, as his sole and separate property"

### 2. Tenancy In Common (Unity of Possession)

*When two or more people own property together with the right to will or sell it (however, without survivorship rights or community property rights), it is called* **TENANCY IN COMMON**. If there is no other agreement, they will each share an equal interest in the property. All tenants in common have **UNITY OF POSSESSION**, *which means they each have the right to occupy the property.* Often, the property is rented to one of the owners or to a tenant. Tenancy in common gives all owners a share of the income and expenses of the property.

Each owner may sell or transfer his or her interest separately from the others. For example, if one of the four owners of a building were to sell his/her one-quarter interest, there would be no restrictions. More commonly, if one of the owners dies, his/her heirs would inherit a one-quarter interest in the property.

If the owners do not agree on the ownership or management, and persistent disagreements exist, it would probably be best to sell the property and divide the profits accordingly. If an agreement cannot be reached by the owners, a court of law will sell the property and decide what is best for all concerned. *When the courts have the responsibility of physically dividing or selling the property, it is referred to as a* **PARTITION ACTION**. It is obviously better for the owners to sell the property themselves, as attorney's fees and court costs would be involved. Furthermore, the court would probably sell the land at a lower price to expedite the sale.

### 3. Joint Tenancy (Right of Survivorship)

**JOINT TENANCY** *occurs when two or more people have identical interests in the whole property with the same right of possession and the right of survivorship.* If one of the joint tenancy owners should die, his or her interest is then split evenly with the surviving owners. Joint tenancy can never be willed.

*Joint tenants have the right of "survivorship." A joint tenancy cannot be willed.*

**Example:** Dick and Jane, brother and sister, own an apartment building in joint tenancy. Dick needs $10,000 to cover unexpected medical expenses, so he borrows the money from a lender, signing a trust deed on the property that was soon recorded in the public records. Forty-five days later, Dick dies. Jane now owns the apartment free and clear of the brother's $10,000 debt.

**Example:** Al and Betty are brother and sister and own an apartment building in joint tenancy. Al having a trust deed or mortgage recorded against his ½ interest in the property would not terminate this joint tenancy.

*A joint tenancy in real property can legally be created with the execution of a deed by a husband and wife to themselves as joint tenants, existing joint tenants to themselves and others as joint tenants, and existing tenants in common to themselves as joint tenants.*

When a joint tenancy is established, there are four necessary unities (**T-Tip**):

T  **1. Title** – All owners are granted title by the same instrument.
T  **2. Time** – All owners obtain title at the same time.
I  **3. Interest** – All owners share an equal interest.
P  **4. Possession** – All owners have an equal right to possess the property.

To create joint tenancy, there must be intention by the owners. If it does not "state" that it is a joint tenancy, joint tenancy does not exist.

If one of the parties should die, the property is automatically transferred to the remaining parties without having to go through the superior court procedure known as *PROBATE (to prove a will)*. The transferred portion conveys the ownership and all debts on the property at the moment of death. Upon death, that debt does not transfer to the surviving joint tenants until it is foreclosed. Although probate costs may be avoided in joint tenancy, the surviving owners may end up paying higher income taxes later.

*Joint tenancy is free of "unsecured debts."*

A joint tenant can sell or transfer his or her ownership interest. Any portion of joint tenancy transferred or sold to a nonowner will bring the nonowner into tenancy in common with the other owners, who remain as joint tenants. If A, B and C own a property together and C sells his interest to D, then D gets only the tenancy in common interest with A and B (who continue to be joint tenants).

Because a corporation could, conceivably, go on forever, it is not permitted to enter into joint tenancies. Such a situation would give corporations an unfair survivorship advantage.

### 4. Tenancy in Partnership

*TENANCY IN PARTNERSHIP refers to two or more people who are co-owners in a business. In a GENERAL PARTNERSHIP, the partners share all profits and losses and share management responsibilities.* All property that general partners bring into the business at the outset, and all that they later acquire (with partnership funds) for the business, is partnership property. All partners must agree to a sale or transfer of real property. Each has a right to possess the partnership property. If a partner should die, his or her interest passes to any heirs who then have a right in the partnership, but not in any particular property. If an agreement cannot be reached with the heirs, the partnership may have to be dissolved.

The amount invested in a partnership need not be equal, but must be agreed upon mutually. The partnership agreement states the amount of money to be contributed by each, the duties of each, and sets the proportional distribution of profits or losses.

A *LIMITED PARTNERSHIP (tax shelter) is one consisting of one or more general partners and limited partners.* A limited partner's losses are limited to the amount of his or her investment. A limited partner does not share management responsibilities.

### 5. Community Property

*COMMUNITY PROPERTY refers to all the property acquired by a husband and wife during their marriage other than separate property.* California is a community property state, which means that any property acquired during a marriage is shared equally. This practice is derived from Spanish law and became incorporated into our legal system when California was a part of Mexico. Both husband and wife must sign all transfer documents to convey community real property. If only one spouse signs a transfer document, the "injured" spouse could void the sale within a one-year period. **As a salesperson, you should make certain that both husband and wife sign all real estate documents, such as listings, purchase agreements, and escrow instructions, if the property being transferred is community property. Both signatures are required when selling, borrowing money, or leasing community property for more than one year**.

*Both husband and wife's signatures are needed to transfer property deeded "Mary Smith, a married woman."*

The right to manage the community property is shared by both the husband and wife. Each can will his or her respective half to whomever he or she wishes. **If there is no will, the half belonging to the deceased would go to the surviving spouse. If willed to an heir, the heir and the remaining spouse would then be tenants in common**.

*Community property (husband and wife) vesting has equal interest.*

Debts of either spouse can become a liability for the community estate if they are incurred before or during marriage. The law also allows some community property to be transferred without going through probate. Questions about debts or probate should be directed to an attorney, as this issue is quite complex.

*Wages (paychecks) earned by either spouse during a marriage are considered "community property."*

Any property obtained by either the husband or wife before marriage may remain as *SEPARATE PROPERTY*. Both may inherit or receive gifts of property during the marriage, which can remain as separate property. **However, any proceeds from the property held separately, such as rents or profit, cannot be commingled with community property, as this would cause them to become community property**.

Do not advise a buyer on how to hold title—that is giving legal advice. However, you can explain the different ways to take title. How a person holds title has a big impact upon income tax planning and estate planning.

*A real estate agent who advises a buyer on how to take title to real property may be liable for practicing law, giving tax advice, and discrimination.*

### 6. Community Property with Right of Survivorship

The California Legislature enacted legislation that allows married couples in California to hold title to real and personal property as "community property with right of survivorship." **COMMUNITY PROPERTY WITH RIGHT OF SURVIVORSHIP** *transfers ownership to the spouse at death, with income tax benefits.* The goal of the legislation was to combine the right of survivorship benefit of joint tenancy with the favorable tax status of community property under federal tax law. The survivorship benefit allows title to pass to the surviving spouse at the death of one spouse. The surviving spouse also gets the benefit of a stepped-up basis for 100% of the property upon the death of a spouse. The surviving spouse may use an affidavit of death of spouse to satisfy title company underwriting requirements to convey or encumber title. Probate proceedings are not necessary to transfer title to the surviving spouse.

# IV. Recording and Acknowledgment

*A deed does NOT have to be "acknowledged" nor "recorded" to be valid, although it is wise to do both.*

## A. RECORDING

**RECORDING** *is the legal process of making an instrument an official part of the records of a county, after it has been acknowledged.* Instruments that affect real property are legal documents, such as deeds, mortgages, trust deeds, leases and contracts of sale. **Recording gives constructive notice** of the existence and content of these instruments to the public.

**CONSTRUCTIVE NOTICE** *is notice of documents presumed by law to have been acquired by a person whether or not they have actually examined them. It can be accomplished by recording a deed or taking possession of the property.* Any recorded notice that can be obtained from the county recorder's office can be considered constructive notice (and therefore public knowledge).

**ACTUAL NOTICE** *is knowing (or one's responsibility for knowing) that a transaction has taken place.* If you have found, for example, that someone other than the owner is living in a house you are buying, you should have been aware of the existence of a signed lease. This is actual notice, whereas public records are representative of constructive notice. The act of taking possession (holding an unrecorded deed) gives constructive notice.

The recording process is a privilege rather than a legal requirement. **Some documents have to be recorded to be valid. These include mechanic's liens and declarations of homestead.** You may record an acknowledged instrument at any time. However, failure to utilize the privilege of recording at the earliest possible date can result in a question of legal or rightful title.

*If the same property is sold to more than one party, the individual who has given constructive notice first (by possession or recordation) will usually be recognized as the rightful owner.*

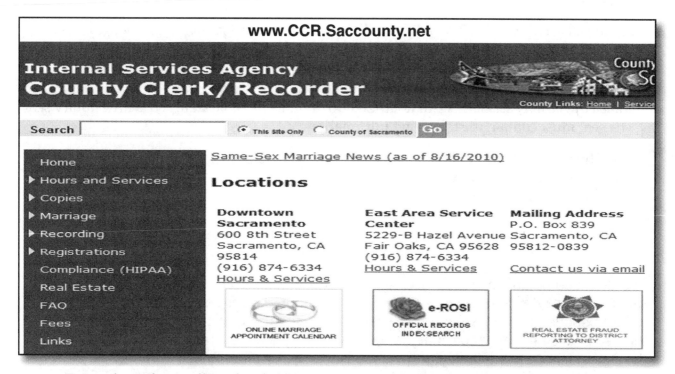

**Example:** When selling his home to John, Bert negotiated a leaseback arrangement in order to continue renting and occupying the property for the next two years. John immediately placed the unrecorded grant deed into a safe deposit box for ultimate security. Two days later, Bert "sold" the home a second time to Julie, who promptly recorded her deed. Julie is the likely owner of the property by virtue of recording her deed first.

In order to establish priority, the documents affecting real property must be recorded by the county recorder in the county where the property is located. If the property is located in two counties, the documents should be recorded in both counties.

## B. PRIORITY OF RECORDING

Under the recording system in California, "The first in time is the first in right." If an owner sells his or her house twice, the first deed recorded usually is considered the valid deed. This person must not have knowledge of the rights of the other party. This is the reward granted in California for recording any real estate transaction. However, there are four exceptions to the rule, including:

1. Government liens, property taxes, and special assessments.
2. Actual or constructive notice of another person's prior rights.
3. Mechanic's liens.
4. Agreements to the contrary.

## C. ACKNOWLEDGMENT (or Notary)

All documents must be acknowledged before they are recorded by the county recorder. *ACKNOWLEDGMENT refers to a signed or verbal statement by the named person that he/she has signed that document of his/her own free will. In other words, that person "acknowledges" his or her signature.* This acknowledgment must be performed in the presence of a witness, usually a notary public, authorized by law to witness acknowledgments.

A **NOTARY PUBLIC** *is a person who is authorized by the Secretary of State to witness the acknowledgment of documents.* All notarized documents must be stamped with a notary seal. The seal must contain the following information:

    1. The word "Notary Public"
    2. The name of the county
    3. The name of the notary
    4. The state seal
    5. The expiration date

In order to be notarized, any person signing a **grant deed**, **quitclaim deed**, or **trust deed** is required to place a right thumb print on the notary's sequential journal. This is because of a high rate of fraud by the use of false deeds. Additionally, a notary must immediately notify the Secretary of State if the notary's sequential journal is stolen, lost, misplaced, destroyed, damaged or otherwise rendered unusable.

*A deed does NOT have to be acknowledged to be valid, but must be acknowledged to be recorded.*

**VERIFICATION** *is an oath or affirmation made before a notary public that the content of an instrument is true.* Notices of completion, nonresponsibility, and the statements used in filing a mechanic's lien are among instruments that must be verified rather than simply acknowledged.

An **AFFIRMATION** *is a solemn and legally binding declaration made under penalty of perjury by a person whose religious or other beliefs prohibit the taking of an oath.*

An **AFFIDAVIT** *is a verified written statement of facts.*

*A notary public does NOT acknowledge a document, but "witnesses" an acknowledgment.*

## D. DO NOT GIVE LEGAL ADVICE

A real estate salesperson or broker may not give legal advice, because the law is a highly complex and specialized profession that requires years of preparation and training. In the state of California, only a licensed attorney who is a member of the State Bar is allowed to practice law. A broker cannot give legal advice, unless he or she is also an attorney.

It is illegal for an agent, except an attorney, to draw up legal documents. For this reason, real estate brokers use preprinted fill-in forms. These standard forms are drawn up by licensed attorneys who are familiar with the legalities involved in contracts.

## V. CHAPTER SUMMARY

An **estate** is an interest, share, right or equity in real estate, and can be either **freehold** (real property) or **less-than-freehold** (personal property). Freehold estates include fee simple estates or life estates.

A **fee simple** (or estate in fee) is the most complete form of ownership as it is of indefinite duration, freely transferable, and inheritable. If a **condition precedent** (before) or **condition subsequent** (future) **condition** is attached to a property's use, it is a **fee simple defeasible estate**.

A **life estate** is a freehold estate with a limited duration based upon someone's lifetime, with the property reverting back to the original owner (who holds an **estate in reversion**) upon the death of the life estate holder. If someone other than the owner is to receive title, that person is said to hold an **estate in remainder**.

A property owner may reserve a life estate for the duration of his or her lifetime. Although the estate is deeded to a designated party, he or she doesn't take possession until the death of the owner.

A **lease** or **rental agreement** is a less-than-freehold estate, where the tenant is given rights to use the real property for a period of time. It's personal property because no real ownership exists. An **estate for years** is a lease for a fixed period of time, agreed to in advance. Other less-than-freehold estates include **estates from period-to-period**, **estates at will**, and **estates at sufferance**.

Property can be sold or transferred by: 1) **deed** (grant deed transfers title); 2) **will** (witnessed or holographic); 3) **probate** (after death through the courts); 4) **intestate succession** (no will, divided among family or state); 5) **accession** (land increases through natural causes); 6) **occupancy** (**abandonment**, **adverse possession**, and **prescription**); and 7) **dedication** (gift to public).

A **grant deed** is a document that transfers title (evidence of the right to possess property). The method of holding title concurrently or in severalty is called **vesting**. The methods of tenancy include **severalty**, **tenants in common**, **joint tenancy**, **tenancy in partnership**, **community property**, and **community property with right of survivorship**.

Although **severalty** means separate ownership, title can be held by an individual or a corporation. When two or more people own property concurrently, it is called a **tenancy in common**, and it, too, can be willed or sold (although there are no survivorship or community property rights).

If there is the right of survivorship it is called **joint tenancy**, and that title cannot be willed. The four unities for joint tenancy are: 1) **title**, 2) **time**, 3) **interest**, and 4) **possession** (**Remember: "T-TIP"**).

TM

---

**Tenancy in partnership** refers to two or more people who are co-owners in a business, and can be a **general partnership** (losses and management duties shared) or **limited partnership** (losses limited and no management duties).

**Community property** refers to all the property acquired by a husband and wife during their marriage, and it can be willed, but if no heir exists, it goes to the remaining spouse. **Community property with right of survivorship** allows the property to pass to the surviving spouse without probate administration, and the property will receive a full step-up basis, which means no capital gains tax to the surviving spouse if the property is sold.

All deeds should be **acknowledged** in the presence of a notary public and recorded with the county. **Generally, the deed recorded first has priority over any that follow.**

---

## VI. TERMINOLOGY

**A.** Abandonment
**B.** Accession
**C.** Actual Notice
**D.** Adverse Possession
**E.** Affirmation, Affidavit, Verification
**F.** Community Property
**G.** Condition Precedent
**H.** Condition Subsequent
**I.** Constructive Notice
**J.** Corporation

**K.** Dedication
**L.** Delivery
**M.** Encroachment
**N.** Escheat
**O.** Freehold Estate
**P.** General and Limited Partnerships
**Q.** Grant Deed
**R.** Holographic Will
**S.** Intestate Succession
**T.** Joint Tenancy

**U.** Life Estate
**V.** Notary Public
**W.** Prescription
**X.** Probate
**Y.** Quitclaim Deed
**Z.** Recording
**AA.** Remainder
**BB.** Reversion
**CC.** Severalty
**DD.** Tenancy in Common
**EE.** Witnessed Will

1.____ The giving of private land by its owner for a public use; most commonly, the developer who gives it to a city.

2.____ The reverting of private property to the state when there are no valid heirs.

3.____ A voluntary association between two or more people to carry on a business with general and limited partners.

4.____ A deed using the word "grant," or like words, containing warranties against prior conveyances and encumbrances. This is the most commonly used deed in California.

5.____ An estate of indeterminable duration, e.g., fee simple or life estate.

6.____ Undivided ownership of a property interest by two or more persons, each of whom has a right to an equal share in the interest and a right of survivorship.

7.____ It is notice that is actually and expressly given or implied.

8.____ A person authorized by the state to witness the signatures of persons executing documents, sign the certificate and affix the official seal.

9.____ An event that must happen before title is passed.

10.____ Documents filed with the County Recorder in such a way as are considered open notice to the world.

11.____ Co-ownership of property by two or more persons who hold undivided interest, without right of survivorship. The interests need not be equal.

12.____An unlawful intrusion onto another's property by making improvements to real property, e.g., a swimming pool built across a property line.

13.____A legal entity, sanctioned by the state, with rights and liabilities, distinct and apart from those of the persons composing it.

14.____The intentional and voluntary relinquishment of any ownership interest (such as an easement) or possession of real property.

15.____The means of acquiring interests in land, usually an easement, by continued use.

16.____A condition attached to an estate whereby the estate is defeated or changed through the failure or non-performance of the condition.

17.____A process of law by which the state lays out the correct succession of inheritance when a person dies without leaving a valid will.

18.____Many different types of statements made before a professional witness.

19.____An estate that reverts back to the grantor after the life of the tenant expires.

20.____The court procedure of proving that a will is valid.

21.____A method of acquiring title to real property, through possession of the property for a statutory period under certain conditions, by a person other than the owner.

22.____A deed to relinquish any interest in property, that the grantor may have, without any warranty of title or interest.

23.____An estate that is transferred to a third party (anyone other than the grantor) upon the death of the life estate holder.

24.____A formal expression of a person's desires, witnessed by others, as to the disposition of his or her property after death.

25.____Property acquired by husband and/or wife during marriage that is not acquired as separate property. Each spouse has equal rights of management, alienation and disposition.

26.____An estate of a single entity held by a single person alone.

27.____An estate or interest in real property that is held for the duration of the life of some certain person. It may be the person holding title to the estate or some other person.

28.____A handwritten expression of a person's desires as to the disposition of their property after death.

29.____Placing a document in the official records of the county.

30.____The act of receiving a deed.

31.____The acquiring of additional property.

# CHAPTER 2

## VII. CHAPTER QUIZ

1. Which of the following is a type of freehold estate?

    a. Probate estate
    b. Leasehold estate
    c. Estate in fee
    d. Estate in sufferance

2. Duke sold his property to Jane with the condition that Jane must never use it for any purpose other than as a private residence. However, after owning the property for several years, Jane decided to start a board and care facility for handicapped adults. What is the status of the estate?

    a. It may revert to Duke because it is a fee simple defeasible estate
    b. It may revert to Duke because it is a fee simple absolute estate
    c. Duke has no claim because his condition is unlawful
    d. Duke has no claim because the statute of limitations ran out on the condition

3. Which of the following is an example of a freehold estate?

    a. The interest created by a trust deed
    b. An estate at will
    c. A life estate
    d. A leasehold estate

4. A seven-year lease would be considered:

    a. an estate for years.
    b. personal property.
    c. chattel real.
    d. all of the above.

5. A tenancy at sufferance would occur when:

    a. a tenant remains in the property after the end of an estate for years and continues to pay rent.
    b. a tenant remains in the property after expiration of a lease without the owner's consent.
    c. a landlord who delivers a 30-day notice to vacate the premises cannot find the tenant.
    d. a landlord cannot obtain a writ of execution from the courts.

6. The owner of property adjacent to the water flow can acquire title to additional land by:

    a. avulsion.
    b. alluvium.
    c. percolation.
    d. accession.

7. Dick and Jane, brother and sister, own an apartment building in joint tenancy. Dick needs $10,000 to cover unexpected medical expenses, so he borrows the money from a lender and signs a trust deed on the property that was soon recorded in the public records. Forty-five days later, Dick dies. Which of the following is most correct?

    a. Jane is now responsible for the entire $10,000.
    b. Jane is now responsible for $5,000.
    c. Jane now owns the apartment building free and clear of her brother's $10,000 debt.
    d. If the loan is not repaid, the lender can foreclose only on Dick's 1/2 interest in the property.

8. Which of the following is needed to transfer property deeded "Mary Smith, a married woman"?

    a. Husband's signature only
    b. Wife's signature only
    c. Both husband and wife's signature
    d. Husband's signature only, if the wife gives verbal consent

9. If a real estate agent advises a buyer how to take title to real property, he/she may be liable for:

    a. practicing law.
    b. giving tax advice.
    c. discrimination.
    d. all of the above.

10. When selling his home to John, Bert negotiated a leaseback arrangement in order to continue renting and occupying the property for the next two years. John immediately placed the unrecorded grant deed into a safe deposit box for ultimate security. Two days later, Bert "sold" the home a second time to Julie who promptly recorded her deed. Which of the following is most correct?

    a. John is the rightful owner of the home provided he can produce this first deed to the property.
    b. Julie is the likely owner of the property because she recorded her deed first.
    c. Bert still owns the home until he vacates.
    d. The title company will decide who is the rightful owner of the property.

*ANSWERS: 1. c; 2. a; 3. c; 4. d; 5. b; 6. d; 7. c; 8. c; 9. d; 10. b*

THE GREAT SEAL OF THE STATE OF

# CHAPTER 3
# *Encumbrances*

## I. Encumbrances – An Overview

The term encumbrance is usually new to the beginner in real estate. An **ENCUMBRANCE** *is a right or interest in real property other than an ownership or tenancy interest*. It is a burden to the property that limits its use and may lessen its value. The two main types of encumbrances, shown in **Figure 3-1** and **Figure 3-3**, are: (1) liens and (2) items that affect the physical condition or use of the property.

**Figure 3-1**

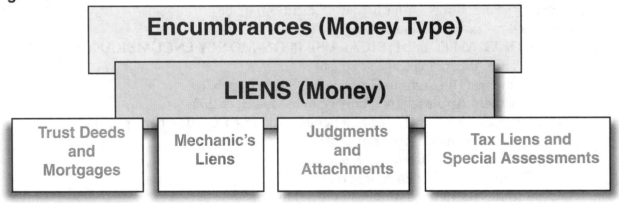

*All liens are encumbrances but NOT all encumbrances are liens.*

When an owner encumbers more than one lot under a single lien, that owner has created a blanket encumbrance. A *BLANKET ENCUMBRANCE/BLANKET TRUST DEED is a voluntary lien (for money owed) placed over more than one parcel*. A *RELEASE CLAUSE releases portions of the property*.

## II. Liens (Money Owed)

A *LIEN is a document that uses a property to secure the payment of a debt or the discharge of an obligation*. It is money owed for one reason or another on a property. Liens include trust deeds or mortgages, tax liens, special assessments, mechanic's liens, judgments, and attachments.

# CHAPTER 3

Liens are either:

1. voluntary or
2. involuntary; and
3. specific or
4. general

## A. VOLUNTARY AND INVOLUNTARY LIENS

*VOLUNTARY LIENS are money debts that an owner agrees to pay.* A lien is created when the buyer takes out a loan to finance the purchase of real estate. He or she voluntarily agrees to allow liens to be placed on the property.

*A voluntary lien does NOT have to be recorded.*

*INVOLUNTARY LIENS are money obligations that create a burden on a property by government taxes or legal action because of unpaid bills.* Both involuntary liens and voluntary liens must be paid, or assumed, in full before the owner can sell or refinance the property.

## B. SPECIFIC AND GENERAL LIENS

*SPECIFIC LIENS are liens against just one property.* Property taxes assessed against real property automatically become a specific lien on only that property on **January 1** of each year.

*GENERAL LIENS are liens on all the properties of the owner, not just one.* Federal or state income taxes and judgment liens can become a general lien on all your real property.

## C. TRUST DEED/DEED OF TRUST (Security Device – Voluntary and Specific)

A *TRUST DEED (Deed of Trust) is a written instrument that makes real property collateral for a loan.* The evidence of debt is created by the promissory note that accompanies the trust deed. The trust deed pledges (hypothecates) the property as collateral, or security, for the note. In California, the trust deed is the usual security device for real property. In eastern states, the mortgage is the typical financing instrument. See Chapter 8 for details on trust deeds.

*A promissory note (which accompanies the trust deed) is evidence of the debt. Trust deeds and mortgages are personal property.*

## D. MORTGAGE (Security Device – Voluntary and Specific)

A *MORTGAGE is a lien that secures real property for the payment of a promissory note (debt).* Mortgages are rarely employed in financing California homes, but because of their wide use in other states, they are emphasized in the real estate licensing examination. In California many people use the term "mortgage" to mean a property loan, but they usually are talking about trust deeds. Therefore, it is essential to understand the difference between mortgages and trust deeds since almost every property transfer in California is financed through a trust deed. Details on mortgages are discussed further in Chapter 8.

## E. MECHANIC'S LIENS (Involuntary and Specific)

*MECHANIC'S LIENS are liens that may be filed against a property by a person who was not paid after furnishing labor or materials for construction work on that property.* The form used to enforce a mechanic's lien action must be recorded to be valid. A mechanic's lien is a lien against the property itself. The property cannot be transferred until the obligation is paid and the title cleared. This gives a subcontractor, craftsman or general contractor, employed by an owner, the right to protect his or her interest. The same right applies to material suppliers who furnish such items as lumber, plumbing or roofing supplies. To determine the start time, the mechanic's lien dates back to the commencement of the project.

*A mechanic's lien is filed against a property and must be recorded to be valid.*

### 1. Preliminary Notice

A **PRELIMINARY NOTICE** *is a written notice that must be given before filing a mechanic's lien and within 20 days of supplying labor or services.* This notice must be given, either by mail or in person, to the owner, general contractor and the lender. The notice must contain a general description of the labor or materials furnished, who supplied them and the person who contracted for these services. Failure to give the preliminary notice within 20 days does not restrict a supplier's right to file, but he or she may have allowed other claimants to file before him or her, which gives those claimants priority. As a matter of good practice, most suppliers include a preliminary notice as part of the original contract.

*If a contractor files a mechanic's lien, it takes priority over all other liens except taxes, special assessments, and trust deeds filed prior to the "start of work."*

### 2. Determining the Start Time for Mechanic's Liens

An important determination when considering a mechanic's lien is the **date that work started on the property**. Mechanic's liens, once recorded, might have priority over all other liens, except property taxes, special assessments, and trust deeds. To lenders, this is critical because lenders want their trust deeds recorded before any work starts. Before they will lend money, lenders will conduct a physical inspection of the property to make sure no construction has started.

*A mechanic's lien dates back to the time work began on the project.*

*A mechanic's lien (labor or materials) dates back to the beginning (commencement) of work on the project. This is known as the* **SCHEME OF IMPROVEMENTS.**

### 3. Notice of Completion and Notice of Cessation (Limits Time to File)

A **"Notice of Completion"** (see **Figure 3-2**), in order to be valid, should be recorded by the owner within 10 days of completion, thereby limiting the general contractor to **60 days** to file a claim and subcontractors to **30 days**. This gives everyone constructive notice. Completion technically occurs when the owner accepts the finished work of the contractor, but in some instances, the job is never completed. **Guidelines have been set up by the state to allow suppliers of services and materials a filing period of up to 90 days if the owner doesn't file a valid notice of completion.** If one of these four alternatives occurs, the work is considered to be complete:

1. Occupation or use by owner after cessation of labor.
2. Acceptance of work improvements by owner.

## Figure 3-2

RECORDING REQUESTED BY

AND WHEN RECORDED MAIL TO:

Name

Street
Address

City &
State

| S | R | U | PAGE | SIZE | DA | MISC | LONG | RFD | COPY |
|---|---|---|------|------|-----|------|------|------|------|
| | | | | | | | | | |
| M | A | L | 465 | 426 | PCOR | NCOR | SMF | NCHG | EXAM |
| | | | | | | T: | CTY | UNI | |

SPACE ABOVE THIS LINE FOR RECORDER'S USE ONLY

### NOTICE OF COMPLETION

Notice is hereby given that:

1.  The undersigned is owner or corporate officer of the owner of the interest or estate stated below in the property hereinafter described:

2.  The full name of the owner is _____

3.  The full address of the owner is _____

4.  The nature of the interest or estate of the owner is in fee.

    *(If other than fee, strike "in Fee" and insert, for example, "purchaser under contract of purchase," or "lessee")*

5.  The full names and full addresses of all persons, if any, who hold title with the undersigned as joint tenants or as tenants in common are:

    NAMES                    ADDRESSES

6.  A work of improvement on the property hereinafter described was completed on _____ . The work done was:

7.  The name of the contractor, if any, for such work of improvement was _____

    *(If no contractor for work of improvement as a whole, insert "none")*          *(Date of Contract)*

8.  The property on which said work of improvement was completed is in the city of _____ ,
    County of _____ , State of California, and is described as follows:_____

9.  The street address of said property is _____
    *(If no street address has been officially assigned, insert "none")*

Dated: _____

_____
Signature of owner of corporate officer of owner
named in paragraph 2 or his agent

### VERIFICATION

I, the undersigned, say: I am the _____ the declarant of the foregoing
*("President of," "Manager of," "A partner of," "Owner of," etc.)*

notice of completion; I have read said notice of completion and know the contents thereof; the same is true of my own knowledge.

I declare under penalty of perjury that the foregoing is true and correct.

Executed on _____ , 20 _____ , at _____ , California.
*(Date of signature)*                              *(City where signed)*

_____
*(Personal signature of the individual who is swearing that the contents of the notice of completion are true)*

3. A cessation of labor for 60 continuous days.

4. A cessation of labor for 30 continuous days if the owner files a "Notice of Cessation" with the county recorder's office.

*A "Completion Bond" may be required by a lender to ensure that an insurance company will complete the job if the contractor cannot.*

### 4. Filing Time (Limited)

The filing period is very important because the rights of a person filing a mechanic's lien are valid for only a short time. A suit can be filed later, but it would not automatically become a lien against the real property. A mechanic's lien may be filed any time after the preliminary notice and until 30 days after completion, if you are a supplier or subcontractor, and 60 days after completion if you are the general contractor. **If there is no notice of completion recorded for the project, all parties (unpaid creditors) have 90 days after completion of the job to file**.

*Filing time = 30 days (subcontractor), 60 days (general contractor), and 90 days (all parties, if no notice of completion).*

### 5. Notice of Non-Responsibility (Must be Recorded and Posted)

An owner may file a notice of non-responsibility within 10 days of discovering that an unauthorized person is performing construction service on his or her property. A recorded and verified *NOTICE OF NON-RESPONSIBILITY is posted on the property stating that the owner is not responsible for the work being done.* This action releases an owner from any liability caused by the unauthorized activity and prevents suppliers from filing a valid mechanic's lien. If a tenant is installing carpet in your apartment without your authorization, filing a notice of non-responsibility with the county recorder's office protects you against the claims of the carpet supplier.

## F. TAX LIENS (Specific or General Liens)

If any government tax is not paid, it may become a lien, through law or a court action, on real property. If the lien is not settled, the property can be sold to pay back-taxes. Tax liens are either: (1) specific liens or (2) general liens.

*The difference between property taxes and special assessments is that special assessments are levied for the cost of specific local improvements, while property tax revenue goes into the general fund.*

## G. SPECIAL ASSESSMENTS

*Local improvements are paid by the property owners in a given district through SPECIAL ASSESSMENTS.* Improvements such as streets, sewers, street lighting and irrigation projects are generally paid for by the property owners who have benefited from the work. If these assessments are not paid, they become a lien against the property. Most special assessments are 10-to-30-year bonds. This allows the property owner a reasonable amount of time to pay them off. The property can be transferred without the assessment being paid. It is best that buyer and seller agree that the buyer will assume the assessment.

*Developers finance roads, schools, and other off-site improvements with "Mello-Roos Bonds," which become a special tax levied against homeowners. Sellers must disclose if their property is subject to a Mello-Roos lien.*

## H. JUDGMENTS (Involuntary and General Liens)

A *JUDGMENT is a court decision determining the rights of the parties involved and the amount of compensation. A judgment can be appealed, and is good for ten years.*

For a judgment to become a lien, an *ABSTRACT OF JUDGMENT, or formal filing of the judgment,* must be recorded. The judgment then becomes a lien upon all nonexempt property of the debtor. It also becomes a lien on all future property he or she later acquires until the lien is paid. A judgment lien is good for ten years. So, if any property is transferred within this ten year period, the lien must first be paid off. Under additional court action, the judgment holder may be able to force the debtor to sell the real property to pay off the lien.

### 1. Small Claims Court ($7,500 Limit)

At this point, it is important that you understand the use of the Small Claims Court. Anyone can take someone else to court regarding civil cases for a $6 filing fee plus the fee for serving the subpoena. Neither party is allowed to be represented in the courtroom by legal counsel. The current maximum amount of a judgment is $7,500. This limit will be adjusted periodically by the state legislature to meet inflationary trends. Night court is also available in some districts, making this process even more accessible. You should be aware, however, that for a plaintiff, the judge's decision in a small claims action is final. The defendant, though, has the right of appeal. This is an excellent way to settle a dispute with a minimal amount of time and expense.

## I. TERMINATION OF JUDGMENT LIEN

Most judgment liens are terminated by the satisfaction of the judgment. A *JUDGMENT IS SATISFIED by the payment of money or the return of property.* A notice that the judgment has been satisfied should be filed with the clerk of the court. It clears the lien from the record. Sometimes certain properties may be released from the judgment, but only with the judgment holder's consent. This partial release enables an owner to sell a property to satisfy a part of the judgment. A judgment may also be terminated if a bond is posted or if the judge grants a new trial.

## J. ATTACHMENT (Court-Seized Property)

*ATTACHMENT (LIEN) is a process of the law that creates a lien. It gives custody of real or personal property to the court to assure payment of a pending lawsuit in that county.* This is to assure that there will be enough property to satisfy the judgment should the plaintiff prevail. The *PLAINTIFF is the person filing a court action to obtain an attachment lien.* The *DEFENDANT is the person who is being sued.* During an unlawful detainer action for collection of past due rents, for instance, it may be advantageous for a plaintiff to obtain an attachment against the defendant. This type of lien is good for three years, and is extended only if the plaintiff wins the court case. Use of the attachment lien is not very common because there are many rules and formalities involved in obtaining this type of lien. This is another area that requires the help of an attorney.

*An attachment is a prejudgment process that creates a lien, good for three years, which does NOT terminate on the death of the property owner.*

### K. LIS PENDENS ("Lawsuit Pending")

**LIS PENDENS** *is the recording of a notice with the county recorder's office warning all persons that a certain type of lawsuit is pending concerning a particular property.* Attorneys often file a lis pendens before a court date is set in order to stop the transfer of the property. A lis pendens places a cloud on the title, and is effective when filed. The property is not marketable until the lis pendens is removed.

*A lis pendens is notice of a pending lawsuit that may affect (cloud) title to real property based on the lawsuit outcome. It remains on the public record (is effective) until the lis pendens is removed, the action is dismissed, or final judgment is rendered.*

### L. SHERIFF'S SALE (Court Order to Sell – Execution)

A **WRIT OF EXECUTION** *(sale) is a court order requiring the sale of certain property to satisfy a judgment.* The writ of execution extends the lien against the real property for one year. If the judgment has already been recorded as a lien on the property, the writ of execution will not create a new lien. The county sheriff, or other local officials, are then ordered to secure and sell the real or personal property to satisfy the lien.

If a person refuses to pay off the judgment, the sheriff's sale is the next step. A **SHERIFF'S SALE** *is the forced sale of a debtor's property to satisfy a judgment under a writ of execution.* In California, the sheriff's sale is the usual method of forcing the sale of property to pay off a judgment.

Mechanic's liens and any previously recorded judgments have priority over paying the expenses of the sale. If these expenses are paid, a first trust deed is next to be satisfied. Any amount left over is applied toward a second trust deed and any subsequent liens, in the order of their recording, until the proceeds are exhausted.

### M. INJUNCTION (Court Order to Stop)

An **INJUNCTION** *is a court order which can restrict a party from doing an act such as violating private deed restrictions.*

**Example:** Mr. Crawford has been burning rubbish on his own property. The neighbors have complained and have secured a court order, ordering Mr. Crawford to stop the offending practice. The court order is called an injunction.

## III. Items That Affect Physical Use (Non-Money Encumbrances)

### A. ITEMS THAT AFFECT PHYSICAL USE

**ITEMS THAT AFFECT PHYSICAL USE** *are non-money encumbrances that affect the physical use of real property.* They include: easements, building restrictions and zoning (such as setback requirements), and encroachments and leases, which are conditions that limit the physical use of the property (see **Figure 3-3**).

**Figure 3-3**

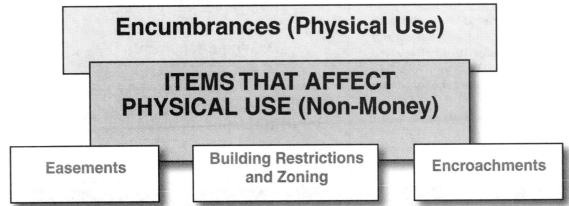

Some encumbrances affect the physical use of the property. They are:

1. Easements
2. Building Restrictions and Zoning
3. Encroachments
4. Leases (see Chapter 6)

### 1. Easements (The Right to Use Another's Land)

*An easement is the right to use another's land; it is an "interest," but NOT an estate. An easement is a non-money encumbrance, but NOT a lien.*

An *EASEMENT is an interest in land owned by another person consisting of the right to use or control the land, or an area above or below it, for a specific, limited purpose. The right to enter is called INGRESS and the right to exit is EGRESS.* Included in this definition is the right to profit from the easement, such as the right to take minerals, oil and gas.

Easements are of two types: (1) easements appurtenant and (2) easements in gross.

#### a. Easement Appurtenant (Runs With the Land)

An *EASEMENT APPURTENANT is an easement "created for and beneficial to" the owner of adjoining or attached lands.* An easement is real property, not personal property, but it is not an estate. In this case there are two parcels of land, with one owner giving another owner an easement. The *DOMINANT TENEMENT is the land that obtains the benefits of an easement.* **Figure 3-4** is an illustration of a driveway easement. Owner A's land is the dominant tenement and Owner B's land is the servient tenement.

*The owner of the servient tenement CANNOT terminate the easement; it must "serve" the dominant tenement.*

**Example:** Able has leased Blackacre for a ten-year term. Baker owns Whiteacre, which is adjacent to Blackacre. Baker requests an easement over Blackacre from Able. Able, the tenant, can legally grant such a right for an indefinite period. A lessee can grant an easement over leased property, but only for the term of the lease. After the lease expires, the easement is no longer valid.

**Figure 3-4**

Property owner B owns the land the easement crosses but cannot block or hinder in any way the right of property owner A to use the driveway for access to his property.

A **SERVIENT TENEMENT** *is the land that gives the easement (use of the land) for the benefit of another.* The appurtenant easement belongs to the land and is transferred with the land. This easement cannot be transferred separately from the land.

*The dominant tenement and the servient tenement do NOT need to physically abut (touch) each other.*

### b. Easement in Gross (Does Not Benefit Adjoining Landowner)

An example of an easement in gross would be an easement for the telephone company (utility company) to enter the property to run telephone lines.

*An "appurtenant easement" goes with the land, whereas an "easement in gross" goes to a person.*

An **EASEMENT IN GROSS** *is not attached to any particular land or dominant tenement. It is an easement created for the benefit of others who do not own adjoining or attached lands. It is a personal property right.* Even though it is a personal right, it is still a servient tenement. An example of an easement in gross would be a utility company or person obtaining the right to run natural gas lines across your land. In this instance your land would become a servient tenement.

**Example:** Landowner Jacobs granted the telephone company the right to erect telephone poles on his land. This easement in gross is an **encumbrance**.

Other not-so-common easements are: rights to take water, wood or minerals; rights to transact business or conduct sports upon the land; rights to receive light, air or heat from the land, and the right to use a wall as a common party wall.

An easement that does not specify a special area for a right-of-way is also valid. *A property owner could give the right to cross his or her land and not limit how or where a person would have to cross. This is known as an **UNLOCATED EASEMENT**.*

*A "license" is permission to use another's property for a certain purpose and period of time. Unlike an easement in gross, it can be revoked at any time.*

### c. Creation of an Easement

Easements are created in three basic ways:

1. Express Grant (in writing)
2. Implication of Law (implied easement)
3. Long Use (prescription)

**1. EXPRESS GRANT (IN WRITING), AS IN A DEED OR CONTRACT.** If a property is transferred as part of the deed, an easement appurtenant to the land would be included in the grant. The same thing is accomplished by transferring a property, but **reserving an easement** over the land. A written contract can create an easement between the parties. For legal protection, this contract should be acknowledged and recorded.

> **Example:** Daniel, who owned two pieces of adjacent land, sold one of them to Charles, reserving an easement for himself at the time. Daniel soon left the state for 21 years, during which time he did not use the easement. When Daniel finally returned to the state, he discovered that the easement was still valid and enforceable.

**2. IMPLICATION OF LAW (IMPLIED EASEMENT).** If an easement is implied in a transfer, or if it is necessary for use of the land, then the easement is said to be implied by law. The right to use the land for obtaining minerals implies that you have the right of surface entry in order to extract the minerals.

*EASEMENT BY NECESSITY (LANDLOCKED) is an easement granted by the court if it is absolutely necessary for access.* If a person is sold property that landlocks that person, he or she may acquire an easement by necessity. When the grantor transfers a portion of his or her land that leaves the grantee totally surrounded by the grantor (transferor), the grantor can be forced to give a necessity easement of access to the grantee. An easement by necessity does not have to be the most convenient way of entering the property. If the grantee later acquires another access to his or her property, the easement by necessity is then terminated.

**3. LONG USE (EASEMENT BY PRESCRIPTION).** *PRESCRIPTION is an easement to continue using land by virtue of having used it for a long period of time.*

Possession for five continuous years can create a prescriptive easement, as long as the use is:

1. Open and notorious;
2. Uninterrupted for five years;
3. Under a claim of right or color of title, and
4. Hostile (without permission of the owner).

An easement obtained by prescription can be terminated if not used for five years.

### d. Transfer of an Easement

Easements are transferred automatically if they are easements appurtenant. Easements in gross can be transferred only by express agreement, providing the easement is not made to a specific individual. An easement should be recorded. If it is not recorded, and the purchaser does not have knowledge of an easement, then the easement may not be considered to have been transferred with the property.

### e. Termination of an Easement

Easements may be terminated in several ways:

**1. EXPRESS RELEASE** – Any written agreement can terminate an easement, but the usual form is a quitclaim deed or release.

*Only the owner of the dominant tenement can release (terminate) an easement, usually by recording a quitclaim deed.*

**2. MERGER OF DOMINANT AND SERVIENT TENEMENTS** – An easement is automatically terminated when the dominant and servient tenements merge into a common, or single, ownership. The easement can be created again if any part of the property is later transferred to a "separate owner."

**3. EXCESSIVE USE** – The courts have held that excessive use of an easement that increases the burden on the servient tenement may be forfeited through a court injunction. If the dominant tenement refuses to correct the excessive use, and misuses of the easement can be established, the easement can be terminated. An example would be a dominant tenement owner allowing the entire neighborhood to use the easement as a through-street.

**4. ABANDONMENT AND NON-USE** – If there is an obvious intent of an easement holder to abandon his or her easement, then that person may lose the easement through court action. In this way, an easement gained through prescription may be extinguished if non-use exists for a period of five continuous years.

*Non-use can only terminate an easement created by prescription.*

**5. DESTRUCTION OF SERVIENT TENEMENT** – When a governing body, by exercising the right of eminent domain, takes servient tenement property for its own use, the dominant tenement easement is considered automatically terminated.

## 2. Building Restrictions (Public and Private)

*PRIVATE DEED RESTRICTIONS limit the use or occupancy of the land.* A typical restriction limits the types of buildings on a given piece of land to single family residences. Also, a restriction might require future construction to meet specific standards. For example, all houses erected on a property must be at least 5,000 square feet.

There are three types of private building restrictions: Covenants, Conditions, and Restrictions (CC&Rs). They are usually included in the deed at the time the property is subdivided, or may be created by a written contract and are listed in the recorded "Declaration of Restrictions." Their main purpose is to keep use of the land uniform throughout certain tracts of land. Subdivisions and condominiums usually include deed restrictions as a method to promote the aesthetics and economics of the project. These private deed restrictions and bylaws are usually recorded separately, and are only referenced in the original grant deeds.

*Private restrictions on the use of land may be created by private land use controls, written agreement, or a developer's general plan restrictions for a subdivision.*

### a. Covenants (Promise Broken, Sue for Damages)

A *COVENANT is a promise to do or not to do a certain thing*. For instance, a property could sell with a covenant stating that the property shall never be used to sell alcoholic beverages. If the covenant is broken, the usual court remedy would be an action for money damages. A court may also grant an injunction requiring compliance with the covenant.

*Only SOME covenants "run with the land," but ALL conditions "run with the land."*

### b. Conditions (More Stringent Than Breaking a Covenant – Can Lose Title)

A *CONDITION is a future and uncertain event which must happen to create an obligation to extinguish an existing obligation.* **The penalty for not following the set conditions is the reversion of the property to the grantor.** This penalty is so stiff that most courts will treat a condition as a covenant unless the terms are clearly stated in the deed or other contract. For a complete discussion of conditions, refer back to Chapter 2.

*A condominium's CC&Rs may prohibit "for sale" signs, but an owner may place a reasonably sized "for sale" sign on the property.*

If a condominium owner breaches a "condition" in the CC&Rs, this would be more stringent than breaching a covenant.

*With regard to CC&Rs, violating a condition can result in loss of title to property, which is more stringent than breaching a covenant.*

### c. Public/Governmental Restrictions (Zoning)

*PUBLIC RESTRICTIONS are limits made by governmental agencies, usually by cities and counties, in the form of zoning.*

*"Public restrictions" promote health, safety, morals, and general welfare of the public. This is the use of "police power."*

**Private restrictions** are made by the present or previous landowners and are created only for their benefit. On the other hand, **zoning restrictions** are created by and for the benefit of the general public to insure its health, safety, comfort, and morals.

*ZONING is the restriction on the use of private property by the local government agency.* Zoning dictates how the property can be used, the **setbacks required,** and the height limit on any structures.

*If public restrictions (zoning) and private restrictions (CC&Rs) differ, the more stringent or rigid will apply.*

> For example, if a developer sets a deed restriction of **at least** 15,000 square feet to a lot, but zoning only allows 10,000 square feet per lot, the deed restriction is more restrictive and would prevail. This area is covered in depth in Chapter 12 under "Government Control."

### d. Race Restrictions (Illegal)

> In 1961, the California State Legislature enacted a law that voided all restrictions as to race. Any race deed restriction before that law or after that law is now void. It is illegal to restrict the right of an individual to sell, rent, lease, use or otherwise occupy a property because of race or membership in a certain ethnic group.

*Race restrictions on a property by a grantor (past or present) are unenforceable and illegal. The courts can remove race restrictions from a deed.*

### 3. Encroachments (Three Years to Act)

> As stated earlier, an *ENCROACHMENT is the wrongful, unauthorized placement of improvements or permanent fixtures on property by a nonowner of that property.* You must pursue the right to have an encroachment removed within three years or lose your right. If someone encroaches on your property, he or she is limiting the use of your property.

> **Example:** If your neighbor builds a driveway over your property, it is considered an encroachment, which is a form of "trespass." You have three years to sue your neighbor to have the encroachment removed.

> Often fences, walls, or buildings may extend over the recognized boundary line. The encroaching party may possibly gain legal title to the property through adverse possession, or legal use through an easement by prescription, if there is legal justification. In any event, an encroachment may legally limit the use of your property.

## IV. Homesteading Your Residence (Protects Against Judgment Liens)

*A lease is an encumbrance and a homestead is NOT considered an encumbrance.*

Although a homestead **is not an encumbrance**, it is appropriately discussed at this point. A *HOMESTEAD is a special provision of the California law that allows homeowners to protect their homes from forced sale to satisfy their debts, within certain limits.* There are two types of homesteads: (1) Head of the household and (2) Federal Homestead Act of 1862, whereby the government encouraged settlements (gave land free to those who made certain improvements—this is not discussed here). It is basic to our society that a homeowner should have some protection against losing his or her home because of debts. A homestead consists of the house and adjoining dwellings in which the owner resides. This can include condominiums, farm and life estates.

A homestead cannot include "unimproved" land such as vacant lots or a residence under construction.

## A. DECLARATION OF HOMESTEAD

*The first $75,000 of a home's value may NOT be used to satisfy a judgment against a head of household.*

A **DECLARATION OF HOMESTEAD** *is the recorded document that protects a homeowner from foreclosure by certain judgment creditors* (see **Figure 3-5**). This protects individuals for $75,000, couples for $100,000, and seniors (over 65), disabled or over 55 with limited income, for $175,000. If the equity exceeds the exemption, the home may be sold to satisfy creditors, but the exemption amount is protected for six months for reinvestment in another home.

*A homestead does NOT protect a homeowner against foreclosure on a trust deed, mechanic's lien, or lien filed prior to the filing of the homestead.*

In order for a declaration of homestead to be valid, there are certain requirements that must be met. Omissions of any one of these will make the homestead void. The requirements are:

1. A statement showing the claimant is the head of a family and stating the name of the spouse. "Head of family" may be anyone who lives in the home and provides for any relative living in the same house.

2. A statement that the claimant is residing on the premises and claims it as his or her homestead.

3. A description of the premises and an estimate of cash value.

4. It further provides that the declaration of homestead may need to contain a statement as to the character of the property; that no former declaration has been made and that it is within the limits prescribed by law.

The homeowner has time to file a declaration of homestead prior to court approval for a writ of execution. As part of the judicial process, the defendant must be informed of his or her right to file a declaration of homestead. This law, in effect, reduces the necessity of filing a homestead declaration until the homeowner is in financial trouble.

*A recorded homestead would have the least impact on property taxes.*

## B. TERMINATION OF HOMESTEAD

*The usual methods for termination of homestead are the sale of the property or the filing of a declaration of abandonment.*

A homestead may be terminated by a **DECLARATION OF ABANDONMENT**. The declaration of abandonment must be acknowledged and recorded by the involved parties. A sale or other conveyance of the property also terminates the homestead. The removal or destruction of the dwelling does not terminate the homestead. The reason for abandoning a homestead is to allow the homeowner the privilege of obtaining another homestead on a new residence.

**Figure 3-5**

RECORDING REQUESTED BY

AND WHEN RECORDED MAIL TO:

NAME

STREET
ADDRESS

CITY, STATE &
ZIP CODE

| S | R | U | PAGE | SIZE | DA | MISC | LONG | RFD | COPY |
|---|---|---|------|------|------|------|------|------|------|
| M | A | L | 465 | 426 | PCOR | NCOR | SMF | NCHG | EXAM |
| | | | | | T: | | CTY | UNI | |

SPACE ABOVE THIS LINE FOR RECORDER'S USE ONLY

# HOMESTEAD DECLARATION

I,_____,
(FULL NAME OF DECLARANT)

do hereby certify and declare as follows:

(1)  I hereby claim as a declared homestead the premises located in the City of _____

County of _____, State of _____ commonly known as

_____
(STREET ADDRESS)

and more particularly described as follows: [Give complete legal description]

(2)  I am the declared homestead owner of the above declared homestead.

(3)  I own the following interest in the above declared homestead:

(4)  The above declared homestead is [strike inapplicable clause]    my principal dwelling
       the principal dwelling of my spouse    and

[strike inapplicable clause]   I am / my spouse is   currently residing on that declared homestead.

(5)  The facts stated in this Declaration are true as of my personal knowledge.

Dated: _____, _____      _____
(SIGNATURE OF DECLARANT)

_____

STATE OF CALIFORNIA            }
COUNTY OF _____ }

On _____ before me, _____, personally appeared
(here insert name and title of the officer)

_____,
who proved to me on the basis of satisfactory evidence to be the person(s) whose name(s) is/are subscribed to the within instrument and acknowledged to me that he/she/they executed the same in his/her/their authorized capacity(ies), and that by his/her/their signature(s) on the instrument the person(s), or the entity upon behalf of which the person(s) acted, executed the instrument.

I certify under PENALTY OF PERJURY under the laws of the State of California that the foregoing paragraph is true and correct.

WITNESS my hand and official seal.           (SEAL)

SIGNATURE _____

Before you use this form, fill in all blanks, and make whatever changes are appropriate and necessary to your particular transaction. Consult a lawyer if you doubt the form's fitness for your purpose and use.

A homestead is terminated by 1) Declaration of Abandonment or 2) the sale of the homesteaded property.

While the typical homeowner need not file a declared homestead to enjoy basic homestead protection, homeowners who are in financial trouble, or who expect to be in financial trouble, probably should file a homestead declaration, just to be on the safe side.

---

## V. CHAPTER SUMMARY

An **encumbrance** is a burden to a property that limits its use by either 1) money owed (liens) or 2) items that affect the physical use of the property (non-money). All liens are "encumbrances," but not all encumbrances are liens. A **blanket encumbrance** is a voluntary lien placed over more than one property, and usually has a **release clause** for one or more of the parcels.

A **lien** is a document that uses a property to secure the payment of a debt or the discharge of an obligation. Liens are either 1) **voluntary** or 2) **involuntary**, and 3) **specific** or 4) **general**.

**Trust deeds** and **mortgages** (mortgages are rare in California) are security devices that make property security for a debt and are considered personal property. The accompanying **promissory note** is the evidence of the debt.

If the people who supply labor or materials for construction on a property are not paid, they can file a **mechanic's lien** against that individual property. It is a **specific and involuntary lien** and, once recorded, has priority over all other liens except taxes, special assessments, and trust deeds filed prior to the "start of work." Before filing a mechanic's lien, **Preliminary Notice** must be given (within 20 days of supplying labor or services).

It is important to establish the starting time and completion date of the work or materials supplied. A **Notice of Completion** should be recorded by the owner within ten days of completion, or a **Notice of Cessation** within 30 days of cessation of labor.

If a person is unauthorized to do construction on a property, an owner needs to file and post a **Notice of Non-Responsibility** on the property, releasing him or her from liability and preventing suppliers from filing a valid mechanic's lien.

Property taxes and mechanic's liens are **specific liens**, meaning liens against just one property, whereas income taxes and judgments are **general liens**, covering all the properties of an owner. A **judgment** is a **general and involuntary lien** against all real property in the county in which the judgment is recorded, and is good for ten years. A **satisfaction of judgment** is made by payment of money or return of property and clears the lien from the record.

An **attachment (lien)**, which is good for three years, creates a **specific and involuntary lien** on one property to assure payment of a pending lawsuit. A **lis pendens** is a notice of a pending lawsuit that affects (**clouds**) title and remains on the public record until the lis pendens is removed, the action is dismissed, or final judgment is rendered. If a person does not pay off a judgment, he or she may be forced to sell the property in a **sheriff's sale** under a court order called a **Writ of Execution**.

Items that affect **physical use** of a property are **non-money encumbrances** and include: 1) **easements**, 2) **restrictions**, 3) **encroachments**, and 4) **leases**.

An **easement** is the right to enter, use and exit another person's land for certain purpose. If it runs with the land it is an **easement appurtenant**. The **dominant tenement** is the land that benefits from the easement that the **servient tenement** gives up. An **easement in gross** benefits others who do not own adjoining or attached lands (like a utility company running a gas line across a property).

Easements can be created by 1) **deed** (writing), 2) **implication of law** (implied easement or easement by necessity), or 3) **prescription** (long use). They can also be terminated in several ways, including: 1) **express release**, 2) **merger** of dominant and servient tenements, 3) **excessive use**, 4) **abandonment and non-use**, and 5) **destruction of servient tenement**.

**Restrictions** can be private deed restrictions, or public restrictions. **Covenants, conditions, and restrictions (CC&Rs)** are private building restrictions. **Public restrictions** are limits made by governmental agencies and are meant to promote health, safety, morals, and general welfare of the public (**police power**). **Zoning** is a public restriction dictating how property can be used, including setback requirements. An **encroachment** is the wrongful, unauthorized placement of improvements or permanent fixtures on a property by a non-owner, which must be removed by the owner within three years.

A **homestead** is not an encumbrance, but a special provision of California law that allows homeowners to protect their homes from forced sale to satisfy their debts. A homestead is terminated by: 1) **declaration of abandonment**, or 2) **the sale of the homesteaded property**.

## VI. TERMINOLOGY

A. Abstract of Judgment
B. Attachment
C. Blanket Encumbrance
D. Conditions
E. Covenant
F. Declaration of Abandonment
G. Declaration of Homestead
H. Defendant
I. Dominant Tenement
J. Easement

K. Easement Appurtenant
L. Easement in Gross
M. Encroachment
N. Encumbrance
O. General Lien
P. Homestead
Q. Lien
R. Lis Pendens
S. Mechanic's Lien
T. Mortgage

U. Notice of Non-Responsibility
V. Plaintiff
W. Preliminary Notice
X. Restrictions
Y. Satisfaction
Z. Servient Tenement
AA. Sheriff's Sale
BB. Specific Lien
CC. Trust Deed
DD. Writ of Execution

1.____ A right, limited to a specific use, that one party has in the land of another.

2.____ A statutory protection of a home from the claims of certain creditors and judgments up to a specified amount.

3.____ Anything that affects or limits the fee simple title to, or value of, property, e.g., mortgages or easements.

4.____ A notice, recorded and posted by the property owner to relieve them of responsibility for the cost of unauthorized work done on his or her property or materials furnished.

5.____ A limitation on the use of real property. These limitations fall into two general classifications: public and private. Zoning ordinances are public, while a clause in the deed requiring the roof to be made of Spanish red title would be a private limitation.

6.____ The process by which real or personal property is seized by the court for the purpose of assuring payment.

7.____ A form of encumbrance that usually makes specific property security for the payment of a debt.

8.____ Discharge of a mortgage or trust deed from the records upon payment of the debt. Make sure you receive a Deed of Reconveyance to prove that you paid off the deed of trust.

9.____ A limiting restriction stating that upon the happening or not happening of some stated event, the estate shall be changed in some manner.

10.____ A promise to do or not to do a particular thing.

11.____ A person against whom a civil or criminal action is taken.

12.____ An instrument, recognized by law, by which property is hypothecated to secure the payment of a debt. This instrument is not commonly used in California, but is popular on the east coast.

13.____ In a court action, the one who sues; the complainant.

14.____ A recorded document of the essential provisions of a court judgment.

15.____ A lien, created by statute, which exists against real or personal property in favor of persons who have performed work or furnished materials for the improvement of real property.

16.____ A legal document by which a borrower pledges certain real property as collateral for the repayment of a loan. In addition to the buyer and seller, there is a third party to the transaction known as a trustee.

17.____ A formal statement that protects the head of the household from losing the property to the claims of creditors, usually up to a set maximum amount.

18.____ A lien, usually a trust deed in California, covering more than one property of the borrower.

19.____ A notice that informs or warns owners, lenders and general contractors that subcontractors have been hired, or materials have been supplied to a particular job site.

20.____ A statement declaring the intent to give up a homestead, usually to declare a homestead on a new residence.

21.____A court ordered sale of real or personal property by the sheriff pursuant to the execution of a judgment.

22.____The construction of improvements on the property of another.

23.____An easement for the benefit of the owner of an adjacent parcel of land.

24.____Real property that benefits from an easement.

25.____A writ to carry out a court order, usually arising from a judgment.

26.____A property that is burdened by an easement.

27.____An easement for the benefit of a person or utility company rather than for the benefit of adjacent landowners.

28.____A notice filed or recorded for the purpose of warning all persons that the title to certain real property is in litigation.

29.____A lien such as a tax lien or judgment lien that attaches to all property of the debtor rather than a specific property.

30.____A lien that attaches to a specific property rather than all the property of the debtor.

## VII. CHAPTER QUIZ

1. When a project of improvement on real property has been completed and the owner has not filed a "notice of completion," how many days do claimants have to file mechanic's liens?

    a. 30 days
    b. 60 days
    c. 90 days
    d. Unlimited

2. The difference between property taxes and special assessments is that:

    a. assessment liens are always subordinate to property tax liens.
    b. assessment liens can only be levied by local improvement districts.
    c. foreclosure of assessment liens can only be achieved by court foreclosure.
    d. special assessments are levied for the cost of specific local improvements, while property tax revenue goes into the general fund.

3. A lis pendens:

    a. may affect title to the property, based upon the results of the lawsuit.
    b. allows real property to be reassessed when it is sold.
    c. means "and wife."
    d. none of the above.

4. Which of the following is a court order restricting a party from doing an act such as violating private deed restrictions?

    a. Writ of execution
    b. Writ of possession
    c. Injunction
    d. Quiet title action

5. Which of the following will terminate an easement?

    a. Dominant tenant records a quitclaim deed

    b. Servient tenant records a grant deed

    c. The owner of the servient tenement records a grant deed

    d. The owner of the dominant tenement records a quitclaim deed

6. Landowner Jacobs granted the telephone company the right to erect telephone poles on his land. Which of the following best describes this situation?

    a. An encroachment

    b. An encumbrance

    c. An appurtenance

    d. Accession

7. Daniel, who owned two pieces of adjacent land, sold one of them to Charles reserving an easement for himself at the time. Daniel soon left the state for 21 years during which time he did not use the easement. When Daniel finally returned to the state he discovered that:

    a. the easement was terminated after 5 years of non-use.

    b. the easement was still valid and enforceable.

    c. the owner of the servient tenement had died leaving Daniel with no easement rights at all.

    d. easements cannot be created by "reservation."

8. A condominium's CC&Rs prohibit "for sale" signs. The owner may:

    a. sue the condo assocation.

    b. place a reasonably sized "for sale" sign on the property.

    c. not place a "for sale" sign on the property.

    d. none of the above.

9. If a condominium owner breaches a "condition" in the CC&Rs this would be:

    a. enforced by the local building department.

    b. the same as violating a health code regulation.

    c. more stringent than breaching a covenant.

    d. the same as breaching a public restriction.

10. Which of the following would have the least impact on property taxes?

    a. Selling price

    b. Market value

    c. A recorded homestead

    d. Tax deferment

**ANSWERS:** 1. c; 2. d; 3. a; 4. c; 5. d; 6. b; 7. b; 8. b; 9. c; 10. c

# CHAPTER 4
## Agency and Its Responsibility

**www.dre.ca.gov**
California Department of Real Estate (DRE)
**www.car.org**
California Association of REALTORS®
**www.inman.com**
Inman News Features

# I. Agency – An Overview

## A. AGENT, PRINCIPAL, AND THIRD PARTY

*The seller gives the right to represent him/her in the sale of property and the broker agrees to use diligence in obtaining a purchaser. This is called "agency."*

### 1. Agent

*AGENCY is the authority (or power) to act in place of another, a principal (person who hires), to do a specified act for a stated period of time. An AGENT is one who acts for and with authority from another, called the principal.*

Agents (brokers) usually select and control their own professional approach to selling a property. Sellers are responsible for their representations to the buyer. While brokers share this responsibility, they also have a responsibility for their individual representations. Agency is a fiduciary relationship based on trust. The agent representing the seller must disclose all pertinent facts to the seller and must not take advantage of, or gain from, this relationship in an unethical manner.

*A "dual agent" is a broker acting as an agent for both the seller and the buyer in the same transaction, with the informed consent of both parties.*

### 2. Principal

A *PRINCIPAL (CLIENT) is a person who hires or employs an agent to work for him or her.* If the principal is a buyer, the agent represents the buyer. On the other hand, if the principal is a seller, the agent represents the seller.

# CHAPTER OUTLINE

### 3. Third Party

A **THIRD PARTY** *is the other person in a contractual negotiation, other than the principal and his or her agent.* If an agent works for the seller, the third party is the buyer. But if the agent works for the buyer, the third party is the seller. In effect, the agent is the second party to the transaction.

In the agency relationship, the broker and other salespeople are required to make certain disclosures about the property they are selling. They are expected to do what is necessary, proper, and usual to sell the real estate being offered. They must also make truthful representations to the buyer as to the condition of the property that may materially affect the value or desirability of the property and the terms of the sale. This is spelled out in the Disclosure Regarding Real Estate Agency Relationships Form (discussed later).

*The broker, as agent of the seller, owes the buyer the duty of honest and fair dealing.*

**OSTENSIBLE** or **IMPLIED AUTHORITY** *is the authority that a third person reasonably believes an agent possesses because of the acts or omissions of the principal.* This authority is conferred when a principal gives a third party reason to believe that another person is his or her agent. If the third party accepts this as true, the principal may well be bound by the acts of that person.

**Example:** As an owner, if you tell a prospective buyer to see Agent Ramos about seeing your property even though the listing has expired and Ramos sells the house, the buyer has every reason to believe that Miss Ramos had the authority as your agent to sell the home.

# AGENT, BROKER, SALESPERSON, ASSOCIATE
## Who Holds a Real Estate License?

### REAL ESTATE AGENT

A **REAL ESTATE AGENT** is a person licensed by the Department of Real Estate (DRE) who holds either a broker's or salesperson's license and negotiates sales for other people.

### REAL ESTATE BROKER AND SALESPERSON

A **REAL ESTATE BROKER** is a broker's license holder (boss/owner) and therefore permitted by law to employ those individuals holding a salesperson's license (or another broker). A **REAL ESTATE SALESPERSON** is an individual holding a salesperson's license who must be employed by a real estate broker to perform any of the activities of a real estate broker.

### REAL ESTATE ASSOCIATE

A **REAL ESTATE ASSOCIATE** or **ASSOCIATE LICENSEE** is another name for a real estate salesperson. An associate works for a broker as either an employee or an independent contractor.

*An agent or licensee is either a broker or a salesperson who works for a broker.*

## DEPARTMENT OF REAL ESTATE (DRE)
### Checking the Status of a Real Estate Salesperson or Broker

To check the status of a real estate salesperson or broker, access the following Department of Real Estate Internet address:

**www.dre.ca.gov/lic_status_inquiries.html**
**Department of Real Estate - Licensee Status Inquiries**

Click on LICENSE RECORDS ON-LINE and enter the name or license number, and the DRE will do the rest.

An agency relationship may also come about by estoppel or ratification, although it is **not** advisable. *ESTOPPEL prohibits the principal from denying that a person is his or her agent if the principal has misled another to his prejudice into believing that person is the agent.* Agency can't be created by estoppel, just ratified. In the above example, you, the owner, would be "estopped" from denying that Miss Ramos was your agent, based on your past actions or words. *RATIFICATION is approval (confirmation) of a transaction which has already taken place.* For example, when you authorize a broker to act for you after he or she has already done so, the action is called ratification.

*The best way to establish an agency relationship is through written agreement.*

In California, most real estate transactions involve the use of a broker and his or her salespeople. To run a real estate office, a broker's license is required, and a licensed salesperson can only work for a licensed real estate broker (one broker at a time). In California, any person in real estate who is acting in return for compensation from others must have a Department of Real Estate license to:

1. Sell or offer to sell.
2. Buy or offer to buy.
3. Solicit prospective buyers or sellers.
4. Negotiate the purchase, sale, loan, or exchange of business opportunities or real estate.
5. Negotiate leases and collect rents.

Real estate license requirements are explained fully in Chapter 14.

## B. LAW OF AGENCY

*The Law of Agency is found in the Civil Code.*

Real estate brokers are agents because they represent an interest other than their own (buyer's or seller's). A written agency contract (listing) exists, for which they may receive compensation if there is a sale. Whenever one person represents another in a business transaction, the "Law of Agency" applies.

*An agency relationship requires the parties to be fiduciary and competent. It does NOT require payment of "consideration."*

Because the real estate broker is an agent, the California Civil Code governing the Law of Agency,defines his or her duties and responsibilities. Further, since the broker is a licensed real estate agent, he or she must comply with the rules and regulations of the California Real Estate Commissioner, which are enforced by the Commissioner. Both codes and regulations can be enforced against all brokers and their salespeople. Throughout this chapter, when we speak of a broker we are also referring to any salesperson (or broker) who may be working for that company broker.

## C. RESPONSIBILITIES OF AGENCY

In the California Civil Code, the law of agency boils down to three basic rules applying to licensed brokers and licensed salespeople:

1. The agent must inform the principal of all material facts pertaining to the handling of the principal's property. The agent must put client's interest above interest of self or others.

2. The agent may not gain any monetary interest in the property without the principal's prior consent.

3. An agent may not use the principal's property to his or her own advantage.

### 1. Fiduciary Relationship

A *FIDUCIARY is a person acting in a position of trust and confidence in a business relationship. A FIDUCIARY RELATIONSHIP requires the highest good faith from the agent to his or her principal.* An agent must act as though he or she is the principal and always seek to represent the principal's best interest. In this case, the agent takes on the responsibility of diligently finding a buyer or seller (see **Figure 4-1**).

**Figure 4-1**

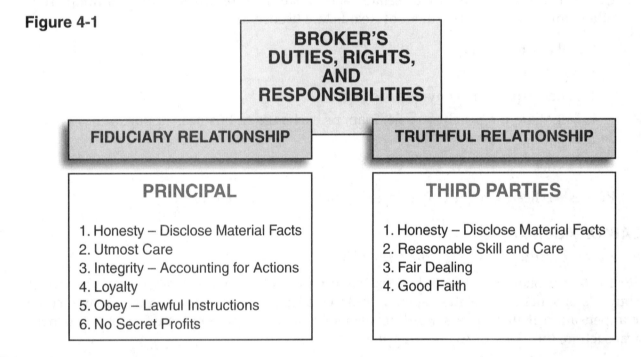

The broker (agent) works for the principal and forms a fiduciary relationship with him or her. The broker also must maintain an honest and truthful relationship with the third party (including full disclosure of material facts affecting value or desirability).

*If the seller's agent informs the buyer that the seller will take less than the list price, the agent violates the fiduciary duty of confidentiality to the seller.*

An agent must exercise honesty, reasonable skill and care, fair dealing and good faith in dealing with a third party. An agent of the principal must disclose to the third party any facts known to the agent that could materially affect the value or desirability of the property.

**TOP AGENTS HIRE TOP ASSISTANTS**

It is estimated that 80 percent of the real estate business is handled by 10 percent of the agents. To handle the workload, more top agents are hiring personal assistants to take over the day-to-day brokerage chores, leaving the agents free to concentrate on sales. **PERSONAL ASSISTANTS** *handle such things as clerical tasks, paperwork, marketing, tickler files, and conduct computer research.* More and more real estate licensees are working as assistants. The growth in personal assistants is not without criticism. Among the complaints are that using assistants entrusts too many high-level tasks to unskilled employees and makes the agents inaccessible. It is important that the broker establish who is employing the assistants, and that unlicensed assistants do not act as agents. There is a wealth of educational materials available to improve the quality of real estate assistants.

### D. LISTING AND SELLING AGENTS

When a salesperson obtains a listing agreement to sell a particular property, he or she is referred to as the "listing salesperson." That salesperson's broker is referred to as the "listing broker." A salesperson employed by a listing broker is an agent of the owner/seller. If a different brokerage company negotiates the sale, that agency is the "selling broker" and "selling salesperson." A broker or salesperson who both lists and sells the same property is referred to as the "listing and selling broker or salesperson."

# II. Real Estate Agency Relationship Disclosure

*The Real Estate Agency Relationship Disclosure Act (Civil Code) became law in 1988.*

### A. AGENCY DISCLOSURE LAW

According to the Disclosure Regarding Real Estate Agency Relationships form, the first thing the agent must do is establish if he or she is an agent for the seller, buyer, or both.

*The three steps of agency disclosure are: disclose, elect, and confirm.*

The Disclosure Regarding Real Estate Agency Relationships form states that both the listing broker and the selling broker must declare in writing, as soon as possible, whom they represent:

1. The seller/owner (seller's agency)
2. The buyer (buyer's agency) or
3. Both the seller and buyer (dual agency).

The only requirement is that the listing broker must at least represent the seller (owner). **This law applies to all sales of residential property of from one-to-four units.**

**Real Estate license number:** Business cards, stationary, advertising materials, websites, email, and regular mail, must include your real estate license number and it must be disclosed at the first point of contact with a consumer, including any purchase agreements.

### THE GROWTH OF "BUYER BROKERAGES"

A large number of brokers are responding to a need that a buyer be represented diligently by offering exclusive buyer's services. More than a fad, it is estimated that buyer's agents will represent 25% or more of the industry within the next ten years.

It is believed that good buyer representation will cut down on disputes and lawsuits. In the future, the trend will be toward brokers working for either the seller or buyer, not just the seller. No longer do brokers have to exclude themselves from one entire side of the market.

*In a "buyer's agency," the agent represents the buyer only.*

*A real estate agency disclosure form must be given to all parties when the transaction involves the sale of a residential triplex.*

**Figure 4-2** shows a Disclosure Regarding Real Estate Agency Relationships form used by the California Association of REALTORS® (CAR). Civil law requires that both parties to a transaction be informed of the various options they have regarding agency representation. Both the buyer and the seller must sign the lower part of this form as an acknowledgment that they understand their rights and have received a copy of this disclosure. In addition, agency disclosure must again be confirmed on the Residential Purchase Agreement (see Chapter 5). If it is not confirmed on the Residential Purchase Agreement, then it must be confirmed on a separate form. This confirmation will protect the licensee against any future charges of misrepresentation in the agency relationship. It should be completed as soon as possible.

*The seller's agent cannot keep silent about any material facts that affect the value of the property (for example, the property is in an earthquake zone or backs up to a freeway or school).*

But, the seller's agent cannot tell the buyer that the seller is insolvent because this would lower the offering price, violating the duty of loyalty in a fiduciary relationship.

Traditionally, the principal was usually a seller. Brokers are now free to represent the buyer, the seller, and sometimes both. **Figure 4-3** illustrates the agency options.

*"Dual agency" occurs when a broker represents both the buyer and the seller in a real estate transaction.*

**Example:** A broker holds a purchase-option on land owned by Nelson. When exercising the option to purchase, the broker must disclose to Seller Nelson that the broker is the principal.

As you can see from Figure 4-3, there may be several brokers involved in a single transaction. In California, the seller (owner) and the buyer are usually represented by different brokers. The listing broker always represents the seller but may represent both. Traditionally, the selling broker, who procures the buyer, customarily represents the buyer. In some other states, all the brokers and salespeople represent only the seller (owner).

*If an agent does not disclose dual agency to both parties, he or she may be disciplined, not receive a commission, and it may be grounds for either party to rescind the contract.*

**Figure 4-2**

CALIFORNIA
ASSOCIATION
OF REALTORS®

## DISCLOSURE REGARDING
## REAL ESTATE AGENCY RELATIONSHIP
(Listing Firm to Seller)
(As required by the Civil Code)
(C.A.R. Form AD, Revised 11/09)

When you enter into a discussion with a real estate agent regarding a real estate transaction, you should from the outset understand what type of agency relationship or representation you wish to have with the agent in the transaction.

### SELLER'S AGENT

A Seller's agent under a listing agreement with the Seller acts as the agent for the Seller only. A Seller's agent or a subagent of that agent has the following affirmative obligations:
To the Seller: A Fiduciary duty of utmost care, integrity, honesty and loyalty in dealings with the Seller.
To the Buyer and the Seller:
  (a) Diligent exercise of reasonable skill and care in performance of the agent's duties.
  (b) A duty of honest and fair dealing and good faith.
  (c) A duty to disclose all facts known to the agent materially affecting the value or desirability of the property that are not known to, or within the diligent attention and observation of, the parties. An agent is not obligated to reveal to either party any confidential information obtained from the other party that does not involve the affirmative duties set forth above.

### BUYER'S AGENT

A selling agent can, with a Buyer's consent, agree to act as agent for the Buyer only. In these situations, the agent is not the Seller's agent, even if by agreement the agent may receive compensation for services rendered, either in full or in part from the Seller. An agent acting only for a Buyer has the following affirmative obligations:
To the Buyer: A fiduciary duty of utmost care, integrity, honesty and loyalty in dealings with the Buyer.
To the Buyer and the Seller:
  (a) Diligent exercise of reasonable skill and care in performance of the agent's duties.
  (b) A duty of honest and fair dealing and good faith.
  (c) A duty to disclose all facts known to the agent materially affecting the value or desirability of the property that are not known to, or within the diligent attention and observation of, the parties.
An agent is not obligated to reveal to either party any confidential information obtained from the other party that does not involve the affirmative duties set forth above.

### AGENT REPRESENTING BOTH SELLER AND BUYER

A real estate agent, either acting directly or through one or more associate licensees, can legally be the agent of both the Seller and the Buyer in a transaction, but only with the knowledge and consent of both the Seller and the Buyer.
In a dual agency situation, the agent has the following affirmative obligations to both the Seller and the Buyer:
  (a) A fiduciary duty of utmost care, integrity, honesty and loyalty in the dealings with either the Seller or the Buyer.
  (b) Other duties to the Seller and the Buyer as stated above in their respective sections.
In representing both Seller and Buyer, the agent may not, without the express permission of the respective party, disclose to the other party that the Seller will accept a price less than the listing price or that the Buyer will pay a price greater than the price offered.
The above duties of the agent in a real estate transaction do not relieve a Seller or Buyer from the responsibility to protect his or her own interests. You should carefully read all agreements to assure that they adequately express your understanding of the transaction. A real estate agent is a person qualified to advise about real estate. If legal or tax advice is desired, consult a competent professional.
Throughout your real property transaction you may receive more than one disclosure form, depending upon the number of agents assisting in the transaction. The law requires each agent with whom you have more than a casual relationship to present you with this disclosure form. You should read its contents each time it is presented to you, considering the relationship between you and the real estate agent in your specific transaction.
This disclosure form includes the provisions of Sections 2079.13 to 2079.24, inclusive, of the Civil Code set forth on page 2. Read it carefully.
**I/WE ACKNOWLEDGE RECEIPT OF A COPY OF THIS DISCLOSURE AND THE PORTIONS OF THE CIVIL CODE PRINTED ON THE BACK (OR A SEPARATE PAGE).**

☐ Buyer ☐ Seller ☐ Landlord ☐ Tenant _____ Date _____

☐ Buyer ☐ Seller ☐ Landlord ☐ Tenant _____ Date _____

Agent _____ DRE Lic. # _____
           Real Estate Broker (Firm)

By _____ DRE Lic. # _____ Date _____
    (Salesperson or Broker-Associate)

---

AGENCY DISCLOSURE COMPLIANCE (Civil Code §2079.14):
• When the listing brokerage company also represents Buyer/Tenant: The Listing Agent shall have one AD form signed by Seller/Landlord and a different AD form signed by Buyer/Tenant.
• When Seller/Landlord and Buyer/Tenant are represented by different brokerage companies: (i) the Listing Agent shall have one AD form signed by Seller/Landlord and (ii) the Buyer's/Tenant's Agent shall have one AD form signed by Buyer/Tenant and either that same or a different AD form presented to Seller/Landlord for signature prior to presentation of the offer. If the same form is used, Seller may sign here:

(SELLER/LANDLORD: DO NOT SIGN HERE)      (SELLER/LANDLORD: DO NOT SIGN HERE)
Seller/Landlord _____ Date _____    Seller/Landlord _____ Date _____

---

Published and Distributed by:
REAL ESTATE BUSINESS SERVICES, INC.
a subsidiary of the California Association of REALTORS®
525 South Virgil Avenue, Los Angeles, California 90020

Reviewed by _____ Date _____

EQUAL HOUSING
OPPORTUNITY

AD REVISED 11/09 (PAGE 1 OF 2)
**DISCLOSURE REGARDING REAL ESTATE AGENCY RELATIONSHIP (AD PAGE 1 OF 2)**

| Agent: WALT HUBER | Phone: | Fax: | Prepared using zipForm® software |
|---|---|---|---|
| Broker: WALT HUBER REALTOR | | | |

**Figure 4-3**

**BROKER REPRESENTS SELLER**

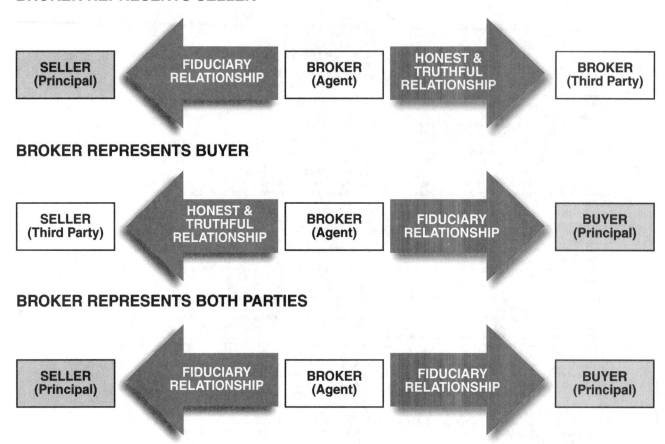

**BROKER REPRESENTS BUYER**

**BROKER REPRESENTS BOTH PARTIES**

# III. Listings and the Multiple Listing Service (MLS)

## A. LISTING AGREEMENTS

The usual way to establish a broker's right to negotiate a sale of property is through a written contract, commonly called a listing. A *LISTING is a contract to employ a broker as an agent, to do certain things for the owner/seller. It is an employment contract for personal service.*

Listings are NOT assignable and death of the seller or broker cancels a listing, unless the broker is a corporation (which may live forever). There are six basic types of listings used in California. They are:

1. Open Listing (non-exclusive)
2. Exclusive Agency Listing
3. Exclusive Right to Sell Listing
4. Net Listing (rare)
5. Option Listing
6. Oral Listing (not discussed here)

*The usual listing contract authorizes a broker to find a purchaser and accept a deposit with an offer to purchase.*

You should also know: all real estate listing agreements or contracts should be in writing, and must be in writing to assure collection of a commission.

*All listings are the property of the broker who employs him/her as a salesperson.*

### 1. Open Listing (Unilateral, Non-Exclusive Contract)

An *OPEN LISTING is an authorization to sell a property. It may be given to several brokers or the property may be sold by the owner.* Only the agent who is the procuring cause earns the commission. If the owner sells the property, he or she is not required to pay a commission. Usually, no time limit is placed on an open listing. A description of the property is included in the agreement along with the selling price and other terms.

Open listings are the simplest form of broker authorization. They can be given to several brokers concurrently, and no notice of sale is required to terminate the listing. A broker should make sure an open listing is still valid before pursuing it. When an open listing is given to more than one broker, the first broker who finds a qualified buyer is entitled to the commission. On the other hand, if an owner finds his or her own buyer, that owner has no obligation to pay a commission to a broker.

**Example:** While prospecting, agent Roberts came upon a homeowner who said he would sell his home if he received the price he wanted. He did not want to list his property with agent Roberts, but said he would listen to any offers that might be presented and pay a commission if he accepted it. This type of listing is an open listing.

Few brokers use this type of listing because of its uncertainty and the expense of advertising when working an open listing.

### 2. Exclusive Agency Listing (No Commission if Owner Sells Privately)

The *EXCLUSIVE AGENCY LISTING is a listing providing that only one agent (the listing broker) has the right to be the only person, other than the owner, to sell the property during a specified period and earn a commission.* The owner, however, still has the right to independently sell the property without paying a commission to the listing broker. The drawback with this type of listing is that the broker is, or could be, in competition with the owner for the sale. These listings are entered into the MLS.

*An exclusive agency listing and exclusive right to sell listing both require a definite termination date.*

**Example:** A broker has listed a seller's home using an exclusive agency listing agreement. The exclusive agreement is for four months. During this time, the broker expends considerable time, effort, and money marketing and advertising on behalf of the seller. Ten days before the date the listing is to expire, the seller decides to sell his home to his next door neighbor. The seller now owes the broker no commission.

## MOBILE DEVICES AND SOCIAL NETWORKING

Access to the Internet revolutionized the real estate industry by allowing the public to transmit loan applications, check credit histories and view photos of properties online. The latest technological trend now includes creating a business presence on Facebook, LinkedIn, and Twitter — the top three online social networking sites. Not yet in the running, but a potential competitor for membership numbers, is Google Me. More than ever, you can see why brokers rely on smartphones, iPads, and other handheld mobile devices.

### 3. Exclusive Right to Sell Listing (Commission if Sold Within the Listing Period)

The most common type of listing is the exclusive right to sell listing. Only the ***EXCLUSIVE RIGHT TO SELL LISTING*** *entitles the listing broker named in the agency contract to a commission even if the owner sells the property.* **Figure 4-4** shows the CAR® Residential Listing Agreement - Exclusive (Exclusive Authorization and Right to Sell).

*With an exclusive agency listing, the broker competes with the owner; with an exclusive right to sell listing, the broker is entitled to a commission even if the owner sells the property privately during the listing period. A seller may revoke an exclusive right to sell listing by sending a written letter to the broker.*

This type of listing often contains a section referred to as a safety clause. A ***SAFETY CLAUSE (Broker Protection Clause)*** *in a listing is a negotiated period (any agreed to time period) after the termination of a listing in which the listing broker may still be entitled to a commission.* To protect themselves, brokers must furnish the owner/seller with a written list of persons to whom they have shown the property during the listing period delivered no later than the listing termination date. If the owner or a new broker sells the property to someone on the list within the negotiated period, the original broker may be entitled to a commission. **If a seller signs, for example, a 90-day exclusive right to sell listing with one broker, cancels it two weeks later, and gives an open listing to another broker who brings in an offer that is accepted, both brokers are entitled to a full commission.**

*An exclusive right to sell listing is a bilateral executory agreement when signed by both seller and broker.*

### 4. Net Listing (Must Be Used With Other Listing – Seldom Used)

A ***NET LISTING*** *is an agreement providing that the agent agrees to sell the owner's property for a set minimum price, any amount over the minimum being retained by the agent as commission.* This authorization to sell must be used with one of the other three listings, taking the form of an open listing, an exclusive agency listing, or an exclusive right to sell listing.

With this type of listing it is imperative for the broker to explain, in writing, the exact meaning of a net listing so that there is no confusion about any earned compensation. Since this is a vague type of listing and the possibility of wide variations in commission, a net listing is seldom used in California.

### 5. Option Listing (Broker has a Reserved Right to Buy)

An ***OPTION LISTING*** *gives the listing broker the right to purchase the property.*

## Figure 4-4

CALIFORNIA
ASSOCIATION
OF REALTORS®

## RESIDENTIAL LISTING AGREEMENT
### (Exclusive Authorization and Right to Sell)
(C.A.R. Form RLA, Revised 2/09)

1. **EXCLUSIVE RIGHT TO SELL:** _____ ("Seller")
hereby employs and grants _____ ("Broker")
beginning (date) _____ and ending at 11:59 P.M. on (date) _____ ("Listing Period")
the exclusive and irrevocable right to sell or exchange the real property in the City of _____ ,
County of _____ , Assessor's Parcel No. _____
California, described as: _____ *123 Sail Avenue* _____ ("Property").

2. **ITEMS EXCLUDED AND INCLUDED:** Unless otherwise specified in a real estate purchase agreement, all fixtures and fittings that are attached to the Property are included, and personal property items are excluded, from the purchase price.
**ADDITIONAL ITEMS EXCLUDED:** _____
**ADDITIONAL ITEMS INCLUDED:** _____
Seller intends that the above items be excluded or included in offering the Property for sale, but understands that: **(i)** the purchase agreement supersedes any intention expressed above and will ultimately determine which items are excluded and included in the sale; and **(ii)** Broker is not responsible for and does not guarantee that the above exclusions and/or inclusions will be in the purchase agreement.

3. **LISTING PRICE AND TERMS:**
   **A.** The listing price shall be: _____
   _____ Dollars ($ _____ ).
   **B.** Additional Terms: _____
   _____

4. **COMPENSATION TO BROKER:**
   Notice: The amount or rate of real estate commissions is not fixed by law. They are set by each Broker individually and may be negotiable between Seller and Broker (real estate commissions include all compensation and fees to Broker).
   **A.** Seller agrees to pay to Broker as compensation for services irrespective of agency relationship(s), either ☐ _____ percent of the listing price (or if a purchase agreement is entered into, of the purchase price), or ☐ $ _____ ,
   AND _____ , as follows:
   **(1)** If during the Listing Period, or any extension, Broker, Seller, cooperating broker, or any other person procures a buyer(s) who offers to purchase the Property on the above price and terms, or on any price and terms acceptable to Seller. (Broker is entitled to compensation whether any escrow resulting from such offer closes during or after the expiration of the Listing Period.)
   **OR (2)** If within _____ calendar days **(a)** after the end of the Listing Period or any extension; or **(b)** after any cancellation of this Agreement, unless otherwise agreed, Seller enters into a contract to sell, convey, lease or otherwise transfer the Property to anyone ("Prospective Buyer") or that person's related entity: **(i)** who physically entered and was shown the Property during the Listing Period or any extension by Broker or a cooperating broker; or **(ii)** for whom Broker or any cooperating broker submitted to Seller a signed, written offer to acquire, lease, exchange or obtain an option on the Property. Seller, however, shall have no obligation to Broker under paragraph 4A(2) unless, not later than **3 calendar days** after the end of the Listing Period or any extension or cancellation, Broker has given Seller a written notice of the names of such Prospective Buyers.
   **OR (3)** If, without Broker's prior written consent, the Property is withdrawn from sale, conveyed, leased, rented, otherwise transferred, or made unmarketable by a voluntary act of Seller during the Listing Period, or any extension.
   **B.** If completion of the sale is prevented by a party to the transaction other than Seller, then compensation due under paragraph 4A shall be payable only if and when Seller collects damages by suit, arbitration, settlement or otherwise, and then in an amount equal to the lesser of one-half of the damages recovered or the above compensation, after first deducting title and escrow expenses and the expenses of collection, if any.
   **C.** In addition, Seller agrees to pay Broker: _____
   **D.** Seller has been advised of Broker's policy regarding cooperation with, and the amount of compensation offered to, other brokers.
   **(1)** Broker is authorized to cooperate with and compensate brokers participating through the multiple listing service(s) ("MLS") by offering MLS brokers either ☐ _____ percent of the purchase price, or ☐ $ _____
   **(2)** Broker is authorized to cooperate with and compensate brokers operating outside the MLS as per Broker's policy.
   **E.** Seller hereby irrevocably assigns to Broker the above compensation from Seller's funds and proceeds in escrow. Broker may submit this Agreement, as instructions to compensate Broker pursuant to paragraph 4A, to any escrow regarding the Property involving Seller and a buyer, Prospective Buyer or other transferee.
   **F.** **(1)** Seller represents that Seller has not previously entered into a listing agreement with another broker regarding the Property, unless specified as follows: _____
   **(2)** Seller warrants that Seller has no obligation to pay compensation to any other broker regarding the Property unless the Property is transferred to any of the following individuals or entities: _____
   **(3)** If the Property is sold to anyone listed above during the time Seller is obligated to compensate another broker: **(i)** Broker is not entitled to compensation under this Agreement; and **(ii)** Broker is not obligated to represent Seller in such transaction.

**RLA REVISED 2/09 (PAGE 1 OF 3)**

Seller acknowledges receipt of a copy of this page.
Seller's Initials ( _____ ) ( _____ )

Reviewed by _____ Date _____

EQUAL HOUSING
OPPORTUNITY

**RESIDENTIAL LISTING AGREEMENT - EXCLUSIVE (RLA PAGE 1 OF 3)**

Agent: WALT HUBER  Phone:  Prepared using zipForm® software
Broker: WALT HUBER REALTOR

Property Address: _123 Sail Avenue_ _____ Date: _____

**5. OWNERSHIP, TITLE AND AUTHORITY:** Seller warrants that: **(i)** Seller is the owner of the Property; **(ii)** no other persons or entities have title to the Property; and **(iii)** Seller has the authority to both execute this Agreement and sell the Property. Exceptions to ownership, title and authority are as follows: _____

**6. MULTIPLE LISTING SERVICE:** All terms of the transaction, including financing, if applicable, will be provided to the selected MLS for publication, dissemination and use by persons and entities on terms approved by the MLS. Seller authorizes Broker to comply with all applicable MLS rules. MLS rules allow MLS data about the Property to be made available by the MLS to additional Internet sites unless Seller gives Broker instructions to the contrary. MLS rules generally provide that residential real property and vacant lot listings be submitted to the MLS within 48 hours or some other period of time after all necessary signatures have been obtained on the listing agreement. However, Broker will not have to submit this listing to the MLS or can prohibit this listing or certain information from or about it from appearing on certain internet sites if, Broker submits to the MLS such an instruction signed by Seller (C.A.R. Form SEL or the locally required form). Information about this listing will be provided to the MLS of Broker's selection unless a form instructing Broker to the contrary is attached to this listing Agreement.

**7. SELLER REPRESENTATIONS:** Seller represents that, unless otherwise specified in writing, Seller is unaware of: **(i)** any Notice of Default recorded against the Property; **(ii)** any delinquent amounts due under any loan secured by, or other obligation affecting, the Property; **(iii)** any bankruptcy, insolvency or similar proceeding affecting the Property; **(iv)** any litigation, arbitration, administrative action, government investigation or other pending or threatened action that affects or may affect the Property or Seller's ability to transfer it; and **(v)** any current, pending or proposed special assessments affecting the Property. Seller shall promptly notify Broker in writing if Seller becomes aware of any of these items during the Listing Period or any extension thereof.

**8. BROKER'S AND SELLER'S DUTIES:** Broker agrees to exercise reasonable effort and due diligence to achieve the purposes of this Agreement. Unless Seller gives Broker written instructions to the contrary, Broker is authorized to order reports and disclosures as appropriate or necessary and advertise and market the Property by any method and in any medium selected by Broker, including MLS and the Internet, and, to the extent permitted by these media, control the dissemination of the information submitted to any medium. Seller agrees to consider offers presented by Broker, and to act in good faith to accomplish the sale of the Property by, among other things, making the Property available for showing at reasonable times and referring to Broker all inquiries of any party interested in the Property. Seller is responsible for determining at what price to list and sell the Property. **Seller further agrees to indemnify, defend and hold Broker harmless from all claims, disputes, litigation, judgments and attorney fees arising from any incorrect information supplied by Seller, or from any material facts that Seller knows but fails to disclose.**

**9. DEPOSIT:** Broker is authorized to accept and hold on Seller's behalf any deposits to be applied toward the purchase price.

**10. AGENCY RELATIONSHIPS:**
   **A. Disclosure:** If the Property includes residential property with one-to-four dwelling units, Seller shall receive a "Disclosure Regarding Agency Relationships" form prior to entering into this Agreement.
   **B. Seller Representation:** Broker shall represent Seller in any resulting transaction, except as specified in paragraph 4F.
   **C. Possible Dual Agency With Buyer:** Depending upon the circumstances, it may be necessary or appropriate for Broker to act as an agent for both Seller and buyer, exchange party, or one or more additional parties ("Buyer"). Broker shall, as soon as practicable, disclose to Seller any election to act as a dual agent representing both Seller and Buyer. If a Buyer is procured directly by Broker or an associate-licensee in Broker's firm, Seller hereby consents to Broker acting as a dual agent for Seller and such Buyer. In the event of an exchange, Seller hereby consents to Broker collecting compensation from additional parties for services rendered, provided there is disclosure to all parties of such agency and compensation. Seller understands and agrees that: **(i)** Broker, without the prior written consent of Seller, will not disclose to Buyer that Seller is willing to sell the Property at a price less than the listing price; **(ii)** Broker, without the prior written consent of Buyer, will not disclose to Seller that Buyer is willing to pay a price greater than the offered price; and **(iii)** except for (i) and (ii) above, a dual agent is obligated to disclose known facts materially affecting the value or desirability of the Property to both parties.
   **D. Other Sellers:** Seller understands that Broker may have or obtain listings on other properties, and that potential buyers may consider, make offers on, or purchase through Broker, property the same as or similar to Seller's Property. Seller consents to Broker's representation of sellers and buyers of other properties before, during and after the end of this Agreement.
   **E. Confirmation:** If the Property includes residential property with one-to-four dwelling units, Broker shall confirm the agency relationship described above, or as modified, in writing, prior to or concurrent with Seller's execution of a purchase agreement.

**11. SECURITY AND INSURANCE:** Broker is not responsible for loss of or damage to personal or real property, or person, whether attributable to use of a keysafe/lockbox, a showing of the Property, or otherwise. Third parties, including, but not limited to, appraisers, inspectors, brokers and prospective buyers, may have access to, and take videos and photographs of, the interior of the Property. Seller agrees: **(i)** to take reasonable precautions to safeguard and protect valuables that might be accessible during showings of the Property; and **(ii)** to obtain insurance to protect against these risks. Broker does not maintain insurance to protect Seller.

**12. KEYSAFE/LOCKBOX:** A keysafe/lockbox is designed to hold a key to the Property to permit access to the Property by Broker, cooperating brokers, MLS participants, their authorized licensees and representatives, authorized inspectors, and accompanied prospective buyers. Broker, cooperating brokers, MLS and Associations/Boards of REALTORS® are **not** insurers against injury, theft, loss, vandalism or damage attributed to the use of a keysafe/lockbox. Seller does (or if checked ☐ does not) authorize Broker to install a keysafe/lockbox. If Seller does not occupy the Property, Seller shall be responsible for obtaining occupant(s)' written permission for use of a keysafe/lockbox.

**13. SIGN:** Seller does (or if checked ☐ does not) authorize Broker to install a FOR SALE/SOLD sign on the Property.

**14. EQUAL HOUSING OPPORTUNITY:** The Property is offered in compliance with federal, state and local anti-discrimination laws.

**15. ATTORNEY FEES:** In any action, proceeding or arbitration between Seller and Broker regarding the obligation to pay compensation under this Agreement, the prevailing Seller or Broker shall be entitled to reasonable attorney fees and costs from the non-prevailing Seller or Broker, except as provided in paragraph 19A.

**16. ADDITIONAL TERMS:** _____
_____
_____

Seller acknowledges receipt of a copy of this page.
Seller's Initials ( _____ ) ( _____ )

**RLA REVISED 2/09 (PAGE 2 OF 3)**

Reviewed by _____ Date _____

EQUAL HOUSING
OPPORTUNITY

**RESIDENTIAL LISTING AGREEMENT - EXCLUSIVE (RLA PAGE 2 OF 3)**

Untitled

*123 Sail Avenue*

Property Address: _____ Date: _____

17. **MANAGEMENT APPROVAL:** If an associate-licensee in Broker's office (salesperson or broker-associate) enters into this Agreement on Broker's behalf, and Broker or Manager does not approve of its terms, Broker or Manager has the right to cancel this Agreement, in writing, within **5 Days** After its execution.

18. **SUCCESSORS AND ASSIGNS:** This Agreement shall be binding upon Seller and Seller's successors and assigns.

19. **DISPUTE RESOLUTION:**

   A. **MEDIATION:** Seller and Broker agree to mediate any dispute or claim arising between them out of this Agreement, or any resulting transaction, before resorting to arbitration or court action, subject to paragraph 19B(2) below. Paragraph 19B(2) below applies whether or not the arbitration provision is initialed. Mediation fees, if any, shall be divided equally among the parties involved. If, for any dispute or claim to which this paragraph applies, any party commences an action without first attempting to resolve the matter through mediation, or refuses to mediate after a request has been made, then that party shall not be entitled to recover attorney fees, even if they would otherwise be available to that party in any such action. THIS MEDIATION PROVISION APPLIES WHETHER OR NOT THE ARBITRATION PROVISION IS INITIALED.

   B. **ARBITRATION OF DISPUTES: (1)** Seller and Broker agree that any dispute or claim in law or equity arising between them regarding the obligation to pay compensation under this Agreement, which is not settled through mediation, shall be decided by neutral, binding arbitration, including and subject to paragraph 19B(2) below. The arbitrator shall be a retired judge or justice, or an attorney with at least 5 years of residential real estate law experience, unless the parties mutually agree to a different arbitrator, who shall render an award in accordance with substantive California law. The parties shall have the right to discovery in accordance with California Code of Civil Procedure §1283.05. In all other respects, the arbitration shall be conducted in accordance with Title 9 of Part III of the California Code of Civil Procedure. Judgment upon the award of the arbitrator(s) may be entered in any court having jurisdiction. Interpretation of this agreement to arbitrate shall be governed by the Federal Arbitration Act.

   **(2) EXCLUSIONS FROM MEDIATION AND ARBITRATION:** The following matters are excluded from mediation and arbitration: (i) a judicial or non-judicial foreclosure or other action or proceeding to enforce a deed of trust, mortgage, or installment land sale contract as defined in California Civil Code §2985; (ii) an unlawful detainer action; (iii) the filing or enforcement of a mechanic's lien; and (iv) any matter that is within the jurisdiction of a probate, small claims, or bankruptcy court. The filing of a court action to enable the recording of a notice of pending action, for order of attachment, receivership, injunction, or other provisional remedies, shall not constitute a waiver of the mediation and arbitration provisions.

   "NOTICE: BY INITIALING IN THE SPACE BELOW YOU ARE AGREEING TO HAVE ANY DISPUTE ARISING OUT OF THE MATTERS INCLUDED IN THE 'ARBITRATION OF DISPUTES' PROVISION DECIDED BY NEUTRAL ARBITRATION AS PROVIDED BY CALIFORNIA LAW AND YOU ARE GIVING UP ANY RIGHTS YOU MIGHT POSSESS TO HAVE THE DISPUTE LITIGATED IN A COURT OR JURY TRIAL. BY INITIALING IN THE SPACE BELOW YOU ARE GIVING UP YOUR JUDICIAL RIGHTS TO DISCOVERY AND APPEAL, UNLESS THOSE RIGHTS ARE SPECIFICALLY INCLUDED IN THE 'ARBITRATION OF DISPUTES' PROVISION. IF YOU REFUSE TO SUBMIT TO ARBITRATION AFTER AGREEING TO THIS PROVISION, YOU MAY BE COMPELLED TO ARBITRATE UNDER THE AUTHORITY OF THE CALIFORNIA CODE OF CIVIL PROCEDURE. YOUR AGREEMENT TO THIS ARBITRATION PROVISION IS VOLUNTARY."

   "WE HAVE READ AND UNDERSTAND THE FOREGOING AND AGREE TO SUBMIT DISPUTES ARISING OUT OF THE MATTERS INCLUDED IN THE 'ARBITRATION OF DISPUTES' PROVISION TO NEUTRAL ARBITRATION."

   Seller's Initials _____ / _____        Broker's Initials _____ / _____

20. **ENTIRE AGREEMENT:** All prior discussions, negotiations and agreements between the parties concerning the subject matter of this Agreement are superseded by this Agreement, which constitutes the entire contract and a complete and exclusive expression of their agreement, and may not be contradicted by evidence of any prior agreement or contemporaneous oral agreement. If any provision of this Agreement is held to be ineffective or invalid, the remaining provisions will nevertheless be given full force and effect. This Agreement and any supplement, addendum or modification, including any photocopy or facsimile, may be executed in counterparts.

**By signing below, Seller acknowledges that Seller has read, understands, received a copy of and agrees to the terms of this Agreement.**

Seller _____ Date _____
Address _____ City _____ State _____ Zip _____
Telephone _____ Fax _____ E-mail _____

Seller _____ Date _____
Address _____ City _____ State _____ Zip _____
Telephone _____ Fax _____ E-mail _____

Real Estate Broker (Firm) _____ DRE Lic. # _____
By (Agent) _____ DRE Lic. # _____ Date _____
Address _____ City _____ State _____ Zip _____
Telephone _____ Fax _____ E-mail _____

THIS FORM HAS BEEN APPROVED BY THE CALIFORNIA ASSOCIATION OF REALTORS® (C.A.R.). NO REPRESENTATION IS MADE AS TO THE LEGAL VALIDITY OR ADEQUACY OF ANY PROVISION IN ANY SPECIFIC TRANSACTION. A REAL ESTATE BROKER IS THE PERSON QUALIFIED TO ADVISE ON REAL ESTATE TRANSACTIONS. IF YOU DESIRE LEGAL OR TAX ADVICE, CONSULT AN APPROPRIATE PROFESSIONAL.

This form is available for use by the entire real estate industry. It is not intended to identify the user as a REALTOR®. REALTOR® is a registered collective membership mark which may be used only by members of the NATIONAL ASSOCIATION OF REALTORS® who subscribe to its Code of Ethics.

Published and Distributed by:
REAL ESTATE BUSINESS SERVICES, INC.
a subsidiary of the California Association of REALTORS®
525 South Virgil Avenue, Los Angeles, California 90020

Reviewed by _____ Date _____        EQUAL HOUSING OPPORTUNITY

**RLA REVISED 2/09 (PAGE 3 OF 3)**

**RESIDENTIAL LISTING AGREEMENT - EXCLUSIVE (RLA PAGE 3 OF 3)**        Untitled

*A broker with an option listing must disclose to prospective buyers that he/she is acting in the dual role of agent and principal, and present all offers to the seller.*

Prior to exercising an option, the broker must disclose any anticipated profit and get the written consent of the seller.

**Example:** Broker Able listed a property from Seller Baker, and reserved an option to purchase the property himself. If Broker Able exercises the option, he must obtain written consent from Seller Baker which discloses the amount of profit or anticipated profit he will receive.

## B. LISTING AGREEMENT COPIES (Give Copy When Signed)

A copy of the listing agreement or any other real estate agreement, including the agency relationship form and the transfer disclosure statement, must be given to the signing party immediately after they are signed. This is a requirement of the Commissioner's Regulations, and a violation could result in license suspension or revocation.

## C. MULTIPLE LISTING SERVICE (MLS) (Subagents and Cooperating Brokers)

A **MULTIPLE LISTING SERVICE (MLS)** *is an association of real estate brokers that provides a pooling of listings, recent sales, and the sharing of commissions on a specified basis.* The advantage to the seller is that his or her home or property will receive wider market exposure because it will be shown by other cooperating brokers.

A **MULTIPLE LISTING** *is a listing, usually an exclusive right to sell, taken by a member of a multiple listing service, with the provision that all members of the multiple listing service have the opportunity to find an interested buyer.* Sometimes in exclusive areas, sellers will request that their listing not be put into the multiple listing service. This would limit the number of people (looky-loos) who just look at their properties for curiosity's sake.

*A "pocket listing" is the unethical practice of not giving a new listing to the MLS until the listing broker first tries to sell that listed property through only the other agents within the company.*

An agent can delegate some authority to his or her salespeople or other brokers and their salespeople. This is known as subagency. A **SUBAGENT** *is a licensed broker or salesperson upon whom some of the powers of an agent have been conferred, not by the principal, but by the agent with the principal's authorization.* The agent can delegate purely mechanical acts such as typing to anyone, but a subagency can only be created with the principal's consent. The subagent has the same duties and responsibilities as the agent.

*When a broker is acting as the subagent of the seller, the subagent is primarily responsible to the seller.*

**Example:** Real estate broker Brown, acting as a subagent of the seller, has a fiduciary duty to the seller and the agent who appointed him as subagent.

*A seller is bound by acts of the seller's broker, listing broker, and any subagent working under his broker. He is NOT bound by acts of the buyer's broker.*

*Generally, real estate agents will have to spend less time with clients who are better informed and have searched the Multiple Listing Services (MLSs).*

The "Internet generation" will probably be searching MLSs on the Net for their "dream home" before they first see a real estate broker or his or her salespeople. Clients can click on **ca.realtor.com** or **realtor.com** to search through every multiple listing service and every listed property in California by region and zip code. Customers can now see on the Internet what agents used to have to wait a week to see when the MLS printed the books of the current listings. The following is only a partial list of MLS websites:

**www.ca.realtor.com (California Living Network)**
**www.car.org (California Association of REALTORS®)**
**www.sucasa.net (California Association of REALTORS®, Spanish Version)**
**www.realtor.com (NAR Home Finder Sites)**

## D. MULTIPLE LISTING SERVICES ON THE INTERNET

Internet Multiple Listing Services are here to stay. Some are independent but most are still controlled by the local Boards of REALTORS®. The California Association of REALTORS® has the most complete system linking the MLS services of the entire state into one Internet address. *CAR.ORG or CA.REALTOR.COM is a source of California Multiple Listing Services' databases that links and provides the largest directory of homes for sale in California.* This has become the main source of available California home listings on the Internet. It breaks down California by regions, maps, and counties in order to help locate the Multiple Listing Service that covers whatever geographical area the user wants. It is the gateway to real estate listing information.

## E. COOPERATING BROKERS

A listing agreement usually authorizes the principal's agent to use cooperating brokers. A *COOPERATING BROKER is a non-listing broker with whom the listing broker agrees to share a commission (not necessarily ½ and ½) if the non-listing broker sells the property.*

*Typically, a cooperating broker, like the listing broker, represents the seller rather than the buyer, which is often a big surprise to the buyer.*

Real estate brokers often belong to a Multiple Listing Service (MLS). Under the terms of MLS membership, when a broker obtains a listing he or she submits it to the MLS. That permits other brokers who belong to the MLS to help find buyer for the listed property. In relation to the listing broker, these other brokers are known as cooperating brokers.

*If a cooperating broker is the procuring cause in bringing about the sale of the property, the listing broker pays the cooperating broker a share of the commission. Agreements between brokers and salespeople must be in writing.*

### 1. Selling in Other States

Since each state has its own licensing laws, how can a cooperating broker sell a property for a commission in another state? The answer is simple. Find a licensed, cooperating broker in that state.

> *"Comps" are the recent sales prices of similar properties in a neighborhood. It's the most important information a real estate salesperson can provide a buyer to pick a "realistic offering price" or a seller to "understand current market pricing."*

A salesperson can quickly obtain a fairly accurate estimate of the probable selling price of a property to be listed or sold by knowing and comparing **recent selling prices (comps)**. Comps are proprietary information, the most comprehensive versions of which are given out only to members of the Multiple Listing Service (MLS) associations. As such, it can be difficult for buyers and sellers to access current comps—although similar information may be obtained by visiting the website listed below.

**Because it can be so difficult to obtain accurate comps, buyers and sellers usually seek out the professional services of real estate salespeople.**

Most sellers are not realistic about the "probable selling price" of their property. Sellers do not always realize that informed buyers will normally purchase only the lowest priced house among similarly priced homes. Comps are used by the buyers as a basis to determine a realistic offering price. Often a property owner mistakenly believes he or she can get 10% or more over what recent comps indicate a property is worth. Realistically, there is little chance a buyer will pay more than 3% over the probable selling price, the result of which is that the overpriced property is often overlooked by brokers and remains unsold for a long period of time.

While the MLS comps may be more accurate and detailed, surfing the Net can turn up alternative methods for finding similar information. The Internet company listed below can give a rough estimate of comps based on secondary sales information statistically averaged by recorded tracts or zip codes. These are "computer-generated" figures, not "cherry-picked" by salespeople, brokers, or appraisers.

**www.zillow.com**
**(Virtual comparables)**

## IV. Commissions (Negotiable)

A *COMMISSION in real estate is a fee paid, usually as a percentage of the selling price, to a broker/ agent as compensation for his or her services.* Traditionally, it is payment from the seller to the agent who finds a ready, willing, and able buyer to purchase the seller's property, according to the listing terms or any other terms acceptable to the seller.

*A broker/agent can pay a finder's fee to an unlicensed individual only for introducing a client to the broker/agent.*

A *COMMISSION SPLIT is a previously agreed split between a broker and his or her salesperson of a commission earned on a sale.* Commission rates vary by negotiation throughout California, but usually range from 3% to 10% of the selling price. The listing agreement states that a commission is to be paid only when all the terms of the listing or other acceptable terms of the sale are met.

*An agent can accept a commission in the form of a note, cash, or personal check.*

# YouTube as a Marketing Tool

*Imagine having an open house where clients can do a "walk through" without personally visiting the property. Streaming video tours on your website or social networking sites like YouTube allow your clients to see the listed properties anytime they want.*

While "virtual tours" on YouTube may never replace a good old fashion walk through, Internet screening may very well eliminate the real estate "drive-by" and "looky-loo" phenomenon. Potential homebuyers no longer need to drive-by a home to get a feel for such things as the neighborhood, condition of the house, curbside appeal, interior layout, spacial relationships, and kitchen design. Because of digital technology, a prospective buyer can zoom in and out, follow the camera to another room, check out the ceiling, and get a 360 degree view of a living room or bedroom. Once clients have seen a video of both the inside and outside of a home, they can decide if they're interested before contacting an agent.

"Streaming video tours" may encompass not only the house for sale, but also show the surrounding area, including schools, churches, shopping districts, and parks. If a picture is worth a thousand words, imagine how valuable a picture tour on a website could be. Picture tours are an effective means to attract both buyers and sellers.

You may want to lend a hand and prepare Web pictures for busy and non-computer oriented salespeople in your office, as it will benefit you and your company in the long run. In fact, many will be willing to pay you for this service. Because you offer picture tours on the Web, sellers will prefer to list properties with you. Not only will your listings increase, but they will also get more attention from buyers.

A real estate licensee who can provide photo or video services to real estate agents will always be in demand. He or she can take digital photos and videos of a property without the listing agent present and speed up the process of getting that property listed on the company's website tours. Panoramic videos are valuable visual aides for a buyer to see size and scale, and a walking video tour provides an unparalleled viewing experience for all to get the feel of space and flow.

**SERVICES**

www.ipix.com (Internet Pictures Corp.)
www.home-view.com/ (HomeView.com)
www.evox.com (eVox Productions)
www.virtualproperties.com (Virtual Tours)

**SOFTWARE**

www.imoveinc.com
  (iMove Spherical Imaging Systems)
www.apple.com/quicktime/
  (Quicktime)

When a broker lists a property for sale and a cooperating broker sells it, the commission is shared. Although the ratio for dividing the commission varies, it is often 50% to the listing broker, and 50% to the selling broker. If a salesperson is involved, he or she shares in the employing broker's part of the commission.

*Salespeople only receive compensation for real estate transactions from their employing brokers. All persons performing real estate activities for compensation must hold a valid real estate license.*

A commission can be earned even if the sale is not finalized. **The broker is entitled to a commission if all the "exact" terms of the listing agreement are met**, provided the buyer is ready, willing, and able to complete the transaction. This is true even if the seller changes his or her mind and refuses to sell. If there is a valid listing agreement and the exact terms are met, the seller is still responsible for the commission. See **Figure 4-5** for facts about commissions from auctions.

> **Example:** Seller Able accepted an offer on his home presented by Broker Baker, and acceptance was communicated back to the buyer. Prior to opening escrow, however, Seller Able received an all cash offer to purchase the property. He decided to cancel the original contract and notified Broker Baker of his decision. Broker Baker has a good legal basis (excellent chance) to collect a commission.

A broker or his or her salesperson must be the procuring cause of a sale to earn a commission. *PROCURING CAUSE is defined as a series of unbroken events that lead to an acceptable agreement with the seller*. If there are several brokers trying to sell the same property, the one who is the procuring cause of the sale is entitled to the selling broker's portion of the commission.

*A listing for a residential building containing 1-4 dwelling units must include a notice that the commission is negotiable.*

# V. Transfer Disclosure Statement

## A. EASTON V. STRASSBURGER

A 1984 California Court of Appeals decision in the case of *Easton v. Strassburger* greatly extended the liability of brokers engaged in real estate sales. **Be warned:** Brokers are required to be aware (or should be aware) of all material facts negatively influencing the value or desirability of the property (**"red flags"**), discoverable by a reasonable visual inspection, and must disclose these facts to all prospective buyers.

*Legally, the listing broker and the buyer's broker must conduct a reasonably competent, diligent, and visual inspection of accessible areas of the property and disclose to a prospective buyer all material facts affecting value and desirability.*

## B. TRANSFER DISCLOSURE STATEMENT (TDS)
### (Seller and Selling Broker Must Provide This Form)

*The law requires sellers of residential property of from one-to-four units (which includes triplexes) to provide prospective buyers with a Real Estate Transfer Disclosure Statement.*

The *REAL ESTATE TRANSFER DISCLOSURE STATEMENT (TDS) identifies items of value attached to the structure or land and states whether these items are operational* (see **Figure 4-6**). It also asks the seller to identify any structural or material defects. This form provides an opportunity for the seller to completely disclose problems of any kind that might adversely affect the value of the property. The obligation to prepare and deliver the Transfer Disclosure Statement to the prospective buyer is imposed upon **the seller and the seller's broker** (see Civil Code Section 1102.6 for exemptions).

*A buyer has two years to sue an agent for failure to make proper disclosures in the Transfer Disclosure Statement.*

---

**Figure 4-5**

## *Real Estate Auction...*
## Another Way to Sell and Receive Commissions

A **REAL ESTATE AUCTION** *is a meeting where interested parties come together and continue to offer higher bids (purchase prices) until only one bidder is left, to whom the property is sold.* The person making the highest bid buys the property. The time and place are always stated on the announcement, but the amount of advertising depends on the type of auction. An **AUCTIONEER** *is a seller.* An auction is one of the quickest ways to unload a piece of property. Auctions are very popular with government agencies and builders in over-built or economically depressed communities. This can be a great way to pick up a real bargain property, as long as you bid using your head, not your heart. Auctions are emotional events where the excitement keeps rising until the property is sold. The best buys are at foreclosure sales, which are put on by public agencies, banks, or savings banks.

An **ABSOLUTE AUCTION** *is an auction where the property must be sold to the highest bidder no matter how low the final bid.* A **NO-SALE AUCTION** *is where there is a minimum bid underlying each property so that a certain price must be reached before the property will be sold.* In legitimate auctions, the starting bid is the minimum bid. But if that fact is not stated, make sure the minimum bid is stated clearly before the auction starts, or do not bid.

*In an "auction without reserve," the auctioneer sets a minimum bid to begin an auction. If someone offers to buy at 10% more than the opening bid, this bid must be accepted, as an auctioneer is required to accept bids in an auction without reserve.*

Do not attend a real property auction if you have not first seen the property and decided what you would be willing to pay for it. The broker auctioneers will be glad to give you maps or help you view the properties. Remember, don't get caught up in auction fever, because you should never go beyond your maximum bid price established well in advance of the auction.

*An auction salesperson represents the seller and is required to have a real estate license.*

**www.cwsmarketing.com (Online Auctions)**
**www.jpking.com (JP King Auction Company)**

*In New Zealand, auctions are the most common method of selling real estate!*

---

## Figure 4-6

**CALIFORNIA ASSOCIATION OF REALTORS®**

**REAL ESTATE TRANSFER DISCLOSURE STATEMENT**
(CALIFORNIA CIVIL CODE §1102, ET SEQ)
(C.A.R. Form TDS, Revised 10/03)

THIS DISCLOSURE STATEMENT CONCERNS THE REAL PROPERTY SITUATED IN THE CITY OF _____ , COUNTY OF _____ , STATE OF CALIFORNIA, DESCRIBED AS _____ *123 Sail Avenue ,* _____ . THIS STATEMENT IS A DISCLOSURE OF THE CONDITION OF THE ABOVE DESCRIBED PROPERTY IN COMPLIANCE WITH SECTION 1102 OF THE CIVIL CODE AS OF (date) _____ . IT IS NOT A WARRANTY OF ANY KIND BY THE SELLER(S) OR ANY AGENT(S) REPRESENTING ANY PRINCIPAL(S) IN THIS TRANSACTION, AND IS NOT A SUBSTITUTE FOR ANY INSPECTIONS OR WARRANTIES THE PRINCIPAL(S) MAY WISH TO OBTAIN.

### I. COORDINATION WITH OTHER DISCLOSURE FORMS

This Real Estate Transfer Disclosure Statement is made pursuant to Section 1102 of the Civil Code. Other statutes require disclosures, depending upon the details of the particular real estate transaction (for example: special study zone and purchase-money liens on residential property).

**Substituted Disclosures:** The following disclosures and other disclosures required by law, including the Natural Hazard Disclosure Report/Statement that may include airport annoyances, earthquake, fire, flood, or special assessment information, have or will be made in connection with this real estate transfer, and are intended to satisfy the disclosure obligations on this form, where the subject matter is the same:

☐ Inspection reports completed pursuant to the contract of sale or receipt for deposit.
☐ Additional inspection reports or disclosures: _____
_____

### II. SELLER'S INFORMATION

The Seller discloses the following information with the knowledge that even though this is not a warranty, prospective Buyers may rely on this information in deciding whether and on what terms to purchase the subject property. Seller hereby authorizes any agent(s) representing any principal(s) in this transaction to provide a copy of this statement to any person or entity in connection with any actual or anticipated sale of the property.

THE FOLLOWING ARE REPRESENTATIONS MADE BY THE SELLER(S) AND ARE NOT THE REPRESENTATIONS OF THE AGENT(S), IF ANY. THIS INFORMATION IS A DISCLOSURE AND IS NOT INTENDED TO BE PART OF ANY CONTRACT BETWEEN THE BUYER AND SELLER.

Seller ☐ is ☐ is not occupying the property.

**A. The subject property has the items checked below (read across)**

| | | |
|---|---|---|
| ☐ Range | ☐ Oven | ☐ Microwave |
| ☐ Dishwasher | ☐ Trash Compactor | ☐ Garbage Disposal |
| ☐ Washer/Dryer Hookups | | ☐ Rain Gutters |
| ☐ Burglar Alarms | ☐ Smoke Detector(s) | ☐ Fire Alarm |
| ☐ T.V. Antenna | ☐ Satellite Dish | ☐ Intercom |
| ☐ Central Heating | ☐ Central Air Conditioning | ☐ Evaporator Cooler(s) |
| ☐ Wall/Window Air Conditioning | ☐ Sprinklers | ☐ Public Sewer System |
| ☐ Septic Tank | ☐ Sump Pump | ☐ Water Softener |
| ☐ Patio/Decking | ☐ Built-in Barbecue | ☐ Gazebo |
| ☐ Sauna | | |
| ☐ Hot Tub ☐ Locking Safety Cover* | ☐ Pool ☐ Child Resistant Barrier* | ☐ Spa ☐ Locking Safety Cover* |
| ☐ Security Gate(s) | ☐ Automatic Garage Door Opener(s)* | ☐ Number Remote Controls |
| Garage: ☐ Attached | ☐ Not Attached | ☐ Carport |
| Pool/Spa Heater: ☐ Gas | ☐ Solar | ☐ Electric |
| Water Heater: ☐ Gas | ☐ Water Heater Anchored, Braced, or Strapped* | |
| Water Supply: ☐ City | ☐ Well | ☐ Private Utility or |
| Gas Supply: ☐ Utility | ☐ Bottled | Other |
| ☐ Window Screens | ☐ Window Security Bars ☐ Quick Release Mechanism on Bedroom Windows* | |

Exhaust Fan(s) in _____ 220 Volt Wiring in _____ Fireplace(s) in _____
☐ Gas Starter _____ ☐ Roof(s): Type: _____ Age: _____ (approx.)
☐ Other: _____
Are there, to the best of your (Seller's) knowledge, any of the above that are not in operating condition? ☐ Yes ☐ No. If yes, then describe. (Attach additional sheets if necessary): _____

**(*see footnote on page 2)**

Buyer's Initials ( _____ )( _____ )
Seller's Initials ( _____ )( _____ )
Reviewed by _____ Date _____

**EQUAL HOUSING OPPORTUNITY**

**TDS REVISED 10/03 (PAGE 1 OF 3)**
**REAL ESTATE TRANSFER DISCLOSURE STATEMENT (TDS PAGE 1 OF 3)**

| Agent: WALT HUBER | Phone: | Prepared using zipForm® software |
|---|---|---|
| Broker: WALT HUBER REALTOR | | |

Property Address: _123 Sail Avenue_ _____ Date: _____

**B.** Are you (Seller) aware of any significant defects/malfunctions in any of the following? ☐ Yes ☐ No. If yes, check appropriate space(s) below.

☐ Interior Walls ☐ Ceilings ☐ Floors ☐ Exterior Walls ☐ Insulation ☐ Roof(s) ☐ Windows ☐ Doors ☐ Foundation ☐ Slab(s)
☐ Driveways ☐ Sidewalks ☐ Walls/Fences ☐ Electrical Systems ☐ Plumbing/Sewers/Septics ☐ Other Structural Components
(Describe: _____
_____
_____ )

If any of the above is checked, explain. (Attach additional sheets if necessary): _____
_____
_____
_____
_____

*This garage door opener or child resistant pool barrier may not be in compliance with the safety standards relating to automatic reversing devices as set forth in Chapter 12.5 (commencing with Section 19890) of Part 3 of Division 13 of, or with the pool safety standards of Article 2.5 (commencing with Section 115920) of Chapter 5 of Part 10 of Division 104 of, the Health and Safety Code. The water heater may not be anchored, braced, or strapped in accordance with Section 19211 of the Health and Safety Code. Window security bars may not have quick release mechanisms in compliance with the 1995 Edition of the California Building Standards Code.

**C.** Are you (Seller) aware of any the following:

1. Substances, materials, or products which may be an environmental hazard such as, but not limited to, asbestos, formaldehyde, radon gas, lead-based paint, mold, fuel or chemical storage tanks, and contaminated soil or water on the subject property . . . . . . . . . . . . . . . . . . . . . . . . . . . . . . . . . . . . . . . . . . . . . . . . . . ☐ Yes ☐ No
2. Features of the property shared in common with adjoining landowners, such as walls, fences, and driveways, whose use or responsibility for maintenance may have an effect on the subject property . . . . . . . . . . . . . . . . . ☐ Yes ☐ No
3. Any encroachments, easements or similar matters that may affect your interest in the subject property . . . . . . . . ☐ Yes ☐ No
4. Room additions, structural modifications, or other alterations or repairs made without necessary permits. . . . . . ☐ Yes ☐ No
5. Room additions, structural modifications, or other alterations or repairs not in compliance with building codes. . . . ☐ Yes ☐ No
6. Fill (compacted or otherwise) on the property or any portion thereof . . . . . . . . . . . . . . . . . . . . . . . . . ☐ Yes ☐ No
7. Any settling from any cause, or slippage, sliding, or other soil problems . . . . . . . . . . . . . . . . . . . . . . . . ☐ Yes ☐ No
8. Flooding, drainage or grading problems . . . . . . . . . . . . . . . . . . . . . . . . . . . . . . . . . . . . . . . . . . . . ☐ Yes ☐ No
9. Major damage to the property or any of the structures from fire, earthquake, floods, or landslides . . . . . . . . . . . . ☐ Yes ☐ No
10. Any zoning violations, nonconforming uses, violations of "setback" requirements . . . . . . . . . . . . . . . . . . . . . . ☐ Yes ☐ No
11. Neighborhood noise problems or other nuisances . . . . . . . . . . . . . . . . . . . . . . . . . . . . . . . . . . . . . . . . ☐ Yes ☐ No
12. CC&R's or other deed restrictions or obligations . . . . . . . . . . . . . . . . . . . . . . . . . . . . . . . . . . . . . . . . ☐ Yes ☐ No
13. Homeowners' Association which has any authority over the subject property . . . . . . . . . . . . . . . . . . . . . . . ☐ Yes ☐ No
14. Any "common area" (facilities such as pools, tennis courts, walkways, or other areas co-owned in undivided interest with others) . . . . . . . . . . . . . . . . . . . . . . . . . . . . . . . . . . . . . . . . . . . . . . . . . . . . . . . . . . ☐ Yes ☐ No
15. Any notices of abatement or citations against the property . . . . . . . . . . . . . . . . . . . . . . . . . . . . . . . . . . ☐ Yes ☐ No
16. Any lawsuits by or against the seller threatening to or affecting this real property, including any lawsuits alleging a defect or deficiency in this real property or "common areas" (facilities such as pools, tennis courts, walkways, or other areas, co-owned in undivided interest with others) . . . . . . . . . . . . . . . . . . . . . . . . . . . . . . . . . . . ☐ Yes ☐ No

If the answer to any of these is yes, explain. (Attach additional sheets if necessary): _____
_____
_____
_____
_____

Seller certifies that the information herein is true and correct to the best of the Seller's knowledge as of the date signed by the Seller.

Seller _____ Date _____

Seller _____ Date _____

Buyer's Initials ( _____ ) ( _____ )

Reviewed by _____ Date _____

**TDS REVISED 10/03 (PAGE 2 OF 3)**

**REAL ESTATE TRANSFER DISCLOSURE STATEMENT (TDS PAGE 2 OF 3)**

Property Address: *123 Sail Avenue* , _____ Date: _____

## III. AGENT'S INSPECTION DISCLOSURE
(To be completed only if the Seller is represented by an agent in this transaction.)

**THE UNDERSIGNED, BASED ON THE ABOVE INQUIRY OF THE SELLER(S) AS TO THE CONDITION OF THE PROPERTY AND BASED ON A REASONABLY COMPETENT AND DILIGENT VISUAL INSPECTION OF THE ACCESSIBLE AREAS OF THE PROPERTY IN CONJUNCTION WITH THAT INQUIRY, STATES THE FOLLOWING:**

☐ Agent notes no items for disclosure.
☐ Agent notes the following items: _____
_____
_____
_____

Agent (Broker Representing Seller) _____ By _____ Date _____
                        (Please Print)                        (Associate Licensee or Broker Signature)

## IV. AGENT'S INSPECTION DISCLOSURE
(To be completed only if the agent who has obtained the offer is other than the agent above.)

**THE UNDERSIGNED, BASED ON A REASONABLY COMPETENT AND DILIGENT VISUAL INSPECTION OF THE ACCESSIBLE AREAS OF THE PROPERTY, STATES THE FOLLOWING:**

☐ Agent notes no items for disclosure.
☐ Agent notes the following items: _____
_____
_____
_____

Agent (Broker Obtaining the Offer) _____ By _____ Date _____
                     (Please Print)                        (Associate Licensee or Broker Signature)

**V. BUYER(S) AND SELLER(S) MAY WISH TO OBTAIN PROFESSIONAL ADVICE AND/OR INSPECTIONS OF THE PROPERTY AND TO PROVIDE FOR APPROPRIATE PROVISIONS IN A CONTRACT BETWEEN BUYER AND SELLER(S) WITH RESPECT TO ANY ADVICE/INSPECTIONS/DEFECTS.**

**I/WE ACKNOWLEDGE RECEIPT OF A COPY OF THIS STATEMENT.**

Seller _____ Date _____ Buyer _____ Date _____

Seller _____ Date _____ Buyer _____ Date _____

Agent (Broker Representing Seller) _____ By _____ Date _____
                        (Please Print)                        (Associate Licensee or Broker Signature)

Agent (Broker Obtaining the Offer) _____ By _____ Date _____
                     (Please Print)                        (Associate Licensee or Broker Signature)

**SECTION 1102.3 OF THE CIVIL CODE PROVIDES A BUYER WITH THE RIGHT TO RESCIND A PURCHASE CONTRACT FOR AT LEAST THREE DAYS AFTER THE DELIVERY OF THIS DISCLOSURE IF DELIVERY OCCURS AFTER THE SIGNING OF AN OFFER TO PURCHASE. IF YOU WISH TO RESCIND THE CONTRACT, YOU MUST ACT WITHIN THE PRESCRIBED PERIOD.**

**A REAL ESTATE BROKER IS QUALIFIED TO ADVISE ON REAL ESTATE. IF YOU DESIRE LEGAL ADVICE, CONSULT YOUR ATTORNEY.**

Published and Distributed by:
REAL ESTATE BUSINESS SERVICES, INC.
*a subsidiary of the California Association of REALTORS®*
525 South Virgil Avenue, Los Angeles, California 90020

TDS REVISED 10/03 (PAGE 3 OF 3)

Reviewed by _____ Date _____

EQUAL HOUSING OPPORTUNITY

**REAL ESTATE TRANSFER DISCLOSURE STATEMENT (TDS PAGE 3 OF 3)**     Untitled

The following sequence of events may help explain how the four parties (seller, seller's agent, buyer, and buyer's agent) fill in and sign the Transfer Disclosure Statement form:

1. The Transfer Disclosure Statement form should be filled out and signed completely by the seller at the time of listing the property. Since the seller is the one most familiar with the property, he or she must be encouraged to be forthright and honest about all known defects.

2. The seller's agent makes a visual, diligent inspection of the property, fills out the appropriate section of the Transfer Disclosure Statement, and signs at the same time the seller lists the property for sale.

*The listing agent can never legally complete the entire Real Property Transfer Disclosure Statement.*

3. The buyer should receive a copy of the Transfer Disclosure Statement and sign that he or she has received it before making a written offer.

4. The buyer's agent must also visually inspect the property, fill out the appropriate section of the statement, and sign it.

5. If the buyer fails to receive the Transfer Disclosure Statement form prior to signing the contractual offer (purchase agreement), he or she has the right to cancel, after receipt of the Transfer Disclosure Statement, for any reason (three days if delivered by hand or five days if mailed). A written notice of termination must be delivered to the seller or to the seller's broker.

*A "TDS" is required for an "as is" sale of a single-family residence by a private person.*

# VI. Broker's Responsibilities

## A. TRUST ACCOUNTS (Other People's Money)

*After reconciliation of a trust account, the client's liabilities should equal the trust account balance.*

A broker accepting a money deposit (and instructions) is required to: 1) give it to the principal; 2) place it in a trust account; or 3) give it to an escrow company. **Deposits other than the initial deposit (usually around $200) to start the account are never the personal property of the broker**. Any moneys accepted should go, within three business days, into an independent bank trust account in the name of the broker as trustee. Most trust accounts are non-interest-bearing because all overages must be explained. Placing a buyer's cash or check in the broker's personal account is called commingling.

*A broker can keep $200 of his/her personal funds in a trust account without being guilty of commingling.*

COMMINGLING *is the mixing together of the funds of a principal and a licensee.* Commingling is a violation of the Commissioner's Regulations. Commingling is the opposite of segregating (keeping separate).

*Commingling is the illegal practice of mixing a client's money with the agent's private funds. By law, each entry in the broker's trust fund account (bank) must be identified.*

*CONVERSION is the unlawful misappropriation and use of a client's funds by a licensee.* A broker, who upon receipt spends his or her principal's deposit without the principal's authorization, has not commingled funds with his or her own funds in a technical sense, but has converted them. This is a much more serious violation than commingling, with heavy criminal penalties.

*An unlicensed employee of a broker who is authorized in writing can make withdrawals from the broker's trust account provided the employee is covered by a "fidelity bond" for at least the amount of funds to which the employee has access at any given time.*

### B. TRANSACTION FILE (Keep for Three Years)

A *TRANSACTION FILE is the file or folder (**all documents**) kept for three years by the broker for each real estate transaction in which the broker or his or her salespeople participated.*

The Commissioner of real estate has the right to inspect this file. Maintaining a complete, up-to-date transaction file is not only good business practice, **it is the law**.

A licensed broker must retain for three years copies of all listings, purchase agreements, canceled checks, trust fund records and other documents executed by the broker or obtained by him or her in connection with any real estate transaction. The retention period shall run from the date of the closing of the transaction or from the date of the listing, if the transaction is not consummated.

*The Real Estate Commissioner requires that all records of a broker or salesperson be kept a minimum of three years.*

## Uniform Electronic Transactions Act (Record Retention)

A real estate broker who obtains documents in any transaction for which a real estate broker license is required, when such documents contain an electronic signature pursuant to the Uniform Electronic Transaction Act, must retain a copy of such documents by: 1) Causing a paper copy of the document to be made or 2) By using electronic image storing media. The broker may retain copies of such documents at a location other than the broker's place of business.

### C. SALESPEOPLE MAY BE INDEPENDENT CONTRACTORS OR EMPLOYEES

*A salesperson cannot act independently of a real estate broker.*

In California, the Department of Real Estate considers a salesperson an employee of the broker for the purpose of the administration of the real estate broker law, even if he or she act as independent contractors for other purposes, such as income tax wage withholding, social security, or medicare coverage. **This makes the broker responsible for the real estate activities of the salesperson.**

An *INDEPENDENT CONTRACTOR sells results rather than time, and his or her physical conduct is not subject to the control of another.* An *EMPLOYEE, on the other hand, works under the direct control (designated hours and breaks) and supervision of the employer.*

A broker who hires an unlicensed person to practice real estate, as well as the unlicensed practitioner, may be fined up to $20,000 each. The county district attorney prosecutes law violations by unlicensed persons.

*Most real estate licensees are considered independent contractors under Federal Income Tax Laws, but according to California Real Estate Law, and the Real Estate Commissioner, they are considered employees of the broker.*

An unlicensed person (like a secretary or bookkeeper) cannot give information regarding a real estate transaction on the phone or in any way practice real estate for compensation. An unlicensed assistant who prepares an advertisement must have prior written approval by the employing broker.

In most real estate offices, the salespeople are treated as independent contractors. They come and go at will, working no fixed hours and paying their own payroll taxes (Federal and State Income Taxes, Social Security, Unemployment Insurance, and State Disability Insurance). More strictly supervised workers, such as secretaries, are generally considered employees. **The broker is required, however, to carry workers' compensation and public liability insurance for salespeople in the same way that they do for employees**.

*Licenses do NOT have to be displayed, but must be kept at the employing broker's main office.*

## D. WRITTEN BROKER-ASSOCIATE CONTRACTS

As required by the Real Estate Commissioner's Regulations, **brokers must have a written contract with each licensed member of the sales staff**. The employment contract shall cover all material aspects of the relationship between the parties, including supervision of licensed activities, duties, and compensation. **A copy of this contract must be retained by all parties for three years from the date of termination**. This is also required of salespeople who are themselves brokers but are working under another broker's license. The agreement shall be dated and signed by the parties and shall cover material aspects of the relationship between the parties, including supervision of licensed activities, duties, and compensation.

*"Broker-salesperson contracts" must be in writing. This contract is NOT required to be approved by the Department of Real Estate.*

**Figure 4-7** shows the three-page CAR® Independent Contractor Agreement (Between Broker and Associate-Licensee). It outlines the duties, responsibilities, and compensation to be provided and must be signed and dated by both the broker and the salesperson.

*Other specific rules and policies for handling procedures at a specific brokerage firm are usually set down in the company POLICY MANUAL. This manual must be read by all salespeople.*

## E. DRE NOTIFICATION

*When a salesperson chooses to leave the employ of a broker, that broker must notify the DRE within 10 days. When a salesperson transfers a license to a new broker, that broker must notify the DRE within 5 days of the new employment.*

If a salesperson is fired for cause, the broker must notify the DRE in writing immediately.

**Figure 4-7**

CALIFORNIA
ASSOCIATION
OF REALTORS®

**INDEPENDENT CONTRACTOR AGREEMENT**
**(Between Broker and Associate-Licensee)**
(C.A.R. Form ICA, Revised 4/09)

This Agreement, dated _____ , is made between _____
_____ ("Broker") and
_____ ("Associate-Licensee").

In consideration of the covenants and representations contained in this Agreement, Broker and Associate-Licensee agree as follows:

1. **BROKER:** Broker represents that Broker is duly licensed as a real estate broker by the State of California, ☐ doing business as _____
_____ (firm name), ☐ a sole proprietorship, ☐ a partnership, or ☐ a corporation.
Broker is a member of the _____
Association(s) of REALTORS®, and a subscriber to the _____ Multiple
Listing Service(s). Broker shall keep Broker's license current during the term of this Agreement.

2. **ASSOCIATE-LICENSEE:** Associate-Licensee represents that: **(i)** he/she is duly licensed by the State of California as a ☐ real estate broker,
☐ real estate salesperson, and **(ii)** he/she has not used any other names within the past five years, except _____
_____. Associate-Licensee shall keep his/her license current during
the term of this Agreement, including satisfying all applicable continuing education and provisional license requirements.

3. **INDEPENDENT CONTRACTOR RELATIONSHIP:**
   A. Broker and Associate-Licensee intend that, to the maximum extent permissible by law: **(i)** This Agreement does not constitute an employment agreement by either party; **(ii)** Broker and Associate-Licensee are independent contracting parties with respect to all services rendered under this Agreement; and **(iii)** This Agreement shall not be construed as a partnership.
   B. Broker shall not: **(i)** restrict Associate-Licensee's activities to particular geographical areas or, **(ii)** dictate Associate-Licensee's activities with regard to hours, leads, open houses, opportunity or floor time, production, prospects, sales meetings, schedule, inventory, time off, vacation, or similar activities, except to the extent required by law.
   C. Associate-Licensee shall not be required to accept an assignment by Broker to service any particular current or prospective listing or parties.
   D. Except as required by law: **(i)** Associate-Licensee retains sole and absolute discretion and judgment in the methods, techniques, and procedures to be used in soliciting and obtaining listings, sales, exchanges, leases, rentals, or other transactions, and in carrying out Associate-Licensee's selling and soliciting activities; **(ii)** Associate-Licensee is under the control of Broker as to the results of Associate-Licensee's work only, and not as to the means by which those results are accomplished; **(iii)** Associate-Licensee has no authority to bind Broker by any promise or representation and **(iv)** Broker shall not be liable for any obligation or liability incurred by Associate-Licensee.
   E. Associate-Licensee's only remuneration shall be the compensation specified in paragraph 8.
   F. Associate-Licensee who only performs as a real estate sales agent, shall not be treated as an employee for state and federal tax purposes. However, an Associate-Licencee who performs loan activity shall be treated as an employee for state and federal tax purposes unless the activity satisfies the legal requirements to establish an independent contractor relationship.
   G. The fact the Broker may carry worker compensation insurance for Broker's own benefit and for the mutual benefit of Broker and licensees associated with Broker, including Associate-Licensee, shall not create an inference of employment.
   **(Workers' Compensation Advisory:** Even though Associate-Licensees may be treated as independent contractors for tax and other purposes, the California Labor and Workforce Development Agency considers them to be employees for workers' compensation purposes. According to that Agency, **(i)** Broker must obtain workers' compensation insurance for Associate-Licensees and **(ii)** Broker, not Associate-Licensees, must bear the cost of workers' compensation insurance. Penalties for failure to carry workers' compensation include, among others, the issuance of stop-work orders and fines of up to $1,000 per agent, not to exceed $100,000 per company.)

4. **LICENSED ACTIVITY:** All listings of property, and all agreements, acts or actions for performance of licensed acts, which are taken or performed in connection with this Agreement, shall be taken and performed in the name of Broker. Associate-Licensee agrees to and does hereby contribute all right and title to such listings to Broker for the benefit and use of Broker, Associate-Licensee, and other licensees associated with Broker. Broker shall make available to Associate-Licensee, equally with other licensees associated with Broker, all current listings in Broker's office, except any listing which Broker may choose to place in the exclusive servicing of Associate-Licensee or one or more other specific licensees associated with Broker. Associate-Licensee shall provide and pay for all professional licenses, supplies, services, and other items required in connection with Associate-Licensee's activities under this Agreement, or any listing or transaction, without reimbursement from Broker except as required by law. Associate-Licensee shall work diligently and with his/her best efforts: **(i)** sell, exchange, lease, or rent properties listed with Broker or other cooperating Brokers; **(ii)** solicit additional listings, clients, and customers; and **(iii)** otherwise promote the business of serving the public in real estate transactions to the end that Broker and Associate-Licensee may derive the greatest benefit possible, in accordance with law. Associate-Licensee shall not commit any unlawful act under federal, state or local law or regulation while conducting licensed activity. Associate-Licensee shall at all times be familiar, and comply, with all applicable federal, state and local laws, including, but not limited to, anti-discrimination laws and restrictions against the giving or accepting of a fee, or other thing of value, for the referral of business to title companies, escrow companies, home inspection companies, pest control companies and other settlement service providers pursuant to the California Business and Professions Code and the Real Estate Settlement Procedures Acts (RESPA). Broker shall make available for Associate-Licensee's use, along with other licensees associated with Broker, the facilities of the real estate office operated by Broker at _____
_____ and the facilities of any other office
locations made available by Broker pursuant to this Agreement.

**ICA REVISED 4/09 (PAGE 1 OF 3)**

Broker's Initials ( _____ ) ( _____ )
Associate-Licensee's Initials ( _____ ) ( _____ )

Reviewed by _____ Date _____

EQUAL HOUSING
OPPORTUNITY

**INDEPENDENT CONTRACTOR AGREEMENT (ICA PAGE 1 OF 3)**

| Agent: WALT HUBER | Phone: | Prepared using zipForm® software |
| Broker: WALT HUBER REALTOR | | |

5. **PROPRIETARY INFORMATION AND FILES:** **(A)** All files and documents pertaining to listings, leads and transactions are the property of Broker and shall be delivered to Broker by Associate-Licensee immediately upon request or termination of this Agreement. **(B)** Associate-Licensee acknowledges that Broker's method of conducting business is a protected trade secret. **(C)** Associate-Licensee shall not use to his/her own advantage, or the advantage of any other person, business, or entity, except as specifically agreed in writing, either during Associate-Licensee's association with Broker, or thereafter, any information gained for or from the business, or files of Broker.

6. **SUPERVISION:** Associate-Licensee, within 24 hours (or ☐ _____ ) after preparing, signing, or receiving same, shall submit to Broker, or Broker's designated licensee: **(i)** all documents which may have a material effect upon the rights and duties of principals in a transaction, **(ii)** any documents or other items connected with a transaction pursuant to this Agreement in the possession of or available to; Associate-Licensee and; **(iii)** all documents associated with any real estate transaction in which Associate-Licensee is a principal.

7. **TRUST FUNDS:** All trust funds shall be handled in compliance with the Business and Professions Code, and other applicable laws.

8. **COMPENSATION:**
   A. **TO BROKER:** Compensation shall be charged to parties who enter into listing or other agreements for services requiring a real estate license:
      ☐ as shown in "Exhibit A" attached, which is incorporated as a part of this Agreement by reference, or
      ☐ as follows: _____
      _____
      Any deviation which is not approved in writing in advance by Broker, shall be: **(1)** deducted from Associate-Licensee's compensation, if lower than the amount or rate approved above; and, **(2)** subject to Broker approval, if higher than the amount approved above. Any permanent change in commission schedule shall be disseminated by Broker to Associate-Licensee.
   B. **TO ASSOCIATE-LICENSEE:** Associate-Licensee shall receive a share of compensation actually collected by Broker, on listings or other agreements for services requiring a real estate license, which are solicited and obtained by Associate-Licensee, and on transactions of which Associate-Licensee's activities are the procuring cause, as follows:
      ☐ as shown in "Exhibit B" attached, which is incorporated as a part of this Agreement by reference, or
      ☐ other: _____
      _____
   C. **PARTNERS, TEAMS, AND AGREEMENTS WITH OTHER ASSOCIATE-LICENSEES IN OFFICE:** If Associate-Licensee and one or more other Associate-Licensees affiliated with Broker participate on the same side (either listing or selling) of a transaction, the commission allocated to their combined activities shall be divided by Broker and paid to them according to their written agreement. Broker shall have the right to withhold total compensation if there is a dispute between associate-licensees, or if there is no written agreement, or if no written agreement has been provided to Broker.
   D. **EXPENSES AND OFFSETS:** If Broker elects to advance funds to pay expenses or liabilities of Associate-Licensee, or for an advance payment of, or draw upon, future compensation, Broker may deduct the full amount advanced from compensation payable to Associate-Licensee on any transaction without notice. If Associate-Licensee's compensation is subject to a lien, garnishment or other restriction on payment, Broker shall charge Associate-Licensee a fee for complying with such restriction.
   E. **PAYMENT:** **(i)** All compensation collected by Broker and due to Associate-Licensee shall be paid to Associate-Licensee, after deduction of expenses and offsets, immediately or as soon thereafter as practicable, except as otherwise provided in this Agreement, or a separate written agreement between Broker and Associate-Licensee. **(ii)** Compensation shall not be paid to Associate-Licensee until both the transaction and file are complete. **(iii)** Broker is under no obligation to pursue collection of compensation from any person or entity responsible for payment. Associate-Licensee does not have the independent right to pursue collection of compensation for activities which require a real estate license which were done in the name of Broker. **(iv)** Expenses which are incurred in the attempt to collect compensation shall be paid by Broker and Associate-Licensee in the same proportion as set forth for the division of compensation (paragraph 8(B)). **(v)** If there is a known or pending claim against Broker or Associate-Licensee on transactions for which Associate-Licensee has not yet been paid, Broker may withhold from compensation due Associate-Licensee on that transaction amounts for which Associate-Licensee could be responsible under paragraph 14, until such claim is resolved. **(vi)** Associate-Licensee shall not be entitled to any advance payment from Broker upon future compensation.
   F. **UPON OR AFTER TERMINATION:** If this Agreement is terminated while Associate-Licensee has listings or pending transactions that require further work normally rendered by Associate-Licensee, Broker shall make arrangements with another associate-licensee to perform the required work, or Broker shall perform the work him/herself. The licensee performing the work shall be reasonably compensated for completing work on those listings or transactions, and such reasonable compensation shall be deducted from Associate-Licensee's share of compensation. Except for such offset, Associate-Licensee shall receive the compensation due as specified above.

9. **TERMINATION OF RELATIONSHIP:** Broker or Associate-Licensee may terminate their relationship under this Agreement at any time, with or without cause. After termination, Associate-Licensee shall not solicit: **(i)** prospective or existing clients or customers based upon company-generated leads obtained during the time Associate-Licensee was affiliated with Broker; **(ii)** any principal with existing contractual obligations to Broker; or **(iii)** any principal with a contractual transactional obligation for which Broker is entitled to be compensated. Even after termination, this Agreement shall govern all disputes and claims between Broker and Associate-Licensee connected with their relationship under this Agreement, including obligations and liabilities arising from existing and completed listings, transactions, and services.

Broker's Initials ( _____ ) ( _____ )
Associate-Licensee's Initials ( _____ ) ( _____ )
Reviewed by _____ Date _____

**ICA REVISED 4/09 (PAGE 2 OF 3)**

**INDEPENDENT CONTRACTOR AGREEMENT (ICA PAGE 2 OF 3)**

Untitled

10. **DISPUTE RESOLUTION:**
   A. **Mediation:** Mediation is recommended as a method of resolving disputes arising out of this Agreement between Broker and Associate-Licensee.
   B. **Arbitration:** All disputes or claims between Associate-Licensee and other licensee(s) associated with Broker, or between Associate-Licensee and Broker, arising from or connected in any way with this Agreement, which cannot be adjusted between the parties involved, shall be submitted to the Association of REALTORS® of which all such disputing parties are members for arbitration pursuant to the provisions of its Bylaws, as may be amended from time to time, which are incorporated as a part of this Agreement by reference. If the Bylaws of the Association do not cover arbitration of the dispute, or if the Association declines jurisdiction over the dispute, then arbitration shall be pursuant to the rules of California law. The Federal Arbitration Act, Title 9, U.S. Code, Section 1, et seq., shall govern this Agreement.

11. **AUTOMOBILE:** Associate-Licensee shall maintain automobile insurance coverage for liability and property damage in the following amounts $ _____ /$ _____ . Broker shall be named as an additional insured party on Associate-Licensee's policies. A copy of the endorsement showing Broker as an additional insured shall be provided to Broker.

12. **PERSONAL ASSISTANTS:** Associate-Licensee may make use of a personal assistant, provided the following requirements are satisfied. Associate-Licensee shall have a written agreement with the personal assistant which establishes the terms and responsibilities of the parties to the employment agreement, including, but not limited to, compensation, supervision and compliance with applicable law. The agreement shall be subject to Broker's review and approval. Unless otherwise agreed, if the personal assistant has a real estate license, that license must be provided to the Broker. Both Associate-Licensee and personal assistant must sign any agreement that Broker has established for such purposes.

13. **OFFICE POLICY MANUAL:** If Broker's office policy manual, now or as modified in the future, conflicts with or differs from the terms of this Agreement, the terms of the office policy manual shall govern the relationship between Broker and Associate-Licensee.

14. **INDEMNITY AND HOLD HARMLESS; NOTICE OF CLAIMS: A.** Regarding any action taken or omitted by Associate-Licensee, or others working through, or on behalf of Associate-Licensee in connection with services rendered or to be rendered pursuant to this Agreement: (i) Associate-Licensee agrees to indemnify, defend and hold Broker harmless from all claims, disputes, litigation, judgments, awards, costs and attorney's fees, arising therefrom and (ii) Associate-Licensee shall immediately notify Broker if Associate-Licensee is served with or becomes aware of a lawsuit or claim regarding any such action. **B.** Any such claims or costs payable pursuant to this Agreement, are due as follows:

☐ Paid in full by Associate-Licensee, who hereby agrees to indemnify and hold harmless Broker for all such sums, or
☐ In the same ratio as the compensation split as it existed at the time the compensation was earned by Associate-Licensee
☐ Other: _____
_____

Payment from Associate-Licensee is due at the time Broker makes such payment and can be offset from any compensation due Associate-Licensee as above. Broker retains the authority to settle claims or disputes, whether or not Associate-Licensee consents to such settlement.

15. **ADDITIONAL PROVISIONS:** _____
_____
_____

16. **DEFINITIONS:** As used in this Agreement, the following terms have the meanings indicated:
   (A) "Listing" means an agreement with a property owner or other party to locate a buyer, exchange party, lessee, or other party to a transaction involving real property, a mobile home, or other property or transaction which may be brokered by a real estate licensee, or an agreement with a party to locate or negotiate for any such property or transaction.
   (B) "Compensation" means compensation for acts requiring a real estate license, regardless of whether calculated as a percentage of transaction price, flat fee, hourly rate, or in any other manner.
   (C) "Transaction" means a sale, exchange, lease, or rental of real property, a business opportunity, or a manufactured home, which may lawfully be brokered by a real estate licensee.

17. **ATTORNEY FEES:** In any action, proceeding, or arbitration between Broker and Associate-Licensee arising from or related to this Agreement, the prevailing Broker or Associate-Licensee shall be entitled to reasonable attorney fees and costs.

18. **ENTIRE AGREEMENT:** All prior agreements between the parties concerning their relationship as Broker and Associate-Licensee are incorporated in this Agreement, which constitutes the entire contract. Its terms are intended by the parties as a final and complete expression of their agreement with respect to its subject matter, and may not be contradicted by evidence of any prior agreement or contemporaneous oral agreement. This Agreement may not be amended, modified, altered, or changed except by a further agreement in writing executed by Broker and Associate-Licensee.

**Broker:**                                                                 **Associate-Licensee:**

_____                        _____
(Brokerage firm name)                                                 (Signature)
By _____
Its ☐ Broker ☐ Office manager (check one)                    _____
                                                                              (Print name)
_____
(Print name)                                                               _____
                                                                              (Address)
_____
(Address)                                                                  _____
                                                                              (City, State, Zip)
_____
(City, State, Zip)                                                         _____
                                                                              (Telephone)                    (Fax)
_____
(Telephone)                    (Fax)

THIS FORM HAS BEEN APPROVED BY THE CALIFORNIA ASSOCIATION OF REALTORS® (C.A.R.). NO REPRESENTATION IS MADE AS TO THE LEGAL VALIDITY OR ADEQUACY OF ANY PROVISION IN ANY SPECIFIC TRANSACTION. A REAL ESTATE BROKER IS THE PERSON QUALIFIED TO ADVISE ON REAL ESTATE TRANSACTIONS. IF YOU DESIRE LEGAL OR TAX ADVICE, CONSULT AN APPROPRIATE PROFESSIONAL.

This form is available for use by the entire real estate industry. It is not intended to identify the user as a REALTOR®. REALTOR® is a registered collective membership mark which may be used only by members of the NATIONAL ASSOCIATION OF REALTORS® who subscribe to its Code of Ethics.

REBS INC. Published and Distributed by:
REAL ESTATE BUSINESS SERVICES, INC.
a subsidiary of the CALIFORNIA ASSOCIATION OF REALTORS®
— 525 South Virgil Avenue, Los Angeles, California 90020

Reviewed by _____ Date _____

ICA REVISED 4/09 (PAGE 3 OF 3)

**INDEPENDENT CONTRACTOR AGREEMENT (ICA PAGE 3 OF 3)**

Untitled

## F. AGENTS WHO BUY AND SELL FOR THEIR OWN ACCOUNT
### (Disclose You Have a Real Estate License)

Many real estate professionals buy and sell property for themselves as part of their own personal investments (acting as a principal and not as an agent). The Real Estate Commissioner created a regulation requiring disclosure of license status (buyer and seller) which has the full force and effect of law. The commissioner has strongly suggested that it would be in the licensee's best interest to disclose this fact, in writing, as soon as possible. This protects the purchasers and others involved. Everyone should be aware that they are dealing with a person knowledgeable in real estate and that he or she is representing his or her own interests.

## G. POWER OF ATTORNEY

A *POWER OF ATTORNEY is an acknowledged, written authorization of one person to act for another.* There are two categories of power of attorney: 1) a general power of attorney, and 2) a special power of attorney.

A *GENERAL POWER OF ATTORNEY allows the person so authorized to perform any act the principal could perform.* The person thus authorized to act on behalf of the principal is called the attorney in fact.

An *ATTORNEY IN FACT under a "general" power of attorney is a person who has been given the right to transact all of a principal's business.* The specific powers conferred must be set down in writing, duly acknowledged and recorded with the county recorder's office in the county where the property is located, in order for the agency to take effect. **Death of either party or an acknowledged declaration from the principal may revoke this power.** An attorney in fact cannot deed his client's property to himself.

A *SPECIAL POWER OF ATTORNEY allows the person so authorized to perform only a specific act (for example, sell your house).* The *ATTORNEY IN FACT, under a "special" power of attorney, has the authorization to perform only a specific act.* A real estate agent under a special power of attorney is an "attorney in fact" who is usually authorized to find a ready, willing, and able buyer.

A listing agreement makes the broker a special agent to perform the authorized act of selling, exchanging, or otherwise transferring real property. Usually, an agent is given expressed authority, by written agreement (listing), to sell a home. If not otherwise expressed in writing, the agent is allowed to delegate parts of that authority under three circumstances:

1. If the act to be performed is purely mechanical, such as typing out a standard form.
2. If the agent is not legally qualified to do something, such as notarizing a document that requires a state license.
3. If it is customary to delegate authority for that task in that business or locality.

## H. TORTS BY AN AGENT (Broker/Salesperson)

A *TORT is any civil injury or wrong committed upon a person or that person's property.* Fraud, misrepresentation, negligence, and secret profit all stem from a breach of an agent's duty. In some cases they can even be considered criminal acts. The broker and his or her salespeople, as professionals, are expected to maintain a high standard of ethics. They are responsible for their own acts and representations even when following the seller's directions.

## I. MISREPRESENTATION OF A MATERIAL FACT

A misrepresentation by a broker or salesperson may be material or immaterial. If the representation is slight, or would not have a measurable effect on the people relying on it, it is not a material fact. When a broker misrepresents his or her authority to act as an agent for someone else, he or she may be liable to the person who relies on the misrepresentation. A statement such as "I think this is the best house on the street" is a statement of opinion (puffing) and is not considered a misrepresentation.

*"Puffing" is a statement of opinion (not fact) that exaggerates a property's benefits. It would only be a misrepresentation if a reasonable person would consider it a statement of fact.*

The misrepresentation of a material fact can financially injure someone and may be punishable under the Civil Code or the Commissioner's Regulations. There are three types of misrepresentations:

1. Innocent Misrepresentations,
2. Negligent Misrepresentations, and
3. Fraudulent Misrepresentations (or nondisclosures).

The first misrepresentation usually has no broker liability. The second and third are subject to civil penalties and the Real Estate Commissioner's actions. ***INNOCENT MISREPRESENTATIONS*** *are false statements that are not known to be false at the time they are made.* These statements do not usually warrant legal liability for the broker but can be the basis for a rescission of any contract. Everyone involved would then be reinstated to their original positions.

*An agent who sells the wrong condo because a prankster switched the condo unit's number is an example of an innocent misrepresentation.*

***NEGLIGENT MISREPRESENTATIONS*** *are false statements believed to be true, but made without reasonable grounds for that belief.* This is breach of duty without fraudulent intent. The broker is liable for any negligent statements made to a buyer or seller. Such statements are in effect a form of deceit.

*An agent mistakenly confirms that a property is within a particular school district without checking. This would be negligent misrepresentation.*

***FRAUDULENT MISREPRESENTATIONS*** *are statements made at a time when the broker knows the statement to be false, or statements in which the broker fails to disclose (conceals) material facts.* This is actual fraud. Any contract made under the influence of fraudulent information may become void, and the person making the fraudulent statements may be liable for civil or even criminal fraud.

*"Intentional deceptions" or the "concealment of material facts" are fraudulent misrepresentations, which are immoral and unlawful.*

**Example:** In July, Baker bought Able's home through Charlie, the listing broker. In November, when the first rain came, the tile roof leaked badly in many places. Baker sued Able and Charlie for the cost of the necessary new roof. Testimony in court showed that Able had mentioned the need of a new roof to Charlie, but Charlie had not mentioned it to Baker because "he had not asked about it." It is likely that Baker will recover damages from Able, who will, in turn, recover from Charlie.

## J. SECRET PROFIT

An agent may not make any secret profit. This is a breach of the fiduciary relationship between the principal and the real estate agent. All financial offers, whether legitimate or not, must be presented to the seller. So, if a real estate agent is offered a secret profit, he or she has a duty to inform his or her principal of this. In addition, the broker may not allow others (friends and relatives) to make a secret profit with his or her knowledge.

**Example:** If a broker presented a full price offer to a seller, which the seller accepted, but the seller discovers during escrow that the buyer is the brother of the broker, the seller can cancel the transaction without any liability for the commission.

*An unlicensed person may make a secret profit on the purchase of real property, but an agent may not.*

## K. WARRANTY OF AUTHORITY

The broker, as an agent, warrants that he or she has the authority to represent another person. *If there is a written listing between the seller and the broker, he or she has an EXPRESS WARRANTY OF AUTHORITY to offer the property for sale.* The problem arises when the broker offers to sell a property, without the listing, to an unsuspecting buyer who relies on the fact that the agent has certain authority. In such cases, the broker could be liable for this untrue representation. A broker gives *IMPLIED WARRANTY OF AUTHORITY to act for a seller by the mere fact that he or she shows the seller's property.*

When a broker represents a seller, he or she does not warrant that the seller has the capacity to sell. If, in fact, the seller does not have the capacity to contract, then the broker is not liable, as long as he or she did not have knowledge of the fact. However, if the broker has knowledge that the seller could not contract, then the broker could be liable to the buyer.

*The prosecution of an unlicensed salesperson, acting as a licensed salesperson, would be handled by the district attorney's office.*

## L. DISCLOSURE OF AIDS AND DEATH

An occupant's death from AIDS or AIDS-related illness, or any other contagious disease, is a highly emotional issue. Brokers must strive to balance the principle of full disclosure against the right to privacy of an AIDS victim. Disclosing casually that a tenant or former tenant (owner or occupant) died, or is dying, from AIDS might very well be in violation of that person's civil rights and might expose the broker to civil or criminal penalties. **By law, sellers, brokers, and landlords have no liability for failure to disclose a prior occupant's**

**death or its cause after three years**. On the other hand, intentional misrepresentation concerning an occupant's death on the property, in response to direct inquiry, is fraud.

# VII. Required Disclosures – Agent Summary (One-to-Four Unit Residential Sales)

## A. VISUAL INSPECTION

**A listing and selling broker must each conduct a reasonably competent and diligent inspection of the property and disclose to the prospective buyer all material facts affecting the value, desirability, and intended use of the property.** The real estate agent does not have to inspect: (a) areas not reasonably accessible; (b) areas off the site of the property; (c) public records or permits concerning the title or use of the property; or (d) in a common interest development where the seller or broker complies by furnishing controlling documents and a financial statement.

> **Example:** Agent Able notices a crack in the wall and the doors are not closing properly. Able should advise the buyer to get a soils report.

## B. DISCLOSURE OF AGENCY RELATIONSHIP

As a real estate agent, you must disclose, in writing, the duties which arise from certain agency relationships, the broker's status as agent of the seller, agent of the buyer, or agent of both the seller and the buyer (dual agent).

## C. DISCLOSURE OF THE NEGOTIABILITY OF REAL ESTATE COMMISSIONS

The listing or sales agreement must contain the following disclosure in not less than 10-point boldface: "**NOTICE:** The rate of real estate commissions is not fixed by law. They are set by each broker individually and may be negotiable between the seller and the broker" (see Chapter 1).

## D. NO DISCLOSURE REQUIRED FOR MANNER/OCCURRENCE OF DEATH; AFFLICTION OF OCCUPANT WITH AIDS

Any death, which occurred within a 3-year period, should be disclosed if it is "material." If the death occurred more than 3 years before the date of the offer to buy, there is no liability for failing to disclose the fact of death. The seller and his/her agent need not voluntarily disclose affliction with AIDS or death from AIDS, but cannot make any misrepresentations to a direct question about death on the property.

# VIII. Terminating an Agency Relationship

## A. REASONS FOR TERMINATION OF AGENCY

An agency relationship between a seller and a real estate broker can be terminated by operation of law or by the acts of either the broker or the seller. **Figure 4-8** shows the seven subcategories of these methods.

---

**Figure 4-8**          **Termination of an Agency Relationship**

| **Operation of Law** | **Acts of the Seller or Broker** |
|---|---|
| a. Expiration of the Agency (Listing) Agreement | a. Agreement by Both Broker and Seller |
| b. Destruction of the Property | b. Renouncement of Listing by the Broker |
| c. Death or Incapacity Broker or Seller (Listing Only) | c. Revocation of Listing by the Seller |
|  | d. Close of Escrow |

---

### 1. Operation of Law

#### a. Expiration of the Agency (Listing) Agreement

The Exclusive Agency Listing Agreement and the Exclusive Authorization and Right to Sell Listing Agreement have a definite termination date. These listings will end automatically on the stated date if not terminated in some other way before that date. The other type of listing, an open listing, does not require a termination date because it can be terminated at any time.

#### b. Destruction of the Property

A house burning down would terminate a listing agreement.

#### c. Death or Incapacity of the Broker or Seller (Listing Only)

*If the broker in a large real estate office dies, all listings are automatically cancelled, and the new broker would need to re-list the properties.*

### 2. Act of the Seller or Broker

#### a. Agreement by Both the Broker and Seller

If both parties to a contract want to end it, it may be terminated by mutual agreement.

#### b. Renouncement of the Listing Agreement by the Broker

The broker can refuse to fulfill the listing agreement, but may be subject to damages for breach of contract.

#### c. Revocation of the Listing Agreement by the Seller

The seller can refuse to sell the listed property, but may be liable for the commission if the broker has found a buyer who is ready, willing and able to purchase the property.

#### d. Close of Escrow

An agency relationship is terminated at the close of escrow.

*A typical agency would be terminated by death of the principal, destruction of the subject property, or mutual consent of the principal and his/her agent. It would NOT be terminated by estoppel.*

## IX. A Brokerage Must be Run Like a Business

*A "company dollar" is the dollar (income and commissions) a broker receives after all salespersons' commissions have been paid.*

A **GROSS DOLLAR** *is all the income that is received by the office before paying out commissions. A* **COMPANY DOLLAR** *is the amount left to management after payment of all commissions, including in-house salespeople and other multiple listings brokers and salespeople (see* **Figure 4-9**). The concept of the company dollar allows the brokerage to examine and focus on how their after-commission income is spent.

**Figure 4-9**

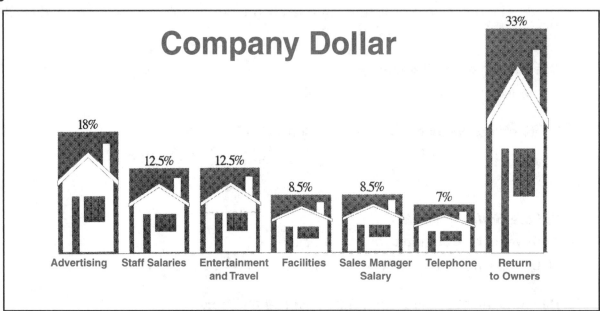

"**TOE**" is the acronym for Total Operating Expense.

T  *Total*
O  *Operating*
E  *Expense*

The **DESK COST** *for a broker is the total operating expenses divided by the number of agents in the office.* The desk cost tells the broker the financial loss caused by an empty desk or an unproductive salesperson.

### A. COMPANY INTERNET AND SOCIAL MEDIA POLICY

All brokerages should establish an **Internet and Social Media Policy** that sets standards for creating, emailing, or publishing content online about company business whether at home, office, or with a mobile device phone. Common forms of online search engines are: Ask, AOL, Bing, Ebay, Facebook, Google, LinkedIn, MySpace, Yahoo, YouTube, and Wikipedia. As soon as salesperson can afford one of the smartphones and monthly contracts, he or she may want to purchase a BlackBerry (RIM), iPhone (Apple), or Android (Google) operating system, or one of the others that are available.

## B. ONE-STOP SHOPPING

When the real estate market goes "soft," it means shrinking profit margins and fewer company dollars. Some brokerages respond to this by offering one-stop shopping. *ONE-STOP SHOPPING means the brokerage is involved in multiple facets of property transactions, including escrow and title services, property management, and mortgage brokerage.*

Small-businesses, like "Real Estate Brokerages," have generated **64 percent of net new jobs** over the past 15 years (see: **sba.gov/advo**).

---

### X. CHAPTER SUMMARY

**Agency** is the relationship between a seller, broker (and his or her salespeople), and a buyer. A **principal** is the person who hires the agent. The agency of a real estate broker may be established by **express agreement**, **implied agreement**, **ratification**, or **estoppel**. The best evidence of an agency relationship is a **written agreement (listing)**.

Agents can be identified as the **listing agents** or **selling agents**. A broker (agent) working for a principal owes him or her a **fiduciary duty**, including honesty, utmost care, integrity, accounting, disclosure, and loyalty. An agent owes a third party (the "other" party in a negotiation) an obligation of honesty and timely disclosure of material facts.

An agent can represent a seller, a buyer, or both **(dual agency)**, if all parties consent to the transaction. The **Disclosure Regarding Real Estate Agency Relationships** Form states that the agency relationship must be disclosed as soon as practical. **Termination of agency** can be by **operation of law** or by **acts of the seller or broker**, but not by estoppel.

Salespeople can be **independent contractors** or **employees**, although the DRE considers them employees of the broker, making the broker responsible for their activities. A broker must immediately notify the DRE in writing of the hiring or firing of a salesperson. Signed **broker-salesperson contracts** must be kept for **three years** after termination of the contract (as well as all transactions files).

A **listing** is a personal service contract between an agent and a principal, creating an **agency relationship**. It may be for any period of time, but must have a definite, final termination date. An **open listing** may be given to several brokers, or the property may be sold by the owner without obligation to pay a commission. It is **unilateral**, because only the seller makes a promise, whereas an **exclusive agency listing** and **exclusive right to sell** are **bilateral** (a promise for a promise).

An **exclusive agency listing** entitles only the listing broker to a commission, unless the owner sells the property, in which case, no commission is owed. An **exclusive right to sell listing** entitles the listing broker to a commission during the listing period even if the owner sells the property.

The rarely used **net listing** sets the broker's commission at whatever amount a property sells for above the asking price set by the owner. A **multiple listing** is an exclusive right to sell held by all the members of a **Multiple Listing Service (MLS)**.

A copy of the **listing agreement** (and any other real estate agreement) should be given to the buyer and seller immediately after signing. All listings belong to the broker, not the salesperson.

An agent can delegate authority to a **subagent** or to a **cooperating agent** or **broker**. While agreements between brokers don't need to be in writing, they must be in writing between brokers and salespeople.

**Real estate commissions** are negotiable. If an offer meets the exact terms of a listing, the agent has earned the commission even if the owner refuses to sell. The agent who is the **procuring cause** (series of unbroken events that lead to an acceptable agreement with the seller) is entitled to the commission.

The *Easton v. Strassburger* case extended the liabilities of brokers to include a duty to inspect and disclose any relevant facts that might materially affect the value or desirability of a property. The **Transfer Disclosure Statement** must be provided by both seller and broker and must be given to the prospective buyer as soon as practicable before or within three days after the **Purchase Agreement** is signed. A broker does not have to disclose a cause of death unless there is a direct inquiry, and no liability to disclose an occupant's cause of death after three years.

When a broker receives a buyer's money deposit, he or she must: 1) place the deposit in escrow, 2) give it to the principal, or 3) put it in the broker's trust fund account. All funds must be kept segregated, as **commingling**, or mixing the client's money with private funds, is illegal.

A real estate agent, under a **special power of attorney** is an **attorney in fact**, authorized to find a ready, willing, and able buyer. As an agent, the broker warrants that he or she has the authority to represent another person. He or she is obligated to maintain a high standard of ethics, and refrain from either material or immaterial misrepresentation. **Misrepresentations** can be innocent, negligent, or fraudulent. Intentional deceptions or concealment of material facts are examples of **fraudulent misrepresentations**. Agents are also prohibited from making **secret profits**.

A brokerage must be run like a business. A **gross dollar** is all the income received by the office, and the **company dollar** is all the money left after paying commissions. **"TOE"** is an easy way to remember **Total Operating Expense**.

## XI. TERMINOLOGY

A. Agency
B. Agency Disclosure Form
C. Commingling
D. Conversion
E. Dual Agency
F. *Easton v. Strassburger*
G. Employee
H. Estoppel
I. Exclusive Agency Listing
J. Exclusive Right to Sell
Listing

K. Fiduciary Relationship
L. Fraudulent
Misrepresentation
M. General Attorney in Fact
N. Independent Contractor
O. Innocent Misrepresentation
P. Multiple Listing Service (MLS)
Q. Negligent Misrepresentation
R. Net Listing
S. Open Listing
T. Policy Manual

U. Principal
V. Ratification
W. Secret Profit
X. Special Attorney in Fact
Y. Subagent
Z. Third Party
AA. Tort
BB. Transfer Disclosure
Statement

1.____ The mixing of funds held in trust with personal funds.

2.____ Authorization from a property owner giving a real estate agent the non-exclusive right to secure a purchaser. Other brokers, or the owners themselves, may also solicit a purchaser.

3.____ The unlawful taking and use of another's property placed in your trust, as an agent, by that person.

4.____ The person(s) who employs a real estate agent, usually through a listing agreement.

5.____ The relationship between the principal and the principal's agent that arises out of a contract, either expressed or implied, written or oral, wherein the agent is employed by the principal to do certain acts dealing with a third party.

6.____ A person upon whom the powers of an agent have been conferred, not by the principal, but by an agent authorized by the principal.

7.____ A civil wrong committed against a person or property, independent of any contractual agreement.

8.____ The theory of law that states a person cannot suddenly assert a legal right when that person has neglected to assert it previously. For example: If someone claims to be your agent and you know about it and don't stop that person, you can't later claim that person was not acting on your behalf.

9.____ A person who acts for another, selling final results and using his or her own judgment to achieve those results.

10.____ The approval of an act performed on behalf of a person without previous authorization, such as the approval by a principal of a previously unauthorized act of an agent.

11.____ An agency relationship in which the agent acts concurrently for both of the principals (buyer and seller), with their consent, in a transaction.

12.____ An association of real estate agents that provides a pooling of listings and the sharing of commissions.

13.____ Any party to a transaction other than the principal with whom you have an agency relationship.

14.____ One who is authorized to perform many acts for another under a power of attorney.

15.____ A listing agreement employing a broker as the sole agent for the seller of real property, under the terms of which the broker is entitled to a commission unless the homeowner sells the property.

16.____ A listing agreement employing a broker to act as an agent for the seller of real property. Under the terms of this agreement, the broker is entitled to a commission if the property is sold during the duration of the listing by the broker or by the owner without an agent.

17.____ A listing that provides for the agent to retain, as compensation for his or her services, all sums received over and above a net price to the owner.

18.____The major court decision which requires an agent to disclose any physical defects or evidence of defects that could affect the value of real property.

19.____An agent's making of additional money in a real estate transaction without disclosing it to the principal and third party.

20.____Knowingly making false and deceptive statements to help sell a property.

21.____Making false statements about a property, without realizing it.

22.____Making false statements regarding a property that could have been checked out or verified.

23.____A form that notifies buyers of any physical defects to a property and requires the seller and the agent to list any evidence of defects of which they are aware.

24.____A form presented to the principal(s) in a transaction stating exactly who the agent is working for: the buyer, the seller, or both.

25.____The relationship between the agent and the principal that requires the highest level of trust and good faith.

26.____One who works directly for another person, is told what to do, and is controlled in how they do it.

27.____A written book of procedures explaining how a broker expects the agents working under him or her to conduct business and handle routine problems.

28.____Someone authorized to represent a principal in a specific task, such as selling a property.

## XII. CHAPTER QUIZ

1. When a seller grants the right to sell and the broker agrees to use diligence in obtaining a purchaser, this is called:

    a. attorney in fact.
    b. power of attorney.
    c. specific performance.
    d. agency.

2. The broker, as agent of the seller, owes the buyer:

    a. only a duty to disclose any item that relates directly to the sales price of the property.
    b. the same fiduciary obligations he or she owes to the seller.
    c. only the duty to answer questions honestly.
    d. the duty of honesty and fair dealing.

3. The best way to establish an agency relationship is through:

    a. written agreement.
    b. oral agreement.
    c. estoppel.
    d. consideration.

4. A salesperson's listings are the property of:

    a. the salesperson.
    b. the salesperson and his/her heirs.
    c. the broker who employs him/her as a salesperson.
    d. the MLS.

5. Seller Skinner signed a 90-day exclusive right to sell listing with Broker Bill. Two weeks later, Skinner cancelled the listing with Bill and gave an open listing to Broker Carl and another open listing to Broker Paul. Three weeks later, Paul presented an offer to Skinner that the seller accepted. Which of the following is most correct?

    a. Broker Bill only is entitled to a full commission

    b. A full commission will be divided equally between Bill, Carl, and Paul

    c. Broker Paul only is entitled to a full commission

    d. Paul is entitled to a full commission and Bill is entitled to a full commission as well

6. Seller signed a 90-day exclusive right to sell listing with Broker Able. When the listing expired, Seller gave an open listing to Broker Baker and Broker Charlie. Three weeks later, Broker Baker presented an offer to the seller which he accepted. Which of the following is most correct?

    a. Broker Able only is entitled to a full commission

    b. A full commission will be divided equally between Able, Baker, and Charlie

    c. Broker Charlie is entitled to a full commission

    d. Broker Baker is the procurring cause of the sale and is entitled to a full commission

7. When inspecting a seller's home the agent discovers several physical defects that the agent fails to disclose to the buyer. The buyer can file civil action against the agent for up to:

    a. 2 years.

    b. 3 years.

    c. 4 years.

    d. 5 years.

8. How much of a broker's personal funds can be kept in his or her trust account without being guilty of commingling?

    a. $100

    b. $200

    c. $400

    d. As much as he/she wants

9. Which of the following is most correct about "puffing?"

    a. It is legal, and proper business tactics

    b. It is usually unethical unless approved by the agent's broker

    c. It is only an "opinion of value" of a specific property as of a given date

    d. It may be misrepresentation if a reasonable person considers it a "statement of fact"

10. The broker in a large real estate office dies. All listings:

    a. usually belong to the subagents according to the terms of the broker/associate contract.

    b. are continued during probate, unless the subagent moves to another firm.

    c. are automatically cancelled and the new broker would need to re-list the properties.

    d. may be cancelled unilaterally by each principal with 24 hours written notice.

**ANSWERS:** 1. d.; 2. d.; 3. a.; 4. c.; 5. d.; 6. d.; 7. a.; 8. b.; 9. d.; 10. c.

# CHAPTER 5
## Contracts

## I. Contracts in General

Nothing is as important to the real estate broker and his/her salespeople than the law of contracts. Because every phase of a real estate transaction involves one or more contracts, it is important to understand the basic rules that govern the creation and life of a contract. This chapter will explain the elements of contracts and illustrate, in detail, the important parts of the Residential Purchase Agreement.

www.leginfo.ca.gov/calaw.html (California Law)
www.leginfo.ca.gov/statute.html (State Statutes)
www.courtinfo.ca.gov (California Courts)
www.ca9.uscourts.gov (9th Circuit Court)
www.calbar.ca.gov (State Bar of California)

A **CONTRACT** *is an agreement to do or not to do a certain act or service*. Every contract consists of a promise or a set of promises that are enforceable by law. These promises may be created in two ways, either in an express manner or in an implied manner.

An **EXPRESS CONTRACT** *describes a contract that is expressed in words, either oral or written*. Listings, purchase agreements, and leases are all express contracts.

On the other hand, an **IMPLIED CONTRACT** *is created when an agreement is made by acts and conduct (implication) rather than by words*. For example, suppose you entered a hardware store where you had an account, picked up an $8 paint brush, and waved it at the clerk as you departed. The clerk, judging from your conduct, would assume that you wanted the paint brush charged to your account and would bill you accordingly. An implied contract was formed. Implied contracts are not used in the practice of real estate.

A **BILATERAL CONTRACT** *is a promise made by one party in exchange for the promise of another party*. It is a promise for a promise. For instance, if a homeowner offers a painter $2,000 to paint his or her garage and the painter agrees to do it, a bilateral contract is formed: The painter promises to paint the garage, while the homeowner promises to give the painter $2,000. *When only one party makes a promise for an act of another, the agreement is called a **UNILATERAL CONTRACT***. It is a promise for an act. If someone acts upon an offer, the one making the offer is obligated to complete his or her promise.

# CHAPTER 5

**Example:** Mr. Bentley offers a reward to any person who can identify the arsonist who set his home on fire. Because this is a unilateral contract, Mr. Bentley is required to give the reward to any person who can fulfill the obligation.

## A. CLASSIFICATION OF CONTRACTS

Some of the ways in which contracts may be classified include the following.

### 1. Valid

A fully operative contract that is binding and enforceable in a court of law is "valid." **If a buyer and seller signed a contract and the seller died, there is a valid contract.**

### 2. Voidable

A "voidable" contract can be affirmed or rejected at the option of a party. The victim can rescind, cancel, or annul. A voidable contract remains binding until it is rescinded.

### 3. Void

A "void" contract has no legal force or effect. It does not exist. It lacks one of the essential elements of a contract. A contract with an illegal purpose is void.

### 4. Unenforceable

An "unenforceable" contract is a valid contract that for some reason cannot be enforced in court (proved or sued upon).

## B. LIFE OF A CONTRACT (Three Phases)

### 1. Phase 1 – Negotiation

During the **negotiation period**, the buyer and seller discuss the possibility of a contract. If there is mutual interest between the parties, then an offer, or perhaps several offers, can be made. The offer becomes a contract when accepted, provided that all the other elements necessary for the creation of a contract are present.

### 2. Phase 2 – Performance

An *EXECUTORY CONTRACT is a legal agreement, the provisions of which have yet to be completely performed.* A purchase agreement is executory until payment is made and title is transferred. Then it becomes executed. A land contract might be executory for years.

*An exclusive listing signed solely by an owner is an example of an express, bilateral, executory contract.*

### 3. Phase 3 – Completion

**This stage occurs after a contract has been completed.** An *EXECUTED CONTRACT is one that has either been discharged or performed.* After a contract has been completed, there is the warranty that every aspect of the contract has been properly performed.

This term should not be confused with the execution of a contract. To *EXECUTE a contract is to sign a contract*, while the *EXECUTION of a contract is the act of performing or carrying out the contract.*

*A contract to be performed is called "executory"; a completely performed contract has been "executed." The contract lives on until the time to bring legal action has expired. This is called the "statute of limitations."*

# II. Elements of a Contract

According to the California Civil Code, there must be four elements to any valid contract whether it involves real estate or not. However, in real estate, contracts generally must be in writing, which becomes a fifth element (see **Figure 5-1**).

*These are the four elements of any contract: 1) capacity, 2) mutual consent, 3) legality, and 4) consideration. Often, in real estate, a proper writing is required, making this the fifth element.*

*The following are NOT essential elements of a valid contract: 1) money (can be other consideration), 2) writing (except for real estate contracts which frequently require it), and 3) performance.*

## A. CAPACITY

For a contract to be valid, there must be two or more parties who have the legal capacity to contract. Everyone is capable of contracting, except for the following persons: 1) minors, 2) incompetents, and 3) convicts.

### 1. Minor

A *MINOR is a person under the age of eighteen.* A minor cannot make contracts relating to real property or property not in his or her immediate possession or control, and

**Figure 5-1**

## Elements of a Contract

I.
CAPACITY

II.
MUTUAL CONSENT

III.
LEGALITY

IV.
CONSIDERATION

V.
WRITING SOMETIMES REQUIRED
(Statute of Frauds)

does not have the right to employ an agent, **unless the minor is emancipated**. An *EMANCIPATED MINOR is one who has the contractual rights of an adult*. The three ways that a minor becomes emancipated are:

1. through marriage,
2. as a member or former member of the armed forces, and
3. when declared to be self-supporting by the courts.

A minor who has been "emancipated" has legal capacity. Once emancipated, always emancipated. Otherwise, a contract or deed signed by a minor would be void. Any minor can acquire property by gift or inheritance.

*A person under the age of 18 and divorced has the capacity to contract.*

A contract with a minor is void because a minor cannot delegate authority. A guardian may, however, buy and sell real estate on behalf of a minor if the action is given court approval.

*Both minors and incompetents may acquire real property by gift or inheritance.*

### 2. Incompetent

An *INCOMPETENT is a person who is judged to be of unsound mind*. Such a person has no capacity (power) to contract; any contract made is void. In real estate transactions with incompetents, it is necessary to have the guardian's decision approved by the court. However, both minors and incompetents may acquire real property by gift or inheritance.

*If a buyer and seller enter into a valid binding contract and one of the parties dies or becomes incompetent, the contract is valid if it was signed before the party died or became incompetent.*

### 3. Convicts

*CONVICTS are persons who have lost their civil rights during their imprisonment.* Convicts are incapable of contracting, but they do not forfeit any property in their possession. They may acquire property by gift, inheritance, or will, but can only convey property if the action is ratified by the California Adult Authority.

**ALIENS** are not citizens of the United States, but they have the right to own property in California. This surprises some people, but it is true that any person, whether he or she is a U.S. citizen or not, may buy, hold or transfer real property.

## B. MUTUAL CONSENT

*"Mutual consent" is a genuine offer by one party and a genuine acceptance by the other party.*

This acceptance need not be a true "meeting of the minds" of the parties because they are bound only by an objective standard (their apparent intentions as evidenced by words or acts). Since courts cannot read minds, any secret or unexpressed intentions are immaterial. The consent must be genuine and free from fraud or mistake, and there must be a true intention to be obligated, or it may be voidable by one or both of the parties.

**Example:** Two days after entering into a binding purchase contract, the buyer and seller decided to mutually surrender the contract. With respect to the deposit, the agent representing both parties must return the entire deposit to the buyer immediately.

### 1. The Offer

An *OFFER expresses a person's willingness to enter into a contract. The **OFFEROR** is the person (buyer) who has made the offer, and the **OFFEREE** is the person (seller) to whom the offer has been made.* The offer made by the offeror must be communicated to the offeree. Every offer must have contractual intent. *CONTRACTUAL INTENT exists when a party communicates an offer to another with the intention of forming a binding contract.* For example, a social invitation to attend a party is not meant to be a contract and, therefore, lacks contractual intent. Likewise, an advertisement in the newspaper is not an offer, but merely an invitation to deal.

*A buyer can withdraw his or her offer at any time prior to receiving communication (in writing, personally, or by registered mail) of its acceptance and receive a refund of the money deposited.*

Finally, offer terms must be definite and certain. *DEFINITE AND CERTAIN means that the precise acts to be performed must be clearly stated.* A court can neither create contracts for parties nor fix the terms and conditions of any contract. An *ILLUSORY CONTRACT is one in which the terms are not definite and certain, therefore the contract is unenforceable.*

## 2. Acceptance

*ACCEPTANCE is the consent to the terms by the offeree.* Acceptance of an offer must be in the manner specified in the offer, but if no particular manner of acceptance is specified, then acceptance may be made by any reasonable or usual mode.

*On a purchase contract, the date of the contract is the date the seller's acceptance of the buyer's offer is communicated back to the buyer.*

Silence cannot be interpreted as an acceptance of an offer because an acceptance must be communicated. One cannot say "If I do not hear from you in 10 days, the offer is considered accepted." There must be a communicated acceptance of an offer in writing.

*A seller may accept a buyer's offer by fax (facsimile documents are legally binding).*

The acceptance must be absolute and unqualified: If it modifies the terms of the offer, it becomes a counter offer. A *COUNTER OFFER is the rejection of an original offer and the proposal of a new offer.* The offeree rejects the offer, then becomes the offeror of the counter offer. **Once there is a counter offer, the previous offer is automatically terminated**. The counter offer is discussed later in the chapter (see Counter Offer form, **Figure 5-8**).

## 3. Termination of an Offer

The hope of the offeror is that the other party will accept and that a contract will be formed, but most initial offers are rejected. Here are six ways an offer can be terminated:

1. **Lapse of Time.** The offer is terminated if the offeree fails to accept within a prescribed period.
2. **Communication of Revocation.** An offer can be withdrawn any time before the other party has communicated his or her acceptance.
3. **Failure of Offeree to Fulfill a Condition.** A specified condition must be satisfied in a prescribed manner or the offer is terminated.
4. **Rejection.** If the offer is rejected, it is terminated.
5. **Death or Insanity of the Offeror or Offeree.** This voids the offer. The death of the offeror or offeree constitutes a revocation of the offer prior to acceptance—the offer died with the death of the offeror.
6. **Illegality of Purpose.** If the conditions or the purpose of a contract are illegal, then the contract is terminated.

## 4. Genuine Consent (Contract is Void or Voidable by Victim)

The final requirement for mutual consent is that the offer and acceptance must be real or genuine (freely given). If not, the contract is void or voidable by the victim. Genuine consent does not exist if any of the following conditions are present:

1. *FRAUD occurs when a person misrepresents a material fact, knowing it is not true, or is carelessly indifferent to the truth of the stated facts.* The contract is void or voidable, depending on the degree of fraud.

2. *MUTUAL MISTAKE exists when both parties are mistaken as to the matter of the agreement, or where the subject matter of the contract ceases to exist. A mistake is also void or voidable.*

> **Example:** A buyer made an offer to purchase a property through a real estate agent. The seller represented that the property was in a good school district. During escrow, the school district boundaries were changed and the seller's home became part of a poor school district. The buyer would probably be able to get out of the transaction because the contract between buyer and seller lacked mutual consent.

3. *DURESS is the unlawful detention of a person and/or that person's property.*
4. *MENACE is a threat to commit duress,* but it also can be a threat of unlawful violent injury to a person and/or his or her character as a party to the contract.
5. *UNDUE INFLUENCE occurs when a person in a position of authority uses that authority to an unfair advantage.* This is usually found in a confidential relationship.

*If a contract was entered into under duress, it is voidable.*

## C. LEGALITY

*A contract based on an unlawful consideration is void.*

A contract must be legal in its formation and operation. **Both the consideration and its objective must also be lawful.** The objective refers to what the contract requires the parties to do or not to do. If the contract consists of a single objective that is unlawful in whole or in part, then the contract is void. If there are several objectives, the contract is normally valid as to those parts that are lawful.

The law will not enforce an illegal contract. If an illegal contract is not completed, the courts will not force its completion.

> **Example:** A contract to bribe a city building inspector to accept substandard work for $5,000 is illegal and void.

## D. CONSIDERATION (Anything of Value)

*VALUABLE CONSIDERATION in a contract is anything of value given by one party to another party to make the agreement binding.* A valid contract must have sufficient consideration, which is any amount of valued consideration. Consideration need not be money. It may: (1) benefit the person making the contract or another person; (2) be a loss suffered or agreed to be suffered; or (3) be an agreement not to bring a legal suit. If the price paid is a promise, consideration may be a promise for a promise. The important point is that the consideration must be of some value.

Some rare types of contracts require that consideration be adequate. In such contracts the condition of adequate consideration must be met for those contracts to be enforceable. Other contracts, without such a condition, are enforceable no matter what the consideration is, as long as it is agreed on by all parties.

*Payment of money is NOT needed as consideration. "Adequate, valuable, good, and sufficient" relate to consideration.*

## E. PROPER WRITING (Real Estate Contracts)

All contracts may be oral except those specifically required by the Statute of Frauds to be in writing. A contract for personal property can be oral or written, but the Statute of Frauds requires that most real estate contracts be in writing (see **Figure 5-2**).

A listing agreement must be in writing to enforce the payment of a commission. Oral agreements between brokers to share commissions are binding.

*Personal property contracts, like rental agreements, for one year or less need not be in writing. Any contract that can't be performed within a year from the date of signing must be in writing.*

### 1. Parol Evidence Rule

*PAROL EVIDENCE refers to prior oral or written agreements of the parties, or even oral agreements made concurrently (contemporaneously) with a written contract.* Under the "parol evidence rule," a contract expressed in writing is intended to be the complete and final expression of the rights and duties of the contracting parties. The parol evidence rule means that prior oral or written agreements of the parties cannot be introduced as evidence to contradict or modify the terms of the written contract. The courts, however, will permit such outside evidence to be introduced when the written contract is incomplete, ambiguous, or it is necessary to show that the contract is not enforceable because of mistake or fraud.

Rarely will the courts allow prior "oral parts or an entire oral contract" to be substituted for a later written contract. The courts would be jammed with people who wanted to rewrite their contracts. So do it properly. Make only written real estate contracts. Many real estate contracts contain preprinted clauses and spaces for which information is to be handwritten.

*In a legal dispute, when there is a conflict between the preprinted clauses and the handwritten information in a real estate contract, the handwritten information takes precedence.*

# III. Performance, Discharge, and Breach of Contract

*TIME IS OF THE ESSENCE refers to acts described in a contract that must be performed within time limits described in the contract.* Most contracts are properly performed and discharged without any legal complications. If difficulties do arise, the parties, either by themselves or with the aid of legal counsel, usually work out an agreeable settlement. If there is no settlement, the courts are available for the resolution of any contractual conflicts.

*The "time is of the essence" clause applies to the entire contract.*

## A. PERFORMANCE OF A CONTRACT

*PERFORMANCE is the successful completion of a contractual duty, usually resulting in the performer's release from any past or future liability.* Sometimes with performance of a contract, one of the parties would prefer to drop out of the picture without terminating the contract. He or she may, under proper circumstances, accomplish this by assignment.

---

**Figure 5-2**

## STATUTE OF FRAUDS

Most contracts, which by statute are required to be in writing, are found under the Statute of Frauds. The Statute of Frauds was first adopted in England in 1677 and became part of English common law. Subsequently, it was introduced into this country and has become part of California's codified law. The main purpose of this law is to prevent forgery, perjury, and dishonest conduct by unscrupulous people, thus improving the existence and terms of certain important types of contracts.

The statute provides that certain contracts are invalid unless those contracts are in writing and signed by either the parties to be charged or their agents. Under California's Civil Code, the following contracts must be in writing:

1. Any agreement where the terms will not be performed within one year following the making of the contract.

2. A special promise to answer for the debt, default, or nonperformance of another, except in cases provided for by the Civil Code.

3. Agreement made upon the consideration of marriage, other than a mutual promise to marry.

4. An agreement for the leasing of real property for a period longer than one year (one year and one day), or for the sale of real property or of interest therein. It also applies to any agreement authorizing an agent to perform the above acts.

5. An agreement authorizing or employing an agent, broker, or any other person to purchase, sell, or lease real estate for more than one year. It is also an agreement to find a buyer, seller, or lessee for more than one year, in return for compensation.

6. An agreement, which by its terms is not to be performed during the lifetime of the promisor, or an agreement that devises or bequeaths any property, or makes provision for any reason by will.

7. An agreement by a purchaser of real estate to pay a debt secured by a trust deed or mortgage upon the property purchased, unless assumption of that debt by the purchaser is specifically provided for in the conveyance of such property.

**The Statute of Frauds also applies to personal property. If the sales price of an item is more than $500, the contract must be in writing. Furthermore, if several items are purchased with the intent that the agreement be a single contract, the contract should be in writing if the total sales price is $500 or more.**

---

An *ASSIGNMENT is the transfer of a person's right in a contract to another party. An* assignment happens when the *ASSIGNOR, the party to the original contract, transfers his or* her rights in the contract to another party, called an *ASSIGNEE.*

Any contract, unless it calls for some personal service, can be assigned if the contract does not state otherwise. For example, listings are not assignable because they are personal service contracts. If the assignee does not perform, the assignor remains liable (secondary liability) for the contract.

In some cases, the original contracting party may want to drop out of the contract completely. This can be done by novation. A *NOVATION is the substitution or exchange (by mutual agreement of the parties) of a new obligation or contract for an existing one with intent to cancel the old contract.*

*Novation is the substitution, by agreement, of a new contract for an old one.*

Time is often significant in a contract and is usually stated in the contract. By statute, if no time is specified for the performance of an act, a reasonable time is allowed. If an act, by its nature, can be done instantly (such as the payment of money) it must be done. If the last day for the performance of an act falls upon a holiday or weekend, the period is extended to include the next business day. *REVOCATION is the cancelling of an offer to contract by the the original offeror.*

## B. DISCHARGE OF A CONTRACT

The *DISCHARGE OF A CONTRACT occurs when the contract has been terminated.* Contracts can be discharged in many ways, from the extreme of full performance (which is the usual pattern) to breach of contract (nonperformance). **Figure 5-3** illustrates these extremes and the variety of possibilities that may exist between them. A brief description of these possibilities follows.

**Figure 5-3**

### 1. Full Performance

The contract is completed according to the terms specified in the original agreement.

### 2. Substantial Performance

Sometimes one party attempts to discharge a contract when the contract has almost, but not entirely, been completed. In certain cases the courts will accept this as a discharge of the contract. Otherwise, there are usually slight monetary charges for damages.

### 3. Partial Performance

If both parties agree to accept the value of the work partially completed, the contract is discharged. This agreement should be in writing. However, if a dispute arises, the courts will determine the obligations of the defaulting party. Damages are one of the hardest things to prove, and the courts usually lean towards the non-defaulting party. A judge will most likely award the non-defaulting party any amount necessary to complete the contract.

### 4. Impossibility of Performance

Under certain circumstances, the contract, for one reason or another, may be impossible to perform. An obvious example is where a painting contractor can no longer paint a house because it was destroyed by fire. In other cases, legality of the purpose may be challenged.

### 5. Agreement Between the Parties

If a contract is not completed, the usual way to discharge the contract is by mutual agreement (agree to disagree). A mutual agreement not to complete the contract is also a contract. Most knowledgeable contractors include ways for the contract to be discharged if one of the parties defaults on the original contract.

*When a contract is mutually rescinded, the deposit must be returned to the buyer immediately.*

### 6. Operation of Law (According to Statutes)

The law may excuse parties from contract performance because of: 1) illegality, 2) impossibility of performance, 3) rejection by bankruptcy, 4) failure of key contingency, and 5) statute of limitations.

### 7. Acceptance of a Breach

A **BREACH** *is the failure to perform a contract, in part or in whole, without legal excuse.* Sometimes a person will accept a breach. If time is important, the anxious party will usually discharge the contract and try to find a new party to perform the task. Contesting the contract sometimes only creates more problems, such as expensive interruption of work in progress and postponement of other contracts.

### 8. Breach (Nonperformance)

This is the nonperformance by one of the contracting parties. The performing party has his or her choice of several legal remedies.

The most common breaches, from the agent's point of view, are: (1) the buyer who decides not to buy after signing the purchase agreement or (2) the seller who decides not to sell after signing the listing and/or purchase agreement.

*One week after entering into a legally binding purchase contract, the buyer backed out of the agreement. The seller can sue the buyer for money damages, must return the deposit to the buyer, and must attempt to resell the property to another buyer in an attempt to minimize damages.*

### a. Statute of Limitations (Time Limit for Civil Action)

According to the Statute of Limitations, a civil action for a breach of contract must be started within a certain period of time. If the civil action has not been started within that given time, no legal recourse will be possible. This policy of law states that a person who "sleeps upon his rights" may find himself barred from any legal action (see **Figure 5-5**).

# IV. Remedies for Breach of a Contract

A breach of contract occurs when one party fails to perform his or her contractual obligations. By law, the party who has been wronged has only four choices. Action for dollar damages is the most common remedy for breach of a contract because most people prefer to receive money (cash) for their damages. **Figure 5-4** illustrates the four alternatives.

**Figure 5-4**

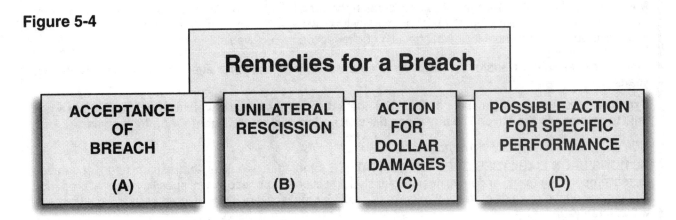

**Remedies for a Breach**

| ACCEPTANCE OF BREACH (A) | UNILATERAL RESCISSION (B) | ACTION FOR DOLLAR DAMAGES (C) | POSSIBLE ACTION FOR SPECIFIC PERFORMANCE (D) |

## A. ACCEPTANCE OF BREACH

A discharge of a contract may be simply the acceptance of the breach. In an *ACCEPTANCE OF BREACH, the wronged party does not pursue legal action.* Sometimes he or she may feel that the damages recoverable are too limited to justify litigation. Perhaps the person considers the other party judgment-proof, which means that the other party does not have enough assets available to satisfy a judgment. Moreover, the legal cost of a lawsuit, the time, the effort, and the psychological effect may not be worth the possible outcome.

## B. UNILATERAL RESCISSION

In a **UNILATERAL RESCISSION** *the wronged party (1) discloses the wrong and (2) restores everything of value to the offending party.* The legal grounds for a rescission are: fraud, mistake, duress, menace, undue influence, and faulty consideration. Rescission is possible when the contract is unlawful for causes not apparent on its face, when the parties are not equally at fault, or when the public interest would be hurt. Minors or incompetents may generally rescind their contracts.

**Figure 5-5**

# STATUTE OF LIMITATIONS

### Actions Which Must Be Brought Within 90 Days:

CIVIL ACTION FOR THE RECOVERY OF PERSONAL PROPERTY, such as trunks or baggage left in a hotel or other furnished establishment, must be started within 90 days after being left by the owner of the personal property.

### Within Six Months:

AN ACTION AGAINST AN OFFICER TO RECOVER ANY GOODS, WAGES, MERCHANDISE, OR OTHER PROPERTY seized by any officer in his or her official capacity as tax collector must be started within six months.

### Within One Year:

AN ACTION FOR LIBEL, SLANDER, INJURY, OR DEATH caused by the neglect of another or against a bank for the payment of a forged check must be started within one year of the alleged wrong.

### Within Two Years:

ACTION MUST BE TAKEN WITHIN TWO YEARS UPON CONTRACTS OR OBLIGATIONS THAT WERE NOT MADE IN WRITING. Actions against contracts that have been founded on title insurance policies, certificates, or abstracts of title for real property must be made within two years from the date the cause of these actions is discovered. This does not include contracts made for accounts receivable.

Action for **misleading transfer disclosure statements** made by broker or agent must be taken within two years.

**Example: When inspecting a seller's home, the agent discovers several physical defects which the agent fails to disclose to the buyer. The buyer can file civil action against the agent for up to two years.**

### Within Three Years (Attachments):

ACTIONS UPON LIABILITIES CREATED BY STATUTE (other than penalties) for trespass upon, or damage to, real property; for taking or damaging goods (including action for the recovery of specific personal property); and actions on the grounds of fraud or mistake caused before discovery by the injured party must be brought within three years.

### Within Four Years (Listings and Purchase Agreements):

ACTIONS WHICH MUST BE MADE ON ANY WRITTEN CONTRACT WITHIN FOUR YEARS include most real estate contracts such as purchase agreements and listings, except for notes or obligations of publicly held corporations (where the limit is specified as being six years). Other exceptions exist when specific limitations are written into a contract. These exceptions include actions on a money judgment for the balance due upon a trust deed or mortgage, actions following the exercise of the power of sale (which may not be brought later than three months after the sale), and actions to recover upon accounts receivable.

### Within Five Years:

ANY ACTION FOR INTERMEDIATE PROFITS OF REAL ESTATE from wrongful occupancy and any action for the recovery of real property may be started anytime within five years.

### Within Ten Years (Judgments):

AN ACTION UPON A JUDGMENT OF ANY COURT OF THE UNITED STATES or of any state within the United States must be brought within ten years.

## C. ACTION FOR DOLLAR DAMAGES

An *ACTION FOR DOLLAR DAMAGES occurs when a court suit for a breach requests payment of a fixed amount of money as compensation.* If a party to a contract causes you to lose money, it is only fair for you to receive compensation. In most purchase agreements (contract to purchase), there is usually a liquidated damages agreement. A *LIQUIDATED DAMAGES AGREEMENT sets, in advance, a specified amount of money as compensation if there is a breach.* This clause is used because it is usually impractical or difficult to determine the actual damages caused by a breach.

> **Example:** Seller Charlie sold his home through a real estate broker. The broker agreed verbally with Charlie that he would find him an acceptable place to live when the sale was completed. The home sold, but the broker does not keep his promise to the seller. Under these circumstances, the seller has the option of trying to recover damages in a court action against the broker.

*The current award for liquidated damages on a purchase agreement form is a maximum of 3% (by law) of the home purchase price.*

## D. SPECIFIC PERFORMANCE

The final remedy for a breach of contract is specific performance. *SPECIFIC PERFORMANCE means that the party causing the breach is, through court action, forced to perform the terms of the contract.* For the most part, courts are skeptical of forcing a person to sell their real property and as a result this type of remedy is seldom used. Courts of equity will consider this action only if dollar damages cannot provide an adequate remedy. If specific performance is ordered, the remedy must be mutual. That is, neither party to a contract can be compelled specifically to perform unless the other party has performed or is also specifically compelled to perform.

To obtain specific performance, the plaintiff must show that the contract was just and reasonable. The contract must have been based on adequate consideration, meaning that the price received for the property must have been fair and reasonable. In addition, specific performance cannot be forced against a party if the contract was obtained by misrepresentation, concealment, circumvention, or any other unfair practice.

# V. The Residential Purchase Agreement

## A. THE OFFER AND ACCEPTANCE (With Deposit)

*A promissory note secured by a deed of trust, a postdated check, or an unsecured promissory note could be used by a buyer as an earnest money deposit in purchasing real property.*

The purchase agreement is the most important contract in the real estate field! Previously known as the **"Deposit Receipt,"** the *CALIFORNIA RESIDENTIAL PURCHASE AGREEMENT AND JOINT ESCROW INSTRUCTIONS is an offer and deposit to purchase a specific property on certain terms and conditions.* When acceptance is communicated to the buyer, this becomes a binding contract on the buyer and seller, and, generally, this becomes the date of the purchase agreement. Acceptance is communicated in writing, in person, by mail, or by fax.

In addition, the purchase agreement discloses (as in the listing agreement) the percentage of commission to be paid to the brokers involved (see **Figure 5-6**, CAR® California Residential Purchase Agreement and Joint Escrow Instructions).

The purchase agreement is neater and more polished if it is typed, but there is nothing wrong with filling it in with a pen. Each form has three copies: a master copy, a buyer's copy, and a seller's copy.

**NOTE: When using preprinted forms, the handwritten parts have control over the printed parts, and all corrections must be initialed by both parties.**

### B. THE DEPOSIT (Consideration for the Purchase Agreement)

The deposit is collected as consideration from a prospective buyer on behalf of the seller for the purchase agreement contract. Suppose the seller accepts the offer on the CAR® Purchase Agreement form and the buyer later defaults on the transaction. If the liquidated damages clause is initialed by both the buyer and seller, the seller may retain the deposit (up to three percent of the sale price). This would then be split 50-50 between the seller and the listing broker, unless otherwise stated in the purchase agreement.

*If a seller rescinds a contract because a buyer defaults, the earnest money deposit must be returned to the buyer if the parties did NOT initial the liquidated damages clause in the purchase contract.*

#### 1. Covenants (A Promise in the Purchase Agreement)

*COVENANTS are promises between the parties to a contract.* Covenants represent promises, obligations and considerations exchanged to fulfill a contract.

Failure to perform a stipulated covenant does not release either party from his or her responsibility. The contract is still in effect, although the offended party may sue for damages.

#### 2. Contingencies, Conditions, or Subject To (An "If" Clause in the Purchase Agreement)

*CONTINGENCIES, CONDITIONS or SUBJECT TO are provisions by which all parties are released from any obligations of a contract if some stated condition occurs or fails to occur.* For example, purchase offers may be made contingent upon the availability of financing, or subject to the successful sale of another property. If the contingency falls through, the contract is voidable by the buyer. Items that are usually found in contingency clauses include:

1. Obtaining financing at a certain interest rate or less.
2. Subject to the approval of my CPA and attorney within 20 days.
3. Conditional upon inspection and approval of each apartment.
4. Subject to property appraisal at no less than the specified price.

## Figure 5-6

**CALIFORNIA**
**RESIDENTIAL PURCHASE AGREEMENT**
**AND JOINT ESCROW INSTRUCTIONS**
For Use With Single Family Residential Property — Attached or Detached
(C.A.R. Form RPA-CA, Revised 4/10)

Date _June 14, 20xx_

1. **OFFER:**
   A. **THIS IS AN OFFER FROM** _Walter Buyer, Debbie Buyer_ ("Buyer").
   B. **THE REAL PROPERTY TO BE ACQUIRED** is described as _264 Beach Lane, Costa Mesa CA 92627_
      _____, Assessor's Parcel No. _____, situated in
      _Costa Mesa_, County of _Orange_, California, ("Property").
   C. **THE PURCHASE PRICE** offered is _Eight Hundred Thousand_
      _____ (Dollars $ _800,000.00_ ).
   D. **CLOSE OF ESCROW** shall occur on _____ (date) (or ☒ _90_ **Days** After Acceptance).
2. **AGENCY:**
   A. **DISCLOSURE:** Buyer and Seller each acknowledge prior receipt of a "Disclosure Regarding Real Estate Agency Relationships" (C.A.R. Form AD).
   B. **POTENTIALLY COMPETING BUYERS AND SELLERS:** Buyer and Seller each acknowledge receipt of a disclosure of the possibility of multiple representation by the Broker representing that principal. This disclosure may be part of a listing agreement, buyer representation agreement or separate document (C.A.R. Form DA). Buyer understands that Broker representing Buyer may also represent other potential buyers, who may consider, make offers on or ultimately acquire the Property. Seller understands that Broker representing Seller may also represent other sellers with competing properties of interest to this Buyer.
   C. **CONFIRMATION:** The following agency relationships are hereby confirmed for this transaction:
      Listing Agent _Sail Realty_ (Print Firm Name) is the agent
      of (check one): ☒ the Seller exclusively; or ☐ both the Buyer and Seller.
      Selling Agent _Ramos Realty_ (Print Firm Name) (if not the same as the Listing Agent) is the agent of (check one): ☒ the Buyer exclusively; or ☐ the Seller exclusively; or ☐ both the Buyer and Seller. Real Estate Brokers are not parties to the Agreement between Buyer and Seller.
3. **FINANCE TERMS:** Buyer represents that funds will be good when deposited with Escrow Holder.
   A. **INITIAL DEPOSIT:** Deposit shall be in the amount of . . . . . . . . . . . . . . . . . . . . . $ _10,000.00_
      (1) Buyer shall deliver deposit directly to Escrow Holder by personal check, ☐ electronic funds transfer, ☐ Other _____ within 3 business days after acceptance (or ☐ Other _____ );
      OR (2) (If checked) ☒ Buyer has given the deposit by personal check (or ☐ _____ )
      to the agent submitting the offer (or to ☒ _____ ),
      made payable to _ABC Escrow_ . The deposit shall be held uncashed until Acceptance and then deposited with Escrow Holder (or ☐ into Broker's trust account) within 3 business days after Acceptance (or ☐ Other _____ ).
   B. **INCREASED DEPOSIT:** Buyer shall deposit with Escrow Holder an increased deposit in the amount of . . . . . . . . . . $ _____
      within _____ **Days** After Acceptance, or ☐ _____
      If a liquidated damages clause is incorporated into this Agreement, Buyer and Seller shall sign a separate liquidated damages clause (C.A.R. Form RID) for any increased deposit at the time it is deposited.
   C. **LOAN(S):**
      (1) **FIRST LOAN:** in the amount of . . . . . . . . . . . . . . . . . . . . . . . . . . . . . . . . $ _640,000.00_
         This loan will be conventional financing or, if checked, ☐ FHA, ☐ VA, ☐ Seller (C.A.R. Form SFA), ☐ assumed financing (C.A.R. Form PAA), ☐ Other _____ . This loan shall be at a fixed rate not to exceed _8.000_ % or, ☐ an adjustable rate loan with initial rate not to exceed _____ %. Regardless of the type of loan, Buyer shall pay points not to exceed _2.00_ % of the loan amount.
      (2) ☐ **SECOND LOAN:** in the amount of . . . . . . . . . . . . . . . . . . . . . . . . . . . . . $ _____
         This loan will be conventional financing or, if checked, ☐ Seller (C.A.R. Form SFA), ☐ assumed financing (C.A.R. Form PAA), ☐ Other _____ . This loan shall be at a fixed rate not to exceed _____ % or, ☐ an adjustable rate loan with initial rate not to exceed _____ %. Regardless of the type of loan, Buyer shall pay points not to exceed _____ % of the loan amount.
      (3) **FHA/VA:** For any FHA or VA loan specified above, Buyer has 17 (or ☐ _____ ) **Days After Acceptance** to Deliver to Seller written notice (C.A.R. Form FVA) of any lender-required repairs or costs that Buyer requests Seller to pay for or repair. Seller has no obligation to pay for repairs or satisfy lender requirements unless otherwise agreed in writing.
   D. **ADDITIONAL FINANCING TERMS:** _____
      _____
   E. **BALANCE OF PURCHASE PRICE OR DOWN PAYMENT:** in the amount of . . . . . . . . . . . . . . . $ _150,000.00_
      to be deposited with Escrow Holder within sufficient time to close escrow.
   F. **PURCHASE PRICE (TOTAL):** . . . . . . . . . . . . . . . . . . . . . . . . . . . . . . . . . . . . $ _800,000.00_

Buyer's Initials ( _WB_ )( _DB_ )

Seller's Initials ( _TS_ )( _RJS_ )

**RPA-CA REVISED 4/10 (PAGE 1 OF 8)**

Reviewed by _JR_ Date _6/14/xx_

**CALIFORNIA RESIDENTIAL PURCHASE AGREEMENT (RPA-CA PAGE 1 OF 8)**

| Agent: WALT HUBER | Phone: | Fax: | Prepared using zipForm® software |
| Broker: WALT HUBER REALTOR | | | |

Property Address: *264 Beach Lane*
*Costa Mesa, CA   92627* _____   Date: *June 14, 20xx*

   **G. VERIFICATION OF DOWN PAYMENT AND CLOSING COSTS:** Buyer (or Buyer's lender or loan broker pursuant to 3H(1)) shall, within **7 (or** ☐ _____ ) **Days** After Acceptance, Deliver to Seller written verification of Buyer's down payment and closing costs. (If checked, ☐ verification attached.)

   **H. LOAN TERMS:**
      **(1) LOAN APPLICATIONS:** Within **7 (or** ☐ _____ ) **Days** After Acceptance, Buyer shall Deliver to Seller a letter from lender or loan broker stating that, based on a review of Buyer's written application and credit report, Buyer is prequalified or preapproved for any NEW loan specified in 3C above. (If checked, ☐ letter attached.)
      **(2) LOAN CONTINGENCY:** Buyer shall act diligently and in good faith to obtain the designated loan(s). Obtaining the loan(s) specified above **is a contingency** of this Agreement unless otherwise agreed in writing. Buyer's contractual obligations to obtain and provide deposit, balance of down payment and closing costs **are not contingencies** of this Agreement.
      **(3) LOAN CONTINGENCY REMOVAL:**
         **(i)** Within **17 (or** ☐ _____ ) **Days** After Acceptance, Buyer shall, as specified in paragraph 14, in writing remove the loan contingency or cancel this Agreement;
         **OR (ii)** (if checked) ☐ the loan contingency shall remain in effect until the designated loans are funded.
      **(4)** ☐ **NO LOAN CONTINGENCY** (If checked): Obtaining any loan specified above is NOT a contingency of this Agreement. If Buyer does not obtain the loan and as a result Buyer does not purchase the Property, Seller may be entitled to Buyer's deposit or other legal remedies.

   **I. APPRAISAL CONTINGENCY AND REMOVAL:** This Agreement is (or, if checked, ☐ is NOT) contingent upon a written appraisal of the Property by a licensed or certified appraiser at no less than the specified purchase price. If there is a loan contingency, Buyer's removal of the loan contingency shall be deemed removal of this appraisal contingency (or, ☐ if checked, Buyer shall, as specified in paragraph 14B(3), in writing remove the appraisal contingency or cancel this Agreement within **17 (or** _____ ) **Days** After Acceptance). If there is no loan contingency, Buyer shall, as specified in paragraph 14B(3), in writing remove the appraisal contingency or cancel this Agreement within **17 (or** _____ ) **Days** After Acceptance.

   **J.** ☐ **ALL CASH OFFER** (If checked): Buyer shall, within **7 (or** ☐ _____ ) **Days** After Acceptance, Deliver to Seller written verification of sufficient funds to close this transaction. (If checked, ☐ verification attached.)

   **K. BUYER STATED FINANCING:** Seller has relied on Buyer's representation of the type of financing specified (including but not limited to, as applicable, amount of down payment, contingent or non contingent loan, or all cash). If Buyer seeks alternate financing, (i) Seller has no obligation to cooperate with Buyer's efforts to obtain such financing, and (ii) Buyer shall also pursue the financing method specified in this Agreement. Buyer's failure to secure alternate financing does not excuse Buyer from the obligation to purchase the Property and close escrow as specified in this Agreement.

**4. ALLOCATION OF COSTS** (If checked): Unless otherwise specified in writing, **this paragraph** only determines who is to pay for the inspection, test or service ("Report") mentioned; it **does not determine who is to pay for any work recommended or identified in the Report.**

   **A. INSPECTIONS AND REPORTS:**
      **(1)** ☐ Buyer ☒ Seller shall pay for an inspection and report for wood destroying pests and organisms ("Wood Pest Report") prepared by *Bug B Gone* _____ a registered structural pest control company.
      **(2)** ☐ Buyer ☐ Seller shall pay to have septic or private sewage disposal systems pumped and inspected _____.
      **(3)** ☐ Buyer ☐ Seller shall pay to have domestic wells tested for water potability and productivity _____.
      **(4)** ☐ Buyer ☐ Seller shall pay for a natural hazard zone disclosure report prepared by _____.
      **(5)** ☐ Buyer ☐ Seller shall pay for the following inspection or report _____.
      **(6)** ☐ Buyer ☐ Seller shall pay for the following inspection or report _____.

   **B. GOVERNMENT REQUIREMENTS AND RETROFIT:**
      **(1)** ☐ Buyer ☒ Seller shall pay for smoke detector installation and/or water heater bracing, if required by Law. Prior to Close Of Escrow, Seller shall provide Buyer written statement(s) of compliance in accordance with state and local Law, unless exempt.
      **(2)** ☐ Buyer ☐ Seller shall pay the cost of compliance with any other minimum mandatory government retrofit standards, inspections and reports if required as a condition of closing escrow under any Law. _____.

   **C. ESCROW AND TITLE:**
      **(1)** ☒ Buyer ☒ Seller shall pay escrow fee *50%/50%* _____
         Escrow Holder shall be *ABC Escrow* _____
      **(2)** ☒ Buyer ☐ Seller shall pay for **owner's** title insurance policy specified in paragraph 12E _____
         Owner's title policy to be issued by _____
         (Buyer shall pay for any title insurance policy insuring Buyer's **lender**, unless otherwise agreed in writing.)

   **D. OTHER COSTS:**
      **(1)** ☐ Buyer ☐ Seller shall pay County transfer tax or fee _____.
      **(2)** ☐ Buyer ☐ Seller shall pay City transfer tax or fee _____.
      **(3)** ☐ Buyer ☐ Seller shall pay Homeowner's Association ("HOA") transfer fee _____.
      **(4)** ☐ Buyer ☐ Seller shall pay HOA document preparation fees _____.
      **(5)** ☐ Buyer ☐ Seller shall pay for any private transfer fee _____.
      **(6)** ☐ Buyer ☐ Seller shall pay the cost, not to exceed $ _____ , of a one-year home warranty plan, issued by _____ , with the following optional coverages:
         ☐ Air Conditioner ☐ Pool/Spa ☐ Code and Permit upgrade ☐ Other: _____
         Buyer is informed that home warranty plans have many optional coverages in addition to those listed above. Buyer is advised to investigate these coverages to determine those that may be suitable for Buyer.
      **(7)** ☐ Buyer ☐ Seller shall pay for _____.
      **(8)** ☐ Buyer ☐ Seller shall pay for _____.

Buyer's Initials ( *WB* ) ( *DB* )

Seller's Initials ( *TS* ) ( *RJS* )

**RPA-CA REVISED 4/10 (PAGE 2 OF 8)**

Reviewed by *JR* Date *6/14/xx*

**CALIFORNIA RESIDENTIAL PURCHASE AGREEMENT (RPA-CA PAGE 2 OF 8)**

EQUAL HOUSING OPPORTUNITY

Cal Principles -

Property Address: *264 Beach Lane*
*Costa Mesa, CA    92627*                                    Date: *June 14, 20xx*

**5. CLOSING AND POSSESSION:**

A. Buyer intends (or ☐ does not intend) to occupy the Property as Buyer's primary residence.

B. **Seller-occupied or vacant property:** Possession shall be delivered to Buyer at 5 PM or ( ☒ *11* ☒ AM ☐ PM), on the date of Close Of Escrow; ☐ on _____; or ☐ no later than _____ **Days** After Close Of Escrow. If transfer of title and possession do not occur at the same time, Buyer and Seller are advised to: **(i)** enter into a written occupancy agreement (C.A.R. Form PAA, paragraph 2); and **(ii)** consult with their insurance and legal advisors.

C. **Tenant-occupied property:**

(i) **Property shall be vacant at least 5 (or ☐ _____ ) Days** Prior to Close Of Escrow, unless otherwise agreed in writing. **Note to Seller: If you are unable to deliver Property vacant in accordance with rent control and other applicable Law, you may be in breach of this Agreement.**

OR **(ii)** (if checked) ☐ **Tenant to remain in possession.** (C.A.R. Form PAA, paragraph 3)

D. At Close Of Escrow, **(i)** Seller assigns to Buyer any assignable warranty rights for items included in the sale, and **(ii)** Seller shall Deliver to Buyer available Copies of warranties. Brokers cannot and will not determine the assignability of any warranties.

E. At Close Of Escrow, unless otherwise agreed in writing, Seller shall provide keys and/or means to operate all locks, mailboxes, security systems, alarms and garage door openers. If Property is a condominium or located in a common interest subdivision, Buyer may be required to pay a deposit to the Homeowners' Association ("HOA") to obtain keys to accessible HOA facilities.

**6. STATUTORY DISCLOSURES (INCLUDING LEAD-BASED PAINT HAZARD DISCLOSURES) AND CANCELLATION RIGHTS:**

A. **(1)** Seller shall, within the time specified in paragraph 14A, Deliver to Buyer, if required by Law: **(i)** Federal Lead-Based Paint Disclosures (C.A.R. Form FLD) and pamphlet ("Lead Disclosures"); and **(ii)** disclosures or notices required by sections 1102 et. seq. and 1103 et. seq. of the Civil Code ("Statutory Disclosures"). Statutory Disclosures include, but are not limited to, a Real Estate Transfer Disclosure Statement ("TDS"), Natural Hazard Disclosure Statement ("NHD"), notice or actual knowledge of release of illegal controlled substance, notice of special tax and/or assessments (or, if allowed, substantially equivalent notice regarding the Mello-Roos Community Facilities Act and Improvement Bond Act of 1915) and, if Seller has actual knowledge, of industrial use and military ordnance location (C.A.R. Form SPQ or SSD).

**(2)** Buyer shall, within the time specified in paragraph 14B(1), return Signed Copies of the Statutory and Lead Disclosures to Seller.

**(3)** In the event Seller, prior to Close Of Escrow, becomes aware of adverse conditions materially affecting the Property, or any material inaccuracy in disclosures, information or representations previously provided to Buyer, Seller shall promptly provide a subsequent or amended disclosure or notice, in writing, covering those items. **However, a subsequent or amended disclosure shall not be required for conditions and material inaccuracies** of which Buyer is otherwise aware, or which are **disclosed in reports provided to or obtained by Buyer or ordered and paid for by Buyer.**

**(4)** If any disclosure or notice specified in 6A(1), or subsequent or amended disclosure or notice is Delivered to Buyer after the offer is Signed, Buyer shall have the right to cancel this Agreement within **3 Days** After Delivery in person, or **5 Days** After Delivery by deposit in the mail, by giving written notice of cancellation to Seller or Seller's agent.

**(5) Note to Buyer and Seller: Waiver of Statutory and Lead Disclosures is prohibited by Law.**

B. **NATURAL AND ENVIRONMENTAL HAZARDS:** Within the time specified in paragraph 14A, Seller shall, if required by Law: **(i)** Deliver to Buyer earthquake guides (and questionnaire) and environmental hazards booklet; **(ii)** even if exempt from the obligation to provide a NHD, disclose if the Property is located in a Special Flood Hazard Area; Potential Flooding (Inundation) Area; Very High Fire Hazard Zone; State Fire Responsibility Area; Earthquake Fault Zone; Seismic Hazard Zone; and **(iii)** disclose any other zone as required by Law and provide any other information required for those zones.

C. **WITHHOLDING TAXES:** Within the time specified in paragraph 14A, to avoid required withholding, Seller shall Deliver to Buyer or qualified substitute, an affidavit sufficient to comply with federal (FIRPTA) and California withholding Law, (C.A.R. Form AS or QS).

D. **MEGAN'S LAW DATABASE DISCLOSURE:** Notice: Pursuant to Section 290.46 of the Penal Code, information about specified registered sex offenders is made available to the public via an Internet Web site maintained by the Department of Justice at www.meganslaw.ca.gov. Depending on an offender's criminal history, this information will include either the address at which the offender resides or the community of residence and ZIP Code in which he or she resides. (Neither Seller nor Brokers are required to check this website. If Buyer wants further information, Broker recommends that Buyer obtain information from this website during Buyer's inspection contingency period. Brokers do not have expertise in this area.)

**7. CONDOMINIUM/PLANNED DEVELOPMENT DISCLOSURES:**

A. **SELLER HAS: 7 (or ☐ _____ ) Days** After Acceptance to disclose to Buyer whether the Property is a condominium, or is located in a planned development or other common interest subdivision (C.A.R. Form SPQ or SSD).

B. If the Property is a condominium or is located in a planned development or other common interest subdivision, Seller has 3 (or ☐ _____ ) **Days** After Acceptance to request from the HOA (C.A.R. Form HOA): **(i)** Copies of any documents required by Law; **(ii)** disclosure of any pending or anticipated claim or litigation by or against the HOA; **(iii)** a statement containing the location and number of designated parking and storage spaces; **(iv)** Copies of the most recent 12 months of HOA minutes for regular and special meetings; and **(v)** the names and contact information of all HOAs governing the Property (collectively, "CI Disclosures"). Seller shall itemize and Deliver to Buyer all CI Disclosures received from the HOA and any CI Disclosures in Seller's possession. Buyer's approval of CI Disclosures is a contingency of this Agreement as specified in paragraph 14B(3).

**8. ITEMS INCLUDED IN AND EXCLUDED FROM PURCHASE PRICE:**

A. **NOTE TO BUYER AND SELLER:** Items listed as included or excluded in the MLS, flyers or marketing materials are **not** included in the purchase price or excluded from the sale unless specified in 8B or C.

B. **ITEMS INCLUDED IN SALE:**

(1) All EXISTING fixtures and fittings that are attached to the Property;

(2) EXISTING electrical, mechanical, lighting, plumbing and heating fixtures, ceiling fans, fireplace inserts, gas logs and grates, solar systems, built-in appliances, window and door screens, awnings, shutters, window coverings, attached floor coverings, television antennas, satellite dishes, private integrated telephone systems, air coolers/conditioners, pool/spa equipment, garage door openers/remote controls, mailbox, in-ground landscaping, trees/shrubs, water softeners, water purifiers, security systems/alarms; (If checked ☐ stove(s), ☐ refrigerator(s)) and

(3) The following additional items: _____

(4) Seller represents that all items included in the purchase price, unless otherwise specified, are owned by Seller.

(5) All items included shall be transferred free of liens and without Seller warranty.

C. **ITEMS EXCLUDED FROM SALE:** Unless otherwise specified, audio and video components (such as flat screen TVs and speakers) are excluded if any such item is not itself attached to the Property, even if a bracket or other mechanism attached to the component is attached to the Property; and _____

Buyer's Initials ( *WB* )( *DB* )

Seller's Initials ( *TS* )( *RJS* )

Reviewed by _*JR*_ Date *6/14/xx*

**RPA-CA REVISED 4/10 (PAGE 3 OF 8)**

**CALIFORNIA RESIDENTIAL PURCHASE AGREEMENT (RPA-CA PAGE 3 OF 8)**

Cal Principles -

Property Address: 264 Beach Lane
Costa Mesa, CA  92627                                    Date: June 14, 20xx

9. **CONDITION OF PROPERTY:** Unless otherwise agreed: **(i)** the Property is sold **(a)** in its **PRESENT** physical **("as-is")** condition as of the date of **Acceptance** and **(b)** subject to Buyer's Investigation rights; **(ii)** the Property, including pool, spa, landscaping and grounds, is to be maintained in substantially the same condition as on the date of Acceptance; and **(iii)** all debris and personal property not included in the sale shall be removed by Seller by Close Of Escrow.

   A. Seller shall, within the time specified in paragraph 14A, DISCLOSE KNOWN MATERIAL FACTS AND DEFECTS affecting the Property, including known insurance claims within the past five years, and make any and all other disclosures required by law.

   B. Buyer has the right to inspect the Property and, as specified in paragraph 14B, based upon information discovered in those inspections: (i) cancel this Agreement; or (ii) request that Seller make Repairs or take other action.

   C. **Buyer is strongly advised to conduct investigations of the entire Property in order to determine its present condition. Seller may not be aware of all defects affecting the Property or other factors that Buyer considers important. Property improvements may not be built according to code, in compliance with current Law, or have had permits issued.**

10. **BUYER'S INVESTIGATION OF PROPERTY AND MATTERS AFFECTING PROPERTY:**

   A. Buyer's acceptance of the condition of, and any other matter affecting the Property, is a contingency of this Agreement as specified in this paragraph and paragraph 14B. Within the time specified in paragraph 14B(1), Buyer shall have the right, at Buyer's expense unless otherwise agreed, to conduct inspections, investigations, tests, surveys and other studies ("Buyer Investigations"), including, but not limited to, the right to: **(i)** inspect for lead-based paint and other lead-based paint hazards; **(ii)** inspect for wood destroying pests and organisms; **(iii)** review the registered sex offender database; **(iv)** confirm the insurability of Buyer and the Property; and **(v)** satisfy Buyer as to any matter specified in the attached Buyer's Inspection Advisory (C.A.R. Form BIA). Without Seller's prior written consent, Buyer shall neither make nor cause to be made: **(i)** invasive or destructive Buyer Investigations; or **(ii)** inspections by any governmental building or zoning inspector or government employee, unless required by Law.

   B. Seller shall make the Property available for all Buyer Investigations. Buyer shall **(i)** as specified in paragraph 14B, complete Buyer Investigations and, either remove the contingency or cancel this Agreement, and **(ii)** give Seller, at no cost, complete Copies of all Investigation reports obtained by Buyer, which obligation shall survive the termination of this Agreement.

   C. Seller shall have water, gas, electricity and all operable pilot lights on for Buyer's Investigations and through the date possession is made available to Buyer.

   D. **Buyer indemnity and Seller protection for entry upon property:** Buyer shall: **(i)** keep the Property free and clear of liens; **(ii)** repair all damage arising from Buyer Investigations; and **(iii)** indemnify and hold Seller harmless from all resulting liability, claims, demands, damages and costs of Buyer's investigations. Buyer shall carry, or Buyer shall require anyone acting on Buyer's behalf to carry, policies of liability, workers' compensation and other applicable insurance, defending and protecting Seller from liability for any injuries to persons or property occurring during any Buyer Investigations or work done on the Property at Buyer's direction prior to Close Of Escrow. Seller is advised that certain protections may be afforded Seller by recording a "Notice of Non-responsibility" (C.A.R. Form NNR) for Buyer Investigations and work done on the Property at Buyer's direction. Buyer's obligations under this paragraph shall survive the termination or cancellation of this Agreement and Close of Escrow.

11. **SELLER DISCLOSURES; ADDENDA; ADVISORIES; OTHER TERMS:**

   A. **Seller Disclosures (if checked):** Seller shall, within the time specified in paragraph 14A, complete and provide Buyer with a:
      - ☒ Seller Property Questionnaire (C.A.R. Form SPQ)  **OR**  ☐ Supplemental Contractual and Statutory Disclosure (C.A.R. Form SSD)

   B. **Addenda (if checked):**
      - ☐ Addendum # _____ (C.A.R. Form ADM)
      - ☐ Wood Destroying Pest Inspection and Allocation of Cost Addendum (C.A.R. Form WPA)
      - ☒ Purchase Agreement Addendum (C.A.R Form PAA)
      - ☐ Septic, Well and Property Monument Addendum (C.A.R. Form SWPI)
      - ☐ Short Sale Addendum (C.A.R. Form SSA)
      - ☐ Other

   C. **Advisories (if checked):**
      - ☐ Probate Advisory (C.A.R. Form PAK)
      - ☒ Buyer's Inspection Advisory (C.A.R. Form BIA)
      - ☐ Trust Advisory (C.A.R. Form TA)
      - ☒ Statewide Buyer and Seller Advisory (C.A.R. Form SBSA)
      - ☐ REO Advisory (C.A.R. Form REO)

   D. **Other Terms:**

12. **TITLE AND VESTING:**

   A. Within the time specified in paragraph 14, Buyer shall be provided a current preliminary title report, which shall include a search of the General Index. Seller shall within 7 Days After Acceptance give Escrow Holder a completed Statement of Information. The preliminary report is only an offer by the title insurer to issue a policy of title insurance and may not contain every item affecting title. Buyer's review of the preliminary report and any other matters which may affect title are a contingency of this Agreement as specified in paragraph 14B.

   B. Title is taken in its present condition subject to all encumbrances, easements, covenants, conditions, restrictions, rights and other matters, whether of record or not, as of the date of Acceptance except: **(i)** monetary liens of record unless Buyer is assuming those obligations or taking the Property subject to those obligations; and **(ii)** those matters which Seller has agreed to remove in writing.

   C. Within the time specified in paragraph 14A, Seller has a duty to disclose to Buyer all matters known to Seller affecting title, whether of record or not.

   D. At Close Of Escrow, Buyer shall receive a grant deed conveying title (or, for stock cooperative or long-term lease, an assignment of stock certificate or of Seller's leasehold interest), including oil, mineral and water rights if currently owned by Seller. Title shall vest as designated in Buyer's supplemental escrow instructions. THE MANNER OF TAKING TITLE MAY HAVE SIGNIFICANT LEGAL AND TAX CONSEQUENCES. CONSULT AN APPROPRIATE PROFESSIONAL.

   E. Buyer shall receive a CLTA/ALTA Homeowner's Policy of Title Insurance. A title company, at Buyer's request, can provide information about the availability, desirability, coverage, survey requirements, and cost of various title insurance coverages and endorsements. If Buyer desires title coverage other than that required by this paragraph, Buyer shall instruct Escrow Holder in writing and pay any increase in cost.

13. **SALE OF BUYER'S PROPERTY:**

   A. This Agreement is NOT contingent upon the sale of any property owned by Buyer.

   **OR B.** ☐ (If checked): The attached addendum (C.A.R. Form COP) regarding the contingency for the sale of property owned by Buyer is incorporated into this Agreement.

Buyer's Initials ( _WB_ )( _DB_ )                    Seller's Initials ( _TS_ )( _RJS_ )

Copyright © 1991-2010, CALIFORNIA ASSOCIATION OF REALTORS®, INC

**RPA-CA REVISED 4/10 (PAGE 4 OF 8)**

Reviewed by _JR_ Date _6/14/xx_     EQUAL HOUSING OPPORTUNITY

**CALIFORNIA RESIDENTIAL PURCHASE AGREEMENT (RPA-CA PAGE 4 OF 8)**     Cal Principles -

132

Property Address: 264 Beach Lane
Costa Mesa, CA    92627           Date: *June 14, 20xx*

**14. TIME PERIODS; REMOVAL OF CONTINGENCIES; CANCELLATION RIGHTS:** The following time periods may only be extended, altered, modified or changed by mutual written agreement. Any removal of contingencies or cancellation under this paragraph by either Buyer or Seller must be exercised in good faith and in writing (C.A.R. Form CR or CC).

    **A. SELLER HAS: 7 (or ☐ _____ ) Days** After Acceptance to Deliver to Buyer all Reports, disclosures and information for which Seller is responsible under paragraphs 4, 6A, B and C, 7A, 9A, 11A and B, and 12. Buyer may give Seller a Notice to Seller to Perform (C.A.R. Form NSP) if Seller has not Delivered the items within the time specified.

    **B. (1) BUYER HAS: 17 (or ☐ _____ ) Days** After Acceptance, unless otherwise agreed in writing, to:
        **(i)** complete all Buyer Investigations; approve all disclosures, reports and other applicable information, which Buyer receives from Seller; and approve all other matters affecting the Property; and
        **(ii)** Deliver to Seller Signed Copies of Statutory and Lead Disclosures Delivered by Seller in accordance with paragraph 6A.
      **(2)** Within the time specified in 14B(1), Buyer may request that Seller make repairs or take any other action regarding the Property (C.A.R. Form RR). Seller has no obligation to agree to or respond to Buyer's requests.
      **(3)** Within the time specified in 14B(1) (or as otherwise specified in this Agreement), Buyer shall Deliver to Seller either (i) a removal of the applicable contingency (C.A.R. Form CR), or (ii) a cancellation (C.A.R. Form CC) of this Agreement based upon a contingency or Seller's failure to Deliver the specified items. However, if any report, disclosure or information for which Seller is responsible is not Delivered within the time specified in 14A, then Buyer has **5 (or ☐ _____ ) Days** After Delivery of any such items, or the time specified in 14B(1), whichever is later, to Deliver to Seller a removal of the applicable contingency or cancellation of this Agreement.
      **(4) Continuation of Contingency:** Even after the end of the time specified in 14B(1) and before Seller cancels this Agreement, if at all, pursuant to 14C, Buyer retains the right to either (i) in writing remove remaining contingencies, or (ii) cancel this Agreement based upon a remaining contingency or Seller's failure to Deliver the specified terms. Once Buyer's written removal of all contingencies is Delivered to Seller, Seller may not cancel this Agreement pursuant to 14C(1).

    **C. SELLER RIGHT TO CANCEL:**
      **(1) Seller right to Cancel; Buyer Contingencies:** If, within time specified in this Agreement, Buyer does not, in writing, Deliver to Seller a removal of the applicable contingency or cancellation of this Agreement then Seller, after first Delivering to Buyer a Notice to Buyer to Perform (C.A.R. Form NBP) may cancel this Agreement. In such event, Seller shall authorize return of Buyer's deposit.
      **(2) Seller right to Cancel; Buyer Contract Obligations:** Seller, after first Delivering to Buyer a NBP may cancel this Agreement for any of the following reasons: (i) if Buyer fails to deposit funds as required by 3A or 3B; (ii) if the funds deposited pursuant to 3A or 3B are not good when deposited; (iii) if Buyer fails to Deliver a notice of FHA or VA costs or terms as required by 3C(3) (C.A.R. Form FVA); (iv) if Buyer fails to Deliver a letter as required by 3H; (v) if Buyer fails to Deliver verification as required by 3G or 3J; (vi) if Seller reasonably disapproves of the verification provided by 3G or 3J; (vii) if Buyer fails to return Statutory and Lead Disclosures as required by paragraph 6A(2); or (viii) if Buyer fails to sign or initial a separate liquidated damage form for an increased deposit as required by paragraphs 3B and 25. In such event, Seller shall authorize return of Buyer's deposit.
      **(3) Notice To Buyer To Perform:** The NBP shall: (i) be in writing; (ii) be signed by Seller; and (iii) give Buyer at least **2 (or ☐ _____ ) Days** After Delivery (or until the time specified in the applicable paragraph, whichever occurs last) to take the applicable action. A NBP may not be Delivered any earlier than **2 Days** Prior to the expiration of the applicable time for Buyer to remove a contingency or cancel this Agreement or meet an obligation specified in 14C(2).

    **D. EFFECT OF BUYER'S REMOVAL OF CONTINGENCIES:** If Buyer removes, in writing, any contingency or cancellation rights, unless otherwise specified in a separate written agreement between Buyer and Seller, Buyer shall with regard to that contingency or cancellation right conclusively be deemed to have: (i) completed all Buyer Investigations, and review of reports and other applicable information and disclosures; (ii) elected to proceed with the transaction; and (iii) assumed all liability, responsibility and expense for Repairs or corrections or for inability to obtain financing.

    **E. CLOSE OF ESCROW:** Before Seller or Buyer may cancel this Agreement for failure of the other party to close escrow pursuant to this Agreement, Seller or Buyer must first give the other a demand to close escrow (C.A.R. Form DCE).

    **F. EFFECT OF CANCELLATION ON DEPOSITS:** If Buyer or Seller gives written notice of cancellation pursuant to rights duly exercised under the terms of this Agreement, Buyer and Seller agree to Sign mutual instructions to cancel the sale and escrow and release deposits, if any, to the party entitled to the funds, less fees and costs incurred by that party. Fees and costs may be payable to service providers and vendors for services and products provided during escrow. **Release of funds will require mutual Signed release instructions from Buyer and Seller, judicial decision or arbitration award. A Buyer or Seller may be subject to a civil penalty of up to $1,000 for refusal to sign such instructions if no good faith dispute exists as to who is entitled to the deposited funds (Civil Code §1057.3).**

**15. REPAIRS:** Repairs shall be completed prior to final verification of condition unless otherwise agreed in writing. Repairs to be performed at Seller's expense may be performed by Seller or through others, provided that the work complies with applicable Law, including governmental permit, inspection and approval requirements. Repairs shall be performed in a good, skillful manner with materials of quality and appearance comparable to existing materials. It is understood that exact restoration of appearance or cosmetic items following all Repairs may not be possible. Seller shall: (i) obtain receipts for Repairs performed by others; (ii) prepare a written statement indicating the Repairs performed by Seller and the date of such Repairs; and (iii) provide Copies of receipts and statements to Buyer prior to final verification of condition.

**16. FINAL VERIFICATION OF CONDITION:** Buyer shall have the right to make a final inspection of the Property within **5 (or ☐ _____ ) Days** Prior to Close Of Escrow, NOT AS A CONTINGENCY OF THE SALE, but solely to confirm: (i) the Property is maintained pursuant to paragraph 9; (ii) Repairs have been completed as agreed; and (iii) Seller has complied with Seller's other obligations under this Agreement (C.A.R. Form VP).

**17. PRORATIONS OF PROPERTY TAXES AND OTHER ITEMS:** Unless otherwise agreed in writing, the following items shall be PAID CURRENT and prorated between Buyer and Seller as of Close Of Escrow: real property taxes and assessments, interest, rents, HOA regular, special, and emergency dues and assessments imposed prior to Close Of Escrow, premiums on insurance assumed by Buyer, payments on bonds and assessments assumed by Buyer, and payments on Mello-Roos and other Special Assessment District bonds and assessments that are a current lien. The following items shall be assumed by Buyer WITHOUT CREDIT toward the purchase price: prorated payments on Mello-Roos and other Special Assessment District bonds and assessments and HOA special assessments that are a current lien but not yet due. Property will be reassessed upon change of ownership. Any supplemental tax bills shall be paid as follows: (i) for periods after Close Of Escrow, by Buyer; and (ii) for periods prior to Close Of Escrow, by Seller (see C.A.R. Form SPT or SBSA for further information). TAX BILLS ISSUED AFTER CLOSE OF ESCROW SHALL BE HANDLED DIRECTLY BETWEEN BUYER AND SELLER. Prorations shall be made based on a 30-day month.

Buyer's Initials ( *WB* )( *DB* )

Copyright © 1991-2010, CALIFORNIA ASSOCIATION OF REALTORS®, INC.
**RPA-CA REVISED 4/10 (PAGE 5 OF 8)**

Seller's Initials ( *TS* )( *RJS* )

Reviewed by *JR* Date *6/14/xx*

**CALIFORNIA RESIDENTIAL PURCHASE AGREEMENT (RPA-CA PAGE 5 OF 8)**      Cal Principles -

Property Address: **264 Beach Lane**
**Costa Mesa, CA    92627**             Date: **June 14, 20xx**

**18. SELECTION OF SERVICE PROVIDERS:** Brokers do not guarantee the performance of any vendors, service or product providers ("Providers"), whether referred by Broker or selected by Buyer, Seller or other person. Buyer and Seller may select ANY Providers of their own choosing.

**19. MULTIPLE LISTING SERVICE ("MLS"):** Brokers are authorized to report to the MLS a pending sale and, upon Close Of Escrow, the sales price and other terms of this transaction shall be provided to the MLS to be published and disseminated to persons and entities authorized to use the information on terms approved by the MLS.

**20. EQUAL HOUSING OPPORTUNITY:** The Property is sold in compliance with federal, state and local anti-discrimination Laws.

**21. ATTORNEY FEES:** In any action, proceeding, or arbitration between Buyer and Seller arising out of this Agreement, the prevailing Buyer or Seller shall be entitled to reasonable attorney fees and costs from the non-prevailing Buyer or Seller, except as provided in paragraph 26A.

**22. DEFINITIONS:** As used in this Agreement:

    A. **"Acceptance"** means the time the offer or final counter offer is accepted in writing by a party and is delivered to and personally received by the other party or that party's authorized agent in accordance with the terms of this offer or a final counter offer.

    B. **"C.A.R. Form"** means the specific form referenced or another comparable form agreed to by the parties.

    C. **"Close Of Escrow"** means the date the grant deed, or other evidence of transfer of title, is recorded.

    D. **"Copy"** means copy by any means including photocopy, NCR, facsimile and electronic.

    E. **"Days"** means calendar days. However, After Acceptance, the last **Day** for performance of any act required by this Agreement (including Close Of Escrow) shall not include any Saturday, Sunday, or legal holiday and shall instead be the next Day.

    F. **"Days After"** means the specified number of calendar days after the occurrence of the event specified, not counting the calendar date on which the specified event occurs, and ending at 11:59PM on the final day.

    G. **"Days Prior"** means the specified number of calendar days before the occurrence of the event specified, not counting the calendar date on which the specified event is scheduled to occur.

    H. **"Deliver", "Delivered" or "Delivery",** regardless of the method used (i.e. messenger, mail, email, fax, other), means and shall be effective upon (i) personal receipt by Buyer or Seller or the individual Real Estate Licensee for that principal as specified in paragraph D of the section titled Real Estate Brokers on page 8; OR (ii) if checked, ☐ per the attached addendum (C.A.R. Form RDN).

    I. **"Electronic Copy" or "Electronic Signature"** means, as applicable, an electronic copy or signature complying with California Law. Buyer and Seller agree that electronic means will not be used by either party to modify or alter the content or integrity of this Agreement without the knowledge and consent of the other party.

    J. **"Law"** means any law, code, statute, ordinance, regulation, rule or order, which is adopted by a controlling city, county, state or federal legislative, judicial or executive body or agency.

    K. **"Repairs"** means any repairs (including pest control) alterations, replacements, modifications or retrofitting of the Property provided for under this Agreement.

    L. **"Signed"** means either a handwritten or electronic signature on an original document, Copy or any counterpart.

**23. BROKER COMPENSATION:** Seller or Buyer, or both, as applicable, agrees to pay compensation to Broker as specified in a separate written agreement between Broker and that Seller or Buyer. Compensation is payable upon Close Of Escrow, or if escrow does not close, as otherwise specified in the agreement between Broker and that Seller or Buyer.

**24. JOINT ESCROW INSTRUCTIONS TO ESCROW HOLDER:**

    A. **The following paragraphs, or applicable portions thereof, of this Agreement constitute the joint escrow instructions of Buyer and Seller to Escrow Holder,** which Escrow Holder is to use along with any related counter offers and addenda, and any additional mutual instructions to close the escrow: 1, 3, 4, 6C, 11B and D, 12, 13B, 14F, 17, 22, 23, 24, 25, 30, and paragraph D of the section titled Real Estate Brokers on page 8. If a Copy of the separate compensation agreement(s) provided for in paragraph 23, or paragraph D of the section titled Real Estate Brokers on page 8 is deposited with Escrow Holder by Broker, Escrow Holder shall accept such agreement(s) and pay out of Buyer's or Seller's funds, or both, as applicable, the respective Broker's compensation provided for in such agreement(s). The terms and conditions of this Agreement not specifically referenced above, in the specified paragraphs are additional matters for the information of Escrow Holder, but about which Escrow Holder need not be concerned. Buyer and Seller will receive Escrow Holder's general provisions directly from Escrow Holder and will execute such provisions upon Escrow Holder's request. To the extent the general provisions are inconsistent or conflict with this Agreement, the general provisions will control as to the duties and obligations of Escrow Holder only. Buyer and Seller will execute additional instructions, documents and forms provided by Escrow Holder that are reasonably necessary to close the escrow.

    B. A Copy of this Agreement shall be delivered to Escrow Holder within 3 business days after Acceptance (or ☐ _____ ). Escrow Holder shall provide Seller's Statement of Information to Title company when received from Seller. Buyer and Seller authorize Escrow Holder to accept and rely on Copies and Signatures as defined in this Agreement as originals, to open escrow and for other purposes of escrow. The validity of this Agreement as between Buyer and Seller is not affected by whether or when Escrow Holder Signs this Agreement.

    C. Brokers are a party to the escrow for the sole purpose of compensation pursuant to paragraphs 23 and paragraph D of the section titled Real Estate Brokers on page 8. Buyer and Seller irrevocably assign to Brokers compensation specified in paragraphs 23, respectively, and irrevocably instruct Escrow Holder to disburse those funds to Brokers at Close Of Escrow or pursuant to any other mutually executed cancellation agreement. Compensation instructions can be amended or revoked only with the written consent of Brokers. Buyer and Seller shall release and hold harmless Escrow Holder from any liability resulting from Escrow Holder's payment to Broker(s) of compensation pursuant to this Agreement. Escrow Holder shall immediately notify Brokers: **(i)** if Buyer's initial or any additional deposit is not made pursuant to this Agreement, or is not good at time of deposit with Escrow Holder; or **(ii)** if either Buyer or Seller instruct Escrow Holder to cancel escrow.

    D. A Copy of any amendment that affects any paragraph of this Agreement for which Escrow Holder is responsible shall be delivered to Escrow Holder within **2** business days after mutual execution of the amendment.

Buyer's Initials ( _WB_ )( _DB_ )             Seller's Initials ( _TS_ )( _RJS_ )

Reviewed by _JR_ Date _6/14/xx_

EQUAL HOUSING OPPORTUNITY

**CALIFORNIA RESIDENTIAL PURCHASE AGREEMENT (RPA-CA PAGE 6 OF 8)**      Cal Principles -

Property Address: *264 Beach Lane*
*Costa Mesa, CA 92627*          Date: *June 14, 20xx*

25. **LIQUIDATED DAMAGES:** If Buyer fails to complete this purchase because of Buyer's default, Seller shall retain, as liquidated damages, the deposit actually paid. If the Property is a dwelling with no more than four units, one of which Buyer intends to occupy, then the amount retained shall be no more than 3% of the purchase price. Any excess shall be returned to Buyer. Release of funds will require mutual, Signed release instructions from both Buyer and Seller, judicial decision or arbitration award. **AT TIME OF THE INCREASED DEPOSIT BUYER AND SELLER SHALL SIGN A SEPARATE LIQUIDATED DAMAGES PROVISION FOR ANY INCREASED DEPOSIT. (C.A.R. FORM RID).**

| Buyer's Initials *WB* / *DB* | Seller's Initials *TS* / *RJS* |
|---|---|

26. **DISPUTE RESOLUTION:**

A. **MEDIATION:** Buyer and Seller agree to mediate any dispute or claim arising between them out of this Agreement, or any resulting transaction, before resorting to arbitration or court action. **Buyer and Seller also agree to mediate any disputes or claims with Broker(s), who, in writing, agree to such mediation prior to, or within a reasonable time after, the dispute or claim is presented to the Broker.** Mediation fees, if any, shall be divided equally among the parties involved. If, for any dispute or claim to which this paragraph applies, any party (i) commences an action without first attempting to resolve the matter through mediation, or (ii) before commencement of an action, refuses to mediate after a request has been made, then that party shall not be entitled to recover attorney fees, even if they would otherwise be available to that party in any such action. **THIS MEDIATION PROVISION APPLIES WHETHER OR NOT THE ARBITRATION PROVISION IS INITIALED. Exclusions from this mediation agreement are specified in paragraph 26C.**

B. **ARBITRATION OF DISPUTES:**

Buyer and Seller agree that any dispute or claim in Law or equity arising between them out of this Agreement or any resulting transaction, which is not settled through mediation, shall be decided by neutral, binding arbitration. **Buyer and Seller also agree to arbitrate any disputes or claims with Broker(s), who, in writing, agree to such arbitration prior to, or within a reasonable time after, the dispute or claim is presented to the Broker.** The arbitrator shall be a retired judge or justice, or an attorney with at least 5 years of residential real estate Law experience, unless the parties mutually agree to a different arbitrator. The parties shall have the right to discovery in accordance with Code of Civil Procedure §1283.05. In all other respects, the arbitration shall be conducted in accordance with Title 9 of Part 3 of the Code of Civil Procedure. Judgment upon the award of the arbitrator(s) may be entered into any court having jurisdiction. Enforcement of this agreement to arbitrate shall be governed by the Federal Arbitration Act. Exclusions from this arbitration agreement are specified in paragraph 26C.

"**NOTICE: BY INITIALING IN THE SPACE BELOW YOU ARE AGREEING TO HAVE ANY DISPUTE ARISING OUT OF THE MATTERS INCLUDED IN THE 'ARBITRATION OF DISPUTES' PROVISION DECIDED BY NEUTRAL ARBITRATION AS PROVIDED BY CALIFORNIA LAW AND YOU ARE GIVING UP ANY RIGHTS YOU MIGHT POSSESS TO HAVE THE DISPUTE LITIGATED IN A COURT OR JURY TRIAL. BY INITIALING IN THE SPACE BELOW YOU ARE GIVING UP YOUR JUDICIAL RIGHTS TO DISCOVERY AND APPEAL, UNLESS THOSE RIGHTS ARE SPECIFICALLY INCLUDED IN THE 'ARBITRATION OF DISPUTES' PROVISION. IF YOU REFUSE TO SUBMIT TO ARBITRATION AFTER AGREEING TO THIS PROVISION, YOU MAY BE COMPELLED TO ARBITRATE UNDER THE AUTHORITY OF THE CALIFORNIA CODE OF CIVIL PROCEDURE. YOUR AGREEMENT TO THIS ARBITRATION PROVISION IS VOLUNTARY.**"

"**WE HAVE READ AND UNDERSTAND THE FOREGOING AND AGREE TO SUBMIT DISPUTES ARISING OUT OF THE MATTERS INCLUDED IN THE 'ARBITRATION OF DISPUTES' PROVISION TO NEUTRAL ARBITRATION.**"

| Buyer's Initials *WB* / *DB* | Seller's Initials *TS* / *RJS* |
|---|---|

C. **ADDITIONAL MEDIATION AND ARBITRATION TERMS:**

(1) **EXCLUSIONS:** The following matters shall be excluded from mediation and arbitration: (i) a judicial or non-judicial foreclosure or other action or proceeding to enforce a deed of trust, mortgage or installment land sale contract as defined in Civil Code §2985; (ii) an unlawful detainer action; (iii) the filing or enforcement of a mechanic's lien; and (iv) any matter that is within the jurisdiction of a probate, small claims or bankruptcy court. The filing of a court action to enable the recording of a notice of pending action, for order of attachment, receivership, injunction, or other provisional remedies, shall not constitute a waiver or violation of the mediation and arbitration provisions.

(2) **BROKERS:** Brokers shall not be obligated or compelled to mediate or arbitrate unless they agree to do so in writing. Any Broker(s) participating in mediation or arbitration shall not be deemed a party to the Agreement.

27. **TERMS AND CONDITIONS OF OFFER:**

This is an offer to purchase the Property on the above terms and conditions. The liquidated damages paragraph or the arbitration of disputes paragraph is incorporated in this Agreement if initialed by all parties or if incorporated by mutual agreement in a counter offer or addendum. If at least one but not all parties initial such paragraph(s), a counter offer is required until agreement is reached. Seller has the right to continue to offer the Property for sale and to accept any other offer at any time prior to notification of Acceptance. If this offer is accepted and Buyer subsequently defaults, Buyer may be responsible for payment of Brokers' compensation. This Agreement and any supplement, addendum or modification, including any Copy, may be Signed in two or more counterparts, all of which shall constitute one and the same writing.

28. **TIME OF ESSENCE; ENTIRE CONTRACT; CHANGES:** Time is of the essence. All understandings between the parties are incorporated in this Agreement. Its terms are intended by the parties as a final, complete and exclusive expression of their Agreement with respect to its subject matter, and may not be contradicted by evidence of any prior agreement or contemporaneous oral agreement. If any provision of this Agreement is held to be ineffective or invalid, the remaining provisions will nevertheless be given full force and effect. Except as otherwise specified, this Agreement shall be interpreted and disputes shall be resolved in accordance with the laws of the State of California. **Neither this Agreement nor any provision in it may be extended, amended, modified, altered or changed, except in writing Signed by Buyer and Seller.**

Buyer's Initials ( *WB* )( *DB* )

RPA-CA REVISED 4/10 (PAGE 7 OF 8)

Seller's Initials ( *TS* )( *RJS* )

| Reviewed by *JR* | Date *6/14/xx* |
|---|---|

**CALIFORNIA RESIDENTIAL PURCHASE AGREEMENT (RPA-CA PAGE 7 OF 8)**     Cal Principles -

Property Address: *264 Beach Lane*
*Costa Mesa, CA  92627*                                                                    Date: *June 14, 20xx*

**29. EXPIRATION OF OFFER:** This offer shall be deemed revoked and the deposit shall be returned unless the offer is Signed by Seller and a Copy of the Signed offer is personally received by Buyer, or by _____, who is authorized to receive it, by 5:00 PM on the third Day after this offer is signed by Buyer (or, if checked, ☐ by _____ ☐ AM ☐ PM, on _____ (date)).

Buyer has read and acknowledges receipt of a Copy of the offer and agrees to the above confirmation of agency relationships.

Date *June 14, 20xx*                                                          Date *June 14, 20xx*

BUYER *Walter Buyer*                                                        BUYER *Debbie Buyer*

*Walter     Buyer*                                                              *Debbie        Buyer*
**(Print name)**                                                                 **(Print name)**
*100 Boat Avenue, Marina del Rey CA 90292*
**(Address)**
☐ Additional Signature Addendum attached (C.A.R. Form ASA).

**30. ACCEPTANCE OF OFFER:** Seller warrants that Seller is the owner of the Property, or has the authority to execute this Agreement. Seller accepts the above offer, agrees to sell the Property on the above terms and conditions, and agrees to the above confirmation of agency relationships. Seller has read and acknowledges receipt of a Copy of this Agreement, and authorizes Broker to Deliver a Signed Copy to Buyer.

☐ (If checked) **SUBJECT TO ATTACHED COUNTER OFFER (C.A.R. Form CO) DATED:** _____

Date *June 15, 20xx*                                                          Date *June 15, 20xx*

SELLER *Tony Seller*                                                        SELLER *Ramona J. Seller*

*Tony      Seller*                                                                *Ramona    J.        Seller*
**(Print name)**                                                                 **(Print name)**
*264 Beach Lane, Costa Mesa, CA  92627*
**(Address)**
☐ Additional Signature Addendum attached (C.A.R. Form ASA).

( *WB* / *DB* )   **CONFIRMATION OF ACCEPTANCE:** A Copy of Signed Acceptance was personally received by Buyer or Buyer's authorized
**(Initials)**   agent on (date) ___ *June 15, 20xx* ___ at ___ *11* ___ ☒ AM ☐ PM. A binding Agreement is created when a Copy of Signed Acceptance is personally received by Buyer or Buyer's authorized agent whether or not confirmed in this document. Completion of this confirmation is not legally required in order to create a binding Agreement. It is solely intended to evidence the date that Confirmation of Acceptance has occurred.

**REAL ESTATE BROKERS:**
A. Real Estate Brokers are not parties to the Agreement between Buyer and Seller.
B. Agency relationships are confirmed as stated in paragraph 2.
C. If specified in paragraph 3A(2), Agent who submitted the offer for Buyer acknowledges receipt of deposit.
D. **COOPERATING BROKER COMPENSATION:** Listing Broker agrees to pay Cooperating Broker **(Selling Firm)** and Cooperating Broker agrees to accept, out of Listing Broker's proceeds in escrow: (i) the amount specified in the MLS, provided Cooperating Broker is a Participant of the MLS in which the Property is offered for sale or a reciprocal MLS; or (ii) ☐ (if checked) the amount specified in a separate written agreement (C.A.R. Form CBC) between Listing Broker and Cooperating Broker. Declaration of License and Tax (C.A.R. Form DLT) may be used to document that tax reporting will be required or that an exemption exits.

Real Estate Broker (Selling Firm) *Ramos Realty*                                         DRE Lic. # *00 000 000*
By *Joseph Ramos* *Joseph Ramos* DRE Lic. # *00 000 000* Date *06/14/20xx*
Address *777 Newport Blvd.* City *Newport Beach* State *CA* Zip *92663*
Telephone *(714)647-0000* Fax *(714)647-0001* E-mail *jr@ramosrealty.com*

Real Estate Broker (Listing Firm) *Sail Realty*                                            DRE Lic. # *00 000 000*
By *Carmen Caro* *Carmen Caro* DRE Lic. # *00 000 000* Date *06/15/20xx*
Address *227 Harbor Blvd.* City *Costa Mesa* State *CA* Zip *92627*
Telephone *(714)626-2828* Fax *(714)626-2829* E-mail *carmen@sailrealty.com*

**ESCROW HOLDER ACKNOWLEDGMENT:**
Escrow Holder acknowledges receipt of a Copy of this Agreement, (if checked, ☐ a deposit in the amount of $ _____ ), counter offer numbered _____, ☐ Seller's Statement of Information and ☐ Other _____, and agrees to act as Escrow Holder subject to paragraph 24 of this Agreement, any supplemental escrow instructions and the terms of Escrow Holder's general provisions if any.
Escrow Holder is advised that the date of Confirmation of Acceptance of the Agreement as between Buyer and Seller is _____.
Escrow Holder _____                                                          Escrow # _____
By _____                                                                              Date _____
Address _____
Phone/Fax/E-mail _____
Escrow Holder is licensed by the California Department of ☐ Corporations, ☐ Insurance, ☐ Real Estate. License # _____

**PRESENTATION OF OFFER:** ( _____ ) Listing Broker presented this offer to Seller on _____ (date).
                                      Broker or Designee Initials

**REJECTION OF OFFER:** ( _____ ) ( _____ ) No counter offer is being made. This offer was rejected by Seller on _____ (date).
                                 Seller's Initials

Reviewed by _____
Broker or Designee *JR* Date *6/15/xx*

**REVISION DATE 4/10**

CALIFORNIA RESIDENTIAL PURCHASE AGREEMENT (RPA-CA PAGE 8 OF 8)                     Cal Principles -

## California Residential Purchase Agreement and Joint Escrow Instructions – Highlights

1. Includes fixed times for delivery of disclosures and removal of contingencies.
2. Allows Buyer to cancel within a set time without first requesting Seller to make repairs.
3. Requires written removal of contingencies.
4. Requires Seller to give Notice to Buyer to Perform before Seller may cancel.
5. Gives Seller a cancellation right if Buyer does not meet certain contractual obligations.
6. Refers to separate agreement for broker compensation.
7. No pre-allocation of costs to cure problems with wood destroying pests.
8. Use of addendum required to accommodate pre-allocation requests.

**Example:** An offer made by a prospective buyer was contingent on the sale of the buyer's current residence. Seller Billings made a counter offer accepting the offer provided the seller could continue to market the home in an attempt to obtain a better offer while granting the buyer a "first right of refusal" to remove the sale contingency if another offer was presented. The buyer accepted the terms and immediately listed his current residence for sale. One week later, Billings notified the buyer that a better offer with no contingencies was "on the table." The agent representing the buyer should advise the buyer about the advantages and disadvantages of removing the contingency feature at this time.

## C. THE PURCHASE AGREEMENT ADDENDUM

The *PURCHASE AGREEMENT ADDENDUM form is used as an addendum to either the Residential Purchase Agreement, another offer form, or the counter offer form.* Only the paragraphs that are checked are included as part of the contract. The CAR® two-page addendum (see **Figure 5-7**) covers six separate topics that are occasionally relevant to a transaction:

1. The cancellation of prior sale; back-up offers.
2. Seller to remain in possession after close of escrow.
3. Tenant to remain in possession.
4. Junior or assumed financing.
5. Short pay.
6. Court confirmation.

*ERRORS AND OMISSIONS INSURANCE is the liability insurance (usually paid for by the salesperson at close of escrow) that brokers and salespeople should carry in order to pay for any costly lawsuits.*

## D. THE COUNTER OFFER (Replaces Original Offer with Changes in Terms)

*A counter offer automatically cancels the original offer if terms of the new offer vary from the original.*

**Figure 5-7**

CALIFORNIA ASSOCIATION OF REALTORS®

**PURCHASE AGREEMENT ADDENDUM No. _____**
(May Also Be Used With Counter Offer)
(C.A.R. Form PAA, Revised 4/08)

This is an addendum to the ☐ California Residential Purchase Agreement, ☐ Counter Offer No. _____, ☐ Other _____
_____, ("Agreement"), dated _____, on
property known as _____123 Sail Avenue,_____ ("Property"),
between _____ ("Buyer"),
and _____ ("Seller").
(The definitions in the California Residential Purchase Agreement are applicable to this Purchase Agreement Addendum.)

1. ☐ **CANCELLATION OF PRIOR SALE; BACK-UP OFFER** (If checked): This Agreement is in back-up position number _____,
   and is contingent upon written cancellation of any prior contracts and related escrows ("Prior Contracts") between Seller and other
   buyers. Seller and other buyers may mutually agree to modify or amend the terms of Prior Contracts. Buyer may cancel this
   Agreement in writing at any time before Seller provides Buyer Copies of written cancellations of Prior Contracts Signed by all parties
   to those contracts. If Seller is unable to provide such written Signed cancellations to Buyer by _____ (date),
   then either Buyer or Seller may cancel the Agreement in writing.
   **A. BUYER'S DEPOSIT CHECK** shall be: **(i)** held uncashed until Copies of the written cancellations Signed by all parties to the Prior
   Contracts are provided to Buyer; OR **(ii)** (if checked) ☐ immediately handled as provided in the Agreement.
   **B. TIME PERIODS** in the Agreement for Investigations, contingencies, covenants and other obligations **(i)** shall begin on the Day
   After Seller provides Buyer Copies of Signed cancellations of Prior Contracts; OR **(ii)** (if checked) ☐ all time periods shall begin
   as provided in this Agreement. However, if the date for Close Of Escrow is a specific calendar date, that date shall NOT be
   extended, unless agreed to in writing by Buyer and Seller.

2. ☐ **SELLER TO REMAIN IN POSSESSION AFTER CLOSE OF ESCROW** (If checked): This provision is intended for short-term
   occupancy (i.e. less than 30 Days). If occupancy is intended to be for 30 Days or longer, use Residential Lease After Sale (C.A.R.
   Form RLAS). **Note:** Local rent control or other Law regarding tenant's rights may impact Buyer's and Seller's rights and
   obligations.
   **A. TERM:** Seller to remain in possession of Property for _____ **Days** After Close Of Escrow (or ☐ _____).
   Seller has no right to remain in possession beyond this term and may be responsible for court awarded damages if Seller does
   remain.
   **B. COMPENSATION:** Seller agrees to pay Buyer **(i)** for the term specified in 2A, $ _____ per Day (or ☐
   _____), and **(ii)** a security deposit in the amount of $ _____. Seller shall deposit
   such funds with escrow holder prior to Close Of Escrow or such funds shall be withheld from Seller's proceeds. At Close Of
   Escrow, security deposit will be released to Buyer (or ☐ held in escrow).
   **C. LATE CHARGE/NSF CHECKS:** If any payment from Seller to Buyer is required outside of escrow, and any such payment is not
   received by Buyer within **5** (or ☐ _____) **Days** After date due, Seller shall pay to Buyer an additional sum of
   $ _____ as a Late Charge. If a check is returned for non-sufficient funds ("NSF"), Seller shall pay to
   Buyer $25.00 as an NSF charge. Seller and Buyer agree that these charges represent a fair and reasonable estimate of the costs
   Buyer may incur by reason of Seller's late or NSF payment. Buyer's acceptance of any Late Charge or NSF fee shall not
   constitute a waiver as to any default by Seller.
   **D. UTILITIES:** Seller agrees to pay for all utilities and services, and the following charges: _____
   _____ except _____, which shall be paid for by Buyer.
   **E. ENTRY:** Seller shall make Property available to Buyer for the purpose of entering to make necessary or agreed repairs, or to
   supply necessary or agreed services, or to show Property to prospective or actual purchasers, tenants, mortgagees, lenders,
   appraisers or contractors. Buyer and Seller agree that 24 hours notice (oral or written) shall be reasonable and sufficient notice.
   In an emergency, Buyer may enter Property at any time without notice.
   **F. MAINTENANCE:** Seller shall maintain the Property, including pool, spa, landscaping and grounds, and all personal property
   included in the sale in substantially the same condition as on the date of Acceptance of the Agreement. Except as provided in the
   Agreement, Seller shall not make alterations to the Property without Buyer's written consent.
   **G. ASSIGNMENT; SUBLETTING:** Seller shall not assign or sublet all or any part of the Property, or assign or transfer the right to
   occupy the Property. Any assignment, subletting or transfer of the Property by voluntary act of Seller, by operation of Law or
   otherwise, without Buyer's prior written consent shall give Buyer the right to terminate Seller's right to possession.
   **H. SELLER'S OBLIGATIONS UPON DELIVERY OF POSSESSION:** Upon delivery of possession to Buyer, Seller shall deliver the
   Property in the condition and on the terms provided in the Agreement.
   **I. INSURANCE:** Seller's personal property (including vehicles) is not insured by Buyer, and, if applicable, owner's association,
   against loss or damage due to fire, theft, vandalism, rain, water, criminal or negligent acts of others, or any other cause. Seller is
   to carry Seller's own insurance to protect Seller from such loss.
   **J. WAIVER:** The waiver of any breach shall not be construed as a continuing waiver of the same or any subsequent breach.
   **K. OTHER TERMS AND CONDITIONS/SUPPLEMENTS:** _____
   _____
   _____

**PAA REVISED 4/08 (PAGE 1 OF 2)**

Buyer's Initials ( _____ ) ( _____ )
Seller's Initials ( _____ ) ( _____ )
Reviewed by _____ Date _____

EQUAL HOUSING OPPORTUNITY

**PURCHASE AGREEMENT ADDENDUM (PAA PAGE 1 OF 2)**

Agent: WALT HUBER     Phone:     Fax:     Prepared using WINForms® software
Broker: WALT HUBER REALTOR

Property Address: *123 Sail Avenue,* _____ Date: _____

3. ☐ **TENANT TO REMAIN IN POSSESSION** (If checked): Buyer shall take Property subject to the rights of existing tenants. Seller shall, within **7 (or ☐** _____ **) Days** After Acceptance, deliver to Buyer Copies of all: estoppel certificates sent to and received back from tenants; leases; rental agreements; and current income and expense statements ("Rental Documents"). Seller shall give Buyer written notice of any changes to existing leases or tenancies or new agreements to lease or rent ("Proposed Changes") at least **7 (or ☐** _____ **) Days** prior to any Proposed Changes. Buyer's approval of the Rental Documents and Proposed Changes is a contingency of the Agreement. Buyer shall, within **5 (or ☐** _____ **) Days** After receipt of Rental Documents or Proposed Changes remove the applicable contingency or cancel the Agreement. Seller shall transfer to Buyer, through escrow, all unused tenant deposits. No warranty is made concerning compliance with governmental restrictions, if any, limiting the amount of rent that can lawfully be charged, and/or the maximum number of persons who can lawfully occupy the Property, unless otherwise agreed in writing.

4. ☐ **SECONDARY OR ASSUMED LOAN** (If checked): Obtaining the secondary loan or assumption below and approval of such financing is a contingency of this Agreement. Buyer shall act diligently and in good faith to obtain the designated financing.
   A. ☐ **SECONDARY LOAN:**
   　(1) New second deed of trust in favor of LENDER encumbering the Property, securing a note payable at maximum interest of _____ % fixed rate or _____ % initial adjustable rate, with a maximum interest rate of _____ %, balance due in _____ years. Buyer shall pay loan fees/points not to exceed _____ . (These terms apply whether the designated loan is conventional, FHA or VA.)
   　(2) Within **17 (or** _____ **Days)** After Acceptance, Buyer shall, as specified in the Agreement, remove this contingency or cancel this Agreement; OR (if checked) ☐ secondary loan contingency shall remain in effect until the loan is funded.
   B. ☐ **ASSUMPTION OF EXISTING LOAN:**
   　(1) Assumption of existing deed of trust encumbering the Property, securing a note payable at maximum interest of _____ % fixed rate or _____ % initial adjustable rate, with a maximum interest rate of _____ %, balance due in _____ years. Buyer shall pay loan fees/points not to exceed _____ . Seller shall, within **5 (or ☐** _____ **) Days** After Acceptance, request from Lender, and upon receipt provide to Buyer, Copies of all applicable notes and deeds of trust, loan balances and current interest rates. Differences between estimated and actual loan balances shall be adjusted at Close Of Escrow by cash down payment. Impound accounts, if any, shall be assigned and charged to Buyer and credited to Seller. If this is an assumption of a VA Loan, the sale is contingent upon Seller being provided a release of liability and substitution of eligibility, unless otherwise agreed in writing.
   　(2) Within **17 (or ☐** _____ **) Days** After Acceptance, Buyer shall, as specified in the Agreement, remove this contingency or cancel this Agreement. However, if the assumed loan documents are not provided to Buyer within **7 Days After Acceptance**, Buyer has **5 (or ☐** _____ **) Days** After receipt of these documents, or the fixed time specified in 4B(2), whichever occurs last, to remove this contingency or cancel the Agreement; OR (if checked) ☐ assumed loan contingency shall remain in effect until the assumption is approved.

5. ☐ **COURT CONFIRMATION** (If checked): This Agreement is contingent upon court confirmation on or before _____ (date). If court confirmation is not obtained by that date, Buyer may cancel this Agreement in writing. Court confirmation may be required in probate, conservatorship, guardianship, receivership, bankruptcy or other proceedings. The court may allow open, competitive bidding, resulting in Property being sold to the highest bidder. Broker recommends that Buyer appear at the court confirmation hearing. Buyer understands that **(i)** Broker and others may continue to market the Property and **(ii)** Broker may represent other competitive bidders prior to and at the court confirmation.

By signing below Buyer and Seller acknowledge that each has read, understands, received a copy of and agrees to the terms of this Purchase Agreement Addendum.

Date _____ 　　Date _____

Buyer _____ 　　Seller _____

Buyer _____ 　　Seller _____

Published and Distributed by:
REAL ESTATE BUSINESS SERVICES, INC.
*a subsidiary of the California Association of REALTORS®*
525 South Virgil Avenue, Los Angeles, California 90020
**PAA REVISED 4/08 (PAGE 2 OF 2)**

Reviewed by _____ Date _____

**PURCHASE AGREEMENT ADDENDUM (PAA PAGE 2 OF 2)**

Produced with ZipForm™ by RE FormsNet, LLC 18025 Fifteen Mile Road, Clinton Township, Michigan 48035　www.zipform.com 　　　　Untitled

Rather than preparing a whole new purchase agreement when presenting a counter offer, most sellers prefer to use a standard counter offer form like the sample CAR® form shown in **Figure 5-8**. This form is used to change some of the terms of the original purchase agreement and allows the seller and buyer to accept the remaining agreed-to terms and conditions of the original agreement. Plenty of blank space is provided to list these exceptions that formally amend the purchase agreement without the necessity of completing an entirely new purchase agreement.

*In a counter offer, the offeree becomes the offeror.*

If there is only a minor change in a term (like sale's price), the counter offer can be written on the back of the original purchase agreement and signed by the buyer and seller. **The seller can never change the purchase agreement on its face by crossing out sections or adding new information**. The counter offer must contain a clause stating that all of the conditions of the original purchase agreement are acceptable except for the listed new terms. If there are major changes, the formal counter offer form may be required. Finally, if there are significant changes it is better to start the process again by filling out a new purchase agreement.

**Example:** A buyer made an offer to purchase a property and placed $5,000 as an earnest money deposit. The seller amended the offer with some terms of her own and did not change the amount of the earnest money deposit. The buyer then changed the amount of the earnest money deposit to $1,000. The buyer's change is considered a counter offer, a contract has not been formed, and the seller must accept the buyer's change in the amount of the earnest money deposit.

*When accepting an offer on her home, the seller changed one of the terms of the buyer's offer. This is best described as a counter offer.*

### E. INSPECTION ADVISORY FOR BUYERS

Property inspection is important. The physical condition of the land and improvements being purchased are not guaranteed by either sellers or brokers, except as specifically set forth in the purchase agreement. For this reason, most salespeople are required by their brokers to "advise" buyers of their right to have a personal and professional inspection of the property they are purchasing. Furthermore, brokers have been advised by their attorneys to have potential buyers sign the Buyer's Inspection Advisory Form to protect the salesperson and broker. This form expressly states in bold print:

**"YOU ARE STRONGLY ADVISED TO INVESTIGATE THE CONDITION AND SUITABILITY OF ALL ASPECTS OF THE PROPERTY.  IF YOU DO NOT DO SO, YOU ARE ACTING AGAINST THE ADVICE OF BROKERS."**

As professionals, we have a duty to advise buyers to exercise reasonable care to protect themselves. The buyer acknowledges receipt of a copy of the Buyer's Inspection Advisory CAR® form by signing a copy (see **Figure 5-9**).

*If an agent fails to disclose known defects in a property to the buyer, the buyer can file civil action against the agent within two years.*

## Figure 5-8

**COUNTER OFFER No. _____**
For use by Seller or Buyer. May be used for Multiple Counter Offer.
(C.A.R. Form CO, Revised 10/04)

Date _____, at _____, California.
This is a counter offer to the: ☐ California Residential Purchase Agreement, ☐ Counter Offer, or ☐ Other _____ ("Offer"),
dated _____ , on property known as *123 Sail Avenue* _____ ("Property"),
between _____ ("Buyer") and
_____ ("Seller").

1. **TERMS:** The terms and conditions of the above referenced document are accepted subject to the following:
   A. **Paragraphs in the Offer that require initials by all parties, but are not initialed by all parties, are excluded from the final agreement unless specifically referenced for inclusion in paragraph 1C of this or another Counter Offer.**
   B. **Unless otherwise agreed in writing, down payment and loan amount(s) will be adjusted in the same proportion as in the original Offer.**
   C. _____
   _____
   _____
   _____
   _____
   _____
   _____
   D. The following attached supplements are incorporated into this Counter Offer: ☐ Addendum No. _____
   ☐ _____ ☐ _____

2. **RIGHT TO ACCEPT OTHER OFFERS:** Seller has the right to continue to offer the Property for sale or for other transaction, and to accept any other offer at any time prior to notification of acceptance, as described in paragraph 3. If this is a Seller Counter Offer, Seller's acceptance of another offer prior to Buyer's acceptance and communication of notification of this Counter Offer, shall revoke this Counter Offer.

3. **EXPIRATION:** This Counter Offer shall be deemed revoked and the deposits, if any, shall be returned unless this Counter Offer is signed by the Buyer or Seller to whom it is sent and a Copy of the signed Counter Offer is personally received by the person making this Counter Offer or _____,
   who is authorized to receive it, by 5:00 PM on the third Day After this Counter Offer is made or, (if checked) by ☐ _____
   (date), at _____ ☐ AM ☐ PM. This Counter Offer may be executed in counterparts.

4. ☐ **(If checked:) MULTIPLE COUNTER OFFER:** Seller is making a Counter Offer(s) to another prospective buyer(s) on terms that may or may not be the same as in this Counter Offer. Acceptance of this Counter Offer by Buyer shall **not** be binding unless and until it is subsequently re-Signed by Seller in paragraph 7 below and a Copy of the Counter Offer Signed in paragraph 7 is personally received by Buyer or by _____, who is authorized to receive it, by 5:00PM
   on the third Day after this Counter Offer is made or, (if checked by ☐ _____ (date), at _____ ☐ AM ☐ PM.
   Prior to the completion of all of these events, Buyer and Seller shall have no duties or obligations for the purchase or sale of the Property.

5. **OFFER:** ☐ **BUYER** OR ☐ **SELLER MAKES THIS COUNTER OFFER ON THE TERMS ABOVE AND ACKNOWLEDGES RECEIPT OF A COPY.**
   _____ Date _____
   _____ Date _____

6. **ACCEPTANCE: I/WE** accept the above Counter Offer **(If checked** ☑ **SUBJECT TO THE ATTACHED COUNTER OFFER)** and acknowledge receipt of a Copy.
   _____ Date _____ Time _____ ☐ AM ☐ PM
   _____ Date _____ Time _____ ☐ AM ☐ PM

7. **MULTIPLE COUNTER OFFER SIGNATURE LINE:** By signing below, Seller accepts this Multiple Counter Offer.
   **NOTE TO SELLER: Do NOT sign in this box until after Buyer signs in paragraph 6. (Paragraph 7 applies only if paragraph 4 is checked.)**
   _____ Date _____ Time _____ ☐ AM ☐ PM
   _____ Date _____ Time _____ ☐ AM ☐ PM

8. (_____ / _____) **(Initials) Confirmation of Acceptance:** A Copy of Signed Acceptance was personally received by the maker of the Counter Offer, or that person's authorized agent as specified in paragraph 3 (or, if this is a Multiple Counter Offer, the Buyer or Buyer's authorized agent as specified in paragraph 4) on (date) _____ , at _____ ☐ AM ☐ PM. **A binding Agreement is created when a Copy of Signed Acceptance is personally received by the the maker of the Counter Offer, or that person's authorized agent (or, if this is a Multiple Counter Offer, the Buyer or Buyer's authorized agent) whether or not confirmed in this document. Completion of this confirmation is not legally required in order to create a binding Agreement; it is solely intended to evidence the date that Confirmation of Acceptance has occurred.**

Published and Distributed by:
REAL ESTATE BUSINESS SERVICES, INC.
*a subsidiary of the California Association of REALTORS®*
525 South Virgil Avenue, Los Angeles, California 90020

Reviewed by _____ Date _____

EQUAL HOUSING OPPORTUNITY

CO REVISED 10/04 (PAGE 1 OF 1)

**COUNTER OFFER (CO PAGE 1 OF 1)**

Agent: WALT HUBER    Phone:    Fax:    Prepared using zipForm® software
Broker: WALT HUBER REALTOR

## Figure 5-9

CALIFORNIA
ASSOCIATION
OF REALTORS®

**BUYER'S INSPECTION ADVISORY**
(C.A.R. Form BIA-A, Revised 10/02)

Property Address: _264 Beach Lane, Costa Mesa  CA   92627_____ ("Property").

**A. IMPORTANCE OF PROPERTY INVESTIGATION:** The physical condition of the land and improvements being purchased is not guaranteed by either Seller or Brokers. For this reason, you should conduct thorough investigations of the Property personally and with professionals who should provide written reports of their investigations. A general physical inspection typically does not cover all aspects of the Property nor items affecting the Property that are not physically located on the Property. If the professionals recommend further investigations, including a recommendation by a pest control operator to inspect inaccessible areas of the Property, you should contact qualified experts to conduct such additional investigations.

**B. BUYER RIGHTS AND DUTIES:** You have an affirmative duty to exercise reasonable care to protect yourself, including discovery of the legal, practical and technical implications of disclosed facts, and the investigation and verification of information and facts that you know or that are within your diligent attention and observation. The purchase agreement gives you the right to investigate the Property. If you exercise this right, and you should, you must do so in accordance with the terms of that agreement. This is the best way for you to protect yourself. It is extremely important for you to read all written reports provided by professionals and to discuss the results of inspections with the professional who conducted the inspection. You have the right to request that Seller make repairs, corrections or take other action based upon items discovered in your investigations or disclosed by Seller. If Seller is unwilling or unable to satisfy your requests, or you do not want to purchase the Property in its disclosed and discovered condition, you have the right to cancel the agreement if you act within specific time periods. If you do not cancel the agreement in a timely and proper manner, you may be in breach of contract.

**C. SELLER RIGHTS AND DUTIES:** Seller is required to disclose to you material facts known to him/her that affect the value or desirability of the Property. However, Seller may not be aware of some Property defects or conditions. Seller does not have an obligation to inspect the Property for your benefit nor is Seller obligated to repair, correct or otherwise cure known defects that are disclosed to you or previously unknown defects that are discovered by you or your inspectors during escrow. The purchase agreement obligates Seller to make the Property available to you for investigations.

**D. BROKER OBLIGATIONS:** Brokers do not have expertise in all areas and therefore cannot advise you on many items, such as soil stability, geologic or environmental conditions, hazardous or illegal controlled substances, structural conditions of the foundation or other improvements, or the condition of the roof, plumbing, heating, air conditioning, electrical, sewer, septic, waste disposal, or other system. The only way to accurately determine the condition of the Property is through an inspection by an appropriate professional selected by you. If Broker gives you referrals to such professionals, Broker does not guarantee their performance. You may select any professional of your choosing. In sales involving residential dwellings with no more than four units, Brokers have a duty to make a diligent visual inspection of the accessible areas of the Property and to disclose the results of that inspection. However, as some Property defects or conditions may not be discoverable from a visual inspection, it is possible Brokers are not aware of them. If you have entered into a written agreement with a Broker, the specific terms of that agreement will determine the nature and extent of that Broker's duty to you. **YOU ARE STRONGLY ADVISED TO INVESTIGATE THE CONDITION AND SUITABILITY OF ALL ASPECTS OF THE PROPERTY. IF YOU DO NOT DO SO, YOU ARE ACTING AGAINST THE ADVICE OF BROKERS.**

**E. YOU ARE ADVISED TO CONDUCT INVESTIGATIONS OF THE ENTIRE PROPERTY, INCLUDING, BUT NOT LIMITED TO THE FOLLOWING:**

1. **GENERAL CONDITION OF THE PROPERTY, ITS SYSTEMS AND COMPONENTS:** Foundation, roof, plumbing, heating, air conditioning, electrical, mechanical, security, pool/spa, other structural and non-structural systems and components, fixtures, built-in appliances, any personal property included in the sale, and energy efficiency of the Property. (Structural engineers are best suited to determine possible design or construction defects, and whether improvements are structurally sound.)

2. **SQUARE FOOTAGE, AGE, BOUNDARIES:** Square footage, room dimensions, lot size, age of improvements and boundaries. Any numerical statements regarding these items are APPROXIMATIONS ONLY and have not been verified by Seller and cannot be verified by Brokers. Fences, hedges, walls, retaining walls and other natural or constructed barriers or markers do not necessarily identify true Property boundaries. (Professionals such as appraisers, architects, surveyors and civil engineers are best suited to determine square footage, dimensions and boundaries of the Property.)

3. **WOOD DESTROYING PESTS:** Presence of, or conditions likely to lead to the presence of wood destroying pests and organisms and other infestation or infection. Inspection reports covering these items can be separated into two sections: Section 1 identifies areas where infestation or infection is evident. Section 2 identifies areas where there are conditions likely to lead to infestation or infection. A registered structural pest control company is best suited to perform these inspections.

4. **SOIL STABILITY:** Existence of fill or compacted soil, expansive or contracting soil, susceptibility to slippage, settling or movement, and the adequacy of drainage. (Geotechnical engineers are best suited to determine such conditions, causes and remedies.)

Buyer's Initials ( _WB_ )( _DB_ )
Seller's Initials ( _TS_ )( _RJS_ )
Reviewed by _JR_  Date _/14/xx_

EQUAL HOUSING
OPPORTUNITY

**BIA-A REVISED 10/02 (PAGE 1 OF 2)**

**BUYER'S INSPECTION ADVISORY (BIA-A PAGE 1 OF 2)**

| Agent: WALT HUBER | Phone: | Fax: | Prepared using zipForm® software |
|---|---|---|---|
| Broker: WALT HUBER REALTOR | | | |

Property Address: _264 Beach Lane, Costa Mesa  CA  92627_ _____ Date: _June 14, 20xx_ _____

5. **ROOF:** Present condition, age, leaks, and remaining useful life. (Roofing contractors are best suited to determine these conditions.)
6. **POOL/SPA:** Cracks, leaks or operational problems. (Pool contractors are best suited to determine these conditions.)
7. **WASTE DISPOSAL:** Type, size, adequacy, capacity and condition of sewer and septic systems and components, connection to sewer, and applicable fees.
8. **WATER AND UTILITES; WELL SYSTEMS AND COMPONENTS:** Water and utility availability, use restrictions and costs. Water quality, adequacy, condition, and performance of well systems and components.
9. **ENVIRONMENTAL HAZARDS:** Potential environmental hazards, including, but not limited to, asbestos, lead-based paint and other lead contamination, radon, methane, other gases, fuel oil or chemical storage tanks, contaminated soil or water, hazardous waste, waste disposal sites, electromagnetic fields, nuclear sources, and other substances, materials, products, or conditions (including mold (airborne, toxic or otherwise), fungus or similar contaminants). (For more information on these items, you may consult an appropriate professional or read the booklets "Environmental Hazards: A Guide for Homeowners, Buyers, Landlords and Tenants," "Protect Your Family From Lead in Your Home" or both.)
10. **EARTHQUAKES AND FLOODING:** Susceptibility of the Property to earthquake/seismic hazards and propensity of the Property to flood. (A Geologist or Geotechnical Engineer is best suited to provide information on these conditions.)
11. **FIRE, HAZARD AND OTHER INSURANCE:** The availability and cost of necessary or desired insurance may vary. The location of the Property in a seismic, flood or fire hazard zone, and other conditions, such as the age of the Property and the claims history of the Property and Buyer, may affect the availability and need for certain types of insurance. Buyer should explore insurance options early as this information may affect other decisions, including the removal of loan and inspection contingencies. (An insurance agent is best suited to provide information on these conditions.)
12. **BUILDING PERMITS, ZONING AND GOVERNMENTAL REQUIREMENTS:** Permits, inspections, certificates, zoning, other governmental limitations, restrictions, and requirements affecting the current or future use of the Property, its development or size. (Such information is available from appropriate governmental agencies and private information providers. Brokers are not qualified to review or interpret any such information.)
13. **RENTAL PROPERTY RESTRICTIONS:** Some cities and counties impose restrictions that limit the amount of rent that can be charged, the maximum number of occupants; and the right of a landlord to terminate a tenancy. Deadbolt or other locks and security systems for doors and windows, including window bars, should be examined to determine whether they satisfy legal requirements. (Government agencies can provide information about these restrictions and other requirements.)
14. **SECURITY AND SAFETY:** State and local Law may require the installation of barriers, access alarms, self-latching mechanisms and/or other measures to decrease the risk to children and other persons of existing swimming pools and hot tubs, as well as various fire safety and other measures concerning other features of the Property. Compliance requirements differ from city to city and county to county. Unless specifically agreed, the Property may not be in compliance with these requirements. (Local government agencies can provide information about these restrictions and other requirements.)
15. **NEIGHBORHOOD, AREA, SUBDIVISION CONDITIONS, PERSONAL FACTORS:** Neighborhood or area conditions, including schools, proximity and adequacy of law enforcement, crime statistics, the proximity of registered felons or offenders, fire protection, other government services, availability, adequacy and cost of any speed-wired, wireless internet connections or other telecommunications or other technology services and installations, proximity to commercial, industrial or agricultural activities, existing and proposed transportation, construction and development that may affect noise, view, or traffic, airport noise, noise or odor from any source, wild and domestic animals, other nuisances, hazards, or circumstances, protected species, wetland properties, botanical diseases, historic or other governmentally protected sites or improvements, cemeteries, facilities and condition of common areas of common interest subdivisions, and possible lack of compliance with any governing documents or Homeowners' Association requirements, conditions and influences of significance to certain cultures and/or religions, and personal needs, requirements and preferences of Buyer.

Buyer and Seller acknowledge and agree that Broker: **(i)** Does not decide what price Buyer should pay or Seller should accept; **(ii)** Does not guarantee the condition of the Property; **(iii)** Does not guarantee the performance, adequacy or completeness of inspections, services, products or repairs provided or made by Seller or others; **(iv)** Does not have an obligation to conduct an inspection of common areas or areas off the site of the Property; **(v)** Shall not be responsible for identifying defects on the Property, in common areas, or offsite unless such defects are visually observable by an inspection of reasonably accessible areas of the Property or are known to Broker; **(vi)** Shall not be responsible for inspecting public records or permits concerning the title or use of Property; **(vii)** Shall not be responsible for identifying the location of boundary lines or other items affecting title; **(viii)** Shall not be responsible for verifying square footage, representations of others or information contained in investigation reports, Multiple Listing Service, advertisements, flyers or other promotional material; **(ix)** Shall not be responsible for providing legal or tax advice regarding any aspect of a transaction entered into by Buyer or Seller; and **(x)** Shall not be responsible for providing other advice or information that exceeds the knowledge, education and experience required to perform real estate licensed activity. Buyer and Seller agree to seek legal, tax, insurance, title and other desired assistance from appropriate professionals.

**By signing below, Buyer and Seller each acknowledge that they have read, understand, accept and have received a Copy of this Advisory. Buyer is encouraged to read it carefully.**

| _Walter Buyer_ | 06/14/20xx | _Debbie Buyer_ | 06/14/20xx |
|---|---|---|---|
| Buyer Signature | Date | Buyer Signature | Date |
| Walter   Buyer | | Debbie        Buyer | |
| _Tony Seller_ | 6/15/20xx | _Ramona J. Seller_ | 06/15/20xx |
| Seller Signature | Date | Seller Signature | Date |
| Tony       Seller | | Ramona   J.        Seller | |

THIS FORM HAS BEEN APPROVED BY THE CALIFORNIA ASSOCIATION OF REALTORS® (C.A.R.). NO REPRESENTATION IS MADE AS TO THE LEGAL VALIDITY OR ADEQUACY OF ANY PROVISION IN ANY SPECIFIC TRANSACTION. A REAL ESTATE BROKER IS THE PERSON QUALIFIED TO ADVISE ON REAL ESTATE TRANSACTIONS. IF YOU DESIRE LEGAL OR TAX ADVICE, CONSULT AN APPROPRIATE PROFESSIONAL.
This form is available for use by the entire real estate industry. It is not intended to identify the user as a REALTOR®. REALTOR® is a registered collective membership mark which may be used only by members of the NATIONAL ASSOCIATION OF REALTORS® who subscribe to its Code of Ethics.

Published and Distributed by:
REAL ESTATE BUSINESS SERVICES, INC.
a subsidiary of the California Association of REALTORS®
525 South Virgil Avenue, Los Angeles, California 90020

Reviewed by _JR_ Date _6/15/xx_

**BIA-A REVISED 10/02 (PAGE 2 OF 2)**         BUYER'S INSPECTION ADVISORY (BIA-A PAGE 2 OF 2)         Cal Principles -

# VI. Seller/Agent Required Disclosures

*The Transfer Disclosure Statement (TDS) requires the disclosure of the known presence of mold, drug lab use, military ordnance, and Mello-Roos bonds and taxes. Additional disclosures may be needed to further detail this information.*

The following is an alphabetical list of the disclosure forms that may typically be required in a residential real estate transaction:

**Agent's Inspection Disclosure** – Designed for use by agents on properties that are exempt from California Civil Code § 1102.6 (TDS) requirements.

**Buyer's Affidavit (FIRPTA Compliance)** – Documents whether or not federal Foreign Investment in Real Property Tax Act (FIRPTA) withholding is required. Explains the criteria buyer and property must meet.

**Confirmation: Real Estate Agency Relationships** – Used to comply with California Civil Code requirements to confirm agency relationships in a transaction. This clause is preprinted in CAR® Purchase Contracts.

**Data Base Disclosure (Regarding Registered Sex Offenders)** – Complies with requirement that certain printed information regarding registered sex offenders be part of residential real estate contracts and leases.

**Disclosure and Consent For Representation Of More Than One Buyer Or Seller** – This form is used to disclose that a real estate brokerage may represent a buyer or seller that is competing with the broker's principal. It also discloses the possibility that the same real estate brokerage company may represent both buyer and seller in the same transaction.

**Disclosure Regarding Real Estate Agency Relationships** – Used to comply with California Civil Code. Explains types of agency relationships.

**Homeowner's Guide to Earthquake Safety** – The **Alquist-Priolo Earthquake Fault Zoning Act** requires the seller and agent to disclose to the buyer that the property is or may be situated in an earthquake fault zone. (See chapter 12 for more details.)

**Lead-Based Paint and Lead-Based Paint Hazards Disclosure, Acknowledgment, and Addendum for Pre-1978 Housing** – Used to comply with federal requirements for disclosure of any known lead-based paint or lead-based paint hazards on any housing constructed prior to 1978. From seller to buyer or from owner or landlord to tenant.

**Manufactured Home and Mobilehome: Transfer Disclosure Statement** – This is a statutory form required in the sales of manufactured homes.

*The seller is primarily responsible for disclosing the presence of Mello-Roos tax liens or other assessments.*

**Methamphetamine Contamination Notice** – This form is used by a landlord or property owner to notify a tenant or purchaser that the property has been identified as being contaminated by methamphetamine (drug lab).

**Mortgage Loan Disclosure Statement (Borrower)** – Complies with DRE regulations requiring disclosure when a broker is acting as an arranger of credit. Outlines loan terms, costs and expenses.

**Natural Hazard Disclosure Statement** – Used to comply with State requirements when a substituted Zone Disclosure Report is not used.

*The Natural Hazard Disclosure Statement covers six zones: Seismic Hazard Zone, Earthquake Fault Zone, Wildland Fire Zone, State Responsibility Area, Flood Zone, and Dam Inundation Zone.*

**Pest Control Inspection and Certification Report** – Identifies any wood destroying pests (termites) or conditions likely to cause pest infestation. (See Chapter 7 for more details.)

*The Structural Pest Control Board collects termite reports, copies of which can be obtained by anyone upon request for a fee.*

**Radon Gas and Mold Notice and Release Agreement** – As required by HUD, this form gives Buyers of HUD-owned property notice that no representation is made regarding radon gas or mold. In addition, Buyer releases HUD and its agents from any liability associated with either of these substances. The form also advises Buyer to contact a lawyer and have an inspection. (A **spectrometer** is used to measure radon.)

**Real Estate Transfer Disclosure Statement (TDS)** – The property disclosure statement required by law in most residential sales transactions in California. It includes Seller's mandatory disclosure of specified items and any known adverse material conditions, as well as sections for seller's and buyer's agents to comply with diligent visual inspection requirements.

*In addition to disclosing any known environmental hazards on the TDS, the seller and his/her agent should provide the buyer with the pamphlet entitled "Environmental Hazards: a Guide for Homeowners, Buyers, Landlords, and Tenants," which includes sections on asbestos, lead, mold, formaldehyde, and radon. The Environmental Hazards Guide does NOT include fire, flood, or earthquake information.*

**Seller Financing Addendum and Disclosure** – Designed to be used with the financing paragraph of the RPA-CA or RIPA. Contains terms of seller financing and the legally required disclosures. It also grants seller the right to obtain and review buyer's credit report, and requires buyer to complete a loan application.

**Seller's Affidavit of Nonforeign Status and/or California Withholding Exemption** – Used to comply with federal Foreign Investment in Real Property Tax Act (FIRPTA) and California nonresident withholding laws. Documents whether tax withholding is required. Requirements are listed on the reverse. One form is used for each person or entity on title.

**Smoke Detector Statement of Compliance** – Seller uses this form to certify that smoke detectors are properly installed in compliance with state and local laws.

**Statewide Buyer and Seller Advisory** – This document advises both Buyer and Seller of various factors that may affect the decision to buy, different types of inspections that can be obtained and questions to ask about or research and information to be disclosed.

**Supplemental Statutory and Contractual Disclosures** – Provides for delivery and confirmation of receipt of statutory disclosures and contractual disclosures (such as insurance claims affecting the Property) not provided for in the Real Estate Transfer Disclosure Statement (TDS).

**Water Heater Statement of Compliance** – Used by Seller to certify that water heaters are properly installed in compliance with state and local laws.

# VII. Purchase Options

## A. OPTIONS (A Unilateral Contract)

An *OPTION is a right to purchase a property upon specified terms within a specific time period, which is granted in exchange for money* (see **Figure 5-10** for the CAR® three-page Option Agreement). An option is normally purchased to take a property off the open market. The prospective purchaser holds an exclusive right to buy during the option period.

*The optionee owns the option.*

An *OPTIONOR is a property owner who gives an interested buyer an exclusive right to purchase a property. An* **OPTIONEE** *is a potential buyer who purchases an agreed-to amount of time to buy a specific property upon set terms.* The optionee does not have to go through with the purchase.

*It is a good practice to obtain a preliminary title report or otherwise verify that the owner will be able to convey marketable title.*

If the optionee decides to buy the property during his or her option period, the optionor must sell. In this case, the option will become a sales contract and both parties are bound by its terms.

*A salesperson who has a listing and an option to purchase a property, from the seller, must, at the same time, disclose all offers, material information, and obtain consent from the seller of any anticipated profits from the seller before exercising the option to purchase.*

The optionee may also secure another buyer for the property (sell his or her option to another party) during its term. Thus, all rights and interests may be transferred without the consent of the optionor, unless stated otherwise.

If an optionee has, for example, a one-year recorded option and, after six months decides not to exercise his or her option, the property owner should see to it that a quitclaim deed is recorded so that the option might be removed from the records.

It's always advisable to seek the services of a real estate attorney who is knowledgeable in lease options.

*Due to the 2007-2009 credit crunch/slump, option agreements, which can be used with a purchase agreement or a lease, are becoming more popular.*

**Figure 5-10**

**OPTION AGREEMENT**
(To be used with a Purchase Agreement. May also be used with a Lease.)
(C.A.R. Form OA, Revised 4/08)

Date _____ , at _____ , California
_____ ("Optionor"), grants to
_____ , ("Optionee"),
on the following terms and conditions, an option ("Option") to purchase the real property and improvements situated in
(City) _____ , County of _____
California, described as _____ *123 Sail Avenue* _____ ("Property") on the terms and
conditions specified in the attached: ☐ Real Estate Purchase Agreement ☐ Other _____ ,
which is incorporated by reference as a part of this Option.

1. **OPTION CONSIDERATION:**
   A. _____ Dollars ($ _____ ),
      payable upon acceptance of this Option, or, if checked, ☐ _____ ,
      by ☐ cash, ☐ cashier's check, ☐ personal check, or ☐ _____
      made payable to _____ .
   OR B. ☐ (If checked) Mutual execution of the attached lease specified in paragraph 2A.
   OR C. ☐ (If checked) Both 1A and 1B.
2. ☐ **LEASE (If checked):**
   A. The attached Lease Agreement, dated _____ , between Optionee as Tenant and Optionor as Landlord, is
      incorporated by reference as part of this Option.
   B. If the Option is exercised, the lease shall terminate on the earliest of (i) the date scheduled for Close Of Escrow under the
      Purchase Agreement, or as extended in writing, (ii) the Close Of Escrow of the Purchase Agreement, or (iii) mutual cancellation
      of the Purchase Agreement.
3. **OPTION PERIOD:** The Option shall begin on (date) _____ , and shall end at 11:59 p.m.
   (or at ☐ _____ ), on (date) _____ .
4. **MANNER OF EXERCISE:** Optionee may exercise the Option **only** by delivering a written unconditional notice of exercise, signed
   by Optionee, to Optionor, or _____ , who is authorized to receive it.
   A copy of the unconditional notice of exercise shall be delivered to the Brokers identified in this Agreement.
5. **NON-EXERCISE:** If the Option is not exercised in the manner specified, within the option period or any written extension thereof,
   or if it is terminated under any provision of this Option, then:
   A. The Option and all rights of Optionee to purchase the Property shall immediately terminate without notice; and
   B. All Option Consideration paid, rent paid, services rendered to Optionor, and improvements made to the Property, if any, by
      Optionee, shall be retained by Optionor in consideration of the granting of the Option; and
   C. Optionee shall execute, acknowledge, and deliver to Optionor, within 6 (or ☐ _____ ) **calendar Days** of Optionor's request,
      a release, quitclaim deed, or any other document reasonably required by Optionor or a title insurance company to verify the
      termination of the Option.
6. **EFFECT OF DEFAULT ON OPTION:**
   A. Optionee shall have no right to exercise this Option if Optionee has not performed any obligation imposed by, or is in default of,
      any obligation of this Option, any addenda, or any document incorporated by reference.
   B. In addition, if a lease is incorporated by reference in paragraph 2A, Optionee shall have no right to exercise this Option if
      Optionor, as Landlord, has given to Optionee, as Tenant, two or more notices to cure any default or non-performance under
      that lease.
7. **OPTIONOR DISCLOSURE:**
   A. Unless exempt, if the Property contains one-to-four residential dwelling units, Optionor shall within 7 (or _____ ) **Days After**
      entering into this Option provide to Optionee (i) a Real Estate Transfer Disclosure Statement, a Natural Hazard Disclosure
      Statement, a Notice of Private Transfer Fee and other disclosures required by Civil Code §§1102 and 1103 et seq.,
      (ii) ☐ a preliminary title report, and (iii) ☐ _____
   B. If any disclosure or notice specified in 7A is delivered to Optionee after the Option is Signed, Optionee shall have the right to
      cancel this Option within **3 Days After** delivery in person or **5 Days After** delivery by deposit in the mail by giving written notice
      of cancellation to Optionor or Optionor's agent.

Optionee and Optionor acknowledge receipt of copy of this page, which constitutes Page 1 of ____ Pages.
Optionee's Initials ( ____ ) ( ____ ) Optionor's Initials ( ____ ) ( ____ )

**OA REVISED 4/08 (PAGE 1 OF 3)**

Reviewed by _____ Date _____

**OPTION AGREEMENT (OA PAGE 1 OF 3)**

| Agent: WALT HUBER | Phone: | Fax: | Prepared using zipForm® software |
| Broker: WALT HUBER REALTOR | | | |

Property Address: _____ Date: _____

8. **PURCHASE AGREEMENT:**

   A. All of the time limits contained in the attached Purchase Agreement, which begin on the date of Acceptance of the Purchase Agreement, shall instead begin to run on the date the Option is exercised.

   B. If this Option is exercised and Optionee cancels pursuant to any contingency in the attached purchase agreement, including but not limited to any right of inspection or financing provision, all option consideration paid, rent paid, services rendered to Optionor, and improvements to the Property, if any, by Optionee, shall be retained by Optionor in consideration of the granting of the Option.

   C. If this Option is exercised, upon close of escrow of the attached Purchase Agreement, ☐ all, or ☐ $ _____ , of the Option Consideration, and ☐ (if checked) $ _____ per month of rent actually paid by Optionee, shall be applied toward Optionee's down payment obligations under that Agreement. Optionee is advised that the full amount of the option consideration applied toward any down payment may not be counted by a lender for financing purposes.

9. **DISPUTE RESOLUTION:** Optionee and Optionor agree that any dispute or claim arising between them out of this Agreement shall be decided by the same method agreed to for resolving disputes in the attached Purchase Agreement.

10. **DAMAGE OR DESTRUCTION:** If, prior to exercise of this Option, by no fault of Optionee, the Property is totally or partially damaged or destroyed by fire, earthquake, accident or other casualty, Optionee may cancel this Agreement by giving written notice to Optionor, and is entitled to the return of all Option Consideration paid. However, if, prior to Optionee giving notice of cancellation to Optionor, the Property has been repaired or replaced so that it is in substantially the same condition as of the date of acceptance of this Agreement, Optionee shall not have the right to cancel this Agreement.

11. **OPTIONEE INSPECTION:** Optionee ☐ has, ☐ has not conducted inspections, investigations, tests, surveys and other studies of the Property prior to entering into this Option.

12. **RECORDING:** Optionor or Optionee shall, upon request, execute, acknowledge, and deliver to the other a memorandum of this Option for recording purposes. All resulting fees and taxes shall be paid by the party requesting recordation.

13. **OTHER TERMS AND CONDITIONS,** including attached supplements: _____
    _____
    _____
    _____
    _____
    _____
    _____
    _____
    _____
    _____
    _____
    _____

14. **ATTORNEY FEES:** In any action, proceeding, or arbitration between Optionee and Optionor arising out of this Option, the prevailing Optionee or Optionor shall be entitled to reasonable attorney fees and costs from the non-prevailing Optionee or Optionor.

15. **BROKER COMPENSATION FROM OPTIONEE:** If applicable, Optionee agrees to pay compensation to Broker as specified in a separate written agreement between Optionee and Broker.

16. **TIME OF ESSENCE; ENTIRE CONTRACT; CHANGES:** Time is of the essence. All understandings between the parties are incorporated in this Option. Its terms are intended by the parties as a final, complete, and exclusive expression of their agreement with respect to its subject matter, and may not be contradicted by evidence of any prior agreement or contemporaneous oral agreement. **This Agreement may not be extended, amended, modified, altered, or changed, except in writing signed by Optionee and Optionor.**

17. **TERMS AND CONDITIONS OF OFFER:** This is an offer for an option to purchase Property on the above terms and conditions. This Option and any supplement, addendum, or modification, including any photocopy or facsimile, may be signed in two or more counterparts, all of which shall constitute one and the same writing. Optionee has read and acknowledges receipt of a copy of this offer.

Optionee and Optionor acknowledge receipt of copy of this page, which constitutes Page 2 of _____ Pages.

Optionee's Initials ( _____ ) ( _____ )    Optionor's Initials ( _____ ) ( _____ )

**OA REVISED 4/08 (PAGE 2 OF 3)**

Reviewed by _____ Date _____

**OPTION AGREEMENT (OA PAGE 2 OF 3)**

Untitled

Property Address: _____ Date: _____

**18. EXPIRATION OF OFFER:** Unless Acceptance of Offer is signed by Optionor, and a signed copy delivered in person, by mail, or facsimile, and personally received by Optionee, or by _____, who is authorized to receive it, by (date) _____ , at _____ ☐ AM ☐ PM , the offer shall be deemed revoked.

OPTIONEE _____

OPTIONEE
Address _____

Telephone _____ Fax _____

**19. BROKER COMPENSATION FROM OPTIONOR:** If applicable, Optionor agrees to pay compensation to Broker as specified in a separate written agreement between Optionor and Broker.

**20. ACCEPTANCE OF OPTION:** Optionor warrants that Optionor is the owner of the Property or has the authority to execute this Agreement. Optionor accepts and agrees to grant an Option to purchase the Property on the above terms and conditions.

If checked: ☐ **SUBJECT TO ATTACHED COUNTER OFFER, DATED** _____ .

OPTIONOR _____

OPTIONOR
Address _____

Telephone _____ Fax _____

**REAL ESTATE BROKERS:**
A. Real Estate Brokers are not parties to the Agreement between Optionee and Optionor.
B. **COOPERATING BROKER COMPENSATION:** Listing Broker agrees to pay Cooperating Broker and Cooperating Broker agrees to accept, (i) the amount specified in the MLS, provided Cooperating Broker is a Participant of the MLS in which the Property is offered for Option or a reciprocal MLS; or (ii) ☐ (If checked) the amount specified in a separate written agreement (C.A.R. Form CBC) between Listing Broker and Cooperating Broker.

Broker _____ By _____ Date _____

Address _____

Telephone _____ Fax _____

Broker _____ By _____ Date _____

Address _____

Telephone _____ Fax _____

THIS FORM HAS BEEN APPROVED BY THE CALIFORNIA ASSOCIATION OF REALTORS® (C.A.R.). NO REPRESENTATION IS MADE AS TO THE LEGAL VALIDITY OR ADEQUACY OF ANY PROVISION IN ANY SPECIFIC TRANSACTION. A REAL ESTATE BROKER IS THE PERSON QUALIFIED TO ADVISE ON REAL ESTATE TRANSACTIONS. IF YOU DESIRE LEGAL OR TAX ADVICE, CONSULT AN APPROPRIATE PROFESSIONAL
This form is available for use by the entire real estate industry. It is not intended to identify the user as a REALTOR®. REALTOR® is a registered collective membership mark which may be used only by members of the NATIONAL ASSOCIATION OF REALTORS® who subscribe to its Code of Ethics.

Published and Distributed by:
REAL ESTATE BUSINESS SERVICES, INC.
a subsidiary of the California Association of REALTORS®
525 South Virgil Avenue, Los Angeles, California 90020

Reviewed by _____ Date _____

OA REVISED 4/08 (PAGE 3 OF 3)

**OPTION AGREEMENT (OA PAGE 3 OF 3)**

Untitled

## VIII. CHAPTER SUMMARY

A **contract** is an agreement to perform or not perform a certain act or service. It can be **express** (verbal or written) or **implied** (by actions). A **bilateral contract** obligates two people, whereas a **unilateral contract** only obligates one party. A **valid contract** is binding and enforceable, but a **voidable contract** can be disavowed. A contract can also be **void** (no contract exists) and **unenforceable** if, for example, it's now against the law.

A contract has three phases: **negotiation**, **performance**, and **completion**. If some provision of a contract is not yet fulfilled, it's called an **executory contract**. If it has been discharged or performed, it's considered an **executed contract**.

The **four elements of any contract** are 1) **capacity**, 2) **mutual consent**, 3) **legality**, and 4) **consideration**. (Money, writing, and performance are NOT necessary for a contract to be valid.) Real estate contracts, however, are required to be in **writing**, making that a **fifth element**. Every offer must be made with **contractual intent**, although a buyer can withdraw an offer before acceptance. If the offer is rejected and a new offer is proposed, it's known as a **counter offer**, and automatically terminates the previous offer. The **offeree** becomes the **offeror** in a counter offer. If any of the following conditions exist, a contract is void or voidable: **fraud**, **misrepresentation**, **mistake**, **duress**, **menace**, or **undue influence**.

A contract for personal property can be oral or written but the **Statute of Frauds** requires that real estate contracts be in **writing**. Any contract that can't be performed **within a year** from the date of signing must also be in writing.

A contract can be discharged by **performance** (full, substantial, and partial), **impossibility of performance**, **agreement between parties**, **operation of law**, **acceptance of breach**, or **breach**. The remedies for a breach of contract include **acceptance of breach**, **unilateral rescission**, **action for money damages**, and **specific performance**. (The current **liquidated damages** on a CAR purchase agreement form is a maximum of 3% of the home purchase price.) Remedies for a breach must be sought within a certain period of time called the **Statute of Limitations**.

The **California Residential Purchase Agreement and Joint Escrow Instructions** is a contract, and is also called the **"purchase agreement"** or **"purchase contract."** A deposit of money or items of value (always the property of the seller, not the buyer) must accompany a purchase agreement to be a valid offer. The term "deposit receipt" is an outdated reference to the Purchase Agreement, and no longer appropriate in California real estate transactions.

A **covenant** in a purchase agreement is a promise between the parties to contract. A **contingency** clause is an "if" situation, also referred to as **conditions** or **"subject to"** provisions that, if not met, can make the contract voidable.

An **option** allows a prospective purchaser to hold the exclusive right to buy during a specified period, in exchange for money. It cannot be revoked by the **optionor** (seller) who could be forced to sell the property by specific performance to the **optionee** (buyer). To avoid a conflict of interest, an agent with a listing and an option to purchase must disclose all offers, any material information, and obtain consent of any anticipated profits from the seller before exercising the option.

## IX. TERMINOLOGY

A. Acceptance
B. Assignee
C. Assignment
D. Assignor
E. Bilateral Contract
F. Breach
G. Capacity of Parties
H. Consideration
I. Contingencies
J. Contract
K. Counter Offer
L. Covenant
M. Definite and Certain

N. Dollar Damages
O. Execute
P. Executory Contract
Q. Expressed Contract
R. Fraud, Duress, Menace
S. Implied Contract
T. Incompetent
U. Liquidated Damages
V. Minors
W. Mutual Consent
X. Novation
Y. Offer
Z. Offeree

AA. Offeror
BB. Option
CC. Optionee
DD. Optionor
EE. Pest Control Report
FF. Purchase Agreement
GG. Rescission
HH. Specific Performance
II. Undue Influence
JJ. Unilateral Contract
KK. Valid Contract
LL. Void, Voidable, Unenforceable

1.____ A court action to compel the performance of an agreement, e.g., sale of land.
2.____ Anything given or promised by a party to induce another to enter into a contract.
3.____ A contract in which something remains to be done by one or both the parties.
4.____ A right given, for consideration, to purchase a property upon specified terms within a specified time period, without obligating the party to purchase the property.
5.____ A written offer to purchase real property upon stated terms and conditions, accompanied by a deposit toward the purchase price, which becomes the contract for the sale of the property upon acceptance.
6.____ All persons under 18 years of age.
7.____ The act of agreeing or consenting to the terms of an offer, thereby establishing "the meeting of the minds" that is an essential element of a contract; genuine assent from both parties.
8.____ One who assigns his or her right in a contract.
9.____ A person to whom property or interests therein shall have been assigned.
10.____ One who is mentally incapable of managing or taking care of self or property and therefore cannot enter into a contract without a guardian.
11.____ A promise to do or not to do a particular act.
12.____ The substitution or exchange of a new contract for an old one by the mutual agreement of the parties.
13.____ A transfer by a person of that person's rights under a contract.
14.____ An agreement to do or not to do a certain thing. It must have four essential elements: parties capable of contracting, consent of the parties, a lawful object, and consideration.
15.____ The terms and provisions of a contract, which are clear, definite, and set forth.
16.____ A binding contract created by the actions of the principals rather than by written or oral agreement.
17.____ A contract under which the parties enter into mutual promises, such as sales contracts.
18.____ A contract under which only one party expressly makes a promise.
19.____ Having no legal force or binding effect, or cannot be enforced for one reason or another.
20.____ One making an offer.
21.____ One to whom an offer is made.
22.____ A proposal for acceptance, in order to form a contract. It must be definite as to price and terms.
23.____ Voluntarily agreeing to the price and terms of an offer. Offer and acceptance create a contract.
24.____ An offer in response to an offer.
25.____ Failure to perform a contract, in whole or part, without legal excuse.
26.____ Annulling a contract and placing the parties to it in a position as if there had not been a contract.

# CHAPTER 5

27.____ A definite amount of damage, set forth in a contract, to be paid by the party breaching the contract. A predetermined estimate of actual damages from a breach.

28.____ An inspection report required, in the sale of property, to determine if termites are present within a building.

29.____ One who, for consideration, receives an option.

30.____ One who, for consideration, gives an option.

31.____ A contract under which the parties expressly enter into mutual promises.

32.____ The dependence upon a stated event before a contract becomes binding.

33.____ An action that abandons all other remedies and simply asks for money.

34.____ Influence used to destroy the will of another so that any decision is not his or her free act.

35.____ To complete a contract by signing it.

36.____ Legally binding, the terms of which can be sued for in a court of law.

37.____ Deceptive statements or acts used to wrongfully obtain money or property.

38.____ Individuals who have a legal capacity to contract, as opposed to minors, convicts and incompetents.

## X. CHAPTER QUIZ

1. The term "express contract" describes a contract which is expressed:

    a. only orally.

    b. only in writing.

    c. in words, either oral or written.

    d. none of the above.

2. If a buyer and seller enter into a valid binding contract and one of the parties dies or becomes incompetent, the contract is:

    a. void by statute.

    b. valid, if it was signed before the party died or became incompetent.

    c. voidable by one of the parties.

    d. none of the above.

3. A contract based on an unlawful consideration is:

    a. valid, until voided.

    b. void.

    c. legal.

    d. enforceable, if in writing.

4. Novation is:

    a. realization of an unexpected profit.

    b. creation of an existing agreement.

    c. substitution of a new contract for an old one.

    d. modification of a contract.

5. The following could be used by a buyer as earnest money deposit in purchasing real property:

    a. a promissory note secured by a deed of trust.

    b. a postdated check.

    c. an unsecured promissory note.

    d. all of the above.

6. An offer made by a prospective buyer was contingent on the sale of the buyer's current residence. Seller Billings made a counter offer accepting the offer provided the seller could continue to market the home in an attempt to obtain a better offer while granting the buyer a "first right of refusal" to remove the sale contingency if another offer was presented. The buyer accepted the terms and immediately listed his current residence for sale. One week later, Billings notified the buyer that a better offer with no contingencies was "on the table." The agent representing the buyer should:

    a. advise the buyer to immediately remove the sale contingency.

    b. advise the buyer to obtain a bridge loan in order to assure that the escrow will be completed without the need of the contingency.

    c. advise the buyer about the advantages and disadvantages of removing the contingency feature at this time.

    d. under no circumstances give advice about the contingency feature. The buyer must consult an attorney.

7. When accepting an offer on his home, Seller Thomas changed one of the terms of the buyer's offer. This is best described as:

    a. a modification or amendment.

    b. a purchase contract.

    c. an alteration.

    d. a counter offer.

8. The primary responsibility for disclosing any Mello-Roos bonds or assessments to a buyer when a home is sold lies with:

    a. the seller.

    b. the seller's agent.

    c. the buyer's agent.

    d. all of the above.

9. What state agency would a consumer contact in order to obtain a written report disclosing the presence of wood destroying organisms?

    a. Department of Real Estate

    b. Department of Corporations

    c. Structural Pest Control Board

    d. Department of Housing and Community Development

10. In an option agreement, the owner of the option is the:

    a. optionor.

    b. optionee.

    c. property owner.

    d. lender.

ANSWERS: 1. c; 2. b; 3. b; 4. c; 5. d; 6. c; 7. d; 8. a; 9. c; 10. b

# CHAPTER 6
## Landlord and Tenant
## (Lessor and Lessee)

## I. Landlord and Tenant – An Overview

A landlord and tenant relationship is created when the owner gives the possession and use of his or her property to another for rent or other consideration. The *LANDLORD (LESSOR) is the owner of the property being rented or leased.* The landlord, or his or her agent, may lease only the land, the land and buildings, or only the buildings or parts of the buildings. The *TENANT (LESSEE) is the person or persons renting or leasing the property.*

A *LEASE is a contract for a set time, typically one year or longer. A RENTAL AGREEMENT is different in that it is usually made on a monthly basis and is renewable at the end of each period (week-to-week, month-to-month, or any period-to-period up to one year).* Because a rental agreement is a type of lease, the principles are the same as those of the lease, except for the time periods involved.

## II. Leasehold Estates (Less-Than-Freehold)

### A. TYPES OF LEASEHOLD ESTATES (Tenancies)

*A leasehold is a personal property right in real property.*

As discussed before, with less-than-freehold estates, there is no direct ownership of real estate. They are chattel real estates. A *CHATTEL REAL is a personal property estate, such as a lease.* We call this type of interest in a property a lease or leasehold. A *LEASEHOLD is an exclusive right to occupy and use the property on a temporary basis.* There are no ownership rights in real property. The owner has *REVERSIONARY INTEREST, which means that he or she can regain possession at the end of the leasehold period.* **Figure 6-1** shows the four types of leasehold estates.

### 1. Estate For Years (A Lease for a Predetermined Amount of Time)

*A conveyance of an estate in real property, such as a lease, to someone for a certain length of time is called a DEMISE. An ESTATE FOR YEARS is an agreement, in advance, between a lessee and a lessor for use of a property for a fixed (predetermined) period of time.* As stated earlier, a lease is a contractual agreement to possess and use a property for an agreed to (predetermined) period of time. If the lease period is longer than one year from the date of the signing, it must be in writing and signed by the lessor. The *LESSOR is the owner, sometimes referred to as the landlord, and the LESSEE is the tenant.*

# CHAPTER 6

**Figure 6-1**

# Types of Leasehold Estates

| ESTATE FOR YEARS | ESTATE FROM PERIOD-TO-PERIOD | ESTATE AT WILL | ESTATE AT SUFFERANCE |

### 2. Estate From Period-To-Period (Periodic Tenancy – Renewable Each Period)

An *ESTATE FROM PERIOD-TO-PERIOD is periodic tenancy that continues from year-to-year, month-to-month, week-to-week, or from any other designated period-to-period.* This period-to-period tenancy, which is automatically renewable, is called a rental agreement. As previously stated, a rental agreement is an agreement between a tenant and landlord for continuing periods of time, usually from month-to-month. Rental agreements do not expire; notice must be given by one of the parties.

Written rental agreements have become the most commonly used real estate agreements in the United States. They are used frequently when renting apartments, duplexes, houses, condominiums, and other types of residential property. The California Association of REALTORS® (CAR) has a Residential Lease or Month-To-Month Rental Agreement form that covers all the basic conditions desired in such a contract (see **Figure 6-2**). **Figure 6-3** is an Application To Rent, Receipt For Deposit/Screening Fee form to be filled out by the prospective tenant.

A landlord holds a reversionary right to the property. A *REVERSIONARY RIGHT means the landlord grants the tenant the right to occupy (possess) the property, but retains the right to retake possession after the lease or rental term has expired.* Periodic tenancy is usually terminated when the appropriate party gives a 30- or 60-day notice, because most rental agreements are month-to-month. If the rental period is less than one month, then only one period (that is, agreed length of the tenancy) notice is required. For example, if tenancy was from week-to-week, only seven days notice would be necessary.

### 3. Estate At Will (Tenancy at Will – Uncommon)

An *ESTATE AT WILL can be terminated at the will of either the lessor or the lessee, and has no fixed duration period.* By California statute, 1) the parties involved must give a notice of termination and 2) since a periodic tenancy is automatically created when a landlord accepts rent, there is no true estate at will in California.

*An estate at will can be terminated by either the lessor or lessee.*

### 4. Estate At Sufferance (Tenancy at Sufferance)

An *ESTATE AT SUFFERANCE occurs when a lessee, who has rightfully come into possession of the land, retains possession after the expiration of his or her term.* (In other words, the tenant does not leave after expiration of the lease.) An estate at sufferance does not require a notice of termination because the expiration of the lease is an automatic termination. If the landlord accepts any payment of rent, the lease reverts to periodic tenancy.

## Figure 6-2

CALIFORNIA
ASSOCIATION
OF REALTORS®

### RESIDENTIAL LEASE OR
### MONTH-TO-MONTH RENTAL AGREEMENT
(C.A.R. Form LR, Revised 11/08)

Date_____ . _____ ("Landlord") and
_____ ("Tenant") agree as follows:

1. **PROPERTY:**
   A. Landlord rents to Tenant and Tenant rents from Landlord, the real property and improvements described as: _123 Sail Avenue_ ,
   _____ ("Premises").
   B. The Premises are for the sole use as a personal residence by the following named person(s) **only**: _____
   _____
   C. The following personal property, maintained pursuant to paragraph 11, is included: _____
   _____ or ☐ (if checked) the personal property on the attached addendum.

2. **TERM:** The term begins on (date) _____ ("Commencement Date"), **(Check A or B):**
   ☐ A. **Month-to-Month:** and continues as a month-to-month tenancy. Tenant may terminate the tenancy by giving written notice at least 30 days prior to the intended termination date. Landlord may terminate the tenancy by giving written notice as provided by law. Such notices may be given on any date.
   ☐ B. **Lease:** and shall terminate on (date) _____ at _____ ☐ AM/ ☐ PM. Tenant shall vacate the Premises upon termination of the Agreement, unless: **(i)** Landlord and Tenant have extended this agreement in writing or signed a new agreement; **(ii)** mandated by local rent control law; or **(iii)** Landlord accepts Rent from Tenant (other than past due Rent), in which case a month-to-month tenancy shall be created which either party may terminate as specified in paragraph 2A. Rent shall be at a rate agreed to by Landlord and Tenant, or as allowed by law. All other terms and conditions of this Agreement shall remain in full force and effect.

3. **RENT:** "Rent" shall mean all monetary obligations of Tenant to Landlord under the terms of the Agreement, except security deposit.
   A. Tenant agrees to pay $ _____ per month for the term of the Agreement.
   B. Rent is payable in advance on the 1st (or ☐ _____ ) **day** of each calendar month, and is delinquent on the next day.
   C. If Commencement Date falls on any day other than the day Rent is payable under paragraph 3B, and Tenant has paid one full month's Rent in advance of Commencement Date, Rent for the second calendar month shall be prorated based on a 30-day period.
   D. PAYMENT: Rent shall be paid by ☐ personal check, ☐ money order, ☐ cashier's check, or ☐ other _____ , to
   (name) _____ (phone) _____ at
   (address) _____ (or
   at any other location subsequently specified by Landlord in writing to Tenant) (and ☐ if checked, rent may be paid personally **between** the hours
   of _____ and _____ on the following days _____ ). **If** any payments is returned for non-sufficient funds ("NSF") or because tenant stops payment, then, after that: (i) Landlord may, in writing, require Tenant to pay Rent in cash for three months and (ii) all future Rent shall be paid by ☐ money order, or ☐ cashier's check.

4. **SECURITY DEPOSIT:**
   A. Tenant agrees to pay $ _____ as a security deposit. Security deposit will be ☐ transferred to and held by the Owner of the Premises, or ☐ held in Owner's Broker's trust account.
   B. All or any portion of the security deposit may be used, as reasonably necessary, to: **(i)** cure Tenant's default in payment of Rent (which includes Late Charges, NSF fees or other sums due); **(ii)** repair damage, excluding ordinary wear and tear, caused by Tenant or by a guest or licensee of Tenant; **(iii)** clean Premises, if necessary, upon termination of the tenancy; and **(iv)** replace or return personal property or appurtenances. **SECURITY DEPOSIT SHALL NOT BE USED BY TENANT IN LIEU OF PAYMENT OF LAST MONTH'S RENT.** If all or any portion of the security deposit is used during the tenancy, Tenant agrees to reinstate the total security deposit within five days after written notice is delivered to Tenant. Within 21 days after Tenant vacates the Premises, Landlord shall: **(1)** furnish Tenant an itemized statement indicating the amount of any security deposit received and the basis for its disposition and supporting documentation as required by California Civil Code § 1950.5(g); and **(2)** return any remaining portion of the security deposit to Tenant.
   C. **Security deposit will not be returned until all Tenants have vacated the Premises and all keys returned. Any security deposit returned by check shall be made out to all Tenants named on this Agreement, or as subsequently modified.**
   D. No interest will be paid on security deposit unless required by local law.
   E. If the security deposit is held by Owner, Tenant agrees not to hold Broker responsible for its return. If the security deposit is held in Owner's Broker's trust account, **and** Broker's authority is terminated before expiration of this Agreement, **and** security deposit is released to someone other than Tenant, **then** Broker shall notify Tenant, in writing, where and to whom security deposit has been released. Once Tenant has been provided such notice, Tenant agrees not to hold Broker responsible for the security deposit.

5. **MOVE-IN COSTS RECEIVED/DUE:** Move-in funds made payable to _____
   shall be paid by ☐ personal check, ☐ money order, or ☐ cashier's check.

| Category | Total Due | Payment Received | Balance Due | Date Due |
|---|---|---|---|---|
| Rent from _____ to _____ (date) | | | | |
| *Security Deposit | | | | |
| Other _____ | | | | |
| Other _____ | | | | |
| Total | | | | |

*The maximum amount Landlord may receive as security deposit, however designated, cannot exceed two months' Rent for unfurnished premises, or three months' Rent for furnished premises.

Tenant's Initials ( _____ ) ( _____ )
Landlord's Initials ( _____ ) ( _____ )

Reviewed by _____ Date _____

EQUAL HOUSING
OPPORTUNITY

**LR REVISED 11/08 (PAGE 1 OF 6)**

### RESIDENTIAL LEASE OR MONTH-TO-MONTH RENTAL AGREEMENT (LR PAGE 1 OF 6)

| Agent: WALT HUBER | Phone: | Fax: | Prepared using zipForm® software |
|---|---|---|---|
| Broker: WALT HUBER REALTOR | | | |

Premises: 123 Sail Avenue _____ Date: _____

**6. LATE CHARGE; RETURNED CHECKS:**
A. Tenant acknowledges either late payment of Rent or issuance of a returned check may cause Landlord to incur costs and expenses, the exact amounts of which are extremely difficult and impractical to determine. These costs may include, but are not limited to, processing, enforcement and accounting expenses, and late charges imposed on Landlord. If any installment of Rent due from Tenant is not received by Landlord within 5 (or [ ] _____ ) calendar days after the date due, or if a check is returned, Tenant shall pay to Landlord, respectively, an additional sum of $ _____ or _____ % of the Rent due as a Late Charge and $25.00 as a NSF fee for the first returned check and $35.00 as a NSF fee for each additional returned check, either or both of which shall be deemed additional Rent.
B. Landlord and Tenant agree that these charges represent a fair and reasonable estimate of the costs Landlord may incur by reason of Tenant's late or NSF payment. Any Late Charge or NSF fee due shall be paid with the current installment of Rent. Landlord's acceptance of any Late Charge or NSF fee shall not constitute a waiver as to any default of Tenant. Landlord's right to collect a Late Charge or NSF fee shall not be deemed an extension of the date Rent is due under paragraph 3 or prevent Landlord from exercising any other rights and remedies under this Agreement and as provided by law.

**7. PARKING: (Check A or B)**
[ ] A. Parking is permitted as follows: _____
The right to parking [ ] is [ ] is not included in the Rent charged pursuant to paragraph 3. If not included in the Rent, the parking rental fee shall be an additional $ _____ per month. Parking space(s) are to be used for parking properly licensed and operable motor vehicles, except for trailers, boats, campers, buses or trucks (other than pick-up trucks). Tenant shall park in assigned space(s) only. Parking space(s) are to be kept clean. Vehicles leaking oil, gas or other motor vehicle fluids shall not be parked on the Premises. Mechanical work or storage of inoperable vehicles is not permitted in parking space(s) or elsewhere on the Premises.
OR [ ] B. Parking is not permitted on the Premises.

**8. STORAGE: (Check A or B)**
[ ] A. Storage is permitted as follows: _____
The right to storage space [ ] is [ ] is not, included in the Rent charged pursuant to paragraph 3. If not included in the Rent, storage space fee shall be an additional $ _____ per month. Tenant shall store only personal property Tenant owns, and shall not store property claimed by another or in which another has any right, title or interest. Tenant shall not store any improperly packaged food or perishable goods, flammable materials, explosives, hazardous waste or other inherently dangerous material, or illegal substances.
OR [ ] B. Storage is not permitted on the Premises.

**9. UTILITIES:** Tenant agrees to pay for all utilities and services, and the following charges: _____, except _____ which shall be paid for by Landlord. If any utilities are not separately metered, Tenant shall pay Tenant's proportional share, as reasonably determined and directed by Landlord. If utilities are separately metered, Tenant shall place utilities in Tenant's name as of the Commencement Date. Landlord is only responsible for installing and maintaining one usable telephone jack and one telephone line to the Premises. Tenant shall pay any cost for conversion from existing utilities service provider.

**10. CONDITION OF PREMISES:** Tenant has examined Premises and, if any, all furniture, furnishings, appliances, landscaping and fixtures, including smoke detector(s).
(Check all that apply:)
[ ] A. Tenant acknowledges these items are clean and in operable condition, with the following exceptions: _____
[ ] B. Tenant's acknowledgment of the condition of these items is contained in an attached statement of condition (C.A.R. Form MIMO).
[ ] C. Tenant will provide Landlord a list of items that are damaged or not in operable condition within 3 (or [ ] _____ ) days after Commencement Date, not as a contingency of this Agreement but rather as an acknowledgment of the condition of the Premises.
[ ] D. Other: _____

**11. MAINTENANCE:**
A. Tenant shall properly use, operate and safeguard Premises, including if applicable, any landscaping, furniture, furnishings and appliances, and all mechanical, electrical, gas and plumbing fixtures, and keep them and the Premises clean, sanitary and well ventilated. Tenant shall be responsible for checking and maintaining all smoke detectors and any additional phone lines beyond the one line and jack that Landlord shall provide and maintain. Tenant shall immediately notify Landlord, in writing, of any problem, malfunction or damage. Tenant shall be charged for all repairs or replacements caused by Tenant, pets, guests or licensees of Tenant, excluding ordinary wear and tear. Tenant shall be charged for all damage to Premises as a result of failure to report a problem in a timely manner. Tenant shall be charged for repair of drain blockages or stoppages, unless caused by defective plumbing parts or tree roots invading sewer lines.
B. [ ] Landlord [ ] Tenant shall water the garden, landscaping, trees and shrubs, except: _____
C. [ ] Landlord [ ] Tenant shall maintain the garden, landscaping, trees and shrubs, except: _____
D. [ ] Landlord [ ] Tenant shall maintain _____
E. Tenant's failure to maintain any item for which Tenant is responsible shall give Landlord the right to hire someone to perform such maintenance and charge Tenant to cover the cost of such maintenance.
F. The following items of personal property are included in the Premises without warranty and Landlord will not maintain, repair or replace them: _____

Tenant's Initials ( _____ ) ( _____ )
Landlord's Initials ( _____ ) ( _____ )

**RESIDENTIAL LEASE OR MONTH-TO-MONTH RENTAL AGREEMENT (LR PAGE 2 OF 6)**

---

Premises: 123 Sail Avenue _____ Date: _____

**12. NEIGHBORHOOD CONDITIONS:** Tenant is advised to satisfy him or herself as to neighborhood or area conditions, including schools, proximity and adequacy of law enforcement, crime statistics, proximity of registered felons or offenders, fire protection, other governmental services, availability, adequacy and cost of any wired, wireless internet connections or other telecommunications or other technology services and installations, proximity to commercial, industrial or agricultural activities, existing and proposed transportation, construction and development that may affect noise, view, or traffic, airport noise, noise or odor from any source, wild and domestic animals, other nuisances, hazards, or circumstances, cemeteries, facilities and condition of common areas, conditions and influences of significance to certain cultures and/or religions, and personal needs, requirements and preferences of Tenant.

**13. PETS:** Unless otherwise provided in California Civil Code § 54.2, no animal or pet shall be kept on or about the Premises without Landlord's prior written consent, except: _____

**14.** [ ] (if checked) **NO SMOKING:** No smoking is allowed on the Premises. If smoking does occur on the Premises, (i) Tenant is responsible for all damage caused by the smoking including, but not limited to, stains, burns, odors and removal of debris, (ii) Tenant is in breach of this Agreement, (iii) Tenant, Authorized Guests, and all others may be required to leave the Premises; and (iv) Tenant acknowledges that in order to remove odor caused by smoking, Landlord may need to replace carpet and drapes and paint entire Premises regardless of when these items were last cleaned or replaced. Such actions and other necessary steps will impact the return of any security deposit.

**15. RULES/REGULATIONS:**
A. Tenant agrees to comply with all Landlord rules and regulations that are at any time posted on the Premises or delivered to Tenant. Tenant shall not, and shall ensure that guests and licensees of Tenant shall not, disturb, annoy, endanger or interfere with other tenants of the building or neighbors, or use the Premises for any unlawful purposes, including, but not limited to, using, manufacturing, selling, storing or transporting illicit drugs or other contraband, or violate any law or ordinance, or commit a waste or nuisance on or about the Premises.
B. (If applicable, check one)
[ ] 1. Landlord shall provide Tenant with a copy of the rules and regulations within _____ days or _____
OR [ ] 2. Tenant has been provided with, and acknowledges receipt of, a copy of the rules and regulations.

**16.** [ ] (if checked) **CONDOMINIUM; PLANNED UNIT DEVELOPMENT:**
A. The Premises is a unit in a condominium, planned unit development, common interest subdivision or other development governed by a homeowners' association ('HOA'). The name of the HOA is _____ Tenant agrees to comply with all HOA covenants, conditions and restrictions, bylaws, rules and regulations and decisions. Landlord shall provide Tenant copies of rules and regulations, if any. Tenant shall reimburse Landlord for any fines or charges imposed by HOA or other authorities, due to any violation by Tenant, or the guests or licensees of Tenant.
B. (Check one)
[ ] 1. Landlord shall provide Tenant with a copy of the HOA rules and regulations within _____ days or _____
OR [ ] 2. Tenant has been provided with, and acknowledges receipt of, a copy of the HOA rules and regulations.

**17. ALTERATIONS; REPAIRS:** Unless otherwise specified by law or paragraph 29C, without Landlord's prior written consent, (i) Tenant shall not make any repairs, alterations or improvements in or about the Premises including: painting, wallpapering, adding or changing locks, installing antenna or satellite dish(es), placing signs, displays or exhibits, or using screws, fastening devices, large nails or adhesive materials, (ii) Landlord shall not be responsible for the costs of alterations or repairs made by Tenant; (iii) Tenant shall not deduct from Rent the costs of any repairs, alterations or improvements; and (iv) any deduction made by Tenant shall be considered unpaid Rent.

**18. KEYS; LOCKS:**
A. Tenant acknowledges receipt of (or Tenant will receive [ ] prior to the Commencement Date, or [ ] _____ ):
[ ] _____ key(s) to Premises, [ ] _____ remote control device(s) for garage door/gate opener(s),
[ ] _____ key(s) to mailbox, [ ] _____
[ ] _____ key(s) to common area(s), [ ] _____
B. Tenant acknowledges that locks to the Premises [ ] have, [ ] have not, been re-keyed.
C. If Tenant re-keys existing locks or opening devices, Tenant shall immediately deliver copies of all keys to Landlord. Tenant shall pay all costs and charges related to loss of any keys or opening devices. Tenant may not remove locks, even if installed by Tenant.

**19. ENTRY:**
A. Tenant shall make Premises available to Landlord or Landlord's representative for the purpose of entering to make necessary or agreed repairs, decorations, alterations, or improvements, or to supply necessary or agreed services, or to show Premises to prospective or actual purchasers, tenants, mortgagees, lenders, appraisers, or contractors.
B. Landlord and Tenant agree that 24-hour written notice shall be reasonable and sufficient notice, except as follows: 48-hour written notice is required to conduct an inspection of the Premises prior to the Tenant moving out, unless the Tenant waives the right to such notice. Notice may be given orally to show the Premises to actual or prospective purchasers provided Tenant has been notified in writing within 120 days preceding the oral notice that the Premises are for sale and that oral notice may be given to show the Premises. No notice is required: (i) to enter in case of an emergency; (ii) if the Tenant is present and consents at the time of entry or (iii) if the Tenant has abandoned or surrendered the Premises. No written notice is required if Landlord and Tenant orally agree to an entry for agreed services or repairs if the date and time of entry are within one week of the oral agreement.
C. [ ] (if checked) Tenant authorizes the use of a keysafe/lockbox to allow entry into the Premises and agrees to sign a keysafe/lockbox addendum (C.A.R. Form KLA).

**20. SIGNS:** Tenant authorizes Landlord to place FOR SALE/LEASE signs on the Premises.

**21. ASSIGNMENT; SUBLETTING:** Tenant shall not sublet all or any part of Premises, or assign or transfer this Agreement or any interest in it, without Landlord's prior written consent. Unless such consent is obtained, any assignment, transfer or subletting of Premises or this Agreement or tenancy, by voluntary act of Tenant, operation of law or otherwise, shall, at the option of Landlord,

Tenant's Initials ( _____ ) ( _____ )
Landlord's Initials ( _____ ) ( _____ )

**RESIDENTIAL LEASE OR MONTH-TO-MONTH RENTAL AGREEMENT (LR PAGE 3 OF 6)**

*123 Sail Avenue*

Premises: _____  Date: _____

terminate this Agreement. Any proposed assignee, transferee or sublessee shall submit to Landlord an application and credit information for Landlord's approval, and, if approved, sign a separate written agreement with Landlord and Tenant. Landlord's consent to any one assignment, transfer or sublease, shall not be construed as consent to any subsequent assignment, transfer or sublease and does not release Tenant of Tenant's obligations under this Agreement.

22. **JOINT AND INDIVIDUAL OBLIGATIONS:** If there is more than one Tenant, each one shall be individually and completely responsible for the performance of all obligations of Tenant under this Agreement, jointly with every other Tenant, and individually, whether or not in possession.

23. ☐ **LEAD-BASED PAINT (If checked):** Premises was constructed prior to 1978. In accordance with federal law, Landlord gives and Tenant acknowledges receipt of the disclosures on the attached form (C.A.R. Form FLD) and a federally approved lead pamphlet.

24. ☐ **MILITARY ORDNANCE DISCLOSURE:** (If applicable and known to Landlord) Premises is located within one mile of an area once used for military training, and may contain potentially explosive munitions.

25. ☐ **PERIODIC PEST CONTROL:** Landlord has entered into a contract for periodic pest control treatment of the Premises and shall give Tenant a copy of the notice originally given to Landlord by the pest control company.

26. ☐ **METHAMPHETAMINE CONTAMINATION:** Prior to signing this Agreement, Landlord has given Tenant a notice that a health official has issued an order prohibiting occupancy of the property because of methamphetamine contamination. A copy of the notice and order are attached.

27. **MEGAN'S LAW DATABASE DISCLOSURE:** Notice: Pursuant to Section 290.46 of the Penal Code, information about specified registered sex offenders is made available to the public via an Internet Web site maintained by the Department of Justice at www.meganslaw.ca.gov. Depending on an offender's criminal history, this information will include either the address at which the offender resides or the community of residence and ZIP Code in which he or she resides. (Neither Landlord nor Brokers, if any, are required to check this website. If Tenant wants further information, Tenant should obtain information directly from this website.)

28. **POSSESSION:**
    A. Tenant is not in possession of the premises. If Landlord is unable to deliver possession of Premises on Commencement Date, such Date shall be extended to the date on which possession is made available to Tenant. If Landlord is unable to deliver possession within 5 (or ☐ ____) calendar days after agreed Commencement Date, Tenant may terminate this Agreement by giving written notice to Landlord, and shall be refunded all Rent and security deposit paid. Possession is deemed terminated when Tenant has returned all keys to the Premises to Landlord.
    B. ☐ Tenant is already in possession of the Premises.

29. **TENANT'S OBLIGATIONS UPON VACATING PREMISES:**
    A. Upon termination of this Agreement, Tenant shall: (i) give Landlord all copies of all keys or opening devices to Premises, including any common areas; (ii) vacate and surrender Premises to Landlord, empty of all persons; (iii) vacate any/all parking and/or storage space; (iv) clean and deliver Premises, as specified in paragraph C below, to Landlord in the same condition as referenced in paragraph 10; (v) remove all debris; (vi) give written notice to Landlord of Tenant's forwarding address; and (vii)

    B. All alterations/improvements made by or caused to be made by Tenant, with or without Landlord's consent, become the property of Landlord upon termination. Landlord may charge Tenant for restoration of the Premises to the condition it was in prior to any alterations/improvements.

    C. **Right to Pre-Move-Out Inspection and Repairs:** (i) After giving or receiving notice of termination of a tenancy (C.A.R. Form NTT), or before the end of a lease, Tenant has the right to request that an inspection of the Premises take place prior to termination of the lease or rental (C.A.R. Form NRI). If Tenant requests such an inspection, Tenant shall be given an opportunity to remedy identified deficiencies prior to termination, consistent with the terms of this Agreement. (ii) Any repairs or alterations made to the Premises as a result of this inspection (collectively, "Repairs") shall be made at Tenant's expense. Repairs may be performed by Tenant or through others, who have adequate insurance and licenses and are approved by Landlord. The work shall comply with applicable law, including governmental permit, inspection and approval requirements. Repairs shall be performed in a good, skillful manner with materials of quality and appearance comparable to existing materials. It is understood that exact restoration of appearance or cosmetic items following all Repairs may not be possible. (iii) Tenant shall: (a) obtain receipts for Repairs performed by others; (b) prepare a written statement indicating the Repairs performed by Tenant and the date of such Repairs; and (c) provide copies of receipts and statements to Landlord prior to termination. Paragraph 29C does not apply when the tenancy is terminated pursuant to California Code of Civil Procedure § 1161(2), (3) or (4).

30. **BREACH OF CONTRACT; EARLY TERMINATION:** In addition to any obligations established by paragraph 29, in the event of termination by Tenant prior to completion of the original term of the Agreement, Tenant shall also be responsible for lost Rent, rental commissions, advertising expenses and painting costs necessary to ready Premises for re-rental. Landlord may withhold any such amounts from Tenant's security deposit.

31. **TEMPORARY RELOCATION:** Subject to local law, Tenant agrees, upon demand of Landlord, to temporarily vacate Premises for a reasonable period, to allow for fumigation (or other methods) to control wood destroying pests or organisms, or other repairs to Premises. Tenant agrees to comply with all instructions and requirements necessary to prepare Premises to accommodate pest control, fumigation or other work, including bagging or storage of food and medicine, and removal of perishables and valuables. Tenant shall only be entitled to a credit of Rent equal to the per diem Rent for the period of time Tenant is required to vacate Premises.

32. **DAMAGE TO PREMISES:** If, by no fault of Tenant, Premises are totally or partially damaged or destroyed by fire, earthquake, accident or other casualty that render Premises totally or partially uninhabitable, either Landlord or Tenant may terminate this Agreement by giving the other written notice. Rent shall be abated as of the date Premises become totally or partially uninhabitable. The abated amount shall be the current monthly Rent prorated on a 30-day period. If the Agreement is not terminated, Landlord shall promptly repair the damage, and Rent shall be reduced based on the extent to which the damage interferes with Tenant's reasonable use of Premises. If damage occurs as a result of an act of Tenant or Tenant's guests, only Landlord shall have the right of termination, and no reduction in Rent shall be made.

33. **INSURANCE:** Tenant's or guest's personal property and vehicles are not insured by Landlord, manager or, if applicable, HOA, against loss or damage due to fire, theft, vandalism, rain, water, criminal or negligent acts of others, or any other cause. **Tenant is**

Tenant's Initials ( _____ )( _____ )
Landlord's Initials ( _____ )( _____ )

Reviewed by _____ Date _____

**RESIDENTIAL LEASE OR MONTH-TO-MONTH RENTAL AGREEMENT (LR PAGE 4 OF 6)**

---

*123 Sail Avenue*

Premises: _____  Date: _____

advised to carry Tenant's own insurance (renter's insurance) to protect Tenant from any such loss or damage. Tenant may comply with any requirement imposed on Tenant by Landlord's insurer to avoid: (i) an increase in Landlord's insurance premium (or Tenant shall pay for the increase in premium); or (ii) loss of insurance.

34. **WATERBEDS:** Tenant shall not use or have waterbeds on the Premises unless: (i) Tenant obtains a valid waterbed insurance policy; (ii) Tenant increases the security deposit in an amount equal to one-half of one month's Rent; and (iii) the bed conforms to the floor load capacity of Premises.

35. **WAIVER:** The waiver of any breach shall not be construed as a continuing waiver of the same or any subsequent breach.

36. **NOTICE:** Notices may be served at the following address, or at any other location subsequently designated:
    Landlord: _____  Tenant: _____

37. **TENANT ESTOPPEL CERTIFICATE:** Tenant shall execute and return a tenant estoppel certificate delivered to Tenant by Landlord or Landlord's agent within 3 days after its receipt. Failure to comply with this requirement shall be deemed Tenant's acknowledgment that the tenant estoppel certificate is true and correct, and may be relied upon by a lender or purchaser.

38. **TENANT REPRESENTATIONS; CREDIT:** Tenant warrants that all statements in Tenant's rental application are accurate. Tenant authorizes Landlord and Broker(s) to obtain Tenant's credit report periodically during the tenancy in connection with the modification or enforcement of this Agreement. Landlord may cancel this Agreement: (i) before occupancy begins; (ii) upon disapproval of the credit report(s); or (iii) at any time, upon discovering that information in Tenant's application is false. A negative credit report reflecting on Tenant's record may be submitted to a credit reporting agency if Tenant fails to fulfill the terms of payment and other obligations under this Agreement.

39. **MEDIATION:**
    A. Consistent with paragraphs B and C below, Landlord and Tenant agree to mediate any dispute or claim arising between them out of this Agreement, or any resulting transaction, before resorting to court action. Mediation fees, if any, shall be divided equally among the parties involved. If, for any dispute or claim to which this paragraph applies, any party commences an action without first attempting to resolve the matter through mediation, or refuses to mediate after a request has been made, then that party shall not be entitled to recover attorney fees, even if they would otherwise be available to that party in any such action.
    B. The following matters are excluded from mediation: (i) an unlawful detainer action; (ii) the filing or enforcement of a mechanic's lien; and (iii) any matter within the jurisdiction of a probate, small claims or bankruptcy court. The filing of a court action to enable the recording of a notice of pending action, for order of attachment, receivership, injunction, or other provisional remedies, shall not constitute a waiver of the mediation provision.
    C. Landlord and Tenant agree to mediate disputes or claims involving Listing Agent, Leasing Agent or property manager ("Broker"), provided Broker shall have agreed to such mediation prior to or within a reasonable time after, the dispute or claim is presented to such Broker. Any election by Broker to participate in mediation shall not result in Broker being deemed a party to this Agreement.

40. **ATTORNEY FEES:** In any action or proceeding arising out of this Agreement, the prevailing party between Landlord and Tenant shall be entitled to reasonable attorney fees and costs, except as provided in paragraph 39A.

41. **C.A.R. FORM:** C.A.R. Form means the specific form referenced or another comparable form agreed to by the parties.

42. **OTHER TERMS AND CONDITIONS; SUPPLEMENTS:** ☐ Interpreter/Translator Agreement (C.A.R. Form ITA); ☐ Keysafe/Lockbox Addendum (C.A.R Form KLA); ☐ Lead-Based Paint and Lead-Based Paint Hazards Disclosure (C.A.R. Form FLD)

The following ATTACHED supplements are incorporated in this Agreement: _____

43. **TIME OF ESSENCE; ENTIRE CONTRACT; CHANGES:** Time is of the essence. All understandings between the parties are incorporated in this Agreement. Its terms are intended by the parties as a final, complete and exclusive expression of their Agreement with respect to its subject matter, and may not be contradicted by evidence of any prior agreement or contemporaneous oral agreement. If any provision of this Agreement is held to be ineffective or invalid, the remaining provisions will nevertheless be given full force and effect. Neither this Agreement nor any provision in it may be extended, amended, modified, altered or changed except in writing. This Agreement is subject to California landlord-tenant law and shall incorporate all changes required by amendment or successors to such law. This Agreement and any supplement, addendum or modification, including any copy, may be signed in two or more counterparts, all of which shall constitute one and the same writing.

44. **AGENCY:**
    A. **CONFIRMATION:** The following agency relationship(s) are hereby confirmed for this transaction.
       Listing Agent: (Print firm name) _____
       is the agent of (check one) ☐ the Landlord exclusively; or ☐ both the Landlord and Tenant.
       Leasing Agent: (Print firm name) _____
       (if not same as Listing Agent) is the agent of (check one) ☐ the Tenant exclusively; or ☐ the Landlord exclusively; or ☐ both the Tenant and Landlord.
    B. **DISCLOSURE:** ☐ (if checked): The term of this lease exceeds one year. A disclosure regarding real estate agency relationships (C.A.R. Form AD) has been provided to Landlord and Tenant, who each acknowledge its receipt.

45. ☐ **TENANT COMPENSATION TO BROKER:** Upon execution of this Agreement, Tenant agrees to pay compensation to Broker as specified in a separate written agreement between Tenant and Broker.

Tenant's Initials ( _____ )( _____ )
Landlord's Initials ( _____ )( _____ )

Reviewed by _____ Date _____

**RESIDENTIAL LEASE OR MONTH-TO-MONTH RENTAL AGREEMENT (LR PAGE 5 OF 6)**

*123 Sail Avenue*

Premises: _____ Date: _____

46. ☐ **INTERPRETER/TRANSLATOR:** The terms of this Agreement have been interpreted for Tenant into the following language: _____ . Landlord and Tenant acknowledge receipt of the attached interpretor/translator agreement (C.A.R. Form ITA).

47. **FOREIGN LANGUAGE NEGOTIATION:** If this Agreement has been negotiated by Landlord and Tenant primarily in Spanish, Chinese, Tagalog, Korean or Vietnamese. pursuant to the California Civil Code Tenant shall be provided a translation of this Agreement in the language used for the negotiation.

48. **OWNER COMPENSATION TO BROKER:** Upon execution of this Agreement, Owner agrees to pay compensation to Broker as specified in a separate written agreement between Owner and Broker (C.A.R. Form LCA).

49. **RECEIPT:** If specified in paragraph 5, Landlord or Broker, acknowledges receipt of move-in funds.

Landlord and Tenant acknowledge and agree Brokers: **(a)** do not guarantee the condition of the Premises; **(b)** cannot verify representations made by others; **(c)** cannot provide legal or tax advice; **(d)** will not provide other advice or information that exceeds the knowledge, education or experience required to obtain a real estate license. Furthermore, if Brokers are not also acting as Landlord in this Agreement, Brokers: **(e)** do not decide what rental rate a Tenant should pay or Landlord should accept; and **(f)** do not decide upon the length or other terms of tenancy. Landlord and Tenant agree that they will seek legal, tax, insurance and other desired assistance from appropriate professionals.

**Tenant agrees to rent the Premises on the above terms and conditions.**

Tenant _____ Date _____
Address _____ City _____ State _____ Zip _____
Telephone _____ Fax _____ E-mail _____

Tenant _____ Date _____
Address _____ City _____ State _____ Zip _____
Telephone _____ Fax _____ E-mail _____

☐ **GUARANTEE:** In consideration of the execution of this Agreement by and between Landlord and Tenant and for valuable consideration, receipt of which is hereby acknowledged, the undersigned ("Guarantor") does hereby: **(i)** guarantee unconditionally to Landlord and Landlord's agents, successors and assigns, the prompt payment of Rent or other sums that become due pursuant to this Agreement, including any and all court costs and attorney fees included in enforcing the Agreement; **(ii)** consent to any changes, modifications or alterations of any term in this Agreement agreed to by Landlord and Tenant; and **(iii)** waive any right to require Landlord and/or Landlord's agents to proceed against Tenant for any default occurring under this Agreement before seeking to enforce this Guarantee.

Guarantor (Print Name) _____
Guarantor _____ Date _____
Address _____ City _____ State _____ Zip _____
Telephone _____ Fax _____ E-mail _____

**Landlord agrees to rent the Premises on the above terms and conditions.**

Landlord _____ Landlord _____

Address _____
Telephone _____ Fax _____ E-mail _____

**REAL ESTATE BROKERS:**
**A.** Real estate brokers who are not also Landlord under this Agreement are not parties to the Agreement between Landlord and Tenant.
**B.** Agency relationships are confirmed in paragraph 44.
**C.** **COOPERATING BROKER COMPENSATION:** Listing Broker agrees to pay Cooperating Broker (Leasing Firm) and Cooperating Broker agrees to accept: **(i)** the amount specified in the MLS, provided Cooperating Broker is a Participant of the MLS in which the Property is offered for sale or a reciprocal MLS; or **(ii)** ☐ (if checked) the amount specified in a separate written agreement between Listing Broker and Cooperating Broker.

Real Estate Broker (Listing Firm) _____ DRE Lic. # _____
By (Agent) _____ DRE Lic. # _____ Date _____
Address _____ City _____ State _____ Zip _____
Telephone _____ Fax _____ E-mail _____

Real Estate Broker (Leasing Firm) _____ DRE Lic. # _____
By (Agent) _____ DRE Lic. # _____ Date _____
Address _____ City _____ State _____ Zip _____
Telephone _____ Fax _____ E-mail _____

Reviewed by _____ Date _____

**Figure 6-3**

CALIFORNIA
ASSOCIATION
OF REALTORS®

## APPLICATION TO RENT/SCREENING FEE
(C.A.R. Form LRA, Revised 11/09)

### I. APPLICATION TO RENT

**THIS SECTION TO BE COMPLETED BY APPLICANT. A SEPARATE APPLICATION TO RENT IS REQUIRED FOR EACH OCCUPANT 18 YEARS OF AGE OR OVER, OR AN EMANICIPATED MINOR.**

Applicant is completing Application as a (check one) ☐ tenant, ☐ tenant with co-tenant(s) or ☐ guarantor/co-signor.
Total number of applicants _____ .

#### PREMISES INFORMATION

Application to rent property at _____ *123 Sail Avenue ,* _____ ("Premises")
Rent: $ _____ per _____ Proposed move-in date _____

#### PERSONAL INFORMATION

FULL NAME OF APPLICANT _____
Social security No. _____ Driver's license No. _____ State _____ Expires _____
Phone number: Home _____ Work _____ Other _____
Email _____
Name(s) of all other proposed occupant(s) and relationship to applicant _____

Pet(s) or service animals (number and type) _____
Auto: Make _____ Model _____ Year _____ License No. _____ State _____ Color _____
Other vehicle(s): _____
In case of emergency, person to notify _____ Relationship _____
Address _____ Phone _____
Does applicant or any proposed occupant plan to use liquid-filled furniture? ☐ No ☐ Yes Type _____
Has applicant been a party to an unlawful detainer action or filed bankruptcy within the last seven years? ☐ No ☐ Yes
If yes, explain _____
Has applicant or any proposed occupant ever been convicted of or pleaded no contest to a felony? ☐ No ☐ Yes
If yes, explain _____
Has applicant or any proposed occupant ever been asked to move out of a residence? ☐ No ☐ Yes
If yes, explain _____

#### RESIDENCE HISTORY

| Current address _____ | Previous address _____ |
|---|---|
| City/State/Zip _____ | City/State/Zip _____ |
| From _____ to _____ | From _____ to _____ |
| Name of Landlord/Manager _____ | Name of Landlord/Manager _____ |
| Landlord/Manager's phone _____ | Landlord/Manager's phone _____ |
| Do you own this property? ☐ No ☐ Yes | Did you own this property? ☐ No ☐ Yes |
| Reason for leaving current address _____ | Reason for leaving this address _____ |

#### EMPLOYMENT AND INCOME HISTORY

Current employer _____ Supervisor _____ From _____ To _____
Employer's address _____ Supervisor's phone _____
Position or title _____ Phone number to verify employment _____
Employment gross income $ _____ per _____ Other $ _____ per _____ Source _____
Previous employer _____ Supervisor _____ From _____ To _____
Employer's address _____ Supervisor's phone _____
Position or title _____ Employment gross income $ _____ per _____

Applicant's Initials ( _____ ) ( _____ )

Reviewed by _____ Date _____

EQUAL HOUSING OPPORTUNITY

**LRA REVISED 11/09 (PAGE 1 OF 2)**

**APPLICATION TO RENT/SCREENING FEE (LRA PAGE 1 OF 2)**

Agent: WALT HUBER     Phone:     Fax:     Prepared using zipForm® software
Broker: WALT HUBER REALTOR

Property Address: _123 Sail Avenue ,_ _____ Date: _____

## CREDIT INFORMATION

| Name of creditor | Account number | Monthly payment | Balance due |
|---|---|---|---|
| | | | |
| | | | |

| Name of bank/branch | Account number | Type of account | Account balance |
|---|---|---|---|
| | | | |
| | | | |

## PERSONAL REFERENCES

Name _____ Address _____
Phone _____ Length of acquaintance _____ Occupation _____
Name _____ Address _____
Phone _____ Length of acquaintance _____ Occupation _____

## NEAREST RELATIVE(S)

Name _____ Address _____
Phone _____ Relationship _____
Name _____ Address _____
Phone _____ Relationship _____

Applicant understands and agrees: **(i)** this is an application to rent only and does not guarantee that applicant will be **offered the Premises**; and **(ii)** Landlord or Manager or Agent may accept more than one application for the Premises and, using their sole discretion, will select the best qualified applicant.

Applicant represents the above information to be true and complete, and hereby authorizes Landlord or Manager or Agent to: **(i)** verify the information provided; and **(ii)** obtain credit report on applicant.

If application is not fully completed, or received without the screening fee: **(i)** the application will not be processed, and **(ii)** the application and any screening fee will be returned.

Applicant _____ Date _____ Time _____

**Return your completed application and any applicable fee not already paid to:** _____
Address _____ City _____ State ____ Zip _____

## II. SCREENING FEE

**THIS SECTION TO BE COMPLETED BY LANDLORD, MANAGER OR AGENT.**

Applicant has paid a **nonrefundable** screening fee of $ _____ , applied as follows: (The screening fee may not exceed $30.00 adjusted annually from 1-1-98 commensurate with the increase in the Consumer Price Index.) A CPI inflation calculator is available on the Bureau of Labor Statistics website, www.bls.gov. The California Department of Consumer Affairs calculates the applicable screening fee amount to be $37.57 as of 2006.

$ _____ for credit reports prepared by _____ :
$ _____ for _____ (other out-of-pocket expenses); and
$ _____ for processing.

The undersigned has read the foregoing and acknowledges receipt of a copy.

_____ _____
Applicant Signature                                                                        Date

The undersigned has received the screening fee indicated above.

_____ DRE Lic. # _____ _____
Landlord or Manager or Agent Signature                                                          Date

Published and Distributed by:
REAL ESTATE BUSINESS SERVICES, INC.
a subsidiary of the California Association of REALTORS®
525 South Virgil Avenue, Los Angeles, California 90020

**LRA REVISED 11/09 (PAGE 2 OF 2)**

Reviewed by _____ Date _____

EQUAL HOUSING OPPORTUNITY

**APPLICATION TO RENT/SCREENING FEE (LRA PAGE 2 OF 2)**                        Untitled

## B. MINIMUM REQUIREMENTS OF A LEASE (or Rental Agreement)

As long as there is intent to rent property, the creation of a lease requires no particular language and can be either a written or an oral agreement. A lease or rental agreement must, at a minimum, include these four items:

1. **L**ength or duration of the lease.
2. **A**mount of rent.
3. **N**ames of parties.
4. **D**escription of property.

Think of
L.A.N.D. !

Leases for one year or less do not need to be in writing, but it makes good business sense to have all real estate agreements in writing. Under the Statute of Frauds, any lease lasting longer than one year from the date of signing must be in writing. California courts have held that in the event the lease is written, it must be signed by the lessor. It is not necessary for the lessee to sign if the lease has been delivered to, and accepted by, the lessee. The payment of rent and possession of the property is sufficient acceptance. Hotels, motels, and other types of lodging fall into the category of leases, even though the duration of use may be for a much shorter time and eviction or termination is handled differently for these daily or weekly rentals.

*A lease for more than one year must be in writing and signed by the lessor; but if the lessee does not sign, moves in and pays rent, he or she is bound to the terms of the lease.*

## C. RIGHTS AND OBLIGATIONS OF THE PARTIES

In addition to the minimum requirements, a number of contractual matters between a landlord and tenant should be considered before entering into a lease. The importance of these factors increases as the time period covered by the contract increases. Certain points that should be covered are:

1. **duration of lease;**
2. **amount of rent and manner of payment;**
3. **security deposits;**
4. **assignment and subleasing provisions;**
5. **liabilities for injuries and repairs;**
6. **conditions and provisions of a lease;**
7. **termination of a lease or rental agreement, and**
8. **renewal or extension provisions in bold type.**

### 1. Duration of Lease

There are certain statutory restrictions on the terms of certain leases:

1. Agricultural lands cannot be leased for more than 51 years.
2. Property situated in a city or town cannot be leased for more than 99 years.
3. A mineral, oil, or gas lease cannot be longer than 99 years after work begins.
4. A minor or incompetent can possess property only for the time a court has approved.

## 2. Amount of Rent

*RENT is the amount of money paid for the use of a property.* It is important to state both the specific amount of rent and when the rent is to be paid to the landlord. With a periodic tenancy, if the rent is to be paid in advance, or any time other than the end of the term, it should be stated in the agreement. **By law, rent becomes due only at the end of the term, unless the lease agreement states otherwise**. Preprinted lease forms normally specify that rent is due on the first day of each calendar month.

The actual amount of rent to be paid is called contract rent. *CONTRACT RENT is the payment designated in a lease contract, at the time the lease is signed, for the use of the property.* This amount must be distinguished from the economic rent. *ECONOMIC RENT is the amount of rent a property might be expected to yield if it were available for lease in the current market.* The economic rent and contract rent of a given property might differ if the lessor is receiving more or less rent than the property should reasonably yield.

*Rents are prorated in escrow.*

For income tax purposes, the amount of rent paid in advance must be included in the landlord's income for that year. If the landlord collects both the first month's and the last month's rent, both are considered current year income.

## 3. Security Deposits (Refundable)

A *SECURITY DEPOSIT provides the landlord with funds to pay for damages or unpaid rent when the tenant vacates.* It is in the landlord's and tenant's best interests to have an inspection of the premises before the tenant moves in and before the tenant moves out.

A *STATEMENT OF PROPERTY CONDITION is a report filled out by the landlord, in the presence of the tenant, that states the condition of the premises on moving in and moving out.* If both parties to a lease or rental agreement complete this form together, the chances of any disputes arising with regard to damages and the security deposit are greatly reduced.

*The maximum rental agreement security deposits for a residential property (in addition to first month's rent) is 2 months' rent for an unfurnished property and 3 months' rent for a furnished property.*

**Security (and "cleaning") deposits for residential leases in California must be refunded, in full, within twenty-one days of the tenant vacating the premises unless there is damage to the property or required cleaning**. If part (or all) of the security deposit is to be withheld from the tenant, the landlord must furnish the tenant an itemized, written statement within the same twenty-one day period. There are a limited number of areas in California that require a minimal amount of interest to be paid on deposits.

## 4. Assignment and Subleasing Provisions

*A sublease is a transfer of less than the entire leasehold estate to the sublessee.*

The tenant, without a clause to the contrary in the lease, may assign or sublease the property. An *ASSIGNMENT of a lease is a transfer of the entire lease*, whereas a *SUBLEASE is a transfer of less than the entire time or space of the lease.* For example, if there is a two-year lease, then an assignment could be for those two years, or a sublease could be for one year of the two-year lease, as long as it's not forbidden in the lease contract.

**Example:** A tenant signed a written lease for two years on a home. The lease made no mention of assignments and/or subleasing. The tenant may assign or sublease the home since the lease did not address those items.

*In a sublease, the lessee is still obligated for the original lease, whereas in an assignment, all the rights and obligations are transferred to the new tenant (assignee). When a tenant signs an assignment, the assignee who acquired the leasehold estate becomes the tenant.*

When a lessee or sublessee subleases a property, he or she holds a sandwich lease. A *SANDWICH LEASE is a leasehold interest in a property that lies between the primary (ownership) interest and the operating (tenancy) interest.*

*The lessee or sublessee with a sandwich lease is both a tenant and landlord to the same property.*

### 5. Liabilities for Injuries and Repairs

Generally, when the entire property is leased, the landlord is not liable for injuries to the tenant or any guests that resulted from a defective condition on the premises. This is true even if reasonable care would have disclosed the defects. In apartments or situations where the tenant does not lease the entire property, the liability for injury in the common areas belongs to the landlord. Therefore, it is the landlord's responsibility to either repair defective conditions in the common areas or be liable for injuries resulting from them. If a landlord has knowledge of such defects or disrepair but conceals the fact from the tenant, the landlord is liable for any resulting injuries.

It's easy to see why landlords should carry a large amount of liability insurance. Building defects may cause serious injury that could result in a lawsuit against the landlord. The tenant may also carry a renter's liability policy to protect against injuries sustained by others while visiting his or her apartment. This type of protection is usually contained in a "renter's" or "content's" policy, which protects the tenants from most losses, including liability and personal property damages.

### 6. Conditions and Provisions of a Lease

The California State Bar Association, in conjunction with CAR, has developed a standard combination lease and rental agreement form (refer back to Figure 6-2). This lease contains a number of conditions and provisions that both groups believe provide a good lease contract. As well as explaining who is responsible for any breach, this lease covers most of the common problems that may arise.

*If a real estate broker sells a property where the buyer will take possession prior to transferring title, the document he/she would have the buyer and seller execute is called an "interim occupancy agreement."*

## III. Termination of a Lease (or Rental Agreement)

A lease or rental agreement can be terminated for a variety of reasons. **Figure 6-4** lists the seven most common reasons for termination. A lease ends at the expiration of the term and without

**Figure 6-4**

# Termination of a Lease

- EXPIRATION OF THE TERM
- DESTRUCTION OF THE PREMISES
- LACK OF QUIET POSSESSION
- BREACH OF CONDITIONS
- REPAIRS FOR HABITABILITY
- SURRENDER/ ABANDONMENT
- EVICTION OR OPERATION OF LAW

notice. Rental agreements terminate by a written notice that must be at least one rental period in length. For example, if a tenancy is on a two-week basis, and the rent is paid for that period, then two week's notice is required.

## A. TERMINATION: EXPIRATION OF THE TERM (Most Common Reason)

A lease ends, without notice, at the expiration of the term. Rental agreements are usually terminated by either party with a 30-day written notice, unless a longer period is agreed to by both parties. As stated before, if the rental period is less than a month, only that much time is required. "Tenancies at will" require no less than a 30-day written "notice to vacate" to be served upon the tenant, or a 30-day notice given to the landlord by a vacating tenant. The 30-day notice may be made at any time during the rental period, with the balance of the rent due prorated. **Any condition in a rental agreement may be changed with a 30-day written notice.**

## B. TERMINATION: LACK OF QUIET POSSESSION

A tenant is entitled to the quiet possession and enjoyment of the premises without interference. The lease or rental agreement is made with the assumption that the tenant will have use of the premises and enjoy a quiet, uninterrupted stay. The landlord has the responsibility to maintain reasonable quiet on the premises for his or her tenants, and must not harass them unduly. Failure in either responsibility can give a tenant grounds for terminating a lease.

The California Civil Code permits the landlord to enter a tenant's unit under the following conditions:

1. Emergencies
2. Necessary repairs
3. To show premises to prospective tenants, buyers, or appraisers
4. If the tenant has abandoned the premises
5. With a court order to enter

*A landlord can enter the property when the tenant is present.*

No written notice of entry is required if the landlord believes the tenant has abandoned the premises, it is an emergency, if the tenant is present and verbally consents at the time of entry, or if the landlord and tenant agree verbally or in writing that the landlord will enter the property to make agreed upon repairs or supply agreed upon services within one week after the agreement is made. Otherwise, 24 hours is considered sufficient notice.

## C. TERMINATION: REPAIRS FOR HABITABILITY

The landlord of a rented home, whether the home is a house, a condominium or an apartment, has the implied responsibility to keep the premises maintained in a condition that meets at least bare living requirements: Hazardous conditions cannot exist that threaten the tenant's health or safety (see **Figure 6-5**).

If the landlord does not live up to this implied warranty of habitability, the tenant is not obligated to pay all the rent. However, a tenant must give notice of any necessary repairs to the landlord. The landlord has a reasonable amount of time to make any necessary repairs. A "reasonable amount of time" is determined by the type of repair needed. If the landlord, after a reasonable amount of time, has failed to make the necessary repairs, the tenant has two methods of recourse:

1. Spend up to (maximum) one month's rent in repairs, up to twice in a twelve consecutive month period. (A tenant cannot charge for his or her labor.)
2. Abandon the premises, which terminates the lease or rental agreement.

## D. TERMINATION: EVICTION OR OPERATION OF LAW

If a tenant does not pay the rent, or the tenant performs illegal acts on the premises, legal action is available to the landlord. *EVICTION is the legal process of removing a tenant because there is a breach of the lease or rental agreement.* **Figure 6-6** shows the life of an eviction process. An alternative would be for the landlord to sue for each payment (installment) as it becomes due. This is true whether the tenant remains in possession or abandons the premises. But at this point most landlords elect to evict the lessee. If the tenant moves and the landlord leases the property, the landlord can only sue for the rent lost while the property was vacant. A *RETALIATORY EVICTION is the process whereby a landlord evicts a tenant in response to a complaint lodged, or a repair deducted from rent, by the tenant.*

When the tenant refuses to give up possession but does not pay the rent, the landlord normally serves a "three-day notice to pay rent or quit" and, if necessary, files an "unlawful detainer" action. A *THREE-DAY NOTICE TO PAY RENT OR QUIT (Eviction Notice) is a legal document that informs the tenant that he/she has three straight days (excluding weekend days and holidays) to pay all past due rent, vacate the premises, or face an unlawful detainer court action* (see **Figure 6-7**). For example, a notice served on Monday expires at midnight on Thursday, but a notice served on Wednesday does not expire until the following Monday at midnight, unless Monday is a holiday.

An *UNLAWFUL DETAINER is a legal action in which a complaint is filed with the court asserting charges against the tenant.* After it is served, the tenant has five days to surrender possession or answer the complaint, and is no longer entitled to a pre-move out inspection.

**Figure 6-5**

# Habitability Obligations
# (Civil Code Section 1941.1)

## LANDLORD'S LEGAL MINIMUM OBLIGATIONS

The landlord's minimum habitability obligations are:

1. Effective waterproofing of roof and exterior walls, including unbroken windows and doors.
2. Plumbing and gas facilities installation maintained in good working order.
3. A water supply capable of hot and cold running water, fixtures, and connection to a sewage disposal system.
4. Heating facilities maintained in good working order.
5. Electrical lighting maintained in good working order.
6. Building and grounds kept clean and sanitary, free from all accumulations of debris, filth, rubbish, garbage, and rodents.
7. An adequate number of rubbish receptacles.
8. Floors, stairways, and railings maintained in good repair.

*If property is declared "untenable" for 35 days, the landlord can be fined $5,000 if he or she attempts to collect rent, issues a three-day notice to quit, or a notice to increase rent.*

## TENANT'S LEGAL OBLIGATIONS

**Tenant's Legal Obligations for Care of Premises.** A tenant's affirmative obligations to a landlord for reasonable care and habitability are:

1. Keep his or her part of the premises as clean and sanitary as possible.
2. Dispose of garbage and trash in a clean and sanitary manner.
3. Properly use the plumbing, electrical, and gas fixtures and keep them as clean as their condition permits.
4. Not permit any person on the premises to willfully destroy, deface, damage, impair, or remove any part of the structure, facilities, or equipment.
5. Occupy the premises for sleeping, cooking, dining, or other purposes for which they were designed or intended.

**Figure 6-6**

## Life of an Eviction Process

| 3 Days | 5 Days | 5 Days |
|:---:|:---:|:---:|
| Three-Day Notice to Pay Rent or Quit | Unlawful Detainer | Writ of Possession |

**Minimum Time Span**

Along with the unlawful detainer, many landlords caused to be served upon the tenants a *PREJUDGMENT CLAIM OF RIGHT OF POSSESSION, which covers any persons who appear to be or who may claim to have occupied the premises at the time of the filing of the action, even if their names do not appear on the lease (rental) agreement.*

If the tenant loses or does not answer the unlawful detainer complaint (defaults), the clerk of the court may issue a writ of possession. A *WRIT OF POSSESSION is a court order directing the sheriff to remove the tenant from the premises within five days of eviction notice.* Often, the landlord will have to account for the storage of the tenant's personal property. This can be complicated, so a landlord should consult an attorney before obtaining an unlawful detainer or writ of possession. Although an entire eviction process could take only thirteen days, it will most likely take a longer period of time. If the tenant answers the complaint, the matter could take several months.

### E. TERMINATION: SURRENDER/ABANDONMENT

*When a tenant voluntarily gives up a lease before the expiration of its term, it is known as* **SURRENDER**. If the tenant gives up the right of possession and surrenders the property back to the landlord, and the landlord accepts the surrender, the tenant is no longer liable for rent. Leases may be surrendered either by mutual agreement of the parties or through operation of law.

*If a tenant just moves out or vacates the premises without a formal surrender and never returns, it is called "abandonment."*

If a tenant abandons a property without cause, he or she has, by "operation of law," surrendered the property back to the landlord. Any cost for legal action by the landlord, plus the cost of any rental loss, may be charged to the tenant. The losses will be minimized if the landlord recovers possession and re-leases the premises quickly. A landlord can bring a lawsuit against the tenant for the lost rents, advertising expenses, and repairs or cleaning.

If a tenant's rent is 14 days delinquent and the landlord has reasonable cause to believe that the lessee has abandoned the premises, the lessor may bring action to reclaim the property. The lease is terminated 15 days after a **Notice of Belief of Abandonment** was personally served or posted in a conspicuous place (door, window) on the premises or 18 days after the notice was deposited in the mail. This will occur unless the lessee pays the rent or notifies the landlord that the premises has not been abandoned and he or she does not wish to surrender the leasehold estate.

**Figure 6-7**

# 3-DAY NOTICE TO PAY RENT OR QUIT

| | |
|---|---|
| **Plaintiff(s)** | **Owner(s)** |
| **VS.** | |
| | **Tenant(s)** |
| **Defendant(s)** | |
| **and Does 1 to 10 inclusive** | |

TO the above named TENANTS/RESIDENTS AND ALL OTHERS IN POSSESSION. PLEASE TAKE NOTICE, that you are justly indebted to the owner of the herein described premises; and notice is hereby given that pursuant to the lease and/or rental agreement under which you hold possession there is now due, unpaid and delinquent rent.

The total amount owing represents rent due for the following period(s).

| Due from | , 20 | thru | , 20 | $ |
|---|---|---|---|---|
| Due from | , 20 | thru | , 20 | $ |
| Due from | , 20 | thru | , 20 | $ |
| Due from | , 20 | thru | , 20 | $ |

**Total Rent Now Due** $ _____

WITHIN THREE (3) DAYS after service on you of this notice, you are hereby required to pay the amount of the above stated rent in full OR quit the subject premises, move out, and deliver up possession to the owner and/or his authorized agent. **No personal checks will be accepted.**

PLEASE TAKE FURTHER NOTICE that unless you pay the rent in full OR vacate the premises WITHIN THREE (3) DAYS as required by this notice, that the undersigned does hereby elect to declare forfeiture of your lease or rental agreement and institute legal proceedings for an unlawful detainer against you to recover possession of the premises plus court costs, attorney fees, and THREE TIMES THE AMOUNT OF RENT AND DAMAGES due as provided for by California law.

The premises herein referred to which you hold and/or occupied by you are:

Address: _____ Apartment or Suite No.: _____

City: _____ State: _____ Zip: _____

County of: _____

**Location to pay rent:**
Name _____
Address _____
City, State, Zip _____
Usual Days **M-F** Usual Hours **9AM TO 4PM**
Phone Number _____

_____
PERSON AUTHORIZED TO GIVE NOTICE

## PROOF OF SERVICE

I, the undersigned, being at least 18 years of age, declare under penalty of perjury that I served the above notice, of which this is a true copy, on the following tenant(s) in possession in the manner(s) indicated below:

☐ On _____, I handed the notice to the tenant(s) personally.

☐ On _____, after attempting personal service, I handed the notice to a person of suitable age and discretion at the residence/business of the tenant(s), AND I deposited a true copy in the U.S. Mail, in a sealed envelope with postage fully prepaid, addressed to the tenant(s) at his/her/their place of residence (date mailed, if different _____).

☐ On _____, after attempting service in both manners indicated previously, I posted the notice in a conspicuous place at the residence of the tenant(s), AND I deposited a true copy in the U.S. Mail, in a sealed envelope with postage fully prepaid, addressed to the tenant(s) at his/her/their place of residence (date mailed, if different _____).

Executed on _____ Served by _____

This form courtesy of *Express Evictions.com* (800) 491-1951

## F. TERMINATION: BREACH OF CONDITIONS

The violation of any conditions of the lease is a breach of contract and may terminate the agreement. Both the lessee and lessor have the responsibility of being informed of all contractual conditions and understand that violation of the conditions may cause termination.

## G. TERMINATION: DESTRUCTION OF THE PREMISES

If a structure is destroyed, there is usually a clause in the contract that automatically terminates the lease. If the damage is light, the tenant may stay while the landlord makes repairs. The lessee has the right to vacate the lease if the property is condemned.

*Selling an apartment building does NOT terminate the leases of the tenants in possession.*

# IV. Special Purpose Leases

In this section we will cover unique types of leases designed to meet specific needs.

## A. SALE-LEASEBACK

A **SALE-LEASEBACK** *occurs when an owner sells his or her property to another party and leases it back for a stated period of time; the original owner becomes the lessee.* This is also a financing device, but it is used mostly for commercial buildings where large business concerns are involved. The main reason for this type of lease is that a large company usually builds structures to its specifications. A large amount of money is required, therefore the company sells the building to get back most of its invested capital. By doing this, the company increases its working capital.

*The original owner of property in a sale-leaseback becomes the lessee.*

Large investors, such as insurance companies and pension funds, will purchase or build such a property, provided they get a well written, long-term lease. Of course the credit rating and financial position of the lessee must be outstanding. This is one device that nets a high rental income to the investor and allows the business a better cash flow. Chain stores, such as department stores and discount stores, use this device frequently.

*A single line of retail stores located along a major transportation corridor in a commercially zoned area is known as a "strip commercial development."*

## B. LEASE-PURCHASE OPTION

A **LEASE-PURCHASE OPTION** *exists only when a tenant leases a property with the option to purchase it at some later date.* See Chapter 5 for more details.

**Example:** Able holds a two-year lease with an option to purchase and assigns it to Baker. Baker would now hold the option, even if it is not stated in the assignment of the lease.

*The credit crunch/slump in making lease-purchase options more popular as alternative financing methods.*

## C. GROUND LEASE

A *GROUND LEASE is for the exclusive use and possession of a specific parcel of land.*

## D. GRADUATED LEASE

A *GRADUATED LEASE provides for a varying rental rate. It is often based upon future determination, such as periodic appraisals.* (Also called a "stair-step" lease.)

## E. GROSS LEASE (Income Property)

*With a GROSS LEASE, the lessee pays only a rental fee for the use of the property.*

## F. NET LEASE (Income Property)

A *NET LEASE is one where the lessee pays the property taxes, insurance, and other operating costs in addition to rental payments and is commonly used for stores.* The lessor receives only a net amount and does not pay the other related property expenses. Sometimes the net lease is referred to as a **"triple net lease"** because the lessee pays for (1) property taxes, (2) fire and hazard insurance, and (3) assessments or other operating expenses.

*The lessor benefits from a net lease because it generates a fixed income.*

## G. PERCENTAGE LEASE (Retail Sales Property)

A *PERCENTAGE LEASE is a commercial (retail sales) lease in which the lessee pays, or may pay, a certain percentage of the monthly gross sales to the lessor.* The idea is that if the lessee has a good or excellent location, the lessor will also benefit. Most percentage leases are written for a base rental amount, paid in advance, with an additional amount due if a predetermined percentage of the gross income receipts exceeds the base rental amount.

*Percentage lease payments are based upon monthly gross income receipts (with a fixed minimum rental).*

# V. Other Lease/Property Issues

## A. CONSUMER PRICE INDEX (CPI)

The *CONSUMER PRICE INDEX (CPI) is a government indicator (also called the "cost of living index") that shows changes in the cost of living from period-to-period.* As one of the largest expenses for consumers, **housing expenses are one of the largest denominators used when calculating the CPI.** Leases are often tied to the CPI, so that rents will adjust to give the lessor the same relative purchasing power from rents during a period of inflation. Long-term commercial leases generally include an *ESCALATOR CLAUSE whereby rents increase with inflation.*

*The most frequently used standard (index) for making commercial lease adjustments for inflation is the "Consumer Price Index for Wage Earners and Clerical Workers (CPI-W)."*

## B. LICENSE

A *LICENSE is a personal nonownership right to use personal or real property for a specific period of time.* It is nontransferable and can be **revoked**. Think of it as a ticket to a movie.

# VI. Property Management (Real Estate License Required)

In ever growing numbers, real estate brokers are now functioning as real property managers. A **PROPERTY MANAGER** *is a licensed real estate person who is paid to oversee the proper management and operations of rental and commercial property.* A property management company in California must be run by a licensed real estate broker and may include licensed salespeople working as property managers. Property managers include, for example, those who only engage in the management of one- and two-family homes as well as agents who oversee large projects such as office and industrial complexes, apartment buildings, and condominiums.

*The ultimate responsibility for the maintenance of an apartment building rests with the owner.*

Property managers must also be familiar with rent control laws in their city. **RENT CONTROL** *is government regulation of the amount of rent a landlord may charge tenants.* It is usually in the form of restrictions, by percentage, of annual increases in rental payments. Commercial, industrial, and luxury rentals are generally exempt from rent control.

*"Maturity" in property management means income has stabilized.*

## A. MANAGEMENT CONTRACT

It is good business practice for a property manager, managing properties for an owner, to have a well written contract with the property owner that sets forth the responsibilities of both parties (see **Figure 6-8** for the **CAR Property Management Agreement** form). This should include the terms and period of the contract, policies pertaining to the management of the premises, management fees, and the powers granted the agent by the owner.

*Property management contracts usually provide for the property manager to be compensated through a flat fee plus a percentage of the gross income.*

## B. RESIDENTIAL MANAGER

California law requires that rental unit buildings of 16 units or more must have an on-site resident manager in the employ of the owner or property management company living on the premises. **RESIDENTIAL MANAGERS** *are tenants of the property who rent units, handle tenants' complaints, and maintain the premises.* They are not required to have a real estate license.

*An on-site residential manager does NOT need a real estate license to manage a property where he/she is living, but does need a license to manage other properties.*

# VII. Professional Associations

## A. INSTITUTE OF REAL ESTATE MANAGEMENT® (IREM)

The Institute of Real Estate Management® (IREM), created by the National Association of REALTORS® (NAR) bolsters professionalism within the industry by offering qualified candidates the designations of Certified Property Manager® (CPM), Accredited

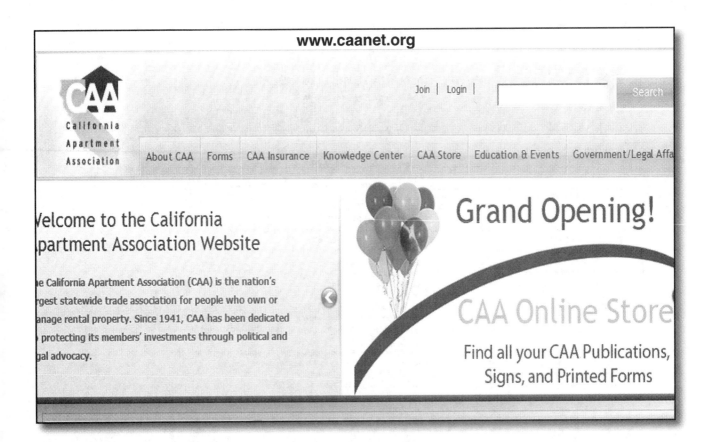

Management Organization® (AMO), and Accredited Resident Managers® (ARM) designation.

**www.irem.org**
Institute of Real Estate Management

## B. CALIFORNIA APARTMENT ASSOCIATION® (CAA)

The California Apartment Association® (CAA) has many local associations to assist property owners with forms and credit checks. Their professional designation for resident managers is Certified Apartment Manager® (CAM) for on-site managers.

**www.caanet.org**
California Apartment Association

*Whether the market is up or down, salespeople are still earning commissions by leasing, property management, and mortgage loan brokering.*

**Figure 6-8**

CALIFORNIA
ASSOCIATION
OF REALTORS®

## PROPERTY MANAGEMENT AGREEMENT
(C.A.R. Form PMA, Revised 4/09)

_____ ("Owner"), and
_____ ("Broker"), agree as follows:

1. **APPOINTMENT OF BROKER:** Owner hereby appoints and grants Broker the exclusive right to rent, lease, operate, and manage the property(ies) known as _____ *123 Sail Avenue* , _____

_____ and any additional property which may later be added to this Agreement ("Property"), upon the terms below, for the period beginning (date) _____ and ending (date) _____ , at 11:59 PM. (If checked:) ☐ Either party may terminate this Property Management Agreement ("Agreement") on at least 30 days written notice _____ months after the original commencement date of this Agreement. After the exclusive term expires, this Agreement shall continue as a non-exclusive agreement that either party may terminate by giving at least 30 days written notice to the other.

2. **BROKER ACCEPTANCE:** Broker accepts the appointment and grant, and agrees to:
   A. Use due diligence in the performance of this Agreement.
   B. Furnish the services of its firm for the rental, leasing, operation and management of the Property.

3. **AUTHORITY AND POWERS:** Owner grants Broker the authority and power, at Owner's expense, to:
   A. **ADVERTISING:** Display FOR RENT/LEASE and similar signs on the Property and advertise the availability of the Property, or any part thereof, for rental or lease.
   B. **RENTAL; LEASING:** Initiate, sign, renew, modify or cancel rental agreements and leases for the Property, or any part thereof; collect and give receipts for rents, other fees, charges and security deposits. Any lease or rental agreement executed by Broker for Owner shall not exceed _____ year(s) or ☐ shall be month-to-month. Unless Owner authorizes a lower amount, rent shall be: ☐ at market rate; OR ☐ a minimum of _____ per _____ ; OR ☐ see attachment.
   C. **TENANCY TERMINATION:** Sign and serve in Owner's name notices that are required or appropriate; commence and prosecute actions to evict tenants; recover possession of the Property in Owner's name; recover rents and other sums due; and, when expedient, settle, compromise and release claims, actions and suits and/or reinstate tenancies.
   D. **REPAIR; MAINTENANCE:** Make, cause to be made, and/or supervise repairs, improvements, alterations and decorations to the Property; purchase, and pay bills for, services and supplies. Broker shall obtain prior approval of Owner for all expenditures over $ _____ for any one item. Prior approval shall not be required for monthly or recurring operating charges or, if in Broker's opinion, emergency expenditures over the maximum are needed to protect the Property or other property(ies) from damage, prevent injury to persons, avoid suspension of necessary services, avoid penalties or fines, or suspension of services to tenants required by a lease or rental agreement or by law, including, but not limited to, maintaining the Property in a condition fit for human habitation as required by Civil Code §§ 1941 and 1941.1 and Health and Safety Code §§ 17920.3 and 17920.10.
   E. **REPORTS, NOTICES AND SIGNS:** Comply with federal, state or local law requiring delivery of reports or notices and/or posting of signs or notices.
   F. **CONTRACTS; SERVICES:** Contract, hire, supervise and/or discharge firms and persons, including utilities, required for the operation and maintenance of the Property. Broker may perform any of Broker's duties through attorneys, agents, employees, or independent contractors and, except for persons working in Broker's firm, shall not be responsible for their acts, omissions, defaults, negligence and/or costs of same.
   G. **EXPENSE PAYMENTS:** Pay expenses and costs for the Property from Owner's funds held by Broker, unless otherwise directed by Owner. Expenses and costs may include, but are not limited to, property management compensation, fees and charges, expenses for goods and services, property taxes and other taxes, Owner's Association dues, assessments, loan payments and insurance premiums.
   H. **SECURITY DEPOSITS:** Receive security deposits from tenants, which deposits shall be ☐ given to Owner, or ☐ placed in Broker's trust account and, if held in Broker's trust account, pay from Owner's funds all interest on tenants' security deposits if required by local law or ordinance. Owner shall be responsible to tenants for return of security deposits and all interest due on security deposits held by Owner.
   I. **TRUST FUNDS:** Deposit all receipts collected for Owner, less any sums properly deducted or disbursed, in a financial institution whose deposits are insured by an agency of the United States government. The funds shall be held in a trust account separate from Broker's personal accounts. Broker shall not be liable in event of bankruptcy or failure of a financial institution.
   J. **RESERVES:** Maintain a reserve in Broker's trust account of $ _____
   K. **DISBURSEMENTS:** Disburse Owner's funds, held in Broker's trust account, in the following order:
      (1) Compensation due Broker under paragraph 6.
      (2) All other operating expenses, costs and disbursements payable from Owner's funds held by Broker.
      (3) Reserves and security deposits held by Broker.
      (4) Balance to Owner.
   L. **OWNER DISTRIBUTION:** Remit funds, if any are available, monthly (or ☐ _____ ), to Owner.
   M. **OWNER STATEMENTS:** Render monthly, (or ☐ _____ ), statements of receipts, expenses and charges for each Property.
   N. **BROKER FUNDS:** Broker shall not advance Broker's own funds in connection with the Property or this Agreement.
   O. **KEYSAFE/LOCKBOX:** ☐ (If checked) Owner authorizes the use of a keysafe/lockbox to allow entry into the Property and agrees to sign a keysafe/lockbox addendum (C.A.R. Form KLA).

Owner's Initials ( _____ ) ( _____ )
Broker's Initials ( _____ ) ( _____ )

Reviewed by _____ Date _____

EQUAL HOUSING OPPORTUNITY

**PROPERTY MANAGEMENT AGREEMENT (PMA PAGE 1 OF 3)**

Agent: WALT HUBER          Phone:          Fax:          Prepared using zipForm® software
Broker: WALT HUBER REALTOR

Owner Name: _____ Date: _____

4. **OWNER RESPONSIBILITIES:** Owner shall:
   A. Provide all documentation, records and disclosures as required by law or required by Broker to manage and operate the Property, and immediately notify Broker if Owner becomes aware of any change in such documentation, records or disclosures, or any matter affecting the habitability of the Property.
   B. Indemnify, defend and hold harmless Broker, and all persons in Broker's firm, regardless of responsibility, from all costs, expenses, suits, liabilities, damages, attorney fees and claims of every type, including but not limited to those arising out of injury or death of any person, or damage to any real or personal property of any person, including Owner, for: **(i)** any repairs performed by Owner or by others hired directly by Owner; or **(ii)** those relating to the management, leasing, rental, security deposits, or operation of the Property by Broker, or any person in Broker's firm, or the performance or exercise of any of the duties, powers or authorities granted to Broker.
   C. Maintain the Property in a condition fit for human habitation as required by Civil Code §§ 1941 and 1941.1 and Health and Safety Code §§ 17920.3 and 17920.10 and other applicable law.
   D. Pay all interest on tenants' security deposits if required by local law or ordinance.
   E. Carry and pay for: **(i)** public and premises liability insurance in an amount of no less than $1,000,000; and **(ii)** property damage and worker's compensation insurance adequate to protect the interests of Owner and Broker. Broker shall be, and Owner authorizes Broker to be, named as an additional insured party on Owner's policies.
   F. Pay any late charges, penalties and/or interest imposed by lenders or other parties for failure to make payment to those parties, if the failure is due to insufficient funds in Broker's trust account available for such payment.
   G. Immediately replace any funds required if there are insufficient funds in Broker's trust account to cover Owner's responsibilities.
5. **DISCLOSURE:**
   A. **LEAD-BASED PAINT**
      (1) ☐ The Property was constructed on or after January 1, 1978.
      OR (2) ☐ The Property was constructed prior to 1978.
         (i) Owner has no knowledge of lead-based paint or lead-based paint hazards in the housing except: _____
         _____
         (ii) Owner has no reports or records pertaining to lead-based paint or lead-based hazards in the housing, except the following, which Owner shall provide to Broker: _____ .
   B. **POOL/SPA DRAIN**
      Any pool or spa on the property does (or, ☐ does not) have an approved anti-entrapment drain cover, device or system.
6. **COMPENSATION:**
   A. Owner agrees to pay Broker fees in the amounts indicated below for:
      (1) Management: _____ .
      (2) Renting or Leasing: _____ .
      (3) Evictions: _____ .
      (4) Preparing Property for rental or lease: _____ .
      (5) Managing Property during extended periods of vacancy: _____ .
      (6) An overhead and service fee added to the cost of all work performed by or at the direction of, Broker: _____ .
      (7) Other: _____ .
   B. This Agreement does not include providing on-site management services, property sales, refinancing, preparing Property for sale or refinancing, modernization, fire or major damage restoration, rehabilitation, obtaining income tax, accounting or legal advice, representation before public agencies, advising on proposed new construction, debt collection, counseling, attending Owner's Association meetings or _____
      _____
      If Owner requests Broker to perform services not included in this Agreement, a fee shall be agreed upon before these services are performed.
   C. Broker may divide compensation, fees and charges due under this Agreement in any manner acceptable to Broker.
   D. Owner further agrees that:
      (1) Broker may receive and keep fees and charges from tenants for: **(i)** requesting an assignment of lease or sublease of the Property; **(ii)** processing credit applications; **(iii)** any returned checks and/or ☐ if checked) late payments; and **(iv)** any other services that are not in conflict with this Agreement.
      (2) Broker may perform any of Broker's duties, and obtain necessary products and services, through affiliated companies or organizations in which Broker may own an interest. Broker may receive fees, commissions and/or profits from these affiliated companies or organizations. Broker has an ownership interest in the following affiliated companies or organizations: _____
         _____
         Broker shall disclose to Owner any other such relationships as they occur. Broker shall not receive any fees, commissions or profits from unaffiliated companies or organizations in the performance of this Agreement, without prior disclosure to Owner.
      (3) Other: _____
7. **AGENCY RELATIONSHIPS:** Broker shall act, and Owner hereby consents to Broker acting, as dual agent for Owner and tenant(s) in any resulting transaction. If the Property includes residential property with one-to-four dwelling units and this Agreement permits a tenancy in excess of one year, Owner acknowledges receipt of the "Disclosure Regarding Agency Relationships" (C.A.R. Form AD). Owner understands that Broker may have or obtain property management agreements on other property, and that potential tenants may consider, make offers on, or lease through Broker, property the same as or similar to Owner's Property. Owner consents to Broker's representation of other owners' properties before, during and after the expiration of this Agreement.
8. **NOTICES:** Any written notice to Owner or Broker required under this Agreement shall be served by sending such notice by first class mail or other agreed-to delivery method to that party at the address below, or at any different address the parties may later designate for this purpose. Notice shall be deemed received three (3) calendar days after deposit into the United States mail OR ☐ _____

Owner's Initials ( _____ ) ( _____ )
Broker's Initials ( _____ ) ( _____ )

**PMA REVISED 4/09 (PAGE 2 OF 3)**

Reviewed by _____ Date _____

EQUAL HOUSING OPPORTUNITY

Untitled

**PROPERTY MANAGEMENT AGREEMENT (PMA PAGE 2 OF 3)**

Owner Name: _____ Date: _____

**9. DISPUTE RESOLUTION**

　　**A. MEDIATION:** Owner and Broker agree to mediate any dispute or claim arising between them out of this Agreement, or any resulting transaction before resorting to arbitration or court action, subject to paragraph 9B(2) below. Paragraph 9B(2) below applies whether or not the arbitration provision is initialed. Mediation fees, if any, shall be divided equally among the parties involved. If, for any dispute or claim to which this paragraph applies, any party commences an action based on a dispute or claim to which this paragraph applies, without first attempting to resolve the matter through mediation, or refuses to mediate after a request has been made, then that party shall not be entitled to recover attorney fees, even if they would otherwise be available to that party in any such action. THIS MEDIATION PROVISION APPLIES WHETHER OR NOT THE ARBITRATION PROVISION IS INITIALED.

　　**B. ARBITRATION OF DISPUTES: (1) Owner and Broker agree that any dispute or claim in law or equity arising between them regarding the obligation to pay compensation under this agreement, which is not settled through mediation, shall be decided by neutral, binding arbitration, including and subject to paragraph 9B(2) below. The arbitrator shall be a retired judge or justice, or an attorney with at least 5 years of residential real estate law experience, unless the parties mutually agree to a different arbitrator, who shall render an award in accordance with substantive California Law. The parties shall have the right to discovery in accordance with Code of Civil Procedure § 1283.05. In all other respects, the arbitration shall be conducted in accordance with Title 9 of Part III of the California Code of Civil Procedure. Judgment upon the award of the arbitrator(s) may be entered in any court having jurisdiction. Interpretation of this agreement to arbitrate shall be governed by the Federal Arbitration Act.**

　　**(2) EXCLUSIONS FROM MEDIATION AND ARBITRATION:** The following matters are excluded from mediation and arbitration hereunder: **(i)** a judicial or non-judicial foreclosure or other action or proceeding to enforce a deed of trust, mortgage, or installment land sale contract as defined in Civil Code § 2985; **(ii)** an unlawful detainer action; **(iii)** the filing or enforcement of a mechanic's lien; and **(iv)** any matter that is within the jurisdiction of a probate, small claims, or bankruptcy court. The filing of a court action to enable the recording of a notice of pending action, for order of attachment, receivership, injunction, or other provisional remedies, shall not constitute a waiver of the mediation and arbitration provisions.

　　**"NOTICE: BY INITIALING IN THE SPACE BELOW YOU ARE AGREEING TO HAVE ANY DISPUTE ARISING OUT OF THE MATTERS INCLUDED IN THE 'ARBITRATION OF DISPUTES' PROVISION DECIDED BY NEUTRAL ARBITRATION AS PROVIDED BY CALIFORNIA LAW AND YOU ARE GIVING UP ANY RIGHTS YOU MIGHT POSSESS TO HAVE THE DISPUTE LITIGATED IN A COURT OR JURY TRIAL. BY INITIALING IN THE SPACE BELOW YOU ARE GIVING UP YOUR JUDICIAL RIGHTS TO DISCOVERY AND APPEAL, UNLESS THOSE RIGHTS ARE SPECIFICALLY INCLUDED IN THE 'ARBITRATION OF DISPUTES' PROVISION. IF YOU REFUSE TO SUBMIT TO ARBITRATION AFTER AGREEING TO THIS PROVISION, YOU MAY BE COMPELLED TO ARBITRATE UNDER THE AUTHORITY OF THE CALIFORNIA CODE OF CIVIL PROCEDURE. YOUR AGREEMENT TO THIS ARBITRATION PROVISION IS VOLUNTARY."**

　　**"WE HAVE READ AND UNDERSTAND THE FOREGOING AND AGREE TO SUBMIT DISPUTES ARISING OUT OF THE MATTERS INCLUDED IN THE 'ARBITRATION OF DISPUTES' PROVISION TO NEUTRAL ARBITRATION."**

| Owner's Initials _____ / _____ | Broker's Initials _____ / _____ |

**10. EQUAL HOUSING OPPORTUNITY:** The Property is offered in compliance with federal, state and local anti-discrimination laws.

**11. ATTORNEY FEES:** In any action, proceeding or arbitration between Owner and Broker regarding the obligation to pay compensation under this Agreement, the prevailing Owner or Broker shall be entitled to reasonable attorney fees and costs from the non-prevailing Owner or Broker, except as provided in paragraph 9A.

**12. ADDITIONAL TERMS:** ☐ Keysafe/Lockbox Addendum (C.A.R. Form KLA) ☐ Lead-Based Paint and Lead-Based Paint Hazards Disclosure (C.A.R. Form FLD)

**13. TIME OF ESSENCE; ENTIRE CONTRACT; CHANGES:** Time is of the essence. All understandings between the parties are incorporated in this Agreement. Its terms are intended by the parties as a final, complete and exclusive expression of their Agreement with respect to its subject matter, and may not be contradicted by evidence of any prior agreement or contemporaneous oral agreement. If any provision of this Agreement is held to be ineffective or invalid, the remaining provisions will nevertheless be given full force and effect. Neither this Agreement nor any provision in it may be extended, amended, modified, altered or changed except in writing. This Agreement and any supplement, addendum or modification, including any copy, may be signed in two or more counterparts, all of which shall constitute one and the same writing.

Owner warrants that Owner is the owner of the Property or has the authority to execute this contract. Owner acknowledges Owner has read, understands, accepts and has received a copy of the Agreement.

Owner _____ Date _____
Owner _____ Date _____
　　　 Print Name 　　　　　　　　　　　　　　　　　　　　Social Security/Tax ID # (for tax reporting purposes)
Address _____ City _____ State _____ Zip _____
Telephone _____ Fax _____ E-mail _____

Owner _____ Date _____
Owner _____ Date _____
　　　 Print Name 　　　　　　　　　　　　　　　　　　　　Social Security/Tax ID # (for tax reporting purposes)
Address _____ City _____ State _____ Zip _____
Telephone _____ Fax _____ E-mail _____

Real Estate Broker (Firm) _____ Date _____
By (Agent) _____ DRE Lic. #: _____
Address _____ City _____ State _____ Zip _____
Telephone _____ Fax _____ E-mail _____

Published and Distributed by:
REAL ESTATE BUSINESS SERVICES, INC.
*a subsidiary of the California Association of REALTORS®*
525 South Virgil Avenue, Los Angeles, California 90020
**PMA REVISED 4/09 (PAGE 3 OF 3)**

| Reviewed by _____ Date _____ | EQUAL HOUSING OPPORTUNITY |

**PROPERTY MANAGEMENT AGREEMENT (PMA PAGE 3 OF 3)**

Untitled

## VIII. CHAPTER SUMMARY

A **less-than-freehold** (chattel) estate is a **personal property** estate in real property, with no ownership rights, such as a lease or leasehold. A **leasehold** is an exclusive right to occupy and use a property on a temporary basis. The types of leasehold estates include: 1) an **estate for years**; 2) an **estate from period-to-period**; 3) an **estate at will**; and 4) an **estate at sufferance**.

The minimum requirements of a lease (or rental agreement) can be remembered by the acronym **LAND**, for: 1) **length** of time or duration of lease; 2) **amount** of rent; 3) **names** of parties; and 4) **descriptions** of property.

**Contract rent** is actual rent, whereas **economic rent** is the amount a property might get if it were for lease in the current market. **Rent control** is a governmental regulation of the amount of rent a landlord may charge tenants.

A tenant may be required to pay a **security deposit** of two months' rent for an unfurnished property (three months for furnished) to cover any damage repair necessary when he or she moves out. A **statement of property** condition ensures that both parties are aware of the condition of the premises before the tenant moves in.

Without a clause disallowing it, a tenant may **assign** (transfer entire lease) or **sublease** (for less than the entire time or space) to another. If the tenant (**assignor**) signs a new valid lease with an **assignee**, the assignee is the tenant. An owner who is a landlord and a tenant (like a developer who rents out his apartment complex) has a **sandwich lease**. **Possessory rights** belong to the lessee, **reversionary rights** to the lessor.

A lease or rental agreement can be terminated by: 1) **expiration of the term**; 2) **lack of quiet possession**; 3) **repairs for habitability**; 4) **eviction** or **operation of law**; 5) **destruction of the premises**; 6) **breach of conditions**; or 7) **surrender/abandonment**. A landlord has a legal minimum obligation to maintain habitability, and a tenant has a legal obligation to care for the premises. Selling an apartment does not terminate a lease.

In the case of **eviction**, it is unlawful for a landlord to lock out tenants, take their property, remove doors, shut off utilities, or trespass. First, the landlord must give a **3-Day Notice to Pay or Quit** (eviction notice), then file an **unlawful detainer** with the court, who issues a **writ of possession**, directing the sheriff to remove the tenant in five days.

**Sale-leasebacks, lease-purchase options, ground leases, graduated leases, gross leases, net leases,** and **percentage leases** are all specialty leases.

A **property manager** is a licensed real estate person paid to oversee the proper management and operations of rental and commercial property. A **residential manager** is a tenant of the property, and as an **on-site manager**, does not need to have a real estate license. The **Institute of Real Estate Management (IREM)** offers the designation of **Certified Property Manager (CPM), Accredited Management Organization (AMO),** and **Accredited Resident Manager (ARM).**

# CHAPTER 6

## IX. TERMINOLOGY

A. Assignment
B. Contract Rent
C. Economic Rent
D. Estate at Sufferance
E. Estate at Will
F. Estate for Years
G. Estate From Period-to-Period
H. Eviction Process
I. Ground Lease

J. Landlord
K. Lease
L. Lease-Purchase Option
M. Lessee
N. Lessor
O. Net Lease
P. Percentage Lease
Q. Rent
R. Rent Control

S. Rental Agreement
T. Sale-Leaseback
U. Sandwich Lease
V. Sublease
W. Surrender
X. Tenant
Y. Unlawful Detainer or Notice
  to Quit
Z. Writ of Possession

1.____ A financial arrangement in which, at the time of sale, the seller retains occupancy by concurrently agreeing to lease the property back from the purchaser.

2.____ One who pays rent under a lease agreement.

3.____ Lease on the property, the rental payment for which is determined by a percentage of gross receipts from the business.

4.____ The amount of rent expected if the property were currently available for renting.

5.____ One who rents his or her property to another under a lease or rental agreement.

6.____ An owner who enters into a lease agreement with a tenant.

7.____ A lease requiring a lessee to pay charges against the property, such as taxes, insurance, and maintenance costs, in addition to rental payments.

8.____ The party who pays rent for a lease or rental agreement.

9.____ An agreement for the use of the land only.

10.____ The occupation of property by a tenant for an indefinite period, terminable by one or both parties (not common in California).

11.____ The general name of the process, from beginning to end, that serves to remove a person from the possession of real property.

12.____ A lease given by a lessee.

13.____ A leasehold interest that lies between the primary lease and the operating lease.

14.____ The concept of possessing an interest in real property by virtue of a contract for a fixed and definite period of time.

15.____ A transfer of a person's entire rights under a contract.

16.____ An estate contract between owner and tenant, setting forth conditions of a period-to-period tenancy.

17.____ A contract between an owner and tenant, setting forth conditions of tenancy for a fixed period of time.

18.____ An estate arising when the tenant wrongfully holds over after the expiration of the term.

19.____ A contract for the monthly rental of residential property.

20.____ Consideration paid for the occupancy and use of real property.

21.____ Rent paid under a lease; the actual rent as opposed to the market rental value of the property.

22.____ The name of the legal process to initiate the removal of a tenant.

23.____ The giving up of an estate, such as a lease. A contractual agreement, having the consent of both parties, such as lessor and lessee, as opposed to abandonment.

24.____ A legal maximum on rental price.

25.____ The court order physically expelling a tenant.

26.____ A lease that includes the right to purchase later.

## X. CHAPTER QUIZ

1. An estate at will can be ended by:
   a. the buyer.
   b. the seller.
   c. the lessor or lessee.
   d. only the lessee.

2. If a real estate broker sells a property where the buyer will take possession prior to transferring title, the document he would have the buyer and seller execute is called:
   a. an option.
   b. an interim occupancy agreement.
   c. a quitclaim deed.
   d. a land contract of sale.

3. Which of the following is usually prorated in escrow?
   a. Purchase price
   b. Rents
   c. Documentary transfer tax
   d. City transfer tax

4. The maximum deposit that can be collected and held for an unfurnished apartment is:
   a. 2 months.
   b. 3 months.
   c. 1 month.
   d. 4 months.

5. The maximum deposit that can be collected and held for a furnished apartment is:
   a. 2 months.
   b. 3 months.
   c. 1 month.
   d. 4 months.

6. A tenant signed a written lease for two years on a home. The lease made no mention of assignments and/or subleasing. The tenant may:
   a. assign or sublease the home since the lease did not address those items.
   b. not assign or sublease the home to another tenant.
   c. only assign or sublease the home with the landlord's prior written approval.
   d. assign the lease to an assignee, but cannot sublease the home to another tenant.

7. Able holds a two-year lease with an option to purchase and assigns it to Baker. Which of the following is correct?

    a. Baker would not hold the option.
    b. Able would continue to hold the option.
    c. This is not permissible.
    d. Baker would now hold the option.

8. Which of the following is a benefit of a net lease?

    a. Lessee receives net income
    b. Lessee does not have to pay taxes, maintenance, and insurance
    c. Lessor receives net income
    d. Lessor pays taxes, maintenance, and insurance

9. A single line of retail stores located along a major transportation corridor in a commercially zoned area would be known as a:

    a. street commercial zone development.
    b. commercial cluster center.
    c. strip commercial development.
    d. commercial redevelopment zone.

10. Which of the following is often used when a commercial lease contains an escalator clause to adjust the rental amount periodically (usually annually) for inflation?

    a. Average commercial rental rates in an area
    b. The Consumer Price Index (CPI)
    c. General economic indicators averaged over the past 12 months
    d. Standard and Poor's statistics of 500 individuals

**ANSWERS:** 1. c; 2. b; 3. b; 4. a; 5. b; 6. a; 7. d; 8. c; 9. c; 10. b

TM

# CHAPTER 7
## *Escrows and Title Insurance*

## I. Escrows in General

*The purpose of an escrow is to ensure that the terms of the transaction are met.*

An **ESCROW** *is created when a separate written agreement instructs a neutral third party to hold funds and only proceed when all the agreed to conditions have been performed.* In California, an escrow is usually a requirement for the sale of a home or any other real estate. Although it is not always required by law, it is an indispensable process by which an independent third party handles the legal paperwork of a real estate sale. An escrow is not only an effective tool for handling normal real estate transactions like sales or refinancing, but is also for the sale of trust deeds, exchanges, and transfer of liquor licenses, businesses, securities, and court-required transfers. The legally required and recommended uses of an escrow are illustrated in **Figure 7-1**.

**Figure 7-1**

| Highly Recommended | Required by Law |
|---|---|
| 1. Sales of Real Property | 1. Liquor License Transfers |
| 2. Loans | 2. Security Sales (Impound Accounts) |
| 3. Exchanges | 3. Court-Ordered Transfers (Probate Sales) |

### A. REQUIREMENTS FOR A VALID ESCROW

*The Escrow Act is found in the Financial Code.*

The three requirements for a valid escrow are:

1. Signed escrow instructions, forming a binding contract between two or more parties (usually a buyer and seller).

2. A neutral party, which is the escrow company, acting as a dual agent of the buyer and seller.

# CHAPTER 7

3. Conditional delivery of funds and documents when all the conditions in the escrow are met.

*When escrow closes, dual agency (representing both parties, usually buyers and sellers, at once) changes to separate agency (handling each party's separate paperwork requirements).*

An escrow may be initiated with a written contract, such as a purchase agreement, or through oral instructions. It is important to have agreed upon the written instructions drawn by the escrow company. Since this may be a new experience for most people, the escrow agent will, when necessary, explain each step to a buyer or seller. **A helpful escrow officer can point out possible problems, suggest alternatives, but cannot give legal advice.**

## B. ESCROW OFFICER

An escrow holder can be: 1) a corporation, 2) an attorney, or 3) a real estate broker who acts as a real estate agent in the transaction.

A *NEUTRAL DEPOSITORY is an escrow business conducted by a licensed escrow holder*. An *ESCROW OFFICER, HOLDER, or AGENT, though not licensed by the state, is an employee of a escrow company who acts as the agent*. Escrow law is found in the California Financial Code. An independent escrow corporation must be licensed by the Department of Corporations to handle escrows. Corporations that are exempt from the escrow law but can handle escrows include: banks, savings banks, and title insurance companies, because they are under the supervision of their respective authorizing agencies.

There are two other types of escrow holders: attorneys who perform escrow duties as a part of their practice, and real estate brokers who handle their own escrows (must be the broker in the transaction). Regardless of the type of escrow company, each performs three essential duties (diagrammed in **Figure 7-2**).

**Figure 7-2**

| Conditional | Confidentiality | Deposit Holder |
|---|---|---|
| Delivery of all funds and documents when the conditions of the escrow have been met. | All escrow instructions are confidential, and disclosure can be authorized only by the buyer or seller. | The escrow company can disburse funds and documents only when all conditions have been met and both parties have reached an agreement. |

The complete sequence of events in an escrow is:

1. Preliminary title search and report
2. Lender's demand (amount owed, pay-off statement)
3. Request for new loan documents
4. Completion of conditions and depositing of funds
5. Adjustments and prorations

6. Transfer of existing fire policies or creation of new ones
7. Recording and issuing of title policy
8. Disbursement of funds
9. Escrow statement sent to each party

After these steps have been completed and all other escrow conditions have been met, the closing of an escrow is usually routine (see **Figure 7-3**). The escrow agent is authorized to call for a buyer's documents and funds.

## C. REAL ESTATE BROKERS CAN CONDUCT ESCROWS

*As a licensed broker, you can handle an escrow for a fee if you are acting as a broker in that real estate transaction.*

This is your personal right, and you shall not delegate any duties other than escrow duties normally performed under the direct supervision of the broker.

All written escrow instructions executed by a buyer or seller must contain a statement, in not less than 10-point type, that includes the licensee's name and the fact that he or she is licensed by the Department of Real Estate.

*If a dispute arose during escrow regarding the distribution of funds, a broker might file an interpleader action.*

# II. How Escrows Work

*Escrow amendments must be signed by the parties to change the escrow.*

## A. ESCROW RULES

Once the escrow instructions have been drawn from the original contract (purchase agreement) and signed by each party, neither party may change the escrow instructions without the written agreement of the other. (All time frames commence from the time the contract became binding; usually the purchase agreement has a provision for escrow to acknowledge receipt of this document.) The escrow is complete when: 1) all conditions of the escrow have been met; 2) all conditions of the parties have been met; and 3) the parties have received an accounting of the procedure. If both parties mutually agree to change the instructions, the change can be put into effect at any time. However, if a dispute should arise, the escrow company will not proceed until both parties come to terms. If the parties cannot agree to terms, an escrow company will bring an interpleader action (court action) to determine where the money or consideration goes. **Figure 7-4** illustrates the three ways in which an escrow can be terminated.

*If there is a disagreement between buyer and seller during escrow, the escrow officer may disburse funds as a result of a judgment between buyer and seller, if the parties to the escrow agree, and if a binding arbitrator settles the matter.*

## B. WHO SELECTS THE ESCROW COMPANY?

Selection of an escrow company and an escrow officer are part of the negotiation between buyer and seller. Like any other item in a real estate transaction, it is part of the negotiated agreement. Either one of the parties may suggest the escrow company, which should be

**Figure 7-3**

## California Customs (North vs. South) for Escrow Services and Title Insurance

### When are signed escrow instructions delivered?

Customarily, in Southern California, the (bilateral) escrow instructions are signed by both the buyer and seller just after the **start of escrow**.

Customarily, in Northern California, the (unilateral) escrow instructions are given to the escrow officer just before the **close of escrow**.

### Who performs the escrow services?

Escrow services in Southern California are traditionally performed by **independent escrow companies (corporations)** or **financial institutions**.

Escrow services in Northern California are traditionally performed by **title insurance companies**.

### Who pays the escrow fees?

Escrow service fees in Southern California are usually **split 50-50 between the buyer and the seller**.

Escrow service fees in Northern California are usually **paid for by the buyer**.

### Who traditionally pays title insurance fees?

Customarily in Southern California, the **seller pays for the California Land Title Association (CLTA) policy (standard policy)**.

Customarily in Northern California, the **buyer pays for the California Land Title Association (CLTA) policy (standard policy)**.

In both the North and the South, the buyers pay for any coverage **above** the California Land Title Insurance (CLTA) policy.

explained when completing the purchase agreement. The salesperson may certainly make suggestions as to a preferred escrow company for both the buyer and seller. When the escrow company is named in the purchase agreement, the real estate listing agent cannot change the escrow company without the mutual consent of the buyer and seller. If the buyer and seller each desire a different escrow company, then the salesperson must work for a mutual agreement before there can be an offer and acceptance of the sale.

**Figure 7-4**

**Three Ways to Terminate an Escrow**

| Complete Escrow | Mutual Agreement | Court Action "Interpleader" |

It is imperative that you, as the salesperson, disclose in writing any shared interest that you or your broker have with the selected escrow company. This disclosure must be made either at the time of listing or whenever the escrow company is selected. Disciplinary action will be taken against any salesperson or broker who, in bad faith and against the wishes of the buyer and seller, attempts to force the use of a particular escrow company.

*A real estate licensee is prohibited by law from receiving any "kickback" for solicitation of escrow business.*

### C. ESCROW INSTRUCTIONS

*ESCROW INSTRUCTIONS are formal instructions drawn from the information contained in the original agreement, usually the signed purchase agreement.* When these instructions are drawn and signed, they become an enforceable contract binding on all parties.

Since the escrow instructions supplement the original contract, both are interpreted together whenever possible. If a conflict should arise between the content of the instructions and the original contract, the instructions will usually prevail. **Therefore, all parties to the escrow should read the escrow instructions very carefully, and sign them only after every detail is absolutely correct and the terms meet with their approval.**

### D. FINANCING IS AN IMPORTANT ASPECT OF THE ESCROW

Most escrows for the sale of a home include obtaining a new loan and the payoff or assumption of an old loan. The brokers and their salespeople can be helpful to the buyer obtaining new financing by providing the necessary loan documentation to the escrow company in a timely manner. Keeping the buyer and seller informed about the progress of the financing and escrow helps to maintain good client-agent communication and trust.

The *PAYOFF DEMAND STATEMENT is a formal demand statement from the lender that details the amounts owed, as calculated by the lender, for the purpose of **paying off the loan in full***. The failure to obtain a payoff or beneficiary statement in a timely manner could hold up the escrow. A payoff demand statement is different from a beneficiary's statement. A *BENIFICIARY'S (LENDER'S) STATEMENT is a demand statement by a lender, under a deed of trust, that provides information, such as the unpaid balance, monthly payment, and interest rate, necessary **if the loan is to be assumed***. The lender may charge up to $100 for furnishing the payoff or beneficiary statement, except when the loan is insured by the FHA or guaranteed by the VA.

## E. ESCROW EXAMPLE

To help illustrate the closing statements used in a simple escrow, we'll assume the following facts.

**Figure 7-5** illustrates the buyer's escrow statement, and **Figure 7-6** illustrates the seller's statement. These statements include many other miscellaneous costs that are a usual part of the escrow.

### An Escrow Example

| | | |
|---|---|---|
| BUYER | John Buyer and Jane Buyer | |
| SELLER | John Seller and Jane Seller | |
| SALES PRICE | | $800,000 |
| 1ST TRUST DEED | | $640,000 |
| 2ND TRUST DEED | | $80,000 |
| DOWN PAYMENT | | $80,000 |
| BROKER | J.Q. Smart | $48,000 |
| EXISTING LIENS | | |
| 1) 1ST TRUST DEED | | $290,000 |
| 2) STREET ASSESSMENT BOND | | $1,300 |
| CLTA TITLE POLICY PAID BY SELLER | | $2,165 |
| Date of Closing is June 1, 2020 | | |

**(Next Page)**

## F. CLOSING DATE IS THE DATE OF RECORDATION

The **CLOSING DATE** *is the date that the documents are recorded.* Escrow usually approximates the closing date, but the actual date is when all the conditions of the escrow have been completed, the buyer's remaining money (cashier's checks) is received, and when all the documents are recorded. Most escrows are for handling the paperwork of property sale and loan financing, but escrows can be for almost any purpose.

*In closing statements, the buyer's and seller's totals are usually different. However, each closing statement must balance within itself. In the buyer's closing statement, the purchase price is debited.*

# III. Proration

*Property taxes, interest, fire insurance, and rents are prorated. Title insurance would NOT be prorated in escrow.*

**PRORATION** *is the process of proportionately dividing expenses or income to the precise date that escrow closes, or any other date previously agreed upon.* It enables the buyer and seller to pay or receive their proportionate share of expenses or income. Items that are commonly prorated include:

1. property taxes,
2. fire insurance,
3. interest, and
4. rents.

**Figure 7-5**

601 East Glenoaks Blvd. Suite 210
Glendale, CA 91207
P.O. Box 433 Glendale, CA 91209-0433
Tel: (818) 500-1633
Fax: (818) 500-0862

### BUYER FINAL SETTLEMENT STATEMENT

PROPERTY: 123 Purchase Lane
                Glendale, CA
BUYER:    John Buyer and Jane Buyer

CLOSING DATE: 06/01/20
ESCROW NO.: 1-10533

| | DEBITS | CREDITS |
|---|---|---|
| **FINANCIAL** | | |
| Total Consideration | $ 800,000.00 | $ |
| Cash Deposit | | 5,000.00 |
| Cash Deposit | | 86,000.00 |
| New 1st Trust Deed | | 640,000.00 |
| New 2nd Trust Deed | | 80,000.00 |
| **PRORATIONS AND ADJUSTMENTS** | | |
| Taxes at 4000.00/6 mo. from 06/01/20 to 07/01/20 | 666.67 | |
| **OTHER DISBURSEMENTS** | | |
| Property Insurance, Inc. for Fire Insurance | 1,000.00 | |
| **TITLE CHARGES TO AMERICAN COAST TITLE** | | |
| Title Policy Premium | 628.50 | |
| Sub Escrow Fee | 75.00 | |
| Recording Grant Deed | 8.00 | |
| Recording Trust Deed(s) | 20.00 | |
| Title Endorsement Fee(s) | 50.00 | |
| **ESCROW CHARGES TO COLONIAL ESCROW, INC.** | | |
| Escrow Fee | 900.00 | |
| Messenger Fee | 50.00 | |
| Loan Tie In Fee | 125.00 | |
| **NEW 1ST TRUST DEED TO GET SMART SAVINGS AND LOAN** | | |
| Loan Fees | 6,400.00 | |
| Credit Report | 45.00 | |
| Appraisal | 350.00 | |
| Tax Service | 89.00 | |
| Document Fee | 250.00 | |
| Interest at 7.5000% from 05/31/20 to 06/01/20 | 131.51 | |
| **REFUND** | 211.32 | |
| **TOTALS** | 811,000.00 | 811,000.00 |

SAVE FOR INCOME TAX PURPOSES

**Figure 7-6**

601 East Glenoaks Blvd. Suite 210
Glendale, CA 91207
P.O. Box 433 Glendale, CA 91209-0433
Tel: (818) 500-1633
Fax: (818) 500-0862

## SELLER FINAL SETTLEMENT STATEMENT

PROPERTY: 123 Purchase Lane      CLOSING DATE: 06/01/20
          Glendale, CA            ESCROW NO.:   1-10533
SELLER:   John Seller and Jane Seller

| | DEBITS | CREDITS |
|---|---|---|
| **FINANCIAL** | | |
| Total Consideration | $ | $ 800,000.00 |
| **New 2nd Trust Deed** | **80,000.00** | |
| **PRORATIONS AND ADJUSTMENTS** | | |
| Taxes at 4000.00/6 mo. from 06/01/20 to 07/01/20 | | 666.67 |
| **PAYOFF CHARGES TO MOST SUPERIOR** | | |
| **SAVINGS AND LOAN** | | |
| Principal Balance | 490,000.00 | |
| Interest on Principal Balance at 10.0000% from 05/01/20 to 06/01/20 | 4,161.64 | |
| Forwarding Fee | 50.00 | |
| Reconveyance Fee | 60.00 | |
| **OTHER DISBURSEMENTS** | | |
| Pest Control, Inc. for Termite Report/Work | 1,000.00 | |
| Home Warranty, Inc. for Home Protection Policy | 400.00 | |
| **COMMISSION** | | |
| Listing Broker: J. Q. Smart | 48,000.00 | |
| **TITLE CHARGES TO AMERICAN COAST** | | |
| **TITLE** | | |
| Title Policy Premium | 2,165.00 | |
| Sub Escrow Fee | 75.00 | |
| Documentary Transfer Tax | 880.00 | |
| Recording Reconveyance | 5.00 | |
| Street Assessment Bond | 1,300.00 | |
| **ESCROW CHARGES TO COLONIAL ESCROW, INC.** | | |
| Escrow Fee | 900.00 | |
| Processing Demands | 35.00 | |
| Document Fee | 85.00 | |
| **NET PROCEEDS** | 171,550.03 | |
| **TOTALS** | 800,666.67 | 800,666.67 |

SAVE FOR INCOME TAX PURPOSES

*Proration of prepaid taxes is a credit to the seller.*

### A. 30 DAYS IS THE BASIS FOR PRORATION

**All escrow companies use 30 days as a base month.** For example, if an escrow closes on the 10th day of the month, all prepaid rents for that month would constitute 9/30 of the rent left for the seller, and 21/30 of the rent would go to the buyer. If the rent is $2,000, the seller's portion would be 9/30 of $2,000, or $600, and the buyer's portion would be 21/30 of $2,000, or $1,400. (Rents belong to the buyer as of the closing date.)

*Property tax prorations are based on the amount of tax the seller is paying. Escrow uses the old assessed valuation when prorating.*

The date used in calculating proration is usually assumed to be the date of closing, but any date may be used if agreed upon by all parties. This is the case when the possession date differs from the closing date.

Taxes are prorated either from July 1, which marks the beginning of the county fiscal year, or January 1, the middle of the fiscal year. If the property taxes on a home, amounting to $2,400 per year, have been paid up to July 1, what is the proration if escrow is to be closed on June 1? In this case, the buyer would reimburse the seller for one month's taxes (or $2,400 divided by twelve months, equaling $200 per month). The seller would then be credited for the $200 in property taxes that he or she had already paid in advance.

## Escrow Company Reports Information to the I.R.S.

All real estate transactions must be reported to the Internal Revenue Service. This is done by the escrow company or whoever handles the closing. A 1099 Form is required for any sale or exchange.

*Escrow reports real estate transactions to the I.R.S. using the seller's social security number.*

# IV. Termites and Other Problems

### A. STRUCTURAL PEST CONTROL CERTIFICATION REPORT (Report and Clearance)

Pest control inspection reports are not required by law in California, but many lenders will require this report. A *STRUCTURAL PEST CONTROL CERTIFICATION REPORT is a written report given by a licensed pest control company identifying any wood-destroying pests or conditions likely to cause pest infestation. The report states the condition and correction cost of any pest, dry rot, excessive moisture, earth-wood contacts, or fungus damage in accessible areas of a structure.* Who pays for the (1) pest control inspection report and (2) any required or recommended repair work is up to the buyer and seller, although they are usually paid for by the seller. There may sometimes be a local custom that dictates who will pay, while in other instances financial institutions or financing agencies will decide which one of the parties will pay.

The escrow officer accepts and holds the pest control report and awaits further instructions from both parties.

*If there is Section I infestation damage (required work), it is usually paid for by the seller. If there is only Section II potential for infestation damage (recommended work), the extent of repairs is up to the parties.*

Most lenders require a pest control inspection report before making a loan, and every VA and FHA loan application requires an inspection report. The usual cost for an inspection report is about $65. The cost, in some areas, may be as high as $175 to $195.

If escrow holds two pest control reports, escrow will notify the broker and get instructions from both buyer and seller.

The question of which party pays for any necessary repairs to obtain a "Notice of Work Completed" report is also a matter of local custom. In most areas the seller usually pays. However, FHA and VA termite certificates and repairs are always paid for by the seller. The seller is allowed to include a clause stating what the maximum cost of repairs will be as a condition of the sale.

The best time for a seller to have a termite report issued is before the sale of the property.

When a structural pest control company is hired, it is accountable to both the buyer and seller, regardless of who pays for the inspection. It is required to furnish the person who ordered the inspection with a copy of the report within ten business days. For a few dollars, any person may request certified copies of any certificate inspection report, filed during the preceding two years, from the State Structural Pest Control Board.

## B. BROKER MAINTAINS PEST CONTROL DOCUMENTATION

The Civil Code requires that the broker shall deliver a copy of the Structural Pest Control Certification Report and Notice of Work Completed to the buyer, seller, and lender, if such a report is a condition of the purchase agreement or is a requirement imposed as a condition of financing. If more than one broker is acting as an agent in the transaction, the broker who obtained the offer (selling broker) made by the buyer shall deliver the required documents.

# V. Fire Insurance

*When one party agrees to indemnify another for loss in return for periodic premium payments, it is called "insurance."*

## A. FIRE INSURANCE . . . A MUST!

Fire insurance is very inexpensive compared to the possible dollar loss due to fire, and all property owners should have this financial protection. A lending institution will require coverage for the amount of its loan. However, it is in the owner's best interest to carry sufficient fire insurance to replace the structure if it is totally destroyed. It is only necessary to insure the current replacement value of the dwelling, since the land itself cannot be destroyed by fire.

The *CALIFORNIA STANDARD FORM FIRE INSURANCE POLICY insures the dwelling against (1) fire and (2) lightning.* If you so desire, you may procure an *EXTENDED COVERAGE ENDORSEMENT that will insure you against the additional perils of windstorm, explosion, hail, aircraft, smoke, riot, and vehicles not attributed to a strike or civil commotion.* Other types of endorsements may insure you against vandalism, malicious mischief, floods, and other damage. Coverage depends on your needs and the perils common to your area.

## B. FIRE INSURANCE PRORATION

*Fire insurance coverage protects an owner of real property. When filing a claim, he or she will neither gain nor lose.*

When purchasing property, a buyer usually obtains a new policy. **If the seller/owner has filed an insurance claim during the previous three years, he or she must disclose this to the buyer in writing.** This may cause some hardship to the new owner/buyer in obtaining his or her own insurance. Cancellation of the seller's insurance must be initiated by the seller after close of escrow, with any unused premium to be prorated and reimbursed to the seller. It is always the buyer's choice to select his or her own house insurance. Condo insurance is chosen by the association.

An insurance company may short-rate fire insurance. A *SHORT RATE CANCELLATION FEE is a fee/penalty charged to the seller who cancels the policy before it expires.* The money returned is the unused premium minus administrative expenses.

## C. COINSURANCE CLAUSE

A *COINSURANCE CLAUSE is a provision in an insurance policy requiring a property owner to carry separate insurance up to an amount stated in the policy to qualify for full coverage. That amount is usually 80% of the value of the dwelling in order to receive full insurance benefits.* The percentage paid represents the actual percentage of insurance carried (up to 80%), which is then divided by the required 80% (see **Figure 7-7**).

---

**Figure 7-7**

### HOW NONRESIDENTIAL COINSURANCE WORKS

| | | |
|---|---|---|
| 1. Actual value of your improvements | = | $200,000 |
| 2. 80% coinsurance clause requires you to carry fire insurance on 80% of the actual value of the dwelling. (80% of $200,000) | = | $160,000 |
| 3. Amount of fire insurance carried (Face amount on your policy) | = | **$120,000** |
| 4. Ratio of loss payment<br>$120,000 (actual amount)<br>$160,000 (required amount) | = | 75% |
| 5. If your actual fire loss is | = | $80,000 |
| 6. Your insurance would pay 75% of actual loss (75% of $80,000) | = | $60,000 |
| 7. Your out-of-pocket cost would be the loss less insurance payments ($80,000 - $60,000) | = | **$20,000** |

---

## VI. Title Insurance

### A. CHAIN OF TITLE (Recorded Public History)

*Every recorded change of ownership and/or claim of ownership on a property is in the abstract of title.*

If one person sells a property to another person, *a recorded public history of a specific property called the CHAIN OF TITLE* is compiled. These public records include files at the county recorder's office, various tax agencies, federal court clerk, and the Secretary of State. *All such information about people and their real property is stored in computers (within a grantor-grantee index) and is referred to as a TITLE PLANT.*

A title insurance company is primarily concerned with a search of the public records, which includes: the Federal Court Clerk, the County Clerk's Office, the County Recorder's Office, and other sources. This search establishes what is called the "chain of title."

### B. TITLE INSURANCE (Has Four Functions)

Title insurance companies are regulated by the California Insurance Commissioner. Fee schedules must be available to the general public upon request. To guarantee solvency, each title insurance company must set aside reserves.

*TITLE INSURANCE insures a lender (and property owner for an additional fee) against losses that result from imperfections in title.* Title insurance companies examine the records documenting chain of title, review any risks that might not be found in the public records, interpret legality, help the seller correct any defects, and insure marketable title to the property. Title insurance is only paid once, unlike auto or fire insurance, which must be paid annually. **Figure 7-8** emphasizes the four most important functions of title insurance.

**Figure 7-8**

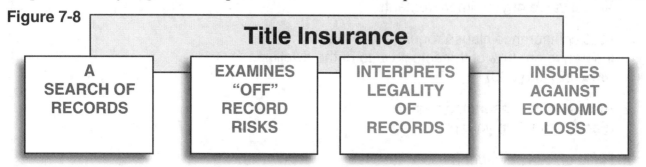

### Title Insurance

| A SEARCH OF RECORDS | EXAMINES "OFF" RECORD RISKS | INTERPRETS LEGALITY OF RECORDS | INSURES AGAINST ECONOMIC LOSS |

## C. PRELIMINARY TITLE REPORT (Ordered First)

The first step in a title search is for the escrow officer to order the preliminary title report. After the buyer or borrower completes a **Statement of Information**, a title search can begin (see **Figure 7-9**). A *PRELIMINARY TITLE REPORT is a report showing the condition of title before a sale or loan transaction.* After completion of the transaction, a title insurance policy is issued. The preliminary title report consists of the following items:

1. The name of the owner and a description of the property.
2. A list of any outstanding taxes, bonds, or other assessments.
3. The identity of any covenants, conditions or restrictions.
4. Any recorded liens or other encumbrances must be eliminated before any loan is made.

# VII. Types of Title Insurance Policies

## A. CALIFORNIA LAND TITLE ASSOCIATION (CLTA)
### (Standard Coverage Policy)

In California, the standard title insurance policy is the CLTA. The *CALIFORNIA LAND TITLE ASSOCIATION (CLTA) policy is the basic title insurance policy.* It may be issued to insure a lender only, or an owner only, or it may insure both the lender and the owner (a joint-protection standard coverage policy). This standard policy insures the lender only, unless the owner requests and pays for owner coverage.

**Figure 7-10** is a sample of a standard CLTA policy form.

*The standard coverage CLTA title insurance policy is most often used.*

Besides insuring against all items of record, the CLTA policy offers protection against many off-record risks. Some of these off-record risks include forgeries, acts of minors and incompetents, acts of an agent whose authority has terminated, invalid deed delivery, unrecorded federal estate tax liens, undisclosed rights of husband and wife when the chain of title states "unmarried," and the expenses (including attorneys' fees) incurred in defending title.

**Figure 7-9**

## Complete, Sign and Return

STATEMENT OF INFORMATION

Order No. 52-78

To expedite the completion of your escrow, please fill out and return this form at your earliest convenience. This information is for confidential use by North American Title Company in searching the land records in connection with the order number shown above. Further explanation of the need for this information is printed on the reverse side of this form.

Please Print all information

### PERSONAL IDENTIFICATION

Name

_____
FIRST NAME                         FULL MIDDLE NAME—IF NONE, INDICATE                  LAST NAME

Year of Birth _____ Birthplace _____ Social Security No. _____

Full name of Husband/Wife _____
FIRST NAME                    FULL MIDDLE NAME—IF NONE, INDICATE           LAST NAME

Year of Birth _____ Birthplace _____ Social Security No. _____

We were married on _____ at _____
DATE                                         CITY AND STATE

Wife's maiden name _____

### RESIDENCES DURING PAST 10 YEARS

| NUMBER AND STREET | CITY | FROM (DATE) | TO (DATE) |
|---|---|---|---|
| | | | |
| NUMBER AND STREET | CITY | FROM (DATE) | TO (DATE) |
| NUMBER AND STREET | CITY | FROM (DATE) | TO (DATE) |

(If more space is needed, use reverse side of form)

### OCCUPATIONS DURING PAST 10 YEARS

Husband's

| OCCUPATION | FIRM NAME | STREET AND CITY | FROM (DATE) TO (DATE) |
|---|---|---|---|
| OCCUPATION | FIRM NAME | STREET AND CITY | FROM (DATE) TO (DATE) |
| OCCUPATION | FIRM NAME | STREET AND CITY | FROM (DATE) TO (DATE) |

Wife's

| OCCUPATION | FIRM NAME | STREET AND CITY | FROM (DATE) TO (DATE) |
|---|---|---|---|
| OCCUPATION | FIRM NAME | STREET AND CITY | FROM (DATE) TO (DATE) |

(If more space is needed, use reverse side of form)

### FORMER MARRIAGE(S), IF ANY

If no former marriages, write "None" _____ Otherwise, please complete the following:

Name of former wife _____

Deceased ☐    Divorced ☐    When _____ Where _____

Name of former husband _____

Deceased ☐    Divorced ☐    When _____ Where _____

(If more space is needed, use reverse side of form)

Buyer intends to reside on the property in this transaction    Yes ☐    No ☐

### THIS PORTION IS TO BE COMPLETED BY THE SELLER

The Street Address of the property in this transaction is _____
(LEAVE BLANK IF NONE)

The land is unimproved ☐  or improved with a structure of the following type;

IMPROVEMENTS:  ☐ SINGLE RESIDENCE OR 1-4 FAMILY  ☐ MULTIPLE RESIDENCE  ☐ COMMERCIAL

OCCUPIED BY:  ☐ OWNER  ☐ LESSEE  ☐ TENANTS

ANY PORTION OF NEW LOAN FUNDS TO BE USED FOR CONSTRUCTION

IMPROVEMENTS, REMODELING OR REPAIRS TO THIS PROPERTY HAVE BEEN MADE WITHIN THE PAST SIX MONTHS  ☐ YES  ☐ NO

IF YES,

HAVE ALL COSTS FOR LABOR AND MATERIALS ARISING IN CONNECTION THEREWITH BEEN PAID IN FULL?  ☐ YES  ☐ NO

The undersigned declare, under penalty of perjury, that the foregoing is true and correct.

DATE _____      _____

HOME PHONE _____  BUSINESS PHONE _____

_____
(IF MARRIED, BOTH HUSBAND AND WIFE SHOULD SIGN)

NAT 44 (5/88)

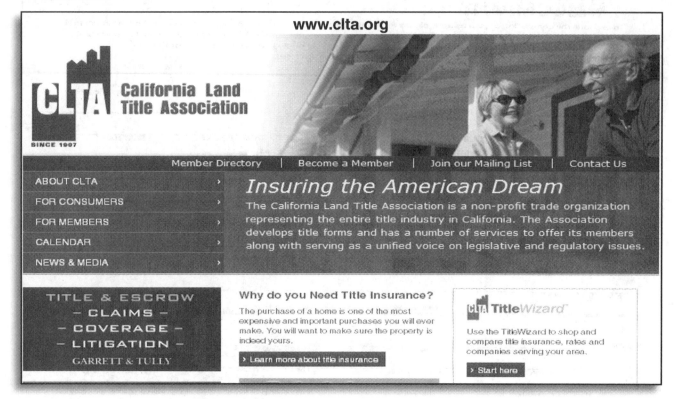

It is very important to note those items NOT included in the standard policy. The items not included are:

1. Easements, encumbrances, and liens that are not shown by the public record. (CLTA, no – ALTA, yes)

2. Rights or claims of persons in physical possession of the land. (CLTA, no – ALTA, yes)

3. Unrecorded claims not shown by the public record that could be ascertained by physical inspection or correct survey. ((CLTA, no – ALTA, yes)

4. Mining claims, reservations in patents, water rights, and government actions, such as zoning ordinances. (CLTA, no – ALTA, yes)

*Standard title insurance (CLTA) does NOT insure against undisclosed liens placed on a property by a grantor (although it is warranted in a grant deed). NO title insurance policy covers everything.*

A warranty is found in a grant deed, which is not covered by a CLTA standard coverage title policy, if there are no undisclosed encumbrances on the property.

## B. AMERICAN LAND TITLE ASSOCIATION (ALTA)
### (Extended Coverage Policy - Survey Included)

The *AMERICAN LAND TITLE ASSOCIATION (ALTA) policy is an extended coverage policy that insures against many exclusions of the standard coverage (CLTA) policy.* The ALTA policy (which includes a competent survey or physical inspection) is usually required by California lenders and by out-of-state lenders who are not able to make a personal physical inspection of the property.

**Figure 7-10**

# POLICY OF TITLE INSURANCE

### ISSUED BY

**NORTH AMERICAN TITLE INSURANCE COMPANY**

C

SUBJECT TO THE EXCLUSIONS FROM COVERAGE, THE EXCEPTIONS FROM COVERAGE CONTAINED IN SCHEDULE B AND THE CONDITIONS AND STIPULATIONS, NORTH AMERICAN TITLE INSURANCE COMPANY, a California corporation, herein called the Company, insures, as of Date of Policy shown in Schedule A, against loss or damage, not exceeding the Amount of Insurance stated in Schedule A, sustained or incurred by the insured by reason of:

1. Title to the estate or interest described in Schedule A being vested otherwise than as stated therein;
2. Any defect in or lien or encumbrance on such title;
3. Unmarketability of the title;
4. Lack of a right of access to and from the land;
5. The invalidity or unenforceability of the lien of the insured mortgage upon the title;
6. The priority of any lien or encumbrance over the lien of the insured mortgage;
7. Lack of priority of the lien of the insured mortgage over any statutory lien for services, labor or material:
   (a) arising from an improvement or work related to the land which is contracted for or commenced prior to Date of Policy; or
   (b) arising from an improvement or work related to the land which is contracted for or commenced subsequent to Date of Policy and which is financed in whole or in part by proceeds of the indebtedness secured by the insured mortgage which at Date of Policy the insured has advanced or is obligated to advance.
8. Any assessments for street improvements under construction or completed at Date of Policy which now have gained or hereafter may gain priority over the insured mortgage; or
9. The invalidity or unenforceability of any assignment of the insured mortgage, provided the assignment is shown in Schedule A, or the failure of the assignment shown in Schedule A to vest title to the insured mortgage in the named insured assignee free and clear of all liens.

The Company will also pay the costs, attorneys' fees and expenses incurred in defense of the title or the lien of the insured mortgage, as insured, but only to the extent provided in the Conditions and Stipulations.

Y

**NORTH AMERICAN TITLE INSURANCE COMPANY**

BY *Gerald B Beery* PRESIDENT

ATTEST _____ SECRETARY

NORTH AMERICAN TITLE INSURANCE COMPANY
INCORPORATED
SEPT 18, 1958
CALIFORNIA

POLICY NO. 116823                          FILE NO.:  14-15360-63

AMOUNT OF INSURANCE: $296,800.00            PREMIUM: $1,161.75

DATE OF POLICY:  JULY 22, 1992 AT  8:00 A.M.


1.  **NAME OF INSURED:**


SYCAMORE FINANCIAL GROUP, INC., A CALIFORNIA CORPORATION


2.  **THE ESTATE OR INTEREST IN THE LAND WHICH IS ENCUMBERED BY THE INSURED MORTGAGE IS:**


A CONDOMINIUM, AS DEFINED IN SECTION 783 OF THE CALIFORNIA CIVIL CODE, IN FEE


3.  **TITLE TO THE ESTATE OR INTEREST IN THE LAND IS VESTED IN:**


WALTER ROY HUBER AND DEBBIE R. HUBER, HUSBAND AND WIFE AS COMMUNITY PROPERTY


4.  **THE INSURED MORTGAGE AND ASSIGNMENTS THEREOF, IF ANY, ARE DESCRIBED AS FOLLOWS:**

A DEED OF TRUST TO SECURE AN INDEBTEDNESS IN THE AMOUNT SHOWN BELOW AND ANY OTHER OBLIGATIONS SECURED THEREBY:

RECORDED:      JULY 22, 1992 AS INSTRUMENT NO. 92-1329290 OF
               OFFICIAL RECORDS
AMOUNT:        $296,800.00
DATED:         JULY 13, 1992
TRUSTOR:       WALTER ROY HUBER AND DEBBIE R. HUBER, HUSBAND AND
               WIFE AS COMMUNITY PROPERTY
TRUSTEE:       UTICA ESCROW INC., A CALIFORNIA CORPORATION
BENEFICIARY:   SYCAMORE FINANCIAL GROUP, INC., A CALIFORNIA
               CORPORATION

5.  **THE LAND REFERRED TO IN THIS POLICY IS DESCRIBED AS FOLLOWS:**


PARCEL 1:

THAT PORTION OF PARCEL A OF PARCEL MAP L.A. NO. 3111, IN THE  CITY OF LOS ANGELES, COUNTY OF LOS ANGELES, STATE OF CALIFORNIA, AS PER MAP  FILED IN BOOK 72 PAGE 26 OF PARCEL MAPS, IN THE OFFICE OF THE COUNTY RECORDER OF SAID COUNTY, SHOWN AND DEFINED AS  UNIT  1  AND AIR SPACE A ON THE CONDOMINIUM PLAN, RECORDED DECEMBER 17, 1976 AS INSTRUMENT NO. 5334, OF OFFICIAL RECORDS OF SAID COUNTY.

PARCEL 2:

AN  UNDIVIDED  1/4  INTEREST IN AND TO PARCEL A OF SAID PARCEL MAP LOS ANGELES NO. 3111.

EXCEPT THEREFROM THOSE PORTIONS SHOWN AND DEFINED AS UNITS 1 TO  4 AND AIR SPACE A AND B ON SAID CONDOMINIUM PLAN.

## EXCLUSIONS FROM COVERAGE

The following matters are expressly excluded from the coverage of this policy and the Company will not pay loss or damage, costs, attorneys' fees or expenses which arise by reason of:

1. (a) Any law, ordinance or governmental regulation (including but not limited to building and zoning laws, ordinances, or regulations) restricting, regulating, prohibiting or relating to (i) the occupancy, use, or enjoyment of the land; (ii) the character, dimensions or location of any improvement now or hereafter erected on the land; (iii) a separation in ownership or a change in the dimensions or area of the land or any parcel of which the land is or was a part; or (iv) environmental protection, or the effect of any violation of these laws, ordinances or governmental regulations, except to the extent that a notice of the enforcement thereof or a notice of a defect, lien or encumbrance resulting from a violation or alleged violation affecting the land has been recorded in the public records at Date of Policy.

   (b) Any governmental police power not excluded by (a) above, except to the extent that a notice of the exercise thereof or a notice of a defect, lien or encumbrance resulting from a violation or alleged violation affecting the land has been recorded in the public records at Date of Policy.

2. Rights of eminent domain unless notice of the exercise thereof has been recorded in the public records at Date of Policy, but not excluding from coverage any taking which has occurred prior to Date of Policy which would be binding on the rights of a purchaser for value without knowledge.

3. Defects, liens, encumbrances, adverse claims or other matters:
   (a) created, suffered, assumed or agreed to by the insured claimant;
   (b) not known to the Company, not recorded in the public records at Date of Policy, but known to the insured claimant and not disclosed in writing to the Company by the insured claimant prior to the date the insured claimant became an insured under this policy;
   (c) resulting in no loss or damage to the insured claimant;
   (d) attaching or created subsequent to Date of Policy (except to the extent that this policy insures the priority of the lien of the insured mortgage over any statutory lien for services, labor or material or the extent insurance is afforded herein as to assessments for street improvements under construction or completed at Date of Policy); or
   (e) resulting in loss or damage which would not have been sustained if the insured claimant had paid value for the insured mortgage.

4. Unenforceability of the lien of the insured mortgage because of the inability or failure of the insured at Date of Policy, or the inability or failure of any subsequent owner of the indebtedness, to comply with applicable doing business laws of the state in which the land is situated.

5. Invalidity or unenforceability of the lien of the insured mortgage, or claim thereof, which arises out of the transaction evidenced by the insured mortgage and is based upon usury or any consumer credit protection or truth in lending law.

6. Any statutory lien for services, labor or materials (or the claim of priority of any statutory lien for services, labor or materials over the lien of the insured mortgage) arising from an improvement or work related to the land which is contracted for and commenced subsequent to Date of Policy and is not financed in whole or in part by proceeds of the indebtedness secured by the insured mortgage which at Date of Policy the insured has advanced or is obligated to advance.

7. Any claim, which arises out of the transaction creating the interest of the mortgagee insured by this policy, by reason of the operation of federal bankruptcy, state insolvency, or similar creditors' rights laws.

## CONDITIONS AND STIPULATIONS

### 1. DEFINITION OF TERMS.
The following terms when used in this policy mean:

(a) "insured": the insured named in Schedule A. The term "insured" also includes
   (i) the owner of the indebtedness secured by the insured mortgage and each successor in ownership of the indebtedness except a successor who is an obligor under the provisions of Section 12(c) of these Conditions and Stipulations (reserving, however, all rights and defenses as to any successor that the Company would have had against any predecessor insured, unless the successor acquired the indebtedness as a purchaser for value without knowledge of the asserted defect, lien, encumbrance, adverse claim or other matter insured against by this policy as affecting title to the estate or interest in the land);
   (ii) any governmental agency or governmental instrumentality which is an insurer or guarantor under an insurance contract or guaranty insuring or guaranteeing the indebtedness secured by the insured mortgage, or any part thereof, whether named as an insured herein or not;
   (iii) the parties designated in Section 2(a) of these Conditions and Stipulations.

(b) "insured claimant": an insured claiming loss or damage.

(c) "knowledge" or "known": actual knowledge, not constructive knowledge or notice which may be imputed to an insured by reason of the public records as defined in this policy or any other records which impart constructive notice of matters affecting the land.

(d) "land": the land described or referred to in Schedule (A), and improvements affixed thereto which by law constitute real property. The term "land" does not include any property beyond the lines of the area described or referred to in Schedule (A), nor any right, title, interest, estate or easement in abutting streets, roads, avenues, alleys, lanes, ways or waterways, but nothing herein shall modify or limit the extent to which a right of access to and from the land is insured by this policy.

(e) "mortgage": mortgage, deed of trust, trust deed, or other security instrument.

(f) "public records": records established under state statutes at Date of Policy for the purpose of imparting constructive notice of matters relating to real property to purchasers for value and without knowledge. With respect to Section 1(a)(iv) of the Exclusions From Coverage, "public records" shall also include environmental protection liens filed in the records of the clerk of the United States district court for the district in which the land is located.

(g) "unmarketability of the title": an alleged or apparent matter affecting the title to the land, not excluded or excepted from coverage, which would entitle a purchaser of the estate or interest described in Schedule A or the insured mortgage to be released from the obligation to purchase by virtue of a contractual condition requiring the delivery of marketable title.

### 2. CONTINUATION OF INSURANCE.
(a) After Acquisition of Title. The coverage of this policy shall continue in force as of Date of Policy in favor of (i) an insured who acquires all or any part of the estate or interest in the land by foreclosure, trustee's sale, conveyance in lieu of foreclosure, or other legal manner which discharges the lien of the insured mortgage; (ii) a transferee of the estate or interest so acquired from an insured corporation, provided the transferee is the parent or wholly-owned subsidiary of the insured corporation, and their corporate successors by operation of law and not by purchase, subject to any rights or defenses the Company may have against any predecessor insureds; and (iii) any governmental agency or governmental instrumentality which acquires all or any part of the estate or interest pursuant to a contract of insurance or guaranty insuring or guaranteeing the indebtedness secured by the insured mortgage.

settlement, and (ii) in any other lawful act which in the opinion of the Company may be necessary or desirable to establish the title to the estate or interest or the lien of the insured mortgage, as insured. If the Company is prejudiced by the failure of the insured to furnish the required cooperation, the Company's obligations to the insured under the policy shall terminate, including any liability or obligation to defend, prosecute, or continue any litigation, with regard to the matter or matters requiring such cooperation.

### 5. PROOF OF LOSS OR DAMAGE.
In addition to and after the notices required under Section 3 of these Conditions and Stipulations have been provided the Company, a proof of loss or damage signed and sworn to by the insured claimant shall be furnished to the Company within 90 days after the insured claimant shall ascertain the facts giving rise to the loss or damage. The proof of loss or damage shall describe the defect in, or lien or encumbrance on the title, or other matter insured against by this policy which constitutes the basis of loss or damage and shall state, to the extent possible, the basis of calculating the amount of the loss or damage. If the Company is prejudiced by the failure of the insured claimant to provide the required proof of loss or damage, the Company's obligations to the insured under the policy shall terminate, including any liability or obligation to defend, prosecute, or continue any litigation, with regard to the matter or matters requiring such proof of loss or damage.

In addition, the insured claimant may reasonably be required to submit to examination under oath by any authorized representative of the Company and shall produce for examination, inspection and copying, at such reasonable times and places as may be designated by any authorized representative of the Company, all records, books, ledgers, checks, correspondence and memoranda, whether bearing a date before or after Date of Policy, which reasonably pertain to the loss or damage. Further, if requested by any authorized representative of the Company, the insured claimant shall grant its permission, in writing, for any authorized representative of the Company to examine, inspect and copy all records, books, ledgers, checks, correspondence and memoranda in the custody or control of a third party, which reasonably pertain to the loss or damage. All information designated as confidential by the insured claimant provided to the Company pursuant to this Section shall not be disclosed to others unless, in the reasonable judgment of the Company, it is necessary in the administration of the claim. Failure of the insured claimant to submit for examination under oath, produce other reasonably requested information or grant permission to secure reasonably necessary information from third parties as required in this paragraph, unless prohibited by law or governmental regulation, shall terminate any liability of the Company under this policy as to that claim.

the insured was and continued to be obligated to advance at and after Date of Policy.

### 9. REDUCTION OF INSURANCE; REDUCTION OR TERMINATION OF LIABILITY.
(a) All payments under this policy, except payments made for costs, attorneys' fees and expenses, shall reduce the amount of the insurance pro tanto. However, any payments made prior to the acquisition of title to the estate or interest as provided in Section 2(a) of these Conditions and Stipulations shall not reduce pro tanto the amount of the insurance afforded under this policy except to the extent that the payments reduce the amount of the indebtedness secured by the insured mortgage.

(b) Payment in part by any person of the principal of the indebtedness, or any other obligation secured by the insured mortgage, or any voluntary partial satisfaction or release of the insured mortgage, to the extent of the payment, satisfaction or release, shall reduce the amount of insurance pro tanto. The amount of insurance may thereafter be increased by accruing interest and advances made to protect the lien of the insured mortgage and secured thereby, with interest thereon, provided in no event shall the amount of insurance be greater than the amount of insurance stated in Schedule A.

(c) Payment in full by any person or the voluntary satisfaction or release of the insured mortgage shall terminate all liability of the Company except as provided in Section 2(a) of these Conditions and Stipulations.

### 10. LIABILITY NONCUMULATIVE.
If the insured acquires title to the estate or interest in satisfaction of the indebtedness secured by the insured mortgage, or any part thereof, it is expressly understood that the amount of insurance under this policy shall be reduced by any amount the Company may pay under any policy insuring a mortgage to which exception is taken in Schedule B or to which the insured has agreed, assumed, or taken subject, or which is hereafter executed by an insured and which is a charge or lien on the estate or interest described or referred to in Schedule A, and the amount so paid shall be deemed a payment under this policy.

### 11. PAYMENT OF LOSS.
(a) No payment shall be made without producing this policy for endorsement of the payment unless the policy has been lost or destroyed, in which case proof of loss or destruction shall be furnished to the satisfaction of the Company.

(b) When liability and the extent of loss or damage has been definitely fixed in accordance with these Conditions and Stipulations, the loss or damage shall be payable within 30 days thereafter.

(b) **After Conveyance of Title.** The coverage of this policy shall continue in force as of Date of Policy in favor of an insured only so long as the insured retains an estate or interest in the land, or holds an indebtedness secured by a purchase money mortgage given by a purchaser from the insured, or only so long as the insured shall have liability by reason of covenants of warranty made by the insured in any transfer or conveyance of the estate or interest. This policy shall not continue in force in favor of any purchaser from the insured of either (i) an estate or interest in the land, or (ii) an indebtedness secured by a purchase money mortgage given to the insured.

(c) **Amount of Insurance:** The amount of insurance after the acquisition or after the conveyance shall in neither event exceed the least of:

(i) the amount of insurance stated in Schedule A;

(ii) the amount of the principal of the indebtedness secured by the insured mortgage as of Date of Policy, interest thereon, expenses of foreclosure, amounts advanced pursuant to the insured mortgage to assure compliance with laws or to protect the lien of the insured mortgage prior to the time of acquisition of the estate or interest in the land and secured thereby and reasonable amounts expended to prevent deterioration of improvements, but reduced by the amount of all payments made; or

(iii) the amount paid by any governmental agency or governmental instrumentality, if the agency or instrumentality is the insured claimant, in the acquisition of the estate or interest in satisfaction of its insurance contract or guaranty.

### 3. NOTICE OF CLAIM TO BE GIVEN BY INSURED CLAIMANT.

The insured shall notify the Company promptly in writing (i) in case of any litigation as set forth in Section 4(a) below, (ii) in case knowledge shall come to an insured hereunder of any claim of title or interest which is adverse to the title to the estate or interest or the lien of the insured mortgage, as insured, and which might cause loss or damage for which the Company may be liable by virtue of this policy, or (iii) if title to the estate or interest or the lien of the insured mortgage, as insured, is rejected as unmarketable. If prompt notice shall not be given to the Company, then as to the insured all liability of the Company shall terminate with regard to the matter or matters for which prompt notice is required; provided, however, that failure to notify the Company shall in no case prejudice the rights of any insured under this policy unless the Company shall be prejudiced by the failure and then only to the extent of the prejudice.

### 4. DEFENSE AND PROSECUTION OF ACTIONS; DUTY OF INSURED CLAIMANT TO COOPERATE.

(a) Upon written request by the insured and subject to the options contained in Section 6 of these Conditions and Stipulations, the Company, at its own cost and without unreasonable delay, shall provide for the defense of an insured in litigation in which any third party asserts a claim adverse to the title or interest as insured, but only as to those stated causes of action alleging a defect, lien or encumbrance or other matter insured against by this policy. The Company shall have the right to select counsel of its choice (subject to the right of the insured to object for reasonable cause) to represent the insured as to those stated causes of action and shall not be liable for and will not pay the fees of any other counsel. The Company will not pay any fees, costs or expenses incurred by the insured in the defense of those causes of action which allege matters not insured against by this policy.

(b) The Company shall have the right, at its own cost, to institute and prosecute any action or proceeding or to do any other act which in its opinion may be necessary or desirable to establish the title to the estate or interest or the lien of the insured mortgage, as insured, or to prevent or reduce loss or damage to the insured. The Company may take any appropriate action under the terms of this policy, whether or not it shall be liable hereunder, and shall not thereby concede liability or waive any provision of this policy. If the Company shall exercise its rights under this paragraph, it shall do so diligently.

(c) Whenever the Company shall have brought an action or interposed a defense as required or permitted by the provisions of this policy, the Company may pursue any litigation to final determination by a court of competent jurisdiction and expressly reserves the right, in its sole discretion, to appeal from any adverse judgment or order.

(d) In all cases where this policy permits or requires the Company to prosecute or provide for the defense of any action or proceeding, the insured shall secure to the Company the right to so prosecute or provide defense in the action or proceeding, and all appeals therein, and permit the Company to use, at its option, the name of the insured for this purpose. Whenever requested by the Company, the insured, at the Company's expense, shall give the Company all reasonable aid (i) in any action or proceeding, securing evidence, obtaining witnesses, prosecuting or defending the action or proceeding, or effecting

### 6. OPTIONS TO PAY OR OTHERWISE SETTLE CLAIMS; TERMINATION OF LIABILITY.

In case of a claim under this policy, the Company shall have the following options:

(a) To Pay or Tender Payment of the Amount of Insurance or to Purchase the Indebtedness.

(i) to pay or tender payment of the amount of insurance under this policy together with any costs, attorneys' fees and expenses incurred by the insured claimant, which were authorized by the Company, up to the time of payment or tender of payment and which the Company is obligated to pay; or

(ii) to purchase the indebtedness secured by the insured mortgage for the amount owing thereon together with any costs, attorneys' fees and expenses incurred by the insured claimant which were authorized by the Company up to the time of purchase and which the Company is obligated to pay.

If the Company offers to purchase the indebtedness as herein provided, the owner of the indebtedness shall transfer, assign, and convey the indebtedness and the insured mortgage, together with any collateral security, to the Company upon payment therefor.

Upon the exercise by the Company of either of the options provided for in paragraphs a(i) or (ii), all liability and obligations to the insured under this policy, other than to make the payment required in those paragraphs, shall terminate, including any liability or obligation to defend, prosecute, or continue any litigation, and the policy shall be surrendered to the Company for cancellation.

(b) To Pay or Otherwise Settle With Parties Other than the Insured or With the Insured Claimant.

(i) to pay or otherwise settle with other parties for or in the name of an insured claimant any claim insured against under this policy, together with any costs, attorneys' fees and expenses incurred by the insured claimant which were authorized by the Company up to the time of payment and which the Company is obligated to pay; or

(ii) to pay or otherwise settle with the insured claimant the loss or damage provided for under this policy, together with any costs, attorneys' fees and expenses incurred by the insured claimant which were authorized by the Company up to the time of payment and which the Company is obligated to pay.

Upon the exercise by the Company of either of the options provided for in paragraphs b(i) or (ii), the Company's obligations to the insured under this policy for the claimed loss or damage, other than the payments required to be made, shall terminate, including any liability or obligation to defend, prosecute or continue any litigation.

### 7. DETERMINATION AND EXTENT OF LIABILITY.

This policy is a contract of indemnity against actual monetary loss or damage sustained or incurred by the insured claimant who has suffered loss or damage by reason of matters insured against by this policy and only to the extent herein described.

(a) The liability of the Company under this policy shall not exceed the least of:

(i) the amount of insurance stated in Schedule A, or, if applicable, the amount of insurance as defined in Section 2 (c) of these Conditions and Stipulations;

(ii) the amount of the unpaid principal indebtedness secured by the insured mortgage as limited or provided under Section 8 of these Conditions and Stipulations or as reduced under Section 9 of these Conditions and Stipulations, at the time the loss or damage insured against by this policy occurs, together with interest thereon; or

(iii) the difference between the value of the insured estate or interest as insured and the value of the insured estate or interest subject to the defect, lien or encumbrance insured against by this policy.

(b) In the event the insured has acquired the estate or interest in the manner described in Section 2(a) of these Conditions and Stipulations or has conveyed the title, then the liability of the Company shall continue as set forth in Section 7(a) of these Conditions and Stipulations.

(c) The Company will pay only those costs, attorneys' fees and expenses incurred in accordance with Section 4 of these Conditions and Stipulations.

### 8. LIMITATION OF LIABILITY.

(a) If the Company establishes the title, or removes the alleged defect, lien or encumbrance, or cures the lack of a right of access to or from the land, or cures the claim of unmarketability of title, or otherwise establishes the lien of the insured mortgage, all as insured, in a reasonably diligent manner by any method, including litigation and the completion of any appeals therefrom, it shall have fully performed its obligations with respect to that matter and shall not be liable for any loss or damage caused thereby.

(b) In the event of any litigation, including litigation by the Company or with the Company's consent, the Company shall have no liability for loss or damage until there has been a final determination by a court of competent jurisdiction, and disposition of all appeals therefrom, adverse to the title or to the lien of the insured mortgage, as insured.

(c) The Company shall not be liable for loss or damage to any insured for liability voluntarily assumed by the insured in settling any claim or suit without the prior written consent of the Company.

(d) The Company shall not be liable for:

(i) any indebtedness created subsequent to Date of Policy except for advances made to protect the lien of the insured mortgage and secured thereby and reasonable amounts expended to prevent deterioration of improvements; or

(ii) construction loan advances made subsequent to Date of Policy, except construction loan advances made subsequent to Date of Policy for the purpose of financing in whole or in part the construction of an improvement to the land which at Date of Policy were secured by the insured mortgage and which

### 12. SUBROGATION UPON PAYMENT OR SETTLEMENT.

(a) The Company's Right of Subrogation.

Whenever the Company shall have settled and paid a claim under this policy, all right of subrogation shall vest in the Company unaffected by any act of the insured claimant.

The Company shall be subrogated to and be entitled to all rights and remedies which the insured claimant would have had against any person or property in respect to the claim had this policy not been issued. If requested by the Company, the insured claimant shall transfer to the Company all rights and remedies against any person or property necessary in order to perfect this right of subrogation. The insured claimant shall permit the Company to sue, compromise or settle in the name of the insured claimant and to use the name of the insured claimant in any transaction or litigation involving these rights or remedies.

If a payment on account of a claim does not fully cover the loss of the insured claimant, the Company shall be subrogated to all rights and remedies of the insured claimant after the insured claimant shall have recovered its principal, interest, and costs of collection.

(b) The Insured's Rights and Limitations.

Notwithstanding the foregoing, the owner of the indebtedness secured by the insured mortgage, provided the priority of the lien of the insured mortgage or its enforceability is not affected, may release or substitute the personal liability of any debtor or guarantor, or extend or otherwise modify the terms of payment, or release a portion of the estate or interest from the lien of the insured mortgage, or release any collateral security for the indebtedness.

When the permitted acts of the insured claimant occur and the insured has knowledge of any claim of title or interest adverse to the title to the estate or interest or the priority or enforceability of the lien of the insured mortgage, as insured, the Company shall be required to pay only that part of any losses insured against by this policy which shall exceed the amount, if any, lost to the Company by reason of the impairment by the insured claimant of the Company's right of subrogation.

(c) The Company's Rights Against Non-insured Obligors.

The Company's right of subrogation against non-insured obligors shall exist and shall include, without limitation, the rights of the insured to indemnities, guaranties, other policies of insurance or bonds, notwithstanding any terms or conditions contained in those instruments which provide for subrogation rights by reason of this policy.

The Company's right of subrogation shall not be avoided by acquisition of the insured mortgage by an obligor (except an obligor described in Section 1(a)(ii) of these Conditions and Stipulations) who acquires the insured mortgage as a result of an indemnity, guarantee, other policy of insurance, or bond and the obligor will not be an insured under this policy, notwithstanding Section 1(a)(i) of these Conditions and Stipulations.

### 13. ARBITRATION.

Unless prohibited by applicable law, either the Company or the insured may demand arbitration pursuant to the Title Insurance Arbitration Rules of the American Arbitration Association. Arbitrable matters may include, but are not limited to, any controversy or claim between the Company and the insured arising out of or relating to this policy, any service of the Company in connection with its issuance or the breach of a policy provision or other obligation. All arbitrable matters when the Amount of Insurance is $1,000,000 or less shall be arbitrated at the option of either the Company or the insured. All arbitrable matters when the Amount of Insurance is in excess of $1,000,000 shall be arbitrated only when agreed to by both the Company and the insured. Arbitration pursuant to this policy and under the Rules in effect on the date the demand for arbitration is made or, at the option of the insured, the Rules in effect at Date of Policy shall be binding upon the parties. The award may include attorneys' fees only if the laws of the state in which the land is located permit a court to award attorneys' fees to a prevailing party. Judgment upon the award rendered by the Arbitrator(s) may be entered in any court having jurisdiction thereof.

The law of the situs of the land shall apply to an arbitration under the Title Insurance Arbitration Rules.

A copy of the Rules may be obtained from the Company upon request.

### 14. LIABILITY LIMITED TO THIS POLICY; POLICY ENTIRE CONTRACT.

(a) This policy together with all endorsements, if any, attached hereto by the Company is the entire policy and contract between the insured and the Company. In interpreting any provision of this policy, this policy shall be construed as a whole.

(b) Any claim of loss or damage, whether or not based on negligence, and which arises out of the status of the lien of the insured mortgage or of the title to the estate or interest covered hereby or by any action asserting such claim, shall be restricted to this policy.

(c) No amendment of or endorsement to this policy can be made except by a writing endorsed hereon or attached hereto signed by either the President, a Vice President, the Secretary, an Assistant Secretary, or validating officer or authorized signatory of the Company.

### 15. SEVERABILITY.

In the event any provision of this policy is held invalid or unenforceable under applicable law, the policy shall be deemed not to include that provision and all other provisions shall remain in full force and effect.

### 16. NOTICES, WHERE SENT.

All notices required to be given the Company and any statement in writing required to be furnished the Company shall include the number of this policy and shall be addressed to the Company at 114 East Fifth Street, Santa Ana, California 92701, or to the office which issued this policy.

Purchasers should note that there are still certain exceptions to the CLTA standard policy and even to the ALTA extended policy. There is no insurance coverage for the following:

1. Defects known to the insured at the time the policy was issued, but not designated in writing, and

2. Government regulations regarding occupancy and use (zoning).

*A CLTA standard title insurance policy does NOT require an on-site inspection, but an ALTA extended policy does.*

## C. ALTA-R (One-to-Four Residential Units)

The **ALTA-R POLICY** *is recommended by title companies for one-to-four unit owner-occupied residential dwellings.* It doesn't include a survey because the property lines are already established by a recorded subdivision map. Since the title company does not have to do a survey, it gives the buyer more coverage for the same price. The CAR® California Residential Purchase Agreement and Joint Escrow Instructions form includes the ALTA-R as the preferred residential title policy choice.

## D. WHO PAYS TITLE INSURANCE FEES?

Title insurance fees are a part of the escrow closing costs. Title insurance companies are required to publish rate schedules and charge according to the published rates. Who assumes payment of the fees, however, varies depending upon the area in which one lives.

In Southern California it is customary for the seller to pay the title fees, whereas in Northern California it is usually the buyer who assumes the cost. Because there is no law determining who must pay, it should be stated in the purchase agreement to prevent any misunderstanding. This, however, covers only the standard CLTA policy. The additional cost of the ALTA extended policy is usually charged to the party purchasing the property (the buyer).

### E. TITLE INSURANCE DISCLOSURE

In any escrow transaction for the purchase or exchange of real property where a title insurance policy will not be issued to the buyer (or exchanger), the buyer (or exchanger) must sign and acknowledge a disclosure statement stating that it may be advisable to obtain title insurance.

# VIII. Real Estate Settlement Procedures Act (RESPA)

*RESPA (enforced by HUD) allows borrowers to shop for settlement services. The law covers first loans on one-to-four unit residential dwellings.*

The **REAL ESTATE SETTLEMENT PROCEDURES ACT (RESPA)** *is a law for the sale or transfer of one-to-four residential units requiring: 1) specific procedures and 2) forms for settlements (closing costs) involving most home loans from financial institutions with federally insured deposits, including FHA and VA loans.*

This law, although amended several times, states that the closing settlement cost of a real estate transaction must be made known to the borrower, on or before the settlement date, although, at the buyer's request, it must be provided one business day before escrow closes. Before this law was passed, buyers were unaware of the exact amount needed until the actual escrow closing day. Sometimes the buyers were surprised to find that more money than expected was needed to complete the procedure. The current law alleviates this problem.

*Under RESPA, a lender has three business days from the date the lender receives the borrower's loan application to provide a booklet entitled "Settlement Costs and You."*

Other provisions required by the Real Estate Settlement Procedures Act include the following:

1. At the time of loan application, or within three business days, the lender must give a good faith estimate of the total closing charges to the borrower.
2. At the same time, the lender must furnish the buyer with an information booklet.
3. The escrow agent must give a uniform settlement statement to the borrower, the seller, and the lender. **Figure 7-11** illustrates the settlement statement. It must be furnished by the time of settlement, except when the borrower waives it, or in areas where the HUD (Department of Housing and Urban Development) permits a later date for supplying it.

*The Uniform Settlement Statement must be delivered or mailed to the borrower on or before the date of settlement, at no charge. The buyer can request it one business day before closing.*

4. Individuals are prohibited from receiving kickbacks and unearned fees. Payments to cooperating brokerages and referral agreements between brokers are exempt.

# Figure 7-11

| A. | B. TYPE OF LOAN |
|---|---|
| U.S. DEPARTMENT OF HOUSING AND URBAN DEVELOPMENT | 1. [ ] FHA  2. [ ] FmHA  3. [X] Conv. unis |
| | 4. [ ] VA  5. [ ] Conv. ins |
| SETTLEMENT STATEMENT | 6. ESCROW NUMBER: 1-10533 · 7. LOAN NUMBER: |
| | 8. MORTGAGE INSURANCE NUMBER: |

THIS NOTE IS FURNISHED TO GIVE YOU A STATEMENT OF THE ACTUAL SETTLEMENT COSTS.  AMOUNTS PAID TO AND BY THE SETTLEMENT AGENT ARE SHOWN.  ITEMS MARKED "(P.O.C.)" WERE PAID OUTSIDE OF THE CLOSING;  THEY ARE SHOWN HERE FOR INFORMATIONAL PURPOSES AND ARE NOT INCLUDED IN THE TOTALS.

| D. NAME OF BORROWER: | E. NAME OF SELLER: | F. NAME OF LENDER: |
|---|---|---|
| JOHN BUYER | JOHN SELLER | GET SMART SAVINGS AND LOAN |
| JANE BUYER | JANE SELLER | 123 Lending Lane |
| 123 Purchase Lane | | Beverly Hills, CA  91020 |
| Glendale, CA | | |

| G. PROPERTY LOCATION: | H. SETTLEMENT AGENT: COLONIAL ESCROW, INC. | I. SETTLEMENT DATE: |
|---|---|---|
| 123 PURCHASE LANE | PLACE OF SETTLEMENT: | |
| GLENDALE, CA | 601 EAST GLENOAKS BLVD. SUITE 210 | 06/01/20 |
| | GLENDALE, CA  91207 | |
| | P.O. BOX 433 GLENDALE, CA  91209-0433 | |

| J. SUMMARY OF BORROWER'S TRANSACTIONS | | K. SUMMARY OF SELLER'S TRANSACTIONS | |
|---|---|---|---|
| **100. GROSS AMOUNT DUE FROM BORROWER** | | **400. GROSS AMOUNT DUE TO SELLER** | |
| 101. CONTRACT SALES PRICE | 800,000.00 | 401. CONTRACT SALES PRICE | 800,000.00 |
| 102. PERSONAL PROPERTY | | 402. PERSONAL PROPERTY | |
| 103. SETTL. CHRGS. TO BORROWER (LINE 1400) | 10,122.01 | 403. DEPOSITS | |
| 104. | | 404. | |
| 105. | | 405. | |
| Adjustments: items paid by seller in advance | | Adjustments: items paid by seller in advance | |
| 106. CITY/TOWN TAXES | | 406. CITY/TOWN TAXES | |
| 107. COUNTY TAXES | | 407. COUNTY TAXES | |
| 108. ASSESSMENTS | | 408. ASSESSMENTS | |
| 109. TAXES : 06/01/20 TO 07/01/20 | 666.67 | 409. TAXES : 06/01/20 TO 07/01/20 | 666.67 |
| 110. | | 410. | |
| 111. | | 411. | |
| 112. | | 412. | |
| 120. GROSS AMOUNT DUE FROM BORROWER | 810,788.68 | 420. GROSS AMOUNT DUE TO SELLER | 800,666.67 |
| **200. AMOUNTS PAID BY OR IN BEHALF OF BORROWER** | | **500. REDUCTIONS IN AMOUNT DUE TO SELLER** | |
| 201. DEPOSITS | 91,000.00 | 501. EXCESS DEPOSIT | |
| 202. PRINCIPAL AMOUNT OF NEW LOAN(S) | 640,000.00 | 502. SETTL. CHRGS. TO SELLER (LINE 1400) | 54,845.00 |
| 203. EXISTING LOAN(S) TAKEN SUBJECT TO | | 503. EXISTING LOAN(S) TAKEN SUBJECT TO | |
| 204. NEW 2ND TRUST DEED | 80,000.00 | 504. PAYOFF TO MOST SUPERIOR SAVINGS AND L | 490,000.00 |
| 205. | | 505. INTEREST FROM 05/01/20 TO 06/01/20 | 4,161.64 |
| 206. | | 506. FORWARDING FEE | 50.00 |
| 207. | | 507. RECONVEYANCE FEE | 60.00 |
| 208. | | 508. NEW 2ND TRUST DEED | 80,000.00 |
| 209. | | 509. | |
| Adjustments: Items unpaid by seller | | Adjustments: Items unpaid by seller | |
| 210. CITY/TOWN TAXES | | 510. CITY/TOWN TAXES | |
| 211. COUNTY TAXES | | 511. COUNTY TAXES | |
| 212. ASSESSMENTS | | 512. ASSESSMENTS | |
| 213. | | 513. | |
| 214. | | 514. | |
| 215. | | 515. | |
| 216. | | 516. | |
| 217. | | 517. | |
| 218. | | 518. | |
| 219. | | 519. | |
| 220. TOTAL PAID BY/FOR BORROWER | 811,000.00 | 520. TOTAL REDUCTION AMOUNT DUE SELLER | 629,116.64 |
| **300. CASH AT SETTLEMENT FROM/TO BORROWER** | | **600. CASH AT SETTLEMENT TO/FROM SELLER** | |
| 301. Gross amounts due from borrower (line 120) | 810,788.68 | 601. Gross amount due to seller (line 420) | 800,666.67 |
| 302. Less amounts paid by/for borrower (line 220) | 811,000.00 | 602. Less reductions in amount due seller (line 520) | 629,116.64 |
| 303. CASH FROM[ ] TO[X] BORROWER | 211.32 | 603. CASH FROM[ ] TO[X] SELLER | 171,550.03 |

207

## L. SETTLEMENT STATEMENT

| | PAID FROM BORROWER'S FUNDS AT SETTLEMENT | PAID FROM SELLER'S FUNDS AT SETTLEMENT |
|---|---|---|
| **700. TOTAL SALES/BROKER'S COMMISSION** | | |
| BASED ON PRICE $ 800,000.00 @ 6.00% | | |
| 701.BROKER: J. Q. SMART  48,000.00 | | |
| 702. | | |
| 703. | | |
| 704.COMMISSIONS PAID AT SETTLEMENT | | 48,000.00 |
| **800. ITEMS PAYABLE IN CONNECTION WITH LOAN** | | |
| 801.LOAN FEE | 6,400.00 | |
| 802.LOAN DISCOUNT | | |
| 803.APPRAISAL | 350.00 | |
| 804.CREDIT REPORT | 45.00 | |
| 805.LENDER'S INSPECTION FEE | | |
| 806.MORTGAGE INSURANCE APPLICATION FEE | | |
| 807.ASSUMPTION FEE | | |
| 808.TAX SERVICE | 89.00 | |
| 809.DOCUMENT FEE | 250.00 | |
| 810. | | |
| 811. | | |
| **900. ITEMS REQUIRED BY LENDER TO BE PAID IN ADVANCE** | | |
| 901.INTEREST AT 7.5000% FROM 05/31/20 TO 06/01/20 | 131.51 | |
| 902.MORTGAGE INSURANCE | | |
| 903.PROPERTY INSURANCE, INC. FOR FIRE INSURANCE | 1,000.00 | |
| 904. | | |
| 905. | | |
| **1000. RESERVES DEPOSITED WITH LENDER** | | |
| 1001.HAZARD INSURANCE | | |
| 1002.MORTGAGE INSURANCE | | |
| 1003.CITY PROPERTY TAXES | | |
| 1004.COUNTY PROPERTY TAXES | | |
| 1005.ANNUAL ASSESSMENTS | | |
| 1006. | | |
| 1007. | | |
| 1008. | | |
| **1100. ESCROW AND TITLE CHARGES** | | |
| 1101.ESCROW FEE TO COLONIAL ESCROW, INC. | 900.00 | 900.00 |
| 1102.ABSTRACT OR TITLE SEARCH | | |
| 1103.TITLE EXAMINATION | | |
| 1104.TITLE INSURANCE BINDER | | |
| 1105.DOCUMENT PREPARATION TO COLONIAL ESCROW, INC. | | |
| 1106.MESSENGER FEE TO COLONIAL ESCROW, INC. | 50.00 | |
| 1107.ATTORNEY'S FEES | | |
| 1108.TITLE POLICY TO AMERICAN COAST TITLE | 628.50 | 2,165.00 |
| 1109.  LENDERS COVERAGE  $ 640,000.00 | | |
| 1110.  OWNERS  COVERAGE  $ 800,000.00 | | |
| 1111.PROCESSING DEMANDS TO COLONIAL ESCROW, INC. | | 35.00 |
| 1112.DOCUMENT FEE TO COLONIAL ESCROW, INC. | | 85.00 |
| 1113.LOAN TIE IN FEE TO COLONIAL ESCROW, INC. | 125.00 | |
| **1200. GOVERNMENT RECORDING AND TRANSFER CHARGES** | | |
| 1201.RECORDING FEES:DEED $8.00;MORTGAGE $20.00;RELEASES $5.00 | 28.00 | 5.00 |
| 1202.DOCUMENTARY TRANSFER TAX | | 880.00 |
| 1203.STATE TAX/STAMPS | | |
| 1204. | | |
| 1205. | | |
| **1300. ADDITIONAL SETTLEMENT CHARGES** | | |
| 1301.SURVEY | | |
| 1302.PEST CONTROL, INC. FOR TERMITE REPORT/WORK | | 1,000.00 |
| 1303.SUB ESCROW FEE TO AMERICAN COAST TITLE | 75.00 | 75.00 |
| 1304.TITLE ENDORSEMENT FEE(S) TO AMERICAN COAST TITLE | 50.00 | |
| 1305.STREET ASSESSMENT BOND TO AMERICAN COAST TITLE | | 1,300.00 |
| 1306.HOME WARRANTY, INC. FOR HOME PROTECTION POLICY | | 400.00 |
| 1307. | | |
| **1400. TOTAL SETTLEMENT CHARGES** | | |
| (ENTER ON LINES 102 SECTION J AND 501, SECTION K) | 10,122.01 | 54,845.00 |

5. No seller may require a buyer to purchase title insurance from any particular company as a condition of sale.

*There are penalties for "kickbacks" and unearned fees. The seller may request a specific title insurer, but only the buyer can require a specific insurance company.*

It is not permissible for a title company to accept or pay referral fees to or from an agent.

*It is permissible for a title company to refer clients to a real estate broker.*

# IX. California Escrow Association

The California Escrow Association has developed a statewide program to promote professional service and educational opportunities for its members. Many community colleges have also adopted certificate courses for escrow personnel and real estate brokers to provide a better understanding of the highly technical escrow field.

## X. CHAPTER SUMMARY

An **escrow** is created when a written agreement (usually from a **Purchase Agreement**) instructs a **neutral third party** to hold funds and proceed only when all the agreed to conditions have been completed. An escrow is strongly recommended in connection with real estate sales, loan agreements, or exchanges made in California. But escrows are required for liquor license transfers, security sales, and court ordered transfers (**probate sales**).

A valid escrow requires: 1) signed escrow instructions (a written escrow contract) between the buying and selling parties; 2) a neutral escrow company acting as a dual agent for the buyer and the seller; and 3) conditional delivery of funds until the escrow conditions are completed.

An **escrow holder** can be a corporation, an attorney, or a real estate broker acting as a real estate agent in the transaction. An escrow officer, holder, or agent, though not licensed by the state, must be an employee of a licensed escrow company acting as agent. The **duties of an escrow company** include **conditional delivery of funds** until escrow conditions are met, **confidentiality of escrow instructions**, and **acting as a deposit holder** until funds are disbursed when escrow closes.

A real estate broker can handle escrow for a fee, but only if the broker acts as a real estate agent in that transaction, or if the broker is a principal (buyer or seller).

The escrow is complete when: 1) all escrow conditions of the parties have been met and 2) the parties have received an accounting of the procedure. Escrows can be terminated in three ways: by **completion**, **mutual agreement**, or court action **interpleader**.

**Amendments** changing escrow instructions must be signed by both parties. The seller cannot rescind escrow without consent of the buyer. **Selection of an escrow company and officer is negotiated between buyer and seller, but the salesperson may recommend an escrow company**. It is illegal for a real estate licensee to receive a **kickback** for solicitation of escrow business.

**Escrow instructions** for the sale of a house are formal instructions drawn from the information contained in the purchase agreement. Most escrows for home sales include getting a new loan and the payoff or assumption of an old one. The **payoff demand statement** details the lender's calculations of the amounts owed for the purpose of paying off the loan in full. If a loan is to be assumed, a **beneficiary's (lender's) statement** under a deed of trust provides information, such as the unpaid balance, monthly payment, and interest rate.

**Closing escrow** is the process of signing various documents, transfer of documents, recordation of deed and trust deeds, and distribution of funds. The **closing date** is the date that the documents are recorded.

**Proration** is the process of dividing expenses or income proportionately between buyer and seller to the precise date that escrow closes, or an agreed date. Items commonly prorated include: **property taxes (credit to seller)**, **fire insurance**, **interest**, and **rents (debit to seller)**. All escrow companies use **30 days as a "base month."** The two important dates in determining proration amounts are the dates escrow closes and when the item is paid.

A **Structural Pest Control Report** (termite report) is usually a condition of the escrow. This report is given by a licensed pest control company to identify any wood-destroying pests or conditions likely to cause pest infestation. It also states the conditions and correction costs of any pest, dry rot, excessive moisture, earth-wood contacts, or fungus damage in accessible areas of a structure. Payment for the report is negotiated between parties, but is usually made by the seller, as indicated in the allocation of costs signed by both parties. **Required repairs** are usually paid for by the seller, then a notice of work completed is obtained. But **recommended repairs** are negotiated between the parties.

Most lenders require a pest control inspection before making a loan. Every VA and FHA loan application requires one. A copy of the pest control report and **notice of work completed** must be delivered to the buyer if it's a condition of the purchase agreement or financing.

**Fire insurance** is a necessity. A lending institution requires fire coverage for the amount of its loan. **California Standard Form Fire Insurance Policy** insures the dwelling **only against fire and lightning**. An **Extended Coverage Endorsement** insures against windstorms, explosions, hail, aircraft, smoke, riot, and vehicles not attributed to a strike or civil commotion. Buyers usually obtain new fire insurance policies. A **coinsurance clause** in a policy requires that 80% of the value of a commercial dwelling be insured or only a percentage of the insurance value will be payable.

**Chain of title** is the recorded public history of a specific property. Information about people and their real property is stored in computers in a grantor-grantee index and referred to as a **title plant**. Title insurance companies examine chain of title records, review any risks not found in public records, seek legal interpretation of deeds or other real estate documents, help the seller correct any defects, and insure marketable title to the property.

A **preliminary title report** is the first step in a title search. It shows the condition of title before a sale or loan transaction.

Title insurance policies in California include the **California Land Title Association (CLTA) Policy**, the more comprehensive **American Land Title Association (ALTA) Policy**, or the **ALTA-R Policy**.

The **CLTA policy** is the most common and basic title insurance policy. The standard CLTA policy insures only the lender, unless the owner pays for "owner" coverage. It protects against lack of capacity of a party in the chain of title, deeds not properly delivered, and forgery.

The **ATLA policy** is an extended coverage policy that insures against many exclusions in the standard coverage (CLTA) policy. The ALTA policy (which includes a competent survey or physical inspection) is usually required by California lenders and out of state lenders unable to make personal inspections of the property. Neither ALTA nor CLTA covers unwritten **title defects known** to the insured at the time of policy issuance or **zoning changes**.

The **ALTA-R policy** is recommended by title companies for one-to-four owner-occupied residential dwellings. It offers more coverage for the same money because no survey is necessary.

Payment for the CLTA policy insurance fees is negotiable, but the purchase agreement must state who pays the insurance fees to prevent any misunderstanding. In Southern California, the seller customarily pays for the CLTA policy. In Northern California, the buyer pays. The fees to upgrade the coverage from a CLTA to an ALTA policy are paid by the buyer in either part of the state.

Escrow service fees are usually split 50-50 in Southern California. The buyer usually pays in Northern California.

The **Real Estate Settlement Procedures Act (RESPA)** involves most federally insured home loans. It is a federal law relating to the sale or transfer of one-to-four residential units requiring specific procedures and forms for settlements closing costs. All settlement closing costs must be disclosed to the borrower one business day before escrow closes.

## XI. TERMINOLOGY

A. ALTA
B. Chain of Title
C. CLTA
D. Coinsurance
E. Date of Closing

F. Escrow
G. Escrow Instructions
H. Escrow Officer
I. Payoff Demand Statement
J. Pest Control Report

K. Preliminary Title Report
L. Proration
M. RESPA
N. Title Insurance
O. Title Plant

1.____ Insurance to protect a real property owner or lender up to a specified amount against certain types of loss; e.g., defective or unmarketable title.

2.____ The process of depositing instruments, funds, and instructions, with a third neutral party who finalizes the transaction.

3.____ A history of conveyances and encumbrances affecting the title from the time the original patent was granted, or as far back as records are available, used to determine how title came to be vested in current owner.

4.____ Adjustments of interest, taxes, and insurance, etc., on a prorated basis as of the closing or agreed upon date.

5.____ The person at the escrow company who handles the paperwork of the escrow.

6.____ The written instructions of the escrow, prepared by the escrow officer and approved by both the buyer and the seller.

7.____ The most all inclusive title insurance policy; it requires a property survey and is usually required by most lenders.

8.____ The minimum standard title insurance policy in California that does NOT require a property survey.

9.____ The requirement by a lender that a property be insured up to its full value, or only a proportion of any loss will be reimbursed.

10.____ A report from a structural pest control company stating the termite or other type of pest damage found and the cost of repairing it.

11.____ The date documents are recorded and title insurance is written.

12.____ A federal statute requiring disclosure of certain costs in the sale of residential property.

13.____ A report showing the condition of title before a sale or loan transaction.

14.____ Written instructions by a lender stating and demanding the amount necessary to pay off a loan.

15.____ A filing of all recorded information to real property.

## XII. CHAPTER QUIZ

1. The Escrow Act is found in the:

    a. Business Code.
    b. Civil Code.
    c. Administrative Code.
    d. Financial Code.

2. An interpleader action is:

    a. a court action.
    b. a formal written protest to the seller.
    c. a formal written apology to the buyer.
    d. none of the above.

3. If there is a disagreement between the buyer and seller during escrow, the escrow officer may disburse funds:

    a. as a result of a judgment between the buyer and seller.
    b. if the parties to the escrow agree.
    c. if a binding arbitrator settles the matter.
    d. all of the above would allow the escrow officer to disburse funds.

4. Which of the following would not be prorated in escrow?

    a. Rents
    b. Impounds
    c. Title insurance premium
    d. Property taxes

5. A partial premium refund on fire insurance is called:

    a. a short rate.
    b. an impound.
    c. title insurance.
    d. all of the above.

6. Every recorded change of ownership and/or claim of ownership on a property is in the:

    a. grant deed.
    b. abstract of title.
    c. title insurance policy.
    d. preliminary title report.

7. What type of title insurance policy is most often used?

    a. State coverage
    b. Standard coverage (CLTA)
    c. ALTA
    d. Extended-coverage

8. A loan officer gives a broker a small referral fee in return for his referral of a client looking to purchase a single-family home. Under RESPA:

    a. this is legal, if disclosures are made to all parties.
    b. this is forbidden.
    c. this is illegal if this fact is not disclosed to the buyer.
    d. this is legal.

9. Under RESPA, a lender cannot charge for:

    a. appraisal fees.
    b. loan documents.
    c. credit reports.
    d. uniform settlements statements (HUD-1).

10. RESPA requires that the Uniform Settlement Statement be delivered or mailed to the borrower no later than:

    a. at or before the date of settlement.
    b. 3 days after signing the loan application.
    c. at the time the mortgage loan disclosure statement is signed.
    d. at the time the loan application is made.

**ANSWERS:** 1. d; 2. a; 3. d; 4. c; 5. a; 6. b; 7. b; 8. b; 9. d; 10. a

# CHAPTER 8
## Real Estate Finance

*The Financial crisis was caused by lax loan standards.*

Real estate is expensive compared to most other possessions. A person or business seldom has enough cash to buy the real estate outright, and therefore must borrow the necessary money to help finance the transaction. If a buyer makes a cash down payment of 20% for example, he or she must then obtain a loan for the remaining 80% of the purchase price. Most buyers must finance at least part of the purchase, so a good rule to remember is, "If you can't finance a property, you probably can't sell it later." If a property can't be easily financed, don't waste time with it: find another, more easily financed property.

*To utilize the "principle of leverage,"an investor would use the maximum amount of borrowed money.*

Even buyers with large amounts of cash rarely purchase real estate outright. An investment principle known as "leverage" favors buying real estate using borrowed funds. *LEVERAGE is the practice of purchasing real estate using a small amount of your own money and a larger proportion of borrowed funds.* The more money borrowed to buy a property, the greater the leverage.

Employing leverage makes it possible for real estate investors to reap the same profits as those buying entirely with their own funds without having to tie up as much cash. This chapter explores the different ways in which real estate can be financed. Each type of financing instrument will be discussed, including the many clauses in the note and trust deed.

## I. Hypothecation (Property as Collateral)

Real estate finance is based on the principle of hypothecation. To *HYPOTHECATE is to provide title to a property as security for a loan without giving up possession.* Although one can hypothecate or "pledge" stocks as security for a bank loan, most real property buyers hypothecate their property as security for a real estate loan. In neither case does the person surrender the use or possession of the property. The hypothecation principle is fundamental to the major instruments of real estate finance: the trust deed in California and the less common mortgage. Each of these instruments uses the promissory note as the primary evidence of debt, which creates a lien on the property.

*Interest rates will remain at relatively low levels, enabling more affordable (lower for the area) home loan payments.*

# CHAPTER 8

# II. The Promissory Note

A **PROMISSORY NOTE** *is the basic instrument used to **evidence** the obligation or debt.* It is an unconditional promise in writing by one person to another to pay on demand, or over a fixed determinable time, a certain sum of money. Borrowers hypothecate real property as security for payment of the promissory note. The trust deed or mortgage is used with the promissory note to hypothecate the property as security for the note.

A loan payment on a note is made up of principal and interest. **PRINCIPAL** *is the dollar amount of the loan.* Commonly we call it the amount of money remaining to be paid off on a promissory note (the loan balance). **INTEREST** *is the rent charged for the use of money.*

*Interest on most real estate loans is "simple interest," paid only on the principal amount owed.*

**Figure 8-1** illustrates the three basic kinds of promissory notes that affect real estate financing.

219

**Figure 8-1**

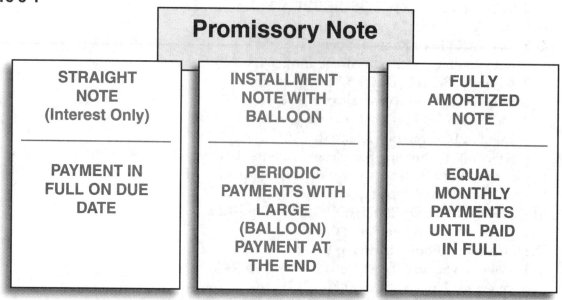

## A. STRAIGHT NOTE (Interest Only)

A *STRAIGHT NOTE is a promissory note in which a borrower repays the principal in one lump sum, at maturity, while interest is paid in installments or at maturity, all due at once.* The parties could agree that interest be paid monthly, quarterly, annually, or any agreed-to term, but the principal is a lump sum payment. In real estate, this type of note is usually for relatively small amounts of money being borrowed for a short time.

## B. INSTALLMENT NOTE WITH A BALLOON PAYMENT

An *INSTALLMENT NOTE WITH A BALLOON PAYMENT (PARTIALLY AMORTIZED NOTE) is a promissory note with periodic payments of principal and interest and a large payment at the end (maturity date or due date).* This type of note and the straight note are usually in the form of secondary financing (second trust deeds). See **Figure 8-2**.

## C. FULLY AMORTIZED INSTALLMENT NOTE
### (Level Payment – Most Common)

A *FULLY AMORTIZED INSTALLMENT NOTE is a promissory note for which both the principal and interest are paid in equal installments until the debt is paid in full.* Installments make it easy to pay off a note, and there is no balloon payment at the end of the loan period.

For real estate financing in California, the fully amortized installment note is the most commonly used type of note. Loan payments are either fixed or adjustable.

A fully amortized loan has equal monthly payments except for the last payment, which is slightly higher or lower. With *EQUAL MONTHLY PAYMENTS, the monthly payment amount, including principal and interest, is constant, but as the loan is paid off, the amount of the payment attributed to interest decreases and the amount attributed to principal increases.*

*A "promotional note" is a short-term note of up to and including a term of 36 months. A "seasoned note" is longer than 36 months.*

**Figure 8-2**      Installment Note with a Balloon Payment

$_____ _____, California_____, 20_____

    In installments as herein stated, for value received, I promise to pay to_____

_____, or order,

at_____

the sum of _____ DOLLARS.

with interest from_____on unpaid principal at the

rate of_____per cent per annum; principal and interest payable in installments of

_____ Dollars

or more on the_____day of each _____month, beginning

on the_____ day of _____, 20 _____ . _____

_____

_____

_____ and continuing until said principal and interest have been paid.

    Each payment shall be credited first on interest then due and the remainder on principal; and interest shall thereupon cease upon the principal so credited. Should default be made in payment of any installment when due the whole sum of principal and interest shall become immediately due at the option of the holder of this note. Principal and interest payable in lawful money of the United States. If action be instituted on this note I promise to pay such sum as the Court may fix as attorney's fees. I promise to pay Servicing Agent a late payment charge of $5 or 10% of installment due of principal and interest, whichever is greater. For First Trust Deed loans of $16,000 or more; and for Junior Lien loans of $8,000 or more, the following clause governs: $5 or 6% of installment due of principal and interest, whichever is greater. For all loans, regardless of principal amount, no late payment charge will be made if the installment is paid or tendered in full within 10 days after its scheduled

due date. This note is secured by a DEED OF TRUST to _____

_____        _____

_____        _____

_____        _____

DEED OF TRUST NOTE-INSTALLMENT NOTE-WOLCOTTS FORM 1458 REV.

# III. Negotiable Instruments

## A. PROMISSORY NOTES, CHECKS, OTHERS

A *NEGOTIABLE INSTRUMENT is any financial document (promissory note, check or other) that can be passed easily from one person to another, if it meets certain legal requirements.* Any promissory note may be a negotiable instrument that is freely transferable. A negotiable instrument must be:

1. an unconditional promise,
2. in writing,
3. made by one person to another,
4. signed by the maker,
5. payable on demand or on a set date,
6. for a set amount of money.

Promissory notes are negotiable instruments, and easily transferable. The most common example is a personal check.

### B. HOLDER IN DUE COURSE (No Knowledge of Defect)

A *HOLDER IN DUE COURSE is one who has taken a negotiable instrument from another, in good faith, without knowledge of defect.*

# IV. Important Clauses in Financial Instruments

The following financial instrument clauses are the most commonly used terms, and they have definite meanings that affect the financial obligations of both a lender and borrower.

### A. ACCELERATION CLAUSE (Entire Amount Due)

In an *ACCELERATION CLAUSE, upon the occurrence of a specific event, the lender has the right to demand immediate payment of the entire note.* An acceleration clause is used to demand immediate payment in full because of a default in loan payments, property taxes, fire insurance, or upon the transfer of property. The main purpose of an acceleration clause is to make the entire balance of the loan due and payable at once. A *LATE PAYMENT is a payment that is, unless otherwise stated, more than ten days past due.*

*An "acceleration clause" is always found in a trust deed.*

### B. ALIENATION CLAUSE (Due on Sale)

An *ALIENATION CLAUSE is a form of the acceleration clause, stating that the entire loan becomes due and payable when the property is sold, assigned, transferred, or otherwise alienated.* The lender, whether a financial institution or a private party, is given the right to full payment when the original borrower transfers the property. This is also commonly referred to as a **"due on sale"** clause. If the loan contains an alienation clause, it would be found in both the trust deed as well as the promissory note.

*An "alienation (due on sale) clause" is enforceable and benefits the lender.*

### C. ASSUMPTION

If a buyer *ASSUMES a loan on a property that is already encumbered, he or she accepts responsibility, with the lender's consent, for the full payment of the loan.* The name on the loan is changed to that of the buyer. With a true assumption, the seller has **secondary responsibility**. To end his or her liability and put the loan in the name of the buyer, the seller files a Substitution of Liability form.

Taking title *SUBJECT TO a prior loan constitutes an agreement to take over and make the payments or lose the property.* The current seller (the buyer to whom the loan was originally made) remains legally responsible for the note, but the new buyer makes the payments.

*A seller is protected from liability for payments on an existing loan when the buyer "assumes" the trust deed (and note liability). In a "subject to" loan takeover, the seller remains liable.*

### D. SUBORDINATION CLAUSE (Current Loan Stands Still; New Loan Moves Ahead)

A *SUBORDINATION CLAUSE is part of a trust deed or mortgage that allows for a future change in the priority of financial liens.* It is used when the buyer wants future financial liens to have priority over a lien he or she is now acquiring. The seller of vacant land will sometimes lend money to the buyer as part of the transaction and will allow the subordination of that loan to any new construction loans.

The subordination clause is used to change the priority on one or more financial liens, but the terms of a subordination clause must be clear and definite. The courts are skeptical about loosely written subordination clauses. Subordination clauses are not used that often, but a salesperson must know and understand them.

### E. PREPAYMENT PENALTIES (Fee for Early Payment)

A *PREPAYMENT PENALTY is a charge to the borrower for paying off all or part of a loan balance before the due date.*

Most financial institutions use a prepayment penalty clause on fixed rate loans, but they are rarely employed with the adjustable rate loans. A prepayment penalty is only enforceable during the first five years of a (one-to-four unit) home loan. The penalty is usually six months' interest on the amount prepaid (each year) that exceeds 20% of the original principal amount of the loan. However, penalties do vary among lenders. **After negotiating, a lender may sometimes waive the prepayment penalty if the borrower obtains a new loan from that institution, or if the money market is tight and the lender needs to use the money to lend out at a higher interest rate**.

*According to the Business and Professions Code, a prepayment penalty is only enforceable during the first five years of a one-to-four unit home loan.*

### F. IMPOUND ACCOUNTS (Reserves)

*IMPOUND ACCOUNTS (RESERVES) are moneys collected in advance from borrowers to assure the payment of recurring costs, such as property taxes and fire insurance.* Some lenders require impound accounts. Impound accounts are especially appropriate when there is a relatively low down payment.

### G. ASSIGNMENT OF RENTS (Take Possession)

An *ASSIGNMENT OF RENTS CLAUSE allows a lender, upon default of the borrower, to take possession of the property, collect rents, and pay expenses.* It benefits the lender.

## V. Interest and Types of Loans

### A. INTEREST (Simple Interest)

*INTEREST is the charge for borrowing money.* In real estate we use simple interest, not compound interest. Interest can be thought of as a rental charge for the use of money.

The *NOMINAL INTEREST RATE is the rate stated in the note.* The *EFFECTIVE INTEREST RATE is the rate the borrower is actually paying (including interest, points, and loan fees).*

The formula for calculating interest is:

$$I = P \times R \times T$$
or
Interest = Principal x Rate x Time

To find the interest on an $80,000 loan at 12 percent interest for 3 years, we would make the following calculation:

$$I = P \times R \times T$$
$$\$28,800 = \$80,000 \times .12 \times 3 \text{ years}$$

(See Chapter 15 for a more detailed discussion of interest calculations.)

## B. FIXED INTEREST RATES (Fixed Rate)

A *FIXED INTEREST RATE LOAN is a loan for which the payments are the same each month for the life of the loan.* The equal monthly payment includes both the principal and the interest. A loan with this kind of fixed rate of interest is said to be a "fully amortized fixed rate loan."

## C. AMORTIZATION PAYMENTS

*AMORTIZATION is the repaying of a loan (principal and interest), in regular payments, over the term of the loan.* This repayment is usually in monthly payments but can be paid quarterly or semi-annually. Amortization is the liquidation of a note including principal and interest.

*NEGATIVE AMORTIZATION means the interest rate charges are higher than the monthly payment.* Negative amortization means that the loan payment does not cover the interest charges, and the amount of unpaid interest is added to the unpaid loan balance.

Real estate salespeople should always have amortization books handy so that they can figure out the monthly payment on any loan. The *AMORTIZATION (SCHEDULE) BOOK shows the monthly payments necessary to amortize a loan, over a given number of years, at different interest rates and for different loan amounts.* This amortization table book is usually given free, upon request, to salespeople by title insurance companies or financial institutions. Salespeople can also use specially programmed, hand-held calculators to instantly determine the monthly payment amount.

**Figure 8-3** is an example of an amortization table at 7% interest per annum for 20, 25, 30, and 40 years at different loan amounts. The loan amounts range from $100 to $100,000, but any loan amount can be obtained by adding the necessary increments. If, for example, we want to determine the monthly payments for a $155,000 loan at 7% interest for 30 years, this is what we would do:

1. Check the 30 years' column for the monthly payment on $100,000.

2. Next, determine the monthly payment for $50,000 and $5,000 using the same method.

3. Lastly, add the monthly payment amounts together.

| Amount | Payment |
|---|---|
| $100,000.00 | $665.30 |
| 50,000.00 | 332.65 |
| 5,000.00 | 33.27 |

**TOTAL LOAN $155,000.00**     **$1,031.22 Monthly Payment**

*Lenders determine monthly payments by using amortization tables and charts.*

**Figure 8-3**

# Monthly Payments Necessary to Amortize a Loan

## 7%

| TERM AMOUNT | 20 YEARS | 25 YEARS | 30 YEARS | 40 YEARS |
|---|---|---|---|---|
| $100 | 0.78 | 0.71 | 0.67 | 0.62 |
| 200 | 1.55 | 1.41 | 1.33 | 1.24 |
| 300 | 2.33 | 2.12 | 2.00 | 1.86 |
| 400 | 3.10 | 2.83 | 2.66 | 2.49 |
| 500 | 3.88 | 3.53 | 3.33 | 3.11 |
| 600 | 4.65 | 4.24 | 3.99 | 3.73 |
| 700 | 5.43 | 4.95 | 4.66 | 4.35 |
| 800 | 6.20 | 5.65 | 5.32 | 4.97 |
| 900 | 6.98 | 6.36 | 5.99 | 5.59 |
| 1,000 | 7.75 | 7.07 | 6.65 | 6.21 |
| 2,000 | 15.51 | 14.14 | 13.31 | 12.43 |
| 3,000 | 23.26 | 21.20 | 19.96 | 18.64 |
| 4,000 | 31.01 | 28.27 | 26.61 | 24.86 |
| 5,000 | 38.76 | 35.34 | 33.27 | 31.07 |
| 6,000 | 46.52 | 42.41 | 39.92 | 37.29 |
| 7,000 | 54.27 | 49.47 | 46.57 | 43.50 |
| 8,000 | 62.02 | 56.54 | 53.22 | 49.71 |
| 9,000 | 69.78 | 63.61 | 59.88 | 55.93 |
| 10,000 | 77.53 | 70.68 | 66.53 | 62.14 |
| 20,000 | 155.06 | 141.36 | 133.06 | 124.29 |
| 30,000 | 232.59 | 212.03 | 199.59 | 186.43 |
| 40,000 | 310.12 | 282.71 | 266.12 | 248.57 |
| 50,000 | 387.65 | 353.39 | 332.65 | 310.72 |
| 100,000 | 775.30 | 706.78 | 665.30 | 621.43 |

www.bankrate.com/gookeyword/mortgage-calculator.asp
Bankrate.com Mortgage calculator
www.interest.com/hugh/calc/
Hugh's Mortgage and Financial Calculators

## D. ADJUSTABLE RATE MORTGAGE (ARM)

Many lenders will allow the borrower a choice of either 1) a fixed interest rate loan or 2) an adjustable rate mortgage (ARM) loan. An ARM allows the interest rate to fluctuate (go up or down) depending on money market conditions. Rather than making equal monthly payments as with a fixed rate loan, the ARM payments will vary over the term of the loan.

An ***ADJUSTABLE RATE MORTGAGE "ARM" (OR TRUST DEED)*** *is a loan in which the interest rate fluctuates periodically, based on a specific index, which makes the payment amount* *also change.* Each lending institution has its own ARM terms and provisions. **Figure 8-4** illustrates how an adjustable rate mortgage (ARM) works. The interest rate, and therefore

---

**Figure 8-4**

# How ARMs Work

### THE INDEX

The **INDEX** *is the starting interest rate used as the indicator so that changes from it can be calculated.* If the index rises 1%, the ARM interest rate you pay goes up 1%. The index must be: 1) beyond the control of the lender, and 2) available and verifiable by the public. Examples of indexes used are the Cost of Living Index, the 11th District Cost of Funds Index, the One Year T-Bill, and the London Interbank Offered Rate (LIBOR).

### THE ADJUSTABLE INTERVAL

The **ADJUSTABLE INTERVAL** *is the frequency with which interest rates are reset.* This period can be monthly, quarterly, every six months, or even once a year. If the index has risen .3% by the end of the interval period, the interest rate you pay goes up .3%.

### THE CAP

The **CAP** *is a percentage rate ceiling or restriction on the 1) periodic (adjustable) interval; and 2) lifetime change in interest rates or payments.* An adjustable interval cap limits the percentage of change upward or downward to, for example, 1/2% every quarter. The lifetime cap is often around a maximum of 5% above or below the initial agreed-to contract rate.

### THE MARGIN

The **MARGIN** *is the spread between the index rate and the initial contract rate from which the lender will make a profit and cover its costs.* It is the agreed to, in advance, amount of profit for the lender. If the index rate is 4% and the margin is 3%, then the current interest rate paid by the borrower is 7%. Even if the index rate moves up to 5%, the margin will always remain at 3% and the new interest rate will be 8%. Some adjustables have **teaser rates** that are even below the starting rate to entice the borrower into the transaction. The borrower is qualified based on the teaser rate, which only lasts for a short period of time and then goes up to the agreed upon rate.

### ADVANTAGES OF ARMs

The main advantage of an ARM is a lower interest rate than can be found with a fixed rate loan because the lender is protected if interest rates rise over the loan period. This makes an ARM more affordable, thus more people can qualify for it. An assumption is usually permitted if the new buyer meets credit standards. ARMs benefit first-time buyers and short-term investors who just want a lower interest rate, because interest rates are initially lower.

---

the payments, will change often over the term of the loan. ARM lenders attempt to make this type of loan attractive to a potential borrower by starting it out at a low **teaser rate**. The following are helpful nonprofit debt counselors who can negotiate with home lenders:

1. **Acorn Housing:** 888-409-3557
2. **Homeownership Preservation:** 888-995-4673
3. **HUD:** www.hud.gov

## E. SOME SPECIAL PURPOSE TYPES OF LOANS

### 1. Graduated Payment Mortgage (GPM/GPAM) (For First Time Buyers)

A *GRADUATED PAYMENT MORTGAGE (GPM/GPAM) (TRUST DEED) is a type of fixed interest rate loan for which the monthly payments start out lower and then gradually increase (for example, after five years the payments will be higher for the remainder of the loan payment).* The difference in monthly payments must be disclosed. Although the final level of payments is higher than the payments would have been had the loan been fully amortized, the initial payments are much lower than the fully amortized rate.

### 2. Biweekly Mortgage (26 Payments)

A *BIWEEKLY mortgage (trust deed) is a fixed interest rate loan for which the payments are made every two weeks, but each payment is one-half the amount of a regular monthly payment.* Since there are 52 weeks in a year, the borrower pays a total of 26 payments.

### 3. 15-Year Fixed and Adjustable Rate Loans

Fifteen-year fixed-rate loans are gaining in popularity because, for a slight increase in the monthly payment, the loan can be paid off in only 15 years, usually at a lower interest rate than 30-year loans.

### 4. Reverse Mortgage Loans (Seniors Who Need Income)

A *REVERSE MORTGAGE, also known as a reverse annuity mortgage (RAM), enables older homeowners (62+) to convert their home equity into tax-free income without having to sell their home, give up title, or take on a mortgage.*

The loan is not repaid until the last owner dies or the property is sold, at which time it is paid back through probate. This type of loan is good for senior citizens who need a monthly income and have a large amount of equity in their homes. The senior citizens can pay off the FHA-backed loans earlier if they so desire.

# VI. Discount Points, Loan Fees, and Usury

## A. DISCOUNT POINTS (1 Point = 1% of the Loan Amount)

A *DISCOUNT POINT is an origination fee of 1% of the amount borrowed, charged by the lender.* Most financial institutions charge the borrower points when he or she obtains a new loan. Points vary, but generally range from 1% to 7% of the loan amount. They are usually paid by the buyer but, if so negotiated, the seller may also pay.

If you purchase a home for $150,000 and obtain a loan for $120,000 plus two points, the loan points will cost you $2,400 ($120,000 x .02). These points are an additional cost and are added to the down payment and other closing costs required to complete the transaction at the time of purchase.

Points paid are usually adjustments to the interest rate. If the interest rate quoted is lower than what is currently being charged, more points are charged to make up the difference, which is paid to the lender. If a savings bank wants to quote a lower interest rate, the borrower can expect a larger point charge.

## B. LOAN FEES

There is usually a loan fee in addition to points. A **LOAN FEE** *is the fee charged by the lender in order to apply for a loan.* This charge usually runs about $250 to $400. Other charges may include the appraisal and credit report.

*The FHA charges a 1 percent loan fee, which is usually paid by the seller.*

## C. USURY

**USURY** *is charging more than the legally allowed percentage of interest.* In California, the maximum interest rate charged for various loans is set by law. Anyone charging more than the designated rate is committing usury and is breaking the law. In determining whether an interest charge is usurious or not, all loan fees and points are added to the interest rate. Prepayment penalties are not included in the usury law test.

The constitutional usury rate in California is ten percent, or five percent above the discount rate charged by the Federal Reserve Bank of San Francisco, whichever is higher. This limit only applies to lenders who are not exempt from the law. Nearly every conventional source of real estate financing, however, has been exempted from the usury limit. Banks, savings banks, and other institutional lenders are all exempt. Sellers carrying back a purchase money trust deed as part of their equity in a real estate sale are exempt. **Any transaction made through a licensed broker is also exempt from usury laws.** The problem arises when a private individual lends money to another private individual. Check with an attorney first.

**www.frbsf.org** (Federal Reserve Bank of San Francisco, 12th District)
**www.fdic.gov** (Federal Deposit Insurance Corporation - FDIC)

# VII. Security Devices

**SECURITY DEVICES (FINANCIAL INSTRUMENTS)** *are written documents that pledge real property as security for a promissory note.*

*The three financial instruments (security devices to collateralize real property) used in California are: mortgages, trust deeds, and land contracts.*

In California we have three common types of security devices (financing instruments). See **Figure 8-5.** Any of the three previously mentioned notes may be used in conjunction with these financial instruments.

**Figure 8-5**

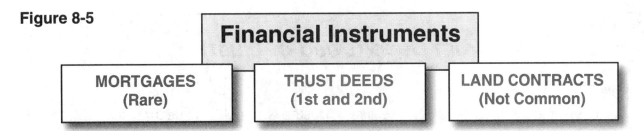

**Financial Instruments**

| MORTGAGES (Rare) | TRUST DEEDS (1st and 2nd) | LAND CONTRACTS (Not Common) |

## A. MORTGAGES

A *MORTGAGE is a financial instrument in the form of a lien that secures a property for payment of a promissory note.* It is not common in California. The *MORTGAGOR is the buyer/owner who is borrowing,* and the *MORTGAGEE is the lender.*

### Mortgage: A General Term

Although mortgages are rarely used in California, the term "mortgage" is so ingrained in the tradition of lending that often trust deeds and other loans are referred to as "mortgages." Adjustable Rate Mortgages and Fixed Rate Mortgages, for example, are deeds of trust. We will use the general words mortgage and deed of trust interchangeably, but mortgagee or mortgagor refer only to mortgages and trustee, trustor, and beneficiary refer only to trust deeds.

If the mortgagor defaults in his or her payments, a foreclosure action may be started. After the foreclosure sale, the borrower has one year to redeem (buy back) the property, pay all the accumulated charges, or pay the mortgagee rent. **Figure 8-6** is a two-page comparison of the differences between mortgages and trust deeds (deeds of trust).

### 1. Power of Sale Clause

Some mortgages have a power of sale clause. A *POWER OF SALE CLAUSE allows the mortgagee to sell the property without a court proceeding (much like a trustee's sale) if the mortgagor is in default.* But it still requires a lengthy proceeding. If there is no power of sale clause, court (judicial) action is required for a foreclosure.

*In a trust deed, the "power of sale" clause is given from the trustor to the trustee.*

### 2. Mortgages Compared to Trust Deeds

#### a. Parties

In a mortgage there are two parties: the mortgagor (borrower) and the mortgagee (lender). The deed of trust has three: trustor (borrower), trustee (third party), and beneficiary (lender).

#### b. Title

A mortgage does not convey title; it creates a lien. In a deed of trust the title is conveyed to a trustee (third party) for the benefit of the lender (beneficiary) and is in effect a lien.

**Figure 8-6**

# Trust Deed (Deed of Trust)

**1. Parties:**

    **a. Trustor** – Borrower who conveys title to trustee who holds as security for debt.

    **b. Trustee** – Receiver of naked legal title who will reconvey it when debt is paid or will sell if foreclosure necessary (must be a corporation or division of an escrow company).

    **c. Beneficiary** – Lender who holds note and trust deed.

**2. Legal Title** – Conveyed to trustee with trustor retaining possession of the property.

**3. Statute of Limitations** – Since security for the debt (title) is held by trustee, rights of creditor are not ended when statute has run out on note.

**4. Remedy for Default** – Foreclosure can be instituted through:

    **a. Trustee's Sale**, or

    **b. Court Foreclosure**.

**5. Right of Redemption** – When title has been sold by trustee at Trustee's Sale, no right of redemption previously existed, but in rare cases the courts now say it does.

**6. Satisfaction** – Trustor has beneficiary send original note and trust deed to trustee with request for full reconveyance. Upon payment of fees, trustee issues reconveyance deed, which must be recorded.

**7. Foreclosure by Trustee's Sale:**

    **a. Beneficiary notifies trustee of default**, who in turn notifies trustor and also records notice. Anyone with recorded "Request for Notice of Default" must also be notified.

    **b. Trustee waits at least three months.** During three-month period, trustor can reinstate loan.

    **c. Trustee advertises "Notice of Sale"** once a week for three weeks and posts notice on property.

    **d. Trustee conducts sale** and issues Trustee's Deed to highest bidder.

**8. Deficiency Judgment** – No judgment available:

    **a. if foreclosure by Trustee's Sale**.

    **b. on purchase money trust deeds**, even if by court foreclosure. (Deficiency judgments may be obtained on FHA and VA first purchase money trust deeds.)

▼

# *Mortgage*

**1. Parties:**

 a. **Mortgagor** – Borrower who retains title but gives lender a lien on the property as the security for debt.

 b. **Mortgagee** – Lender who holds the mortgage.

**2. Title** – Retained by mortgagor together with possession.

**3. Statute of Limitations** – Foreclosure is barred if no action is taken within four years of delinquency. Mortgage is said to have "outlawed."

**4. Remedy for Default** – Court foreclosure is usually the only remedy.

**5. Right of Redemption** – Mortgagor has one year to redeem following court foreclosure; called "Equity of Redemption."

**6. Satisfaction of Mortgage** – Upon final payment and on demand, mortgagee signs certificate that debt is satisfied. Certificate or release is recorded.

**7. Foreclosure by Court:**

 a. **Court action commenced by mortgagee**. Court issues decree of foreclosure and order of sale.

 b. **Commissioner appointed by court sells to highest bidder** after publication and posting of sale notice.

 c. **Certificate of Sale issued by Commissioner**. Mortgagor has one year to redeem property and to remain in possession.

 d. **Sheriff's Deed issued after one year**.

**8. Deficiency Judgment** – Available in court foreclosure unless mortgage was purchase money mortgage as noted below.

**Note: Purchase money is defined as:**

 1. Mortgage or trust deed or real property sales contract given to seller as part of purchase price, or

 2. Mortgage or trust deed given to lender to finance purchase of owner-occupied dwelling of four or fewer units.

### c. Statute of Limitations

In a mortgage, an action to foreclose is subject to the statute of limitations. Since it is a promissory note, the mortgagee has four years from the date of the last payment to start foreclosure. With a trust deed, there is no time limit because the third party (trustee) has title and power of sale.

### d. Remedy for Default

In a mortgage, the only remedy of the mortgagee (lender) is judicial (court) foreclosure, unless the mortgage contains a power of sale clause. Although the actual mortgage foreclosure takes a short period of time, the redemption period is very long (1 year). The *REDEMPTION PERIOD is the legally acceptable time period for buying back one's property after a judicial sale.* In a deed of trust the entire process, including any redemption or sale, requires a short period of time (4 months).

## 3. Trust Deeds are Preferred to Mortgages

In California, the trust deed is preferred to the mortgage as the usual financing device. The lender has fewer restrictions when using a trust deed. There is: 1) A short period to reinstate prior to the sale and the fact that the sale, once made, is usually absolute. The purchaser can take possession at once, which is not true for a mortgage; 2) The ease and convenience, without having to resort to court action, with which the property may be sold to satisfy the debt if the borrower defaults. California laws favor lenders who use the trust deed, which allows them more freedom in granting loans to deserving buyers.

## B. TRUST DEEDS (DEEDS OF TRUST)

### 1. Trust Deeds are Used in California

*Trust deeds (deeds of trust loans) are personal property.*

In California the trust deed, sometimes called a deed of trust, is the usual financing instrument. The *TRUST DEED (DEED OF TRUST) is a security device that makes the real property collateral for the promissory note.* **Figure 8-7** shows a copy of a trust deed.

*A trust deed needs a note for security, but a note does NOT need a trust deed. A trust deed is not a negotiable instrument; the note is. If the conditions of a note and the trust deed are in conflict, the note prevails.*

### 2. Parties to a Trust Deed

In a trust deed there are three parties. The *TRUSTOR is usually the party that is borrowing the money.* This is often the buyer, but may also be the owner if the property is being refinanced. The *BENEFICIARY is the lender who is lending money for the purchase of real property.* Home lenders in California are usually savings banks, but may also be commercial banks. The *TRUSTEE is the third, disinterested party (usually a corporation) who holds naked legal title to the property, but only in so far as the trustee may have to sell the property for the beneficiary, should the trustor default.* This is normally a title insurance company. **Figure 8-8** illustrates this three-party relationship.

# Figure 8-7

RECORDING REQUESTED BY

ORDER #
APN

WHEN RECORDED MAIL TO

Name
Street
Address
City &
State

———————— SPACE ABOVE THIS LINE FOR RECORDER'S USE ————————

## SHORT FORM DEED OF TRUST AND ASSIGNMENT OF RENTS

ALL    PTN.

This Deed of Trust, made this _____ day of _____ , between

_____ , herein called TRUSTOR,

whose address is _____

| (number and street) | (city) | (state) | (zip) |

**OLD REPUBLIC TITLE COMPANY**, a California corporation, herein called TRUSTEE, and

_____ , herein called BENEFICIARY,

Witnesseth: That Trustor IRREVOCABLY GRANTS, TRANSFERS AND ASSIGNS TO TRUSTEE IN TRUST, WITH POWER OF SALE, that property in _____ County, California, described as:

TOGETHER WITH the rents, issues and profits thereof, SUBJECT, HOWEVER, to the right, power and authority given to and conferred upon Beneficiary by paragraph (10) of the provisions incorporated herein by reference to collect and apply such rents, issues and profits.

For the Purpose of Securing: 1. Performance of each agreement of Trustor incorporated by reference or contained herein. 2. Payment of the indebtedness evidenced by one promissory note of even date herewith, and any extension or renewal thereof, in the principal sum of $_____ executed by Trustor in favor of Beneficiary or order. 3. Payment of such further sums as the then record owner of said property hereafter may borrow from Beneficiary, when evidenced by another note (or notes) reciting it is so secured.

To Protect the Security of This Deed of Trust, Trustor Agrees: By the execution and delivery of this Deed of Trust and the note secured hereby, that provisions (1) to (14), inclusive, of the fictitious deed of trust recorded in Santa Barbara County and Sonoma County October 18, 1961, and in all other counties October 23, 1961, in the book and at the page of Official Records in the office of the county recorder of the county where said property is located, noted below opposite the name of such county, viz.:

| COUNTY | BOOK | PAGE | COUNTY | BOOK | PAGE | COUNTY | BOOK | PAGE | COUNTY | BOOK | PAGE |
|---|---|---|---|---|---|---|---|---|---|---|---|
| Alameda | 435 | 684 | Kings | 792 | 833 | Placer | 895 | 301 | Sierra | 29 | 335 |
| Alpine | 1 | 250 | Lake | 362 | 39 | Plumas | 151 | 5 | Siskiyou | 468 | 181 |
| Amador | 104 | 348 | Lassen | 171 | 471 | Riverside | 3005 | 523 | Solano | 1105 | 182 |
| Butte | 1145 | 1 | Los Angeles | T2055 | 899 | Sacramento | 4331 | 62 | Sonoma | 1851 | 689 |
| Calaveras | 145 | 152 | Madera | 810 | 170 | San Benito | 271 | 383 | Stanislaus | 1715 | 456 |
| Colusa | 296 | 617 | Marin | 1508 | 339 | San Bernardino | 5567 | 61 | Sutter | 572 | 297 |
| Contra Costa | 3978 | 47 | Mariposa | 77 | 292 | San Francisco | A332 | 905 | Tehama | 401 | 289 |
| Del Norte | 78 | 414 | Mendocino | 579 | 530 | San Joaquin | 2470 | 311 | Trinity | 93 | 366 |
| El Dorado | 568 | 456 | Merced | 1547 | 538 | San Luis Obispo | 1151 | 12 | Tulare | 2294 | 275 |
| Fresno | 4626 | 572 | Modoc | 184 | 851 | San Mateo | 4078 | 420 | Tuolumne | 135 | 47 |
| Glenn | 422 | 184 | Mono | 52 | 429 | Santa Barbara | 1878 | 860 | Ventura | 2062 | 386 |
| Humboldt | 657 | 527 | Monterey | 2194 | 538 | Santa Clara | 5336 | 341 | Yolo | 653 | 245 |
| Imperial | 1091 | 501 | Napa | 639 | 86 | Santa Cruz | 1431 | 494 | Yuba | 334 | 486 |
| Inyo | 147 | 598 | Nevada | 305 | 320 | Shasta | 684 | 528 | | | |
| Kern | 3427 | 60 | Orange | 5889 | 611 | San Diego | Series 2 | Book 1961, | Page 183887 | | |

( which provisions, identical in all counties, are printed on the reverse hereof) hereby are adopted and incorporated herein and made a part hereof as fully as though set forth herein at length; that he will observe and perform said provisions; and that the references to property, obligations, and parties in said provisions shall be construed to refer to the property, obligations, and parties set forth in this Deed of Trust.

The undersigned Trustor requests that a copy of any Notice of Default and of any Notice of Sale hereunder be mailed to him at his address hereinbefore set forth.

STATE OF CALIFORNIA
COUNTY OF _____ } SS.

On _____ before me, the undersigned,
a Notary Public in and for said State, personally appeared

_____ ,

personally known to me (or proved to me on the basis of satisfactory evidence) to be the person(s) whose name(s) is/are subscribed to the within instrument and acknowledged to me that he/she/they executed the same in his /her /their authorized capacity(ies), and that by his/her/their signature(s) on the instrument the person(s), or the entity upon behalf of which the person(s) acted, executed the instrument.
    WITNESS my hand and official seal.

Signature _____

_____
Name (Typed or Printed)

(Seal)

ORT 100

The following is a copy of provisions (1) to (14) inclusive, of the fictitious Deed of Trust, recorded in each county in California, as stated in the foregoing Deed of Trust and incorporated by reference in said Deed of Trust as being a part thereof as if set forth at length therein.

To Protect the Security of This Deed of Trust, Trustor Agrees:

1. To keep said property in good condition and repair; not to remove or demolish any building thereon; to complete or restore promptly and in good and workmanlike manner any building which may be constructed, damaged or destroyed thereon and to pay when due all claims for labor performed and materials furnished therefor; to comply with all laws affecting said property or requiring any alterations or improvements to be made thereon; not to commit or permit waste thereof; not to commit, suffer or permit any act upon said property in violation of law; to cultivate, irrigate, fertilize, fumigate, prune and do all other acts which from the character or use of said property may be reasonably necessary, the specific enumerations herein not excluding the general.

2. To provide, maintain and deliver to Beneficiary fire insurance satisfactory to and with loss payable to Beneficiary. The amount collected under any fire or other insurance policy may be applied by Beneficiary upon any indebtedness secured hereby and in such order as Beneficiary may determine, or at option of Beneficiary the entire amount so collected or any part thereof may be released to Trustor. Such application or release shall not cure or waive any default or notice of default hereunder or invalidate any act done pursuant to such notice.

3. To appear in and defend any action or proceeding purporting to affect the security hereof or the rights or powers of Beneficiary or Trustee; and to pay all costs and expenses, including cost of evidence of title and attorney's fees in a reasonable sum, in any such action or proceeding in which Beneficiary or Trustee may appear, and in any suit brought by Beneficiary to foreclose this Deed.

4. To pay: at least ten days before delinquency all taxes and assessments affecting said property, including assessments on appurtenant water stock; when due, all encumbrances, charges and liens, with interest, on said property or any part thereof, which appear to be prior or superior hereto; all costs, fees and expenses of this Trust.
   Should Trustor fail to make any payment or to do any act as herein provided, then Beneficiary or Trustee, but without obligation so to do and without notice to or demand upon Trustor and without releasing Trustor from any obligation hereof, may: make or do the same in such manner and to such extent as either may deem necessary to protect the security hereof, Beneficiary or Trustee being authorized to enter upon said property for such purposes; appear in and defend any action or proceeding purporting to affect the security hereof or the rights or powers of Beneficiary or Trustee; pay, purchase, contest or compromise any encumbrance, charge or lien which in the judgment of either appears to be prior or superior hereto; and, in exercising any such powers, pay necessary expenses, employ counsel and pay his reasonable fees.

5. To pay immediately and without demand all sums so expended by Beneficiary or Trustee, with interest from date of expenditure at the amount allowed by law in effect at the date hereof, and to pay for any statement provided for by law in effect at the date hereof regarding the obligation secured hereby any amount demanded by the Beneficiary not to exceed the maximum allowed by law at the time when said statement is demanded.

6. That any award of damages in connection with any condemnation for public use of or injury to said property or any part thereof is hereby assigned and shall be paid to beneficiary who may apply or release such moneys received by him in the same manner and with the same effect as above provided for disposition of proceeds of fire or other insurance.

7. That by accepting payment of any sum secured hereby after its due date, Beneficiary does not waive his right either to require prompt payment when due of all other sums so secured or to declare default for failure so to pay.

8. That at any time or from time to time, without liability therefor and without notice, upon written request of Beneficiary and presentation of this Deed and said note for endorsement, and without affecting the personal liability of any person for payment of the indebtedness secured hereby, Trustee may: reconvey any part of said property; consent to the making of any map or plat thereof; join in granting any easement thereon; or join in any extension agreement or any agreement subordinating the lien or charge thereof.

9. That upon written request of Beneficiary stating that all sums secured hereby have been paid and upon surrender of this Deed and said note to Trustee for cancellation and retention and upon payment of its fees, Trustee shall reconvey, without warranty the property then held hereunder. The recitals in such reconveyance of any matters or facts shall be conclusive proof of the truthfulness thereof. The Grantee in such reconveyance may be described as "the person or persons legally entitled thereto." Five years after issuance of such full reconveyance, Trustee may destroy said note and this Deed (unless directed in such request to retain them).

10. That as additional security, Trustor hereby gives to and confers upon Beneficiary the right, power and authority, during the continuance of these trusts, to collect the rents, issues and profits of said property, reserving unto Trustor the right, prior to any default by Trustor in payment of any indebtedness secured hereby or in performance of any agreement hereunder, to collect and retain such rents, issues and profits as they become due and payable. Upon any such default, Beneficiary may at any time without notice, either in person, by agent or by a receiver to be appointed by a court, and without regard to the adequacy of any security for the indebtedness hereby secured, enter upon and take possession of said property or any part thereof, in his own name sue for or otherwise collect such rents, issues and profits, including those past due and unpaid, and apply the same, less costs and expenses of operation and collection, including reasonable attorney's fees, upon any indebtedness secured hereby, and in such order as Beneficiary may determine. The entering upon and taking possession of said property, the collection of such rents, issues and profits and the application thereof as aforesaid, shall not cure or waive any default or notice of default hereunder or invalidate any act done pursuant to such notice.

11. That upon default by Trustor in payment of any indebtedness secured hereby or in performance of any agreement hereunder, Beneficiary may declare all sums secured hereby immediately due and payable by delivery to Trustee of written declaration of default and demand for sale and of written notice of default and of election to cause to be sold said property, which notice Trustee shall cause to be filed for record. Beneficiary also shall deposit with Trustee this Deed, said note and all documents evidencing expenditures secured hereby.
    After the lapse of such time as may then be required by law following the recordation of said notice of default and notice of sale having been given as then required by law, Trustee, without demand on Trustor, shall sell said property at the time and place fixed by it in said notice of sale, either as a whole or in separate parcels, and in such order as it may determine, at public auction to the highest bidder for cash in lawful money of the United States, payable at time of sale. Trustee may postpone sale of all or any portion of said property by public announcement at such time and place of sale, and from time to time thereafter may postpone such sale by public announcement at the time fixed by the preceding postponement. Trustee shall deliver to such purchaser its deed conveying the property so sold but without any covenant or warranty, express or implied. The recitals in such deed of any matters or facts shall be conclusive proof of the truthfulness thereof. Any person, including Trustor, Trustee, or Beneficiary as hereinafter defined, may purchase at such sale.
    After deducting all costs, fees and expenses of Trustee and of this Trust, including cost of evidence of title in connection with sale, Trustee shall apply the proceeds of sale to payment of: all sums expended under the terms hereof, not then repaid, with accrued interest at the amount allowed by law in effect at the date hereof; all other sums then secured hereby; and the remainder, if any, to the person or persons legally entitled thereto.

12. Beneficiary, or any successor in ownership of any indebtedness secured hereby, may from time to time, by instrument in writing, substitute a successor or successors to any Trustee named herein or acting hereunder, which instrument, executed by the Beneficiary and duly acknowledged and recorded in the office of the recorder of the County or Counties where said property is situated, shall be conclusive proof of proper substitution of such successor Trustee or Trustees, who shall, without conveyance from the Trustee predecessor, succeed to all its title, estate, rights, powers and duties. Said instrument must contain the name of the original Trustor, Trustee and Beneficiary hereunder, the book and page where this Deed is recorded and the name and address of the new Trustee.

13. That this Deed applies to, inures to the benefit of, and binds all parties hereto, their heirs, legatees, devisees, administrators, executors, successors and assigns. The term Beneficiary shall mean the owner and holder, including pledgees, of the note secured hereby, whether or not named as Beneficiary herein. In this Deed, whenever the context so requires, the masculine gender includes the feminine and/or neuter, and the singular number includes the plural.

14. That Trustee accepts this Trust when this Deed, duly executed and acknowledged, is made a public record as provided by law. Trustee is not obligated to notify any party hereto of pending sale under any other Deed of Trust or of any action or proceeding in which Trustor, Beneficiary or Trustee shall be a party unless brought by Trustee.

## REQUEST FOR FULL RECONVEYANCE

To be used only when note has been paid.

Dated_____

**To OLD REPUBLIC TITLE COMPANY, Trustee:**

The undersigned is the legal owner and holder of all indebtedness secured by the within Deed of Trust. All sums secured by said Deed of Trust have been fully paid and satisfied; and you are hereby requested and directed, on payment to you of any sums owing to you under the terms of said Deed of Trust, to cancel all evidences of indebtedness, secured by said Deed of Trust, delivered to you herewith together with said Deed of Trust, and to reconvey, without warranty, to the parties designated by the terms of said Deed of Trust, the estate now held by you under the same.

Mail Reconveyance To:

_____

_____

_____          By_____

_____          By_____

Do not lose or destroy this Deed of Trust OR THE NOTE which it secures. Both must be delivered to the Trustee for cancellation before reconveyance will be made.

OLD REPUBLIC TITLE COMPANY

SHORT FORM DEED OF TRUST AND ASSIGNMENT OF RENTS

234

**Figure 8-8**

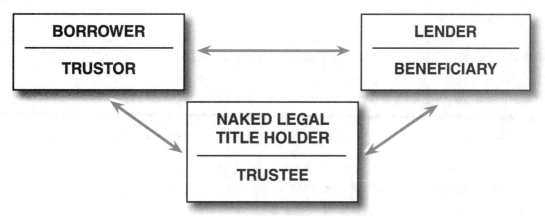

*The trustor (borrower) signs the promissory note and trust deed, as he or she owes the debt. The lender is also known as the beneficiary.*

A trust deed conveys bare (or naked) legal title (but not possession) of a property to a trustee as security for a loan. **A trust deed differs from other deeds in that the legal title only is thus conveyed.** A trust deed is a security device in the nature of a lien and differs in one respect from other deeds in that the trust deed and the promissory note for which it was given may be assigned.

*When a real estate broker negotiates a loan on real property and creates a new trust deed, he/she must record the trust deed within 10 days.*

A trust deed must have all three parties: trustor, trustee, and beneficiary. The trust deed and note form the lien, which conveys the "bare" or "naked" legal title of the property to the trustee, to be held until the trust deed is paid in full, at which time the title is reconveyed to the trustor through a reconveyance. If the trustor defaults in payments, the beneficiary will instruct the trustee to start the default period, which could ultimately lead to a trustee foreclosure sale.

*EQUITABLE TITLE is held by a trustor while he or she is repaying a trust deed and note. It is* **true ownership** *in that the trustor may enjoy all customary rights of title and possession.*

*LEGAL TITLE, "Bare or Naked Legal Title," is held by a trustee until the terms of a trust deed and note have been fulfilled.* When the trustor has paid the note in full, the trustee will reconvey the naked legal title.

### 3. Deed of Reconveyance (Proof of Payment in Full)

A *DEED OF RECONVEYANCE (Full Reconveyance) provides proof that a promissory note and the accompanying trust deed have been paid in full.* When the note has been paid in full, the beneficiary requests the trustee to grant a full reconveyance, which makes the trustor's legal title a part of the public record and gives evidence that the debt has been paid off. A full reconveyance must be recorded to give public notice, in the county records, that it has been paid. The reconveyance is paid for by the trustor.

*When a debt has been paid in full, the trustee will record a deed of reconveyance to remove the lien of a trust deed from the public record.*

See **Figure 8-9** for more information about a deed of reconveyance and **Figure 8-10** for an example.

---

**Figure 8-9**  **Full Reconveyance**

A full reconveyance is a simple written document that offers proof that a loan on real property has been paid off in full. If a trust deed (loan on real property) is to be paid off in full, a request for full reconveyance is to be signed by the beneficiary and sent to the trustee for recording.

The trustor (borrower), who is in the process of paying off a loan secured by a note and deed of trust on a certain piece of real property, wants the following:

1. The return of the original note,
2. The return of the original trust deed, and
3. A "Reconveyance deed" should be recorded in the county recorder's office where the deed of trust is recorded.

When the trustor originally borrowed the money to purchase property or later obtained a loan secured by the property, he or she signed a promissory note and a trust deed. This trust deed, when recorded, became a specific lien. If the trustor tries to sell or refinance the property, this lien will show up on all title searches or title reports until the deed of trust has been "reconveyed."

So it is extremely important for the trustor to have the deed of trust and note returned along with having the beneficiary sign a "Request for Full Reconveyance." Under California Civil Code Section 2941, the beneficiary must forward a deed of reconveyance, within 90 days of receiving the "Request for Full Reconveyance," to the trustee. Violation of this law is a misdemeanor punishable by a $300 fine, plus damages, and/or six months in jail.

---

# VIII. Default and Foreclosure of a Trust Deed

## A. DEFAULT ON A TRUST DEED

In California, the procedure and remedy for nonpayment of a trust deed is well established by law. The trust deed is a lien on the property involved. The lender has the legal right to receive the trust deed payment on time. By law the lender can start default action after the 10- to 15-day grace period. A *GRACE PERIOD is a set number of days in which a lender will allow a payment to be late without any penalty.* The lender, at any time after the grace period, may start default action/foreclosure against the trustor. **Figure 8-11** shows the sequence of events that will follow if the trustor does not make the trust deed payments.

When a borrower defaults on his or her payments under the trust deed and note, the beneficiary's remedy is to start default action. The beneficiary notifies the trustee of the trustor's failure to make the payments. **The trustee then records a notice of default, which will start the foreclosure action.**

When the trustee is notified by the lender (beneficiary) of the trustor's nonpayment, the trustee records a "notice of default" (see Figure 8-12). This notice contains all the pertinent

**Figure 8-10**

RECORDING REQUESTED BY

AND WHEN RECORDED MAIL TO

| S | R | U | PAGE | SIZE | DA | MISC | LONG | RFD | COPY |
|---|---|---|------|------|-----|------|------|------|------|
|   |   |   |      |      |     |      |      |      |      |
| M | A | L | 465 | 426 | PCOR | NCOR | SMF | NCHG | EXAM |
|   |   |   |     |     | T: |      | CTY | UNI |      |

Escrow No.
Order No.

SPACE ABOVE THIS LINE FOR RECORDER'S USE ONLY

## FULL RECONVEYANCE

as trustee, or Successor Trustee, or Substituted Trustee, under Deed of Trust dated
executed by

Trustor, and recorded as Instrument No.                     on                          , of
Official Records in the office of the Recorder of
County, California, describing land therein as:

**MORE FULLY DESCRIBED IN SAID DEED OF TRUST**

having received from holder of the obligations thereunder a written request to reconvey, reciting that all sums secured by said Deed of Trust have been fully paid, and said Deed of Trust and the note or notes secured thereby having been surrendered to said Trustee for cancellation, does hereby RECONVEY, without warranty, to the person or persons legally entitled thereto, the estate no held by it thereunder.

Date _____

STATE OF CALIFORNIA                    }
COUNTY OF _____ }

On _____ before me,

_____ ,
(here insert name and title of the officer)

personally appeared _____

_____ ,

who proved to me on the basis of satisfactory evidence to be the person(s) whose name(s) is/are subscribed to the within instrument and acknowledged to me that he/she/they executed the same in his/her/their authorized capacity(ies), and that by his/her/their signature(s) on the instrument the person(s), or the entity upon behalf of which the person(s) acted, executed the instrument.

I certify under PENALTY OF PERJURY under the laws of the State of California that the foregoing paragraph is true and correct.

WITNESS my hand and official seal.

Signature _____

By: _____
Trustee

Print Name: _____

(SEAL)

**Figure 8-11**

| PAYMENT PAST DUE | 3 MONTHS MINIMUM | 21 DAYS MINIMUM | 1 DAY |
|---|---|---|---|
| NOTICE OF DEFAULT RECORDED | REINSTATEMENT PERIOD (up to 5 days before sale) | PUBLISHING PERIOD (3 weeks) | TRUSTEE'S SALE |

information about the default. Within 10 days after the recording, the borrower (trustor) and all people who have filed a "request for notice," such as junior lienholders, will receive (by certified or registered mail) notification from the trustee of the default. In addition, the notice of default must be published in a newspaper of general circulation once a week for three weeks.

*A seller who agrees to carry back a second trust deed has a "request for notice of default" recorded to protect his or her interests as a beneficiary of the second trust deed.*

## B. TRUSTOR'S RIGHT OF REINSTATEMENT

### 1. Reinstatement Period (Three Months)

During the three-month reinstatement period after the"notice of default" is filed, the trustor may reinstate the loan. The **REINSTATEMENT PERIOD** *is the time within which the trustor may pay all past due payments*. To do this, the trustor must pay the beneficiary the following:

1. All past due payments, penalties, taxes, and interest.
2. Any other costs to the beneficiary.
3. All costs and fees owed to the trustee.

*The trustor can reinstate a loan up until five days prior to foreclosure (the trustee's sale). If reinstated, it is again in good standing.*

If the trustor does not pay the past due payments, taxes, interest, and other charges within the three-month reinstatement period, the reinstatement rights are lost. This reinstatement period runs until five days before the date of sale. Sometimes in special circumstances, and always at the discretion of the lender, the trustor may still be allowed to reinstate the loan after this period. If the beneficiary decides to foreclose, however, he or she will start the process by recording a "notice of sale."

### 2. Notice Of Sale (21 Days/3 Weeks)

*After recording a "notice of default," a trustee must wait three months (90 days) before publishing a "notice of sale."*

The **NOTICE OF SALE** *is a recorded notice stating the time, place, property description, and type of sale*. See **Figure 8-12**, the notice of default. It also serves as the notice of sale. **The notice must be published in a newspaper of general circulation once a week during the 21-day (3-week) publishing period.** A copy of the notice must also be

# Figure 8-12

RECORDING REQUESTED BY


WHEN RECORDED MAIL TO

*Name*

*Street*
*Address*

*City &*
*State*

|  |  | SPACE ABOVE THIS LINE FOR RECORDER'S USE |
|--|--|--|
| TITLE ORDER NO. | T.S. NO. | COMPUTER NO. |
| LOAN NO. | OTHER REF. | T.S. NO. |

### NOTICE OF DEFAULT AND ELECTION TO SELL UNDER DEED OF TRUST
### IMPORTANT NOTICE
### IF YOUR PROPERTY IS IN FORECLOSURE BECAUSE YOU ARE BEHIND
### IN YOUR PAYMENTS, IT MAY BE SOLD WITHOUT ANY COURT ACTION,

and you may have the legal right to bring your account in good standing by paying all of your past due payments plus permitted costs and expenses within the time permitted by law for reinstatement of your account which is normally five business days prior to the date set for the sale of your property. No sale date may be set until three months from the date this notice of default may be recorded (which date of recordation appears on this notice).

This amount is                              as of                              and will increase until your account becomes current.

While your property is in foreclosure, you still must pay other obligations (such as insurance and taxes) required by your note and deed of trust or mortgage. If you fail to make future payments on the loan, pay taxes on the property, provide insurance on the property, or pay other obligations as required in the note and deed of trust or mortgage, the beneficiary or mortgagee may insist that you do so in order to reinstate your account in good standing. In addition, the beneficiary or mortgagee may require as a condition to reinstatement that you provide reliable written evidence that you paid all senior liens, property taxes, and hazard insurance premiums.

Upon your written request, the beneficiary or mortgagee will give you a written itemization of the entire amount you must pay. You may not have to pay the entire unpaid portion of your account, even though full payment was demanded, but you must pay all amounts in default at the time payment is made. However, you and your beneficiary or mortgagee may mutually agree in writing prior to the time the notice of sale is posted (which may not be earlier than the end of the three-month period stated above) to, among other things, (1) provide additional time in which to cure the default by transfer of the property or otherwise; or (2) establish a schedule of payments in order to cure your default; or both (1) and (2).

Following the expiration of the time period referred to in the first paragraph of this notice, unless the obligation being foreclosed upon or a separate written agreement between you and your creditor permits a longer period, you have only the legal right to stop the sale of your property by paying the entire amount demanded by your creditor.

To find out the amount you must pay, or to arrange for payment to stop the foreclosure, or if your property is in foreclosure for any other reason, contact:

Name of Beneficiary or Mortgagee:

Phone:

If you have any questions, you should contact a lawyer or the Governmental agency which may have insured your loan.

Notwithstanding the fact that your property is in foreclosure, you may offer your property for sale, provided the sale is concluded prior to the conclusion of the foreclosure.

Remember, YOU MAY LOSE LEGAL RIGHTS IF YOU DO NOT TAKE PROMPT ACTION.

NOTICE IS HEREBY GIVEN: CHICAGO TITLE COMPANY, a California Corporation, is duly appointed Trustee under a Deed of Trust dated                                    executed by

                                    as Trustor, to secure certain obligations

in favor of                                    ,as beneficiary,


recorded                        as instrument no.                in book            page

of Official Records in the Office of the Recorder of                        County, California, describing the land therein as


said obligations including                        note(s) for the                        sum of $


that a breach of, and default in, the obligations for which such Deed of Trust is security has occurred in that payment has not been made of:


that by reason thereof, the undersigned, present beneficiary under such Deed of Trust, has executed and delivered to said duly appointed Trustee, a written Declaration of Default and Demand for Sale, and has deposited with said duly appointed Trustee, such Deed of Trust and all documents evidencing obligations secured thereby, and has declared and does hereby declare all sums secured thereby immediately due and payable and has elected and does hereby elect to cause the trust property to be sold to satisfy the obligations secured thereby.

THIS NOTICE MUST BE RECORDED BY
CHICAGO TITLE COMPANY, a
California Corporation

Dated _____                    _____

posted on the property and in a public place, such as the city hall. Most title insurance companies also post a copy if they are acting as trustee.

### 3. The Trustee's Sale (Foreclosure Sale)

The trustee's sale is held at the time and place stated in the notice of sale. At the public sale, the trustee states the purpose of the sale and describes the property to be sold. All bids must be in the form of cash or cashier's checks.

The first deed holder may bid up to the total amount of the debt without cash. Because it costs the first trust deed holder nothing more than what he or she is already owed, that person will usually make the first bid. The highest bidder obtains the property and will be issued a trustee's deed. Any money more than the amount owed is reimbursed to the trustor. The new owner is entitled to immediate possession.

*A trustee's sale is a nonjudicial foreclosure under the "power of sale" clause in the deed of trust and promissory note.*

### 4. Judicial Court Foreclosure for a Trust Deed (Rare)

In rare cases, a beneficiary (lender) in California may want to foreclose by court action instead of the simpler trustee's sale. The reason would be to obtain a **deficiency judgment** if it was not a purchase money trust deed. See the purchase money section below.

### 5. Deed in Lieu of Foreclosure

A *DEED IN LIEU OF FORECLOSURE is a deed given by an owner (borrower) to a lender to prevent the lender from bringing foreclosure proceedings.* **The lender (beneficiary) becomes the new owner of the property and takes responsibility for any junior liens (loans) on the property.** It is up to the lender to accept or reject such an offer. This could save the borrower's credit in some circumstances.

### 6. Short Sale (Increasing Foreclosure Alternative Due to 2007-2009 Credit Crunch)

A *SHORT SALE is when a lender will accept less than the amount owed on a debt if the property is sold.* This arrangement must be approved by the lender who knows the borrower has financial problems (see **Figure 8-13**, CAR Short Sale Listing Addendum).

*If you convince your lender to mark a short sale as paid, it may not affect your credit as badly as a foreclosure. See an attorney for advice.*

### C. LIENS NOT ELIMINATED BY FORECLOSURE SALE

Most junior liens are eliminated by foreclosure. The following liens might not be eliminated:

1. Federal tax liens
2. State, county, and city taxes or assessments
3. Mechanic's liens for work begun before the trust deed was recorded

### D. PURCHASE MONEY TRUST DEED OR MORTGAGE

A *PURCHASE MONEY INSTRUMENT is a trust deed or mortgage obtained during the purchase of a home (1-to-4 units, owner-occupied).* It is called a purchase money instrument **only when**

**Figure 8-13**

## SHORT SALE LISTING ADDENDUM
(C.A.R. Form SSL, 8/07)

This is an addendum to the ☐ Residential Listing Agreement, ☐ Other _____ ,
("Agreement"), dated _____ on property known as *123 Sail Avenue* , _____
_____ ("Property"), between
_____ ("Seller"),
and _____ ("Broker").

1. **SHORT SALE LISTING:** Broker has advised Seller that the amount of money necessary to pay in full all loans and other debt or obligations that are secured by a lien(s), including any IRS liens, on the Property (Loans/Liens) as well as Broker commissions and other costs of sale may exceed the current market value of the Property. Accordingly, in order to sell the Property, Seller may be required to: (1) deposit his/her own funds into escrow, (2) obtain the agreement of secured lender(s) or creditor(s) (Lender) to accept, as payment in full, less money than they are owed (Short Sale), and/or (3) pay back some or all of the shortage after the sale is complete. Broker has advised Seller that other options, such as, but not limited to, negotiating a modification of existing Loans/Liens, refinancing, bankruptcy, foreclosure, or deed in lieu of foreclosure may be more appropriate for Seller. Any sale of the Property will be contingent on Lender approval (C.A.R. Form SSA).
2. **TAX CONSEQUENCES:** Broker has advised Seller that if Lender agrees to accept less than full payment, the difference may result in taxable income to Seller even though Seller does not receive any cash proceeds from the sale. Seller may also be taxed on the gain in value of the Property from the date of Seller's purchase to the date of sale, regardless of the amount of any existing Loans/Liens.
3. **CREDIT CONSEQUENCES:** A Short Sale may have a negative impact on Seller's credit rating even if a foreclosure process has not officially begun or once begun, is not completed.
4. **LENDER CONSIDERATIONS:** Seller acknowledges that a Short Sale is subject to Lender approval. Lender is not obligated to accept a Short Sale. Lender may impose conditions prior to consideration or approval of a Short Sale, such as obtaining a new appraisal, or requiring Seller to demonstrate hardship or provide copies of tax returns, pay stubs, assets, or other financial information. Lender may inform the IRS or credit reporting companies of the payment shortage. Broker has no control over Lender's decisions. Accordingly, Seller agrees to hold Broker harmless for acts or omissions of Lender.
5. **BROKER AUTHORITY:** Seller authorizes Broker to: (1) market the Property for sale, (2) contact Lender concerning Lender's approval of a Short Sale (C.A.R. Form ARC) and Seller agrees to give Broker any necessary information to negotiate with Lender, and (3) advertise in the MLS and other advertising medium that the Property transfer, sales price and payment of commissions are subject to Lender approval. If Lender will not cooperate, Broker may cancel this listing agreement.
6. **TAX AND LEGAL ADVICE:** Broker has advised Seller to consult with legal and tax counsel, prior to signing this listing, regarding the decision to seek a Short Sale. Broker cannot give legal or tax advice.

**By signing below, Seller acknowledges that Seller has read, understands and received a copy of this Short Sale Listing Addendum. Seller is encouraged to read it carefully.**

Date _____ Date _____
SELLER _____ SELLER _____

(Print name) _____ (Print name) _____

(Address) _____
Real Estate Broker (Listing Firm) _____ DRE Lic. # _____
By _____ DRE Lic. # _____ Date _____

Address _____ City _____ State ____ Zip _____
Telephone _____ Fax _____ E-mail _____

Published and Distributed by:
REAL ESTATE BUSINESS SERVICES, INC.
a subsidiary of the California Association of REALTORS®
525 South Virgil Avenue, Los Angeles, California 90020

Reviewed by _____ Date _____

SSL 8/07 (PAGE 1 OF 1) **SHORT SALE LISTING ADDENDUM (SSL PAGE 1 OF 1)**

Agent: WALT HUBER  Phone:  Fax:  Prepared using zipForm® software
Broker: WALT HUBER REALTOR

it is obtained at the time of purchase, **not on a refinanced loan**. It is an automatic protection given to homeowners (nothing is signed and nothing is mentioned). This is important because if the property is forced into foreclosure, a purchase money trust deed holder, or mortgage lender, cannot obtain a deficiency judgment. (Deficiency judgments may be obtained on **FHA and VA home loans** because federal law supercedes state law.)

A *DEFICIENCY JUDGMENT is given when the security pledged for a loan does not satisfy the debt upon its default*. If a home was sold at a court foreclosure sale for $217,000 and $240,000 was owed on the property, a lender would have a $23,000 deficiency judgment against the borrower. If it were a purchase money instrument, however, there would be no deficiency judgment.

**The purchase money instrument only protects owners of residential dwellings of 1-to-4 units where the owner lives in one unit.** Owners of properties having more than four units or properties that do not have a purchase money instrument are not protected against possible deficiency judgments. **Remember:** deficiency judgments can be obtained only if the owner doesn't have a purchase money instrument and is foreclosed upon in a court foreclosure sale.

# IX. Second Trust Deeds (Junior TDs)

*A seller may have to take back a second trust deed as part of his or her equity in order to make the sale.*

Even if a buyer qualifies for a loan to cover 80% of the cost of a home, he or she may still have a difficult time scraping together the 20% needed for the down payment. **When a buyer does not have enough cash to cover the gap between the sales price and the loan amount, another loan, or "second" trust deed, is sometimes obtained (often from the seller) and the interest charged the buyer is not governed by the usury law (10% is common).**

## A. JUNIOR LIENS ("Private Parties")

Besides seconds, it is also possible for borrowers who qualify to obtain "third" or "fourth" trust deeds, but they are all commonly referred to as second trust deeds or junior liens. They all may be called second trust deeds but their priority is determined by the order in which they were recorded. *Any loan on real property obtained after the first trust deed and secured by a second, third, or subsequent trust deed, is known as a JUNIOR LIEN*. The most senior lien, on the other hand, is the first trust deed.

> **Example:** Smith is buying a house with a sale's price of $250,000. She assumes the seller's loan on the property of $200,000. She applies to her company credit union and is given a second trust deed of $30,000, so all she needs is a cash down payment of $20,000, plus closing costs, to complete the transaction.

## B. HOMEOWNER EQUITY LOANS

Second trust deeds are not only obtainable as part of the financing package when a property is first being purchased. Seconds and other junior liens may be arranged any time a qualified borrower wants to borrow money, for whatever reason, as long as there is sufficient equity and enough ready income to support the payments. *EQUITY is the fair market value of a property, minus the amount of money owed to lenders and all other lienholders. HOMEOWNER EQUITY LOANS are loans based on the homeowner's increase in equity caused by inflation, rising property values, and the reduction, by payments, of the existing loan balance.*

Let's suppose Smith, who purchased that new home for $250,000, finds herself in need of money after a few years. Fortunately, her property has increased in market value and is now worth more than $300,000. Even though Smith is already mortgaged up to her ears, she can borrow on her equity; the difference between what she owes and what her property is worth.

Homeowner equity loans are generally secured by second (junior) trust deeds. They are available from institutional lenders, small finance companies, and individuals who specialize in this area. Lenders will charge a higher interest rate on seconds and other junior trust deeds because they are less secure than primary financing.

## C. HOLDER OF A SECOND TRUST DEED (Lender)

Sometimes when purchasing a property, additional funds will be required beyond the cash down payment and the first trust deed. As a result, the seller may loan the buyer more money through the use of a second trust deed. Usually the second trust deed has a higher rate of interest and a shorter payoff period because of the higher risk involved. The usual monthly payment is one percent of the loan.

Second trust deeds often require a balloon payment at the end of the term because they are not fully amortized. The holder of a second trust deed or any junior trust deed has the same rights as does the holder of the first deed of trust. He or she is entitled to his or her payment each month, as is the first trust deed holder. If the trustor defaults on the second, the second trust deed holder, just like the first trust deed holder, can start default action. In addition, if the trustor defaults on the first trust deed, the second trust deed holder can reinstate the first trust deed and start default action against the trustor. If the property's market value is higher than the total amount owed on the first trust deed, it is a wise move for the second trust deed holder to start his or her own default and sale action.

## D. REQUEST FOR NOTICE OF DEFAULT

When a *REQUEST FOR NOTICE OF DEFAULT is recorded, the trustee is required to notify all persons who request notice if a "notice of default" is recorded on a particular property* (see **Figure 8-14**). Any person who has an interest in a particular trust deed, usually a second or third trust deed holder, should want to be informed if the buyer is not paying on the first deed of trust. This information not only informs the junior deed holders of nonpayment on the first trust deed, but it also allows them time to prepare to purchase the trust deed at the forthcoming trustee's sale. It will also give them time to start default actions on their own junior trust deeds.

This request for notice is recorded in the county recorder's office where the property is located. If a seller takes back a second or even a third trust deed, thereby becoming a junior trust deed holder on the property that person has just sold, that person would be wise to record a request for notice. Some request for notice forms are incorporated into the trust deed form, so the request for notice is automatically filed.

**Figure 8-14**

————— SPACE ABOVE THIS LINE FOR RECORDER'S USE —————

# REQUEST FOR NOTICE

In accordance with section 2924b, Civil Code, request is hereby made that a copy of any notice of default

and a copy of any notice of sale under the deed of trust recorded          19

in Book      page      of official records of      County, (or filed for record

with recorder's serial No.

        County) California, executed by

as trustor in which

is named as beneficiary and

as trustee be mailed to                   whose

address is

Signature ...........................................

FOR NOTARY SEAL OR STAMP

STATE OF CALIFORNIA

COUNTY OF                     SS.

On this the      day of      19   , before me,
the undersigned, a Notary Public in and for said County and State,
personally appeared

                     , personally known
to me or proved to me on the basis of satisfactory evidence to be the
person      whose      name      subscribed to the within
instrument and acknowledged that
executed the same.

NOTARY SIGNATURE

Title Order No.             Escrow No.

SAFECO Stock No. **CAL-0038**

STATE OF CALIFORNIA

COUNTY OF                          

On this the      day of      19    before
me, the undersigned, a Notary Public in and for said County and State,
personally appeared                      

                    , personally
known to me or proved to me on the basis of satisfactory evidence to
be the      President, and            

                    , personally
known to me or proved to me on the basis of satisfactory evidence to
be      Secretary of the corporation that executed the
within instrument on behalf of the corporation therein named, and
acknowledged to me that such corporation executed the within instrument pursuant to its by-laws or a resolution of its board of directors.

NOTARY SIGNATURE

244

### E. WRAPAROUND – ALL INCLUSIVE TRUST DEEDS (AITD)

An *ALL INCLUSIVE TRUST DEED (WRAPAROUND)* is a second trust deed with a face value of both the new amount it secures and the balance due under the first trust deed. A wraparound trust deed can take the form of a land contract or a deed of trust. The wraparound is seldom used except when a property is difficult to sell or credit is tight (high interest rates). This form of security may be used to increase the lender's (seller's) yield upon the sale of property and to provide easy financing for the buyer. Rather than having a new buyer assume an existing loan, the seller carries back a wraparound trust deed at a higher rate of interest (if the loan is assumable). The seller continues to pay off the old trust deed out of the payment received from the buyer. Since these payments are larger, the seller gets a margin of profit. The buyer, in turn, gets easy financing and avoids the new loan fees charged by institutional lenders. As always, an attorney should be consulted because wraparound contracts may require special handling and will not be available with all loans.

# X. Land Contract
# (Conditional Installment Sales Contract)

*A buyer purchasing a home under a valid land sales contact holds equitable title, and is entitled to full use and enjoyment of the property.*

The *LAND CONTRACT is an instrument of finance in which the seller retains legal ownership of the property until the buyer has made the last payment.* It is usually called a land contract in California, but may also be referred to as a "contract of sale," "agreement of sale," "conditional sales contract," "installment sales contract," or a "property sales contract." Since this is a contract between the buyer and seller, the requirements as to the down payment and other conditions of the land contract are negotiable.

*A vendee (buyer) under a land contract should record the land contract for his/her protection.*

When financing is hard to obtain, this can be an alternative to the usual financing methods. Although it is not widely used, it is a valid financing device (see **Figure 8-15**).

*With a land contract, the seller keeps legal title to the property until the last payment is made.*

*An owner selling under a land contract is known as a **VENDOR**. A **VENDEE** is a buyer using a land contract.* A vendor can sell his or her store (real property) and store fixtures (personal property) to a vendee by use of a land contract. A land contract is a common way to sell a business.

With a land contract the buyer holds **equitable title**, like a borrower purchasing under a trust deed. He or she is entitled, though, to the full use and enjoyment of the property. Legal title is held by the seller until the land contract terms have been completely fulfilled. A grant deed to the property is given only when the land contract is paid off in full.

Land contracts should be recorded. If the buyer were to default, his or her interest would show as a cloud on the title. To protect his or her interests, the vendee (buyer) should record the land contract.

*If a buyer (vendee) defaults on a recorded land contract, the seller (vendor) should file a "quiet title action" to remove the "cloud on title."*

**Figure 8-15**

RECORDING REQUESTED BY

AND WHEN RECORDED MAIL TO

SPACE ABOVE THIS LINE FOR RECORDER'S USE

### LONG FORM SECURITY (INSTALLMENT) LAND CONTRACT WITH POWER OF SALE AND REQUEST FOR NOTICE OF DEFAULT (PRIOR LOAN PAYMENTS *NOT* INCLUDED)

THIS AGREEMENT, made and entered into this                    day of                    between

herein called VENDOR, and

herein called VENDEE, and

STEWART TITLE OF CALIFORNIA, INC., a California corporation, herein called TRUSTEE.

The signature of Vendor and Vendee of this contract shall also constitute their signature of the

### REQUEST FOR NOTICE OF DEFAULT

In accordance with California Civil Code section 2924(b), request is hereby made by the undersigned Vendor and Vendee that: (1) a copy of any Notice of Default and a copy of any Notice of Sale under Deed of Trust recorded _____, in Book _____ Page _____, Document No. _____ Official Records of _____ County, California, as affecting the herein described property, executed by _____

as Trustor, in which _____
is named as Beneficiary, and _____ as Trustee,
be mailed to Vendor and Vendee at address immediately below; and (2) a copy of any Notice of Default and a copy of any Notice of Sale under Deed of Trust recorded _____ in Book _____,
Page _____, Document No. _____, Official Records of_____County,
California, as affecting the herein described property, executed by_____
as Trustor, in which _____ is named as
Beneficiary, and _____Trustee,
be mailed to Vendor and Vendee at address below.

Vendee                                            Vendor

Address                                           Address

LANDContract.doc

246

Land contracts are legal documents that should be drawn by and discussed with an attorney before use. Legal problems associated with a land contract are: obtaining marketable title, non-recorded status, intervening liens, foreclosure, and quiet title action. As you can see, legal advice is necessary.

# XI. Truth in Lending Act (Regulation Z) and Other Acts

*Regulation Z applies to 1-4 residential units, NOT to agricultural, business, or commercial loans.*

## A. TRUTH IN LENDING

The *TRUTH IN LENDING ACT, known as Regulation Z, was enacted to protect the consumer by requiring that the lender (creditor) tell the borrower how much he or she is paying for credit.* This enables the consumer to make comparisons between various credit sources. Regulation Z also states that the lender (creditor) must express all related financing costs as a percentage, known as the annual percentage rate (APR).

Regulation Z is enforced by the Federal Trade Commission (FTC). The CAR® 3-page Mortgage Loan Disclosure Statement is used to implement Regulation Z (see **Figure 8-16**). See **Figure 8-17** for an example of the CAR® Seller Financing Addendum and Disclosure form.

*A low down payment and a long-term loan will increase the total financing cost.*

### 1. Annual Percentage Rate (APR)

*APR is the measure or "relative cost of credit" expressed as an annual rate. If the APR appears in an advertisement, NO other disclosure of terms need be stated because it includes all credit costs.*

The *ANNUAL PERCENTAGE RATE (APR) represents the relationship between the total of the finance charges (interest rate, points, and the loan fee) and the total amount financed, expressed as a percentage.* It must be computed to the nearest one-quarter of one percent and must be printed on the loan form more conspicuously than the rest of the printed material.

Interest rates can be calculated by many different methods that can be very confusing to the borrower. The APR standardizes these figures, calculating all rates by the same formula. Borrowers should look for the APR figure (usually in a box) to compare and find the best APR available.

*According to the Federal Truth in Lending Act, the lender must disclose the annual percentage rate of a loan, which is the cost of credit, including interest and other financing costs, expressed as an annual rate.*

### 2. Advertising Terms May Require Additional Disclosures

Anyone placing an advertisement for consumer credit must comply with the advertising requirements of the Truth in Lending Act. Disclosures must be made "clearly and conspicuously." **If only the annual percentage (APR) rate is disclosed, additional**

## Figure 8-16

CALIFORNIA
ASSOCIATION
OF REALTORS®

## MORTGAGE LOAN DISCLOSURE STATEMENT
### (BORROWER)
(As required by the Business and Professions Code §10241
and Title 10, California Administrative Code, §2840)
(C.A.R. Form MS, Revised 08/08)

_____
(Name of Broker/Arranger of Credit)

_____
(Business Address of Broker)

I. <u>SUMMARY OF LOAN TERMS</u>
  A. PRINCIPAL AMOUNT . . . . . . . . . . . . . . . . . . . . . . . . . . . . . . . . . . . . . . . . . . . . . . . . . . . . . . $ _____
  B. ESTIMATED DEDUCTIONS FROM PRINCIPAL AMOUNT
    1. Costs and Expenses (See Paragraph III-A) . . . . . . . . . . . . . . . . . . . . . . . . . . . $ _____
    2. Broker Commission/Origination Fee (See Paragraph III-B) . . . . . . . . . . . . . . . $ _____
    3. Lender Origination Fee/Discounts (See Paragraph III-B) . . . . . . . . . . . . . . . . . $ _____
    4. Additional compensation will/may be received from lender not deducted from loan proceeds.
       ☐ YES  $ _____ (if known) or ☐ NO
    5. Amount to be Paid on Authorization of Borrower (See Paragraph III-C) . . . . . . . . . . $ _____
  C. ESTIMATED CASH PAYABLE TO BORROWER (A less B) . . . . . . . . . . . . . . . . . . . . . . $ _____
II. <u>GENERAL INFORMATION ABOUT LOAN</u>
  A. PROPOSED LOAN INFORMATION
    1. Proposed loan term _____  ☐ Years  ☐ Months

| ☐ FIXED RATE LOAN | ☐ ADJUSTABLE RATE LOAN (EXAMPLE 6-MONTH ARM; 1-YEAR ARM) |
|---|---|
| Fixed rate loan _____ % payable at $ _____ month | Proposed interest rate _____ % |
| | Fully indexed rate _____ % |
| | Proposed monthly payment: $ _____ |
| | Maximum interest rate _____ % |
| | Interest rate can increase _____ % each _____ months |
| | Maximum loan payment can be $ _____ after _____ months |
| ☐ INITIAL FIXED RATE LOAN (EXAMPLE 2/28, 3/1, 5/1) | ☐ INITIAL ADJUSTABLE RATE LOAN (EXAMPLE LOW ENTRY RATE ARM) |
| Proposed initial fixed interest rate _____ % | Proposed initial adjustable interest rate _____ % |
| Initial fixed interest rate in effect for _____ months | Initial fixed interest rate in effect for _____ months |
| Proposed initial monthly payment: $ _____ | Proposed initial monthly payment: $ _____ |
| Adjustable interest rate of _____ % will begin after fixed rate period ends | Fully indexed rate _____ % |
| Monthly payment can increase to $ _____ after fixed rate period ends | Maximum interest rate _____ % |
| Fully indexed rate _____ % | Interest rate can increase _____ % each _____ months |
| Maximum interest rate _____ % | Monthly payment can increase to $ _____ after initial adjustable rate period ends |
| Interest rate can increase _____ % each _____ months | Maximum loan payment can be $ _____ after |
| Maximum loan payment can be $ _____ after _____ months | _____ months |

    2. This loan is based on limited or no documentation of your income and/or assets and may have a higher interest rate, or more points or fees than other products requiring documentation:  ☐ No  ☐ Yes.
    3. The loan is subject to a balloon payment:  ☐ No  ☐ Yes. If Yes, the following paragraph applies and a final balloon payment of $ _____ will be due on _____ [estimated date (month/day/year)].

    **NOTICE TO BORROWER:** IF YOU DO NOT HAVE THE FUNDS TO PAY THE BALLOON PAYMENT WHEN IT COMES DUE, YOU MAY HAVE TO OBTAIN A NEW LOAN AGAINST YOUR PROPERTY TO MAKE THE BALLOON PAYMENT. IN THAT CASE, YOU MAY AGAIN HAVE TO PAY COMMISSIONS, FEES AND EXPENSES FOR THE ARRANGING OF THE NEW LOAN. IN ADDITION, IF YOU ARE UNABLE TO MAKE THE MONTHLY PAYMENTS OR THE BALLOON PAYMENT, YOU MAY LOSE THE PROPERTY AND ALL OF YOUR EQUITY THROUGH FORECLOSURE. KEEP THIS IN MIND IN DECIDING UPON THE AMOUNT AND TERMS OF THIS LOAN.

  B. This loan will be evidenced by a promissory note and secured by a deed of trust on property identified as (street address or legal description):
    _123 Sail Avenue_ , _____

Buyer's Initials (_____)(_____)
Seller's Initials (_____)(_____)

Reviewed by _____ Date_____

EQUAL HOUSING OPPORTUNITY

**MS REVISED 08/08 (PAGE 1 OF 3)**
**MORTGAGE LOAN DISCLOSURE STATEMENT (MS PAGE 1 OF 3)**

| Agent: WALT HUBER | Phone: | Fax: | Prepared using zipForm® software |
|---|---|---|---|
| Broker: WALT HUBER REALTOR | | | |

C. 1. Liens presently against this property (do not include loan being applied for):

| Nature of Lien | Priority | Lienholder's Name | Amount Owing |
|---|---|---|---|
| | | | |
| | | | |
| | | | |

   2. Liens that will remain against this property after the loan being applied for is made or arranged (include loan being applied for):

| Nature of Lien | Priority | Lienholder's Name | Amount Owing |
|---|---|---|---|
| | | | |
| | | | |
| | | | |

**NOTICE TO BORROWER:** Be sure that you state the amount of all liens as accurately as possible. If you contract with the broker to arrange this loan, but it cannot be arranged because you did not state these liens correctly, you may be liable to pay commissions, fees and expenses even though you do not obtain the loan.

D. Prepayments: The proposed loan has the following prepayment provisions:
  ☐ No prepayment penalty (you will not be charged a penalty to pay off or refinance the loan before maturity)
  ☐ You will have to pay a prepayment penalty if the loan is paid off or refinanced in the first _____ years. The prepayment penalty could be as much as $ _____ . Any prepayment of principal in excess of 20% of the
      ☐ original loan balance or
      ☐ unpaid balance
  for the first _____ years will include a penalty not to exceed _____ months interest at the note interest rate but not more than the interest you would be charged if the loan were paid to maturity.
  ☐ Other - you will have to pay a prepayment penalty if the loan is paid off or refinanced in the first _____ years as follows: _____

E. Taxes and Insurance:
  ☐ There will be an impound (escrow) account which will collect approximately $ _____ a month in addition to your principal and interest payments for the payment of ☐ county property taxes** ☐ hazard insurance ☐ mortgage insurance ☐ flood insurance ☐ other _____
  ☐ If there is no impound (escrow) account or if your escrow (impound) account does not include one or more of the payments described above, you will have to plan for the payment of ☐ county property taxes** ☐ hazard insurance of approximately $ _____ per year.
  **In a purchase transaction, county property taxes are calculated based on the sales price of the property and may require the payment of an additional (supplemental) tax bill from the county tax authority by your lender (if escrowed) or you (if not escrowed).**
F. Late Charges: ☐ YES, see loan documents or ☐ NO
G. The purchase of credit life and/or credit disability insurance by a borrower is not required as a condition of making this loan.

**III. DEDUCTIONS FROM LOAN PROCEEDS**
  A. Estimated Maximum Costs and Expenses of Arranging the Loan to be Paid Out of Loan Principal:

| | PAYABLE TO Broker | Others |
|---|---|---|
| 1. Appraisal fee ................................................. | | |
| 2. Escrow fee ................................................... | | |
| 3. Title insurance policy ...................................... | | |
| 4. Notary fees .................................................. | | |
| 5. Recording fees .............................................. | | |
| 6. Credit investigation fees ................................... | | |
| 7. Other costs and expenses: | | |
| | | |
| | | |
| Total Costs and Expenses ..................................... | $ | |
| B. Compensation ............................................... | $ | |
| 1. Brokerage Commission/Origination Fee ................ | $ | |

Buyer's Initials ( _____ )( _____ )
Seller's Initials ( _____ )( _____ )

MS REVISED 08/08 (PAGE 2 OF 3)

Reviewed by _____ Date _____

**MORTGAGE LOAN DISCLOSURE STATEMENT (MS PAGE 2 OF 3)**

Untitled

2.  Lender Origination Fee/Discounts ............................. $ _____

C.  Estimated Payment to be Made out of Loan Principal on
Authorization of Borrower

PAYABLE TO

| | Broker | Others |
|---|---|---|
| 1.  Fire or other hazard insurance premiums ................ | _____ | _____ |
| 2.  Credit life or disability insurance premiums (See Paragraph II-G) ....... | _____ | _____ |
| 3.  Beneficiary statement fees ................................ | _____ | _____ |
| 4.  Reconveyance and similar fees ............................ | _____ | _____ |
| 5.  Discharge of existing liens against property: | | |
| | _____ | _____ |
| | _____ | _____ |
| 6.  Other: | | |
| | _____ | _____ |
| | _____ | _____ |

Total to be Paid on Authorization of Borrower ..................... $ _____

Article 7 Compliance: If this loan is secured by a first deed of trust on dwellings in a principal amount of less than $30,000 or secured by a junior lien on dwellings in a principal amount of less than $20,000, the undersigned licensee certifies that the loan will be made in compliance with Article 7 of Chapter 3 of the Real Estate Law.

This loan **may / will / will not** (delete two) be made wholly or in part from broker-controlled funds as defined in Section 10241(j) of the Business and Professions Code.

**IV. NOTICES TO BORROWER:**

1. This disclosure statement may be used if the Broker is acting as an agent in arranging the loan by a third person or if the loan will be made with funds owned or controlled by the broker. If the Broker indicates in the Article 7 Compliance immediately above, that the loan "may" be made out of Broker-controlled funds, the Broker must notify the borrower prior to the close of escrow if the funds to be received by the Borrower are in fact Broker-controlled funds.

2. THIS IS NOT A LOAN COMMITMENT. Do not sign this statement until you have read and understood all of the information in it. All parts of this form must be completed before you sign. Borrower hereby acknowledges the receipt of a copy of this statement.

_____   _____   _____   _____
Name of Broker             License Number   Broker Representative   License Number

_____
Broker's Address

OR

_____   _____   _____   _____
Signature of Broker        Date      Signature of Representative   Date

_____   _____   _____   _____
Borrower                   Date      Borrower                      Date

The Department of Real Estate License Information phone number is 916-227-0931, or check license status at www.dre.ca.gov.

Published and Distributed by:
REAL ESTATE BUSINESS SERVICES, INC.
a subsidiary of the California Association of REALTORS®
525 South Virgil Avenue, Los Angeles, California 90020

**MS REVISED 08/08 (PAGE 3 OF 3)**

Reviewed by _____ Date_____

**MORTGAGE LOAN DISCLOSURE STATEMENT (MS PAGE 3 OF 3)**

Untitled

**Figure 8-17**

CALIFORNIA
ASSOCIATION
OF REALTORS®

## SELLER FINANCING ADDENDUM AND DISCLOSURE
(California Civil Code §§2956-2967)
(C.A.R. Form SFA, Revised 10/02)

This is an addendum to the ☐ Residential Purchase Agreement, ☐ Counter Offer, or ☐ Other _____
_____ , ("Agreement"), dated _____
On property known as _____ 123 Sail Avenue , _____ ("Property"),
between _____ ("Buyer"),
and _____ ("Seller").
Seller agrees to extend credit to Buyer as follows:

1. **PRINCIPAL; INTEREST; PAYMENT; MATURITY TERMS:** ☐ Principal amount $ _____ , interest at _____ % per annum,
   payable at approximately $ _____ per ☐ month, ☐ year, or ☐ other _____ , remaining principal
   balance due in _____ years.

2. **LOAN APPLICATION; CREDIT REPORT:** Within 5 (or _____ ) Days After Acceptance: **(a)** Buyer shall provide Seller a completed loan
   application on a form acceptable to Seller (such as a FNMA/FHLMC Uniform Residential Loan Application for residential one to four unit properties);
   and **(b)** Buyer authorizes Seller and/or Agent to obtain, at Buyer's expense, a copy of Buyer's credit report. Buyer shall provide any supporting
   documentation reasonably requested by Seller. Seller, after first giving Buyer a Notice to Buyer to Perform, may cancel this Agreement in writing and
   authorize return of Buyer's deposit if Buyer fails to provide such documents within that time, or if Seller disapproves any above item within 5 (or
   ☐ _____ ) Days After receipt of each item.

3. **CREDIT DOCUMENTS:** This extension of credit by Seller will be evidenced by: ☐ Note and deed of trust; ☐ All-inclusive note and deed of trust;
   ☐ Installment land sale contract; ☐ Lease/option (when parties intend transfer of equitable title); OR ☐ Other (specify) _____
   _____

**THE FOLLOWING TERMS APPLY ONLY IF CHECKED. SELLER IS ADVISED TO READ ALL TERMS, EVEN THOSE NOT CHECKED, TO
UNDERSTAND WHAT IS OR IS NOT INCLUDED, AND, IF NOT INCLUDED, THE CONSEQUENCES THEREOF.**

4. ☐ **LATE CHARGE:** If any payment is not made within _____ Days After it is due, a late charge of either $ _____ , or
   _____ % of the installment due, may be charged to Buyer. **NOTE:** on single family residences that Buyer intends to occupy, California
   Civil Code §2954.4(a) limits the late charge to no more than 6% of the total monthly payment due and requires a grace period of no less than 10
   days.

5. ☐ **BALLOON PAYMENT:** The extension of credit will provide for a balloon payment, in the amount of $ _____ , plus any accrued
   interest, which is due on _____ (date).

6. ☐ **PREPAYMENT:** If all or part of this extension of credit is paid early, Seller may charge a prepayment penalty as follows (if applicable):
   _____ . Caution: California Civil Code §2954.9 contains limitations on
   prepayment penalties for residential one-to-four unit properties.

7. ☐ **DUE ON SALE:** If any interest in the Property is sold or otherwise transferred, Seller has the option to require immediate payment of the entire
   unpaid principal balance, plus any accrued interest.

8.* ☐ **REQUEST FOR COPY OF NOTICE OF DEFAULT:** A request for a copy of Notice of Default as defined in California Civil Code §2924e will be
   recorded. **If not,** Seller is advised to consider recording a Request for Notice of Default.

9.* ☐ **REQUEST FOR NOTICE OF DELINQUENCY:** A request for Notice of Delinquency, as defined in California Civil Code §2924e, to be signed and
   paid for by Buyer, will be made to senior leinholders. **If not,** Seller is advised to consider making a Request for Notice of Delinquency. Seller is
   advised to check with senior leinholders to verify whether they will honor this request.

10.* ☐ **TAX SERVICE:**
   A. If property taxes on the Property become delinquent, tax service will be arranged to report to Seller. **If not,** Seller is advised to consider
      retaining a tax service, or to otherwise determine that property taxes are paid.
   B. ☐ Buyer, ☐ Seller, shall be responsible for the initial and continued retention of, and payment for, such tax service.

11. ☐ **TITLE INSURANCE:** Title insurance coverage will be provided to both Seller and Buyer, insuring their respective interests in the Property. **If not,**
   Buyer and Seller are advised to consider securing such title insurance coverage.

12. ☐ **HAZARD INSURANCE:**
   A. The parties' escrow holder or insurance carrier will be directed to include a loss payee endorsement, adding Seller to the Property insurance
      policy. **If not,** Seller is advised to secure such an endorsement, or acquire a separate insurance policy.
   B. Property insurance **does not** include earthquake or flood insurance coverage, unless checked:
      ☐ Earthquake insurance will be obtained; ☐ Flood insurance will be obtained.

13. ☐ **PROCEEDS TO BUYER:** Buyer will receive cash proceeds at the close of the sale transaction. The amount received will be approximately
   $ _____ , from _____ (indicate source of proceeds). Buyer represents
   that the purpose of such disbursement is as follows: _____

14. ☐ **NEGATIVE AMORTIZATION; DEFERRED INTEREST:** Negative amortization results when Buyer's periodic payments are less than the amount
   of interest earned on the obligation. Deferred interest also results when the obligation does not require periodic payments for a period of time. In
   either case, interest is not payable as it accrues. This accrued interest will have to be paid by Buyer at a later time, and may result in Buyer owing
   more on the obligation than at its origination. The credit being extended to Buyer by Seller will provide for negative amortization or deferred
   interest as indicated below. (Check A, B, or C. CHECK ONE ONLY.)
   ☐ A. All negative amortization or deferred interest shall be added to the principal _____ (e.g., annually, monthly, etc.),
      and thereafter shall bear interest at the rate specified in the credit documents (compound interest);
   OR ☐ B. All deferred interest shall be due and payable, along with principal, at maturity;
   OR ☐ C. Other _____

*(For Paragraphs 8-10) In order to receive timely and continued notification, Seller is advised to record appropriate notices and/or to notify appropriate
parties of any change in Seller's address.

Buyer's Initials ( _____ ) ( _____ )
Seller's Initials ( _____ ) ( _____ )

Reviewed by _____ Date _____

EQUAL HOUSING
OPPORTUNITY

SFA REVISED 10/02 (PAGE 1 OF 3)

**SELLER FINANCING ADDENDUM AND DISCLOSURE (SFA PAGE 1 OF 3)**

| Agent: WALT HUBER | Phone: | Fax: | Prepared using zipForm® software |
|---|---|---|---|
| Broker: WALT HUBER REALTOR | | | |

Property Address: _123 Sail Avenue_ , _____ Date: _____

15. ☐ **ALL-INCLUSIVE DEED OF TRUST; INSTALLMENT LAND SALE CONTRACT:** This transaction involves the use of an all-inclusive (or wraparound) deed of trust or an installment land sale contract. That deed of trust or contract shall provide as follows:
    A. In the event of an acceleration of any senior encumbrance, the party responsible for payment, or for legal defense is: ☐ Buyer ☐ Seller ;
      OR ☐ **Is not** specified in the credit or security documents.
    B. In the event of the prepayment of a senior encumbrance, the responsibilities and rights of Buyer and Seller regarding refinancing, prepayment penalties, and any prepayment discounts are: _____ ;
      OR ☐ **Are not** specified in the documents evidencing credit.
    C. Buyer will make periodic payments to _____ (Seller, collection agent, or any neutral third party), who will be responsible for disbursing payments to the payee(s) on the senior encumbrance(s) and to Seller.
      **NOTE:** The Parties are advised to designate a neutral third party for these purposes.
16. ☐ **TAX IDENTIFICATION NUMBERS:** Buyer and Seller shall each provide to each other their Social Security Numbers or Taxpayer Identification Numbers.
17. ☐ **OTHER CREDIT TERMS:** _____
18. ☐ **RECORDING:** The documents evidencing credit (paragraph 3) will be recorded with the county recorder where the Property is located. **If not,** Buyer and Seller are advised that their respective interests in the Property may be jeopardized by intervening liens, judgments, encumbrances, or subsequent transfers.
19. ☐ **JUNIOR FINANCING:** There will be additional financing, secured by the Property, junior to this Seller financing. Explain: _____
20. **SENIOR LOANS AND ENCUMBRANCES:** The following information is provided on loans and/or encumbrances that will be **senior** to Seller financing. **NOTE:** The following are estimates, unless otherwise marked with an asterisk (*). If checked: ☐ A separate sheet with information on additional senior loans/encumbrances is attached.

| | 1st | 2nd |
|---|---|---|
| A. Original Balance | $ _____ | $ _____ |
| B. Current Balance | $ _____ | $ _____ |
| C. Periodic Payment (e.g. $100/month) | $ _____ | $ _____ / |
|     Including Impounds of | $ _____ | $ _____ / |
| D. Interest Rate (per annum) | _____ % | _____ % |
| E. Fixed or Variable Rate: | _____ | _____ |
|     If Variable Rate: Lifetime Cap (Ceiling) | _____ | _____ |
|     Indicator (Underlying Index) | _____ | _____ |
|     Margins | _____ | _____ |
| F. Maturity Date | _____ | _____ |
| G. Amount of Balloon Payment | $ _____ | $ _____ |
| H. Date Balloon Payment Due | _____ | |
| I. Potential for Negative Amortization? (Yes, No, or Unknown) | _____ | |
| J. Due on Sale? (Yes, No, or Unknown) | _____ | |
| K. Pre-payment penalty? (Yes, No, or Unknown) | _____ | |
| L. Are payments current? (Yes, No, or Unknown) | _____ | |

21. **BUYER'S CREDITWORTHINESS:** (CHECK EITHER A OR B. Do not check both.) In addition to the loan application, credit report and other information requested under paragraph 2:
    A.   ☐ No other disclosure concerning Buyer's creditworthiness has been made to Seller;
OR B.   ☐ The following representations concerning Buyer's creditworthiness are made by Buyer(s) to Seller:

| **Borrower** _____ | **Co-Borrower** _____ |
|---|---|
| 1. Occupation _____ | 1. Occupation _____ |
| 2. Employer _____ | 2. Employer _____ |
| 3. Length of Employment _____ | 3. Length of Employment _____ |
| 4. Monthly Gross Income _____ | 4. Monthly Gross Income _____ |
| 5. Other _____ | 5. Other _____ |

22. **ADDED, DELETED OR SUBSTITUTED BUYERS:** The addition, deletion or substitution of any person or entity under this Agreement or to title prior to close of escrow shall require Seller's written consent. Seller may grant or withhold consent in Seller's sole discretion. Any additional or substituted person or entity shall, if requested by Seller, submit to Seller the same documentation as required for the original named Buyer. Seller and/or Brokers may obtain a credit report, at Buyer's expense, on any such person or entity.

Buyer's Initials ( _____ ) ( _____ )
Seller's Initials ( _____ ) ( _____ )

**SFA REVISED 10/02 (PAGE 2 OF 3)**

| Reviewed by _____ Date _____ |

EQUAL HOUSING OPPORTUNITY

**SELLER FINANCING ADDENDUM AND DISCLOSURE (SFA PAGE 2 OF 3)**

Untitled

Property Address: _123 Sail Avenue_ , _____ Date: _____

23. **CAUTION:**
  A. If the Seller financing requires a balloon payment, Seller shall give Buyer written notice, according to the terms of Civil Code §2966, at least 90 and not more than 150 days before the balloon payment is due if the transaction is for the purchase of a dwelling for not more than four families.
  B. If **any** obligation secured by the Property calls for a balloon payment, Seller and Buyer are aware that refinancing of the balloon payment at maturity may be difficult or impossible, depending on conditions in the conventional mortgage marketplace at that time. There are no assurances that new financing or a loan extension will be available when the balloon prepayment, or any prepayment, is due.
  C. If **any** of the existing or proposed loans or extensions of credit would require refinancing as a result of a lack of full amortization, such refinancing might be difficult or impossible in the conventional mortgage marketplace.
  D. In the event of default by Buyer: (1) Seller may have to reinstate and/or make monthly payments on any and all senior encumbrances (including real property taxes) in order to protect Seller's secured interest; (2) Seller's rights are generally limited to foreclosure on the Property, pursuant to California Code of Civil Procedure §580b; and (3) the Property may lack sufficient equity to protect Seller's interests if the Property decreases in value.

If this three-page Addendum and Disclosure is used in a transaction for the purchase of a dwelling for not more than four families, it shall be prepared by an Arranger of Credit as defined in California Civil Code §2957(a). (The Arranger of Credit is usually the agent who obtained the offer.)

Arranger of Credit - (Print Firm Name) _____ By _____ Date _____

Address _____ City _____ State _____ Zip _____

Phone _____ Fax _____

BUYER AND SELLER ACKNOWLEDGE AND AGREE THAT BROKERS: (A) WILL NOT PROVIDE LEGAL OR TAX ADVICE; (B) WILL NOT PROVIDE OTHER ADVICE OR INFORMATION THAT EXCEEDS THE KNOWLEDGE, EDUCATION AND EXPERIENCE REQUIRED TO OBTAIN A REAL ESTATE LICENSE, OR (C) HAVE NOT AND WILL NOT VERIFY ANY INFORMATION PROVIDED BY EITHER BUYER OR SELLER. BUYER AND SELLER AGREE THAT THEY WILL SEEK LEGAL, TAX, AND OTHER DESIRED ASSISTANCE FROM APPROPRIATE PROFESSIONALS. BUYER AND SELLER ACKNOWLEDGE THAT THE INFORMATION EACH HAS PROVIDED TO THE ARRANGER OF CREDIT FOR INCLUSION IN THIS DISCLOSURE FORM IS ACCURATE. BUYER AND SELLER FURTHER ACKNOWLEDGE THAT EACH HAS RECEIVED A COMPLETED COPY OF THIS DISCLOSURE FORM.

Buyer _____ Date _____
(signature)
Address _____ City _____ State _____ Zip _____
Phone _____ Fax _____ E-mail _____

Buyer _____ Date _____
(signature)
Address _____ City _____ State _____ Zip _____
Phone _____ Fax _____ E-mail _____

Seller _____ Date _____
(signature)
Address _____ City _____ State _____ Zip _____
Phone _____ Fax _____ E-mail _____

Seller _____ Date _____
(signature)
Address _____ City _____ State _____ Zip _____
Phone _____ Fax _____ E-mail _____

Published and Distributed by:
REAL ESTATE BUSINESS SERVICES, INC.
a subsidiary of the California Association of REALTORS®
525 South Virgil Avenue, Los Angeles, California 90020

Reviewed by _____ Date _____

EQUAL HOUSING OPPORTUNITY

SFA REVISED 10/02 (PAGE 3 OF 3)

**SELLER FINANCING ADDENDUM AND DISCLOSURE (SFA PAGE 3 OF 3)**

Untitled

**disclosures are not required.** If, however, an advertisement contains any one of the following terms, then the ad must also disclose other credit terms:

1. The amount or percentage of any down payment
2. The number of payments or period of repayment
3. The amount of any payment
4. The amount of any finance charge

*When advertising a graduated payment loan, differences in monthly payments must be disclosed.*

## B. RIGHT TO CANCEL (Federal Notice of Right to Cancel)

*Loans subsequent (future loans) have a 3-day right of rescission by the borrower (not original first trust deeds).*

The **RIGHT TO CANCEL** *is the federal law that gives a borrower the right to rescind (cancel) any loan transaction only if it is a business loan or a second trust deed secured by the borrower's home.*

*The right to rescind lasts for three business days from the last of the following events: 1) delivery of the notice of right to rescind; 2) signing of the transaction; or 3) delivery of the truth in lending disclosure.*

A first trust deed loan to finance the purchase of the borrower's home carries no right of rescission. However, a first loan secured on the borrower's home for any other purpose, including refinancing, or a **second loan on the same home, may be cancelled within 3 business days** (see **Figure 8-18**).

*The borrower has the right to rescind when a loan is secured by a junior trust deed on an owner-occupied single-family residence already owned by the borrower (refinancing).*

## C. EQUAL CREDIT OPPORTUNITY ACT

The **EQUAL CREDIT OPPORTUNITY ACT** *is a federal law prohibiting those who lend money from discriminating against borrowers based on their race, sex, color, religion, national origin, age, or marital status.* It is specifically designed to come to the aid of low income group members (who receive income from public assistance programs), women, and the elderly. This law limits the lender's access to personal information regarding:

1. marriage and divorce,
2. receipt of alimony and child support, and
3. birth control and child bearing.

It can also require lenders to consider individuals on the merits of their personal credit, as distinct from the bad credit history of a joint account. It also insists that lenders respond quickly to loan applications and be prepared to explain any loan refusal.

**Figure 8-18**

# NOTICE OF RIGHT TO CANCEL
## Notice of Cancellation - Notice of Rescission
(California Civil Code 1689.7)

NAME _____     JOB CONTRACT NO. _____

ADDRESS _____     TRANSACTION DATE _____

CITY _____ STATE _____ ZIP _____

## THREE-DAY RIGHT TO CANCEL

You, the buyer, have the right to cancel this contract within three business days. You may cancel by e-mailing, mailing, faxing, or delivering a written notice to the contractor at the contractor's place of business by midnight of the third business day after you received a signed and dated copy of the contract that includes this notice. Include your name, your address, and the date you received the signed copy of the contract and this notice.

If you cancel, the contractor must return to you anything you paid within 10 days of receiving the notice of cancellation. For your part, you must make available to the contractor at your residence, in substantially as good condition as you received it, any goods delivered to you under this contract or sale. Or, you may, if you wish, comply with the contractor's instructions on how to return the goods at the contractor's expense and risk. If you do make the goods available to the contractor and the contractor does not pick them up within 20 days of the date of your notice of cancellation, you may keep them without any further obligation. If you fail to make the goods available to the contractor, or if you agree to return the goods to the contractor and fail to do so, then you remain liable for performance of all obligations under the contract."

I, _____ (Buyer) hereby acknowledge that on _____ (Date) I was provided this document entitled "Three-Day Right to Cancel."

_____
(Buyer's Signature)

## NOTICE OF CANCELLATION
DATE _____

You may cancel this transaction, without any penalty or obligation, within three business days from the above date.

If you cancel, any property traded in, any payments made by you under the contract or sale, and any negotiable instrument executed by you will be returned within 10 days following receipt by the seller of your cancellation notice, and any security interest arising out of the transaction will be cancelled.

If you cancel, you must make available to the seller at your residence, in substantially as good condition as when received, any goods delivered to you under this contract or sale, or you may, if you wish, comply with the instructions of the seller regarding the return shipment of the goods at the seller's expense and risk.

If you do make the goods available to the seller and the seller does not pick them up within 20 days of the date of your notice of cancellation, you may retain or dispose of the goods without any further obligation. If you fail to make the goods available to the seller, or if you agree to return the goods to the seller and fail to do so, then you remain liable for performance of all obligations under the contract.

To cancel this transaction, mail or deliver a signed and dated copy of this cancellation notice, or any other written notice, or send a FAX to _____ at _____ not later than midnight of _____
            (Name of Seller)      (Address of Sellers Place of Business)      (Date)

**I hereby cancel this transaction** _____     _____
                                       (Buyer's Signature)        (Date)

### SENDER'S FILE RECORD OF CANCELLATION

Date sent: _____

### METHOD OF COMMUNICATION

❏ U.S. Mail   ❏ First Class   ❏ Certified   ❏ Registered

❏ United Parcel Service   ❏ Federal Express   ❏ Personal Delivery   ❏ FAX # _____

## D. SERVICE MEMBERS CIVIL RELIEF ACT OF 2003

The **SERVICE MEMBERS CIVIL RELIEF ACT OF 2003** *is a law that was passed by Congress to protect persons serving in the military, and their dependents, from loss of real property through foreclosure.*

In general, the law prohibits the sale or foreclosure of real estate owned by a military person without his or her expressed approval or a court order. It also extends foreclosure proceedings and the mortgage redemption period. Career soldiers are exempt.

---

## XII. CHAPTER SUMMARY

**Leverage** is the practice of purchasing real estate using a small amount of your own money and a larger proportion of borrowed funds. Buyers generally **hypothecate** their property as security for a real estate loan, meaning they provide title as security for the loan, without giving up possession.

A **promissory note** is the basic instrument used to evidence the obligation or debt and can be a **straight note**, an **installment note with a balloon payment**, or the most commonly used in California, a **fully amortized note**.

With the proper requirements, a promissory note can be a **fully negotiable instrument**, like a check, easily transferred to an innocent third party known as a **holder in due course**.

An **acceleration clause** speeds up the balance due based on the occurrence of a specific event. A buyer can assume a loan on a property by accepting responsibility (with the lender's consent) for the full payment of the loan, but cannot assume an existing loan that contains an **alienation clause** (where the entire balance becomes due when the property is sold, assigned, or transferred). A **subordination clause** allows a borrower to obtain additional loans on the property that have a higher priority. A **prepayment penalty** may only be charged during the first five years of a one-to-four unit home loan.

Real estate loans involve **simple interest**. The **nominal interest rate** is stated in the note, whereas the **effective interest rate** includes interest, points, and loan fees. The formula for finding interest is:

$$\text{Interest} = \text{Principal} \times \text{Rate} \times \text{Time}$$

With a **fixed interest rate loan**, the payments are the same for the life of the loan. **Amortization** is the repaying of a loan (principal and interest), in regular payments over the term of the loan. If the interest rate charges are higher than the monthly payment, it's called **negative amortization**. An **adjustable rate mortgage ("ARM" or trust deed)** has a fluctuating interest rate based on a specific index, meaning the payment amounts may also change.

A **point** equals 1% of the loan amount. **Usury** is charging more than the legally allowed percentage of interest.

The **three financial instruments (security devices)** used in California are: 1) **mortgages** (rare), 2) **trust deeds** (1st and 2nds are common), and 3) **land contracts** (uncommon). In California, the terms mortgage and trust deed are often used interchangeably, but in reality we are usually referring to trust deeds.

A **trust deed** (deed of trust loan) is personal property, and needs a **note** for security. It is not a negotiable instrument, but the note is. The **trustor** borrows the money from the **beneficiary**, who is the lender. A **trustee** is the third, disinterested party (usually a corporation) who holds title to the property on the condition it may have to be sold for the beneficiary if the trustor defaults. **Equitable title** is held by the trustor while repaying the trust deed and note in full, at which time he or she receives the **"bare"** or **"naked"** legal title. A full reconveyance provides proof that a promissory note and trust deed have been paid in full.

If a borrower defaults on a trust deed and note, the remedy is to start a **default action** (after a 10-15 day grace period). The sequence of events includes: 1) the recording of the default, 2) a 3-month minimum reinstatement period, 3) a three consecutive week minimum publishing period, and 4) a one-day trustee's sale (**foreclosure**).

Any loan on real property secured by a second, third, or subsequent trust deed is known as a **junior lien**. The best sources for junior liens are **private lenders**.

**Homeowner equity loans** are based on the increase in equity caused by inflation, rising property values, and the reduction, by payments, of the existing loan balance. They are generally secured by second (junior) trust deeds.

A **land contract** is also called a real property sales contract, an agreement of sale, an agreement to purchase, or an installment sales contract. It is an instrument of finance in which the **vendor** (seller) retains legal ownership of property until the **vendee** (buyer) has made the last payment. A **wraparound**, or all **inclusive trust deed (AITD)**, is a second trust deed with a face value of both the new amount it secures and the balance due under the first trust deed.

The **Truth in Lending Act (Regulation Z)** requires lenders to disclose the costs of credit terms to borrowers within three business days of receiving a loan application. The two most important terms are the **Annual Percentage Rate (APR)** and amount financed. APR is the "cost of credit" expressed in percentage terms.

A borrower has the right to rescind within three days when a loan is secured by a second trust deed and on an owner-occupied, single-family residence already owned by the borrower.

The **Equal Credit Opportunity Act** is a federal law prohibiting money lenders from discriminating against borrowers based on race, sex, color, religion, national origin, age, or marital status. The **Service Members Civil Relief Act of 2003** protects military personnel and their dependents from foreclosure.

# CHAPTER 8

## XIII. TERMINOLOGY

A. Acceleration Clause
B. Adjustable Rate Mortgage
C. Alienation Clause
D. Amortization
E. Amortization Chart
F. Annual Percentage Rate
G. Assumption
H. Beneficiary
I. Default
J. Deficiency Judgment
K. Equal Credit Opportunity
L. Equitable Title
M. Equity
N. Grace Period
O. Graduated Payment Mortgage

P. Holder in Due Course
Q. Hypothecation
R. Interest
S. Junior Lien or Second Trust Deed
T. Land Contract
U. Legal Title
V. Leverage
W. Point
X. Prepayment Penalty
Y. Promissory Note
Z. Purchase Money Instrument
AA. Reconveyance Deed
BB. Reinstatement Period
CC. Request for Notice of Default

DD. Right to Cancel
EE. Straight Note
FF. Subordination Clause
GG. Trust Deed
HH. Trustee
II. Trustee's Sale
JJ. Trustor
KK. Truth in Lending Act
LL. Usury
MM. Vendee
NN. Vendor
OO. Wraparound Trust Deed

1._____ An instrument used to transfer title back from a trustee to the equitable owner of real estate.

2._____ A second trust deed for which the monthly payment includes the amount of monthly payment on the existing first trust deed.

3._____ Federal law granting women financial independence and preventing lenders from considering such negative credit aspects as the possibility of a woman having children and dropping out of the labor market.

4._____ A mortgage or deed of trust for which the payments increase over the term of the loan. The payments may increase as the buyer's earnings increase.

5._____ The amount for which the borrower is personally liable on a note and mortgage if the foreclosure sale does not bring enough to cover the debt.

6._____ A penalty under a note, mortgage, or deed of trust imposed when the loan is paid before it is due.

7._____ The total cost of financing expressed as one simple annual percentage rate. This rate must be clearly expressed on any loan agreement.

8._____ A promise in writing to pay a specified amount during a limited time, or on demand, to a named person.

9._____ Clause used in a deed of trust that gives the lender the right to demand payment in full upon the happening of a certain event.

10._____ Ownership by one who does not have legal title, such as a vendee under a land contract or, technically, a trustor under a deed of trust.

11._____ A sale at auction by a trustee under a deed of trust, pursuant to foreclosure proceedings.

12._____ A type of lien that is subordinate to a prior lien.

13._____ An instrument used in place of a mortgage in most western states that is based on the Spanish legal tradition. Property is transferred to a trustee by the borrower (trustor) in favor of the lender (beneficiary) and reconveyed upon payment in full.

14._____ A type of acceleration clause, calling for a debt under a mortgage or deed of trust, to be due in its entirety upon transfer of ownership.

15._____ The use of financing to allow a small amount of cash to purchase and control a large property investment.

16._____ A period of time past the due date for a payment (mortgage, insurance, etc.) during which a payment may be made and not considered delinquent.

17.\_\_\_\_Purchaser or buyer, especially on a land contract.

18.\_\_\_\_A nonamortized note for which the principal is due in a lump sum upon maturity.

19.\_\_\_\_Charging an illegal rate or amount of interest on a loan.

20.\_\_\_\_Payment of debt in regular, periodic installments of principal and interest, as opposed to interest-only payments.

21.\_\_\_\_The seller of property under a land contract.

22.\_\_\_\_The kind of title held by the vendor under a land contract and the trustee under a deed of trust. They are still owed money by the buyer.

23.\_\_\_\_An installment contract for the sale of land. The seller (vendor) has legal title until paid in full. The buyer (vendee) has equitable title during the contract term.

24.\_\_\_\_A financing charge equal to one percent of the amount of the loan.

25.\_\_\_\_Money charged for the use of money.

26.\_\_\_\_A failure to perform the financial obligation to pay under a loan.

27.\_\_\_\_A holder of a check or note who takes the note in good faith, on the assumption it is valid.

28.\_\_\_\_The borrower under a deed of trust.

29.\_\_\_\_In a deed of trust, the person who acts as an intermediary between the trustor and the beneficiary.

30.\_\_\_\_A lender for whose benefit a trust is created in those states where trust deeds are commonly used instead of mortgages.

31.\_\_\_\_The ownership interest in real property; it is the market value minus any unpaid loan amount.

32.\_\_\_\_Agreement by the buyer to take over the financial responsibility for real property under the existing note and trust deed.

33.\_\_\_\_An agreement by which a lender substitutes a junior loan position for a senior loan position.

34.\_\_\_\_A schedule of monthly payments that varies according to interest rates and number of monthly payments.

35.\_\_\_\_Mortgage loans on which the interest rate is periodically adjusted to more closely coincide with current rates.

36.\_\_\_\_Regulation Z under the Federal Reserve regulations that requires a credit purchaser be advised, in writing, of all costs connected with the credit portion of their purchase.

37.\_\_\_\_The principle of using real property as security for a debt while the borrower retains possession.

38.\_\_\_\_A recorded form requiring the trustee to notify other creditors in the event of a default on the deed of trust to a property.

39.\_\_\_\_A limited amount of time during which the trustor has the right to pay all past due payments and charges due on a loan to bring it current.

40.\_\_\_\_Part of the Truth in Lending Law that allows a borrower to rescind a loan transaction until midnight of the third business day, on business loans and second trust deeds secured by a borrower's residence.

41.\_\_\_\_The original loan taken out when purchasing a property, not a refinanced or junior loan.

# CHAPTER 8

## XIV. CHAPTER QUIZ

**1.** Amortization tables are used to calculate:

    a. the annual payment.

    b. the monthly payment.

    c. only interest due with each payment.

    d. the amount of a straight loan.

**2.** The 1% loan fee on FHA loans is usually paid by the:

    a. borrower.

    b. seller.

    c. lender.

    d. PMI.

**3.** In a deed of trust, the power of sale in event of foreclosure is given from the:

    a. trustee to the trustor.

    b. beneficiary to the trustor.

    c. trustor to the trustee.

    d. trustee to the beneficiary.

**4.** Which of the following is a true statement regarding recording a trust deed?

    a. A trust deed conveys bare legal title (but not possession) of a property to a trustee (third party) as security for a loan.

    b. A trust deed differs from other deeds in that the legal title only is thus conveyed.

    c. A trust deed is a security device in the nature of a lien and differs in one respect from other deeds in that the trust deed and the promissory note for which it was given may be assigned.

    d. All of the above.

**5.** A request for notice of default is recorded to protect:

    a. the beneficiary on the first loan.

    b. the beneficiary on the second loan/trust deed.

    c. trustor on the first loan.

    d. trustor on the second loan.

**6.** If a lender accepts a deed in lieu of foreclosure:

    a. the trustor under certain circumstances assumes the deed and any liens.

    b. the beneficiary may assume any junior loans/liens on the property.

    c. the trustee will assume any junior liens on the property.

    d. any of the three parties depending on the value of the property and the amount of any liens on the property may assume any junior encumbrance on the property.

7. A vendee (buyer) under a land contract should:

    a. record the land contract for his/her protection.

    b. hold legal title in a safe deposit box.

    c. obtain a CLTA title insurance policy to assure that the vendor cannot encumber the property.

    d. have a reconveyance deed held in escrow.

8. According to Federal Truth in Lending, the lender must disclose the annual percentage rate of a loan, which is:

    a. the nominal interest rate.

    b. the cost of credit, including interest and other financing costs, expressed as an annual rate.

    c. the yearly compounded interest rate.

    d. none of the above.

9. The right to rescind lasts for 3 days from the last of these events to occur:

    a. delivery of the notice of right to rescind.

    b. signing of the transaction.

    c. delivery of the truth in lending disclosure.

    d. all of the above.

10. A lender would not be exempt from the requirement of providing the borrower with a Federal Right to Rescind Notice when the:

    a. loan is for more than $25,000 and is not secured by the borrower's personal residence.

    b. security for the loan is commercial property.

    c. loan is for business expansion.

    d. borrower is refinancing his personal residence.

**ANSWERS:** 1. b; 2. b; 3. c; 4. d; 5. b; 6. b; 7. a; 8. b; 9. d; 10. d

# CHAPTER 9
## Financial Institutions

The real estate money market, like any other commodity market, changes constantly. Money for financing real estate may be plentiful in one month or quarter, then scarce and expensive in the next. The money market is no longer national, it has become a global market. A broker must be able to finance real estate transactions every month if he or she expects to remain in business. Because of this, a broker must be able to use all the standard financing methods and any unconventional methods that may fit the time and situation.

*Before you advertise a property or present it to a prospect, try to visualize all the ways the property may be financed. The more alternatives available, the more likely you are to negotiate a sale. Real estate finance continues to become more variable and more complex as time goes on. This chapter will explain the sources of funds available from financial institutions, the government's role, and other creative prospects and information that will assist you when offering financing.*

## I. Our Ever Changing Economy (Economic Cycles)

*With regard to inflation, market value increases and sales price increases. When the general level of prices decreases, the value of money increases.*

Because our government's spending and taxing policies shift with every new election, our economy is in a constant state of transition. From month-to-month, it is difficult to predict what amount of financing money will be available and what rate of interest will be charged. These influences, multiplied over a period of years, make it nearly impossible to accurately project long-term trends in the money supply.

*INFLATION is the result of too much money chasing too few goods.* When the economy is going very well, most people are making more money and spending it too freely, thereby driving up the price of real estate and other goods. The Fed, sensing that inflation is out of control, starts applying the brakes and starts restricting the amount of money available. This and higher interest rates decrease borrowing. If the Fed is forced to apply the brakes hard, deflation will occur. *DEFLATION is when prices of real estate, goods, and services go down.*

# CHAPTER OUTLINE

*A "seller's market" is when prices rise due to shortages of available properties, and a "buyer's market" is when prices fall.*

It is a **BUYER'S MARKET** *when the prices of real estate are down; terms are easy and there is usually a great deal of real estate listed for sale or rent.* Buyers have a choice; there is more to pick and choose from, at lower prices. In a **SELLER'S MARKET**, *the prices of real estate are up and there is less real estate listed for sale or rent.* This is due to increased demand and lagging supplies.

## A. THE FEDERAL RESERVE BANKING SYSTEM ("Fed")

The Federal Reserve Banking System is the single greatest influence on the cost and supply of money for real estate loans. It is the link between America's private financial institutions and the taxing and spending policies of the federal government. The **FEDERAL RESERVE BANKING SYSTEM (The "Fed")** *is the nation's central banking authority.* If the Fed makes money tight, thus restricting the amount of available loan funds, demand for the available funds increases, pushing interest rates higher. Conversely, if the Fed increases the amount of money in circulation, interest rates go down. In this way they keep centralized control over the interest rates for not only banks, but for all lending institutions.

*When the federal reserve wants to create a tight money market, it raises the discount rate and sells government bonds. When the federal reserve wants a "loose" money market, it buys back bonds and lowers reserve requirements of banks.*

These operations and the other important functions of the Federal Reserve System are supervised by the Federal Reserve Board. The *FEDERAL RESERVE BOARD is a committee appointed by the President, but is politically independent*. In regulating the amount and flow of loan money available to banks, the board has indirect but far-reaching influence over all lending institutions and the economy as a whole. The Federal Reserve's monetary policies influence the supply of money by:

1. buying and selling government T-bonds and T-securities;
2. raising and lowering the reserve requirement;
3. raising and lowering the discount rate to member banks; and
4. margin requirements (percentage loaned on stocks and bonds).

**www.federalreserve.gov/sitemap.htm** (Federal Reserve Board)
**www.ustreas.gov** (U.S. Treasury)
**www.occ.treas.gov** (Office of the Comptroller of the Currency)
**www.frbsf.org** (Federal Reserve Bank of San Francisco - 12th District)

### B. GROSS DOMESTIC PRODUCT (GDP) (Measures Economic Activity)

We can monitor growth in our economy and the influence of the Fed by watching closely any changes in the gross domestic product. The *GROSS DOMESTIC PRODUCT (GDP) is the total value of all goods and services produced by an economy during a specific period of time*. It serves as a kind of monetary barometer that shows us the rate and areas of greatest growth.

*Depression, recession, expansion, and prosperity represent four phases of the business cycle.*

### C. CHANGING INTEREST RATES (Affect Real Estate)

The economy goes in cycles. Interest rates go up and down. When interest rates go down, people will buy more homes. When interest rates go up, people will buy fewer homes, and have a harder time selling their homes. When interest rates go down, homes become more affordable.

If a homeowner has a high interest rate and the rate goes down, he or she may choose to refinance. *REFINANCING is the process of obtaining a new loan to pay off the old loan*. If interest rates fall dramatically, it is wise to consider refinancing.

*In a tight money market, lenders may waive prepayment penalties in order to lend out that money at a higher rate than old loans.*

## II. Shopping for a Loan

All the variables of our changing economy come home in a very personal way when a borrower goes out to look for a loan. For the average person, borrowing the money necessary to buy a house is the largest financial obligation he or she is likely to assume in his or her lifetime. It's an extremely important decision, second only to the selection of the property itself. The salesperson should advise caution and careful consideration before a promissory note is signed. Shopping around for a loan from several different loan sources is an excellent idea.

Even if the borrower has found financing that he or she feels is acceptable, talking to other lenders should never be discouraged. **Figure 9-1** provides a detailed discussion of the steps in obtaining a loan.

### A. LOAN TO VALUE (Percent of Appraised Value Lender Will Loan)

*LOAN TO VALUE is the percentage of sale price or appraised value, whichever is lower, the lender will loan to the borrower to purchase the property.* It is abbreviated as L-T-V or L to V. The lower the L to V, the higher the down payment has to be. The lower the L to V, the more equity is required.

### B. ESTIMATE OF SETTLEMENT COSTS (RESPA)

The lender must give the applicant the HUD booklet *Settlement Costs and You* that explains closing costs and has until **three business days after receipt of a loan application** to provide a good faith estimate of the actual settlement costs to the borrower. The Real Estate Settlement Procedures Act (RESPA) disclosure must include:

1. the rate of interest;
2. points to be charged;
3. any additional loan fees and charges, and
4. escrow, title, and other allowable costs, which could add up to $1,000 or more above lender's estimates.

The idea is to alert the borrower, at the beginning of the loan process, to how much cash besides the down payment will be needed to close escrow. Usually the lender will provide the complete estimated settlement cost form along with the loan application.

### C. CREDIT SCORING (Access to Credit Profile)

*CREDIT SCORING gives lenders a fast, objective measurement of your ability to repay a loan or make timely credit payments.* It is based solely on information in consumer credit reports maintained at one of the credit reporting agencies. Factors comprising a credit score include:

1. **Payment History** – What is your track record?
2. **Amounts Owed** – How much is too much?
3. **Length of Credit History** – How established is yours?
4. **New Credit** – Are you taking on more debt?
5. **Types of Credit Use** – Is it a "healthy" mix?

*The most widely used credit bureau scores are developed by Fair, Isaac and Company. These are known as FICO SCORES.* See **Figure 9-2** for a fuller description of credit scoring, which is often difficult to explain.

*If a credit agency refuses to provide a copy of a credit report to an applicant who is denied credit, the applicant can:*

1. *file civil action against the credit agency;*
2. *negotiate a settlement, or*
3. *require the credit agency to pay all legal fees.*

**Figure 9-1**

# Steps in Obtaining a Loan

## 1. Application

After deciding that a real estate loan is necessary, the first step in obtaining the loan is filling out a loan application. It would be a good idea to shop around and check for the best rate and terms at various savings institutions before applying because, despite what many people suspect, every lender is different. Finding the right loan is as important as finding the right piece of real estate. The application will request detailed information regarding both the property and the borrower.

## 2. Analysis

The application generally receives a preliminary screening to determine if there are any obvious and glaring reasons why either the prospective borrower or the property could not qualify for a loan. This process is accomplished by credit scoring. This analysis is followed by a professional appraisal of the property and an in-depth investigation into the credit background of the applicant (in addition to credit scoring). The lender wants to know how likely the borrower is to meet monthly payments and pay back the loan. This is analyzed with reference to the borrower's "capacity" and "desire" to pay.

*CAPACITY is determined based upon a borrower's savings, valuable property, and income, and is evaluated in terms of the reliability of these assets. Excellent evidence of capacity would be good collateral. COLLATERAL is valuable property pledged as a guarantee for payment of a loan. DESIRE (to pay) is demonstrated by a good credit history reflecting the discipline to make monthly payments on time.* A background of late payments and loan defaults would make it difficult to get loan approval.

## 3. Processing

If loan analysis proves favorable and financing terms are acceptable to all parties, it is then time to get the terms of the agreement down on paper. Processing involves typing up the loan documents, preparing necessary disclosure statements, and issuing instructions to the escrow holder.

## 4. Escrow

All the paperwork of the loan transaction ends up in escrow along with all the other contracts involved in the purchase of real property. The trust deed and promissory note are signed and passed along to the escrow company where the deal is closed.

## 5. Servicing

Loan servicing involves mailing monthly loan statements, collecting payments, and seeing to it that all records are kept up to date. Some lenders service their own loans while others hire independent mortgage companies to handle the paperwork for them. Loan servicing also involves all correspondence for late and delinquent payments.

▼

## Qualifying for a Loan

All lenders set their own standards for evaluating who qualifies and who does not qualify for loan money. These standards are reflected in the interest rates charged. Some lenders have very strict requirements, while others will take a greater risk but charge a higher rate of interest—especially on second trust deeds. Real estate agents can obtain more specific guidelines simply by contacting local lenders.

Traditionally, lending institutions decided whether or not a borrower was qualified based upon a simple formula: the property should not cost more than two-and-a-half times the borrower's annual income. Today, however, many lenders recognize that this method can be very inadequate. It fails to take into account other debts that the borrower might be paying off and doesn't give the middle income property buyer, or those entering the housing market for the first time, much of a chance with today's high-cost real estate.

New rules of thumb consider a borrower's other debts along with the housing payments. Long term debts are added to these payments, and the sum is referred to as the borrower's total monthly expenses.

One standard rule was that a borrower's monthly expenses should be no more than 25 percent of all total monthly income. Now, in California, it is closer to 3½ to 1 ratio. Another rule, which is applied to borrowers who are not heavily in debt elsewhere, requires that their annual income be approximately 30 percent of the cost of the property. This is a variation on the traditional formula reflecting a more realistic attitude on the part of lenders.

## Appraisal of the Property

Just as the borrower is evaluated during the loan process, lenders evaluate the property being purchased. They want to be certain that the price being paid reflects a fair market value. If a property is overpriced and the borrower defaults, it might be difficult for the lender to recoup the amount of the loan. This process of determining a property's fair market value is known as appraisal and is discussed in detail in Chapters 10 and 11.

Institutional lenders are not likely to lend the entire amount needed for the purchase of a property. Most often they will determine the fair market value and lend a set percentage of that amount. This "loan to value ratio" (L-T-V) is generally 80 percent to 90 percent at banks and savings banks and 70 percent if the loan comes from an insurance company. Collateral is required but most often the property itself (including any structures) is used as security for the loan.

*The lower the L-T-V, the greater the down payment required.*

**Figure 9-2**

# Credit Scoring

A credit score is a three-digit number assigned to consumers based on credit history that is used by lenders to determine the level of risk they maybe taking if they lend to someone. The system awards points based on information in the credit report, and compared to others with similar profiles, lenders can use this information to predict how likely someone is to repay a loan and make payments on time – and therefore decide whether or not to make a loan and at what interest rate.

Credit scores are often referred to as FICO scores due to the fact that Fair Isaac and Company was the first company to develop a mathematical credit scoring model based on selected criteria in a credit report. The following are the systems now used:

**Experian – Experian/Fair Isaac system**
**TransUnion – Empirica system**
**Equifax – Beacon system**

FICO scores, which still dominate the industry, range from 300 to 850. Any score under 620 is considered high risk, and subject to higher interest rates, and anything over 720 qualifies for the best interest rate.

Loan applicants are entitled to know the specific credit scores and the "reason codes" used in determining their scores. Reason codes may include too high a debt-to-credit limit ratio, late payments, or too short a credit history.

In addition to a consumer's right to receive a free credit report from each of the three national credit reporting agencies once a year, by law, credit reporting agencies are required to correct inaccurate information in a timely manner, and are subject to legal recourse if inaccurate information continues to be reported once they are made aware of mistakes.

**www.experian.com**
Experian
**www.transunion.com**
TransUnion
**www.equifax.com**
Equifax

Once popular ALT-A programs (where applicants with good credit couldn't document their income) used only the last 12 to 24 months' personal bank statements to support the income stated on the loan application.

**SUBPRIME LOANS** *are generally made to borrowers with less than excellent credit scores*. Due to higher risk, they are generally charged higher interest rates, points, fees, and prepayment penalties. After initial **TEASER RATES**, *where low ARM loan interest rates accelerate after two years*, many subprime borrowers are now faced with difficulty making much higher payments and face foreclosure.

### D. THE LOAN APPLICATION

The lender needs a loan application from the borrower so that the borrower's financial condition can be analyzed. **Figure 9-3** shows two pages of the FHLMC/FNMA application form that is used by most financial institutions. The application provides the lender with the following:

1. Information about property being financed
2. Information about borrower (and co-borrower, if any)
3. Sources of income and analysis
4. Monthly housing expenses (present and proposed)
5. Balance sheet
6. Other information relevant to the borrower's financial status

*If a loan application section requests information regarding marital status or race, the applicant can refuse to complete this section.*

### E. EQUITY (Market Value Less Debt)

When shopping for a loan, the lender wants to determine your worth, or equity, so they will require you to fill out an accounting balance sheet as part of the application. *EQUITY is your net worth; it is the amount that is left after subtracting all that you owe (debt) from what you own (assets).* Lenders want to see your equity on paper. Equity shows them your ability to make the down payment and meet other expenses. It is common practice to ask buyers what the equity is in their current home in order to determine if they financially qualify for the price of a new home.

*Equity in real property is the difference between mortgage indebtedness and market value of the property.*

### F. LIQUIDITY (Convert Assets into Cash)

*LIQUIDITY is the ease and rate with which an asset can be converted into a medium of exchange (like cash).* It is not enough to make money; there also must be the ability to pay bills on time. Real estate has very little liquidity. Depending on market conditions, it could take a very long time to sell a piece of real estate. On the other hand, income property may bring in more cash monthly than goes out for expenditures.

### G. OPPORTUNITY COST (Cost of Non-Liquidity)

*OPPORTUNITY COST is the lost profit one could have made by the alternative investment action not taken.* It is the cost of non-liquidity. If you own a home, the lost return on that equity is referred to as opportunity cost.

# III. Sources of Real Estate Funds

The remainder of this chapter will deal with the different institutions that lend money to finance the purchase of real property. Details concerning the types of lenders and how they make loans will be explained and different kinds of government loan participation are compared and discussed. In addition, the responsibilities of a broker acting as a loan agent or security dealer are outlined.

# Figure 9-3

## Uniform Residential Loan Application

This application is designed to be completed by the applicant(s) with the lender's assistance. Applicants should complete this form as "Borrower" or "Co Borrower", as applicable. Co-Borrower information must also be provided (and the appropriate box checked) when ☐ the income or assets of a person other than the "Borrower" (including the Borrower's spouse) will be used as a basis for loan qualification or ☐ the income or assets of the Borrower's spouse will not be used as a basis for loan qualification, but his or her liabilities must be considered because the Borrower resides in a community property state, the security property is located in a community property state, or the Borrower is relying on other property located in a community property state as a basis for repayment of the loan.

### I. TYPE OF MORTGAGE AND TERMS OF LOAN

| Mortgage Applied for: | ☐ VA ☐ FHA | ☐ Conventional ☐ FmHA | ☐ Other: | Agency Case Number | Lender Case No. |
|---|---|---|---|---|---|

| Amount $ | Interest Rate % | No. of Months | Amortization Type: | ☐ Fixed Rate ☐ GPM | ☐ Other (explain): ☐ ARM (type): |
|---|---|---|---|---|---|

### II. PROPERTY INFORMATION AND PURPOSE OF LOAN

| Subject Property Address (street, city, state, & ZIP) | No. of Units |
|---|---|

| Legal Description of Subject Property (attach description if necessary) | Year Built |
|---|---|

| Purpose of Loan | ☐ Purchase ☐ Refinance | ☐ Construction ☐ Construction-Permanent | ☐ Other (explain): | Property will be: ☐ Primary Residence | ☐ Secondary Residence | ☐ Investment |
|---|---|---|---|---|---|---|

**Complete this line if construction or construction-permanent loan.**

| Year Lot Acquired | Original Cost $ | Amount Existing Liens $ | (a) Present Value of Lot $ | (b) Cost of Improvements $ | Total (a + b) $ |
|---|---|---|---|---|---|

**Complete this line if this is a refinance loan.**

| Year Acquired | Original Cost $ | Amount Existing Liens $ | Purpose of Refinance | Describe Improvements ☐ made ☐ to be made Cost: $ |
|---|---|---|---|---|

| Title will be held in what Name(s) | Manner in which Title will be held | Estate will be held in: ☐ Fee Simple ☐ Leasehold (show expiration date) |
|---|---|---|

Source of Down Payment, Settlement Charges and/or Subordinate Financing (explain)

### III. BORROWER INFORMATION

| Borrower | Co-Borrower |
|---|---|
| Borrower's Name (include Jr. or Sr. if applicable) | Co-Borrower's Name (include Jr. or Sr. if applicable) |

| Social Security Number | Home Phone (incl. area code) | Age | Yrs. School | Social Security Number | Home Phone (incl. area code) | Age | Yrs. School |
|---|---|---|---|---|---|---|---|

| ☐ Married ☐ Separated ☐ Unmarried (include single, divorced, widowed) | Dependents (not listed by Co-Borrower) no. ages | ☐ Married ☐ Separated ☐ Unmarried (include single, divorced, widowed) | Dependents (not listed by Borrower) no. ages |
|---|---|---|---|

| Present Address (street, city, state, ZIP) ☐ Own ☐ Rent ____ No. Yrs. | Present Address (street, city, state, ZIP) ☐ Own ☐ Rent ____ No. Yrs. |
|---|---|

**If residing at present address for less than two years, complete the following:**

| Former Address (street, city, state, ZIP) ☐ Own ☐ Rent ____ No. Yrs. | Former Address (street, city, state, ZIP) ☐ Own ☐ Rent ____ No. Yrs. |
|---|---|

| Former Address (street, city, state, ZIP) ☐ Own ☐ Rent ____ No. Yrs. | Former Address (street, city, state, ZIP) ☐ Own ☐ Rent ____ No. Yrs. |
|---|---|

### IV. EMPLOYMENT INFORMATION

| Borrower | Co-Borrower |
|---|---|
| Name & Address of Employer ☐ Self Employed | Yrs. on this job | Name & Address of Employer ☐ Self Employed | Yrs. on this job |

| | Yrs. employed in this line of work/profession | | Yrs. employed in this line of work/profession |
|---|---|---|---|

| Position/Title/Type of Business | Business Phone (incl. area code) | Position/Title/Type of Business | Business Phone (incl. area code) |
|---|---|---|---|

**If employed in current position for less than two years or if currently employed in more than one position, complete the following:**

| Name & Address of Employer ☐ Self Employed | Dates (from - to) | Name & Address of Employer ☐ Self Employed | Dates (from - to) |
|---|---|---|---|

| | Monthly Income $ | | Monthly Income $ |
|---|---|---|---|

| Position/Title/Type of Business | Business Phone (incl. area code) | Position/Title/Type of Business | Business Phone (incl. area code) |
|---|---|---|---|

| Name & Address of Employer ☐ Self Employed | Dates (from - to) | Name & Address of Employer ☐ Self Employed | Dates (from - to) |
|---|---|---|---|

| | Monthly Income $ | | Monthly Income $ |
|---|---|---|---|

| Position/Title/Type of Business | Business Phone (incl. area code) | Position/Title/Type of Business | Business Phone (incl. area code) |
|---|---|---|---|

Freddie Mac Form 65

Fannie Mae Form 1003

## V. MONTHLY INCOME AND COMBINED HOUSING EXPENSE INFORMATION

| Gross Monthly Income | Borrower | Co-Borrower | Total | Combined Monthly Housing Expense | Present | Proposed |
|---|---|---|---|---|---|---|
| Base Empl. Income * | $ | $ | $ | Rent | $ | |
| Overtime | | | | First Mortgage (P&I) | | $ |
| Bonuses | | | | Other Financing (P&I) | | |
| Commissions | | | | Hazard Insurance | | |
| Dividends/Interest | | | | Real Estate Taxes | | |
| Net Rental Income | | | | Mortgage Insurance | | |
| Other (before completing, see the notice in "describe other income," below) | | | | Homeowner Assn. Dues | | |
| | | | | Other: | | |
| Total | $ | $ | $ | Total | $ | $ |

\* Self Employed Borrower(s) may be required to provide additional documentation such as tax returns and financial statements.

**Describe Other Income** *Notice: Alimony, child support, or separate maintenance income need not be revealed if the Borrower (B) or Co-Borrower (C) does not choose to have it considered for repaying this loan.*

| B/C | | Monthly Amount |
|---|---|---|
| | | $ |

## VI. ASSETS AND LIABILITIES

This Statement and any applicable supporting schedules may be completed jointly by both married and unmarried Co-Borrowers if their assets and liabilities are sufficiently joined so that the Statement can be meaningfully and fairly presented on a combined basis; otherwise separate Statements and Schedules are required. If the Co-Borrower section was completed about a spouse, this Statement and supporting schedules must be completed about that spouse also. Completed ☐ Jointly ☐ Not Jointly

| ASSETS Description | Cash or Market Value | LIABILITIES (List the creditor's name, address and account number for all outstanding debts) | Monthly Payt. & Mos. Left to Pay | Unpaid Balance |
|---|---|---|---|---|
| Cash deposit toward purchase held by: | $ | Name and address of Company | $ Payt./Mos. | $ |
| *List checking and savings accounts below* | | | | |
| Name and address of Bank, S&L, or Credit Union | | Acct. no. | | |
| | | Name and address of Company | $ Payt./Mos. | $ |
| Acct. no. | $ | | | |
| Name and address of Bank, S&L, or Credit Union | | Acct. no. | | |
| | | Name and address of Company | $ Payt./Mos. | $ |
| Acct. no. | $ | | | |
| Name and address of Bank, S&L, or Credit Union | | Acct. no. | | |
| | | Name and address of Company | $ Payt./Mos. | $ |
| Acct. no. | $ | | | |
| Name and address of Bank, S&L, or Credit Union | | Acct. no. | | |
| | | Name and address of Company | $ Payt./Mos. | $ |
| Acct. no. | $ | | | |
| Stocks & Bonds (Company name/number & description) | $ | Acct. no. | | |
| | | Name and address of Company | $ Payt./Mos. | $ |
| Life insurance net cash value | $ | | | |
| Face amount: $ | | | | |
| **Subtotal Liquid Assets** | $ | | | |
| Real estate owned (enter market value from schedule of real estate owned) | $ | Acct. no. | | |
| Vested interest in retirement fund | $ | Name and address of Company | $ Payt./Mos. | $ |
| Net worth of business(es) owned (attach financial statement) | $ | | | |
| Automobiles owned (make and year) | $ | Acct. no. | | |
| | | Alimony/Child Support/Separate Maintenance Payments Owed to: | $ | |
| Other Assets (Itemize) | $ | Job Related Expense (child care, union dues, etc.) | $ | |
| | | Total Monthly Payments | $ | |
| Total Assets a. | $ | Net Worth (a minus b) ► $ | Total Liabilities b. | $ |

Freddie Mac Form 65

Fannie Mae Form 1003

*The three areas of demand for borrowing money are:*

1. *Construction funds to build*
2. *Financing a purchase*
3. *Refinancing*

# IV. Institutional Lenders

**INSTITUTIONAL LENDERS** *are very large corporations that lend the money of their depositors to finance real estate transactions.* Their principal function is to act as financial intermediaries; to transfer money from those who have funds to those who wish to borrow. **Figure 9-4** illustrates which groups are institutional and which are noninstitutional lenders.

**Figure 9-4**

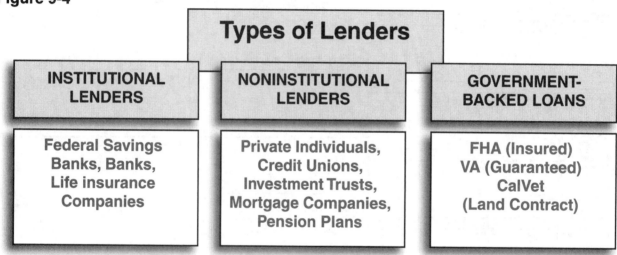

| **Types of Lenders** | | |
| --- | --- | --- |
| **INSTITUTIONAL LENDERS** | **NONINSTITUTIONAL LENDERS** | **GOVERNMENT-BACKED LOANS** |
| Federal Savings Banks, Banks, Life insurance Companies | Private Individuals, Credit Unions, Investment Trusts, Mortgage Companies, Pension Plans | FHA (Insured) VA (Guaranteed) CalVet (Land Contract) |

## A. FEDERAL DEPOSIT INSURANCE CORPORATION (FDIC)

The **FEDERAL DEPOSIT INSURANCE CORPORATION (FDIC)** *is a government corporation that, for a fee, insures each account of a depositor up to $250,000.* All the deposits in savings banks and banks in California are insured by the FDIC because they pay for the premiums. If a depositor has more than the insured $250,000 in any one account, then he or she may lose that amount in excess of $250,000 if there is a savings bank or bank failure. It would be wise to put any excess in a different account or financial institution.

**www.fdic.gov**
Federal Deposit Insurance Corp.

## B. FEDERAL SAVINGS BANKS (Greatest Source of Money for Home Loans)

In California, most of the home purchases are financed by federal savings banks. They make more real estate loans than any other financial institution. This is because until recently all the money that savings banks lent out was in the form of real estate loans. Even with current changes in the banking industry, savings banks are still the primary home mortgage lenders. Savings banks are either federally or state licensed.

## How Financial Institutions Determine Interest Rates

Financial institutions obtain funds from their depositors and pay a modest return in the form of interest or dividends to keep their depositors money invested with them. In order to make money, the spread that a financial institution must make between the interest rate it charges on loans and the interest rate paid to its depositors must be at least 2%. So if a bank pays 7% to depositors, it must make loans at 9% or higher in order to stay in business.

This is a brief description of how a federal savings bank works: A person wishing to deposit funds in exchange for interest would open an account (i.e., savings, money market, or checking) at a federal savings bank. These funds would then be invested in real estate loans, which yield higher rates of interest for the institution than is being paid out to depositors. This system allows savers to obtain interest from federal savings bank accounts and at the same time provide a source of loan funds to home buyers. All federal savings banks can make 80% loans on any amount that is acceptable to them. Federal savings banks will occasionally make 90 and 95 percent (loan-to-value) loans if the loans are covered by private mortgage insurance.

Federal savings banks primarily make loans on single-family homes or condos that are owner-occupied. They will also make loans on apartment buildings and manufactured homes. Larger federal savings banks will often make construction loans for a tract and then supply each owner with permanent, long-term financing.

Federal savings banks, like banks and insurance companies, charge points and loan fees. Points will range from one to five percent (points) of the total loan amount. Loan fees are usually $300 to $500 while appraisal costs start at $200, but vary depending on the property. All institutional lenders tend to charge comparable points and fees according to economic conditions in the market place.

_Federal savings banks are primary sources for residential loans because they invest most of their money in home loans._

**Institutions that specialize in making home loans obtain their funds mainly from individual savings**.

**Figure 9-5** compares the lending priorities of federal savings banks with banks and life insurance companies.

### C. BANKS

Banks are _GENERAL PURPOSE LENDERS, which means they lend money for anything from real estate to sailboats._ Even so, they are the second largest lenders for real estate in California. All national banks are required to be members of the Federal Reserve System, while a state bank may be a member by choice. There is no great difference between real estate loans that a state bank makes and loans that the federal banks make. Interest rates and other loan terms are comparable to those offered by mutual savings banks.

Any commercial bank may lend money on real property if it is a first loan on that property. In general, there are four types of real estate financing:

1. **First Trust Deed Loans** – The bank finances long-term loans for existing land and the buildings.

**Figure 9-5**

# Priorities of Institutional Lenders

| Federal Savings Banks (Residential Lenders) | Banks (General Purpose Lenders) | Life Insurance Companies (Big Money Lenders) |
|---|---|---|
| 1. Single-family homes and condos | 1. Business and auto loans | 1. Large shopping centers and office buildings |
| 2. Apartment buildings | 2. Conventional home loans | 2. Hotels and industrial properties |
| 3. Home improvement loans | 3. Government-backed FHA and VA home loans | 3. FHA and VA home loans through mortgage companies (Government-backed loans) |
| 4. Manufactured homes | 4. Credit cards | |
| | 5. Construction loans | |

2. **Construction Loans (or Interim Loans)** – Money is provided for the construction of a building, to be repaid when the construction is complete.

*Construction loan and interim loan are synonymous.*

3. **Take-Out Loans (Repayment of Interim Loan)** – Permanent long-term loans are made to pay off the interim lender upon completion of construction of commercial or apartment projects and are called "takeout loans" because they take out the interim lender.

4. **Home Improvement Loans** – This type of loan is for repairing and modernizing existing buildings.

## D. LIFE INSURANCE COMPANIES

Life insurance companies have more money to lend than either a bank or a savings bank. They are more conservative lenders and specialize in large loans for commercial projects, but they also make conventional loans on residential property. These companies supply most of the loan funds for properties where a great deal of capital is required (such as high-rise office buildings, shopping centers, industrial properties, and hotels).

Life insurance companies also invest large amounts of money in trust deeds that are either insured by the FHA or guaranteed by the VA. Mortgage companies make such loans for insurance companies. Quite often, these mortgage companies, in return for a servicing fee, collect the loan payments for the insurance company.

*An insurance company is the least likely source to refinance an existing home loan.*

## Truth in Savings Act

**"Annual Percentage Yield" defined as APY**

The Truth in Savings Act requires depository institutions to furnish "clear, complete, and uniform disclosures" of the terms of their savings and checking deposit accounts. It also requires institutions to pay interest on the consumer's daily balance. Certain practices are no longer permitted, such as advertising "Free Accounts" and then charging maintenance or per-check fees, or requiring minimum balances.

This Act introduces a standard method of expressing interest paid to depositors called "Annual Percentage Yield" or APY. This new method takes into account the interest rate and also the compounding. So if the APY is 4.46 percent, a hundred dollars will earn $4.46 in one year. The higher the APY, the more interest is paid.

Life insurance companies are governed by the laws of the state in which they are incorporated, as well as the laws of the states in which they do business. There is no state restriction concerning the number of years for which a loan can be made. However, company policy usually restricts the term to no more than 30 years and requires a loan to be amortized.

When making loans, life insurance companies in California are restricted to a 75 percent maximum of market value of any given property. This is not a requirement if the loan is insured by the Federal Housing Administration (FHA) or guaranteed by the Veterans Administration (VA).

# V. Noninstitutional Lenders

*Noninstitutional lenders are smaller lenders, including: credit unions, investment trusts, pension plans, and mortgage companies.*

**NONINSTITUTIONAL LENDERS** *are individuals and organizations that lend on a private or individual basis.* Both institutional and noninstitutional lenders make loans that may be or may not be backed by one of the government loan programs.

*CONVENTIONAL LOANS are loans that are not insured or guaranteed by the United States government.*

## A. PRIVATE INDIVIDUALS

Any real estate loan by an individual is considered a private individual loan. Most individuals who lend money on real estate are sellers who take back a second trust deed as part of the real estate transaction. The seller will be a likely lender when the buyer needs a little more money to purchase a property. Most second trust deed loans are of this type and are the most important type of secondary financing in California.

*When the current money market is tight, it often means that a seller will have to take back a second trust deed as part of the equity in his/her home. Many second loans on real estate, called junior loans (second trust deeds), are obtained from private parties.*

# CHAPTER 9

Common second trust deed terms are:

1. The loan amount is usually relatively small (under $50,000).

2. There is a relatively high interest rate (8% to 15%).

3. The loan term is usually from 3 to 7 years, with payments on a monthly basis.

4. Loan payments are usually 1% of the original loan, and there is usually a balloon payment at the end of the term (if more than six years).

5. There is usually an acceleration clause that makes the entire loan due if any payment is missed or the property is transferred.

## B. CREDIT UNIONS

A **CREDIT UNION** *is a co-operative association organized to promote thrift among its members and provide them with a source of credit.*

Under the Federal Credit Union Act of 1934, a credit union charter may be given to any group having a common bond of association or occupation—a factory, store, office, church, trade group, club, or fraternal organization.

Although there are thousands of credit unions across the country, they play a much smaller role than banks, savings banks, and insurance companies in financing real estate. The typical credit union is smaller than the average commercial bank or savings bank.

Most credit unions are incorporated and accumulate funds by selling shares to members. From this pool of funds, loans are made at an interest rate equal to or below the current market rate. Low interest rate loans to members are a big plus for credit unions.

The modern credit union offers savings plans, credit cards, ATM cards, travelers' checks, vehicle loans, signature loans, and real estate loans. All deposit accounts have National Credit Union Administration (NCUA) insurance up to $250,000.

Recent changes in the law have enabled credit unions to make not only second trust deed loans, but also first trust deed loans. This source of real estate funding is expected to grow and expand in coming years.

## C. REAL ESTATE INVESTMENT TRUST (REIT)

A **REAL ESTATE INVESTMENT TRUST (REIT)** *is a type of company that sells securities to invest in real estate properties.* If the company distributes 95 percent or more of its income to its shareholders, it does not pay federal income taxes on that distribution. Because of these formalities, a real estate investment trust is taxed like any other real estate investment.

An **EQUITY TRUST** *is a company that invests in real estate itself or several real estate projects.* The **MORTGAGE TRUST** *is a company that invests in mortgages and other types of real estate loans or obligations.* Now there are even combination trusts that invest in real estate and lend money in the form of real estate mortgages.

## D. PENSION PLANS

A **PENSION PLAN** *is an investment organization that obtains funds from people before they retire and invests this money for their clients' retirement.* Company pension plans have become a popular source of real estate funds and are expected to grow even larger in the future.

Enormous amounts of money, gathered through deductions from each pay period, are held by these plans. Those who administer pension money are becoming more and more inclined to invest it directly in large real estate projects rather than investing in the stock market or simply investing in savings institutions and insurance companies.

### E. MORTGAGE BANKERS (COMPANIES) – Secondary Mortgage Market

*MORTGAGE BANKERS (COMPANIES) usually lend their own money or roll it over so they can originate, finance, and close first trust deeds or mortgages secured by real estate. They then sell the loans to institutional investors and service the loans through a contractual relationship with the investors.*

*Mortgage loan brokers (correspondents) are licensed by the DRE as real estate brokers and/or by the Department of Corporations as Residential Mortgage Lenders (RML) or California Finance Lenders (CFL).*

In California, the brokerage function is one of the prime sources for loans on homes and income property, and they are the largest originator of FHA and VA trust deeds or mortgages. Sometimes private mortgage insurance is necessary to make a loan.

*"Warehousing" is the action of a mortgage banker collecting loans in a package prior to sale.*

### F. PRIVATE MORTGAGE INSURANCE (PMI)

*PRIVATE MORTGAGE INSURANCE is a guarantee to lenders that the upper portion of a conventional loan will be repaid if a borrower defaults and a deficiency occurs at the foreclosure sale.*

**Example:** Smith is buying a property for $300,000 but he has only $15,000 for a down payment. He approaches lender Jones for financing. Lender Jones is eager to see this sale go through but he does not feel entirely comfortable putting up $285,000 when normally he would limit the loan to 80%, or $240,000. He is uncomfortable lending Smith the extra $45,000. He agrees to make the loan if Smith will pay for private mortgage insurance to cover the upper portion ($45,000) of the $285,000 loan.

Private mortgage insurance is obtainable on properties with one-to-four units and generally covers the top 20% of the loan amount. The borrower generally pays an initial premium or an annual fee of one-half of one percent on the remaining principal balance.

# VI. Government-Backed Loans

The government is very involved in helping people obtain homes. The three programs we will discuss have already helped millions to enjoy "owning a home," the American dream. FHA insurance (part of Housing and Urban Development – HUD) and VA guarantees are federal programs. They approve loans made by private lenders, but lend no actual money. The CalVet program makes direct loans to qualified borrowers from the state of California (see **Figure 9-6** and the chart in **Figure 9-7**).

**Figure 9-6**

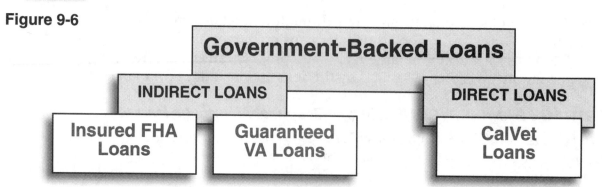

## A. FHA INSURED LOANS (A Division of HUD)

*Unlike conventional lenders, the Federal Housing Administration (FHA) does not make loans, but insures them.*

The FHA has two main programs that affect California homeowners and buyers: 1) Title I home improvement loans, and 2) Title II (Section 203b) purchase and construction loans. There are other types of FHA financing available. For information, contact a lender who specializes in FHA loans (see Figure 9-7).

**www.hud.gov**
Housing and Urban Development
**www.oig.hhs.gov**
Office of The Inspector General - OIG

*The main purpose of FHA is to promote home ownership by insuring loans made by approved lenders.*

### 1. FHA Title I:  Home Improvement Loans

The FHA can make home improvement loans to a maximum of $25,000. The funds can be used only for home improvement purposes.

### 2. FHA Title II:  Home Purchase or Build Loans

The maximum FHA loan amount varies from area-to-area in California and could change each year if median home prices change or Federal National Mortgage Association (FNMA) loan amounts change. The maximum loan amount is determined as follows:

1. On homes sold at over $125,000, the maximum loan-to-value ratio is 97.15%.
2. On homes from $50,000 to $125,000, the maximum loan-to-value ratio is 97.65%.
3. On homes below $50,000, the maximum loan-to-value ratio is 98.75%.

Obviously, different geographical areas warrant different maximum loans based on the median home values. Accessing the HUD's website at **hud.gov** will give the agent the latest quotes for the various counties.

**www.comerica.com**
Independent FHA Lender

## Minimum Property Requirements (MPRs)

All of these government-backed finance programs have increased the number of houses and condominiums that people in California can afford to buy. They also have an indirect influence on the quality of homes constructed because they require that the home involved meet minimum property requirements as a prerequisite to financing. Minimum Property Requirements (MPRs) are set standards of materials and construction required for FHA and VA loans. These requirements are often more restrictive than the building codes. As a real estate licensee, you should be familiar with the basic financing programs and qualification requirements. In addition, most mortgage companies will help you qualify the buyer and complete the necessary forms for FHA and VA loans.

*Minimum Property Requirements (or MPRs) are minimum quality standards established by the FHA and VA.*

www.quickenloans.com/home-buying/learn/loans/fha-loans-for-home-buying
Independent FHA lender

All FHA home buyers must obtain loans at an approved lender's office. The approved local lender (such as banks, insurance companies, and mortgage companies) will make the loan if the FHA qualifies the buyer. The FHA has many requirements for its different loan programs. Both the borrower and the property must meet these criteria. If either the borrower or the property does not meet the minimum standards, it would probably be better to look for a lender who deals in conventional rather than FHA loans.

The FHA does not lend the money. It only insures the approved lender against foreclosure loss. The FHA collects a percentage of the loan for this insurance called the mortgage insurance premium. The *MORTGAGE INSURANCE PREMIUM (MIP), also called mutual mortgage insurance, is the protection for the FHA that insures the lender for any loss if there is a foreclosure*. It is an up-front fee (paid by the borrower) in cash, or through insurance as part of the loan. If there is a foreclosure, FHA will take over the property and reimburse the lender for the cost of default.

An *FHA MORTGAGE LOAN CORRESPONDENT is a mortgagee approved by the Secretary of the Department Housing and Urban Development*. The loan correspondent has as his or her principal activity either 1) the origination of mortgages for sale or transfer to a sponsor or sponsors, or 2) satisfies the definition of a supervised mortgagee contained in the regulations of the Secretary of the Department of Housing and Urban Development.

### 3. Advantages and Disadvantages of FHA Financing

The advantages and disadvantages of FHA financing include the following.

#### a. Advantages

1. Low down payment compared to conventional loans.
2. Loans are assumable. Loans require approval of the FHA and non-owner-occupied are permitted under some circumstances.

**Figure 9-7**

## Federal Housing Administration (FHA 203b "basic")

| | |
|---|---|
| **ELIGIBILITY** | Anyone residing in the United States |
| **SOURCE OF FUNDS** | Approved Lenders |
| **LOAN INSTRUMENT** | **Trust Deed or Mortgage** |
| **TERM** | 30 years |
| **INTEREST RATE** | Current interest rates plus mortgage insurance premiums paid up front, prior to close of escrow |
| **MAXIMUM PURCHASE** | **No Maximum** |
| **MAXIMUM LOAN AMOUNTS** (For high cost areas) (Alaska & Hawaii up to 150% higher) | 97% of the maximum for the county average: house-condo $729,750; 2-unit $934,200; 3-unit $1,129,500, and 4-unit $1,403,400 |
| **DOWN PAYMENT** | 3.5% minimum cash investment; 100% over appraisal |
| **SECONDARY FINANCING** | **Allowed** |
| **PREPAYMENT PENALTY** | None (30-days' notice) |
| **ASSUMABLE** | After 2 years, if owner occupant |
| **POINTS PAID BY** | **Buyer or Seller** |
| **BORROWER'S MONTHLY PAYMENT** | Monthly principal and interest 29% to 41% of annual gross income |
| **MONTHLY SALARY (AFTER FEDERAL TAXES)** | Approximately 3 times total monthly payment |

| Department of Veterans Affairs VA | State of California CalVet |
|---|---|
| W.W. II, Korean Conflict, Vietnam Era, Persian Gulf War, or continuous active duty for 90 days (181 days peacetime) | 90 day's active duty and received a discharge classified as Honorable or Under Honorable Conditions |
| Approved Lenders | California Bond Issues |
| **Trust Deed or Mortgage** | **Conditional Sales Contract** |
| 30-year maximum | 30-year maximum |
| Set by VA | Set by California, but may increase later |
| **No Maximum by VA (Restricted by Guarantee)** | **None** |
| 1-to-4 units, owner occupied, up to CRV. No loan maximum, but usually under $962,500; Guaranty Maximum is 25% of loan amount | Mauufactured Home – $175,000 (in Mobile Park) (on owned lot – $521,250) House – $521,250 |
| None required, lender may require down payment | Manufactured Home – 3% to 20% House – 3% to 20% |
| **Only up to amount of CRV** | **Under Certain Ciscumstances** |
| None | None |
| Subject to VA approval of assumer's credit | To a CalVet, YES |
| **Buyer or Seller** | **Buyer** |
| Monthly principal and interest 29% to 41% of annual gross income | Monthly principal and interest 28% to 50% of annual gross income |
| Approximately 3 times total monthly payment | Approximately 2 times total monthly payment |

## CHAPTER 9

3. No prepayment penalty is allowed by the FHA.

4. Minimum property requirements (MPRs) give the buyer a quality home.

5. A seller receives all cash because of the high loan-to-value ratio.

*FHA-backed loans generally have lower interest rates than conventional loans. There are NO prepayment penalties on FHA loans.*

### b. Disadvantages

1. Lots of processing time and red tape.

2. Existing properties may require repairs necessary to meet minimum property requirements.

## B. DEPARTMENT OF VETERANS AFFAIRS (VA)

### 1. VA Loans (Loan Guarantees to Approved Lenders)

The Congress of the United States has passed legislation to assist veterans in obtaining housing. A *VA LOAN is not a loan, but rather a guarantee to an approved institutional lender.*

### a. Veteran's Eligibility

Veterans are eligible for a Department of Veterans Affairs (VA) loan guarantee if they served on active duty for 90 days or more (181 days during certain peacetime periods) and were honorably discharged.

American citizens who served in the armed forces of our Allies in World War II may also apply. Widows or widowers of service people or veterans who were eligible at the time of death, but did not use their benefits, may apply to use their husbands' or wives' benefits. Also, the VA Adjudication Board, at its discretion, may give eligibility to any veteran who received other than an honorable discharge.

### b. Veterans May be Entitled to More Than One Loan

A veteran may restore his or her eligibility and apply for an additional loan if the previous home was sold and its loan paid in full. Other veterans who are eligible for a new VA loan program may apply even if they have a prior VA loan, if the prior loan is not in default and if the veteran no longer owns the property. The previous VA loan need not be paid off. The veteran who purchased a home under a previous program may be eligible again under a new program.

### 2. Certificate of Reasonable Value (CRV)

A *CERTIFICATE OF REASONABLE VALUE (CRV) is an appraisal of the property to be purchased by the veteran.* The property is appraised by an independent fee appraiser who is appointed by the Department of Veterans Affairs. Although the appraisal may be paid for by the veteran, it may also be paid for by the seller. The CRV appraisal expires after six months.

*The amount of down payment required for a VA loan is determined by the CRV.*

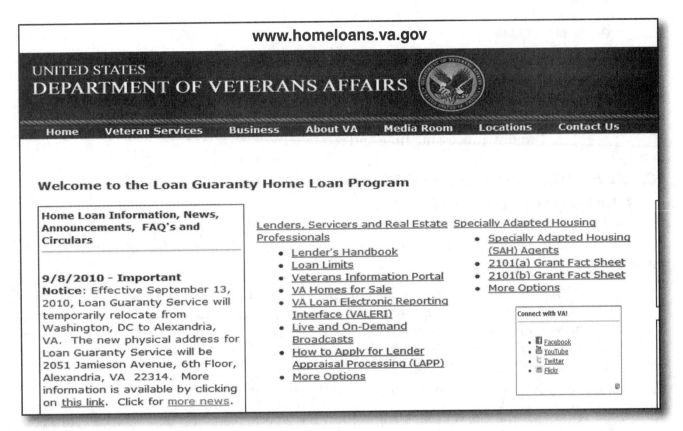

### 3. VA Loan Provisions

*VA loans require NO down payment (100% financing), and NO prepayment penalties.*

No down payment VA loans can be for any amount, but California lenders will only make a loan up to $417,000.

The veteran has the choice of several types of VA loans. They include fixed-rate mortgages, graduated payment mortgages, growing equity mortgages, and buy-down loans. The duration of a VA loan is generally 30 years. Discount points charged sellers and interest rates vary according to the current economic conditions. **The main advantage to the veteran is that no down payment is needed**, unless the property's price exceeds the VA's appraisal. This "no money down" feature is unique among government programs. Loans can be above the $417,000 guaranteed maximum loan amount, but require that the difference between the $417,000 maximum and the actual loan be in the form of a cash down payment.

### 4. Advantages and Disadvantages of VA Financing

The advantages and disadvantages of VA financing include the following.

#### a. Advantages

1. **No down payment**, but a funding fee is paid by the veteran.

2. **Low interest rate** because of the VA loan guarantee.

3. **No prepayment penalty** is allowed by the VA.

CHAPTER 9

### b. Disadvantages

1. Buyer's creditworthiness is a requirement for assumption; VA must approve credit and a fee of up to $500 is required; assumption only after one year if owner-occupied or after two years if investor owned.

2. Buyer or seller can pay discount points.

3. Lengthy processing time and red tape.

## C. CALIFORNIA DEPARTMENT OF VETERAN'S AFFAIRS (CalVet)

### 1. CalVet (Land Contract – Direct Loans)

*Land contracts (contracts of sale or real property sales contracts) are used by the California Department of Veterans Affairs, who retains legal title until the loan is paid in full.*

The *CALVET loan program is administered by the California Department of Veterans Affairs.* As part of its comprehensive veterans program, the State of California has developed and operates a program to assist its veterans in purchasing a farm, home, or manufactured home. Home property must be a single-family dwelling, condominium unit or apartment townhouse.

*CalVet will NOT loan on rental property purchases, but FHA-backed lenders will.*

Funds for the CalVet loans come from the sale of Veterans Bonds, voted into law by the people of California. All money lent to veterans is repaid through installments (including principal, property taxes, insurance, and interest) at a rate to cover all operating costs. The bonds are retired at maturity from veterans' loan payments without cost to the State of California.

Funds may not be immediately available for loans to all applicants. The availability of these funds is limited, therefore wartime veterans (especially those disabled with war-connected injuries) may be given higher priority when applying for these loans.

A veteran who intends to obtain a CalVet loan should contact a representative of the Department of Veterans Affairs for complete California Farm and Home Purchase Plan information before committing to purchase a property. To apply for a loan, he or she should obtain the necessary information and forms from one of the California Department of Veterans Affairs offices throughout the state.

The CalVet maximum for the purchase of a home is $521,250 and up to $625,500 for a farm. A farm loan, however, may not exceed 95 percent of the CalVet appraisal. The veteran must pay to the seller the difference between the sales price and the CalVet loan.

The loan term is determined by the amount of the loan and the age and income of each applicant. Most loans are for 30 years. New loan interest rates are usually lower than current market rates, but may vary according to economic conditions during the life of the loan.

A loan may be paid in full at any time. A CalVet loan can be obtained for a manufactured home if the ownership of the land is included. The maximum manufactured home loan is $125,000 in a park and $250,000 on a single-family lot.

*CalVet has NO points and no prepayment penalties.*

286

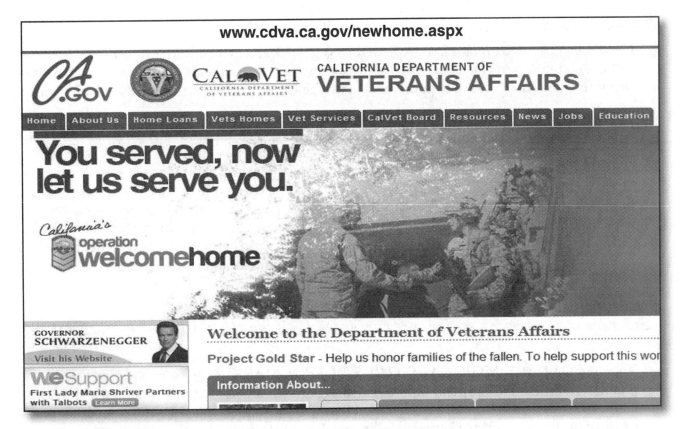

### a. Eligibility

There is no residency requirement. All veterans are eligible for the CalVet program.

To qualify, a California veteran must have served a minimum of 90 days active duty (not including active duty for training purposed only), and received a discharge classified as Honorable or Under Honorable Conditions. Recent changes in the Military and Veterans Code and CalVet Home Loan funding policies have made most veterans eligible under state law, including those whose entire active service was during peacetime.

There are exceptions to the 90 days service requirement for veterans who:

1. were discharged sooner due to a service-connected disability; or

2. are eligible to receive a U.S. campaign or expeditionary medal, or

3. were called to active duty from the Reserves or National Guard due to a Presidential Executive Order.

Current members of the California National Guard or the U.S. Military Reserves who have served a minimum of one year of a six-year obligation are also eligible provided they qualify as first time home buyers or purchase properties located in certain Targeted Areas.

A qualified veteran must apply for a CalVet loan within 30 years following release from active military duty. However, those who were wounded or disabled during war or who were prisoners of war have an indefinite period in which to apply.

### D. CALIFORNIA HOUSING FINANCE AGENCY (Cal HFA)

*CALIFORNIA HOUSING FINANCE AGENCY (Cal HFA) is a state agency that sells bonds so that it can provide funds for low-income family housing on a project or individual home basis.* It is self-supporting and has political support across party lines. **Figure 9-8** explains Cal HFA in detail.

# VII. Lending Corporations and the Secondary Mortgage Market

## A. PRIVATE AND QUASI-GOVERNMENTAL CORPORATIONS

There were once three federal corporations that used cash to buy and sell trust deeds between financial institutions. These corporations are now either private or quasi-governmental and provide stability and flexibility for real estate financing in the United States. Each has different programs and areas of focus, but all work together to keep sufficient financing money available at lending institutions so they can make home loans.

## B. SECONDARY MORTGAGE (TRUST DEED) MARKET

*Lenders in the secondary market are concerned with the "liquidity and marketability" of loans.*

The *SECONDARY MORTGAGE (TRUST DEED) MARKET provides an opportunity for financial institutions to buy from, and sell first mortgages (trust deeds) to, other financial institutions.* California has a growing real estate market that will pay higher interest rates than other parts of the country. Therefore, California's financial institutions will make trust deed loans and sell them to other institutions for a profit. The secondary mortgage market enables lenders to keep an adequate supply of money for new loans.

*The secondary mortgage market provides additional funds to mortgage lenders.*

### 1. Federal National Mortgage Association (Fannie Mae – Federal Conservatorship)

*Fannie Mae is not a demand source to borrow money.*

The Federal National Mortgage Association (FNMA), which is commonly referred to as Fannie Mae, dominates the secondary mortgage market. Originally it bought and sold only FHA and VA trust deeds. In 1968 it became a private corporation and now sells securities over the stock exchange to get money so that it can buy and sell conventional loans in addition to government-backed notes. **It is not a demand source**.

*Fannie Mae is the largest investor in the secondary market. It was created to increase the amount of money available for credit financing of houses.*

www.fanniemae.com
Fannie Mae

### 2. Government National Mortgage Association (Ginnie Mae)

The Government National Mortgage Association (GNMA) is a government corporation referred to as Ginnie Mae. It sells secondary mortgages to the public and provides the federal government with cash. These trust deeds are grouped together in pools, and

**Figure 9-8**

# Cal HFA
## *California Housing Finance Agency*

1121 "L" STREET 7TH FLOOR · SACRAMENTO, CA 95814 · (916) 322-3991

The **California Housing Finance Agency** is an exciting program providing real estate funds for low-income families, encouraging homeownership over a wider spectrum than has been possible in recent years. This plan is being hailed as a boon from all quarters because it provides a desperately needed funding source and helps stimulate the real estate industry. At the same time, it is entirely self-supporting.

### Bonds Issued

Seb Sterpa, past president of CAR, is credited with originating the idea for this program and promoting it to the governor and house speaker. The money for these loans is provided by the issuance of tax-free bonds by the state. These bonds sell quickly at a very favorable rate. Because this rate is below the current level, it enables approved lenders to provide loans with affordable rates of interest and still make a reasonable return.

### Entirely Self-Supporting

Everyone benefits from this program. Housing in California has become more accessible to buyers with restricted resources. Young couples starting out are now able to enter the housing market. The market is stimulated by the influx of new participants. Investors who purchase the bonds enjoy this profitable form of investment. No tax money is involved and the program is entirely self-supporting.

### Support Across Party Lines

Because of the universal benefits, this program claims support across traditional party lines. Democrats favor this program because of the opportunity it offers to the economically disadvantaged. Many Republicans in the state are delighted because of the boost these loans bring to the real estate industry and the state economy in general.

**www.calhfa.ca.gov**

shares are sold on the stock market exchange. All shares are federally guaranteed, making this one of the safest investments available.

### 3. Federal Home Loan Mortgage Corporation (Freddie Mac - Federal Conservatorship)

The Federal Home Loan Mortgage Corporation (FHLMC), commonly known as Freddie Mac, is a government corporation that issues preferred stock to the public. It is supervised by the Federal Home Loan Bank Board. It helps savings banks maintain a stable and adequate money supply by purchasing their home loan mortgages and repackaging them for sale to investors. The savings banks use the money obtained to make new loans available for home buyers.

*The Federal Home Loan Mortgage Corporation, commonly called "Freddie Mac," increases the availability of funds through its involvement in the maintenance of the secondary mortgage market.*

www.ginniemae.gov
Ginnie Mae
www.freddiemac.com
Freddie Mac

> Because Fannie and Freddie were losing $40 billion a year, they were effectively taken over by the federal government in 2008. The "conservatorship" is administered by the Federal Housing Finance Agency (FHFA).

### C. FINAL WORD ON CONVENTIONAL LOANS
### (Risk – Loans Without Government Backing)

Since conventional loans are loans made without government backing or guarantees, they are riskier. Even if conventional loans have lower loan-to-value (LTV) ratios, which make them safer, government-backed loans are the safest. Because the government will pay off if there is a foreclosure, Fannie Mae and Freddie Mac currently have loan limits of $729,750 (expected to increase) for a single-family house or condo. *If the requested loan amount is higher than the Fannie Mae and Freddie Mac loan limit, it is called a JUMBO LOAN.*

# VIII. Real Estate Broker Can Make Loans

The broker or salesperson, as part of most real estate transactions, may help the buyer fill out a loan application for a financial institution or arrange financing for the buyer. In either case, there are certain restrictions that apply to a real estate licensee acting as a loan broker in buying, selling, or exchanging loans. Most of these loans are in the form of a trust deed since it is the usual financing instrument in California.

*Advertising criteria (pertinent information) ensures that advertisements are not misleading.*

The "Mortgage Loan Broker Law," sections 10240-10248 of Article 7 of the Business and Professions Code, requires loan brokers to give a Mortgage Loan Disclosure Statement to all borrowers before they become obligated for the loan.

A new real estate license endorsement is required from the DRE in order to engage in the business as a mortgage loan originator. A *MORTGAGE LOAN ORIGINATOR is an individual who takes a residential mortgage loan application or offers or negotiates terms of a residential mortgage loan for compensation or gain.*

## A. MORTGAGE LOAN DISCLOSURE STATEMENT
### (Keep on File for Three Years)

A real estate licensee negotiating a loan for a prospective borrower must present to that person a completed loan disclosure statement. This statement must be given to the borrower prior to his or her signing the loan documents. It is usually referred to as the Mortgage Loan Disclosure Statement.

A **MORTGAGE LOAN DISCLOSURE STATEMENT** *is a form that completely and clearly states all the information and charges connected with a particular loan.* Nontraditional mortgage product information must be disclosed to the borrower. It must be kept on file for three years (see Figure 9-10). Expect more changes to this form. Besides providing the borrower with the disclosure statement, the broker is prohibited from doing certain things and is restricted as to the amount of commission that he or she may charge the borrower. The broker's (fiduciary) obligation is to fully explain the terms of a loan to the borrower.

Anyone negotiating real estate loans (fiduciary relationship) must be a real estate licensee with an Endorsement and a Unique Identifier Number from the Nationwide Mortgage Licensing System and Registry (NMLS&R) in accordance with the SAFE Act. If you make collections on real estate loans and you make more than ten a year, or collect more than $40,000, you must also be a licensed real estate broker. Many brokers establish a regular, ongoing business relationship with individuals or financial institutions that will loan money to prospective buyers.

www.calbankers.com
California Bankers Association
www.mortgage.nationwidelicensingsystem.org
NMLS Resource Center

## B. BUSINESS AND PROFESSIONS CODE – Division 4 – Real Estate
### (Commissions and Other Requirements)

#### 1. Article 7 – Loan Broker Laws ($20,000 – $30,000)

Brokers negotiating trust deed loans are subject to certain limitations regarding commissions and expenses and must meet other requirements set out by the real estate commissioner (see **Figure 9-9**). Legislation also requires that brokers provide both the borrower and the lender, on property for first trust deed loans under $30,000 and seconds under $20,000, with copies of the appraisal report.

*Anyone performing these services, whether soliciting borrowers or lenders in home loans secured by real property must have a real estate license. This restriction applies even if no advance fee is paid.*

Loans on owner-occupied homes negotiated by brokers for a term of six years or less may not have a balloon payment. If a home is nonowner occupied, loans are exempt from balloon payments when the term is less than three years. Neither of these restrictions apply to transactions where the seller extends credit to the buyer. When such transactions have balloon payments, the seller is obligated to notify the buyer 60 to 150 days before the payment is due. Also, the broker is obligated to inform the buyer regarding the likelihood of obtaining new financing.

# CHAPTER 9

**Figure 9-9**

## Loan Broker Commission Limits

| | Loans for Less Than 2 Years | Loans for 2 Years and Less Than 3 Years | Loans for 3 Years and Over | Transactions That are Exempt (No Limit on Commission) |
|---|---|---|---|---|
| **First Trust Deeds** | 5% | 5% | 10% | Loans of $30,000 and over |
| **Junior Trust Deeds** | 5% | 10% | 15% | Loans of $20,000 and over |

### a. Threshold Reporting (Big Lending – $2,000,000)

*THRESHOLD REPORTING is the requirement of reporting annual and quarterly loan activity (review of trust fund) to the Department of Real Estate if, within the past 12 months, the broker has negotiated any combination of 20 or more loans to a subdivision or a total of more than $2,000,000 in loans.* In addition, advertising must be submitted to the DRE for review. This regulation is intended to protect the public by overseeing the loan activity of big lenders who are using their real estate broker's licenses.

## 2. Article 5 – Broker Restrictions

The licensee is prohibited from pooling funds. A broker may not accept funds except for a specifically identified loan transaction. Before accepting a lender's money, the broker must:

1. Own the loan or have an unconditional written contract to purchase a specific note.

2. Have the authorization from a prospective borrower to negotiate a secured loan.

## 3. Article 6 – Real Property Securities Dealer

**A DRE broker's license and endorsement are required: A $100 fee plus a $10,000 surety bond. DRE permit is required to sell specific security.**

No real estate investment type security shall be sold to the public without first obtaining a permit from the Commissioner. A *COMMISSIONER'S PERMIT is the approval of the proposed real property security and plan of distribution.* If, in the commissioner's opinion, the security and proposed plan of distribution is fair, just, and equitable, he or she will authorize the sale, subject to any limiting conditions. A permit is not an endorsement or recommendation of the security; it is only a permit to sell. The application for the permit is extensive and may require supplementary filings. The duration of the permit is one year, and the permit may not be used in advertising unless it is used in its entirety. **A Commissioner's permit requires a $10,000 surety bond.**

**Figure 9-10**

CALIFORNIA
ASSOCIATION
OF REALTORS®

**MORTGAGE LOAN DISCLOSURE STATEMENT**
**(BORROWER)**
(As required by the Business and Professions Code §10241
and Title 10, California Administrative Code, §2840)
(C.A.R. Form MS, Revised 08/08)

_____
(Name of Broker/Arranger of Credit)

_____
(Business Address of Broker)

**I. SUMMARY OF LOAN TERMS**
A. PRINCIPAL AMOUNT . . . . . . . . . . . . . . . . . . . . . . . . . . . . . . . . . $ _____
B. ESTIMATED DEDUCTIONS FROM PRINCIPAL AMOUNT
   1. Costs and Expenses (See Paragraph III-A) . . . . . . . . . . . . . . . . . . $ _____
   2. Broker Commission/Origination Fee (See Paragraph III-B) . . . . . . . . $ _____
   3. Lender Origination Fee/Discounts (See Paragraph III-B) . . . . . . . . . . $ _____
   4. Additional compensation will/may be received from lender not deducted from loan proceeds.
     ☐ YES $ _____ (if known) or ☐ NO
   5. Amount to be Paid on Authorization of Borrower (See Paragraph III-C) . . . . $ _____
C. ESTIMATED CASH PAYABLE TO BORROWER (A less B) . . . . . . . . . . . $ _____

**II. GENERAL INFORMATION ABOUT LOAN**
A. PROPOSED LOAN INFORMATION
   1. Proposed loan term     ☐ Years     ☐ Months

☐ **FIXED RATE LOAN**
Fixed rate loan _____ % payable at $ _____ month

☐ **ADJUSTABLE RATE LOAN (EXAMPLE 6-MONTH ARM; 1-YEAR ARM)**
Proposed interest rate _____ %
Fully indexed rate _____ %
Proposed monthly payment: $ _____
Maximum interest rate _____ %
Interest rate can increase _____ % each _____ months
Maximum loan payment can be $ _____ after _____ months

☐ **INITIAL FIXED RATE LOAN (EXAMPLE 2/28, 3/1/5/1)**
Proposed initial fixed interest rate _____ %
Initial fixed interest rate in effect for _____ months
Proposed initial monthly payment: $ _____
Adjustable interest rate of _____ % will begin after fixed rate period ends
Monthly payment can increase to $ _____ after fixed rate period ends
Fully indexed rate _____ %
Maximum interest rate _____ %
Interest rate can increase _____ % each _____ months
Maximum loan payment can be $ _____ after _____ months

☐ **INITIAL ADJUSTABLE RATE LOAN (EXAMPLE LOW ENTRY RATE ARM)**
Proposed initial adjustable interest rate _____ %
Initial fixed interest rate in effect for _____ months
Proposed initial monthly payment: $ _____
Fully indexed rate _____ %
Maximum interest rate _____ %
Interest rate can increase _____ % each _____ months
Monthly payment can increase to $ _____ after initial adjustable rate period ends
Maximum loan payment can be $ _____ after _____ months

   2. This loan is based on limited or no documentation of your income and/or assets and may have a higher interest rate, or more points or fees than other products requiring documentation: ☐ No ☐ Yes.
   3. The loan is subject to a balloon payment: ☐ No ☐ Yes. If Yes, the following paragraph applies and a final balloon payment of $ _____ will be due on _____ [estimated date (month/day/year)].

**NOTICE TO BORROWER: IF YOU DO NOT HAVE THE FUNDS TO PAY THE BALLOON PAYMENT WHEN IT COMES DUE, YOU MAY HAVE TO OBTAIN A NEW LOAN AGAINST YOUR PROPERTY TO MAKE THE BALLOON PAYMENT. IN THAT CASE, YOU MAY AGAIN HAVE TO PAY COMMISSIONS, FEES AND EXPENSES FOR THE ARRANGING OF THE NEW LOAN. IN ADDITION, IF YOU ARE UNABLE TO MAKE THE MONTHLY PAYMENTS OR THE BALLOON PAYMENT, YOU MAY LOSE THE PROPERTY AND ALL OF YOUR EQUITY THROUGH FORECLOSURE. KEEP THIS IN MIND IN DECIDING UPON THE AMOUNT AND TERMS OF THIS LOAN.**

B. This loan will be evidenced by a promissory note and secured by a deed of trust on property identified as (street address or legal description):
_123 Sail Avenue ,_ _____

Buyer's Initials (_____)(_____)
Seller's Initials (_____)(_____)

Reviewed by _____ Date _____

EQUAL HOUSING OPPORTUNITY

MS REVISED 08/08 (PAGE 1 OF 3)
**MORTGAGE LOAN DISCLOSURE STATEMENT (MS PAGE 1 OF 3)**

| Agent: WALT HUBER | Phone: | Fax: | Prepared using zipForm® software |
|---|---|---|---|
| Broker: WALT HUBER REALTOR | | | |

C. 1. Liens presently against this property (do not include loan being applied for):

| Nature of Lien | Priority | Lienholder's Name | Amount Owing |
|---|---|---|---|
| _____ | _____ | _____ | _____ |
| _____ | _____ | _____ | _____ |

2. Liens that will remain against this property after the loan being applied for is made or arranged (include loan being applied for):

| Nature of Lien | Priority | Lienholder's Name | Amount Owing |
|---|---|---|---|
| _____ | _____ | _____ | _____ |
| _____ | _____ | _____ | _____ |

**NOTICE TO BORROWER:** Be sure that you state the amount of all liens as accurately as possible. If you contract with the broker to arrange this loan, but it cannot be arranged because you did not state these liens correctly, you may be liable to pay commissions, fees and expenses even though you do not obtain the loan.

D. Prepayments: The proposed loan has the following prepayment provisions:

☐ No prepayment penalty (you will not be charged a penalty to pay off or refinance the loan before maturity)

☐ You will have to pay a prepayment penalty if the loan is paid off or refinanced in the first _____ years. The prepayment penalty could be as much as $ _____ . Any prepayment of principal in excess of 20% of the

    ☐ original loan balance or

    ☐ unpaid balance

for the first _____ years will include a penalty not to exceed _____ months interest at the note interest rate but not more than the interest you would be charged if the loan were paid to maturity.

☐ Other - you will have to pay a prepayment penalty if the loan is paid off or refinanced in the first _____ years as follows: _____

_____

_____

E. Taxes and Insurance:

☐ There will be an impound (escrow) account which will collect approximately $ _____ a month in addition to your principal and interest payments for the payment of ☐ county property taxes** ☐ hazard insurance ☐ mortgage insurance ☐ flood insurance ☐ other _____ .

☐ If there is no impound (escrow) account or if your escrow (impound) account does not include one or more of the payments described above, you will have to plan for the payment of ☐ county property taxes** ☐ hazard insurance of approximately $ _____ per year.

**In a purchase transaction, county property taxes are calculated based on the sales price of the property and may require the payment of an additional (supplemental) tax bill from the county tax authority by your lender (if escrowed) or you (if not escrowed).

F. Late Charges: ☐ YES, see loan documents or ☐ NO

G. The purchase of credit life and/or credit disability insurance by a borrower is not required as a condition of making this loan.

III. **DEDUCTIONS FROM LOAN PROCEEDS**

A. Estimated Maximum Costs and Expenses of Arranging the Loan to be Paid Out of Loan Principal:

| | PAYABLE TO | |
|---|---|---|
| | Broker | Others |
| 1. Appraisal fee | _____ | _____ |
| 2. Escrow fee | _____ | _____ |
| 3. Title insurance policy | _____ | _____ |
| 4. Notary fees | _____ | _____ |
| 5. Recording fees | _____ | _____ |
| 6. Credit investigation fees | _____ | _____ |
| 7. Other costs and expenses: | | |
| | _____ | _____ |
| | _____ | _____ |
| Total Costs and Expenses | $ _____ | |
| B. Compensation | $ _____ | |
| 1. Brokerage Commission/Origination Fee | $ _____ | |

MS REVISED 08/08 (PAGE 2 OF 3)

Buyer's Initials ( _____ )( _____ )
Seller's Initials ( _____ )( _____ )

Reviewed by _____ Date_____

**MORTGAGE LOAN DISCLOSURE STATEMENT (MS PAGE 2 OF 3)**

Untitled

2. Lender Origination Fee/Discounts .............................. $ _____

C. Estimated Payment to be Made out of Loan Principal on Authorization of Borrower

PAYABLE TO

| | Broker | Others |
|---|---|---|
| 1. Fire or other hazard insurance premiums .................... | _____ | _____ |
| 2. Credit life or disability insurance premiums (See Paragraph II-G) ........ | _____ | _____ |
| 3. Beneficiary statement fees .................... | _____ | _____ |
| 4. Reconveyance and similar fees .................... | _____ | _____ |
| 5. Discharge of existing liens against property: | _____ | _____ |
| | _____ | _____ |
| 6. Other: | _____ | _____ |
| | _____ | _____ |

Total to be Paid on Authorization of Borrower ...................... $ _____

Article 7 Compliance: If this loan is secured by a first deed of trust on dwellings in a principal amount of less than $30,000 or secured by a junior lien on dwellings in a principal amount of less than $20,000, the undersigned licensee certifies that the loan will be made in compliance with Article 7 of Chapter 3 of the Real Estate Law.

This loan **may / will / will not** (delete two) be made wholly or in part from broker-controlled funds as defined in Section 10241(j) of the Business and Professions Code.

**IV. NOTICES TO BORROWER:**

1. This disclosure statement may be used if the Broker is acting as an agent in arranging the loan by a third person or if the loan will be made with funds owned or controlled by the broker. If the Broker indicates in the Article 7 Compliance immediately above, that the loan "may" be made out of Broker-controlled funds, the Broker must notify the borrower prior to the close of escrow if the funds to be received by the Borrower are in fact Broker-controlled funds.

2. THIS IS NOT A LOAN COMMITMENT. Do not sign this statement until you have read and understood all of the information in it. All parts of this form must be completed before you sign. Borrower hereby acknowledges the receipt of a copy of this statement.

_____  _____  _____  _____
Name of Broker           License Number    Broker Representative      License Number

_____
Broker's Address

OR

_____  _____  _____  _____
Signature of Broker      Date              Signature of Representative Date

_____  _____  _____  _____
Borrower                 Date              Borrower                   Date

The Department of Real Estate License Information phone number is 916-227-0931, or check license status at www.dre.ca.gov.

**REBS INC** Published and Distributed by:
REAL ESTATE BUSINESS SERVICES, INC.
a subsidiary of the California Association of REALTORS®
525 South Virgil Avenue, Los Angeles, California 90020

Reviewed by _____ Date _____

**MS REVISED 08/08 (PAGE 3 OF 3)**

**MORTGAGE LOAN DISCLOSURE STATEMENT (MS PAGE 3 OF 3)**

Untitled

### a. Real Property Securities Dealer Endorsement

A *REAL PROPERTY SECURITIES DEALER (RPSD) is any person acting as principal or agent who engages in the business of selling real property securities (such as promissory notes or sales contracts).* These dealers also accept or offer to accept funds for reinvestment in real property securities or for placement in an account. Before a licensed real estate broker may act in this capacity, he or she must obtain an RPSD endorsement on his or her broker's license. To obtain an RPSD endorsement on a broker's license, submit the appropriate endorsement fee ($100) along with proof of a properly executed $10,000 surety bond. (For information on Real Property Securities, call the DRE.)

---

# "Equity Sharing"

## A Different Financing and Ownership Idea

*EQUITY SHARING (SHARED EQUITY FINANCING) is a contractual arrangement whereby an investor shares any equity gain with a homeowner.* Since California has high housing costs that require a large down payment, many potential homeowners cannot qualify or do not have the cash for a down payment. The concept is that an investor puts up most of the down payment, and receives no interest deductions but shares in any equity gain when the property is sold. The homeowner gets his or her home quickly with a minimum down payment, with relaxed credit, and with full income tax write-offs. Consult an attorney or CPA before investing.

---

## IX. CHAPTER SUMMARY

**Inflation** (when prices appreciate) protects both lender and trustor because there will be more equity protecting the lender in the case of a default. When prices decrease, the value of money increases and vice versa. In a **seller's market**, prices rise due to a shortage of properties available, whereas in a **buyer's market**, prices fall, terms are easy and properties plentiful.

The **Federal Reserve (Fed)** is the nation's central banking authority and controls the availability of loan funds, but has nothing to do with raising or lowering interest rates. The Fed's influence on the economy is evidenced by changes in the **Gross Domestic Product (GDP)**.

The three areas of demand for borrowing money are: construction funds, financing a purchase, and refinancing. Most lenders request an 80% **L-T-V (loan to value) ratio**. The lower the L-T-V, the greater the down payment.

The primary purpose of **RESPA** is to require lenders to make special disclosures, without cost to the borrower, for loans involving the sale or transfer of one-to-four residential dwellings.

Large **institutional lenders** who pool funds to lend to individual borrowers, include: **insurance companies, savings banks,** and **banks**. Depositor's accounts in savings banks and banks are insured up to $100,000 by the **Federal Deposit Insurance Corporation (FDIC)**. Savings banks have the highest percentage of funds invested in real estate loans, followed by banks, which are **general purpose lenders**.

Smaller, **noninstitutional lenders** include: private lenders, mortgage companies, investment trusts, pension plans and credit unions. Private investors make many of the **second (junior) loans** on real estate. **Real estate investment trusts (REITs)** sell securities specializing in real estate ventures, and are of two types, 1) **equity trust** and 2) **mortgage trust**.

**Mortgage bankers (companies)** like to make loans that can be sold easily on the **secondary mortgage market**, which is a resale marketplace for smaller lenders to sell their loans to larger lenders. Buyers may be required to obtain **private mortgage insurance (PMI)** to protect the lender in case of default.

The **Federal Housing Administration (FHA)** is a division of **HUD** that **insures loans** but does not make them. **FHA Title 1** involves home improvement loans and **FHA Title II** insures home loan purchase or building loans. The **Mortgage Insurance Premium (MIP)** is the FHA insurance protection against owner default (also called mutual mortgage insurance).

Veterans may qualify for a **Department of Veterans Affairs (VA) Loan**, which is not really a loan, but a **loan guarantee** to approved institutional lenders. The amount of down payment on a VA loan is determined by the **Certificate of Reasonable Value (CRV)**. Vets may be required to pay origination fees and discount points. On the state level, **CalVet**, administered by the California Department of Veteran Affairs, will purchase a **land contract (contract of sale or real property sales contract)** and hold legal title to a property until the veteran pays off the loan in full.

The **secondary mortgage (trust deed) market** is the market where lenders buy and sell mortgages. **Fannie Mae (FNMA)** buys and sells conventional loans. It helps set loan standards and maintain the secondary market, but is not a demand source to borrow money. **Freddie Mac (FHLMC)** purchases home loan mortgages and repackages them for sale to investors, freeing up savings banks to make new loans. Conventional loans are riskier than FHA loans; the higher the risk the higher the interest rates.

**Ginnie Mae (GNMA)** sells secondary mortgages to the public and provides the federal government cash.

A loan broker must provide a borrower with a **Mortgage Loan Disclosure Statement**, clearly stating all information and charges connected with a loan, and keep it on file for three years. Brokers negotiating trust deed loans (fiduciary relationship) may charge whatever commission the buyer will pay on loans of $30,000+ for first trust deeds and $20,000+ for junior deeds of trust.

# CHAPTER 9

A broker must make a **threshold report** if he or she negotiates more than $2 million in loans or 20+ subdivision loans. Other broker restrictions are covered by **Article 5**.

A **real property securities dealer (RPSD)** acts as a principal or agent engaged in the business of selling real property securities such as promissory notes or sales contracts. A DRE broker's license and endorsement are required including a $10,000 surety bond.

## X. TERMINOLOGY

**A.** Buyer's Market
**B.** California Housing Financing Agency (Cal HFA)
**C.** CalVet Loans
**D.** Certificate of Reasonable Value (CRV)
**E.** Collateral
**F.** Conventional Loans
**G.** Credit Union
**H.** Equity Investment Trust
**I.** Fannie Mae

**J.** FDIC
**K.** Federal Reserve Board
**L.** Federal Reserve System (The "Fed")
**M.** Freddie Mac
**N.** Ginnie Mae
**O.** Gross Domestic Product (GDP)
**P.** Institutional Lender
**Q.** Minimum Property Requirements (MPRs)
**R.** Mortgage Banker

**S.** Mortgage Company
**T.** Mortgage Investment Trust
**U.** Mortgage Loan Disclosure Statement
**V.** Noninstitutional Lender
**W.** Private Mortgage Insurance (PMI)
**X.** Seller's Market
**Y.** Soft Money Financing
**Z.** VA Loans

1.____ A company providing mortgage financing with its own funds rather than simply bringing together lender and borrower, as does a mortgage broker. The mortgages are sold to investors within a short time.

2.____ (FHLMC) Federal Home Loan Mortgage Corporation. A federal agency purchasing first mortgages, both conventional and federally insured, from savings banks.

3.____ A company authorized to service real estate loans, charging a fee for this service.

4.____ The federal corporation that insures against loss of deposits in banks, up to a maximum amount (currently $250,000).

5.____ Insurance issued by a private insurance company against a loss by a lender in the event of default by a borrower (mortgagor). The premium is paid by the borrower and is included in the mortgage payment.

6.____ Loans made under a land contract directly from the California Department of Veterans Affairs, which has its own specific qualifications.

7.____ A mortgage or deed of trust not obtained under a government insured or guaranteed program.

8.____ The money value of all goods and services produced by a nation's economy for a given period of time.

9.____ Government National Mortgage Association: A federal corporation, working with the FHA, which offers special assistance in obtaining mortgages and purchases mortgages in the secondary market.

10.____ Banks, savings banks, loan associations, and other businesses that make loans to the public in the ordinary course of business, rather than individuals, or companies that may make loans to employees.

11.____Housing loans to veterans by banks, savings banks, or other lenders that are guaranteed by the Veteran's Administration, enabling veterans to buy a residence with little or no down payment.

12.____A private corporation that acts as a secondary market for the purchase of existing first mortgages, at a discount.

13.____The central banking system that controls the amount of money and the rate of interest in the United States.

14.____The powerful nine-member banking panel which controls the destiny of the United State's monetary system. Along with the President of the United States, the Chairman is one of the most powerful positions in the country.

15.____A form that California law requires be given to the borrower, breaking down all the costs and fees of securing a loan.

16.____An agency, sponsored by the state of California, which sponsors special housing projects and certain types of loans.

17.____The real estate pledged to back up a loan. The value of the real estate should be worth substantially more than the loan amount.

18.____Smaller lenders such as sellers, credit unions, and pension plans that lend money on real estate.

19.____An appraisal document stating the fair market value of real estate under a VA loan.

20.____The minimal property standards for a property to qualify for an FHA loan.

21.____A loan made by the seller to the buyer as part of the purchase transaction.

22.____A market condition favoring the seller, when fewer homes are for sale than there are interested buyers.

23.____A trust company specializing in making mortgages as an investment.

24.____A trust company that specializes in taking an ownership position in other projects.

25.____A market condition favoring the buyer, when more homes are for sale than there are interested buyers.

26.____An organization whose members often have a common bond of occupation. Considered a growing source of real estate funds.

# CHAPTER 9

## XI. CHAPTER QUIZ

1. With regard to inflation:
   - a. market value increases and sales price increases.
   - b. sales price increases and market value decreases.
   - c. market value decreases and sale price decreases.
   - d. sale price decreases and market value increases.

2. When the general level of prices decreases:
   - a. the value of money decreases.
   - b. the value of money increases.
   - c. inflation increases.
   - d. the GDP increases/market value increases.

3. When the federal reserve wants a "loose" money market:
   - a. the fed buys back bonds and lowers reserve requirements of banks.
   - b. the fed sells bonds and increases the reserve requirements of banks.
   - c. the fed sells bonds and keeps the reserve requirements the same.
   - d. none of the above.

4. Recession, depression, expansion, and prosperity represent four phases of:
   - a. the elements of value.
   - b. the right of survivorship.
   - c. joint tenancy.
   - d. the business cycle.

5. If a loan application includes a section requesting information about marital status and race, an applicant may:
   - a. sue the lender for fraud.
   - b. file a complaint under The Housing Financial Discrimination Act of 1977.
   - c. refuse to complete this section of the application.
   - d. all of the above.

6. For financing the purchase of residential properties, the principal lender of money is:
   - a. Federal National Mortgage Association.
   - b. federal savings banks.
   - c. insurance companies.
   - d. commercial banks.

7. Institutions that specialize in making home loans most commonly get their funds from:
   - a. mortgage bankers.
   - b. mortgage brokers.
   - c. individual savings.
   - d. Federal Reserve.

8. Which of the following are synonymous?

    a. Interim loan/take out loan

    b. Take out loan/construction loan

    c. Construction loan/interim loan

    d. None of the above

9. For which of the following is an FHA loan available, but not a Cal-Vet loan?

    a. A loan to purchase a single-family dwelling to be rented to a tenant

    b. A loan to purchase a business opportunity

    c. A loan to purchase agricultural land

    d. A loan to purchase farm equipment

10. Many lenders consider the liquidity and marketability of loans to be very important when they make a loan secured by a mortgage. The importance of liquidity and marketability relates to:

    a. activities of the secondary mortgage markets.

    b. desirability of fixed rate loans over adjustable rate loans.

    c. ability to resell homes.

    d. the mix of loans made by banks only.

**ANSWERS:** 1. a; 2. b; 3. a; 4. d; 5. c; 6. b; 7. c; 8. c; 9. c; 10. a

TM

# CHAPTER 10
## *Appraisal Basics*

# I. What is an Appraisal?

An *APPRAISAL is an opinion as to the monetary value of a particular property at a given date.* One of the most important factors for you to consider in deciding whether to sell or buy a home or any specific piece of real estate is its selling price. Each parcel of land (and the buildings on it) is unique. No two are exactly alike, so prices vary. The *MARKET PRICE (SELLING PRICE) is the total price, including down payment and financing, that a property actually brought when sold.* Market price is what it sold for, whereas market value is what it should have sold for in a competitive market.

The market value is what the property is actually worth. *MARKET VALUE is the price that a willing buyer will pay and a willing seller accept, both being fully informed and with the sale property exposed for a reasonable period.* The courtroom definition is even more technical:

> *"The highest price, estimated in terms of money, that a property will bring if it is exposed for sale in the open market, allowing a reasonable length of time to find a buyer who buys with full knowledge of all the uses to which it is adapted and for which the property is capable of being used."*

*Appraisers are required to consider the impact of financing terms and "creative financing" when determining price or value.*

**IMPROVED VALUE OF LAND** *is the market value of the land and any improvements.*

*In comparing real property price to value, a change in financing terms will affect price and value for extreme "creative financing."*

Current market value is not affected in any way by the original cost of the property. The market value of a particular property is an opinion of value, by an appraiser, based on analysis of actual and relevant data, as of a given date. Appraisers must have the required experience, education, and have passed one of the three California State Appraisal Exams (see end of Chapter 11).

*Market value is primarily based upon the "willing buyer and willing seller" concept.*

## A. FOUR ESSENTIAL ELEMENTS OF VALUE

*VALUE is a relationship between the thing desired and a potential purchaser.* Four elements must be present to create and maintain value. The four essential elements of value are:

# CHAPTER OUTLINE

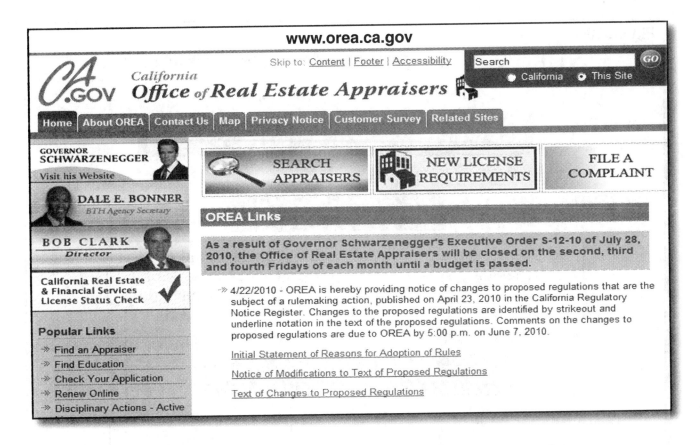

D  **1. Demand** – the desire, need, and ability to purchase

U  **2. Utility** – usefulness; ability to instill a desire for possession

S  **3. Scarcity** – in short supply, usually more expensive

T  **4. Transferability** – can change ownership, as with a deed.

*Elements of value include demand, utility, scarcity, and transferability (DUST). Neither cost nor expectation is an element of value.*

## II. The Appraisal Process (Four Logical Steps)

An appraisal is the solution to the problem of determining value. To solve this problem, an orderly procedure has been developed; it is called the appraisal process. The *APPRAISAL PROCESS is an orderly program by which the problem is defined, the work is planned, and the data is gathered, analyzed, and correlated to estimate the value.* Although the characteristics of real property differ, this is an orderly procedure for solving any appraisal problem (see **Figure 10-1**). The appraisal process consists of four logical steps:

1. Defining and clarifying the problem (Chapter 10)
2. Gathering the data (Chapter 10)
3. Performing the three appraisal methods (Chapter 11)
4. Correlating the three methods and determining the final opinion of value. (Chapter 11)

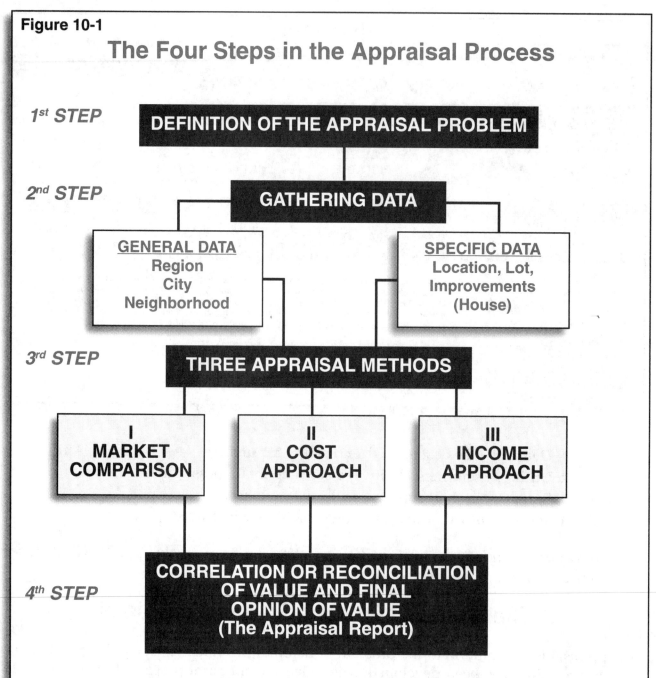

**Figure 10-1**

## The Four Steps in the Appraisal Process

*1st* STEP — **DEFINITION OF THE APPRAISAL PROBLEM**

*2nd* STEP — **GATHERING DATA**

**GENERAL DATA**
Region
City
Neighborhood

**SPECIFIC DATA**
Location, Lot,
Improvements
(House)

*3rd* STEP — **THREE APPRAISAL METHODS**

I
**MARKET
COMPARISON**

II
**COST
APPROACH**

III
**INCOME
APPROACH**

*4th* STEP — **CORRELATION OR RECONCILIATION
OF VALUE AND FINAL
OPINION OF VALUE
(The Appraisal Report)**

This correlation or reconciliation is never an averaging of the three approaches. For instance, in a single-family residential appraisal, the Income Approach is not as valuable as the Market Comparison Approach. This is one of the reasons why the experience and knowledge of the appraiser is so important in any appraisal.

## A. DEFINITION OF THE APPRAISAL PROBLEM (1st Step in the Appraisal Process)

The first step in the appraisal process must include a definition of what questions are to be answered during the appraisal. To begin with, the precise location of the property must be established. Next, the extent of ownership (fee simple or partial) to be appraised must be identified. The date and purpose of the appraisal (usually to establish market value) is then determined. Any limiting conditions (facts unknown to the appraiser) must be clarified. Finally, the appraiser will determine the fee for his or her services.

### 1. Purpose of an Appraisal

An appraisal can serve several purposes. Here is a partial list of the kinds of appraisals that you, as an owner or a potential owner (or as a broker representing an owner or potential owner), may need:

1. Market Value
2. Insurance Value
3. Loan Value
4. Tax Assessment Value
5. Rental Value
6. Value for certain Internal Revenue Service Purposes
7. Settlements
8. Salvage Value
9. Other

### 2. Highest and Best Use

*The primary purpose of a site analysis by an appraiser is to determine highest and best use. Land is always appraised separately as if vacant and available for highest and best use.*

Before we can properly appraise a property, we must determine its highest and best use. *HIGHEST AND BEST USE is the use that will produce the maximum amount of profit or net return.* For example, should we build a house or an apartment on an available piece of land? From the standpoint of economics, it would be best to build that which brings the highest net return.

*When the current use is expected to soon change to the property's highest and best use, the current use is called the "interim use."*

## B. GATHERING DATA (2nd Step in the Appraisal Process)

There are logical reasons why one home is worth more than another that appears comparable and why the choice of a neighborhood is as important, or even more important, than the house itself. There are also differences in location within a neighborhood that must be taken into account. Differences in the actual building construction must also be considered. The background information needed for real estate appraisal is very broad, but there is a simple, sensible way to make a wise decision about buying a home or investment property. Start with the largest aspects and work toward the details. Look at:

# CHAPTER 10

## 1. GENERAL DATA

a. Region
b. City
c. Neighborhood

## 2. SPECIFIC DATA (Site Analysis)

a. Location
b. Lot
c. Improvements (House)

### 1. General Data (Region, City, Neighborhood)

The gathering of general data (regional, city or county, and neighborhood information) allows us to understand whether the area is prospering, holding its own, or declining and, if so, why.

#### a. Region (State is Divided Into Regions)

The condition of the nation's economy can be reflected in the California real estate market and can affect the ease with which financing is available. But real estate markets are essentially regional and local. If the regional or local economy is expanding, people are working and can afford to buy homes because lending institutions are eager to grant loans. In a recession, jobs are less secure, confidence is low, and financing may not be as easy to obtain. So, the economic mood of the nation as a whole can indirectly affect the economic mood in California, but it is the local and regional economy that directly affects the mood in a particular real estate market.

A regional economy is affected by upturns and also downtrends. Not only do large areas reflect the national picture, but they also respond to more localized forces, such as the rapid growth of large cities and industrial complexes and the downsizing of defense-related industries or even the weather in agricultural areas. California is divided into north and south regions and many subregions and cities.

California, like most large states, is a very geographically diverse state. Geographical considerations can easily affect an entire region. For example, if an area has snow for eight months of the year, the value of the property may be reduced when compared to regions that have year-round moderate or sunny climates.

#### b. City (or County)

A desirable city or county is a growing area where people can get good jobs and where people want to live. If the city is undesirable or even unsafe, people want to leave. Features to look for in cities, besides the availability of work and safety, are good public facilities, parks, good school systems, and active citizens who care and take part in the city's affairs.

#### c. Neighborhood

A residential **NEIGHBORHOOD** *is normally a limited area where the homes are physically similar and where the occupants have a certain degree of social and economic* *background in common.* It may cover a few square miles or it may be only one block square. Boundaries may be defined by physical, social, or economic differences. The important thing is that your neighborhood is the environment in which you live day-in and day-out. **The neighborhood in which you live is usually a more important factor than the house itself!** This is because the surroundings of a house influence the property value even more than the house itself does.

Neighborhoods influence homeowners' location decisions more than renters'. The reason is that many people rent apartments in neighborhoods in which they would never think of buying, because they plan to stay there for only a short time. Renters may rent in a less desirable area, but when they buy they will select a neighborhood they like.

*Owner-occupied homes lend economic stability to a neighborhood, as owners tend to take better care of property than renters. The most important factor influencing value is location, location, location.*

The selection or acceptance of a neighborhood should come before the actual decision of whether to buy a particular house or not. The four primary forces that affect value of a neighborhood are shown in **Figure 10-2**.

Neighborhoods are always changing, sometimes at a fast pace, but usually at a slow, steady pace. The four considerations discussed in Figure 10-2 can change a prestigious area to a shabby neighborhood or vice versa. Each consideration can change the outlook for any neighborhood.

*Social forces, economic influences, and political influences are all forces affecting value. Private deed restrictions may be (in an appraiser's opinion) a force affecting value.*

### 2. Specific Data (Property Itself)

There is plenty of land in the world, but the exact location of each parcel makes it unlike any other on earth. Its location is the major factor that determines its value.

#### a. Location

A *SITE is a particular parcel within a neighborhood.* Since each parcel is unique, the individual site that one selects for a home should be chosen with care. There are several site selection factors that affect the value of the home, but the personal needs and objectives of the buyer should be of the utmost concern.

*Site: the location of a plot of ground for a building.*

#### b. Lot (Types)

There are six major types of lots (see **Figure 10-3**):

1. Cul-de-sac (**Lot A**)
2. Corner (**Lot B**)
3. Key (**Lot C**)
4. T-Intersection (**Lot D**)
5. Interior (**Lot E**)
6. Flag (**Lot F**)

**Figure 10-2**

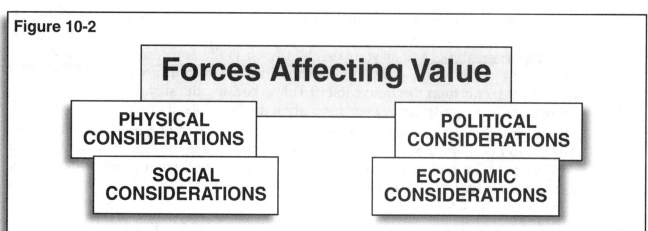

## PHYSICAL CONSIDERATIONS

A neighborhood that is close to a commercial area is generally highly desirable. Being close to downtown areas, employment centers, and major shopping areas only adds to this desirability, as long as an owner is not located right next to such a facility. If the street patterns are curved and there are wide boulevards, the neighborhood also looks more attractive.

Access to transportation is necessary. The availability of freeways, transit systems, and convenient parking is an important consideration in making comparisons between various areas. However, this factor is less important in high-value suburban areas where estate living is desirable.

### Balanced Land Use

The best efficiency and highest value come when there is a balance between different types of use. A city is a naturally attractive environment when it has a proper balance between residential, commercial, industrial, and recreational space.

Families are attracted to a neighborhood with good schools. Certain private or parochial schools may create a demand for homes in that area. Churches are also a definite benefit. Other institutions such as libraries, colleges, and universities may also enhance a community.

The first trip into a neighborhood may be impressive, or, on the other hand, it may be depressing. First impressions are important: the landscaping, architectural style, and the streets can create either impression. Well-maintained buildings create enhanced marketability.

Physical conditions such as lakes, beaches, rivers, or hilly areas may be either advantageous or disadvantageous depending on where they are. A feature such as a wooded hillside or lake front property would probably enhance a neighborhood, but a river that frequently floods the surrounding area is a disadvantage.

▼

Invasion of a residential area by commercial or industrial usage around it is usually a disadvantage, especially if the neighborhood is exposed to noise or odors. A bar located across from a home is usually a devaluing factor. Some areas may be hazardous because of landslides or simply from heavy truck and auto traffic.

## SOCIAL CONSIDERATIONS

Neighborhoods often consist of persons of similar income, education, cultural background and lifestyle. As such, the neighborhood may or may not appeal to certain individual buyers. Could a change in the social makeup of a neighborhood affect values? Whether or not such a change has any influence either positive or negative and the effect of any change is a field of inquiry that must be left to sociologists. Appraisers, lenders, and real estate agents are forbidden by both federal and state law to consider race, religion, sex, ethnicity, or lifestyle as factors of value. Only economic factors may be considered by real estate professionals.

*BLIGHT occurs as a result of a lack of property maintenance in a neighborhood.* This is generally due to an economic inability to provide maintenance on the part of the owners. The result is lowered property values.

*GENTRIFICATION is the rehabilitation of a blighted neighborhood.* It is generally a result of low property values attracting buyers who are economically able to upgrade and maintain the properties in the neighborhood.

## POLITICAL CONSIDERATIONS

Property tax rates vary from area to area. Wealthy, more stable economic areas usually have a slightly higher tax rate because the residents are willing and have the ability to pay for more public services. In areas where the taxes are very high, potential buyers are often scared off. Special assessments for lighting, sewers, and street improvements may temporarily turn some people away, but they generally add to the property's total value.

Some cities use **zoning** and **building codes** as devices to ensure the continued stability of a neighborhood. If the desirability of the neighborhood warrants such regulation, then the city will continue to be a growing one. In the end, most city leaders politically control changes in their cities by enacting zoning and building codes.

## ECONOMIC CONSIDERATIONS

Population growth is an indication of the economic health of a neighborhood. If more people want to live in an area, then it must be desirable: an economically alive neighborhood has well-maintained lawns and buildings, whereas in a deteriorating neighborhood the lack of maintenance is obvious and so is the lowered value of the homes.

The rents charged and income levels of the people indicate a community's prestige (or lack of it). **The larger the percentage of home ownership versus those renting, the more economically stable the area is.** If many rentals are vacant, you can surmise that renters are not interested in the area. New construction, on the other hand, indicates that the area is growing and its value is increasing.

### 1. Cul-De-Sac Lot

The *CUL-DE-SAC LOT is a lot facing the turnaround portion of a dead-end street.* Figure 10-3 shows that Lot A is a cul-de-sac. The main advantage of a cul-de-sac lot is privacy and lack of traffic one gets by living on a "not a through" street. Due to its pie-shaped design, it has the disadvantage of a small front yard, but this is offset by generally having a large backyard. The design makes it more secluded and limits through traffic from both autos and pedestrians. Limited parking and front yard space does not stop it from rivaling the corner lot as one of the most desirable types of lots. A cul-de-sac lot's desirability may vary due to view, size, area, and family characteristics. **Figure 10-3, Lot A, Cul-de-sac.**

**Figure 10-3**

### 2. Corner Lot

The *CORNER LOT is a lot that is located at the intersection of two streets.* A corner site frequently has a higher value than a lot fronting only on one street. The appraiser must be careful to look at the local market in determining the actual effects of a corner influence on the surrounding lots. *CORNER INFLUENCE is the theory that a variety of forces affect corner lots (and also lots located near a corner) to a greater degree than most other lots.* A corner lot is generally more desirable for commercial use and undesirable, because of noise and set backs, for residential use. Other people like it because there is more light, fresh air, and also more lot area for gardens and other types of landscaping.

The main disadvantage of a corner lot is the loss of privacy and higher cost, since both sides of the lot require off-site improvements, such as streets, curbs, gutters, and sidewalks. Also, zoning setbacks may reduce the buildable lot space. Usually commercial corner lots benefit because of easy access and added traffic exposure. **Figure 10-3, Lot B, Corner**.

### 3. Key Lot

A **KEY LOT** *is a lot that is bordered on the side by the back of other lots that front on another street.* Key lots are the least desirable lots because of the lack of privacy caused by the close proximity of several neighbors abutting the side of the property. **Figure 10-3, Lot C, Key**.

### 4. T-Intersection Lot

The **T-INTERSECTION LOT** *is an interior lot that is faced head-on by a street; it is the lot at the end of a dead-end street.* The streets form a "T" shape. It is an interior lot with one advantage and two disadvantages. The advantage is a clear view down the street, which gives a more spacious feeling. Intersection noise and annoying headlights at night are its disadvantages. **Figure 10-3, Lot D, T-Intersection**.

### 5. Interior Lot

An **INTERIOR LOT** *is a lot generally surrounded by other lots on three sides.* It is usually in the shape of a rectangle, but can be almost any shape. It is the most common type of lot and it is preferred by most people. Interior lots have larger backyards than corner lots, which make them much better for recreational purposes. Since the front yards are smaller than those found on corner lots, they require less yard maintenance and benefit from less intersection noise. Because of typical long block design, interior lots are by far the most numerous. The disadvantages are limited backyard access and three or more adjoining neighbors. **Figure 10-3, Lot E, Interior**.

### 6. Flag Lot

A **FLAG LOT** *is a rear lot, in back of other lots, with a long, narrow access driveway.* This type of lot takes on the shape a flag. The flag lot's shape allows for a maximum of privacy and can be easily gated. In hilly areas, flag lots have some of the better views, while others can be pushed up against a steep mountain side. The value of a flag lot verses other types of lots depends on the circumstances. The same can be said about all other types of lots: their value depends on the specifics of each lot and the local market conditions. But it is up to the salesperson to gain a working knowledge of lot shapes and the pluses and minuses attributed to each type of lot. **Figure 10-3, Lot F, Flag**.

### c. Physical Aspects of a Lot

The major physical aspects of the actual site are:

1. Size and shape
2. Slope, drainage, and soil (lot design layouts)

3. View, exposure to sun, and weather

4. Improvements (on-site and off-site)

### 1. Size and Shape of Lot

Lots or parcels can be subdivided into almost any shape imaginable, but most lots are rectangular and front onto a street. Any lot is valuable if it offers enough area to build a house that is compatible with the surroundings. In general, the more land or frontage on the street, the higher the value of the land. An example of a depth table will explain this concept. A *DEPTH TABLE is a percentage table that illustrates how the highest value is located in the front part of a lot.* **Figure 10-4** is an example of the "4-3-2-1" depth table. The "4-3-2-1 rule" is best used by appraisers to determine the value of commercial properties on which the lots vary in depth.

**Figure 10-4**

# The "4-3-2-1" Depth Table

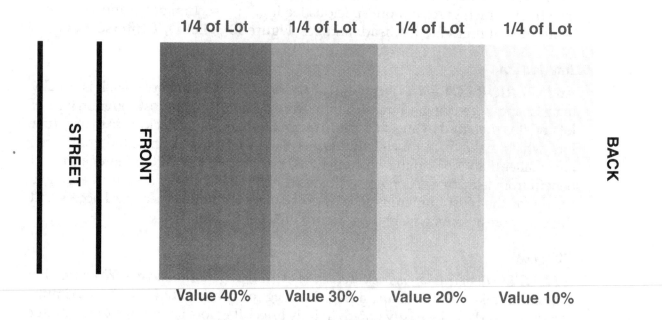

The percentage of value for each ¼ or 25% section of the lot varies: 40%, 30%, 20%, to 10% in value for each quarter back from the front.

In Figure 10-4, the highest value is in the front portion of the lot. For example, a small backyard will not affect the value of the property as much as a small front yard. This is especially true with commercial property such as shopping centers where there is plenty of parking in the back, but most people prefer to park in the front. Remember, though, that the percentage and values of a depth table vary from property to property.

Since the front portion of the lot has the most value, the more frontage there is, the better. *FRONT FOOTAGE is the width of the property in the front, along the street.* Generally speaking, we can say that a house with a large front yard is worth more than the same house with a large backyard. But people do have different preferences, such as large backyards for swimming pools, tennis courts, or other recreational activities.

*When two or more contiguous properties are joined to make one property, and become more valuable than the sum of the properties separately, it is called "plottage."*

### 2. Lot Design Layouts

There are several ways to lay out lots in a parcel of land being subdivided. Zoning regulations usually state the minimum amount of square feet a lot can have, but a developer can get better prices if he or she divides the land wisely. **Figure 10-5** shows the same parcel of land twice. **Plan 1** is a good design, giving a variety of desirable lots. **Plan 2** is a poor design, giving too little variation, too little front area and too much depth.

The layout of lots in a large subdivision is illustrated in **Figure 10-6**. Often a subdivision tract with fewer, well-planned lots will bring a higher total sales price than a poorly designed tract with more lots. The best tract layout is the one that considers all the costs involved and the marketability of all the lots. This kind of planning is not easy and requires the services of a specialist.

### 3. Slope, Drainage, and Soil

The slope of a lot will lower its value if it will be costly to improve. A lot that is higher or lower in relation to the street level may be costly to improve because of possible slope and drainage problems. Erosion may also be a part of slope or drainage problems. These problems, however, can be easily offset by an excellent view or location.

The soil composition of a lot may or may not be of any great concern. There are certain types of soil, however, that may create a problem depending on your lifestyle or possible construction needs. In some regions there are certain peat moss areas that must be corrected before a foundation can be poured. In other areas the soil content can destroy a pipeline within 10 years. If you like gardens and plant life, it is wise to see how the plants are growing in the surrounding lots. Some hillside tracts are built on bedrock covered by a thin layer of topsoil; to dig a swimming pool might even require blasting with dynamite, which is very costly.

### 4. View, Exposure to Sun, and Weather (Orientation)

*The south and west sides of streets are preferred by merchants: pedestrians seek the shady side and displayed merchandise is not damaged by the sun. The northeast corner is the least desirable.*

Most people appreciate a good view from their homes; it is pleasant to sit back and enjoy the beautiful surroundings. In a new tract of homes, the lots with the best views usually sell first and apartments with views rent for more. Places like Nob Hill (in San Francisco), Lake Tahoe, and La Jolla are examples of areas that are expensive because of their beautiful views.

**Figure 10-5**

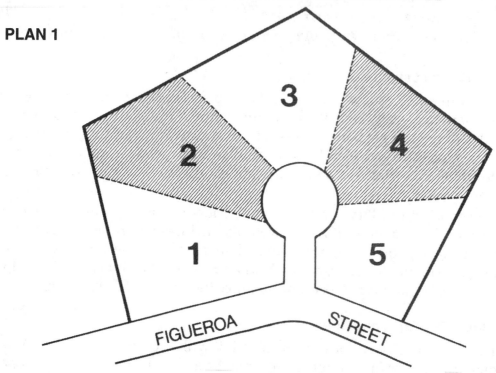

GOOD LAYOUT – LOTS ARE WELL DESIGNED

PLAN 1

FIGUEROA STREET

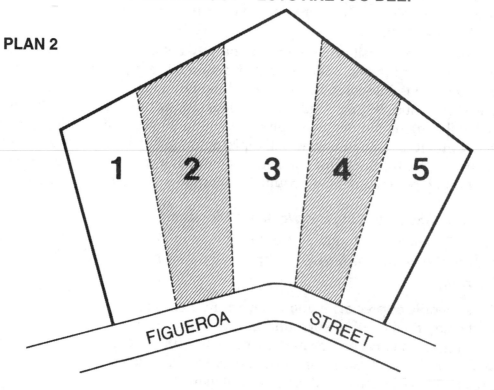

POOR LAYOUT – LOTS ARE TOO DEEP

PLAN 2

FIGUEROA STREET

**Figure 10-6**

### TENTATIVE SUBDIVISION MAP

TENTATIVE TRACT 26158

***ORIENTATION*** *is planning the most advantageous place on a parcel of land for an improvement to be located.* The exposure of a house to the sun and weather elements may influence a person's decision to buy a house. If the wind usually blows from the northwest, it is best for the house to face the northwest. In this case the house can be a shield for backyard entertaining. The exposure to the sun is a different matter. Most people prefer the sun to shine on their backyard, so the backyard should face the south or the west. In this way the backyard receives the best exposure throughout the day. In windy areas on the coast, sheltered patios, away from cold sea breezes, are desirable.

*A map showing the house and its location relating to other plants, buildings, and streets is an example of "orientation."*

***AMENITIES*** *are those improvements or views that increase the desirability or enjoyment rather than the necessities of the residents.* For example, a view of the ocean, mountains, or city lights at night increase the value of a home. Amenity improvements would include jacuzzis, swimming pools, and tennis courts. *Amenity properties are usually single-family residences.*

# III. Improvements

Real estate is logically divided into land (site) and improvements. *IMPROVEMENTS are any buildings, walkways, pools, and other structures. CAPITAL IMPROVEMENTS are permanent improvements made to increase the useful life of the property or increase the property's value. They stay with the property.* These include off-site improvements (streets and utilities) and on-site improvements (buildings). *OFF-SITE IMPROVEMENTS are the improvements made to areas adjoining the parcel that add to the parcel's usefulness and sometimes its value.* Examples of off-site improvements are: streets, street lights, sewers, sidewalks, curbs, and gutters. These items generally add value to urban property but may be of little value in rural areas. Off-site improvements are usually paid for by the homeowners through the levying of special assessments. On the other hand, *ON-SITE IMPROVEMENTS are structures erected permanently for use on a site, such as buildings and fences.*

*The three steps or phases in construction of a home are land acquisition, development, and construction.*

## A. HOUSE STRUCTURE ILLUSTRATED

This section identifies different parts of a house. Figure **10-7** shows roof types. **Figure 10-8** is a diagram of a house that illustrates the 20 most used construction terms. Each part is labeled and defined so that it can be identified. **Figure 10-9** lists construction and other terms.

## B. HOME WARRANTY PLANS

A *WARRANTY PLAN is an insurance plan that provides financial protection against defects in any major home construction.* There are a growing number of such warranty plans in California. These warranty plans insure the new owner of an existing home against such things as malfunction of built-in appliances and defects in major systems such as structure, roof, heating, plumbing, and electrical wiring. For this protection, the previous owner or the buyer pays a fee that varies according to the type of coverage received. Some companies inspect the property (thereby giving notice of any existing defects). The CAR® purchase agreement informs buyers and sellers that there are warranty plans available. But this item, along with who pays for the warranty plan, is negotiable. **Note: All new homes automatically carry a one-year warranty, from the contractor, against labor or material defects**.

# IV. Basic Appraisal Principles

There are several "principles of appraisal." These principles are valid economic concepts that are applied to the appraisal of real estate. A few of the basic principles are explained so that you can understand the logic and reasons why a particular home is worth more than another. **Figure 10-10** shows you seven of the basic appraisal principles.

**Figure 10-7**

# ROOF TYPES

Before purchasing a house, a potential buyer should carefully evaluate the structure, checking to see that its style of architecture is compatible with that of the surrounding neighborhood. This should also be an element of consideration when building a new house or remodeling.

Examining the type of roof, the way it is framed and finished, is one of the simplest ways to assess the architectural compatibility of a given house.

Pictured below are several of the most common roof types. One is likely to see examples of flat, gable, hip, gambrel, mansard, and pyramid roofs throughout California.

*A roof sloping on all four sides is called a "hip roof."*

FLAT  
GABLE (Two Sides)  
HIP (Four Sides)  
GAMBREL (Barn)  
MANSARD  
PYRAMID

**Figure 10-8**

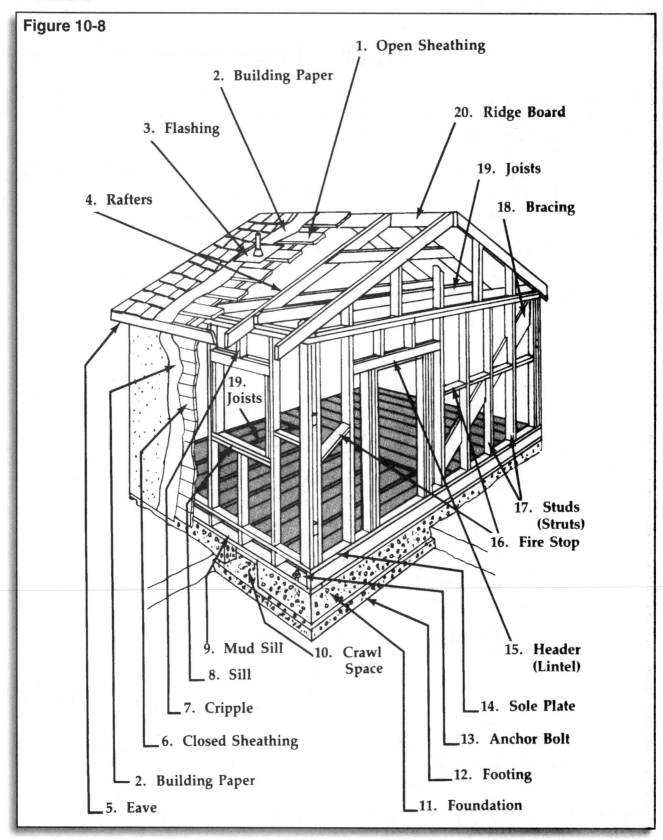

1. Open Sheathing

2. Building Paper

3. Flashing

20. Ridge Board

19. Joists

4. Rafters

18. Bracing

19. Joists

17. Studs (Struts)

16. Fire Stop

9. Mud Sill

10. Crawl Space

8. Sill

15. Header (Lintel)

7. Cripple

14. Sole Plate

6. Closed Sheathing

13. Anchor Bolt

2. Building Paper

12. Footing

5. Eave

11. Foundation

# EXPLANATION OF DIAGRAM DETAILS

1. Open Sheathing

Boards nailed to rafters as foundation for the roof covering. Open sheathing is used with wood shingles.

2. Building Paper

Heavy waterproof paper used between sheathing and roof covering or siding.

3. Flashing

Sheet metal used to protect a roof from seepage.

4. Rafters

Sloping members of a roof used to support the roof boards and shingles (Maximum 24" apart).

5. Eave

Protruding underpart of roof overhanging exterior walls.

6. Closed Sheathing

Boards nailed to studding as foundation for exterior siding. "Closed" means butted together.

7. Cripple

Stud above or below a window opening or above a doorway.

8. Sill

Bottom portion lining doorway or window.

9. Mud Sill

Treated lumber (or redwood) bolted to the foundation.

10. Crawl Space

Unexcavated area under the house (**Minimum 18´**).

11. Foundation

Concrete base of house.

12. Footing

The spreading element that supports a pier, column, wall, or foundation. (**Can be located in the interior of a house**.)

13. Anchor Bolt

Large bolt used for fastening mud sill to foundation. Bolt is anchored into concrete foundation.

14. Sole Plate

Support on which the studs rest.

15. Header (Lintel)

The beam over a doorway or window.

16. Fire Stop

Blocking used to restrict flames from spreading to attic. May be placed horizontally or diagonally.

17. Studs (Struts)

Vertical 2˝ x 4˝ framework in the walls **spaced 16˝ on center**.

18. Bracing

Board running diagonally across the wall framing to prevent sway.

19. Joists

Structural parts supporting floor or ceiling loads. A beam which supports them would be called a girder.

20. Ridge Board

Highest point of construction in a frame building.

**Figure 10-9**

# Construction and Other Terms

**Backfill** – The replacement of excavated earth against a structure (wall). If a property is backfilled, it will fill in around piers, columns, and footings.

*A contractor/builder who buys a large quantity of backfill is probably using it to fill in space around the foundation, retaining wall, or other excavations.*

**Bearing Wall** – A strong wall supporting any vertical load in addition to its own weight, usually a roof or floor above.

**Boardfoot** – 1 board foot = 6 inches x 12 inches x 2 inches. Any 144 cu. ins. of lumber.

**BTU (British Thermal Unit)** – A unit of measurement used to calculate heat - the quantity of heat required to raise one pound of water one degree Fahrenheit.

**Capital Assets** – Expenditures of a permanent nature that increase property values. Examples: buildings and street improvements.

**Cash Flow** – In investment property, the actual cash the investor will receive after deduction of operating expenses and debt servicing (loan payment) from his or her gross income.

**Conduit** – A flexible metal pipe used to protect the electrical wiring inside.

**Dry Wall** – Also known as wallboard or plasterboard; comes in dry sheets (usually 4´ x 8´) of varying thickness: 1/2˝ is standard for most interior walls.

**EER (Energy Efficiency Ratio)** – A measure of energy efficiency; when an air conditioning unit has a higher energy efficiency ratio, the unit is more efficient.

**Elevation Sheet** – A rendering which shows the front and side views of a building; it shows the exterior views.

**Foundation Plan** –  **A plan that refers to piers, columns, footings, and subfloor.**

**H2O Pressure** – Testing water pressure by turning on all faucets and flushing all toilets.

**HVAC – Heating, ventilation, and air conditioning systems in commercial buildings.**

**Hoskold Tables** – Concept of a "sinking fund" as a compound interest-bearing account, into which the portion of the investment returned each year is reinvested immediately.

# Construction and Other Terms

**Inwood Tables** – Concept of using present value of income in a perpetuity table to help appraisers.

**Joists – Parallel wooden members used to support floor and ceiling loads.**

**Kiosk** – An information booth.

**Local Building Inspector** – Person who enforces construction standards.

**Over-Improvement** – An expenditure to a property that doesn't improve its value.

**Percolation Test** – A test to determine how well water is absorbed by the soil. (Used when installing a sewage system.)

**Plot Plan** – The placement of improvements (buildings) on a lot.

**Potable Water** – Drinkable water.

**Property Residual, Building Residual, and Land Residual** – All are methods of working backwards to find the unknown variable when appraising property.

**R-Value** – A measure used to calculate the heat resistance of insulation (the higher the better). Insulation is considered adequate if the temperature on the inside of an exterior wall is the same as the temperature on an interior wall.

**Rehabilitation** – The restoration of a property to a satisfactory condition without changing the interior or exterior design.

**Soil Pipe** – A pipe used to carry waste and sewage from a property.

**Toxic Waste Report** – A report evaluating how harmful the dangerous material is on a property.

**Turnkey Project/Property** – A single-family home ready to move into.

**Unearned Increment** – An increase in value of real estate due to no effort on the part of the owner; often caused by population increase.

**Wainscoting** – The wood lining of the lower portion of an interior wall with the upper portion wallpapered or covered with another material different from the lower portion.

**Figure 10-10**

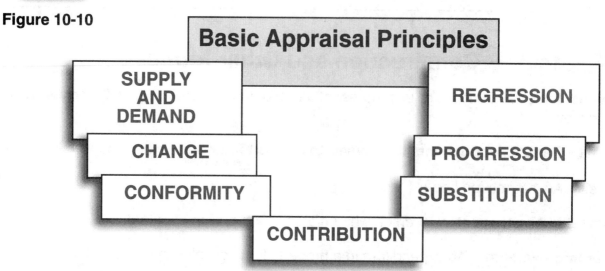

## A. PRINCIPLE OF SUPPLY AND DEMAND

The principle of supply and demand shows why "location" is important. The **PRINCIPLE OF SUPPLY AND DEMAND** *states that as the supply of land decreases, the value of land increases, because more people are competing for the desirable land.* Living next to the Pacific Ocean is expensive because the land is scarce. Even small lots bring very high selling prices in these areas. To beach lovers, these are the most desirable neighborhoods because there are only so many ocean view lots. In areas where there are many lots available, like the desert, the supply is large and the price of a lot can be very low. Downtown high-rise commercial locations in cities like San Francisco, Los Angeles, and San Diego are scarce and therefore expensive.

## B. PRINCIPLE OF CHANGE

The **PRINCIPLE OF CHANGE** *is that real property is constantly changing.* Value is influenced by changes in such things as: population size, shopping centers, schools and colleges, freeways, economic and social trends. It is hard to see change on a day-to-day basis, but if you go back to the area where you grew up, the change is apparent.

The real property life cycle goes through three stages: development, maturity, and decline, which are illustrated in **Figure 10-11**.

### 1. Development (Integration)

This is the stage when the land is subdivided into lots, the streets are paved, and street lights are installed. Soon, homes are built and the community starts. As new people move in, landscaping and fences improve the homes.

*The three steps in construction of a home are land acquistion, development, and construction.*

### 2. Maturity (Equilibrium)

The maturity stage starts when the homes become older and the children grow up and move away. Most of the residents are long-time homeowners and the community has a solid, well-established look.

**Figure 10-11**

**REAL PROPERTY LIFE CYCLE (AGE CYCLE)**

MATURITY
(Values Stable)

DEVELOPMENT
(Values Increase)

DECLINE
(Values Decrease)

### 3. Decline (Disintegration)

In this stage, the buildings show some wear and tear and the oldest buildings are starting to deteriorate. As the useful life of the property declines, lower social or economic groups move into the area. Large homes may be converted into multiple family use.

The life cycle of real property may take a few years, such as that of a mining town going "bust," or may span a century, such as that of a community that constantly revitalizes itself.

## C. PRINCIPLE OF CONFORMITY

The *PRINCIPLE OF CONFORMITY states that the maximum value is obtained when a reasonable degree of building similarity is maintained in the neighborhood.* So, if all the homes in an area are similar (not identical), the maximum value of real property is created. The word "similar" is the key. If all the tract homes are identical, as if they were all made with the same cookie cutter, the maximum value is not present.

*When a residential neighborhood is composed mostly of owner-occupied residential properties, it tends to stabilize values.*

The principle of conformity is one of the primary reasons for zoning regulations (discussed in Chapter 12). They protect the neighborhood from other nonconforming uses and from infiltration of incompatible structures. An attractive neighborhood would quickly decline in value if zoning did not help protect its conformity.

## D. PRINCIPLE OF CONTRIBUTION

The *PRINCIPLE OF CONTRIBUTION states that the value of a particular component is measured in terms of its contribution to the value of the whole property.* Consequently, cost does not necessarily equal value. It either adds more or less to the value of real property.

**Example:** If an apartment building produces a 10% return to investors, a $50,000 investment in a swimming pool, without an equal ($50,000 x 10%) $5,000 or higher increase in rents, would not be a good idea.

Thus, in some cases, a property's market value may not increase even if it has had additions, alterations, or has been rehabilitated. If the swimming pool were added, the property would be considered "over-built." The principle of contribution is also referred to as increasing and (decreasing) "diminishing returns" in economic textbooks.

## E. PRINCIPLE OF SUBSTITUTION

Under the *PRINCIPLE OF SUBSTITUTION, a buyer will not pay more for a particular property if it costs less to buy a similar property of equal utility and desirability.* People prefer the less expensive price if all other things are considered equal. When appraisers use the principle of substitution, they compare properties to adjust for differences. The maximum value of a property tends to be set by the cost of acquiring an equally desirable substitute property.

## F. PRINCIPLE OF REGRESSION (Value Goes Down)

*When a house of greater value is adversely affected by houses of comparably lesser value, it is called the PRINCIPLE OF REGRESSION.* For example, if a house that would easily be worth $790,000 in a neighborhood of similar homes was to be built in a neighborhood of $210,000 homes, it would not sell for $790,000. Anyone in the market for a $790,000 house would not want to live in a tract where the average price of a house was $210,000. Because of its superior quality or size, the house would undoubtedly sell for more than the average house in the tract, but it would not approach $790,000.

The same principle applies to the over-improved home. When owners invest very large sums in major additions, lavish landscaping, and swimming pools, and the other residents do not improve their homes, the house is no longer similar to the others. The owners of the over-built house will not receive the full value for the cost of improvements they have made.

*When the best property in the neighborhood is adversely affected by the presence of a substandard property, it is called regression.*

## G. PRINCIPLE OF PROGRESSION (Value Goes Up)

In the *PRINCIPLE OF PROGRESSION, the value of a lesser residence is increased in value by its location in a neighborhood of better homes.* This is the opposite of the principle of regression. A smaller, unattractive, and poorly maintained home in an exclusive area will sell for much more than if it were located in a comparable neighborhood. People who wish to live in an exclusive area would think of the smaller home as a bargain.

## V. CHAPTER SUMMARY

An **appraisal** is an opinion of value based on judgment and professional experience for a **specific property as of a certain date**. Appraisers, who must be licensed in California, want "open market results," not prudent values or prices. The **value** of a property is determined by the elements of **demand, utility, scarcity,** and **transferability**. Cost and/or expectation are never one of these elements.

The **appraisal process** consists of four steps: 1) **defining the problem**, 2) **gathering the data**, 3) **performing the three appraisal methods**, and 4) **determining the final opinion of value**. Whether the reason for the appraisal is transfer of ownership, obtaining a loan, condemnation, or insurance, the first step is to do a **site analysis** to determine **highest and best use**.

The second step involves gathering data, including **general data** (region, city, and neighborhood) and **specific data** (location, lot, and improvements). The **neighborhood** is the most important general data. The **four forces** affecting value are: **physical, social, economic,** and **political considerations**. The most important economic characteristic is area preference (**location**).

**Front footage** is a pricing tool often used to sell commercial property and a **4-3-2-1 depth table** is used when the lots vary in depth. **Plottage** (assemblage) refers to separately owned, contiguous lots brought under single ownership resulting in increased value. The **shady south and west sides of streets** are preferred by merchants with the northeast corner being the least desirable.

There are several principles of appraisal, including **supply and demand**, and the **principle of change**, which is evident in the **real estate life cycle of development, maturity,** and **decline**. The **principle of conformity** states that the maximum value is obtained when building similarity is maintained in the neighborhood, and is one of the major reasons for **zoning regulations**.

The **principle of contribution** (or diminishing returns) states that the value of a particular component is measured in terms of its contribution to the value of the whole property. The **principle of substitution** states that a buyer will not pay more for a particular property if it costs less to buy a similar property of equal utility and desirability.

The **principle of regression** states that between properties in the same neighborhood, the value of the best property will be negatively affected by the value of the other properties. The opposite of regression is the **principle of progression**, where a lesser residence increases in value by its location in a neighborhood of better homes.

## VI. TERMINOLOGY

**A.** Appraisal
**B.** Appraisal Process
**C.** Change
**D.** Conformity
**E.** Corner Lot
**F.** Cul-de-Sac
**G.** Depth Table
**H.** Flag Lot

**I.** Frontage
**J.** Highest and Best Use
**K.** Interior Lot
**L.** Key Lot
**M.** Market Price
**N.** Market Value
**O.** Neighborhood
**P.** Off-Site Improvements

**Q.** Progression Principle
**R.** Regression Principle
**S.** Site
**T.** Supply and Demand
**U.** T-Intersection Lot
**V.** Warranty Plan

1. ____ The appraisal principle that maintains the maximum value of a property is realized when a reasonable degree of similarity is present in the area where the property is located.

2. ____ The least desirable type of lot because the back ends of other lots face one of its sides.

3. ____ A general term describing people living or working together in an area of similar properties with similar social, economic, and political backgrounds.

4. ____ The highest price a willing buyer would pay and a willing seller accept, both being fully informed, and the property exposed for a reasonable period of time. This value may be different from the price a property can actually be sold for at a given time.

5. ____ Not a corner lot, but an inside lot; the most common type of lot.

6. ____ Development of large parcels into smaller lots suitable for construction. This includes sidewalks, curbs, streets, sewers, streetlights, etc.

7. ____ A lot at the U-shaped end of a street. Even though they are narrower in the front and wider in the back, these lots are popular because the street itself makes the area exclusive.

8. ____ An opinion of real property value based upon a factual analysis by a qualified (licensed) person with education and experience.

9. ____ The use of land that will bring the greatest economic return over a given time.

10. ____ The price a property sells for, which may be higher or lower than its actual market value.

11. ____ The orderly process of determining the fair market value of real property by: 1) defining the problem, 2) gathering the data, 3) applying the three methods of appraisal (cost approach, market comparison approach, income approach), and 4) correlating the information for a final estimate of value.

12. ____ A general term for a lot or plot of land.

13. ____ A lot with both the front and side facing different streets. Such a residential lot is generally more desirable because of its increased exposure to light and fresh air. A commercial lot benefits from better street access and exposure to traffic patterns.

14. ____ An interior lot facing down a street into traffic. Such a lot benefits from the view down the open street but suffers from additional traffic noise and on-coming headlights at night.

15. ____ A lot with a long, narrow entrance, forming the shape of a flag. While it has limited frontage, such a lot can be very desirable if the odd shape is accompanied by a spectacular view in the back.

16. ____ A chart illustrating the principle that the greatest value exists in the front portion of the lot, and the value of the land decreases the further back from the street you go.

17. ____ The linear measure of the front portion of a parcel facing a major street, walkway, lake, or ocean.

18. ____ An insurance plan covering the major systems of a home such as electrical, heating, plumbing, and major appliances.

19. ____ A principle of real estate appraisal suggesting that the value of property increases when there is more demand and a short supply in an area. Conversely, the value decreases when there is an abundant supply and less demand.

20.____The concept that although changes may be imperceptible, neighborhoods are constantly changing. Population shifts and economic changes, along with many other variables, will constantly work to alter the value of property.

21.____The real estate principle that a smaller, low-quality home will gain value if larger, nicer homes are being built in the neighborhood.

22.____The real estate principle that a larger, nicer home will not enjoy its full value if it is located in a neighborhood of smaller, low-quality homes.

## VII. CHAPTER QUIZ

1. In comparing real property price to value, a change in "creative financing" terms will affect:

    a. value and price.
    b. value.
    c. price.
    d. neither price nor value.

2. The primary purpose of a site analysis by an appraiser is to determine the:

    a. applicable zoning laws.
    b. highest and best use.
    c. soil conditions.
    d. available amenities.

3. When the highest and best use of a property is expected to change, the current use is called:

    a. the interim use.
    b. the temporary use.
    c. the transitional use.
    d. the possible use.

4. When two properties are joined to make one property, and becomes more valuable than the sum of the properties separately, it is called:

    a. leverage.
    b. inflation.
    c. plottage.
    d. subdividing.

5. A map shows the house and its location relating to other plants, buildings, and streets. This is an example of:

    a. plottage.
    b. orientation.
    c. elevation.
    d. topography.

# CHAPTER 10

6. Which of the following is one board foot?

    a. Six inches x twelve inches x one foot
    b. Six inches x twelve inches x two inches
    c. Six inches x six inches x two inches
    d. Six inches x twelve inches x one inch

7. When an air conditioning unit has a higher energy efficiency ratio (EER), the:

    a. unit needs more watts of electricity.
    b. unit is more efficient.
    c. unit is less efficient.
    d. BTUs are larger.

8. "HVAC" refers to:

    a. heating, ventilation, and air conditioning systems in commercial buildings.
    b. Home Value After Correlation.
    c. Highest Value Appraising Consideration.
    d. House Vitality Area Consultants.

9. When a residential neighborhood is composed mostly of owner-occupied residential properties it tends to:

    a. attract commercial shopping centers to the neighborhood.
    b. stabilize values.
    c. deteriorate faster than areas with many rental properties.
    d. lower property values.

10. When a house of greater value is adversely affected by houses of comparably lesser value, it is called:

    a. anticipation.
    b. regression.
    c. contribution.
    d. balance.

**ANSWERS:** 1. c; 2. b; 3. a; 4. c; 5. b; 6. b; 7. b; 8. a; 9. b; 10. b

# CHAPTER 11
## Appraisal Methods

Real estate salespeople need to know enough about appraisal techniques and practices so that they can determine, in advance, the approximate selling price of a property. Salespeople have the advantage of determining the "probable" sales price of a property quickly because they see what similar properties in their area sell for each day. They can be on top of the market because of their multiple listing service and close contact with other knowledgeable agents. They are constantly being updated as to the current listing and selling prices.

By completing a **Comparative Market Analysis (CMA)** form and presenting it to a seller, the seller can see at a glance the selling prices of other houses or condos in his/her neighborhood. This enables the sellers to "price their listings" close to a realistic selling price.

An agent can download comparable sales information ("comps") in a variety of forms by accessing an MLS website.

**www.appraisalfoundation.org**
Appraisal Foundation
**www.asfmra.org/**
American Society of Farm Managers and Rural Appraisers (ASFMRA)

The *HOME VALUATION CODE OF CONDUCT (HVCC) is a document that was created jointly by members of Freddie Mac, the Federal Housing Finance Agency (FHFA), and the New York State Attorney General. The document states that, effective May 1, 2009, Freddie Mac will no longer purchase mortgages from Sellers that do not adopt the HVCC with respect to single-family mortgages that are delivered to Freddie Mac.*

A state licensed (expert) appraiser will use all three of the valuation approaches to determine the value of a property, but will emphasize only one to establish the final value. These approaches are:

### I. COMPARISON APPROACH (MARKET DATA METHOD)
### II. COST (REPLACEMENT) APPROACH
### III. CAPITALIZATION (INCOME) APPROACH

The appraisal is also an opinion of a value "range." Let us assume that a range of $450,000 to $500,000 is established from the three appraisal approaches mentioned above. By correlating the economic information from the three approaches, an experienced appraiser can estimate a more precise value. The results of the three approaches can be weighed and it can then be

## CHAPTER OUTLINE

determined which method has provided the best information about the property. In this case, let's say that the appraiser felt he or she should emphasize the market comparison approach that was $490,000. The appraiser would state that, in his or her opinion, the property was worth $490,000; but the value "ranged" from $450,000 to $500,000.

# I. Comparison Approach (Market Data Method)

Of the three approaches previously mentioned, the market comparison method is the one most frequently used. It is easy for an alert student to master this technique within a short time, and it is the most logical way to appraise a house.

The market data method uses the "principle of substitution" to compare similar properties. **A person will not pay more for a property if he/she can buy something similar for less.**

The *MARKET DATA METHOD is a method of appraising real property by comparing the current selling prices of recently sold similar properties and adjusting those prices for any differences.* The comparative (market data method) approach uses the principle of substitution; a person will not pay more for a property if he or she can buy something similar for less.

Simply adjust the value of the comparable sales price. If a house is comparable except that it has a pool, sells for $640,000 and the value of the $40,000 pool is subtracted, the house we are appraising is valued at $600,000.

## A. HOW TO ADJUST FOR A COMPARABLE SALE (Comps)

The market data method is basically common sense. If your neighbor has a similar house to yours that he just sold for $400,000, then yours is worth about $400,000. The only problem is that adjustments must be made for any differences between the houses. For example, if a similar $400,000 house had a fireplace worth $8,000 and yours did not, then your house would be worth $392,000 ($400,000 - $8,000). Adjustments should be made to the selling price of the comparable house for any differences between the properties. **The usual adjustments are made for differences in location, age, lot size, building size, condition of the property, and any time difference between the sales.**

*Subtract or add from/to the selling price of the comparable property to adjust for differences.*

If the comparable property has an item not present in the subject property, the appraiser subtracts the value of the item from the comparable property's selling price. Likewise, if the subject property has an item not present in the comparable property, the appraiser adds the value of the item to the comparable property's selling price. After all these adjustments are made to the comparable selling price, the resulting figure gives the appraiser the subject property's value.

By comparing recent selling prices of properties in the same area, it is easy to see the trends in selling prices and why certain properties sell for more than others. The more comparable sales you gather, the more reliable the results. Real estate salespeople often refer to comparable sales as "comps."

*An appraiser using the market data approach would be most interested in the date that the price was agreed upon.*

Unsold properties are important when using the market data method. If a property has been listed "for sale" for a long time, it is usually overpriced. Such comparable "unsold properties" suggest an upper limit of value. Unsold listings can therefore help establish the highest comparable price. An experienced appraiser can easily estimate the amount of an adjustment. The adjustment is an estimate or opinion determined solely by the appraiser, and reflects his or her broad experience and education.

Comparable sales information can be obtained from many different sources. Brokers and salespeople are familiar with property sales prices in their area, so naturally they are a good source for appraisal data. In addition, most brokers are members of the local multiple listing service and have access to past sales information. Other people in the real estate field, such as loan officers, title insurance agents, and escrow officers can also supply comparable sales information.

It is essential that: 1) the information is from a reliable source; 2) there is an adequate number of comparable sales, and 3) the comparable sales are truly comparable.

*The market data method is the most common approach for houses and condominiums. It is also the best method for appraising lots and vacant land (unimproved property).*

**Figure 11-1** shows the first three pages of the Uniform Residential Appraisal Report (URAR) that is accepted by Fannie Mae and Freddie Mac.

## B. ADVANTAGES OF THE MARKET DATA METHOD

This method is excellent for appraising single family homes. Here are the reasons why:

1. The market data method is easy to learn, and with a little experience it is easy to apply.
2. Since there are usually many recent comparable sales, the required information is readily available.
3. This method is used mostly for houses or condos, which makes this method the most relevant to us as homeowners, salespeople, or investors.

The most difficult part of the market data method is to adjust similar properties for differences. The market data method is limited when market conditions are rapidly changing.

*Marketability and acceptability of a property are the primary concerns when appraising a residential property. Marketability is the ultimate test of functional utility.*

## C. DISADVANTAGES OF THE MARKET DATA METHOD

The disadvantages of using the market data method are concentrated into several areas which are listed below:

1. This method requires many recent comparable sales of similar properties.
2. **This method is least reliable when there are rapid economic changes**. If market prices are increasing rapidly, the comparables, which are based on past sales prices, lag behind. If prices are decreasing rapidly, the comparables, which are based on past sales prices, still remain high.
3. The market data method is less valid with certain income properties because a separate analysis of the income is required.

# Figure 11-1

## Uniform Residential Appraisal Report      File #

The purpose of this summary appraisal report is to provide the lender/client with an accurate, and adequately supported, opinion of the market value of the subject property.

**SUBJECT**

| | | |
|---|---|---|
| Property Address | City | State   Zip Code |
| Borrower | Owner of Public Record | County |
| Legal Description | | |
| Assessor's Parcel # | Tax Year | R.E. Taxes $ |
| Neighborhood Name | Map Reference | Census Tract |

Occupant ☐ Owner ☐ Tenant ☐ Vacant    Special Assessments $         ☐ PUD   HOA $        ☐ per year ☐ per month

Property Rights Appraised ☐ Fee Simple ☐ Leasehold ☐ Other (describe)

Assignment Type ☐ Purchase Transaction ☐ Refinance Transaction ☐ Other (describe)

Lender/Client                          Address

Is the subject property currently offered for sale or has it been offered for sale in the twelve months prior to the effective date of this appraisal? ☐ Yes ☐ No

Report data source(s) used, offering price(s), and date(s).

**CONTRACT**

I ☐ did ☐ did not analyze the contract for sale for the subject purchase transaction. Explain the results of the analysis of the contract for sale or why the analysis was not performed.

Contract Price $         Date of Contract         Is the property seller the owner of public record? ☐ Yes ☐ No  Data Source(s)

Is there any financial assistance (loan charges, sale concessions, gift or downpayment assistance, etc.) to be paid by any party on behalf of the borrower? ☐ Yes ☐ No

If Yes, report the total dollar amount and describe the items to be paid.

**NEIGHBORHOOD**

Note: Race and the racial composition of the neighborhood are not appraisal factors.

| Neighborhood Characteristics | One-Unit Housing Trends | One-Unit Housing | | Present Land Use % | |
|---|---|---|---|---|---|
| Location ☐ Urban ☐ Suburban ☐ Rural | Property Values ☐ Increasing ☐ Stable ☐ Declining | PRICE | AGE | One-Unit | % |
| Built-Up ☐ Over 75% ☐ 25–75% ☐ Under 25% | Demand/Supply ☐ Shortage ☐ In Balance ☐ Over Supply | $ (000) | (yrs) | 2-4 Unit | % |
| Growth ☐ Rapid ☐ Stable ☐ Slow | Marketing Time ☐ Under 3 mths ☐ 3–6 mths ☐ Over 6 mths | Low | | Multi-Family | % |
| Neighborhood Boundaries | | High | | Commercial | % |
| | | Pred. | | Other | % |

Neighborhood Description

Market Conditions (including support for the above conclusions)

**SITE**

| Dimensions | Area | Shape | View |
|---|---|---|---|

Specific Zoning Classification         Zoning Description

Zoning Compliance ☐ Legal ☐ Legal Nonconforming (Grandfathered Use) ☐ No Zoning ☐ Illegal (describe)

Is the highest and best use of the subject property as improved (or as proposed per plans and specifications) the present use? ☐ Yes ☐ No  If No, describe

| Utilities | Public | Other (describe) | | Public | Other (describe) | Off-site Improvements—Type | Public | Private |
|---|---|---|---|---|---|---|---|---|
| Electricity | ☐ | ☐ | Water | ☐ | ☐ | Street | ☐ | ☐ |
| Gas | ☐ | ☐ | Sanitary Sewer | ☐ | ☐ | Alley | ☐ | ☐ |

FEMA Special Flood Hazard Area ☐ Yes ☐ No  FEMA Flood Zone         FEMA Map #         FEMA Map Date

Are the utilities and off-site improvements typical for the market area? ☐ Yes ☐ No  If No, describe

Are there any adverse site conditions or external factors (easements, encroachments, environmental conditions, land uses, etc.)? ☐ Yes ☐ No  If Yes, describe

**IMPROVEMENTS**

| General Description | Foundation | Exterior Description   materials/condition | Interior   materials/condition |
|---|---|---|---|
| Units ☐ One ☐ One with Accessory Unit | ☐ Concrete Slab ☐ Crawl Space | Foundation Walls | Floors |
| # of Stories | ☐ Full Basement ☐ Partial Basement | Exterior Walls | Walls |
| Type ☐ Det. ☐ Att. ☐ S-Det./End Unit | Basement Area          sq. ft. | Roof Surface | Trim/Finish |
| ☐ Existing ☐ Proposed ☐ Under Const. | Basement Finish          % | Gutters & Downspouts | Bath Floor |
| Design (Style) | ☐ Outside Entry/Exit ☐ Sump Pump | Window Type | Bath Wainscot |
| Year Built | Evidence of ☐ Infestation | Storm Sash/Insulated | Car Storage ☐ None |
| Effective Age (Yrs) | ☐ Dampness ☐ Settlement | Screens | ☐ Driveway   # of Cars |
| Attic ☐ None | Heating ☐ FWA ☐ HWBB ☐ Radiant | Amenities ☐ Woodstove(s) # | Driveway Surface |
| ☐ Drop Stair ☐ Stairs | ☐ Other      Fuel | ☐ Fireplace(s) # ☐ Fence | ☐ Garage   # of Cars |
| ☐ Floor ☐ Scuttle | Cooling ☐ Central Air Conditioning | ☐ Patio/Deck ☐ Porch | ☐ Carport   # of Cars |
| ☐ Finished ☐ Heated | ☐ Individual ☐ Other | ☐ Pool ☐ Other | ☐ Att. ☐ Det. ☐ Built-in |

Appliances ☐ Refrigerator ☐ Range/Oven ☐ Dishwasher ☐ Disposal ☐ Microwave ☐ Washer/Dryer ☐ Other (describe)

Finished area **above** grade contains:          Rooms          Bedrooms          Bath(s)          Square Feet of Gross Living Area Above Grade

Additional features (special energy efficient items, etc.)

Describe the condition of the property (including needed repairs, deterioration, renovations, remodeling, etc.).

Are there any physical deficiencies or adverse conditions that affect the livability, soundness, or structural integrity of the property? ☐ Yes ☐ No  If Yes, describe

Does the property generally conform to the neighborhood (functional utility, style, condition, use, construction, etc.)? ☐ Yes ☐ No  If No, describe

| Freddie Mac Form 70  March 2005 | Page 1 of 6 | Fannie Mae Form 1004  March 2005 |
|---|---|---|

**Uniform Residential Appraisal Report**   File #

[Appraisal report form — Page 2 of 6. Sales Comparison Approach grid with columns for FEATURE, SUBJECT, COMPARABLE SALE #1, COMPARABLE SALE #2, COMPARABLE SALE #3, including rows for Address, Proximity to Subject, Sale Price, Sale Price/Gross Liv. Area, Data Source(s), Verification Source(s), VALUE ADJUSTMENTS (Sale or Financing, Concessions, Date of Sale/Time, Location, Leasehold/Fee Simple, Site, View, Design (Style), Quality of Construction, Actual Age, Condition, Above Grade Room Count, Gross Living Area, Basement & Finished Rooms Below Grade, Functional Utility, Heating/Cooling, Energy Efficient Items, Garage/Carport, Porch/Patio/Deck), Net Adjustment (Total), Adjusted Sale Price of Comparables, and research/transfer history sections, Summary of Sales Comparison Approach, Indicated Value by Sales Comparison Approach, Cost Approach, Income Approach.]

Freddie Mac Form 70   March 2005        Page 2 of 6        Fannie Mae Form 1004   March 2005

**Uniform Residential Appraisal Report**   File #

[Appraisal report form — Page 3 of 6. ADDITIONAL COMMENTS section, COST APPROACH TO VALUE (not required by Fannie Mae), INCOME APPROACH TO VALUE (not required by Fannie Mae), PROJECT INFORMATION FOR PUDs (if applicable).]

Freddie Mac Form 70   March 2005        Page 3 of 6        Fannie Mae Form 1004   March 2005

*The effectiveness of the market data approach is limited by economic conditions that change rapidly.*

# II. Cost Approach (Replacement Cost Method)

The **COST APPROACH** *is the process of calculating the cost of the land and buildings (as if they were new today) and then subtracting the accrued depreciation to arrive at the current value of the property.* To use the cost approach, the appraiser must be able to determine the new construction cost of replacing the building today using current construction methods. Depreciation is estimated by the appraiser and is then subtracted from the estimated cost of the new building. The value of the lot and depreciated building is then added to find the market value.

*The cost approach objective is to determine the land value plus the cost to replace the improvements new (minus depreciation) while maintaining the same utility value.*

Of the three approaches, the cost approach tends to set what the appraisers call an "upper limit of value." Most home buyers or investors prefer a newer building over an older one if the price is about the same. The cost approach therefore tends to set the highest price that a knowledgeable person will pay for a property. Why not build if the construction cost of a newer building is close to the sales price of an older building?

The cost approach is most useful when appraising: 1) new buildings and 2) special purpose or unique structures. Estimating depreciation is critical in this approach. As a building gets older, the depreciation becomes more difficult to estimate, eventually making the cost approach impractical. Since newer structures have little depreciation, the cost approach is the most suitable. The cost approach may also be preferred for special purpose or unique structures as they have few, if any, market comparable sales. Special purpose structures, such as an airplane factory, a city hall, or a church, are best appraised by the cost approach.

*The cost approach is more appropriate for new buildings because there is almost no depreciation.*

It is limited in its effectiveness for appraising old buildings because determining depreciation is the most difficult part of the cost approach for the appraiser.

Some properties **require** the use of the cost approach. If, for example, there have been no recent sales in an area, the market comparison approach cannot be used effectively. Furthermore, if there is no income (as for example, from government-owned properties), the appraiser must rely solely on the cost approach.

## A. COSTS ARE BOTH DIRECT AND INDIRECT

Any method used for estimating cost requires the calculation of direct (hard) or indirect (soft) costs. Both types of costs are equally necessary for construction and must be measured accurately.

**DIRECT COSTS** *are expenditures for labor and materials used in the construction of the improvement(s).* A contractor's overhead and profit are generally treated as direct costs.

**INDIRECT COSTS** *are expenditures other than material and labor costs.* Examples are administrative costs, professional fees, financing costs, insurance, and taxes. Indirect costs are usually calculated separately from direct costs.

## B. STEPS IN THE COST APPROACH

The steps used in the cost approach are easy to follow, but studying **Figure 11-2** will help to explain each step.

1. Estimate the value of the land (use the market comparison approach).
2. Estimate the replacement cost of the building as if it were new.
3. Deduct estimated depreciation from the replacement cost of the building.
4. Add the value of the lot (Step 1) and the depreciated cost of the building Steps 2 & 3) to find the total value (Step 4).

**Figure 11-2**

### 1. Step 1 – Appraise the Land (Lot) Separately

Appraise the land (lot) separately. The value of the vacant land is determined by comparing the lot of the property to be appraised with similar lots that have just been sold. The market comparison approach is used by the appraiser to estimate the lot value of the appraised property.

*The cost approach requires the appraiser to identify land values separately by the use of the market data approach.*

### 2. Step 2 – Estimate Replacement Cost

Estimate the replacement cost of the improvements to the land. This includes all the buildings and the landscaping improvements.

*"Replacement cost" is the present cost to build a building having the same amount of utility.*

#### a. Replacement Cost

*REPLACEMENT COST is the cost of building a similar new structure today (of equal utility) using modern construction methods.* These methods may differ from the original building techniques, but are becoming an important factor due to the ever increasing costs of new construction. As construction costs increase for new homes, the replacement cost of existing homes also increases. Therefore, well-located older homes will keep rising in value year after year, no matter how old they are, because the newer substitutes are so costly. This is not necessarily because of excellent upkeep, but because it is becoming impossible to find a newer home with the same features at a reasonable price. *REPRODUCTION or REPLICATION COST is the cost of reproducing a structure (usually destroyed) at current prices using identical (older) style materials and methods as used in the original structure.* This method is rarely used, but it is the type, for example, used by Disneyland to recreate its historical Main Street.

### b. Three Replacement Methods

The *COMPARATIVE-UNIT METHOD is used to derive a cost estimate in terms of dollars per square foot or per cubic foot, based on known costs of similar structures and adjusted for time and physical differences.* The comparative-unit method represents a relatively uncomplicated, practical approach to a cost estimate and is widely used.

The *UNIT-IN-PLACE METHOD employs unit costs for the various building components such as foundations, floors, walls, windows, and roofs as installed and uses square foot, linear foot, or other appropriate units of measurement to estimate each component part.* These estimates include labor and overhead. To use this method, the appraiser must have specialized construction knowledge.

The *QUANTITY SURVEY METHOD involves detailed estimates of the quantities of raw materials used, such as brick, lumber, cement, the price of such materials, and the labor costs.* It is the most comprehensive and accurate method of cost estimating, but too complicated to fully explain here.

Although there are several ways to determine replacement cost, the simplest way is to *measure the outside of the building to determine SQUARE FOOTAGE.* After you determine the square footage, multiply it by the current cost of construction, per square foot, to get the value (as if it were new) of the building.

To determine square feet, use the formula: **LENGTH x WIDTH**

The square foot cost for a smaller house is higher than the square foot cost for a larger house. If other factors are equal, including square footage, the cost of building a two-story house is up to 50% cheaper than a one-story house. A two-story house utilizes 50% less land (foot print).

The cubic foot method is used to appraise warehouses. To determine cubic feet, use the formula: **LENGTH x WIDTH x HEIGHT**

A warehouse building is appraised by the cubic foot but is usually rented by the square foot. **Caution: the industrial land the warehouse is on is appraised by the square foot.**

As construction costs vary from city-to-city and from builder-to-builder, many appraisers use cost engineers to help them determine the square foot cost of different types of construction. One of the most popular building cost information services is Marshall and Swift.

They compile a residential cost handbook that details the current cost of most types of residential construction in California. This is published quarterly.

### 3. Step 3 – Estimate and Deduct Depreciation

*DEPRECIATION is a reduction in the value of a property due to any cause.* The difference between replacement cost of a property and its market value is depreciation.

*Loss of value from any cause is called depreciation.*

Estimate and deduct the depreciation from the replacement cost of the building being appraised. This accumulated depreciation is sometimes called accrued depreciation. Accrued depreciation (observed) is the loss in value of improvements from any cause at the date of the appraisal. Accrued depreciation is what has happened in the past, whereas the accrual for depreciation is the amount of future depreciation. There are five methods of estimating accrued depreciation:

1. Capitalized Income
2. Market
3. Straight-line (Most common and explained below)
4. Engineering
5. Breakdown

The straight-line method is explained here. For information on the other methods, please see Educational Textbook Company's *Real Estate Appraisal – Principles and Procedures*, by Walt Huber, Levin P. Messick, IFAC, and William Pivar (see **Order Form** at back of this book). The *STRAIGHT-LINE METHOD (AGE LIFE) assumes the value declines in equal amounts of depreciation each year, until it reaches zero.* A building with an economic life of 50 years would depreciate 2 percent (100 percent ÷ 50 years = 2 percent) in value each year. Actual age is the current (real) age of the building. When using the age life method, an appraiser will use an age other than the actual age of the building. This is known as the effective age. *EFFECTIVE AGE (vs. actual age) is determined by the condition of the building rather than the actual age.* If a building has been maintained, its effective age may be less than the actual age; if there has been inadequate maintenance, it may be greater. *ECONOMIC LIFE (vs. physical life) is the estimated number of years of anticipated usefulness of the improvements.*

*"Effective age" is determined by the condition and usefulness of the property, not the actual age. The economic life of an improvement is usually shorter than its estimated physical life.*

*ACCRUAL FOR DEPRECIATION is the concept of estimating the amount of depreciation there will be in the future.* The accrual for depreciation is used in the income approach, discussed in the next section.

**Example:** A 19-year-old home looks like it is only 6 years old because it has been well maintained. The estimated life of the home is 40 years. Using the cost approach to appraise the home, the appraiser most likely would use the effective age of the improvements.

To accurately estimate accrued depreciation, the appraiser must have experience, skill, and good judgment. He or she must not only estimate the physical wear and tear on the building, but also the losses in value due to outmoded styles, poor design, and

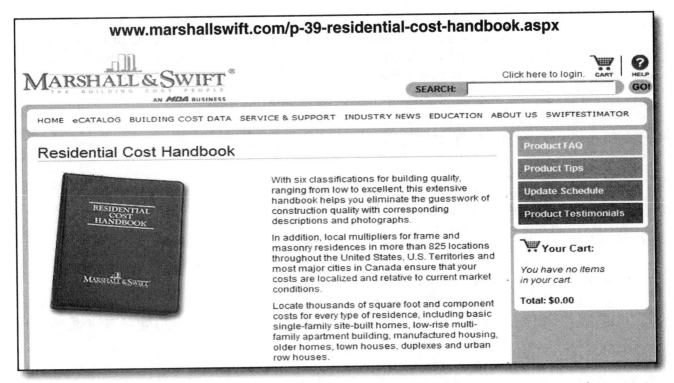

neighborhood changes that tend to reduce the value of the improvements. A property can lose value through three different types of depreciation.

**The three types of depreciation causes are: 1) physical deterioration, 2) functional obsolescence, and 3) economic obsolescence.**

### a. Physical Deterioration (Curable or Incurable)

*PHYSICAL DETERIORATION is the loss in value due to wear and tear.* As a building gets older, its age will start to show visibly. Since most types of physical deterioration (like a deteriorated driveway) can be repaired, we usually think of it as curable depreciation. On the other hand, severe structural deterioration may not be curable. So physical deterioration can be either curable or incurable. *CURABLE DEPRECIATION are repairs that add more to a building's value than they cost. INCURABLE DEPRECIATION refers to repairs that would be so expensive they are not economically feasible.* Examples of physical deterioration (curable or incurable) are:

1. all forms of wear and tear;
2. damage from dry rot and termites;
3. negligent care (deferred maintenance); and
4. depreciation that has already occurred.

*Obsolescence is not a method of calculating depreciation, but is a term meaning a "major cause" of depreciation.*

### b. Functional Obsolescence (Curable or Incurable)

*FUNCTIONAL OBSOLESCENCE is the loss in value due to outmoded style or non-usable space.* Examples of functional obsolescence would be a bedroom that can be reached only by walking through another bedroom. By modern standards this is very inconvenient and reduces the value of the second bedroom. **Another devaluing factor is a home with a single-car garage**. Functional depreciation is hard to cure. If the cost of curing the defect adds at least the same amount to the property's value, then it is worth the investment.

*A one-car garage is an example of functional obsolescence.*

Types of functional obsolescence (curable or incurable) are:

1. an outdated kitchen;
2. antique fixtures;
3. a four-bedroom, one-bath home;
4. a one-car garage, and
5. massive cornices.

### c. Economic Obsolescence (Incurable)

*An appraiser is trying to determine the amount of economic obsolescence when appraising a commercial property. He probably wonders, "Are the tenants in the neighborhood prospering?"*

> **ECONOMIC OBSOLESCENCE (also referred to as SOCIAL OBSOLESCENCE)** is the loss in value due to changes in the neighborhood and is external to the property itself. It is always incurable. If a freeway is built next to your property, your home will decrease in value because of the noise and nuisance factor. On the other hand, if the freeway is three blocks away, your house will increase in value because of improved freeway access. If social or economic factors (such as loss of jobs) cause a neighborhood to become shabby and rundown, the value of your property will decrease accordingly.

*Since economic obsolescence results from "off the property" causes, it is always incurable. Economic (profitable) life remaining is the main concern when purchasing an older property.*

> **Example:** Average priced homes coming into an area of expensive priced homes would cause real estate values to become unstable.

> **Example:** An airport flight pattern is changed and causes the affected homes to decrease in value due to economic obsolescence.

> **Example:** A zoning change would be considered economic obsolescence.

Types of economic obsolescence (incurable) are:

1. an oversupply of similar or competitive units;
2. beyond the confines of the property;
3. aircraft noise;
4. adverse zoning and legislative acts;
5. economic recession;
6. departure of major industries from the area, and
7. number of rental units increases.

### 4. Step 4 – Value of the Property

The last step in the cost approach is to add the depreciated value of any improvements to the value of the land. This figure is the market value of the property using the cost approach.

## C. ADVANTAGES OF THE COST APPROACH

*The main advantages of the cost approach is that it can be used on: 1) newly constructed buildings; 2) unique structures; and 3) public buildings.*

Since there is little depreciation, if any, to calculate on newer buildings and there is available construction cost data, the value can be easily determined using the cost approach. Unique structures, public buildings, and one-of-a-kind structures have no comparables, so the cost approach may be the only logical way to appraise them.

*The best appraisal method for a home built in 1900 is the cost approach.*

## D. DISADVANTAGES OF THE COST APPROACH

The disadvantages of using the cost approach are:

1. There must be an accurate value of the site (land).
2. Since determining depreciation is more difficult as buildings age, the reliability of the depreciation estimate may be questioned.
3. This approach may be difficult to apply to condos or planned unit developments because the land, improvements and marketing costs are not always easy to determine just for appraising one unit.

*Economic obsolescence is the hardest or most difficult to change.*

# III. Capitalization Approach (Income Approach)

*The income approach determines the "present worth of future benefits." Capitalization is the process of converting income into value.*

The **INCOME APPROACH** *is the process of analyzing the future net income from a property to determine its current market value.* Another word for this process is capitalization. The appraiser, when using the income approach, is determining the present property value based upon the information he or she has on future income and expenses of that given property.

The actual process of capitalization is simple. Divide a capitalization rate into the yearly net income; the answer you obtain is the value of the property.

$$\frac{\text{NET INCOME}}{\text{CAPITALIZATION RATE}} = \text{VALUE OF PROPERTY}$$

$$\frac{\$110,000}{10\%} = \$1,100,000$$

# CHAPTER 11

Rent producing (income) properties such as apartments, offices, warehouses, and manufacturing concerns can best be appraised by the income approach. This is because the people who invest in such projects are primarily interested in the income that they will receive. It is only natural that an investor would choose the property producing the highest return. The income approach allows a comparison of different types of income producing real estate and, at the same time, analyzes each as to the return of income to be received from that investment in the future.

## A. STEPS IN THE INCOME APPROACH

There are five basic steps to establish value using the income approach:

1. Calculate the annual effective gross income.
2. Complete an operating expense statement.
3. Deduct related operating expenses from gross income to get net income.
4. Divide net income by the appropriate capitalization rate.
5. Result of dividing net income by capitalization rate.

**Figure 11-3** illustrates the five steps.

**Figure 11-3**

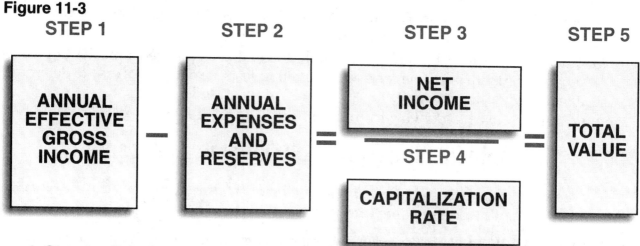

### 1. Step 1 – Calculate the Annual Effective Gross Income

Calculate the annual effective gross income from the investment property. *EFFECTIVE GROSS INCOME is the gross income minus any vacancies or rental losses.* In the case of rental properties, the annual gross rental income will be the annual rent that an owner receives if he or she charges the going rental rates with no vacancies. Sometimes managers charge rents that are below the market level, resulting in a very low number of vacancies. On the other hand, rents that are set too high usually yield a higher vacancy rate. The *VACANCY FACTOR is the loss in rents due to any cause.* This is commonly expressed as a percentage. The vacancy factor increases while trying to find a new tenant or because of cleaning, repairs, or non-paying renters.

### 2. Step 2 – Complete an Operating Expense Statement

Complete an operating expense statement. All of the following would be considered operating expenses when appraising an apartment building:

    1. Property taxes
    2. Insurance and licenses
    3. Manager fees
    4. Utilities
    5. Maintenance, repairs, and services (i.e., gardeners)
    6. Replacement reserves

*Cost of capital (mortgage payments of principal or interest) is NOT an operating expense.*

The expenses listed in the operating statement should represent the actual cost of each item. Though costs may vary, it is the appraiser's responsibility to determine what actual costs are on an annual basis.

An item that may need explanation is the replacement reserve. A *REPLACEMENT RESERVE consists of funds set aside for the purpose of replacing items in the future.* An example of a replacement reserve cost would be a $2,000 water heater with a life expectancy of five years. The replacement reserve for this item would be $400 per year ($2,000 ÷ 5).

*Management fees and replacement reserves must always be included in the basic operating expenses.*

*VARIABLE COSTS are operating expenses that can vary (utilities and repairs). FIXED COSTS remain constant, such as property taxes and fire insurance.*

### 3. Step 3 – Deduct Related Operating Expenses From Gross Income to Get Net Income

To determine net income, simply deduct the related operating expenses (Step 2) from the annual effective gross income (Step 1).

### 4. Step 4 – Divide Net Income by the Appropriate Capitalization Rate

Divide the net income by the appropriate capitalization rate. Selection of a capitalization rate can be a delicate task. A one percent change in the capitalization rate, for example, can alter the estimated value of a property by up to ten percent or more. The capitalization rate is composed of an interest rate return to the investor "on" his or her original investment and "of" the return of the original investment. The higher the rate, the greater the perceived risk is to the investor/owner.

**Example:** An owner of a vacant building is trying to decide whether to lease her building to a hardware store or to a post office. The owner would likely prefer the post office because the post office would probably have a lower risk than the hardware store. Thus, a lower rate would be acceptable.

There are several ways to select the proper capitalization rate. One way of selecting the appropriate capitalization rate is to sample similar recent apartment sales. Simply divide the net income by the sales price to obtain the capitalization rate used in that particular area.

The capitalization rate is composed of two parts: (1) a rate of return "on" the money invested and (2) a return "of" the original investment of money. This latter item is commonly referred to as the recapture rate (see **Figure 11-4**).

**Figure 11-4**

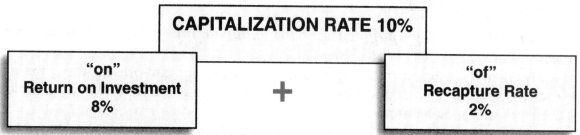

The capitalization rate is composed of two parts: the rate "on" the money invested (expected investor's return) and the annual rate "of" (recapture) of the investment.

*A capitalization rate can be determined by band of investment theory, market data/ comparison, or summation.*

### 5. Step 5 – Result of Dividing Net Income by Capitalization Rate

This is the easiest and final step in the income approach. It is simply the result of dividing net income by the capitalization rate.

*Net Income divided by Capitalization Rate = Market Value*

$$\frac{I}{R} = V$$

$\underline{\text{Net income } \$65,000}$ = $650,000 Estimated Market Value
Capitalization Rate 10% (.10)

**THE MARKET VALUE USING THE INCOME APPROACH IS $650,000**

*The best appraisal approach to use on a shopping center would be the cost-income method.*

### B. GROSS RENT MULTIPLIER – GRM (Rule of Thumb)

*GROSS RENT MULTIPLIER (GRM) is a multiplication rule of thumb used to convert the rental income into market value.* If we use a gross rent multiplier of 125 times the monthly rent of $1,000, the property is worth approximately $125,000 (125 x $1,000). See **Figure 11-5** for more details. This is definitely not an accurate way to appraise a property, but it does give a quick estimate of value. Many professional investors use it as a screening device to eliminate undesirable investment opportunities. This monthly gross multiplier is often used for single-family homes and small apartment buildings.

The *GROSS (RENT) is the money received from a property before any expenses are deducted.* It can be expressed as monthly or annual income, as long as it is applied consistently.

**Example:** A desert cabin which rents for $600 per month just sold for $96,000. A similar property rents for $660 per month, so the market value is most likely to be near $105,600.

In the real estate investment field (commercial and industrial), it is common knowledge that the annual gross income multiplier of "x 6.2" is a good "rule of thumb" for an investment. For example, if the annual gross income from an apartment project is $40,000, its value should be approximately $248,000 ($40,000 x 6.2). The annual gross income multiplier varies from "x 5" to "x 12," depending upon the location of the property and the condition of the individual buildings. Remember: this is an approximation device and should be used only as a quick estimate—not in place of an actual appraisal.

*Gross income changed to value in one operation describes a rent multiplier.*

## C. ADVANTAGES OF THE INCOME APPROACH

The advantage of the income approach method is that no other method focuses solely on determining the present value of the future income stream from the subject property. It is a little different than the other two methods of determining value in that "If the purpose of the property is to generate income, use the income approach." For example a house that is zoned for commercial use may be valued at a much higher amount when used as an insurance office rather than as a house. The location may bring in a great deal of income; as a house the market value is low, but as an income-producing property the market value may be very high.

*The "present worth of future benefits" is what the income approach is all about.*

It is most often used for multi-family residential income property but could be used on any type of property that generates income.

## D. DISADVANTAGES OF THE INCOME APPROACH

The disadvantage of the income approach is that it may be difficult to determine the proper capitalization rate. For example, it may be impossible to ascertain the cap-rate for a theme park or alligator farm. These other items used in the income approach may also be difficult to estimate: vacancy rate, economic rent, operation expenses, and reserve requirements.

# IV. Correlation of Value (Bracketing)

The last and most important part of the appraisal process is the correlation (sometimes referred to as reconciliation) of the three approaches to value. *CORRELATION is the process of selecting the most appropriate approach for the particular appraisal job and giving it the most consideration in pinpointing the final value.* Although all three methods are used in appraisal, one is usually most appropriate for a specific appraisal problem.

*In general, the "market comparison approach" is best for single-family homes or lots; the "cost approach" is best for new, unique or unusual structures; and the "income approach" is best for properties that can be used to generate income.*

**Figure 11-5**

# Gross Rent Multiplier

The **GROSS RENT MULTIPLIER (GRM)** *is a rough, quick way of converting gross monthly rent into market value.* To obtain the gross rent multiplier, divide the "sales" price by the monthly rent. It is not a very accurate method, but it is a good estimator because it is so easy. The gross rent multiplier is best used for single or small multi-family residential properties.

$$\frac{\text{SALES PRICE}}{\text{RENT}} = \text{GROSS RENT MULTIPLIER}$$

*TYPICAL PROBLEMS:*

*If a house that rented for $600 a month sold for $78,000, what is the gross rent multiplier?*

$$\frac{\$78,000 \text{ Sales price}}{\text{Monthly Rent } \$600} = 130 \text{ (Gross Rent Multiplier)}$$

*If a similar house down the street is renting for $690, what would the selling price be?*

**Monthly Rent $690 x 130 (Gross Rent Multiplier) = $89,700**

*CAN ANNUAL RENTS BE USED?*

The gross rent multiplier is not a percentage, so it can be expressed as either a monthly or annual figure. If the above problem were expressed as an annual rent figure, the gross rent multiplier would have to be divided by 12. The annual gross rent multiplier is 10.83 (130 ÷ 12).

*If a house that rents for $72,000 a year sold for $780,000, what is the annual gross multiplier?*

$$\frac{\$780,000 \text{ Sales Price}}{\text{Annual Rent } \$72,000} = 10.83 \text{ Annual Gross Rent Multiplier}$$

**NOTE: Sometimes a different multiplier is used, the Gross Income Multiplier (GIM), when the revenues being considered are not just from rental income (like coin-operated washers and dryers). The GIM is preferred for commercial and income properties.**

# V. Final Estimate of Value (Appraisal Report)

After the appraiser has collected all the data and applied the appropriate appraisal method(s), the next step in the appraisal process is to reconcile or correlate the adjusted sales price of the comparables.

The **APPRAISAL REPORT** *is the documentation of the appraiser's findings*. It can be a prepared fill-in form. However, if it is complicated or subject to close interpretation, the report should be written in a narrative form with supporting data contained in supplemental exhibits. **In practice, most appraisal reports are written**. There are two main types of written appraisal reports:

1. **Short form** (a form with checks and explanations, often used by lenders)

*A short form appraisal report is called a short form, form report, or summary report.*

2. **Narrative report** (most complete and extensive)

*A narrative appraisal report is the most comprehensive and complete and typically contains the headings "Introduction," "Site and Improvement," "Property Description," "Supporting Data," and "Final Value Estimate."*

Whether the report is a simple one-page report or an extensive volume, the following information should be presented:

1. An adequate description for the property that is being appraised.
2. A statement as to the purpose and scope of the appraisal.
3. An adequate description of the neighborhood.
4. The date on which the value is estimated.

*An appraiser's "effective date" is usually the date of the inspection of the property.*

5. The qualifying conditions and assumptions.
6. The factual data, maps, and photos with their analysis and interpretations.
7. The processing of the data by one or more of the three approaches to value (correlation).

*An appraiser's "date signed" is the date of final writing or delivery of the appraisal report.*

8. The estimate of value.
9. The name, address, type of license (and any certifications), and signature of the appraiser.

## A. COST OF AN APPRAISAL

Appraisal costs can vary from relatively small amounts to thousands of dollars. The cost of an appraisal may be affected by its purpose, the qualifications of the appraiser, and how detailed the appraisal. An appraisal used to document a court case could cost several thousand dollars.

It would be impractical to spend thousands of dollars for a home appraisal just to determine a selling price. If you are thinking about selling your home, your local real estate broker will probably do this at no cost. Local brokers are familiar with your area and are knowledgeable about current sales prices of similar homes in your neighborhood. On the other hand, appraisal of large parcels, commercial buildings, and apartment houses, or appraisals to be used in court, may require the services of a highly skilled appraiser. Although the fees are higher, they reflect the experience and ability of the appraiser. The appraisal fee and an outline of what is to be accomplished in the appraisal should be set in advance. It is unethical to set an appraisal fee as a percentage of the determined value. This may influence the appraiser to increase the value.

### Appraisal Report Copies

A lender must provide a notice to a loan applicant stating that the applicant is entitled to a consumer information copy of the appraisal report if the applicant requests and pays for the report.

The notice must be provided on any loan secured by residential property and on purchase money financing (or refinancing of purchase money debt) on nonresidential property.

## VI. Licensing, Fee Appraisers, and Appraisal Organizations

### A. APPRAISAL LICENSE AND CERTIFICATION (California)

All California appraisers are required to be licensed or certified (see **Figure 11-6**). The license/certification categories are:

**1. TRAINEE APPRAISER**

**2. RESIDENTIAL APPRAISER**

**3. CERTIFIED RESIDENTIAL APPRAISER**

**4. CERTIFIED GENERAL APPRAISER**

*A Certified General License would be needed to appraise a strip mall valued at approximately $540,000.*

### B. FEE APPRAISERS

**While the Standards permit an appraiser to appraise a property in which he or she has an interest, as long as the fact is disclosed to the lender/client in writing, it would be highly unusual for it to be accepted by any lender/client.**

A *FEE APPRAISER is an independent, self-employed appraiser; he or she appraises for a fee or charge.* In California a license or certification is required to appraise real estate as a profession. Other appraisers are dependent on large corporations or organizations for their employment. Gas, electric, telephone, and other utility companies have appraisal departments. Banks, savings banks, mortgage companies, and other lenders often have in-house appraisal staffs. Most cities and counties have large appraisal staffs in their assessors' offices. There are also various state agencies, such as Cal-Trans, that maintain appraisal staffs.

**A fee appraiser is self-employed; he/she appraises for a fee or charge. Remember: both appraisers and real estate agents are concerned with the marketability of residential properties.**

## Figure 11-6 CALIFORNIA OFFICE OF REAL ESTATE APPRAISERS (OREA) EDUCATION REQUIREMENTS

### TRAINEE LICENSE AND RESIDENTIAL LICENSE

**150 hours of education.** Qualifying Education hours must include instruction in the following modules:

| | |
|---|---|
| 30 hours | Basic Appraisal Principles |
| 30 hours | Basic Appraisal Procedures |
| 15 hours | The 15-hour National USPAP Course |
| 15 hours | Residential Market Analysis and Highest and Best Use |
| 15 hours | Residential Appraiser Site Valuation and Cost Approach |
| 30 hours | Residential Sales Comparison and Income Approaches |
| 15 hours | Residential Report Writing and Case Studies |

**Note:** *Course work for the Trainee License cannot be taken more than 5 years prior to the application date.*

### CERTIFIED RESIDENTIAL LICENSE

**200 hours of education and an Associate Degree from a Regionally Accredited College.** Qualifying Education hours must include instruction in the following modules:

| | |
|---|---|
| 30 hours | Basic Appraisal Principles |
| 30 hours | Basic Appraisal Procedures |
| 15 hours | The 15-hour National USPAP Course |
| 15 hours | Residential Market Analysis and Highest and Best Use |
| 15 hours | Residential Appraiser Site Valuation and Cost Approach |
| 30 hours | Residential Sales Comparison and Income Approaches |
| 15 hours | Residential Report Writing and Case Studies |
| 15 hours | Statistics, Modeling and Finance |
| 15 hours | Advanced Residential Applications and Case Studies |
| 20 hours | Appraisal Subject Matter Electives. May include hours over the minimum requirement in the above modules or in modules not listed above. |

*\* In lieu of the Associate Degree, an applicant can complete 21 college semester credits in courses covering specific subject matters: English Composition; Principles of Economics (Micro or Macro); Finance; Algebra, Geometry or higher mathematics; Statistics; Introduction to Computers; and Business or Real Estate Law.*

### CERTIFIED GENERAL LICENSE

**300 hours of education and a Bachelors Degree from a Regionally Accredited College or University.** Qualifying Education hours must include instruction in the following modules:

| | |
|---|---|
| 30 hours | Basic Appraisal Principles |
| 30 hours | Basic Appraisal Procedures |
| 15 hours | The 15-hour National USPAP Course |
| 30 hours | General Appraiser Market Analysis and Highest and Best Use |
| 15 hours | Statistics, Modeling and Finance |
| 30 hours | General Appraiser Sales Comparison Approach |
| 30 hours | General Appraiser Site Valuation and Cost Approach |
| 60 hours | General Appraiser Income Approach |
| 30 hours | General Appraiser Report Writing and Case Studies |
| 30 hours | Appraisal Subject Matter Electives. May include hours over the minimum requirement in the above modules or in modules not listed above. |

*\*\* In lieu of the Bachelors Degree, an applicant can complete 30 college semester credits in courses covering specific subject matters: English Composition; Micro Economics; Macro Economics; Finance; Algebra, Geometry or higher mathematics; Statistics; Introduction to Computers; and Business or Real Estate Law; and two elective courses in accounting, geography, ag-economics, business management, or real estate.*

Many community colleges and universities offer courses in appraisal or investment properties to acquaint you with the techniques involved in the income approach.

www.cccco.edu/
Information on the California Community Colleges

## C. PROFESSIONAL APPRAISAL ASSOCIATIONS

**American Society of Appraisers (ASA)**
555 Herndon Parkway, Suite 125
Herndon, VA 20170
**www.appraisers.org**

**American Society of Farm Managers and Rural Appraisers (ASFMRA)**
950 Cherry Street, Suite 508
Denver, CO 80246-2664
**www.asfmra.org**

**Appraisal Institute (AI)**
550 West Van Buren Street, Suite 1000
Chicago, IL 60607
**www.appraisalinstitute.org**

**Appraisal Institute of Canada (AIC)**
403-200 Catherine Street
Ottawa ON K2P 2K9 Canada
**www.aicanada.org**

**International Association of Assessing Officers (IAAO)**
314 West 10th Street
Kansas City, MO 64105-1616
**www.iaao.org**

**International Right of Way Association (IRWA)**
19750 South Vermont Avenue, Suite 220
Torrance, CA 90502-1144
**www.irwaonline.org**

**National Association of Independent Fee Appraisers (NAIFA)**
401 North Michigan Avenue, Suite 2200
Chicago, IL 60611
**www.naifa.com**

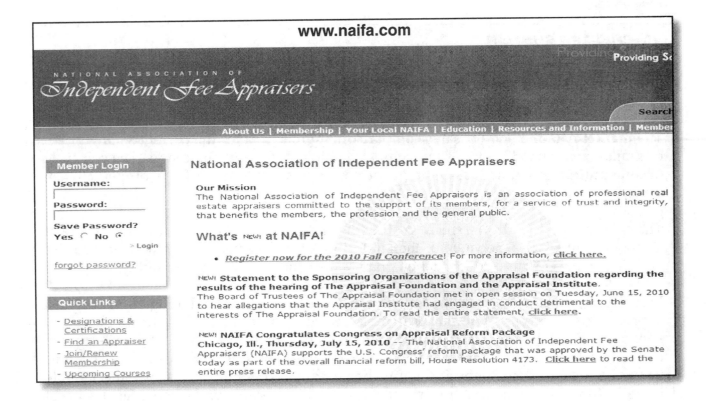

**National Association of Master Appraisers (NAMA)**
303 West Cypress Street
San Antonio, TX 78212-0617
**www.masterappraisers.org.**

## VII. CHAPTER SUMMARY

A **licensed appraiser** will use three different approaches to establish **final value**. These include the: 1) **comparative (market data) approach**; 2) **cost (replacement) approach**; and 3) **capitalization (income) approach**.

The **market data method** (or **sales comparison approach**) takes the current selling prices of similar or comparable properties (comps) and adjusts for any differences. The **principle of substitution** is applied, assuming a person will not pay more for a property when something similar is available for less.

The **cost approach** (or **replacement cost method**) determines the current market value of a property by adding the value of the land plus (+) replacement or reproduction cost of buildings today, minus (-) depreciation, maintaining the same amount of utility.

In step one of the cost approach, the appraiser finds the **value of the land** using the market data approach. In step two, the **reproduction** or **replacement cost** is calculated. The three replacement methods include the **comparative-unit method** (most commonly used), the **unit-in-place method**, and the **quantity survey method**. In step three, **depreciation** is factored in. The three types of depreciation are: 1) **physical**, 2) **functional**, and 3) **economic**, and can be either **curable** (profitable to repair) or **incurable** (unprofitable to repair). In step four the depreciated value of improvements is added to the value of the land to find the **market value** of the property.

The **capitalization** (or **income**) **approach** is concerned with the present worth of future benefits. The basic formula to determine total value is: **Annual effective gross income minus (-) annual expenses and reserves equals (=) net income**. Then **divide the net income by the capitalization rate to find (=) market value**. The **cap rate** is the percentage rate that an investor expects to earn "on" a real estate investment. A quick rule of thumb to convert gross income into approximate value is to use the **gross rent multiplier**, which is based on monthly rent and is used for residential properties. The **gross income multiplier** is based on annual rents and is used for commercial properties.

**Correlation** (or **reconciliation**) is the process of selecting the most appropriate approach for the appraisal job. Generally, the market comparison approach is best for single-family homes or lots; the cost approach is best for new, unique or unusual structures; and the income approach is best for properties that can be used to generate income. The **final estimate of value** (or **appraisal report**) is then generated, the **narrative report** being the most comprehensive and complete.

The **cost of an appraisal** can be effected by its purpose, how detailed it is, and the experience of the appraiser. All appraisers must be licensed or certified, the categories being **trainee license, residential license, certified residential license**, and **certified general license**. A **fee appraiser** is self employed, and charges a fee for his or her services. Although highly unusual, it is technically permissible for a fee appraiser to appraise a property in which he or she owns an interest as long as it is disclosed in writing. It is the **marketability of real property** that concerns appraisers and real estate agents.

## VIII. TERMINOLOGY

A. Accrual for Depreciation
B. Accrued Depreciation
C. Actual Age
D. Correlation
E. Cost Approach
F. Curable Depreciation
G. Depreciation
H. Direct Cost

I. Economic Life
J. Economic Obsolescence
K. Effective Age
L. Effective Gross Income
M. Functional Obsolescence
N. Gross Rent Multiplier
O. Income Approach
P. Incurable Depreciation

Q. Indirect Costs
R. Market Comparison
S. Physical Deterioration
T. Replacement
U. Replacement Reserve
V. Reproduction Cost
W. Square Footage
X. Vacancy Factor

1.____ The estimated percentage of vacancies in a rental property, such as in an apartment building.

2.____ The use of different appraisal methods to reach an estimate of the value of a property. The methods must be weighed as to which is most appropriate for the type of property being appraised.

3.____ The theoretical cost of replacing a building with one of equivalent usefulness.

4.____ A simple method of using gross monthly or yearly rents to obtain an approximate value of an income property.

5.____ The need to replace part of a structure because new improvements have come along that make the older structure inefficient by comparison.  For example, a one-bathroom, eight-bedroom house.

6.____ An appraisal method, estimating the replacement cost of a structure, less depreciation, plus land value.

7.____ Loss of desirability and useful life of a property through economic forces, such as zoning changes, traffic pattern changes, etc., rather than wear and tear.

8.____ A decrease in the value of real property improvements for any reason.

9.____ An appraisal method to determine the present value today of rental property by estimating the income it will generate over the life of the structure.

10.____ A way of measuring real property in 1 ft. by 1 ft. segments.

11.____ The method of estimating the value of real property by adjusting the sales price of comparable properties for differences.

12.____ Gradual physical wear and tear on a structure that decreases its value.

13.____ Periodically setting money aside to replace systems and appliances in a building.  For example, a landlord putting aside a portion of monthly rents toward a new roof or water heater.

14.____ The chronological age of a structure as opposed to its effective or economic life.

15.____ Accumulation of depreciation.

16.____ Construction costs (material and labor).

17.____ The cost of reproducing a property (usually one that has been destroyed) at current prices using the same materials.

18.____ Repairs that would be so expensive they are not economically feasible.

19.____ Age of a structure as estimated by its condition rather than its actual age.

20.____ Repairs that are economically feasible to do.

21.____ Costs other than labor and materials.

22.____ Amount of depreciation in the future, not past.

23.____ The "profitable" life of an improvement.  Generally shorter than the physical life.

24.____ Gross income of a building if fully rented, less an allowance for estimated vacancies.

# CHAPTER 11

## IX. CHAPTER QUIZ

1. An appraiser using the market data approach in appraising would be most interested in the date that:

    a. the offer was written.
    b. the buyer moved into the property.
    c. the price was agreed upon.
    d. recording occurred.

2. The ultimate test of functional utility is:

    a. marketability.
    b. cost of the item.
    c. market cost.
    d. All of the above.

3. A 19 year-old home looks like it is only 6 years old because it has been well maintained. The estimated life of the home is 40 years. Using the cost approach to appraise the home, the appraiser most likely would use the:

    a. effective age of the improvements.
    b. economic age of the improvements.
    c. physical age of the improvements.
    d. chronological age of the improvements.

4. Which of the following would be an example of functional obsolescence?

    a. New zoning laws
    b. Incompatible land use in the neighborhood
    c. A deteriorated driveway
    d. A one-car garage

5. An airport flight pattern is changed and causes the affected homes to decrease in value due to:

    a. economic obsolescence.
    b. aviation obsolescence.
    c. political obsolescence.
    d. functional obsolescence.

6. An appraiser is using the replacement cost approach to appraise a building built in 1901. The appraiser would:

    a. determine the labor cost in 1901 adjusted for inflation based on the consumer price index (CPI) since 1901.
    b. use the cost to build the building in 1901 if the data is available. Otherwise, use the available data from the closest year to 1901.
    c. use the current cost to build the building today and deduct the depreciation over the economic life of the building.
    d. utilize the average labor costs over the building's economic life.

7. When appropriate, an appraiser would use the cost approach to determine the value of:

    a. special purpose property or service buildings.
    b. vacant land.
    c. an expensive family home.
    d. constructing a building.

8. An owner of a vacant building is trying to decide whether to lease his building to a hardware store or to a post office. The owner would likely prefer the post office because the post office would probably:

    a. have a higher capitalization rate than that of the hardware store.
    b. have a lower capitalization rate than that of the hardware store.
    c. provide a higher return for the owner than the hardware store.
    d. sign a longer lease if unemployment rises in the area.

9. A capitalization rate can be determined by:

    a. summation.
    b. band of investment theory.
    c. market data (comparison).
    d. all of the above.

10. Which appraisal report would typically contain the headings, "Introduction," "Site and Improvement," "Property Description," "Supporting Data," and "Final Value Estimate?"

    a. The letter form report
    b. The short form report
    c. The narrative report
    d. The certified general report

**ANSWERS:** 1. c; 2. a; 3. a; 4. d; 5. a; 6. c; 7. a; 8. b; 9. d; 10. c

THE GREAT SEAL OF THE STATE OF
CALIFORNIA

EUREKA

# CHAPTER 12
## *Subdivisions and Government Control*

## I. Doctrine of Police Power

*There are currently over 38 million people in California and we are adding over 1,700 new residents each day.*

With a population of more than thirty-five million people, California has more people than any other state. That means we have approximately 12.5% of the United States population. Since we are such a fast growing and mobile state, the problems encountered can be tremendous. The state and local governments have the responsibility (under the doctrine of police power) to enact and enforce legislative acts to protect the general public. This public protection in the real estate area prevents fraud, misrepresentation, and deceit.

### A. POLICE POWER

*Police power is the right of public officials to control the use of private property for the health, safety, and general welfare of the public.*

> **POLICE POWER** *is the power to make rulings to control the "use and taking of private property" for the protection of the public's health, safety, and welfare.* Police power allows the state, county, or city to protect its citizens by controlling how land is being used.
>
> Police power provides for the regulation of lot design and physical improvements for the orderly and proper development of the community, the construction of streets, highways and parking facilities adequate for our car-oriented society, and the certainty of an adequate water supply. It ensures the protection of life and property by police and firemen, the maintenance of the purity of air we breathe, the control of noise, the disposal of sewage and waste, and the provision under public or private regulation for essential utility services. **Figure 12-1** shows seven basic areas of government control at either the state or local level.

*Zoning, planning, and governmental land use are important examples of the exercise of police power.*

## II. The Basic Subdivision Laws

A **SUBDIVISION** *is a parcel of land divided into smaller parcels with the intent to sell, lease, or finance them now or in the future.* It can also be some form of common or mutual ownership rights in

## CHAPTER 12

**Figure 12-1**

one parcel. A **condominium** is sometimes referred to as a "one lot subdivision." There are two basic laws under which subdivisions are controlled in California:

    **A. Subdivision Map Act** (City or County) – Two or more parcels or lots
    **B. Subdivided Lands Act** (Department of Real Estate) – Five or more parcels or lots

These two laws were enacted for different purposes, and were adopted to achieve the objective for which each was designed.

### A. SUBDIVISION MAP ACT (Enforced by Local City or County)

*The primary objective of the **SUBDIVISION MAP ACT** is to provide an outline of the methods for the subdivision filing procedure at the city or county level and to make sure subdividers comply with* *the city's or county's master plan*. This law permits the local government of the city or county to enact subdivision ordinances. Thus, the direct control of the kind and type of subdivision for each community, and the public physical improvements to be installed, is left to the local city (if incorporated) or county (if unincorporated). This act has two major objectives:

1. To coordinate the subdivision plans including lot design, street patterns, drainage, and sewers with the community pattern (master plan) as laid out by the local planning authorities.

2. To ensure, by the filing of the subdivision maps, that parts of the subdivision area will be dedicated to the city or county for public purposes. These dedications include public streets and other public areas, dedicated by the subdivision so that they will not be an unmanageable future burden upon the taxpayers of the community.

State law now requires that each community (city or county government) shall enact local subdivision ordinances. Before the Department of Real Estate will approve the subdivision, a tentative subdivision map must be approved by the local government.

*The Subdivision Map Act (for two or more parcels or lots) gives local government entities (planning commissions) control over the physical design of a subdivision.*

### B. SUBDIVIDED LANDS ACT (State Law Enforced by the DRE)

This law is statewide in its operation and is directly administered by the California Real Estate Commissioner. The *basic objective of the SUBDIVIDED LANDS ACT is to protect the purchasers of property in new subdivisions from fraud, misrepresentation, or deceit in the marketing of subdivided lots, parcels, condominiums, or other undivided property interests in the state of California.*

No subdivision unit can be offered for sale in California unless the commissioner has issued a subdivision public report. This applies not only to tracts located in California, but also to subdivided lands lying partly outside the state's boundaries. The public report is a factual account of the subdivided property.

The report is not issued until the commissioner is satisfied that the subdivider has met all the statutory requirements, with particular emphasis on the establishment and facilities included in the offering, and demonstrates that the lots or parcels can be used for the purpose for which they are being offered.

*The Subdivided Lands Act (public report) requirements apply when a parcel is divided into five or more lots (units).*

## III. Public Report (Consumer Information)

*The public report (issued by the Department of Real Estate) is required reading by any purchaser.*

As provided by the Subdivided Lands Act, purchasers of a home in a new subdivision must receive a Public Report from the California Real Estate Commissioner's office. A *PUBLIC REPORT is a formal disclosure report of the important facts regarding a subdivision*. It is, in a sense, a developer's "permit" to sell. It is not, however, a recommendation pro or con. The report makes clear the physical characteristics of the land, so that the buyer can know exactly what he or she is buying. The buyer is told the size, arrangement, and location of the lot and exactly what off-site improvements and recreation facilities to expect.

*A subdivider must give a copy of the Commissioner's Public Report to anyone who requests it orally or in writing.*

There may be two public reports. The optional preliminary report may be submitted to the Department of Real Estate for tentative approval. The required final report must be issued and given to the buyer. The ***PRELIMINARY PUBLIC REPORT (PINK)*** *is a tentative public report that must be given to each prospective purchaser*. The report is printed on pink paper, making it easily recognizable. It is given to a buyer when he or she makes a reservation to purchase or lease a lot, unit, or parcel in a subdivision.

*Preliminary reports allow subdividers to obtain reservations only. They cannot sell and the deposit is fully refundable. Any preliminary report issued will expire when the final report is published or after one year passes, whichever is first.*

A prospective purchaser must be given a copy of the preliminary report and sign a receipt to that effect. A copy of the reservation agreement is signed by the prospective buyer and the money deposited with a neutral escrow company. **The reservation to buy or lease must contain a clause allowing the buyer the option to cancel his or her reservation at any time and immediately have the deposit returned**. Any preliminary report issued will expire when the final report is published or after one year passes, whichever occurs first. The subdivider must keep receipts taken for any public report on file for three years.

*A "Desist and Refrain Order" is issued by the Real Estate Commissioner to stop sales for violations.*

The **FINAL PUBLIC REPORT (WHITE),** *"Real Estate Commissioner's Final Subdivision Public Report,"* *is the official report that must be given to the buyer.* The buyer must receive a copy of the final public report even if he or she has a preliminary public report. After having enough time to read it, the buyer must sign a receipt stating that the report has been received. There is a five-year time limit on the report, and it can be updated and renewed.

**Note – The public report process only applies to the first sale of each lot. Later resales are exempt.**

### A. PUBLIC REPORT RECEIPTS

*The subdivider must keep a receipt of the public report for a three-year period.*

The receipt stating that the buyer has received a copy of any public report, and had the opportunity to read it, must be kept on file by the owner, his or her agent, or the subdivider. Receipts for any public reports are subject to inspection by the commissioner for a three-year period. An approved reservation agreement form is furnished by the Department of Real Estate (see **Figure 12-2**). This form, or a form similar to it, is to be used when taking reservations and deposits under a preliminary public report or deposits under the final public report.

*If there is a discrepancy between local and state building codes, the highest standard of safety will prevail. A developer is responsible for streets, curbs, and utilities in a new subdivision.*

### B. MATERIAL CHANGES (Notify Commissioner)

*Change in price is NOT a material fact.*

Any material change in the subdivision or its handling after the filing is made, or the public report is issued, must be reported to the Commissioner of Real Estate. This not only includes physical changes, such as changes in the lot or street lines, but any new condition or development that may affect the value of the subdivision or the terms of how it is offered to the public.

The owner of a standard type subdivision or planned development must report to the commissioner the sale of five or more parcels. The sale to a single purchaser of two or more units in a community apartment, condominium, or stock cooperative project must also be reported. Failure to report material changes not only violates the law, but may furnish a basis for rescission, by court action, of purchases.

If a person purchases, or has an option to purchase, five or more lots in a subdivision, whether contiguous or not, the subdivider must immediately notify the Department of Real Estate with the name and address. The reason for this is that another subdivision has been created within the original subdivision, so a new Final Public Report will be required.

## IV. Subdivision Defined by Law

Although the definitions of the Subdivided Lands Act and the Subdivision Map Act are in many ways similar, there are some differences. Both define a subdivision as **improved or unimproved land divided for the purpose of sale, leasehold, or financing into several parcels.** They are applied not only to residential land, but include lands used for any purpose, including business, industry, recreation, or agriculture.

**Figure 12-2**

REGULATION 2795.1

REQUIRED RECEIPT FOR PUBLIC REPORT

The following form shall be duplicated and used by the owner, subdivider or agent as the prospective purchaser's receipt for the copy of the Public Report which was given to said prospective purchaser.

It shall also be used pertinent to all prospective purchasers who sign a reservation agreement under the authority of a Preliminary Public Report or a Short Form Preliminary Public Report.

The receipt is to be kept on file by the subdivider or his/her representative/agent for three years

---

RECEIPT FOR PUBLIC REPORT

The Laws and Regulations of the Real Estate Commissioner require that you as a prospective purchaser or lessee be afforded an opportunity to read the public report for this subdivision before you make any written offer to purchase or lease a subdivision interest or before any money or other consideration toward purchase or lease of a subdivision interest is accepted from you.

In the case of a preliminary subdivision public report, you must be afforded an opportunity to read the report before a written reservation or any deposit in connection therewith is accepted from you.

DO NOT SIGN· THIS RECEIPT UNTIL YOU HAVE RECEIVED A COPY OF THE REPORT AND HAVE READ IT.

I have read the Commissioner's Public Report on

"CENTURY PARK PLACE"
_____

054916LA-A04                    37164, Phase 4, Lot 1
_____    _____
    (File No.)                  (Tract No. or Name)

I understand the report is not a recommendation or endorsement of the subdivision, but is for information only.

The date of the public report which is received and read
is: ___6/7/XX_____  .

_____*Vic Tester*_____
                      Name
_____*1307 Arden Street*_____
                      Address
_____*6/7/XX*_____
                      Date

There are several differences between the two Acts. In general, the Subdivided Lands Act applies to five or more units while the Subdivision Map Act applies to two or more units.

Full compliance with all the provisions of the Subdivision Map Act and the Subdivided Lands Act is required by law. Subdividers and their professional consultants should be thoroughly familiar with the provisions of the state laws and with the specific city and county provisions that affect the particular community in question. Many variations are found in local subdivision ordinances due to the great diversity of communities and conditions throughout the state (see **Figure 12-3** for a summary of subdivision laws).

**Figure 12-3**

## Subdivision Laws Summarized

| SUBDIVISION MAP ACT | SUBDIVIDED LANDS LAW |
|---|---|
| Two or more lots or parcels | Five or more lots or parcels |
| Land must be contiguous units | No contiguity requirement |
| No exemption for 160 acres and larger | 160 and larger parcels are exempt |
| Administered by local officials | Administered by the California Real Estate Commissioner |
| No public report required | Public report required |

### A. LAND PROJECTS (State Law)

In recent years, lots in some subdivisions located in sparsely populated areas have been sold by intensive promotional efforts that tend to obscure the gamble involved in such speculations. Such subdivisions are referred to as land projects. A **LAND PROJECT** *is a remote subdivision of 50 or more vacant lots in a rural area (having fewer than 1,500 registered voters within two miles).*

Certain laws have been established to protect the public from these risky ventures. By law, any contract to buy or lease in a land project may be rescinded without cause, by written notice, before midnight on the fourteenth day after the sales contract is signed.

### B. OUT-OF-STATE BUYERS (Federal Law)

*Subdividers of large subdivisions to be sold interstate are registered with HUD.*

Under the Federal Interstate Land Sales Full Disclosure Act, such sales are subject to special registration and control. A contract for the purchase or lease of a lot of this kind is voidable at the option of the buyer if the contract is made without prior inspection of the site. The buyer has seven days after receiving the public report to rescind the contract.

# V. Common Interest Development (CID)

A **COMMON INTEREST DEVELOPMENT (CID)** *is a project where there are common areas used by all—excepting separate interests for the use of individual living units and managed by a* *nonprofit association.* The four basic types of common interest ownership, which are defined as subdivisions, include:

A. **Planned Development (PD)**
B. **Community Apartment Project**
C. **Condominiums (including Timesharing)**
D. **Stock Cooperative**

To be defined as subdivisions by the Department of Real Estate as part of the Subdivided Lands Act, a planned unit development must have five or more lots, but all the other types only need two units.

## A. PLANNED DEVELOPMENT (PD)

In a *PLANNED DEVELOPMENT (PD), each resident has separate ownership of his or her house and the lot that it's located on.* How is it different from a standard subdivision of single-family homes? A planned development includes areas or facilities that are either owned by all the homeowners as tenants in common, or that are owned by a community association and maintained for the use of the homeowners. Like the other forms of common interest projects, a planned development project is established by a recorded declaration and plan.

The *COMMON AREA is that part of a lot or unit in a subdivision that is shared equally by all owners (undivided interest).* An *UNDIVIDED INTEREST is the right of any owner to use any part of the project.*

## B. COMMUNITY APARTMENT PROJECTS

*COMMUNITY APARTMENT PROJECTS are two or more apartments, defined as a subdivision, where the operation, maintenance, and control is usually exercised by a governing board elected by the owners of the fractional interests.* An owner receives an undivided interest in the land together with an exclusive leasehold right to occupy a unit. There is only one property tax bill for the entire project.

*Purchasers receive only a right to occupy (leasehold interest) in an apartment unit, while a condo purchaser gets a deed (fee interest) to a unit.*

## C. CONDOMINIUM (Most Common Type)

*A condominium owner gets a deed (fee interest) to a unit and a separate tax bill.*

A *CONDOMINIUM is the ownership of the land and buildings in common with other owners plus the individual ownership of specific air spaces.* A "condominium" is a type of ownership; a "townhouse" is a type of architecture. In a PD, the property owner owns the living unit as well as the lot. Condominiums may be used for residential, industrial, or commercial purposes, although the residential type is most commonly seen in California. Condominium projects having two or more units are defined as subdivisions.

A condominium is the ownership of unit (airspace) and shared ownership of the land and all improvements. Each "condo" has a separate grant deed, trust deed, and tax bill. You "own what you see"; the airspace between the paint on one wall to the paint on the other wall.

In effect, a condominium buyer owns, in fee simple, the air space in which his or her particular unit is situated. He or she receives a separate tax bill for private airspace and percentage share of the common area. Each airspace unit is given a grant deed, and the owner can acquire a title insurance policy. The common area is managed by an elected governing board.

*A copy of the CC&Rs, a copy of the bylaws, and a copy of the most recent financial statement of the condo association must be given to every buyer of a condominium unit.*

### 1. Timesharing

**TIMESHARING** *is a form of ownership where each investor holds a share in a specific unit or home and possesses the right to occupy that home for a specified period each year* (see **Figure 12-4**).

*Fifty-two owners (usually less because of downtime for maintenance) may each own a specific one-week share in one unit at a resort property.*

**Example:** A timeshare company advertises the sale of timeshares on a billboard or the world wide web. If the billboard does not disclose the requirement to listen to a sales presentation in order to receive the promised prize, this is illegal, because the broker did not disclose the requirement to listen to a sales presentation.

### D. STOCK COOPERATIVE (Corporation is the Owner)

A **STOCK COOPERATIVE** *is a corporation that is formed to own the land and improved real property.* A stock cooperative either owns or leases real property. The buyer does not receive a grant deed but owns a share of the corporation and the right to occupy a certain unit. The right to occupy can be transferred only with the share of stock in the corporation.

# VI. Subdivision Advertising

Guidelines for subdividers in advertising and promotions have been developed by the Department of Real Estate. The pamphlet contains filing procedures, requirements and prohibitions on advertising. Since misleading advertising is watched very carefully, it is now a requirement that the public report must be given to each advertising media selected by the subdivider. In addition, a true copy of any advertising proposed for use in connection with a land project offering must be submitted as part of the documentation required prior to the issuance of the public report.

# VII. Environmental Laws

In recent years there has been increasing attention focused on the problems of our environment. These problems include energy, water pollution, air pollution, population growth, preservation of wild life, waste disposal and the quality of life in general. In response, the federal, state and local governments have passed laws and made regulations to help protect us and our environment.

An **ENVIRONMENTAL IMPACT REPORT (EIR)** *is a study of how a subdivision will affect the ecology of a subdivision's surroundings.* An EIR may be required by either city or county authorities prior to their approval of the subdivision map, but some projects may be exempt. In rare cases, the responsibility for the preparation of the EIR will belong to the Department of Real Estate.

**Figure 12-4**

# TIMESHARING:

### *Pro or Con? — You Decide! A chalet at Lake Tahoe...a condo in Palm Springs...beachfront property in La Jolla...*

*TIMESHARING* is a form of ownership where each investor holds a share in a specific unit or home and possesses the right to occupy that home for a specified period each year. For instance, fifty-two owners may each own a one-week share in the property. Each is given a grant deed and each has the right to sell his or her share, rent out the week, or stay there for one seven-day period every year. The ownership week is fixed but it is possible to trade with other owners. Similarly, there are timesharing groups across the country and around the world which allow investors to exchange time with owners of comparable properties in other desirable locations.

## Advantages

The advantages to this kind of ownership are obvious. The buyer has a vacation home without the expense of purchasing the complete home outright. This kind of plan provides access to some of the most unique and scenic property in the world. Once these very special locations are sold, they are gone: they cannot be replaced in the marketplace.

## Disadvantages

On the negative side, these properties tend to be disproportionately high priced. For instance, if you multiplied the cost of one share in a week-based timeshare by an even 50, it would total much more than the market value of the property purchased. Those selling timeshares are burdened with tremendous marketing expenses. Rather than selling once, each property must be sold many times, complete with financing and paperwork.

## Restrictions

A brokerage license is required to sell a timeshare package but, just as with other forms of home sales, owners have the right to transfer their ownership shares without a real estate license and have a 72-hour right of rescission.

*A "Negative Declaration" is a statement by an expert affirming that a new subdivision will have NO negative impact on the environment.*

The voters of California passed Proposition 20 that established the state Coastal Commission to preserve the coastline. This commission has set construction standards for private and public projects within 1,000 yards of the Pacific Ocean or any other body of water. Its purpose is to establish land use planning, which has considerable economic, social, and political overtones.

As part of this law, the commission had to establish a long-range coastal plan. No one seems to agree on the economic effects of Proposition 20, but it did have the result of reducing the number and size of coastal construction projects and required an average of six weeks to pass a project through the commission.

## A. LEAD-BASED PAINT DISCLOSURE (Federal Government)

### Lead-Based Paint Disclosure Pamphlet
### Residential Lead-Based Paint Hazard Reduction Act

The seller or lessor must provide the buyer or lessee with a lead hazard information pamphlet (including disclosure form) and disclose the known presence of any lead-based paint.

The CAR® Residential Purchase Agreement and Joint Escrow Instructions contains a Lead Warning Statement and a statement, to be signed by the buyer, that the buyer has read the warning statement. Also, CAR® has a Lead-Based Paint Hazards Disclosure, Acknowledgment, and Addendum Form (**Figure 12-5**) that can be made a part of a Residential Purchase Agreement, Residential Lease or Month-To-Month Rental Agreement, or some other contract. The EPA's **Lead-Based Paint Renovation, Repair, and Painting Program (RRP)** affects property managers, contractors, and others who disturb painted surfaces. It applies to anyone who performs renovations for compensation in residential houses, apartments, and child-occupied facilities built before 1978. Firms are required to be certified (8-hour training course) and the EPA can impose steep fines or jail time for noncompliance. There *may* be an exception to the training requirement if the property was built after 1978 or the repairs disturb less than six square feet of the interior or twenty square feet of the exterior. Please go to **www.realtor.org/government_affairs/lead_paint_main** for more information.

The agent, on behalf of the seller or lessor, must ensure compliance with the requirements of the law. The purchaser has a **10-day opportunity** to inspect before becoming obligated under the contract.

## B. GEOLOGICAL HAZARD ZONES

Before any real estate development or large structure is built in California, a geological report must be submitted. This report must be compiled by a registered geologist and given to the city in which the development is planned. In the case of a development in an unincorporated area, the report is submitted to the county in which the planned development is located.

If the state geologist approves it, the city or county department may waive such a report as long as there is no earthquake fault activity.

The California Geological Survey (formerly called the Division of Mines and Geology) has mapped every earthquake fault that has hazardous potential or recent activity. These special study zones are found throughout California and new ones are added to the map (see **Figure 12-6**).

Any person buying within such a zone should be informed either by the seller or the real estate licensee of this fact. A buyer who is thinking of building should be cautioned as to the regulations and requirements that may have to be met to develop the land. See **Figure 12-7** for specifics on the Alquist-Priolo Special Studies Zones Act. There are approximately 205 different Geological Survey areas in California. If you want more information about these hazardous zones or copies of the maps, they can be obtained for a small fee.

**Figure 12-5**

CALIFORNIA
ASSOCIATION
OF REALTORS®

### LEAD-BASED PAINT AND LEAD-BASED PAINT HAZARDS DISCLOSURE, ACKNOWLEDGMENT AND ADDENDUM
#### For Pre-1978 Housing Sales, Leases, or Rentals
(C.A.R. Form FLD, Revised 1/03)

The following terms and conditions are hereby incorporated in and made a part of the: ☐ California Residential Purchase Agreement, ☐ Residential Lease or Month-to-Month Rental Agreement, or ☐ other: _____, dated _____, on property known as: _____ ("Property") in

123 Sail Avenue ,

which _____ is referred to as Buyer or Tenant and _____ is referred to as Seller or Landlord.

**LEAD WARNING STATEMENT (SALE OR PURCHASE)** Every purchaser of any interest in residential real property on which a residential dwelling was built prior to 1978 is notified that such property may present exposure to lead from lead-based paint that may place young children at risk of developing lead poisoning. Lead poisoning in young children may produce permanent neurological damage, including learning disabilities, reduced intelligent quotient, behavioral problems and impaired memory. Lead poisoning also poses a particular risk to pregnant women. The seller of any interest in residential real property is required to provide the buyer with any information on lead-based paint hazards from risk assessments or inspections in the seller's possession and notify the buyer of any known lead-based paint hazards. A risk assessment or inspection for possible lead-based paint hazards is recommended prior to purchase.

**LEAD WARNING STATEMENT (LEASE OR RENTAL)** Housing built before 1978 may contain lead-based paint. Lead from paint, paint chips and dust can pose health hazards if not managed properly. Lead exposure is especially harmful to young children and pregnant women. Before renting pre-1978 housing, lessors must disclose the presence of lead-based paint and/or lead-based paint hazards in the dwelling. Lessees must also receive federally approved pamphlet on lead poisoning prevention.

**1. SELLER'S OR LANDLORD'S DISCLOSURE**

I (we) have no knowledge of lead-based paint and/or lead-based paint hazards in the housing other than the following:

_____
_____
_____
_____

I (we) have no reports or records pertaining to lead-based paint and/or lead-based paint hazards in the housing other than the following, which, previously or as an attachment to this addendum have been provided to Buyer or Tenant:

_____
_____
_____

I (we), previously or as an attachment to this addendum, have provided Buyer or Tenant with the pamphlet *"Protect Your Family From Lead In Your Home"* or an equivalent pamphlet approved for use in the State such as *"The Homeowner's Guide to Environmental Hazards and Earthquake Safety."*

For Sales Transactions Only: Buyer has 10 days, unless otherwise agreed in the real estate purchase contract, to conduct a risk assessment or inspection for the presence of lead-based paint and/or lead-based paint hazards.

**I (we) have reviewed the information above and certify, to the best of my (our) knowledge, that the information provided is true and correct.**

_____                                    Date
Seller or Landlord

_____                                    Date
Seller or Landlord

Buyer's Initials ( _____ ) ( _____ )

Reviewed by _____ Date _____

EQUAL HOUSING OPPORTUNITY

**LEAD-BASED PAINT AND LEAD-BASED PAINT HAZARDS DISCLOSURE (FLD PAGE 1 OF 2)**

| Agent: WALT HUBER | Phone: | Fax: | Prepared using zipForm® software |
|---|---|---|---|
| Broker: WALT HUBER REALTOR | | | |

Property Address: _123 Sail Avenue_, _____ Date: _____

## 2. LISTING AGENT'S ACKNOWLEDGMENT

Agent has informed Seller or Landlord of Seller's or Landlord's obligations under §42 U.S.C. 4852d and is aware of Agent's responsibility to ensure compliance.

**I have reviewed the information above and certify, to the best of my knowledge, that the information provided is true and correct.**

_____ By _____
Agent (Broker representing Seller) Please Print     Associate-Licensee or Broker Signature    Date

## 3. BUYER'S OR TENANT'S ACKNOWLEDGMENT

I (we) have received copies of all information listed, if any, in 1 above and the pamphlet *"Protect Your Family From Lead In Your Home"* or an equivalent pamphlet approved for use in the State such as *"The Homeowner's Guide to Environmental Hazards and Earthquake Safety."* **If delivery of any of the disclosures or pamphlet referenced in paragraph 1 above occurs after Acceptance of an offer to purchase, Buyer has a right to cancel pursuant to the purchase contract. If you wish to cancel, you must act within the prescribed period.**

For Sales Transactions Only: Buyer acknowledges the right for 10 days, unless otherwise agreed in the real estate purchase contract, to conduct a risk assessment or inspection for the presence of lead-based paint and/or lead-based paint hazards; OR, (if checked) ☐ Buyer waives the right to conduct a risk assessment or inspection for the presence of lead-based paint and/or lead-based paint hazards.

**I (we) have reviewed the information above and certify, to the best of my (our) knowledge, that the information provided is true and correct.**

_____    _____
Buyer or Tenant      Date      Buyer or Tenant      Date

## 4. COOPERATING AGENT'S ACKNOWLEDGMENT

Agent has informed Seller or Landlord, through the Listing Agent if the property is listed, of Seller's or Landlord's obligations under §42 U.S.C. 4852d and is aware of Agent's responsibility to ensure compliance.

**I have reviewed the information above and certify, to the best of my knowledge, that the information provided is true and correct.**

_____ By _____
Agent (Broker obtaining the Offer)     Associate-Licensee or Broker Signature    Date

**LEAD-BASED PAINT AND LEAD-BASED PAINT HAZARDS DISCLOSURE (FLD PAGE 2 OF 2)**

**Figure 12-6**

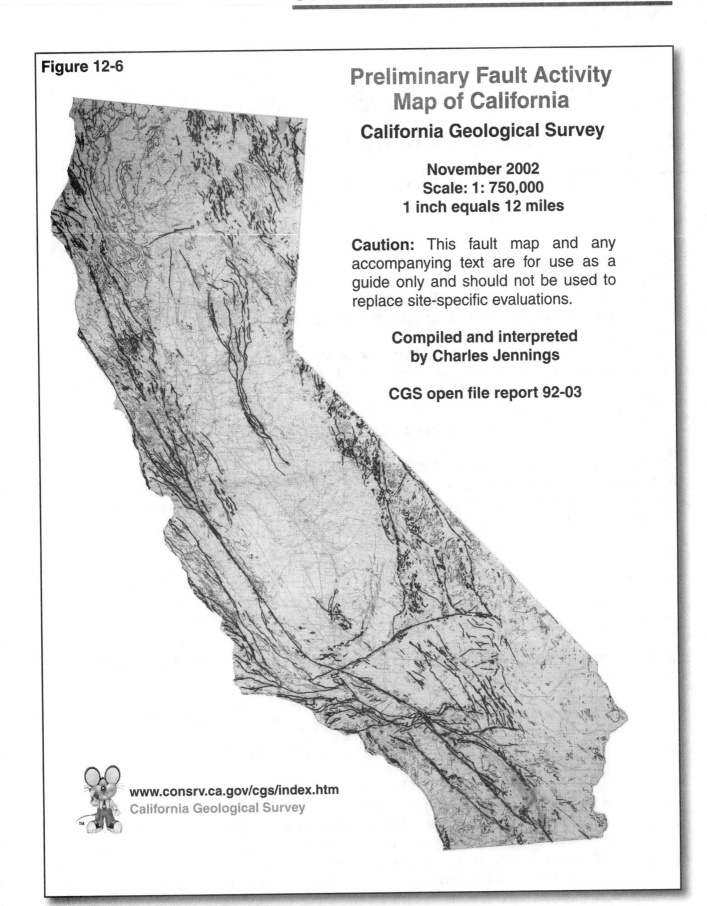

# Preliminary Fault Activity Map of California

## California Geological Survey

November 2002
Scale: 1: 750,000
1 inch equals 12 miles

**Caution:** This fault map and any accompanying text are for use as a guide only and should not be used to replace site-specific evaluations.

**Compiled and interpreted by Charles Jennings**

**CGS open file report 92-03**

www.consrv.ca.gov/cgs/index.htm
California Geological Survey

**Figure 12-7**

# Earthquake Zones

## Alquist-Priolo Special Studies Zones Act

*This is a zoning act designed to control the development in the vicinity (1/4 mile wide strip) of hazardous earthquake faults for the benefit of public safety for the entire state of California.*

The purpose of the Alquist-Priolo Special Studies Zones Act is to assist governmental jurisdictions in the exercise of their responsibility to prohibit the development of structures for human occupancy on top of active earthquakes faults as defined by the state geological survey maps. Developments or structures in existence prior to May 4, 1975, are not affected.

**An earthquake zone normally extends one-quarter of a mile in width**, centered on the trace of a fault, and includes an area that may be hazardous for development or construction of a structure for human occupancy due to surface faulting or fault creep.

### Maps for Special Studies Zone

These maps can be consulted at any district office of the California Geological Survey (formerly named the Division of Mines and Geology). Individuals can obtain copies of these maps at many different local jurisdictions. As a practical matter, the local Multiple Listing Office is one of the most convenient locations to see a map.

*"Any person who is acting as an agent for a seller of real estate that is located within a delineated special studies zone, or the seller who is acting without an agent, shall disclose the fact that the property is located within a delineated special studies zone."*

**Note – Most agents and sellers have a professional company prepare these disclosures for the buyers.**

# VIII. Planning Commission

The primary responsibility of a *CITY or COUNTY PLANNING COMMISSION is to prepare and adopt comprehensive, long-term general plans for the physical development of its area of jurisdiction.* These city or county organizations gather information, cite other examples, and come up with their own innovations in an attempt to make some order out of the chaos into which a city may have fallen. Commissions have discovered that preplanning exactly which types of buildings can go where, before they are constructed, saves more time and money than all the zoning laws made after the building is done. Such planning commissions make predictions to guarantee that today's residential, commercial, and industrial areas will not collide in the future due to expansion of both areas.

*The primary tool used by planning commissions to implement a general plan is zoning.*

## A. MASTER PLAN

Every city and county must have a planning commission. The primary purpose of a Master Plan is to set forth existing and future matters concerning seismic safety, districts, streets, and highways.

Entire new cities can be pre-planned so that zoning laws exist only to enforce and execute the city's master plan. The *MASTER PLAN is a comprehensive guide through which zoning establishes an ideal plan for the city's development in the future. DIRECTIONAL GROWTH is the actual growth path of urban development. Properties in the direction of growth tend to increase in value especially if the growth is steady and rapid.* It is used, by smart investors, to determine where future development will be most profitable. A good example of preplanning is the Irvine Ranch in Orange County, where there is a balance between residential, recreational, commercial, and manufacturing areas. The essential elements of a master plan are:

1. The designation of proposed general distribution, location, and extent of land uses within certain areas.
2. The determination of general traffic patterns, including the extensions of existing and proposed transportation routes, terminals, and other public utility facilities.
3. The setting of standards of population density and building units per acre of various districts and the estimation of future population growth trends. A number of other elements may also be included.

# IX. Zoning (Use)

*Zoning is the city or county exercise of "police power"; rulings are made to control the use of private property for the protection of the public's health, safety, and welfare.*

The power to zone is given by the U.S. Constitution.

*ZONING LAWS regulate the use of property by prescribing what uses that land can be put to and by establishing uniformity throughout the community.* For example, zoning laws may indicate that a specific property can be used only as a single family home, multiple family housing, or for commercial or industrial use. It is possible for the planning commission to change zoning. It can change an area from commercial to residential or change a residential area from R-4 to R-1. This is called down zoning. *DOWNZONING means the land will have less use density.*

*Changing zoning from industrial to residential is called downzoning.*

*INCLUSIONARY ZONING requires builders of new residential housing to provide a certain number of low- and moderate-income units.* No permit will be obtained if the builder does not agree. Sometimes a builder will, in lieu of setting aside inclusionary units, contribute to a fund used to provide low- and moderate-income housing.

# CHAPTER 12

*If zoning conflicts with deed restrictions, the most restrictive controls.*

Zoning laws use the "police power" granted to every county and city to regulate the use, planning, and setbacks of land. Such regulations protect the health, safety, comfort and general welfare of the community. These ordinances are public restrictions to the uses of private property. Counties and cities can set higher standards, which can be much higher than the minimums set by the state. For example, zoning which regulates the use of lands and buildings may specify the following:

1. Location and type of building
2. Height of the structure
3. Size of the building
4. Percentage of a lot the building may occupy
5. Setback requirements from front, back, and sides of the property boundaries.

*Zoning changes can be initiated by local authorities, subdividers, and individuals.*

**Figure 12-8** is an example of a Los Angeles zoning plan. You will notice that there are many symbols that indicate the regulated uses for all the different parts of Los Angeles.

Each symbol represents a different type of zone, but it is possible to make the following generalization about some of the common zoning symbols:

**A** – This symbol usually indicates an *agricultural* area such as farm or ranch land. In a few isolated areas a symbol beginning with "A" stands for an airport.

**C** – The "C" symbol represents *commercial* areas. In these areas anything from an office building to a community shopping center may exist. There are other, more specific, "C" symbols regulating the construction of such commercial properties.

*A "strip commercial development" is a single line of store buildings constructed along a major transportation route.*

**M** – Stands for *manufacturing*. Industrial complexes must be built only in zones classified "M."

*According to local zoning laws, the designation "M" most likely will refer to industrial.*

**P** – Although there are many different interpretations of the "P" symbol, the most important categories it covers are *parking lots* and *parks*.

**R** – The "R" symbol stands for *residential* and is probably the most important symbol to the real estate person. This symbol (and its derivations) designates those areas in which *homes, condominiums,* or *apartments* may be built or maintained.

Each of these symbols is usually followed by a number, for example "R" may be followed by 1, 2, 3, or 4. The number indicates a higher density or use for that particular zone. The following will help explain each use:

**R1** – is for a *single-family* dwelling

**R2** – is for *two dwelling* units

## Figure 12-8

# SUMMARY OF ZONING REGULATIONS
## CITY OF LOS ANGELES

| CLASSIFICATION | ZONE | USE | MAXIMUM HEIGHT STORIES | FEET | REQUIRED YARDS FRONT | SIDE | REAR | MINIMUM AREA PER LOT | PER DWELLING UNIT | MINIMUM LOT WIDTH | PARKING SPACE | EAGLE PRISMACOLOR PENCIL CHART |
|---|---|---|---|---|---|---|---|---|---|---|---|---|
| AGRICULTURAL | A1 | AGRICULTURAL ONE-FAMILY DWELLINGS - PARKS - PLAY-GROUNDS - COMMUNITY CENTERS GOLF COURSES - TRUCK GARDENING - EXTENSIVE AGRICULTURAL USES | 3 | 45 FT. | 25 FT. | 25 FT MAXIMUM 10% LOT WIDTH 3 FT. MINIMUM | 25 FT | 5 ACRES | 2½ ACRES | 300 FT. | TWO SPACES PER DWELLING UNIT | 909 GRASS GREEN |
| | A2 | AGRICULTURAL A1 USES | 3 | 45 FT. | 25 FT. | 25 FT MAXIMUM 10% LOT WIDTH 3 FT. MINIMUM | 25 FT | 2 ACRES | 1 ACRE | 150 FT | TWO SPACES PER DWELLING UNIT | 912 APPLE GREEN |
| | RA | SUBURBAN LIMITED AGRICULTURAL USES | 3 | 45 FT. | 25 FT. | 10'-1&2 STORIES 11'-3 STORIES | 25 FT | 17,500 SQ. FT. ✱ | 17,500 SQ. FT. ✱ | 70 FT. ✱ | TWO GARAGE SPACES PER DWELLING UNIT | 910 TRUE GREEN |
| ONE FAMILY RESIDENTIAL | RE40 | RESIDENTIAL ESTATE ONE-FAMILY DWELLINGS PARKS PLAYGROUNDS COMMUNITY CENTERS TRUCK GARDENING | 3 | 45 FT. | 25 FT | 10 FT | 25 FT | 40,000 SQ. FT. ✱ | 40,000 SQ. FT. ✱ | 80 FT. ✱ | TWO GARAGE SPACES PER DWELLING UNIT | 950 GOLD |
| | RE20 | | | | 25 FT | 10 FT | 25 FT | 20,000 SQ. FT. ✱ | 20,000 SQ. FT. ✱ | 80 FT. ✱ | | |
| | RE15 | | | | 25 FT | 10 FT. MAXIMUM 10% LOT WIDTH 5 FT. MINIMUM | 25 FT | 15,000 SQ. FT. ✱ | 15,000 SQ. FT. ✱ | 80 FT. ✱ | | |
| | RE11 | | | | 25 FT | 5'-1&2 STORIES 6'-3 STORIES | 25 FT | 11,000 SQ. FT. ✱ | 11,000 SQ. FT. ✱ | 70 FT. ✱ | | |
| | RE9 | | | | 25 FT | 5 FT. MAXIMUM 10% LOT WIDTH 3 FT. MINIMUM | 25 FT | 9,000 SQ. FT. ✱ | 9,000 SQ. FT. ✱ | 65 FT. ✱ | | |
| | RS | SUBURBAN ONE-FAMILY DWELLINGS - PARKS PLAYGROUNDS - TRUCK GARDENING | 3 | 45 FT. | 25 FT. | 5'-1&2 STORIES 6'-3 STORIES | 20 FT | 7,500 SQ FT | 7,500 SQ. FT. | 60 FT | TWO GARAGE SPACES PER DWELLING UNIT | 911 OLIVE GREEN |
| | R1 | ONE-FAMILY DWELLING RS USES | 3 | 45 FT. | 20 FT. | 5'-1&2 STORIES 6'-3 STORIES | 15 FT | 5,000 SQ FT | 5,000 SQ. FT. | 50 FT | TWO GARAGE SPACES PER DWELLING UNIT | 916 CANARY YELLOW |
| | RW1 | ONE-FAMILY RESIDENTIAL WATERWAYS ZONE | 3 | 45 FT. | 10 FT. | 4' PLUS 1' EACH STORY ABOVE 2 ½ 10% LOT WIDTH | 15 FT. | 2,300 SQ FT | 2,300 SQ FT | 28 FT | TWO GARAGE SPACES PER DWELLING UNIT | 914 CREAM |
| | RW2 | TWO-FAMILY RESIDENTIAL WATERWAYS ZONE | | | | | | | 1,150 SQ FT | | | |
| MULTIPLE RESIDENTIAL | R2 | TWO-FAMILY DWELLING R1 USES TWO-FAMILY DWELLINGS | 3 | 45 FT. | 20 FT. | 5'-1&2 STORIES 6'-3 STORIES | 15 FT | 5,000 SQ FT | 2,500 SQ FT | 50 FT | TWO SPACES ONE IN A GARAGE | 917 YELLOW ORANGE |
| | RD1.5 | RESTRICTED DENSITY MULTIPLE DWELLING ZONE TWO-FAMILY DWELLING APARTMENT HOUSES MULTIPLE DWELLINGS | HEIGHT DISTRICT NO. 1 3 STORIES 45 FT. HEIGHT DISTRICT NOS 2,3 OR 4 6 STORIES 75 FT. | | 20 FT | 6 FT | 20 FT. | 6,000 SQ FT | 1,500 SQ FT | 60 FT | ONE SPACE EACH DWELLING UNIT OF LESS THAN THREE ROOMS ONE AND ONE HALF SPACES EACH DWELLING UNIT OF THREE ROOMS TWO SPACES EACH DWELLING UNIT OF MORE THEN THREE ROOMS ONE SPACE EACH GUEST ROOM (FIRST THIRTY) | 940 SAND |
| | RD2 | | | | 20 FT | 10 FT | 25 FT. | 8,000 SQ FT | 2,000 SQ FT | 60 FT | | |
| | RD3 | | | | | | | 12,000 SQ FT | 3,000 SQ. FT. | 70 FT | | |
| | RD4 | | | | | | | | 4,000 SQ FT | | | |
| | RD5 | | | | | | | | 5,000 SQ FT | | | |
| | RD6 | | | | | | | | 6,000 SQ. FT. | | | |
| | R3 | MULTIPLE DWELLING R2 USES APARTMENT HOUSES MULTIPLE DWELLINGS | | | 15 FT. | 5'-1&2 STORIE 6'-3 STORIES | 15 FT. | 5,000 SQ. FT. | 800 TO 1,200 SQ. FT. | 50 FT | | 918 ORANGE |
| | R4 | MULTIPLE DWELLING R3 USES CHURCHES HOTELS-SCHOOLS | UNLIMITED ✱ | | 15 FT. | 5' PLUS 1' EACH STORY ABOVE 2½ 16 FT. MAX | 15' PLUS 1' EACH STORY ABOVE 3½ 20 FT. MAX. | 5,000 SQ FT | 400 TO 800 SQ. FT. | 50 FT | | 943 BURNT OCHRE |
| | R5 | MULTIPLE DWELLING R4 USES CLUBS - HOSPITALS LODGES - SANITARIUMS | UNLIMITED ✱ | | 15 FT. | 5' PLUS 1' EACH STORY ABOVE 2½ 16 FT. MAX. | 15' PLUS 1' EACH STORY ABOVE 3½ 20 FT MAX | 5,000 SQ FT | 200 TO 400 SQ. FT. | 50 FT | | 946 DARK BROWN |

✱ SEE HEIGHT DISTRICTS AT THE BOTTOM OF PAGE 2

● FOR TWO OR MORE LOTS THE INTERIOR SIDE YARDS MAY BE ELIMINATED, BUT 4 FT IS REQUIRED ON EACH SIDE OF THE GROUPED LOTS.

✱ "H" HILLSIDE OR MOUNTAINOUS AREA DESIGNATION MAY ALTER THESE REQUIREMENTS IN THE RA-H OR RE-H ZONES.
SUBDIVISIONS MAY BE APPROVED WITH SMALLER LOTS, PROVIDING LARGER LOTS ARE ALSO INCLUDED EACH LOT MAY BE USED
FOR ONLY ONE SINGLE-FAMILY DWELLING SEE MINIMUM WIDTH & AREA REQUIREMENTS BELOW.

| ZONE COMBINATION | MINIMUM TO WHICH NET AREA MAY BE REDUCED | MINIMUM TO WHICH LOT WIDTH MAY BE REDUCED |
|---|---|---|
| RA-H | 14,000 SQ FT | 63 FT |
| RE 9 -H | 7,200 SQ FT | 60 FT |
| RE11 -H, | 8,800 SQ FT | 63 FT |
| RE15 -H | 12,000 SQ FT | 72 FT |
| RE20 -H | 16,000 SQ FT | 72 FT |
| RE 40 -H | 32,000 SQ FT | NO REDUCTION |

SHEET 1 OF 2                    CP FORM 10

PREPARED BY CITY PLANNING DEPARTMENT

# SUMMARY OF ZONING REGULATIONS
## CITY OF LOS ANGELES

| CLASSIFICATION | ZONE | USE | MAXIMUM HEIGHT STORIES | MAXIMUM HEIGHT FEET | REQUIRED YARDS FRONT | REQUIRED YARDS SIDE | REQUIRED YARDS REAR | MINIMUM AREA PER LOT AND UNIT | MINIMUM LOT WIDTH | LOADING SPACE | PARKING SPACE | EAGLE PRISMACOLOR PENCIL CHART |
|---|---|---|---|---|---|---|---|---|---|---|---|---|
| COMMERCIAL (RESIDENTIAL USES (EXCEPT HOTELS) PROHIBITED UNLESS CONDITIONAL USE IS APPROVED BY ZONING ADMINISTRATOR) | CR | LIMITED COMMERCIAL — BANKS, CLUBS, HOTELS, CHURCHES, SCHOOLS, BUSINESS & PROFESSIONAL OFFICES, PARKING AREAS | 6 | 75 FT. | 10 FEET | 5'-10' CORNER LOT, RESIDENTIAL USE OR ADJOINING AN "A" OR "R" ZONE SAME AS R4 ZONE | 15' PLUS 1' EACH STORY ABOVE 3rd OTHERWISE NONE | SAME AS R4 FOR DWELLINGS OTHERWISE NONE | | HOSPITALS, HOTELS INSTITUTIONS, AND WITH EVERY BUILDING WHERE LOT ABUTS ALLEY | ONE SPACE FOR EACH 500 SQ. FT. OF FLOOR AREA | 939 FLESH |
| | C1 | LIMITED COMMERCIAL — LOCAL RETAIL STORES, OFFICES OR BUSINESSES, HOTELS, LIMITED HOSPITALS AND/OR CLINICS, PARKING AREAS | UNLIMITED * | | | 3'-5' CORNER LOT OR ADJOINING AN "A" OR "R" ZONE | 15' PLUS 1' EACH STORY ABOVE 3rd RESIDENTIAL USE OR ABUTTING AN "A" OR "R" ZONE OTHERWISE NONE | SAME AS R3 FOR DWELLINGS EXCEPT 5000 SQ FT PER UNIT IN CI-H ZONES — OTHERWISE NONE | 50 FEET FOR RESIDENCE USE OTHERWISE NONE | MINIMUM LOADING SPACE 400 SQUARE FEET | ONE SPACE FOR EACH 500 SQUARE FEET OF FLOOR AREA IN ALL BUILDINGS ON ANY LOT MUST BE LOCATED WITHIN 750 FEET OF BUILDING | 929 PINK |
| | C1.5 | LIMITED COMMERCIAL — C1 USES — DEPARTMENT STORES, THEATRES, BROADCASTING STUDIOS, PARKING BUILDINGS, PARKS & PLAYGROUNDS | | | | RESIDENTIAL USE SAME AS R4 ZONE | | | | ADDITIONAL SPACE REQUIRED FOR BUILDINGS CONTAINING MORE THAN 50,000 SQUARE FEET OF FLOOR AREA | | 928 BLUSH |
| | C2 | COMMERCIAL — C1.5 USES — RETAIL BUSINESSES WITH LIMITED MANUFACTURING, AUTO SERVICE STATION & GARAGE, RETAIL, CONTRACTORS BUSINESSES, CHURCHES, SCHOOLS | | | NONE | NONE FOR COMMERCIAL BUILDINGS RESIDENTIAL USES — SAME AS IN R4 ZONE | NONE FOR COMMERCIAL BUILDINGS RESIDENTIAL USES — SAME AS IN R4 ZONE | SAME AS R4 FOR DWELLINGS OTHERWISE NONE | | NONE REQUIRED FOR APARTMENT BUILDINGS 20 UNITS OR LESS | SEE CODE FOR ASSEMBLY AREAS, HOSPITALS AND CLINICS | 922 SCARLET RED |
| | C4 | COMMERCIAL — C2 USES — (WITH EXCEPTIONS, SUCH AS AUTO SERVICE STATIONS, AMUSEMENT ENTERPRISES, CONTRACTORS BUSINESSES, SECOND-HAND BUSINESSES) | | | | | | | | | | 924 CRIMSON RED |
| | C5 | COMMERCIAL — C2 USES — LIMITED FLOOR AREAS FOR LIGHT MANUFACTURING OF THE CM-ZONE TYPE | | | | | | | | | | 925 CRIMSON LAKE |
| | CM | COMM'L MANUFACTURING — WHOLESALE BUSINESSES, STORAGE BUILDINGS, CLINICS, LIMITED MANUFACTURING, C2 USES — EXCEPT HOSPITALS, SCHOOLS, CHURCHES | | | | | | SAME AS R3 FOR DWELLINGS OTHERWISE NONE | | | | 905 AQUA-MARINE |
| INDUSTRIAL (RESIDENTIAL USES PROHIBITED IN ALL INDUSTRIAL ZONES) | MR1 | RESTRICTED INDUSTRIAL — CM USES — LIMITED COMMERCIAL & MANUFACTURING USES, HOSPITALS, CLINICS, SANITARIUMS, LIMITED MACHINE SHOPS | UNLIMITED * | | 15 FT. | NONE FOR INDUSTRIAL OR COMMERCIAL BUILDINGS RESIDENTIAL USES — SAME AS IN R4 ZONE | NONE FOR INDUSTRIAL OR COMMERCIAL BUILDINGS RESIDENTIAL USES — SAME AS IN R4 ZONE | | | HOSPITALS, HOTELS INSTITUTIONS, AND WITH EVERY BUILDING WHERE LOT ABUTS ALLEY | ONE SPACE FOR EACH 500 SQUARE FEET OF FLOOR AREA IN ALL BUILDINGS ON ANY LOT | 901 INDIGO BLUE |
| | MR2 | RESTRICTED LIGHT INDUSTRIAL — MR1 USES — ADDITION INDUSTRIAL USES, MORTUARIES, AGRICULTURE | | | | | | SAME AS R4 FOR DWELLINGS OTHERWISE NONE | 50 FEET FOR RESIDENCE USE OTHERWISE NONE | MINIMUM LOADING SPACE 400 SQUARE FEET | MUST BE LOCATED WITHIN 750 FEET OF BUILDING | 906 COPENHAGEN BLUE |
| | M1 | LIMITED INDUSTRIAL — CM USES — LIMITED INDUSTRIAL & MANUFACTURING USES — NO "R" ZONE USES, NO HOSPITALS, SCHOOLS OR CHURCHES | | | NONE | | | | | ADDITIONAL SPACE REQUIRED FOR BUILDINGS CONTAINING MORE THAN 50,000 SQUARE FEET OF FLOOR AREA | | 904 LIGHT BLUE |
| | M2 | LIGHT INDUSTRIAL — M1 USES — ADDITIONAL INDUSTRIAL USES, STORAGE YARDS OF ALL KINDS, ANIMAL KEEPING — NO "R" ZONE USES | | | | | | | | | SEE CODE FOR ASSEMBLY AREAS, HOSPITALS AND CLINICS | 902 ULTRA-MARINE |
| | M3 | HEAVY INDUSTRIAL — M2 USES — ANY INDUSTRIAL USES — NUISANCE USES — 500 FT. FROM ANY OTHER ZONE — NO "R" ZONE USES | | | | NONE | NONE | NONE — NOTE — "R" ZONE USES PROHIBITED | NONE | NONE REQUIRED FOR APARTMENT BUILDINGS 20 UNITS OR LESS | | 931 PURPLE |
| PARKING | P | AUTOMOBILE PARKING — SURFACE & UNDERGROUND — PROPERTY IN A "P" ZONE MAY ALSO BE IN AN "A" OR "R" ZONE. PARKING PERMITTED IN LIEU OF AGRICULTURAL OR RESIDENTIAL USES | | | | | | NONE UNLESS ALSO IN AN "A" OR "R" ZONE | NONE UNLESS ALSO IN AN "A" OR "R" ZONE | | | 967 COLD GREY LIGHT |
| | PB | PARKING BUILDING — AUTOMOBILE PARKING WITHIN OR WITHOUT A BUILDING | ** | — | 0', 5', OR 10' DEPENDING ON ZONING IN BLOCK AND ACROSS STREET | 5' PLUS 1' EACH STORY ABOVE 2nd IF ABUTTING OR ACROSS STREET FROM "A" OR "R" ZONE | 8' PLUS 1' EACH STORY ABOVE 2nd IF ABUTTING AN "A" OR "R" ZONE, TO A 16' MAXIMUM | NONE | NONE | | | 936 SLATE GREY |
| SPECIAL | SL | SUBMERGED LAND ZONE — COMMERCIAL SHIPPING, NAVIGATION, FISHING, RECREATION | | | | | | | | | | 919 SKY BLUE |
| | (T) | TENTATIVE CLASSIFICATION — USED IN COMBINATION WITH ZONE CHANGE ONLY - DELAYS ISSUANCE OF BUILDING PERMIT UNTIL SUBDIVISION OR PARCEL MAP RECORDED | | | | | | | | | | |
| | (F) | FUNDED IMPROVEMENT CLASSIFICATION — AN ALTERNATE MEANS OF EFFECTING ZONE CHANGES AND SECURING IMPROVEMENTS (WHEN NO SUBDIVISION OR DEDICATIONS ARE INVOLVED) | | | | | | | | | | |
| | (Q) | QUALIFIED CLASSIFICATION — USED IN COMBINATION WITH ZONE CHANGES ONLY EXCEPT WITH RA, RE, RS OR R1 ZONES - RESTRICTS USES OF PROPERTY AND ASSURES DEVELOPMENT COMPATIBLE WITH THE SURROUNDING PROPERTY | | | | | | | | | | |

**SUPPLEMENTAL USE DISTRICTS** (ESTABLISHED IN CONJUNCTION WITH ZONES): G ROCK AND GRAVEL • O OIL DRILLING • S ANIMAL SLAUGHTERING • RPD RESIDENTIAL PLANNED DEVELOPMENT • K HORSE-KEEPING

**HEIGHT DISTRICT**

| | |
|---|---|
| Nº 1 | FLOOR AREA OF MAIN BUILDING MAY NOT EXCEED THREE TIMES THE BUILDING AREA OF THE LOT |
| Nº 1L | SAME AS Nº 1 AND MAXIMUM HEIGHT - 6 STORIES OR 75 FT. |
| Nº 1-VL | SAME AS Nº 1 AND MAXIMUM HEIGHT - 3 STORIES OR 45 FT |
| Nº 2 | FLOOR AREA OF MAIN BUILDING MAY NOT EXCEED SIX TIMES THE BUILDABLE AREA OF THE LOT |
| Nº 3 | FLOOR AREA OF MAIN BUILDING MAY NOT EXCEED TEN TIMES THE BUILDABLE AREA OF THE LOT |
| Nº 4 | FLOOR AREA OF MAIN BUILDING MAY NOT EXCEED THIRTEEN TIMES THE BUILDABLE AREA OF THE LOT |

**MAXIMUM PB ZONE HEIGHTS**

| | |
|---|---|
| Nº 1 | 2 STORIES AND ROOF |
| Nº 2 | 6 STORIES |
| Nº 3 | 10 STORIES |
| Nº 4 | 13 STORIES |

NOTE: ALL INFORMATION GENERAL - FOR SPECIFIC DETAILS CHECK WITH DEPARTMENT OF BUILDING AND SAFETY

SHEET 2 OF 2

PREPARED BY CITY PLANNING DEPARTMENT

**R3** – is for *multiple-family dwellings* depending on square footage and height of apartment buildings, condos, etc. **The typical zoning for multiple-family residential units is R-3.**

**R4** – is for *higher density multiple dwellings with certain square footage.*

**R5** – *requirements and maximum height allowable* concerning motels, hotels, and high-rise apartments or condominiums.

*Zoning restrictions reduce the buildable area by requiring setbacks from the front, back, and sides of the lot lines.*

**Figure 12-9** is a math problem using setbacks to determine the buildable area of a lot. Remember that all the above explanations are general and may vary. You should investigate any individual symbol for its exact meaning in your city or county before interpreting it.

*Title insurance does NOT give protection for zoning changes.*

## A. ZONING REGULATION (Controls Use)

*Zoning is police power that controls only the "use" of the property, NOT ownership.*

Most planning commissions, boards, or city councils have an established procedure for a change of zoning. As part of a logical procedure, four steps are usually followed. They are:

1. Giving public notice of any proposed zoning changes.
2. Calling a public hearing where interested people can voice their opinions before any changes are made.
3. Adoption or rejection of a zoning regulation.
4. If rejected, an appeal can be made to the city council, which can overrule the planning commission.

Once zoning regulations are enacted, the objecting parties have the right to appeal to the courts on the basis that the ordinance may be arbitrary or unreasonable. The usual grounds for appeal is equal protection under the ordinance. Zoning ordinances have been held invalid when it was shown that a monopoly would be created, the new ordinance rendered an adjoining lot worthless, or when it prohibited an existing business that did not create a nuisance.

Although the intent of zoning is to create reasonable uniformity, total uniformity is not required. Spot zoning might benefit the public in some cases. *SPOT ZONING is a small area that is zoned differently from the surrounding area.* For example, controlled use of commercial stores and service stations can enhance the value and utility of the residential area.

## B. NONCONFORMING USE

As conditions in the area change, the zoning of existing parcels may also change. The change may cause some of the existing structures to become nonconforming. *NONCONFORMING USE is a property that is not used according to the current zoning, but which existed legally before zoning changes were enacted.* An example of nonconforming use is an apartment building with one parking space per unit where zoning changes require two parking spaces per unit. It is a general policy to let nonconforming uses continue for a time if conformity creates unnecessary hardships. However, the growing trend is for cities to charge large fees for nonconforming properties as a source of income.

**Figure 12-9**

# SETBACK PROBLEM
## *(Zoning Regulations)*

*BUILDABLE AREA is the maximum allowable area of a lot that a city or county allows for a building after deducting setbacks from the front, back, and sides.*

### DETERMINING USABLE AREA

**Question:** What is the buildable space of a lot 150 feet by 50 feet if the city zoning regulation requires deducting a 20-foot setback from the front and deducting 4 feet from each side and the back?

**150 Feet x 50 Feet**

4-Foot Setback

20-Foot Setback      ***Buildable Area?***      4-Foot Setback

4-Foot Setback

### ANSWER:

Width: 50 feet minus (4 feet on both the left and right side) =  ?
50 feet - 8 Feet = **42 feet buildable width**

Length: 150 feet minus (20-foot front setback and a 4-foot rear setback) = ?
150 feet - 24 feet = **126 feet buildable length**

### TOTAL:

Width x Length  = Area
42 feet x 126 feet= Area
42 feet x 126 feet= **5,292 SQUARE FEET**

*A "grandfather" clause is "prearranged" and allows an owner to continue using his or her property in a way prohibited by the new zoning (nonconforming use).*

### C. VARIANCE (For Private Hardship)

One way to provide reasonable conformity is to allow zoning variances. A *VARIANCE is an exception to the existing zoning regulations in cases of special need for circumstances that might create serious hardship for property owners.* Zoning restrictions such as setbacks may be removed by petitioning for a variance.

For example, if an individual wants to construct a building that does not comply with the local zoning rule, he or she may petition for a variance. When filing this petition, the individual must prove that the construction of the building will not be detrimental to the public. Variances are often granted with special conditions such that both plans and construction be approved and initiated within a specified time.

### D. CONDITIONAL USE PERMIT (For Public Benefit)

A *CONDITIONAL USE PERMIT is an exception to the current zoning for the public welfare or benefit.* Variances, on the other hand, are based on hardship.

Since zoning ordinances may be altered, most title insurance policies do not insure against zoning changes. For a small fee, an endorsement may be added to the title insurance policy that covers any losses due to zoning changes. Zoning is an environmental control that attempts to ensure uniform land use while also meeting the occasional special needs of the community.

# X. Housing, Building, and Health Laws

The basic control of housing, building, and health standards is held at the state level. Although building codes and health standards are usually enforced by the local county and city agencies, contractors, factory home builders, and house builders are always regulated at the state level.

*Regulatory authority of the housing and construction industry is accomplished by the state contractor's license laws, the local building codes, and the State Housing Law.*

### A. STATE HOUSING LAW

California has adopted a State Housing Law that sets the minimum construction and occupancy requirements for all apartments, hotels and other dwellings. It should be noted that any city or county may impose more stringent requirements if it so wishes. Construction regulations under this law are handled by local building inspectors. Occupancy and sanitation regulations are enforced by local health officers.

### B. LOCAL BUILDING CODES

*If there is a building code conflict, the highest construction standard controls.*

Most cities and counties have additional, more stringent construction standards than the state. The *BUILDING CODE is the basic minimum construction standard for a structure.* This code includes regulation of all the basic methods, materials, and components of a structure from the foundation to the plumbing and electrical system. Local building inspectors enforce both the state and local building codes.

New construction or building alterations require a building permit. A **BUILDING PERMIT** *is an approved building application that includes plans, specifications, and a plot plan.* After an examination of the application, plans and any revisions of the plans, the building permit is issued. No construction or alteration can be started until the building permit has been issued.

## C. GOVERNMENT FINANCING REQUIREMENTS

To obtain certain forms of government financing toward the purchase of a home, various construction requirements must be met. These **Minimum Property Requirements (MPRs)** are usually more restrictive than state housing or local building codes. This indirect type of regulation must be considered if any FHA, VA, or CalVet financing is needed.

## D. FACTORY-BUILT HOUSING LAW

The state has preempted local building codes concerning factory-built housing (prefabricated homes). These are homes that are built in sections in a factory and assembled on site. Each section is checked at the factory by state inspectors. Local inspectors oversee only the site hookup of water lines and other on-site facilities.

### 1. Manufactured Housing

*A manufactured home is transferred with a certificate of title.*

> **MANUFACTURED HOUSING,** *is a transportable structure in one or more eight-foot (or more) wide by 40-foot (or more) long sections that will cover 320 or more square feet that meets HUD Code Standards.* Built on a permanent chassis, it is designed to be used with or without permanent foundation when connected to the necessary utilities. If sold in California, it must meet the California Department of Housing standards.
>
> Real estate salespeople can also sell, lease, or finance manufactured homes as soon as they have been transformed into real property (wheels removed, placed on a foundation, and having a building permit).

*A broker can sell a manufactured home if it is registered with the Department of Housing and Community Development (HCD).*

> Real Estate brokers can sell manufactured homes once they are considered real property. A real estate broker must report all sales of manufactured homes within ten calendar days to the Department of Housing and Community Development (HCD). Registration cards, title, and fees are also sent there.

*An agent or licensee is able to sell any new manufactured home sold with a deed.*

> A new manufactured home dealer must be licensed by the Department of Housing and Community Development.

*A licensee who sells a personal property manufactured home must notify the local Department of Housing and Community Development in writing within 10 calendar days.*

New manufactured homes, a growing industry, can only be sold by licensed manufactured home dealers. The **Manufactured Home Purchase Agreement and Joint Escrow Instructions** form is available from CAR®. See **Figure 12-10** for page 1 of this 10-page form.

A licensee must withdraw any advertisement of a manufactured home within 48 hours after notice that it is no longer available for sale.

## E. CONTRACTOR'S STATE LICENSE LAW

*Construction work of less than $500 does NOT require a contractor's license.*

Contractors are licensed at the state level by the Contractor's State License Board, whose main purpose is to protect the public against incompetent building contractors and subcontractors. This protection is achieved by requiring construction to be done only by licensed persons. This includes subcontract work as well as general and engineering contract work.

The construction field is divided into general engineering, general building and specialty contracting. A license is required to perform work in any of these categories. Examinations are prepared on legal matters affecting construction and cost estimation. Each applicant is further required to have a certain amount of actual experience in his or her particular field. Only construction work done on one's own home without intent to sell or lease may be undertaken without a license, but still requires a building permit.

The state housing law, administered by the codes and standards division, is designed to provide that minimum construction and occupancy standards are met.

## F. HEALTH AND SANITATION (County Function)

The California State Department of Health regulates a statewide health program. Even though the state regulates it, local health officials are required by law to be appointed in every city or county. These officials enforce either state or local health laws, whichever is stricter. Health inspectors also act as health advisors. They can close down any proposed development that may cause contamination of the water supply or drainage systems, as well as any development that would cause improper sewage disposal. Furthermore, the sanitary condition of all housing is subject to control by the health authorities.

# XI. Eminent Domain

## A. EMINENT DOMAIN (Involuntary Taking – Condemnation)

*INVOLUNTARY CONVERSION is the legal conversion of real property to personal property (money) without the voluntary act of the owner.* This occurs when property is taken by eminent domain (condemnation).

Eminent domain is an involuntary conversion process, which means that the owner receives money and is allowed to buy another property, within three years, without incurring taxes.

The owner is allowed to convert back to real property (buy another property) without paying tax on the gain from the condemnation. This must be done within a three-year period and the prices of the old and new property are considered to form a new tax base. (Tax laws are complicated and subject to change, so professional tax advice is always wise.)

## Figure 12-10

CALIFORNIA
ASSOCIATION
OF REALTORS

**MANUFACTURED HOME PURCHASE AGREEMENT
AND JOINT ESCROW INSTRUCTIONS**
(C.A.R. Form MHPA, Revised 4/10)

Date _____

1. **OFFER:**
   A. **THIS IS AN OFFER FROM** _____ ("Buyer").
   B. **THE MANUFACTURED HOME TO BE ACQUIRED** is described in paragraph 1E and F below ("Property").
   C. **THE PURCHASE PRICE** offered is _____
      _____ (Dollars $ _____ ).
   D. **CLOSE OF ESCROW** shall occur on _____ (date) (or ☐ _____ **Days** After Acceptance).
   E. **TYPE OF MANUFACTURED HOME:** (Check the box below that applies: paragraphs (1)(a), (1)(b) or (2). Check ONLY one.)
      **(1) PERSONAL PROPERTY MANUFACTURED HOME:**
         **(a)** ☐ **A Manufactured Home On Leased Or Rented Land** (complete paragraph F).
            Space Number _____ Park Name _____
         **OR (b)** ☐ **A Manufactured Home To Be Sold With Real Property** (complete paragraph F). Real Property described as _____
            _____
            **PURCHASE PRICE ALLOCATED AS FOLLOWS:** Manufactured Home $ _____ , Land $ _____
      **OR (2)** ☐ **A REAL PROPERTY MANUFACTURED HOME** (complete applicable parts of paragraph F) described as *123 Sail Avenue* _____
         _____
         Assessor's Parcel No. _____ , situated in _____
         _____ , County of _____ , California.
         A real property manufactured home is one that meets the following requirements: **(i)** a building permit is obtained from local authorities pursuant to Health and Safety Code §18551; **(ii)** the manufactured home is affixed to a foundation pursuant to Health and Safety Code §18551; **(iii)** a certificate of occupancy is issued by local authorities; and **(iv)** there is recordation with the local authorities of a form pursuant to Health and Safety Code §18551.
   F. **ADDITIONAL DESCRIPTION:**
      Manufacturer's Name _____ Model _____ Date Of Manufacture _____
      Date Of First Sale _____
      Property is: ☐ On Local Property Tax Roll, ☐ Department of Housing and Community Development ("HCD") registered (use tax applies)
      Approximate Width _____ Approximate Length _____ (Without Hitch) Expando Size _____
      HCD/HUD License/Decal Number _____
      SERIAL NUMBERS:    1. _____    2. _____    3. _____
      HCD/HUD Label/Insignia: 1. _____  2. _____  3. _____
2. **AGENCY:**
   A. **DISCLOSURE:** Buyer and Seller each acknowledge prior receipt of a "Disclosure Regarding Real Estate Agency Relationships" (C.A.R. Form AD).
   B. **POTENTIALLY COMPETING BUYERS AND SELLERS:** Buyer and Seller each acknowledge receipt of a disclosure of the possibility of multiple representation by the Broker representing that principal. This disclosure may be part of a listing agreement, buyer representation agreement or separate document (C.A.R. Form DA). Buyer understands that Broker representing Buyer may also represent other potential buyers, who may consider, make offers on or ultimately acquire the Property. Seller understands that Broker representing Seller may also represent other sellers with competing properties of interest to this Buyer.
   C. **CONFIRMATION:** The following agency relationships are hereby confirmed for this transaction:
      Listing Agent _____ (Print Firm Name) is the agent of (check one):
      ☐ the Seller exclusively; or ☐ both the Buyer and Seller.
      Selling Agent _____ (Print Firm Name) (if not the same as the Listing Agent) is the agent of (check one): ☐ the Buyer exclusively; or ☐ the Seller exclusively; or ☐ both the Buyer and Seller. Real Estate Brokers are not parties to the Agreement between Buyer and Seller.
3. **FINANCE TERMS:** Buyer represents that funds will be good when deposited with Escrow Holder.
   A. **INITIAL DEPOSIT:** Deposit shall be in the amount of . . . . . . . . . . . . . . . . . . . . . . . . . . . . . . . . . . $ _____
      **(1)** Buyer shall deliver deposit directly to Escrow Holder by personal check, ☐ electronic funds transfer, ☐ Other _____ within 3 business days after acceptance for (or ☐ Other _____ ).
      **OR (2)** (If checked) ☐ Buyer has given the deposit by personal check (or ☐ _____ ) to the agent submitting the offer (or to ☐ _____ ), made payable to _____ . The deposit shall be held uncashed until Acceptance and then deposited with Escrow Holder (or ☐ into Broker's trust account) within 3 business days after Acceptance (or ☐ Other _____ ).
   B. **INCREASED DEPOSIT:** Buyer shall deposit with Escrow Holder an increased deposit in the amount of. . . $ _____ within _____ **Days** After Acceptance, or ☐ _____ . If a liquidated damages clause is incorporated into this Agreement, Buyer and Seller shall sign a separate liquidated damages clause (C.A.R. Form RID) for any increased deposit at the time it is deposited.

Buyer's Initials ( _____ ) ( _____ )                    Seller's Initials ( _____ ) ( _____ )

**MHPA REVISED 4/10 (PAGE 1 OF 10)**

Reviewed by _____ Date _____

EQUAL HOUSING
OPPORTUNITY

**MANUFACTURED HOME PURCHASE AGREEMENT AND JOINT ESCROW INSTRUCTIONS (MHPA PAGE 1 OF 10)**

Agent: WALT HUBER          Phone:          Fax:          Prepared using zipForm® software
Broker: WALT HUBER REALTOR

*EMINENT DOMAIN is the right of the federal or state government to take private property from a landowner (with the fair market value paid as compensation to that owner) for the "public good."* The use of the right of eminent domain is often referred to as "condemnation."

*Property taken by the local government under the power of eminent domain must have fair and just compensation to the landowner.*

If a portion of a parcel is condemned, then there may be severance damages. *SEVERANCE DAMAGE is the compensation paid an owner for "devalued remaining property" as the result of an eminent domain action.*

In some instances, the property owner will feel that the property is so devalued that he or she will file an inverse condemnation action. *INVERSE CONDEMNATION is an action whereby the property owner files suit to force the government to purchase all or part of his or her property.*

**Example:** Airplane flight paths cross a person's property and cause a reduction in value. The homeowner forces the government to purchase his property. This is called inverse condemnation.

*The power of eminent domain can be exercised by government entities (cities and counties), utility companies, and school districts.*

A renter may vacate or desert the premises when the building is condemned.

## B. REDEVELOPMENT (City and County Agencies)

*REDEVELOPMENT is the process of purchasing land in a run-down area (blighted) and constructing new buildings, parks, and other new construction.* Early efforts at redevelopment were made by organizations such as syndication groups, realty boards, and large insurance companies. However, the difficulty of assembling the necessary parcels by negotiation alone proved to be an impossible task. There was need for a government agency that could exercise its right of eminent domain to bring, by process of law, the court condemnation orders. Redevelopment organizations have been replaced by redevelopment agencies. *REDEVELOPMENT AGENCIES are city or county-run organizations that direct the spending of federal and state money.* The cities or counties have found a new way to rebuild their areas with government money.

## C. MUTUAL WATER COMPANY

A *MUTUAL WATER COMPANY is organized by water users in a given district to supply ample water at a reasonable rate.* It is usually a corporation in which the owner of each parcel of land is given a share of stock. The stock is appurtenant to the land; that is, each share of stock is attached to the land and cannot be sold separately. This enables the water company to develop uniformity and prevents speculation in the shares of stock.

*Stock in a mutual water company is appurtenant to the land; it is real property.*

No cash dividends are declared by these companies, but credits are given to water users if surpluses occur. On the other hand, assessments may be levied if operating revenues are not sufficient. Directors are elected by the stockholders, who usually employ one officer to operate the company, supervise the clerical help, and advise stockholders regarding any water problems.

# XII. Fair Housing Laws

*California first passed the Unruh Civil Rights Act (no discrimination in business, including real estate agents' services) and then the Fair Employment and Housing Act (no discrimination in housing). These were later reinforced by the Federal Civil Rights Act of 1968.*

**Figure 12-11** describes the different types of civil rights violations.

### A. STATE LAW – UNRUH CIVIL RIGHTS ACT (No Discrimination in Business)

*The Unruh Civil Rights Act was the first civil rights act in California; it prohibits "steering" and "block busting" as a real estate business practice.*

The Unruh Civil Rights Act (California Civil Code Section 51) prohibits business establishments from discriminating on the basis of sex, race, color, religion, ancestry, national origin, disability, or medical condition. Assembly Bill 1400 adds marital status and sexual orientation to the list. California continues to prohibit any arbitrary discrimination.

### B. STATE LAW – FAIR EMPLOYMENT AND HOUSING ACT (FEHA)

*The Fair Employment and Housing Act (FEHA) (no discrimination in housing) established the Commission of Fair Employment and Housing to investigate and take action against property owners, financial institutions, and real estate licensees who engage in discriminatory practices.*

It clearly defines discrimination as the refusal to sell, rent, or lease housing accommodations, including misrepresentation as to availability, offering inferior terms, and cancellations on the basis of race, color, religion, sex, family status, national origin, ancestry, and age. It also outlaws sale or rental advertisements containing discriminatory information.

*Owners of three single-family homes and owner-occupied buildings that are four units or less are exempt from Fair Housing Laws under the "Mom and Pop" provision.*

### C. STATE LAW – HOUSING FINANCIAL DISCRIMINATION ACT

*The Housing Financial Discrimination Act prohibits financial institutions from engaging in discriminatory loan practices called "redlining."*

In remedying such violations, the state may force a landowner to proceed with the rental or sale in question, provide comparable housing accommodations if the original is no longer available or pay punitive damages up to $1,000. Under the **Housing Financial Discrimination Act of 1977**, the practice of redlining is specifically outlawed. *REDLINING is the practice by financial institutions of denying loans or varying finance terms based on the location of a given property, regardless of the credit worthiness of the borrower.* This law explicitly forbids discrimination because of the race of the borrower or the racial composition of the neighborhood in which the borrower's prospective home is located.

The Housing Financial Discrimination Act (no redlining) covers 1-to-4 units (at least one owner-occupied) used for residential purposes, but an owner seeking a home improvement loan need not occupy the property.

---

**Figure 12-11**

# Fair Housing Violations and Possible Remedies

REDLINING _____ The refusal of a loan or insurance based upon a property's location (zip code).

STEERING _____ Showing a client property in only one type of neighborhood, such as a Caucasian buyer in a Caucasian neighborhood, and the refusal to communicate the availability of housing in other neighborhoods.

**OWNER TELLS AGENT NOT TO SHOW PROPERTY TO MINORITY** _____ The agent is relieved of the duty to show the property to anyone, including a minority who has requested to see the property.

**CONTRACT REFUSED TO BUYER BECAUSE OF RACE** _____ ADVISE BUYER of the right to complain to the Fair Employment and Housing (FEH) and WARN SELLER that he or she has violated fair housing laws.

**RACE RESTRICTIONS** _____ Any race restriction is UNENFORCEABLE. It has NO LEGAL effect upon a transaction.

**PANIC SELLING OR BLOCK BUSTING AND PANIC PEDDLING** _____ An agent intentionally incites existing homeowners to sell their properties by saying that property values will fall because persons of a different race or religion have targeted a move into their neighborhood.

**SALE OF PROPERTY (AGENT ASKED TO DISCRIMINATE)** Agent must REFUSE the listing.

---

Lending institutions in violation of the Housing Financial Discrimination Act may be required to pay for damages, limited to $1,000 for each offense.

## D. FEDERAL LAWS (Federal Civil Rights Act of 1968)

Federal law prohibits discrimination on the part of owners of property and their agents based on the U.S. Supreme Court case *Jones v. Mayer* (after the Civil War) and Title VIII of the Civil Rights Act of 1968 (commonly referred to as the Federal Fair Housing Act).

For all practical purposes, discrimination laws evolved from the U.S. Supreme Court Case *Jones v. Mayer*, Title VIII of the Civil Rights Act of 1968 and the 13th Amendment to the U.S. Constitution.

At the federal level, the Federal Civil Rights Act of 1968 reinforced the Unruh and Fair Employment and Housing Acts: 1) Any discrimination that the two acts did not prohibit was explicitly outlawed. **THERE ARE NO EXCEPTIONS**; 2) It makes it illegal for real estate licensees to engage in discriminatory practices regardless of any instructions the agent may have received from the seller or landlord. If asked to discriminate in the sale of a property, the salesperson must refuse to accept the listing; 3) It bars real estate boards or multiple listing services from discriminating by denying participation or restricting terms and conditions of membership; 4) It requires a fair housing poster to be displayed at all real estate offices and subdivision model homes. **The poster (see Figure 12-12) must also be displayed at all financial institutions or by mortgage lenders who make loans to the general public**.

The only time an agent can refuse to show a property to a buyer is when the owner's have informed the agent that they will be out of town and, during their absence, the broker has been instructed not to show the property to anyone.

**Note – A lender who charges an additional fee per annum for processing loans to non-English speaking applicants because the lender must hire non-English speaking employees, is practicing discrimination.**

### 1. Federal Civil Rights Act Expanded in 1988 (HUD Can Initiate Housing Discrimination Cases)

A 1988 federal law allows the U.S. Government to take court action if it believes discrimination exists in home sales or apartment rentals. Landlords are explicitly forbidden to discriminate against families with children under 18 years of age. The only exemptions from this would be in retirement communities where most of the residents are more than 55 years of age.

This federal law also extends protections to handicapped home buyers or tenants. As of 1991, builders of all new apartment buildings were required to include ground floor rooms suitable for use by residents in wheelchairs.

*The Americans With Disabilites Act (ADA) is a federal civil rights law that applies to people with disabilities and protects them from discrimination.*

The Housing and Urban Development (HUD) Department is authorized to bring enforcement action against sellers and landlords who defy this law. Fines of up to $10,000 have been authorized for first time violators, up to $25,000 for a second offense within five years and up to $50,000 for a third offense within seven years. Those accused of violating this tough statute would face an administrative judge unless they specifically requested a jury trial.

Complaints should be filed with Housing and Urban Development (HUD). Fair Employment and Housing will enforce any action.

*When discrimination takes place (under the Civil Rights Act of 1968), the aggrieved party may file civil suit in federal, state, or local court, and file a complaint with HUD.*

**Figure 12-12**

# Equal Housing Lender

**We Do Business In Accordance With The
Federal Fair Housing Law**

**(Title VIII of the Civil Rights Act of 1968,
as Amended by the Housing and Community
Development Act of 1974)**

**IT IS ILLEGAL TO DISCRIMINATE AGAINST ANY PERSON
BECAUSE OF RACE, COLOR, NATIONAL ORIGIN, RELIGION,
SEX, FAMILIAL STATUS (including children under the age of 18 living
with parents or legal custodians, pregnant women, and
people securing custody of children under the age of 18),
and HANDICAP, TO:**

■ Deny a loan for the purpose of purchasing, constructing, improving, repairing or maintaining a dwelling or

■ Discriminate in fixing of the amount, interest rate, duration, application procedures or other terms or conditions of such a loan.

**IF YOU BELIEVE YOU HAVE BEEN DISCRIMINATED
AGAINST, YOU MAY SEND A COMPLAINT TO:**

**U.S. DEPARTMENT OF HOUSING AND URBAN DEVELOPMENT
Assistant Secretary for Fair Housing and Equal Opportunity
Washington, D.C. 20410**

**or call your local HUD Area or Insuring Office.**

### E. THE REAL ESTATE COMMISSIONER AND "NAR" ALSO ENFORCE ANTI-DISCRIMINATION

# The Real Estate Commissioner

## Regulations of the Real Estate Commissioner

**(10177 of the Business and Professions Code)**

Regulations have been issued by the Real Estate Commissioner that cover any discrimination with regard to housing. Disciplinary action will be taken against any real estate licensee who violates these regulations. This could include a suspension, fine, revocation of license, or prosecution by the local district attorney. See Chapter 14 for more about the Commissioner's Regulations.

## The National Association of REALTORS®

## Code of Ethics

The National Association of REALTORS® (NAR) Code of Ethics and Fair Practices forbids discrimination against any minority group. Any violation by a real estate licensee could subject that licensee to disciplinary action from the local board of REALTORS®.

Article 10 states that the REALTOR® shall not deny equal service (or be a party to any plan or agreement to deny service) to any person for reasons of race, color, religion, handicap, family status or national origin.

## XIII. CHAPTER SUMMARY

There are two basic subdivision laws, including the **Subdivision Map Act** (2 or more lots) that gives cities and counties control over the physical design of a subdivision, and the **Subdivided Lands Law** (5 or more lots) that protects the purchasers of property in new subdivisions from fraud, misrepresentation, or deceit in the marketing of subdivisions.

The subdivided lands law requires a subdivider to give a buyer a copy of the public report disclosing important facts about the subdivision. A **preliminary public report** allows property reservations before the final report is issued, and a **final public report**, which must be kept by the subdivider for a three year period, is the official report that must be given to the buyer. In addition to the public reports an **environmental impact report (EIR)** may be necessary and disclosure of location within a **special studies zone** (earthquake zone).

A **master plan** is a comprehensive guide through which zoning establishes an ideal plan for the city's development in the future. **Zoning** is the city or county's exercise of **police power**, which are rulings made to control the use (not the ownership) of private property for the protection of the public's health, safety, and welfare.

**Eminent domain** (or **condemnation**) is the right of the government to take private property from a landowner (in exchange for fair market value) for the "public good." If any remaining property is devalued because of the condemnation, the government may pay severance damage. If the property is so devalued that a property owner feels the government should take all of the property, he or she may file an action called **inverse condemnation**.

California was one of the first states with fair housing laws. These include the **Unruh Civil Rights Act**, which prohibits steering and blockbusting in real estate, and the **Fair Employment and Housing Act (FEHA)**, which established the **Department of Fair Employment and Housing** to address housing discrimination. In addition, the **Housing Financial Discrimination Act of 1977** prohibits financial institutions from engaging in discriminatory loan practices called **redlining**.

Federal law also prohibits discrimination on the part of owners of property and their agents based on the Supreme Court Case *Jones v. Mayer*, **Title VIII of the Civil Rights Act of 1968**, and the **13th Amendment**. In 1988, the Federal Civil Rights Act was expanded to allow HUD to enforce actions against sellers and landlords who defy the law. The **DRE** and **NAR** also enforce anti-discrimination laws.

# CHAPTER 12

## XIV. TERMINOLOGY

A. Building Code
B. Building Permit
C. Civil Rights Act of 1968
D. Common Area
E. Community Apartment Project
F. Conditional Use Permit
G. Condominium
H. Eminent Domain
I. Environmental Impact Report

J. Housing Financial Discrimination Act
K. *Jones v. Mayer*
L. Land Project
M. Manufactured Homes
N. Master Plan
O. Mutual Water Company
P. Nonconforming Use
Q. Planned Development (PD)
R. Planning Commission
S. Public Report

T. Redevelopment Agency
U. Redlining
V. Fair Employment and Housing Act
W. Severance Damages
X. Spot Zoning
Y. Subdivided Lands Act
Z. Subdivision Map Act
AA. Unruh Act
BB. Variance
CC. Zoning Laws

1.____ A comprehensive zoning plan to help a city grow in an orderly and sound manner, both economically and ecologically.

2.____ A water company in which the owners are the customers.

3.____ A permit given by a local government to construct a building or make improvements.

4.____ A report given to a prospective purchaser(s) in a new subdivision.

5.____ Zoning on a parcel-by-parcel basis, rather than a comprehensive general or master plan. Considered poor planning.

6.____ The outlining in red on a map of certain "high risk" areas where lenders will not extend credit, regardless of the qualifications of the applicants (illegal practice).

7.____ The local government board which must approve proposed building projects according to zones; it must answer to the county board or city council.

8.____ A subdivision where there is private ownership of individual lots as well as common ownership of another lot, usually a swimming pool or a recreation room.

9.____ A report of the probable effect of a development on the ecology of the surrounding area. The report is prepared by an independent company and follows federal, state, or local guidelines.

10.____ An isolated rural subdivision, operating under federal guidelines, with certain rights of rescission.

11.____ Permission to change a portion of zoning requirements without changing the entire zoning.

12.____ Loss in value to the remaining property when part of a parcel is condemned and seized by the government for public use.

13.____ A corporation formed for the purpose of holding title to a building. Each shareholder receives the right to occupy a dwelling unit but must pay property taxes and insurance in common with the other owners.

14.____ The area owned in common by all the owners of condominiums or planned unit developments.

15.____ A property that does not conform to the current zoning of the area. Usually, the property was built in conformity and then the zoning was changed.

16.____ A structure of two or more units, the interior spaces of which are individually owned; the balance of the property is owned in common by the owners of the individual units.

17.____ A comprehensive set of laws that control the construction of buildings, including design, materials used, repair, remodeling, and other similar factors.

18.____ Generally, the improvement of land in accordance with a city renewal project.

19.____A governmental right to acquire private property for public use by condemnation, and the payment of just compensation.

20.____Homes that are not truly mobile but are constructed in the same manner as trailers, as opposed to conventional, on-site construction.

21.____Laws that require cities and counties to specify the uses allowable for real property in different areas or zones.

22.____An act requiring developers to obtain local government (city or county) approval for the detailed construction plan of their subdivision.

23.____A specific exception to zoning laws, granted for the general good of the community.

24.____A law requiring an acknowledgment from the Department of Real Estate that a subdivision has met the minimum requirements for filing the necessary reports.

25.____Established far-reaching federal anti-discrimination laws. Requires that fair housing posters be displayed at real estate offices and lending institutions.

26.____Civil War-era court case that was the basis for current civil rights laws.

27.____State fair housing law established to eliminate redlining.

28.____Established the Commission of Fair Employment and Housing.

29.____The state fair housing law that disallowed discrimination in business, including real estate agent's services.

# CHAPTER 12

## XV. CHAPTER QUIZ

1. Zoning, planning and governmental land use are important examples of:

    a. encumbrances.
    b. eminent domain.
    c. deed restrictions.
    d. exercise of police power.

2. After several lots have been sold in a subdivision, the Real Estate Commissioner was informed of misrepresentation being made by a developer. The Commissioner may stop the sale of more lots by:

    a. revoking the final public report.
    b. issuing a writ of prohibition.
    c. issuing a desist and refrain order.
    d. filing an accusation in court.

3. Which of the following must be given to every buyer of a condominium unit?

    a. Copy of the CC&Rs
    b. Copy of the bylaws
    c. Copy of the most recent financial statement of the condo association
    d. All of the above

4. A timeshare company advertises the sale of timeshares on a billboard. If the billboard does not disclose the requirement to listen to a sales presentation in order to receive the promised prize, this is:

    a. legal, if the prospect is notified within 24 hours after purchasing the time share.
    b. illegal, because the broker did not disclose the requirement to listen to a sales presentation in order to receive the prize.
    c. legal.
    d. illegal, only if the timeshare company is a corporation.

5. A "Negative Declaration" is:

    a. part of the agent's section in the Transfer Disclosure Statement (TDS).
    b. issued by the title company if the property is unmarketable due to certain matters of record listed in the abstract of title.
    c. utilized by escrow if there are sufficient funds available to close escrow.
    d. a statement by an expert affirming that a new subdivision will have no significant negative impact on the environment.

6. What is the primary tool used by planning commissions to implement a general plan?

    a. Eminent domain
    b. Adverse possession
    c. Zoning
    d. Master plan

7. A change of zoning from industrial to residential is called:
   a. downzoning.
   b. spotzoning.
   c. upzoning.
   d. crosszoning.

8. What kind of manufactured home can a broker sell?
   a. Certified manufactured home
   b. Registered manufactured home
   c. Licensed manufactured home
   d. All of the above

9. Airplane flight paths cross a person's property and cause a reduction in value. If the homeowner forces the government to purchase his/her property, this is called:
   a. inverse condemnation.
   b. functional obsolescence.
   c. police power.
   d. none of the above.

10. A lender charges an additional fee of 1/8% per annum for processing loans to non-English speaking applicants since the lender must hire non-English speaking employees to communicate with these borrowers. This would be considered:
   a. good business practice.
   b. an unethical business practice as defined in the UCC.
   c. legal in the lender must pay higher wages to accommodate the non-English speaking clients.
   d. a form of illegal discrimination.

*ANSWERS: 1. d; 2. c; 3. d; 4. b; 5. d; 6. c; 7. a; 8. b; 9. a; 10. d*

# CHAPTER 13
## Taxation of Real Estate

Taxes are an important aspect of all real estate transactions. Property owners are taxed annually on the property they own. In addition, there are other state and federal taxes that must be paid in order to buy, sell, or give away real property. **Figure 13-1** illustrates the five taxes with which every taxpayer, investor, and salesperson should be familiar. The amount of tax and who must pay the tax are often major factors to consider in the transfer of real estate.

**Figure 13-1**

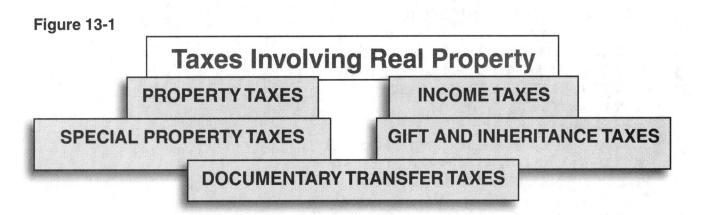

## I. Real Property Taxes

A city or county receives most of its operating revenue from the assessment and collection of real property taxes. *REAL PROPERTY TAXES are taxes determined according to the value of the real property, and are paid annually or semi-annually.* These taxes are called ad valorem taxes. An *AD VALOREM TAX is a tax that is charged in proportion to the value of the property.* Property taxes are based on the concept that taxes should be assessed in accordance with a person's ability to pay. In the case of real estate, the higher the value of the property, the higher the property taxes.

"**Ad valorem" means taxed "according to value."** Real property is reassessed each time it is transferred (sold) at 100% of its selling price (or market value, if it is higher).

## CHAPTER OUTLINE

The **COUNTY ASSESSOR** *is the county officer who has the responsibility of determining the assessed valuation of land, improvements, and personal property used in business.* The county assessor determines the value of both county and city properties, except in a few cities that use their own assessors. In Los Angeles County, the City of Pasadena has its own assessor who assesses the property in that city. San Francisco is unique because the city and county assessor's functions are combined.

*The county assessor accumulates a list of all private owners of real property in his/her jurisdiction. The "assessment roll" is used to establish the tax base for the county.*

www.assessor.lacounty.gov/extranet/default.aspx
L.A. County Assessor

In general all real property, except that which is owned by the government, and all tangible personal property except inventory used in a business, is subject to property tax assessment in California. **Intangible personal property, such as goodwill of a business opportunity, as well as tangible property, such as household furnishings and personal effects of individuals, are not assessed or taxed.**

*County Assessor assesses; County Board of Supervisors sets tax rate.*

The **COUNTY TAX COLLECTOR** *is the county officer who collects the real property taxes.* He or she only collects taxes; the county tax collector has nothing to do with determining how much tax is levied. If the real property taxes are not paid, the county tax collector will eventually require that the property be sold at a tax sale.

www.cacttc.org
List of California County Tax Collectors

## A. PROPOSITION 13

**PROPOSITION 13** *limits the amount of taxes to a maximum of 1%\* of the March 1, 1975, market value of the property plus the cumulative increase of 2% in market value each year thereafter.*

Improvements made after March 1, 1975, are added to the value in the year they are made. If ownership has changed after March 1, 1975, the tax is limited to 1%* of the market value plus the 2% cumulative increase each succeeding year. (In some cases, property values came down, lowering taxes instead of raising them by 2%.) Any state-allowed exemptions are deducted after figuring the basic tax (see **Figure 13-2**).

*Voted indebtedness may increase this rate beyond 1%, from area-to-area, with voter approval.

## B. REAL PROPERTY TAX BASE IS TRANSFERABLE (Props 60 & 90)

Under the following conditions (based on Propositions 60 and 90), homeowners may be permitted to transfer their current Proposition 13 tax base with them when they buy a new home:

1. Homeowners over the age of 55, and
2. Home purchased within two years of original sale, and
3. Replacement home of equal or lesser value, and
4. New home must be in the same county, or another participating county (check first).

Propositions 60 and 90 allow "empty-nesters" to purchase new homes (one at a time) while holding on to their low tax base, thus freeing up larger multiple bedroom homes for younger families.

*ASSESSED VALUATION is set at **100% of the property's selling price or fair market value**, whichever is higher, plus a 2% increase for every year the property has been owned, but only as far back as March 1, 1975. The tax rate is set at 1% of fair market value (or selling price, whichever is higher) plus any voter-approved indebtedness.* Properties that are transferred and new construction are subject to a new appraisal based upon the current market value or selling price, whichever is higher. Existing structures are given a new assessment each year as of January 1. New construction and transfers are assessed immediately upon the first day of the next month. See **Figures 13-3** and **13-4** for an example of a property tax bill.

*Real property is assessed each time it is transferred (sold) at 100% of its selling price (or market value if it is higher). A "change of ownership statement" must be filed with an assessor within 45 days of change.*

## C. PROPERTY TAXES BECOME A SPECIFIC LIEN

Property taxes due upon real property are, in effect, liens against that specific property. Business personal property taxes (trade fixtures) also become liens against that specific real property on the same tax bill. For example, the furniture in furnished apartments is taxed as business personal property and is usually included on the property tax bill.

Property taxes for the following fiscal year become a lien against the real property on January 1 of the current year. Officially, the first installment for half of the taxes becomes due on November 1 and is delinquent after 5 P.M. on December 10. The second installment is due on February 1 and is delinquent if not paid by 5 P.M. on April 10. If either December 10 or April 10 falls on a Saturday, Sunday, or legal holiday, the delinquency date is extended to the close of the next business day.

**Figure 13-2**

# Proposition 13

That Article XII A is added to the Constitution to read:

### Section 1.

(a) The maximum amount of any ad valorem tax on real property shall not exceed one percent (1%)* of the full cash value of such property. The one percent (1%)* tax to be collected by the counties and apportioned according to law to the districts within the counties.

(b) The limitation provided for in subdivision (a) shall not apply to ad valorem taxes or special assessments to pay the interest and redemption charges on any indebtedness approved by the voters prior to the time this section becomes effective.

### Section 2.

(a) The full cash value means the county assessors valuation of real property as shown on the 1975-76 tax bill under "full cash value," or thereafter, the appraised value of real property when purchased, newly constructed, or a change in ownership has occurred after the 1975 assessment. All real property not already assessed up to the 1975-76 tax levels may be reassessed to reflect that valuation.

(b) The fair market value base may reflect from year to year the inflationary rate not to exceed two percent (2%) for any given year or reduction as shown in the consumer price index or comparable data for the area under taxing jurisdiction.

### Section 3.

From and after the effective date of this article, any changes in state taxes enacted for the purpose of increasing revenues collected pursuant thereto whether by increased rates or changes in methods of computation must be imposed by an Act passed by not less than two-thirds of all members elected to each of the two houses of the Legislature, except that no new ad valorem taxes on real property, or sales or transaction taxes on the sales of real property may be imposed.

### Section 4.

Cities, counties, and special districts, by a two-thirds vote of the qualified electors of such district, may impose special taxes on such district, except ad valorem taxes on real property or a transaction tax or sales tax on the sale of real property within such city, county, or special district.

### Section 5.

This article shall take effect for the tax year beginning on July 1 following the passage of this Amendment, except Section 3 which shall become effective upon the passage of this article.

### Section 6.

If any section, part, clause, or phrase hereof is for any reason held to be invalid or unconstitutional, the remaining sections shall not be affected but will remain in full force and effect.

*Voted indebtedness may increase this rate beyond 1% from local area to area with voter approval.*

## Figure 13-3

**2009**       **ANNUAL PROPERTY TAX BILL**       **2009**

CITIES, COUNTY, SCHOOLS AND ALL OTHER TAXING AGENCIES IN LOS ANGELES COUNTY

**SECURED PROPERTY TAX FOR FISCAL YEAR JULY 1, 2009 TO JUNE 30, 2010**

MARK J. SALADINO, TREASURER AND TAX COLLECTOR

FOR ASSISTANCE CALL 1 (213) 974-2111 OR 1 (888) 807-2111, ON THE WEB AT www.lacountypropertytax.com

ASSESSOR'S ID. NO.     CK

DETAIL OF TAXES DUE FOR    **4225 011 081 09 000**   **01**

**PROPERTY IDENTIFICATION**

ASSESSOR'S ID.NO.: 4225 011 081 09 000
OWNER OF RECORD AS OF JANUARY 1, 2009
SAME AS BELOW

**MAILING ADDRESS**

Wolfgang Hubie
100 Internet Highway
Culver City, CA 90230

| AGENCY | AGENCY PHONE NO. | RATE | | AMOUNT |
|---|---|---|---|---|
| GENERAL TAX LEVY | | | | |
| ALL AGENCIES | | 1.000000 | $ | 2,459.40 |
| | | | | |
| VOTED INDEBTEDNESS | | | | |
| CITY-LOS ANGELES | | .041220 | $ | 101.38 |
| METRO WATER DIST | | .004300 | | 10.57 |
| COMMNTY COLLEGE | | .023112 | | 56.84 |
| UNIFIED SCHOOLS | | .151809 | | 373.36 |
| | | | | |
| DIRECT ASSESSMENTS | | | | |
| LA STORMWATER | (213) 485-2402 | | $ | 8.05 |
| CITY 911 FUND | (213) 978-1099 | | | 14.03 |
| FLOOD CONTROL | (626) 458-5165 | | | 10.09 |
| COUNTY PARK DIST | (213) 738-2983 | | | 15.38 |
| LACITY PARK DIST | (213) 473-9702 | | | 14.51 |
| TRAUMA/EMERG SRV | (866) 587-2862 | | | 58.47 |
| LA WEST MOSQ AB | (310) 915-7370 | | | 5.39 |

**ELECTRONIC FUND TRANSFER (EFT) NUMBER**

ID#:19 4225 011 081 9 YEAR:09 SEQUENCE:000 1
PIN: 664860

For **American Express, Mastercard and Visa** payments call 1 (888) 473-0835 and have available the EFT number listed above. Service fees will be charged.

**SPECIAL INFORMATION**

**PROPERTY LOCATION AND/OR PROPERTY DESCRIPTION**

27 KETCH ST NO 1       LOS ANGELE
*TR=P M 72-26-27 CONDOMINIUM*UNITS
1 AND A

**ASSESSOR'S REGIONAL OFFICE**

REGION #07 INDEX:     TRA:00067
WEST DISTRICT OFFICE
6120 BRISTOL PARKWAY
CULVER CITY CA 90230
(310)665-5300

ACCT. NO.:    PRINT NO.: 641621 BILL ID.:

| | |
|---|---|
| **TOTAL TAXES DUE** | **$3,127.47** |
| **FIRST INSTALLMENT TAXES** DUE NOV. 1, 2009 | **$1,563.74** |
| **SECOND INSTALLMENT TAXES** DUE FEB. 1, 2010 | **$1,563.73** |

**VALUATION INFORMATION**

| ROLL YEAR 09-10 | CURRENT ASSESSED VALUE | TAXABLE VALUE |
|---|---|---|
| LAND | 144,772 | 144,772 |
| IMPROVEMENTS | 108,168 | 108,168 |
| TOTAL | | 252,940 |
| LESS EXEMPTION: HOME | | 7,000 |
| NET TAXABLE VALUE | | 245,940 |

## D. PROPERTY TAX TIME TABLE

The city or county fiscal year starts on July 1 and ends on June 30. All revenues and expenditures are planned for this period of time. **Figure 13-5** illustrates all the important dates that are associated with property taxes. Assessable property is evaluated by the assessor on January 1 for the upcoming year in the name of the property's legal owner on that date. Most cities allow the county assessor to evaluate the property in both the county and the incorporated parts of the

**Figure 13-4**

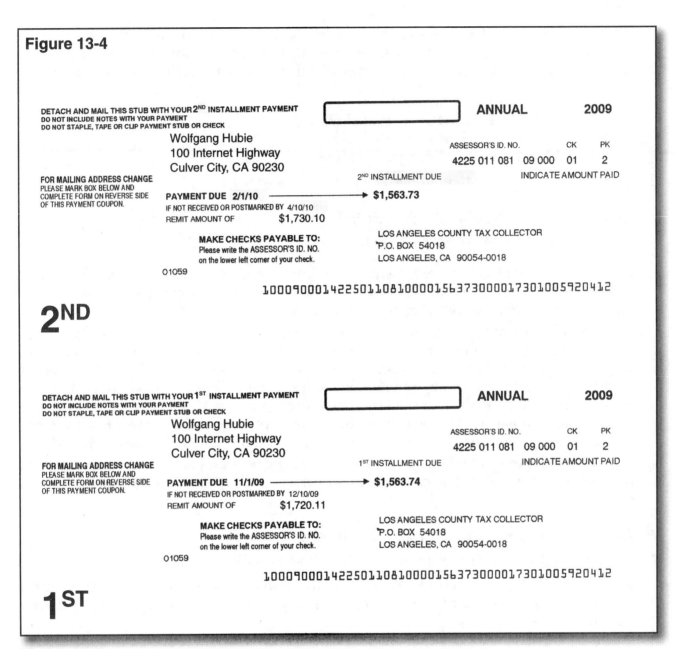

DETACH AND MAIL THIS STUB WITH YOUR 2ND INSTALLMENT PAYMENT
DO NOT INCLUDE NOTES WITH YOUR PAYMENT
DO NOT STAPLE, TAPE OR CLIP PAYMENT STUB OR CHECK

**ANNUAL   2009**

Wolfgang Hubie
100 Internet Highway
Culver City, CA 90230

ASSESSOR'S ID. NO.    CK    PK
4225 011 081  09 000   01     2

2ND INSTALLMENT DUE          INDICATE AMOUNT PAID

FOR MAILING ADDRESS CHANGE
PLEASE MARK BOX BELOW AND
COMPLETE FORM ON REVERSE SIDE
OF THIS PAYMENT COUPON.

**PAYMENT DUE  2/1/10** → **$1,563.73**
IF NOT RECEIVED OR POSTMARKED BY 4/10/10
REMIT AMOUNT OF          **$1,730.10**

**MAKE CHECKS PAYABLE TO:**
Please write the ASSESSOR'S ID. NO.
on the lower left corner of your check.

01059

LOS ANGELES COUNTY TAX COLLECTOR
P.O. BOX 54018
LOS ANGELES, CA  90054-0018

10009000142250110810000156373000017301005920412

**2ND**

DETACH AND MAIL THIS STUB WITH YOUR 1ST INSTALLMENT PAYMENT
DO NOT INCLUDE NOTES WITH YOUR PAYMENT
DO NOT STAPLE, TAPE OR CLIP PAYMENT STUB OR CHECK

**ANNUAL   2009**

Wolfgang Hubie
100 Internet Highway
Culver City, CA 90230

ASSESSOR'S ID. NO.    CK    PK
4225 011 081  09 000   01     2

1ST INSTALLMENT DUE          INDICATE AMOUNT PAID

FOR MAILING ADDRESS CHANGE
PLEASE MARK BOX BELOW AND
COMPLETE FORM ON REVERSE SIDE
OF THIS PAYMENT COUPON.

**PAYMENT DUE  11/1/09** → **$1,563.74**
IF NOT RECEIVED OR POSTMARKED BY 12/10/09
REMIT AMOUNT OF          **$1,720.11**

**MAKE CHECKS PAYABLE TO:**
Please write the ASSESSOR'S ID. NO.
on the lower left corner of your check.

01059

LOS ANGELES COUNTY TAX COLLECTOR
P.O. BOX 54018
LOS ANGELES, CA  90054-0018

10009000142250110810000156373000017301005920412

**1ST**

**Figure 13-5**

## PROPERTY TAX TIME TABLE

| January 1 | July 1 | November 1 | February 1 |
|---|---|---|---|
| Property tax becomes a lien on real property | Fiscal year starts | 1st installment is due and delinquent after December 10 at 5 P.M. | 2nd installment is due and delinquent after April 10 at 5 P.M. |

county, which are the cities. In a few rare cases as stated earlier, cities may use their own assessors. County assessors complete their assessment rolls by July 1, the beginning of the government (fiscal) year. Important tax dates can be remembered by "No Darn Fooling Around" as follows:

**N**  November 1 (first installment)
**D**  December 10 (first installment is delinquent)
**F**  February 1 (second installment)
**A**  April 10 (second installment is delinquent)

*Property taxes become a lien on real property on January 1.*

## E. PROPERTY TAX PRORATION PROBLEM

**Proration question: Who owes whom how much?**

If the seller of the subject property has paid both the 1st and 2nd installments of the property taxes for a total annual bill of $2,760, what is the proration of property taxes for both the seller and buyer if the buyer takes possession on May 1?

**Remember: Escrow prorates property taxes using old (seller's) assessed value (tax bill).**

The first step is to determine the amount of taxes per month. The annual tax bill of $2,760 is divided by 12 months to determine that the monthly tax is $230. Since the seller paid the property taxes through the month of June (the end of the fiscal tax year, which is July 1 through June 30), and the buyer took possession on May 1, two months of paid property taxes are owed the seller. The buyer would owe the seller for two months (May and June) that were already paid by the seller. This amount would be $460 (2 x $230).

When a property is sold, the buyer will receive one new property tax bill, but it may be followed by other updated property tax bills referred to as **supplemental property tax bills** (see **Figure 13-6**).

## F. HOMEOWNER'S PROPERTY TAX EXEMPTION

*Homeowner's property tax exemption is $7,000 of assessed valuation.*

The *HOMEOWNER'S PROPERTY TAX EXEMPTION is a deduction on the property tax bill of the first $7,000 of assessed value of an owner-occupied property.* A homeowner's exemption on your home does the following:

1. All personal property of the homeowner is exempt from property taxes.

2. A resident owner receives a $7,000 homeowner's exemption in assessed value if the property is the principal residence on the 1st of March.

The time to file for the homeowner's exemption is from January 1 to April 15 in order to receive the full exemption. Once the exemption is filed, it remains on the property until the homeowner terminates it. If the exemption is terminated, a new claim form must be obtained from, and filed with, the assessor to regain eligibility.

Qualifying owner-occupied residential property receives a $7,000 homeowner's exemption. For example, an assessed value of $500,000 minus the homeowner's exemption of $7,000 is $493,000. (Prop. 13 tax rate is 1% of the $7,000, so the tax savings, in reality, is only $70.)

### Figure 13-6

## Supplemental Property Tax Bills

The law requires reassessment of property **immediately** when it changes ownership or when new construction is completed. While the amount of the supplemental assessment is still determined in accordance with Proposition 13, the actual effect is to "speed up" reassessment of property. In fact, prior to the change in the law, property was generally not reappraised until January 1.

The Office of Assessor enters the new property value onto the assessment roll as of the first of the month following the month in which the property changes ownership or new construction is completed.

Depending upon the date you purchase property or the date construction is completed, you will receive **one or more** supplemental tax bills in addition to your regular tax bill. Taxes on the supplemental tax roll become a lien against the real property on the date of change in ownership or the date new construction is completed.

### G. HOMEOWNER'S AND RENTER'S PROPERTY TAX REBATE
#### (Senior Citizens and Disabled Persons)

This is a property tax relief law for any resident who is 62 years of age or older as of January 1, and has a household income of not more than $12,000 for the calendar year. The applicant must have owned and occupied his or her home within the fiscal year. Persons under the age of 62 who are totally disabled also qualify for this rebate. A similar program provides a rebate to elderly and disabled persons who rent their homes or apartments.

All relief is in the form of a property tax rebate granted to the applicant. The amount of the property tax rebate is a percentage of household income on the first $8,500 of assessed valuation. The exact amount of rebate is determined by the Senior Citizen's Property Tax Assistance branch of the State Franchise Tax Board.

Rebate applicants pay property taxes as usual during the year and their application must be filed between May 16 and August 31. The claim form is processed and the rebate checks are sent to the applicant. The form may be obtained from the local Franchise Tax Board office.

**SENIOR CITIZEN'S PROPERTY TAX ASSISTANCE**
**P. O. BOX 1588**
**SACRAMENTO, CALIFORNIA 95807**

*Senior citizens may be able to defer the payment of the property taxes on their residence. In order to find out if they qualify for the program, senior citizens should contact the State Franchise Tax Board.*

## H. DISABLED AND SENIOR CITIZEN'S PROPERTY TAX POSTPONEMENT

Seniors who are 62 years of age or older and have a household income of $24,000 or less may qualify for this tax postponement assistance program. This program offers them the option of having the state pay all or part of the taxes on their homes. In return, a lien is placed on the property for the amount that the state has to pay. This specific lien becomes payable when the taxpayer moves or dies. In effect, the homeowner is relieved of his or her tax burden in exchange for a lien on his or her home to be paid upon death. California has extended this program to include persons under the age of 62 who are legally disabled.

## I. VETERAN'S EXEMPTION

Any California resident who served in the military during a time of war is entitled to an annual $4,000 property tax exemption against the assessed value of one property. This exemption also applies to the widow, widowed mother, or pensioned father of a deceased veteran. However, the exempted property is limited to an assessed value of less than $5,000 for a single veteran or $10,000 if he or she is married. For disabled California veterans who qualify, however, the assessment limit can be raised up to $100,000.

## J. TAX EXEMPT PROPERTY

In California there are some properties that are partially or totally tax exempt. All real property that is owned by the federal, state, county, or city government is automatically tax exempt. This is a huge benefit to the federal government, as it owns 45% of California land. Eastern states benefit because only about 10% of their land is owned by the federal government. **A lessee with possessory interest in oil and gas rights on government owned property is not exempt from property taxes**.

Since California has many national and state parks, the majority of land in this state is tax exempt. In addition, 50 percent of all growing crops, young orchard trees, immature timber, and young grapevines are tax exempt.

*Property of nonprofit organizations used for religious, charitable, medical, or educational purposes is tax exempt.*

## K. PROPERTY TAX APPEALS

*Over-assessments can be taken to the appeals board.*

People who feel that the assessment of their property is not correct may appeal the assessment. Appeals would be directed to the Board of Equalization (the property tax assessment appeals board) in the county in which the property is located between July 2 and August 26 (in most counties). After it considers the case, the Board may reduce an assessment, or it may increase it, or it may issue a new assessment if the property has not been assessed before.

In most small and many medium sized counties, the County Board of Supervisors serves as the Board of Equalization. In larger counties with a larger number of properties to assess, a special Tax Appeals Board is usually established. This board has no control over tax rates in general, but is the government body that makes individual assessment decisions on individual properties.

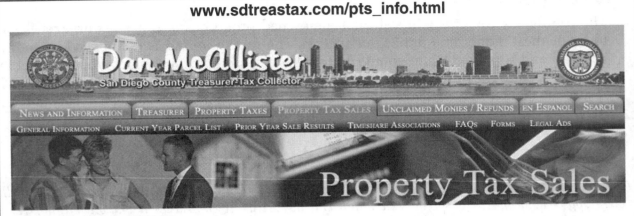

If a property owner wishes to protest the real property tax assessment, he or she can do so by contacting the appeals board office for detailed information. This Board of Equalization agency may reduce an assessed value that has been appealed.

## L. DELINQUENT TAX SALE (Book Sale)

Each year, on or before June 8, the county tax collector publishes a list of tax delinquent properties. This is his or her "notice of intent to sell" all such properties on which the property taxes have not been paid for one year. *Strictly speaking, this is not a true sale but is a formality called a* **BOOK SALE**, *that starts a five-year redemption period*. If the property is not redeemed within five years, it will be deeded over to the state.

Properties may be redeemed by anyone upon the payment of taxes, interest, costs, and redemption penalties. The tax collector gives a receipt called a **"certificate of redemption"** as evidence of payment. If the owner cannot pay for all past due taxes and costs at once, he or she may pay them in five annual installment payments, providing all current taxes are paid.

*If taxes are NOT paid on or before June 30, the property is sold to the state. This sale starts the running of the redemption period, which is five years.*

## M. SECOND SALE (After Five Years)

*After five years, if the property has not been redeemed, the delinquent property is deeded to the state.*

This is the official sale, and the former owner may now redeem the property only if the state has not sold the property at public auction.

### N. SALE TO THE PUBLIC

The county tax collector will sell the state-owned properties to other taxing agencies or to the highest bidder at a public tax auction. The minimum bid is established by the tax collector and approved by the county board of supervisors. All such sales are for cash at the time of the sale. The purchaser then receives a tax deed. Most title insurance companies will insure the tax deed sale after one year has elapsed. But, if any difficulties are encountered, the buyer may clear title through a "quiet title" court action.

## II. Special Assessment Tax

A **SPECIAL ASSESSMENT TAX** *is levied by a city council or a county board of supervisors, with the voters' approval, for the cost of specific local improvements such as streets, sewers, irrigation, or drainage.*

*The difference between property taxes and special assessments is that special assessments are levied for the cost of specific local improvements, while property tax revenue goes into the general fund.*

The official body that levies a special assessment is called a **SPECIAL ASSESSMENT DISTRICT BOARD**. According to state law, any self-governing area such as a city or county may establish a special assessment district for the purpose of levying a special assessment.

As a rule, a district issues its own bonds to finance particular improvements such as water distribution systems, parking facilities, street lighting, and many other types of developments. To repay the funds borrowed through the bonds issued, these districts have the power to assess all lands included in the district on an ad valorem basis. Such loans constitute liens on the land until paid. These liens can be foreclosed by sale similar to a tax sale and have priority over private property interests.

### A. STREET IMPROVEMENT ACT OF 1911

According to the **STREET IMPROVEMENT ACT OF 1911**, *developers can use the Act to construct and improve streets and for sewer construction, however* **they cannot use the Act to purchase land for subdividing.**

### B. THE MELLO-ROOS COMMUNITY FACILITIES ACT

*A seller must disclose the existence of a Mello-Roos bond on the property.*

The Mello-Roos Community Facilities Act is another type of improvement bond. **Figure 13-7** explains Mello-Roos in detail.

> **Example:** A subdivider wanted to subdivide his property into many lots and sell individual lots to potential builders of single-family homes. To finance the off-site improvements, which include streets, sidewalks, and schools, he would institute a Mello-Roos municipal bond.

## III. Documentary Transfer Tax

*$.55 per $500 is paid only on the new amount of money (cash down and new financing), not on any assumed financing.*

**Figure 13-7**

# Mello-Roos Liens
## DISCLOSURE REQUIRED

### Failure to disclose allows buyer a 3-day right of rescission, and results in agent disciplinary action.

*MELLO-ROOS LIENS* are municipal bonds issued to fund streets, sewers, and other infrastructure needs before a housing development is built. This financial device allows developers to raise money to complete off-site improvements in a house or condo subdivision. The developer is usually responsible for making payments on the bond until the home is sold. The homeowner then becomes responsible for payment via a special tax.

The Mello-Roos Community Facilities Act is a way that a city or governmental district can skirt the property tax limitations of Proposition 13. The city can include the cost and maintenance of infrastructure items in the property tax bill as a special tax, which is allowed to go above the limits of Proposition 13.

This has been a boon for developers who need help financing their projects and for municipalities anxious to upgrade new developments under the restrictions of Proposition 13. The downside is that if something goes wrong with the economy or the project, the municipality may have to foreclose on the developer.

**The primary responsibility for disclosure of any Mello-Roos bonds lies with the seller.**

**A broker must disclose to property buyers that a project is subject to a Mello-Roos special tax levy. If the agent fails to provide this disclosure, he or she is subject to discipline by the Real Estate Commissioner. A disclosure notice of the amount assessed and the amount of special tax applicable to the property is required on the sale or lease (for more than five years) of property subject to this lien. Failure to give notice before signing the sales contract permits the buyer or tenant a three-day right of rescission after receipt of the notice.**

**Warning:** Whereas property taxes are totally deductible from state and federal income taxes, Mello-Roos taxes may only be partially deductible depending upon whether they are for maintenance or improvements. Consult with your C.P.A. before claiming such a deduction.

The *DOCUMENTARY TRANSFER TAX is a tax that is applied to the consideration paid or money borrowed when transferring property, except for any remaining loans or liens on the property.* This tax is computed at the rate of 55 cents for each $500 or $1.10 per $1,000 of consideration or any fraction thereof that exceeds $100. The consideration is any amount of cash payment plus any new loans.

However, this tax does not apply to any liens or encumbrances that remain on the property as part of the transfer. If a house were sold for $230,000 and a buyer assumed the old loan of $30,000, the documentary transfer tax would be $220 (only $200,000 is "new money" and taxable).

$$\frac{\$200,000}{\$500} \times \$.55 = \$220 \qquad \text{(Loan Assumptions are not taxed.)}$$

**Example:** A single-family home sold for $90,750 and the buyer assumed an existing $30,000 first deed of trust. The documentary transfer tax is $67.

The documentary transfer tax is charged to the seller and is handled as part of the escrow. According to state law the county is allowed to charge this tax. However, a city within a county can charge that county for one-half of this tax. Therefore, in most cities, the county collects the documentary transfer tax and gives half of it to the city. Based on the information found at the county recorder's office, the documentary transfer tax can be used to determine a previous sale price of a property. Simply divide 55 cents into the amount of the documentary transfer tax and multiply by $500. If any loans have been assumed by the new owner, also add that amount to arrive at the total prior sale price of the property.

If any old loans or liens are to remain on the property, this fact must be stated on the deed or on a separate paper filed with the deed. Then add the value of the cash down payment and any new loans together with any remaining loan on the property to find the total selling price.

## – CITY TRANSFER TAXES –

The city of Los Angeles initiated a transfer tax to be paid by sellers when a property is sold. The current charge is $4.50 per $1,000 of selling price.

### – WATCH FOR A VERSION OF THIS TAX IN YOUR CITY –

# IV. Gift and Estate Taxes

For federal purposes, the transfer of property by a gift or inheritance is taxed. Exemptions may reduce the taxes and sometimes eliminate them. **Figure 13-8** illustrates the federal taxes encountered by transferring property as a gift or by inheritance.

A gift of real estate may avoid federal estate taxes. So if a person wants to give a property away, it will most likely escape (the future) federal estate taxes. But, if you are to avoid federal gift taxes, usually only a fractional interest in the property should be given away each year. For example, you could give a son and daughter each a 1/30 interest in your home every year for 15 years to give the house to your children.

## A. FEDERAL GIFT TAX

Frequently, as an individual family matures, the value of the real property owned by the family increases, and the owning family may consider bestowing it as a gift. When a family gives property, whether real or personal, to another individual, there may be federal gift

**Figure 13-8**

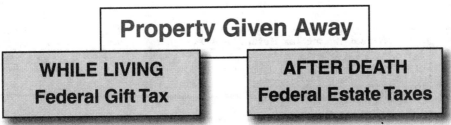

taxes that must be paid. If the value of the property is higher than an exempt amount, the donor must pay a gift tax. A *DONOR is the person or persons giving the property as a gift*. Generally, people give their property away to relatives on a systematic basis so that taxes are avoided. The *DONEE is the person or persons who receive the property as a gift*. The federal gift tax law also provides for an $11,000 annual exemption per donee.

### B. FEDERAL ESTATE TAX

A *FEDERAL ESTATE TAX return must be filed for the estate of every resident of the United States whose gross estate exceeds $1,000,000 ($1,500,000 in 2004, $2,000,000 in 2006) in value at the date of death*. Estate tax exemptions will gradually increase the size of estates that are exempt from $1,000,000 to being repealed in 2010. However, the estate tax can be restored in 2011.

### C. NO STATE GIFT AND INHERITANCE TAXES

The California State Inheritance Tax and the California State Gift Tax were repealed on June 8, 1982.

## V. Federal and State Income Taxes

The annual Federal Income Tax Form 1040 (see **Figure 13-9**) and the State Income Tax Form 540 are bookkeeping or accounting summaries of the prior year's financial facts. These facts are a history and cannot be altered at the time of filing the income tax return.

**www.irs.ustreas.gov**
Internal Revenue Service (IRS)
**www.ftb.ca.gov**
Franchise Tax Board (FTB)

California has both state and federal income taxes (see **Figure 13-10**). That's right! California residents pay both income taxes, which ranks us among the most taxed people in the United States. It is no wonder that Californians are very interested in understanding the effects of income taxes on both their personal residence and income-producing property.

*Under Federal Income Tax Laws, most real estate licensees are considered independent contractors. According to California Real Estate Law, most real estate licensees are considered employees of the broker.*

**Figure 13-9**

Form **1040**   Department of the Treasury—Internal Revenue Service
**U.S. Individual Income Tax Return**   20XX   (99)   IRS Use Only—Do not write or staple in this space

For the year Jan. 1–Dec. 31, 20XX, or other tax year beginning , 20XX, ending , 20XX   OMB No. 1545-0074

**Label**
(See instructions on page 16.)
**Use the IRS label.** Otherwise, please print or type.

L A B E L   H E R E

Your first name and initial   Last name   Your social security number

If a joint return, spouse's first name and initial   Last name   Spouse's social security number

Home address (number and street). If you have a P.O. box, see page 16.   Apt. no.

City, town or post office, state, and ZIP code. If you have a foreign address, see page 16.

▲ You must enter your SSN(s) above. ▲

Checking a box below will not change your tax or refund.

**Presidential Election Campaign** ▶ Check here if you, or your spouse if filing jointly, want $3 to go to this fund (see page 16) ▶ ☐ You ☐ Spouse

**Filing Status**
Check only one box.

1 ☐ Single
2 ☐ Married filing jointly (even if only one had income)
3 ☐ Married filing separately. Enter spouse's SSN above and full name here. ▶
4 ☐ Head of household (with qualifying person). (See page 17.) If the qualifying person is a child but not your dependent, enter this child's name here. ▶
5 ☐ Qualifying widow(er) with dependent child (see page 17)

**Exemptions**

6a ☐ **Yourself.** If someone can claim you as a dependent, **do not** check box 6a
b ☐ **Spouse**

c Dependents:

| (1) First name   Last name | (2) Dependent's social security number | (3) Dependent's relationship to you | (4) ✔ if qualifying child for child tax credit (see page 19) |
|---|---|---|---|
| | | | ☐ |
| | | | ☐ |
| | | | ☐ |
| | | | ☐ |

If more than four dependents, see page 19.

d Total number of exemptions claimed

Boxes checked on 6a and 6b
No. of children on 6c who:
• lived with you
• did not live with you due to divorce or separation (see page 20)
Dependents on 6c not entered above
Add numbers on lines above ▶

**Income**

Attach Form(s) W-2 here. Also attach Forms W-2G and 1099-R if tax was withheld.

If you did not get a W-2, see page 22.

Enclose, but do not attach, any payment. Also, please use Form 1040-V.

7 Wages, salaries, tips, etc. Attach Form(s) W-2 | 7
8a **Taxable** interest. Attach Schedule B if required | 8a
b **Tax-exempt** interest. **Do not** include on line 8a | 8b
9a Ordinary dividends. Attach Schedule B if required | 9a
b Qualified dividends (see page 23) | 9b
10 Taxable refunds, credits, or offsets of state and local income taxes (see page 23) | 10
11 Alimony received | 11
12 Business income or (loss). Attach Schedule C or C-EZ | 12
13 Capital gain or (loss). Attach Schedule D if required. If not required, check here ▶ ☐ | 13
14 Other gains or (losses). Attach Form 4797 | 14
15a IRA distributions | 15a | b Taxable amount (see page 25) | 15b
16a Pensions and annuities | 16a | b Taxable amount (see page 25) | 16b
17 Rental real estate, royalties, partnerships, S corporations, trusts, etc. Attach Schedule E | 17
18 Farm income or (loss). Attach Schedule F | 18
19 Unemployment compensation | 19
20a Social security benefits | 20a | b Taxable amount (see page 27) | 20b
21 Other income. List type and amount (see page 29) | 21
22 Add the amounts in the far right column for lines 7 through 21. This is your **total income** ▶ | 22

**Adjusted Gross Income**

23 Educator expenses (see page 29) | 23
24 Certain business expenses of reservists, performing artists, and fee-basis government officials. Attach Form 2106 or 2106-EZ | 24
25 Health savings account deduction. Attach Form 8889 | 25
26 Moving expenses. Attach Form 3903 | 26
27 One-half of self-employment tax. Attach Schedule SE | 27
28 Self-employed SEP, SIMPLE, and qualified plans | 28
29 Self-employed health insurance deduction (see page 30) | 29
30 Penalty on early withdrawal of savings | 30
31a Alimony paid   b Recipient's SSN ▶ | 31a
32 IRA deduction (see page 31) | 32
33 Student loan interest deduction (see page 33) | 33
34 Tuition and fees deduction (see page 34) | 34
35 Domestic production activities deduction. Attach Form 8903 | 35
36 Add lines 23 through 31a and 32 through 35 | 36
37 Subtract line 36 from line 22. This is your **adjusted gross income** ▶ | 37

For Disclosure, Privacy Act, and Paperwork Reduction Act Notice, see page 78.   Cat. No. 11320B   Form **1040** (2005)

Tax matters should be considered prior to buying and continued during ownership until the estate's ultimate disposition.

We will discuss only the most basic concepts of reducing the income tax bite for the average citizen. A basic knowledge of the requirements necessary to take advantage of federal and state income tax incentives is helpful. Arranging the purchase of real estate in a manner that reduces your personal income taxes is the purpose of tax planning. This may allow you to reduce the income taxes you pay, or at least postpone such taxes.

*Tax shelters are the reduction in income taxes. Now is the time to start tax planning for your future income tax returns.*

---

**Figure 13-10**

## California vs. Federal Income Tax:
### Emphasis is on the Federal

California state income tax laws tend to conform with federal laws in most respects. There are, however, several important income tax exceptions listed below:

1. State does not tax Social Security benefits.
2. State has no capital gains rates; just ordinary income rates.
3. State does not allow tax breaks for IRA plans (simple).
4. State does not tax lottery winnings.

The state taxes at a lower rate (a maximum of 9.3 percent) but tends to be more restrictive on deductions. State taxes paid are themselves deductible from the federal return.

Most state and local tax laws are considered by many insiders to be antiquated. Tax reform on these levels has become a much slower process than that by the federal government. Focus is on the federal government which taxes at higher rates and sets the tone for state and local taxes. For more detailed information on preparing personal income taxes, a tax attorney or CPA should be consulted.

---

**Figure 13-11** shows the five main areas of the federal and state income tax laws that are incentives to owning real estate. Each area will be explained only to give the general concepts or ideas behind the laws. To obtain the exact meaning and clauses of the law, an owner or investor should seek the help of a Certified Public Accountant for advice on the accounting, or an attorney who is familiar with tax problems. Remember, these are only generalizations, and our income tax laws are more complex than the basic concepts presented here.

# VI. Taxes on Personal Residence

Homeowners can deduct these three items from their income taxes based on their personal residence:

1. Mortgage Interest on Loan (Trust Deeds)
2. Property Taxes
3. Prepayment Penalties

**Figure 13-11**

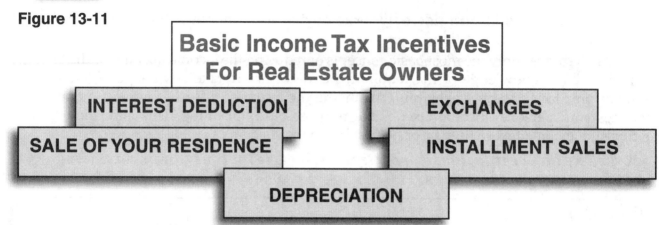

You cannot deduct the cost of personal residence repairs from your federal taxes, except for uninsured casual losses. For example, if your roof blows off and you have no insurance to cover it, the replacement cost can be deducted from your federal income taxes.

*Unlike appraisals, depreciation for tax purposes is NOT based on actual deterioration, but on the calculated useful life of the property.*

### A. DEDUCTION OF INTEREST

Deduction of interest on your home loan from your income taxes is one of the major tax advantages of owning real estate. Buying a first and second home provides the average family with the biggest buffer against income taxes that it is likely to enjoy.

Despite recent income tax reforms, the federal tax laws still provide incentives to those who purchase a first and even a second home. When buying these homes you may finance up to $1 million ($1,000,000) with all the interest paid out during the year fully tax deductible. An additional deduction is available on the interest from home equity loans, taken for any purpose, even buying a second home, of up to $100,000 in principal. The $1,000,000 and $100,000 debit limit is a total applied against both first and second homes together or one owner-occupied home taken separately.

### B. DEDUCTION OF PROPERTY TAXES

Property taxes on your first and second homes are deductible from your income taxes. This makes us feel better about paying local property taxes.

### C. DEDUCTION OF PREPAYMENT PENALTIES

Prepayment penalties are also deductible from your income taxes. If you pay off or drastically reduce your home loan balance, there may be a prepayment penalty.

### D. SALE OF A RESIDENCE

When selling a personal residence, the seller can deduct up to $250,000 ($500,000 if married) of any capital gain. This could be used only once every two years.

*Federal income tax laws allow a taxpayer to exclude up to $250,000 of gain for each individual ($500,000 if married and on the title). This benefit may only be used once every two years for a residence.*

**While the law allows this deduction once every two years, you must reside in the home for two out of the last five years to qualify.** In other words, if you live in the home for a year, then rent it out for three years, you would have to move back in for another year in order to take advantage of this tax break.

The only way to deduct a loss on a personal residence is to turn that property into income-producing property first by renting it. Then any loss based on its sale is deductible because it is income-producing property, not a personal residence.

# VII. Taxes for Income-Producing Properties

Investors of income producing properties can annually deduct these items from income taxes:

1. Mortgage Interest on Loans (no maximum)
2. Property Taxes
3. Prepayment Penalties

In addition they can deduct:

4. Operating Expenses
5. Depreciation of Improvements

## A. DEPRECIATION OF BUSINESS PROPERTY (Federal and State)

*DEPRECIATION FOR TAX PURPOSES is a yearly tax deduction for wear and tear on investment property that is deducted from the taxpayer's income on his or her income tax form.* This deduction applies only to investment property or property used in a business, not on a taxpayer's personal residence. Apartment buildings, commercial buildings, and any building improvements to investment property can be depreciated. The land itself cannot be depreciated.

*Only the buildings and other improvements on income, trade, or business property can be depreciated. Land CANNOT be depreciated under federal income tax law.*

One can only depreciate property that is improved. Since land cannot be depreciated, only the improvements can be depreciated. Currently, the straight-line method is the accepted way to depreciate buildings and other improvements.

*Residential (homes and apartments) property depreciation schedule:*
*Minimum 27.5 years (Straight-line)*
*Commercial improvements depreciation schedule:*
*Minimum 39 years (Straight-line)*

The amount of depreciation must be spread uniformly over the useful life of the property, with the same amount deducted each year (straight-line depreciation). Since most buildings in these inflationary times actually increase in value, depreciation is usually just a technique for postponing income taxes until the property is sold.

**Example:** An apartment building is purchased for $450,000 with land valued at $33,700. Using a 40-year straight-line depreciation schedule, the depreciated book value of the property after 16 years would be $283,480.

## B. ADVANTAGES OF "SALE-LEASEBACK"
### (Buyer Gets to Depreciate New Building Cost)

*In a sale-leaseback for a commercial property, the buyer would be least concerned with the seller's depreciated book value of the property and more concerned with the lease amount the seller is paying, the amount the seller is receiving for the property, and the purchase price of the property.*

If the owner of a business sells his or her building for cash, and then leases it back, the seller becomes a lessee and the buyer the lessor.

**The advantage to the seller:** all lease payments can be deducted from income taxes and he or she receives cash for the building.

**The advantage to the buyer:** he or she can use the purchase price as the new basis for depreciation and establish a new depreciation schedule.

*Seller, now a renter, deducts 100% of future rents paid.*

# VIII. Sale of Real Property

## A. CAPITAL ASSETS (Gains and Losses)

In real estate, a capital asset includes your personal residence (including your second home) and any other real estate because they are long-term investments. When you sell your home or other real estate, there is usually a capital gain or loss. *CAPITAL GAINS are taxed at a lower rate than is ordinary income,* but *CAPITAL LOSSES can be deducted from capital gains.* It is in the public interest to foster investment in land and buildings and other long-term assets so that businesses are encouraged to expand. This in turn creates more job opportunities for everyone.

Congress and President Barrack Obama have passed and established the 2010-2013 capital gains marginal tax rates, based on your taxable income, that range from 10% to 39.6%. This legislation may change.

**www.banks.com/taxes**
U.S. Tax Center

There should be a tax benefit to encourage entrepreneurs to risk investing long-term in things such as equipment, stocks, bonds, and real estate in order to obtain capital gains or losses. Other countries, like Japan and Germany, have very low capital gain tax rates which encourage investment in companies so that more career opportunities are generated for their employees. The size of the nation's "economic pie," which everyone enjoys, increases.

## B. FEDERAL INCOME TAX RATES (Progressive)

As the old saying goes, "Nothing in life is certain, except death and taxes." One other certainty is the constant change in federal tax rates. Income tax rates are progressive. A *PROGRESSIVE TAX is a tax that charges a higher percentage of income as income rises.* So as you make more money, not only does the amount increase, but the rate at which income is taxed also increases. The end effect is that higher income families (the exact ones who usually own businesses and can expand job opportunities) pay most of the income taxes.

The *MARGINAL TAX RATE is the rate that the next dollar earned puts you into. REGRESSIVE TAXES use the same rate no matter how much is spent or earned. Sales tax is an example of a regressive tax.* The rate is the same, so in effect the poor pay a higher percent of their income.

## C. ACCOUNTING FOR THE SALE OF REAL ESTATE

The method of determining a profit or loss on the sale of real property is spelled out by the Internal Revenue Service. Steps 1 and 2 must be completed before determining the profit or loss on a sale (Step 3).

*"Adjusted cost basis" is the base cost, plus capital improvements, minus depreciation and sale expenses.*

| | |
|---|---|
| **(1) Cost Basis (Purchase Price)** | **$500,000** |
| **+ Improvements** | **200,000** |
| | **$700,000** |
| **- Depreciation (tax records)** | **30,200** |
| **= Adjusted Cost Basis** | **$669,800** |
| | |
| **(2) Sale price** | **$1,000,000** |
| **- Sale Expenses** | **32,500** |
| **= Adjusted Sale Price** | **$967,500** |
| **(3) Adjusted Sale Price** | **$967,500** |
| **- Adjusted Cost Basis** | **669,800** |
| **= Gain** | **$297,700** |

# IX. Installment Sales and Exchanges

## A. INSTALLMENT SALES OF REAL ESTATE

An *INSTALLMENT SALE is the sale of real estate in which the payments for the property extend over more than one calendar year.* Installment sales are used to spread a gain over two or more calendar years so that the entire gain is not taxed all in the first year. Our income tax system has progressive rates, which means that the higher the income, the higher the income tax rate for that year. If a person can spread a gain over more than one calendar year, the same income may be taxed at a lower rate.

By doing this the seller avoids the disadvantages of paying for his or her entire gain in one year and thereby has a substantial savings on his or her income taxes. This method is usually used when selling large tracts of land held for a period of time or large buildings owned by one individual.

A sale of a large lot for $100,000 all at once might force you into a higher tax bracket. So by having an installment sale of $25,000 for each of the next four years, you may substantially reduce the total income taxes paid. An installment sale may be a good way to defer income taxes if your income varies from year-to-year; just arrange to get larger installment payments in years when your ordinary income is low.

## B. EXCHANGES TAX-DEFERRED (FEDERAL AND STATE)
### (Section 1031 of the IRS Code)

*In an exchange, the adjusted cost basis of the old property becomes the basis of the new property if there is no boot or mortgage relief.*

An **EXCHANGE** *is a transfer of real estate where one party trades property for another's property.* The property must be of "like kind" in nature or character, not in use, quality, or grade. The exchange may be a straight trade (tax-free) or one party may receive cash in addition to the property (partially tax-free). An exchange can be income tax free, partially taxed, or fully taxed, depending on the cost factors in each particular exchange. Exchanges are too detailed to explain here, but it is a way of deferring or possibly eliminating income taxes on the transfer of real estate.

> **Example:** Able owns an apartment building and undertakes a 1031 exchange. He may exchange his apartment building for one that is more valuable, exchange loans, and pay the balance in cash.

> **Example:** Able owned community property with a cost basis of $95,000 and a fair market value of $125,000. He exchanged this property for another property with a fair market value of $85,000 and received $30,000 cash and a $10,000 promissory note paid over four years. For federal income tax purposes, the entire cash difference of $30,000 is taxable.

To defer all current taxes, a party in an exchange would need to receive a more valuable building with a larger loan on it than the current property and pay compensation to the other party for any difference in the equities. *Any net cash or net mortgage relief that a participant in an exchange might receive in addition to the actual property is known as **BOOT**.* All boot is taxable to the extent of the gain in this partially tax-free exchange (see **Figure 13-12**).

*"Boot" is cash or debt relief. The receiver has recognized gain. If there is no boot in an exchange, the old basis is the new basis.*

Exchanges are popular among apartment owners and commercial property investors. This is because these owners are usually in high-income tax bracket, and exchanging enables them to move up to a more valuable property without paying taxes on the gain. People in higher income tax brackets usually keep their money invested in real estate, and they find exchanges to be a way of selling and buying simultaneously.

**Figure 13-12**

## Tax-Deferred Exchanges

In a "tax-deferred" exchange, boot is defined as cash or mortgage relief given in addition to the property. Boot is the amount received to balance the equities in the exchange. Brokers often encounter the term "boot" when talking with a client about income taxes.

The person receiving boot has a net gain and has to pay taxes on it. When no boot is given or received, then the basis remains the same.

In a tax free exchange, properties must be of a "like kind" in nature or character, not in use, quality, grade, or value. "Tax free" merely means to DEFER the payment of taxes until a later time. Since you can move your equity to another property, it is almost like buying and selling without paying income taxes.

The actual techniques used to understand exchanging are too complex to be explained here, but many six-hour seminars and exchange clubs are available to interested people.

*Exchanges are based on "equity value." Equity is market value minus liens.*

## X. We Are Now Tax Collectors (Federal and State Income Tax Laws – Escrow Usually Takes Care of This)

### A. FEDERAL TAX COLLECTION REQUIREMENTS AND EXEMPTIONS (If a Foreigner) – $300,000 or More

Persons buying property from foreign investors (sellers) are required to set aside 10% of the purchase price for the Internal Revenue Service. This 10% withholding is kept by the IRS to ensure that property capital gains taxes are paid on the transaction. Both the buyer and broker share liability. If this amount is not withheld, the broker may be liable for the full amount of the tax not paid.

In effect, this law holds brokers responsible to check the citizenship of all sellers and see to it that the buyer retains either a 10% deposit, an affidavit from the seller stating that he or she is not a foreigner, or a waiver from the IRS. Residential property purchased for under $300,000 to be used as the buyer's residence is exempted from this withholding. The key points for licensees to remember are these:

1. **Inquire** into the citizenship of all sellers of residential or commercial properties priced at $300,000 or more, even if a foreigner holds only partial or syndicate interest.

2. **Require** a statement of citizenship as part of the listing agreement and then follow up in escrow by having the seller or sellers sign a sworn affidavit.

3. **Do not discriminate.** Require this information of all sellers **in transactions of $300,000 or more**. Even if someone does not appear to be an alien, they might hold foreign citizenship.

The CAR® Seller's Affidavit of Nonforeign Status and/or California Withholding Exemption is a form for the seller to sign swearing that he or she is not a nonresident alien (see **Figure 13-13**). If the seller completes the lower portion of this sworn statement, the buyer and broker may no longer be liable for any portions of unpaid taxes.

**Figure 13-14** shows a Buyer's Affidavit form available from CAR®. This form states that the sales price is less than $300,000 and that the property will be used as a residence. It is signed by the buyer under penalty of perjury. If these two considerations can be met, the buyer is immediately exempted from the withholding requirement. If neither of these forms can truthfully be completed, then the broker should see to it that 10% of the sales price is withheld in escrow or that the proper waiver is obtained from the IRS. The escrow officer will help you with this matter.

### B. STATE TAX COLLECTION REQUIREMENTS AND EXEMPTIONS (If a Foreigner or Resident of Another State) – $100,000 or More

Persons buying property from foreign or out-of-state investors may be required to set aside 3.3% of the sales price for the Franchise Tax Board. If this amount is not withheld, the broker and buyer may be liable for the full amount of income taxes not paid. Escrow usually handles this, but the buyer and broker are responsible.

The exemptions from the buyer withholding 3.3% of the sales price for the Franchise Tax Board are:

1. **Sales price is $100,000 or less**.
2. Property is seller's principle residence, under certain conditions.
3. Seller signs California Residency Declaration.
4. Seller receives a waiver – Franchise Tax Board Form 567A.

# XI. Other Taxes Paid by Brokers

### A. BUSINESS LICENSE TAXES (City Income Taxes)

*A city may levy a tax against real estate brokerage firms, which is based upon the gross receipts, through a **BUSINESS LICENSE TAX**.* In most areas of California, this annual city business license tax is a nominal amount that usually starts at about $100. Other city taxes may also include employee payroll taxes.

### B. SALES TAX

***Sales tax is a tax on only tangible personal property.***

The maximum sales tax penalty is 35% for late filing of sales and use tax, due to fraud or evasion.

## Figure 13-13

CALIFORNIA
ASSOCIATION
OF REALTORS

### SELLER'S AFFIDAVIT OF NONFOREIGN STATUS AND/OR CALIFORNIA WITHHOLDING EXEMPTION
FOREIGN INVESTMENT IN REAL PROPERTY TAX ACT (FIRPTA)
AND CALIFORNIA WITHHOLDING LAW
(Use a separate form for each Transferor)
(C.A.R. Form AS, Revised 11/06)

Internal Revenue Code ("IRC") Section 1445 provides that a transferee of a U.S. real property interest must withhold tax if the transferor is a "foreign person." California Revenue and Taxation Code Section 18662 provides that a transferee of a California real property interest must withhold tax unless an exemption applies.

I understand that this affidavit may be disclosed to the Internal Revenue Service and to the California Franchise Tax Board by the transferee, and that any false statement I have made herein may result in a fine, imprisonment or both.

*123 Sail Avenue*

1. **PROPERTY ADDRESS** (property being transferred): _____ ("Property")
2. **TRANSFEROR'S INFORMATION:** _____ ("Transferor")
   Full Name _____
   Telephone Number _____
   Address _____
   (Use HOME address for individual transferors. Use OFFICE address for an "Entity" i.e.: corporations, partnerships, limited liability companies, trusts and estates.)
   Social Security No., Federal Employer Identification No. or California Corporation No. _____
   **Note: In order to avoid withholding, IRC Section 1445 (b) requires that the Seller (a) provides this affidavit to the Buyer with the Seller's taxpayer identification number ("TIN"), or (b) provides this affidavit, including Seller's TIN, to a "qualified substitute" who furnishes a statement to the Buyer under penalty of perjury that the qualified substitute has such affidavit in their possession. A qualified substitute may be (i) an attorney, title company, or escrow company (but not the Seller's agent) responsible for closing the transaction, or (ii) the Buyer's agent.**
3. **AUTHORITY TO SIGN:** If this document is signed on behalf of an Entity Transferor, THE UNDERSIGNED INDIVIDUAL DECLARES THAT HE/SHE HAS AUTHORITY TO SIGN THIS DOCUMENT ON BEHALF OF THE TRANSFEROR.
4. **FEDERAL LAW:** I, the undersigned, declare under penalty of perjury that, for the reason checked below, if any, I am exempt (or if signed on behalf of an Entity Transferor, the Entity is exempt) from the federal withholding law (FIRPTA):
   ☐ (For individual Transferors) I am not a nonresident alien for purposes of U.S. income taxation.
   ☐ (For corporation, partnership, limited liability company, trust and estate Transferors) The Transferor is not a foreign corporation, foreign partnership, foreign limited liability company, foreign trust or foreign estate, as those terms are defined in the Internal Revenue Code and Income Tax Regulations.
5. **CALIFORNIA LAW:** I, the undersigned, declare under penalty of perjury that, for the reason checked below, if any, I am exempt (or if signed on behalf of an Entity Transferor, the Entity is exempt) from the California withholding law.
   **Certifications which fully exempt the sale from withholding:**
   ☐ The total sales price for the Property is $100,000 or less.
   ☐ The Property qualifies as my principal residence (or the decedent's, if being sold by the decedent's estate) within the meaning of IRC Section 121 (owned and occupied as such for two of the last five years).
   ☐ The Property was last used as my principal residence (or the decedent's, if being sold by the decedent's estate) within the meaning of IRC Section 121 without regard to the two-year time period.
   ☐ The transaction will result in a loss or zero gain for California income tax purposes. (Complete FTB Form 593-E.)
   ☐ The Property has been compulsorily or involuntarily converted (within the meaning of IRC Section 1033) and Transferor intends to acquire property similar or related in service or use to be eligible for non-recognition of gain for California income tax purposes under IRC Section 1033.
   ☐ Transferor is a corporation (or an LLC classified as a corporation) that is either qualified through the California Secretary of State or has a permanent place of business in California.
   ☐ Transferor is a partnership (or an LLC that is not a disregarded single member LLC, classified as a partnership) and recorded title to the Property is in the name of the partnership or LLC. If so, the partnership or LLC must withhold from nonresident partners or members as required.
   ☐ Transferor is exempt from tax under California or federal law.
   ☐ Transferor is an insurance company, qualified pension/profit sharing plan, IRA or charitable remainder trust.
   **Certifications which may partially or fully exempt the sale from withholding:**
   ☐ The Property is being, or will be, exchanged for property of like kind within the meaning of IRC Section 1031.
   ☐ Payments for the Property are being made in installments, the transferor is a non-resident seller and withholding will be applied to each principal payment.
   ☐ As a result of the sale of the Property, Seller's tax liability, calculated at the maximum tax rate regardless of Seller's actual rate, will be less than the 3 1/3% withholding otherwise required. Seller will be required to sign a certification, under penalty of perjury, specifying the amount to be withheld. **(Not to be used for sales closing prior to January 1, 2007)**

By _____ Date _____
(Transferor's Signature) (Indicate if you are signing as the grantor of a revocable/grantor trust.)

_____ _____
Typed or printed name                          Title (If signed on behalf of Entity Transferor)

## Buyer's unauthorized use or disclosure of Seller's TIN could result in civil or criminal liability.

Buyer _____ Date _____
(Buyer acknowledges receipt of a Copy of this Seller's Affidavit)
Buyer _____ Date _____
(Buyer acknowledges receipt of a Copy of this Seller's Affidavit)

Published and Distributed by:
REAL ESTATE BUSINESS SERVICES, INC.
a subsidiary of the California Association of REALTORS®
525 South Virgil Avenue, Los Angeles, California 90020

Reviewed by _____ Date _____

EQUAL HOUSING OPPORTUNITY

AS 11/06 (PAGE 1 OF 2)
**SELLER'S AFFIDAVIT OF NONFOREIGN STATUS AND/OR CALIFORNIA WITHOLDING EXEMPTION (AS PAGE 1 OF 2)**

| Agent: WALT HUBER | Phone: | Fax: | Prepared using zipForm® software |
|---|---|---|---|
| Broker: WALT HUBER REALTOR | | | |

**Figure 13-14**

<table>
<tr><td>

CALIFORNIA
ASSOCIATION
OF REALTORS®

</td><td>

**BUYER'S AFFIDAVIT**
That Buyer is acquiring property for use as a residence
and that sales price does not exceed $300,000.
(FOREIGN INVESTMENT IN REAL PROPERTY TAX ACT)

</td></tr>
</table>

1. I am the transferee (buyer) of real property located at *123 Sail Avenue*,

2. The sales price (total of all consideration in the sale) does not exceed $300,000.

3. I am acquiring the real property for use as a residence. I have definite plans that I or a member of my family will reside in it for at least 50 percent of the number of days it will be in use during each of the first two 12 month periods following the transfer of the property to me. I understand that the members of my family that are included in the last sentence are my brothers, sisters, ancestors, descendents, or spouse.

4. I am making this affidavit in order to establish an exemption from withholding a portion of the sales price of the property under Internal Revenue Code §1445.

5. I understand that if the information in this affidavit is not correct, I may be liable to the Internal Revenue Service for up to 10 percent of the sales price of the property, plus interest and penalties.

Under penalties of perjury, I declare that the statements above are true, correct and complete.

Date _____ Signature _____

Typed or Printed Name _____

Date _____ Signature _____

Typed or Printed Name _____

**IMPORTANT NOTICE:** An affidavit should be signed by each individual transferee to whom it applies. Before you sign, any questions relating to the legal sufficiency of this form, or to whether it applies to a particular transaction, or to the definition of any of the terms used, should be referred to an attorney, certified public accountant, other professional tax advisor, or the Internal Revenue Service.

REBS | Published and Distributed by:
REAL ESTATE BUSINESS SERVICES, INC.
*a subsidiary of the California Association of REALTORS®*
525 South Virgil Avenue, Los Angeles, California 90020

OFFICE USE ONLY
Reviewed by Broker
or Designee _____
Date _____

EQUAL HOUSING OPPORTUNITY

**FORM AB-11 REVISED 2/91**

| Agent: WALT HUBER | Phone: | Fax: | Prepared using zipForm® software |
|---|---|---|---|
| Broker: WALT HUBER REALTOR | | | |

### 1. Successor's Liability

To avoid successor's liability in the sale of a business that collects sales tax, the buyer should be certain to include a provision in the purchase agreement that an amount for any sales tax collected and not yet paid is to be held in escrow until a clearance receipt is received from the State Board of Equalization.

*A buyer is protected from successor's liability by obtaining a "clearance receipt" from the State Board of Equalization.*

---

## XII. CHAPTER SUMMARY

**Real property taxes** are determined by the value of the real property (ad valorem) and are reassessed each time a property is sold at 1% of its selling price. The **County Assessor** assesses taxes, the **County Tax Collector** collects them, and the **County Board of Supervisors** sets the rates. **Proposition 13** limits the amount of taxes to 1% of the 1975 market value of the property plus a cumulative increase of 2% in market value each year thereafter, called **assessed valuation**.

Property taxes due are, in effect, liens against that specific property. Important tax dates include **November 1** (first installment), **December 10** (first installment is delinquent), **February 1** (second installment) and **April 10** (second installment is delinquent), or **No Darn Fooling Around**.

If taxes are not paid on or before June 30, the property is sold to the state, beginning a 5-year **redemption period**. After five years, the delinquent property is deeded to the state and sold at a **public tax auction**.

The **homeowner's property tax exemption** is $7,000 of assessed valuation. And, although California has no exemption for low income families, it does have senior citizen and disabled person tax rebates and postponements, as well as veterans' and non-profit organizations' tax exemptions.

Local improvement taxes for off-site improvements like streets, sewers, irrigation, etc. are called **special assessment taxes**. Additional taxes that may be incurred include: **documentary transfer taxes**, **Mello-Roos liens** (for which disclosure is required), **federal gift taxes**, and **federal estate taxes**.

Interest, property taxes and prepayment penalties paid on a personal residence can be deducted from income taxes. Federal income tax allows a taxpayer to exclude up to $250,000 of gain for each individual ($500,000 if married and on title). When you sell your home (capital asset) a capital gain or loss results. **Capital gains** are taxed at a lower rate than ordinary income tax rates.

A loss on a sale of a personal residence can also be deducted if it is turned into **income producing property** by renting it. Income property owners can deduct **mortgage interest**, **property taxes**, and **prepayment penalties**, as well as **operating expenses** and **depreciation**, but not losses due to vacancies. If a business owner sells a building for cash, then leases it back (a **sale-leaseback**), the seller becomes the lessee and the buyer the lessor, and the seller can deduct 100% of future rents paid.

Federal taxes are **progressive**, meaning the percentage paid increases as the amount to be taxed increases, which is the opposite of sales taxes, which are regressive.

In addition to depreciation, two major tax benefits of owning income-producing property are **installment sales** (gain is only taxed in the year it is received) and **1031 tax-deferred exchanges** (a means of deferring or eliminating income taxes on property transfers). Cash or debt relief gained in a tax-deferred exchange is known as **boot**.

Persons buying property from **foreign investors** are required to set aside 10% of the purchase price for the IRS, to insure the property capital gains taxes are paid on the transaction. An additional 3.3% of the sales price for the Franchise Tax Board may also have to be withheld. In both cases, the burden is on the buyer and broker, not the seller. Brokers may also have to pay a **business license tax**, which is a city tax based on gross receipts.

## XIII. TERMINOLOGY

**A.** Ad Valorem
**B.** Assessed Valuation
**C.** Boot
**D.** County Assessor
**E.** County Collector
**F.** Depreciation for Tax Purposes
**G.** Documentary Transfer Tax
**H.** Donee

**I.** Donor
**J.** Exchange
**K.** Federal and State Income Tax
**L.** Federal Estate Tax
**M.** Federal Gift Tax
**N.** Homeowner's Property Tax Exemption
**O.** Installment Sale

**P.** Proposition 13
**Q.** Real Property Taxes
**R.** Renter's Credit
**S.** Special Assessment
**T.** Two Out of the Last 5 Years
**U.** $250,000

1.____ Value placed upon property, for property tax purposes, by the tax assessor.

2.____ The sale of property in installments that spreads tax on profit from a sale of property over a number of years.

3.____ A tax charged according to the value of the property.

4.____ One who gives a gift.

5.____ A tax against the property of a deceased, based on the value of the estate.

6.____ One who receives a gift.

7.____ In a tax-deferred exchange, any cash or other property included in the transaction to make the exchange an even proposition.

8.____ The trading of parcels of real property to obtain tax benefits that might not be available in a normal sale. Generally considered tax-deferred, not tax-exempt.

9.____ An annual tax that applies to real estate that is based on the assessed valuation of the property.

10.____ The person, in a given political division within a state, who is responsible for collecting property taxes.

11.____ One who estimates the value of property for property tax purposes.

12.____ A renter's deduction allowed from state income taxes payable, under certain conditions.

13.____ A loss in value of improvements as an accounting procedure: used as a deduction on income taxes.

14.____ A lien assessed against real property in a given district, by a public authority to pay costs of special public improvements.

15.____ A tax on the sale of real property, usually based on the sales price and paid on or before the recordation of the deed.

16.____ Federal taxes paid on the giving of real property as a gift, if over an exempted amount.

17.____ Limits the amount of taxes to a maximum of 1% of the March 1, 1975 market value of the property plus the cumulative increase of 2% in market value each year thereafter.

18.____ Personal taxes paid annually on your taxable income.

19.____ A deduction of up to $7,000 from an owner-resident's assessed valuation on his or her property tax bill. Must be filed between March 1 and April 15 each year, to receive the full deduction.

20.____ The length of time a couple must live in their house to qualify for a $500,000 exclusion.

21.____ The amount that is exempt if a single person sells his or her house.

## XIV. CHAPTER QUIZ

1. The county assessor accumulates a list of all private owners of real property in his or her jurisdiction. The assessment roll is used to:

    a. set the tax rate for each year.
    b. establish the tax base for the county.
    c. determine the taxes to be paid by individual property owners.
    d. equalize the assessment throughout the county.

2. Senior citizens may be able to defer the payment of the property taxes on their residence. In order to find out if they qualify for the program, the senior citizen should contact the:

    a. Real Estate Commissioner.
    b. State Franchise Tax Board.
    c. State Housing Authority.
    d. County Tax Assessor.

3. The difference between property taxes and special assessments is that:

    a. assessment liens are always subordinate to property tax liens.
    b. assessment liens can only be levied by local improvement districts.
    c. foreclosure of assessment liens can only be achieved by court foreclosure.
    d. special assessments are levied for the cost of specific local improvements, while property tax revenue goes into the general fund.

4. The Street Improvement Act of 1911 can be used by a developer for all the following, except:

    a. constructing sewers.
    b. improving streets.
    c. constructing streets.
    d. purchase of land for subdividing.

5. The primary responsibility for disclosing any Mello-Roos bonds or assessments to a buyer when a home is sold lies with:

    a. the seller.
    b. the seller's agent.
    c. the buyer's agent.
    d. all of the above.

6. A subdivider wanted to subdivide his property into many lots and sell individual lots to potential builders of single-family homes. To finance the off-site improvements that include streets, sidewalks, and schools he would:

    a. approach the State of California for funding.
    b. ask the local governmental bodies to institute a special assessment to pay for the improvements.
    c. institute a Mello-Roos municipal bond.
    d. obtain a blanket encumbrance.

7. A home sold for $200,000. The buyer assumed an existing loan against the property for $160,000. The documentary transfer tax for this county is $.55 per $500 of consideration. The transfer tax is:

    a. $11.
    b. $22.
    c. $33.
    d. $44.

8. Under Federal Income Tax Laws, most real estate licensees are considered:

    a. employees of the broker.
    b. employees of the seller.
    c. independent contractors.
    d. any of the above.

9. Which of the following is true regarding the depreciation of land under federal income tax law?

    a. Land may be depreciated by the 125% declining balance method.
    b. Owner may deduct the accrued depreciation of land over time.
    c. Land may be depreciated by the sum of the year's digits method.
    d. Land cannot be depreciated under federal income tax law.

10. Able owns an apartment building and undertakes a 1031 exchange. He may:

    a. exchange his apartment building for one more valuable, exchange loans, and pay the balance in cash.
    b. purchase an apartment building of lesser value.
    c. purchase personal property as long as it is lesser value.
    d. none of the above.

**ANSWERS:** 1. b; 2. b; 3. d; 4. d; 5. a; 6. c; 7. d; 8. c; 9. d; 10. a

# CHAPTER 14
# Licensing, Education, and Associations

## I. Department of Real Estate (DRE)

In California, all real estate agreements are under the jurisdiction of the *CALIFORNIA DEPARTMENT OF REAL ESTATE (DRE), which is the regulatory agency for real estate in California.* The main purpose of this department is to protect the public by enactment and enforcement of laws relating to real estate and by establishing requirements for real estate salespersons' or brokers' licenses.

The California Department of Real Estate is responsible for regulating real estate brokerage matters and the enforcement of real estate laws. These laws help protect both the individual citizen and the real estate profession. There are obvious benefits derived by shielding citizens from dishonest or incompetent real estate licensees. The reputation of the real estate profession is upheld by making sure that all practicing salespeople and brokers are both honest and capable of performing their jobs properly.

The California Department of Real Estate is governed by the Real Estate Commissioner. The Commissioner, who sets all the rules and regulations for the Department of Real Estate, receives his or her power from the state legislature. The legislature, in turn, used police power to create the position of Commissioner. *POLICE POWER is the right to enact and enforce laws beneficial to the health, safety, morals, and general welfare of the public.*

### A. REAL ESTATE COMMISSIONER (Appointed by the Governor)

*The Real Estate Commissioner will start an action against a licensee with an accusation.*

**www.ca.gov**
Welcome to California - Online Services

In addition to his/her position as chairperson of the State Real Estate Advisory Commission, the *REAL ESTATE COMMISSIONER is the chief executive of the Department of Real Estate.* It is the Commissioner's duty, therefore, to mold the department's policy, create regulations, and to enforce Real Estate Law (found in the Business and Professions Code) so that both real estate purchasers and real estate licensed agents benefit from his or her rulings.

## CHAPTER OUTLINE

*The Commissioner enforces the Real Estate Law, but does not replace a court of law.*

The Commissioner's other duties include:

1. Deciding the business policy of the State Department of Real Estate.

2. Informing the Governor and other state officials as to what services the department can render to the state and provide them with descriptions of the department's licenses.

3. Recommending changes in policy that may have been deemed necessary for the good of the public and the business of real estate in California.

4. Regulating the sales of subdivisions.

5. Deciding if applicants for real estate licenses have met all the experience and education requirements.

6. Investigating complaints against allegedly incompetent license holders.

7. Investigating complaints against those performing acts without the required license.

*The Commissioner does not give legal advice, and do not settle commission (payment for real estate services) disputes. Commission disputes are settled by arbitration or civil lawsuits in local courts.*

**Example:** At close of escrow the seller decided not to pay the commission. The broker/agent can file civil action in court (or in binding mediation if initialed in listing agreement).

The Real Estate Commissioner has the power to call formal hearings to discuss any issue concerning an applicant for a license, a current license holder, or a subdivider. The Commissioner may subsequently suspend, revoke or deny a license. He or she could also halt sales (desist and refrain order) in a subdivision.

*The maximum fine the Real Estate Commissioner can levy against a broker who pays an unlicensed person for soliciting borrowers or negotiating loans is $20,000.*

# II. Real Estate License Requirements

As mentioned in the preceding section, the Real Estate Commissioner's main purpose is the regulation of the real estate business in the state of California. This regulation is accomplished by imposing mandatory licenses on those individuals who choose to work in the field of real estate. Who is required to have these licenses?

*In short, any person who is actively involved in a real estate transaction at the service of another, in the expectation of receiving a commission, must be licensed.*

## A. WHO MUST HAVE A LICENSE

A person is required to have a license if he or she:

1. sells or offers to sell, buys or offers to buy, and solicits buyers or sellers;
2. solicits or obtains listings;
3. negotiates the purchase, sale, or exchange of real property or business opportunities;
4. leases or rents, collects rents, or negotiates the sale, purchase, or exchange of leases;
5. assists in the purchase of leases on lands owned by the state or federal government;
6. negotiates loans, collects payments, or performs services for borrowers or lenders.

*Any person found to be involved in such actions without a license may be guilty of breaking the Real Estate Law, under which stiff penalties can be imposed.*

## B. WHEN A LICENSE IS NOT REQUIRED

It should be noted that there are a few exceptions to these regulations. The following people, because of the nature of their work, are exempt from the licensing regulations (NO LICENSE REQUIRED):

1. Employees of lending institutions.
2. Lenders making federally insured or guaranteed loans.
3. Certain agricultural associations.
4. Licensed personal property brokers.
5. Cemetery authorities.
6. Collectors of loans made on real property.
7. Certain clerical help.

A individual who is not a real estate salesperson or broker may solicit for the sale of real property (according to Section 10133 of the Real Estate Law) as long as he or she is:

1. the owner.
2. holding power of attorney for the owner.
3. an attorney at law acting on behalf of the owner.
4. a receiver or court appointee.
5. a trustee, selling under a deed of trust.

The **Federal SAFE Act of 2008** requires all persons/entities performing acts such as mortgage loan originations to be registered with and/or licensed through the **Nationwide Mortgage Licensing System and Registry (NMLS/NMLS&R).**

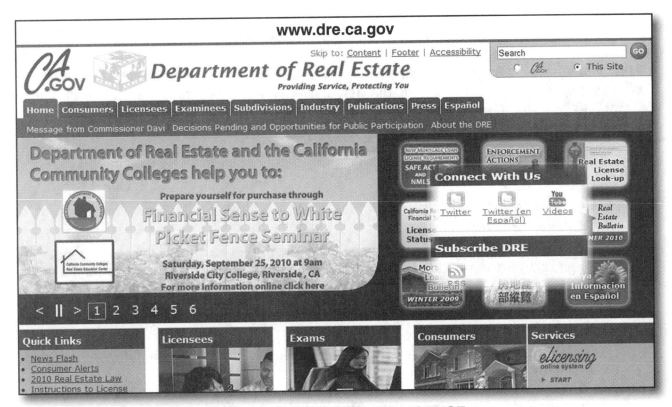

## C. OBTAINING THE FOUR-YEAR SALESPERSON'S LICENSE

To obtain a real estate salesperson license, you must first qualify for and pass a written examination. After passing the exam, a license application must be submitted to and approved by the Department of Real Estate (DRE).

*You are now allowed to file your examination and license application at the same time.*

1. **Age:** You must be 18 years of age to be licensed, but there is no age restriction for taking the exam.

2. **Residence:** Proof of legal presence in the United States is required. If you're not a California resident, refer to "Out-of-State Applicants" on the DRE website.

3. **Honesty:** Applicants must be honest and truthful. Conviction of a crime may result in denial of a license.

4. **Education:** Successful completion of the following college-level courses is required to become a real estate salesperson:

   a. **Real Estate Principles**

   b. **Real Estate Practice**

   c. One additional DRE-approved real estate course

For further information, call or write any district office of the Department of Real Estate. You can access the pamphlet, *Instructions to License Applicants* (see **Figure 14-1**) on the DRE website.

---

## Applicants for the Salesperson's Exam

The original salesperson examination applicants will be required to submit evidence of completion of a three semester, or quarter unit equivalent, college-level course in **Real Estate Principles, Real Estate Practice**, and one additional course which should be chosen from the following list of courses:

| | |
|---|---|
| Legal Aspects of Real Estate | Real Estate Office Administration |
| Real Estate Appraisal | Computer Applications in Real Estate |
| Real Estate Finance | Real Estate Economics |
| Property Management | Business Law |
| Escrows | Accounting |
| Mortgage Loan Brokering and Lending | Common Interest Developments |

---

### 1. DRE and Electronic Exams

The DRE offers an electronic testing system at some DRE testing facilities. Check their website for more information.

### 2. Four-Year Salesperson's License (Regular, Renewable License)

To obtain a regular four-year salesperson's license, the applicant must:

1. complete a college-level **Real Estate Principles course**, a **Real Estate Practice course**, and one other approved college-level (broker-required) course;
2. pass the DRE salesperson's exam, and
3. pay the necessary fees.

### 3. Salesperson's Examination

To pass, an applicant must achieve a score of at least 70% in the three-hour, fifteen-minute salesperson's exam, which has 150 multiple-choice questions. Exams are scheduled during the morning or afternoon. A nonrefundable fee is required to take the test. If you fail, you may take the exam as often as you wish, but you must pay for each exam application. See **Figure 14-2** for the salesperson's and broker's requirements.

*The use of a silent, battery-operated, pocket-sized electronic calculator that is nonprogrammable and does not have a printout capability is permitted.*

### 4. Notification of Examination Results

You will be notified of your examination results by mail, normally within five working days after the examination. You can also check your examination results using the DRE exam website (**dre.ca.gov/elic_exam_services.html**).

To pass the examination, you must correctly answer at least 70% of the questions. The examination is qualifying in nature; applicants who pass are not informed of their score. You will be notified of the actual score and the percentage of questions answered correctly in each of the seven subject areas only when unsuccessful. Those who pass will receive an application for a license. Those who do not receive a passing grade will automatically receive a re-examination form.

*With the implementation of electronic DRE testing, an applicant will know if he or she passed or failed before leaving the testing facility.*

You may not apply for a re-examination until after notification of failure of a prior test. Another application fee payment will be required. There is no limitation to the number of re-examinations you may take during the two-year period following the date of the filing of the original application. If you wish to take additional examinations after the two-year period, you must complete a new application.

*Applicants for the salesperson's license must apply for a license within one year from the exam passing date, NOT the date of notification of passing.*

### 5. Electronic Fingerprint Requirement (Salesperson and Broker)

Applicants for the salesperson's license must apply for a license within one year from the exam date.

If you have taken Principles and Practice, plus one other required course and have passed the examination, you are qualified to apply for a four-year renewable license. You must pay $51 (paid to scan service provider—fee may vary) for the live scan set of your fingerprints.

Upon completion of the real estate license exam, a copy of RE Form 237 (the Live Scan Service Request Form) will be mailed to all applicants. A list of providers of the live scan fingerprinting technique is available through the DRE website (**dre.ca.gov**).

## D. OBTAINING THE BROKER'S LICENSE (Renewable Four-Year License)

A *BROKER'S LICENSE* is required of any individual who wants to operate a real estate office. The candidate for a real estate broker's license examination must:

1. be 18 years of age to apply for a license, although there is no age restriction for taking the exam;
2. provide Proof of Legal Presence in the United States;
3. if not a California resident, refer to "Out-of-State Applicants" on DRE website;
4. have had previous experience (two years or college education);
5. complete the required eight broker courses;
6. be honest and truthful;
7. pass the required DRE examination (Governmental Photo ID required).

### 1. Broker's Qualifying Experience

A candidate must also be able to prove that he or she has experience in real estate before applying for a broker's license. Generally, two years of full-time work (104 forty-hour

**Figure 14-1**

# Department of Real Estate (DRE)

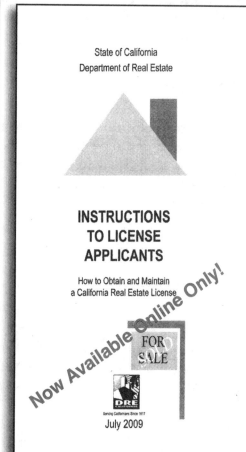

State of California
Department of Real Estate

**INSTRUCTIONS
TO LICENSE
APPLICANTS**

How to Obtain and Maintain
a California Real Estate License

*Now Available Online Only!*

FOR
SALE

July 2009

## *PRINCIPAL OFFICE*

**SACRAMENTO**
2201 Broadway, Sacramento, CA  95818-2500
(916-227-0931)

 www.dre.ca.gov

| **All offices open
8-5 weekdays** |
| --- |

## *DISTRICT OFFICES*

**LOS ANGELES** Suite 350 (213-620-2072)
320 W. 4th St. Los Angeles, CA  90013-1105

**OAKLAND** Suite 702 (510-622-2552)
1515 Clay St., Oakland, CA  94612-1402

**SAN DIEGO** Suite 3064 (619-525-4192)
1350 Front St., San Diego, CA  92101-3687

**FRESNO** Rm. 3070 (559-445-5009)
2550 Mariposa Mall, Fresno, CA  93721-2273

---

## Proof of Legal Presence in the United States

The **Personal Responsibility and Work Opportunity Act** (the "Act") requires states to eliminate a broad array of public benefits for illegal immigrants. The definition of a public benefit includes professional and occupational licenses issued to individuals by state agencies. For purposes of the Department of Real Estate, the term "public benefit" applies to original and renewal real estate salesperson and broker licenses, prepaid rental listing service licenses, and a payment from the Real Estate Recovery Account.

To implement the provisions of the Act, the Department has adopted Regulation 2718. This regulation requires **proof of legal presence in the United States from all applicants for a license**, and from applicants for payment from the Real Estate Recovery Account. This requirement applies to applicants for both original and renewal licenses.

# Figure 14-2

| EXAMINATION SUBJECT AREAS | SALESPERSON EXAM | BROKER EXAM |
|---|:---:|:---:|
| **1. Property Ownership and Land Use Controls and Regulations** | **18%** | **15%** |
| Classes of property; Property characteristics; Encumbrances; Types of ownership; Descriptions of property; Government rights in land; Public controls; Environmental hazards and regulations; Private controls; Water rights; Special categories of land | | |
| **2. Laws of Agency** | **12%** | **12%** |
| Law, definition, and nature of agency relationships, types of agencies, and agents; Creation of agency and agency agreements; Responsibilities of agent to seller/buyer as principal; Disclosure of agency; Disclosure of acting as principal or other interest; Termination of agency; Commission and fees | | |
| **3. Valuation and Market Analysis** | **12%** | **11%** |
| Value; Methods of estimating value | | |
| **4. Financing** | **13%** | **13%** |
| General concepts; Types of loans; Sources of financing; How to deal with lenders; Government programs; Mortgages/deeds of trust/ notes; Financing/credit laws; Loan brokerage | | |
| **5. Transfer of Property** | **9%** | **10%** |
| Title insurance; Deeds; Escrow; Reports; Tax aspects; Special processes | | |
| **6. Practice of Real Estate and Mandated Disclosures** | **24%** | **27%** |
| Trust account management; Fair housing laws; Truth in advertising; Record keeping requirements; Agent supervision; Permitted activities of unlicensed sales assistants; DRE jurisdiction and disciplinary actions; Licensing, continuing education requirements and procedures; California Real Estate Recovery Fund; General ethics; Technology; Property management/landlord-tenant rights; Commercial/industrial/income properties; Specialty areas; Transfer disclosure statement; Natural hazard disclosure statements; Material facts affecting property value; Need for inspection and obtaining/ verifying information | | |
| **7. Contracts** | **12%** | **12%** |
| General; Listing agreements; Buyer broker agreements; Offers/ purchase contracts; Counter offers/multiple counter offers; Leases; Agreements; Promissory notes/securities | | |

**Dept. of Real Estate
% of Exam Questions
Testing Emphasis**

**For more information:**

**www.dre.ca.gov**
(Department of Real Estate Home Page)

**www.dre.ca.gov/exm_content_sales.html**
(Salesperson Examination Content and Test Questions)

---

### Applicants for the Broker's Exam

1. An applicant for the broker's license examination must have completed eight courses in addition to the experience requirements. These eight courses must include the following five:

**Real Estate Practice**
**Legal Aspects of Real Estate**
**Real Estate Finance**

**Real Estate Appraisal**
**Real Estate Economics (or Accounting)**

2. The remaining three courses are to be selected from the following:

**Real Estate Principles**
**Business Law**
**Property Management**
**Escrows**
**Real Estate Office Administration**
**Mortgage Loan Brokering and Lending**

**Advanced Legal Aspects of Real Estate**
**Advanced Real Estate Finance**
**Advanced Real Estate Appraisal**
**Computer Applications in Real Estate**
**Common Interest Development**

---

weeks) as a salesperson is required. This two-year requirement may be replaced by an equivalent amount of part-time salesperson work. Such experience must have been completed within the five years immediately preceding the date of application.

Sometimes the State Real Estate Commissioner will accept experience in fields other than real estate sales. These fields include contract work, lease, escrow, title insurance, bonds, mortgage company, or experience in another area directly involved in real estate.

**Besides direct experience in these fields, education may qualify as full or partial experience. For example, the Commissioner has ruled that any individual with a four-year college degree is exempt from the two-year experience requirement.** But, all candidates must complete the eight required real estate courses, regardless of their educational degree.

All students are encouraged to submit an equivalency request with the Department of Real Estate. All decisions made by the Commissioner are final.

*B.S. or B.A. (four-year degree) = 2 years of experience*

Most California colleges and universities offer courses and majors in real estate (see **Figure 14-3**).

The broker's 200-question exam takes five hours to complete. The applicant must answer 75% of the questions correctly to pass.

### 2. Broker's Required Education (Eight Courses)

Applicants for the real estate broker's license examination must have successfully completed the eight statutory-required, college-level courses. The required salesperson's

**Figure 14-3**

# ADVANCED EDUCATION IN REAL ESTATE

As the study of real estate becomes more complex and more intertwined with other business disciplines, students of real estate find it rewarding to continue their studies beyond those levels required to enter the field as a salesperson or broker. Many real estate professionals, after obtaining their A.A. degrees from one of our 108 community colleges, have gone on to pursue bachelor's and master's degrees.

## CALIFORNIA STATE UNIVERSITY SYSTEM

Bakersfield
Channel Islands
Chico
Dominguez Hills
Fresno
Fullerton
Hayward
Humboldt
Long Beach
Los Angeles
Maritime
Academy
Monterey Bay

Northridge
Pomona*
Sacramento*
San Bernardino
San Diego*
San Francisco
San Jose
San Luis Obispo
San Marcos
Sonoma
Stanislaus

*Regional centers for RELUI
Real Estate and Land Use Institute
Cal State University, Sacramento
Sacramento, CA 95819*

## UNIVERSITY OF CALIFORNIA SYSTEM

Berkeley**
Davis
Irvine
Los Angeles***
Merced

Riverside
San Diego
San Francisco
Santa Barbara
Santa Cruz

*\*\*The U.C. Berkeley Fisher Center for Real Estate and Urban Economics (FCREUE) publishes a newsletter, Quarterly Report, which may be obtained by instructors and school libraries by writing (on college stationery) to, or contacting: Haas Real Estate Group or FCREUE: Haas School of Business, University of California Berkeley, CA 94720-1900; Tel: (510) 643-6105; Fax: (510) 643-7357; Email: creue@haas.berkeley.edu.*

*\*\*\*U.C.L.A. offers information on recent trends in real estate. For more information, contact the Richard S. Ziman Center for Real Estate, 110 Westwood Plaza, Los Angeles, CA 90095; Phone: (310) 206-9424; Fax: (310) 206-5455; ziman.center@anderson.ucla.edu*

## EXTENSION COURSES

The UC and Cal State University campuses also offer extension programs for persons interested in a more in-depth study of certain areas of real estate without the constraints of a degree program. Classes are generally offered in the evening or on weekends.

## Filing a Ficticious Business Name

To file a fictitious business name, the broker must: 1) file a fictitious business name statement in the county where he/she intends to operate; 2) publish the fictitious business name in a newspaper of general circulation; and 3) obtain approval of the name by the Real Estate Commissioner and be issued a license in the name of the fictitious business name.

courses can be found on the list of required broker's courses, but the number of required courses is different: three for the regular salesperson's license and eight for the broker's license. An applicant's choice of eight (broker-required) courses must be taken by all broker candidates.

Once all of these requirements have been completed, a candidate may apply to take the broker's examination. By filing the examination fee, plus proof of 2 years' experience or the equivalent thereof, and transcripts showing that the eight statutory classes have been completed, the applicant will receive his or her admission card for the test. The cost of a broker's license is $165.

*Members of the bar will generally qualify on the basis of their education and experience and are exempt from the college-level course requirements. Law school graduates who are not members of the state bar are required to successfully complete a college-level course in Real Estate Finance and one in Real Estate Appraisal.*

### E. RENEWAL OF LICENSE – EVERY FOUR YEARS (Salesperson and Broker)

*If a real estate license is not renewed, the licensee has a two-year grace period and late renewal fees.*

Once the license has expired, no licensed-required activity can be performed by the salesperson until the license has been renewed. The late renewal period (often referred to as the "grace" period) simply allows the licensee to renew on a late basis without retaking the examination; it does not allow the licensee to conduct license-required activity during the late renewal period. The license renewal fee for a salesperson is $245 if filed on time and $367 if filed late. A broker's renewal costs $300 if on time and $450 if late.

*Whenever a real estate salesperson enters the employ of a real estate broker, or whenever the salesperson is terminated, the broker shall immediately notify the Department of Real Estate in writing.*

### F. CONTINUING EDUCATION (CE) REQUIREMENT
### (45 Hours Every Four Years to Renew Your License)

All real estate licensees are required to attend 45 clock hours of Commissioner-approved courses, seminars, or conferences during the four-year period preceding license renewal. First time renewal for both broker and salesperson requires five separate three-hour courses in the following subjects: Ethics, Agency, Trust Fund Handling, Fair Housing, and Risk Management; a minimum of 18 clock hours of Consumer Protection Courses, and the remaining 15 clock hours related to either Consumer Service or Consumer Protection. **Figure 14-4** shows continuing education requirements for second and subsequent renewals.

---

**Figure 14-4**

## 45 Hours of Required Continuing Education

**The required 45 hours of continuing education for second and subsequent renewals include:**

12 hours of: Ethics, Agency, Trust Fund Handling, and Fair Housing **or** one six-hour course that covers the four mandatory subjects (Ethics, Agency, Trust Fund Handling, and Fair Housing);

One three-hour course in Risk Management, 18 clock hours of consumer protection courses, and the remaining clock hours to complete the 45 hours of continuing education may be related to either Consumer Service or Consumer Protection courses.

---

*18 hours of Consumer Protection, including Agency, Ethics, Trust Fund Handling, Fair Housing, and Risk Management are all included in the required 45 hours of continuing education.*

### 1. "Eight-Hour Continuing Education (CE) Survey" Course

The "Eight-Hour CE Survey" course can replace the 15-hour combination of five separate 3-hour courses (Ethics, Agency, Trust Fund Handling, Fair Housing, and Risk Management), starting with your second license renewal. So if a licensee takes the *Eight-hour CE Survey* course, he or she still needs an additional 30 hours of CE to complete the 45 total hours required every four years at license renewal time.

## G. OTHER REAL ESTATE-RELATED LICENSES

### 1. Prepaid Rental Listing Service License

A *PREPAID RENTAL LISTING SERVICE (PRLS) license is required when running a business that supplies prospective tenants with listings of residential real property for rent or lease while collecting a fee for such service.* Negotiation of the rental of property is not a part of this activity. An individual may obtain, without examination, a two-year license to conduct PRLS activities.

Prior to issuance of the PRLS license, the applicant must submit, and have approved by the DRE, a contract to be entered into between the licensee and client (prospective tenant). Fingerprints and a $2,500 surety bond are required for each business location.

### 2. Real Property Securities Dealer (RPSD) Endorsement

A *REAL PROPERTY SECURITIES DEALER (RPSD) is any person acting as a principal or agent who engages in the business of selling real property securities (such as promissory notes or sales contracts).* RPSDs also accept or offer to accept funds for reinvestment in real property securities or for placement in an account. Before a licensed real estate broker may act in the capacity of an RPSD, he or she must obtain an RPSD endorsement on his or her broker's license. To obtain an RPSD endorsement on a broker's license, submit the appropriate endorsement fee along with proof of a properly executed $10,000 surety bond. (For information on Real Property Securities, see Chapter 9 or call the DRE.)

**www.corp.ca.gov**
Department of Corporations

# III. Business Opportunity Brokerage

In a sale of an existing business (Business Opportunity), the real property is transferred by "deed." If money is owed on the business, the proper financial statements are filed with the Secretary of State's office.

*Personal property is transferred by a "bill of sale."*

Your real estate license also authorizes you to practice in the specialized field of "Business Opportunities." This is a different area of real estate, and requires knowledge and experience beyond that which is needed for real property transactions. The business opportunity broker's transactions usually include the three items shown in **Figure 14-5**.

**www.census.gov**
U.S. Census Bureau
**www.sba.gov**
Small Business Administration

## A. BUSINESS OPPORTUNITY SALE

A common definition of a *BUSINESS is an establishment whose main purpose is the buying and reselling of goods, or the performance of services, with the intention of making a profit. A BUSINESS OPPORTUNITY is the sale or lease of a business, including the goodwill of an existing business.* It involves the sale of personal property and must also conform to the rules and laws that govern the transfer of chattels (personal property). The most common types of business opportunities are small, locally owned neighborhood businesses like grocery stores, liquor stores, laundromats, service stations, and restaurants.

---

**Figure 14-5** **Sale of a Business (3 Assets)**

| 1. REAL PROPERTY | 2. PERSONAL PROPERTY | 3. GOODWILL |
|---|---|---|
| Sale or Lease | Equipment and Trade Fixtures | Reputation and Established Sales |
| | (Tangible) | (Intangible) |

---

The three documents in a personal property security transaction are: 1) a promissory note; 2) a security agreement; and 3) compliance with the UCC-1 financing statement.

## B. BUSINESS OPPORTUNITY LISTING

A business opportunity salesperson should have a working knowledge of business practices and a thorough understanding of accounting or bookkeeping principles. The seller of the business must give you all the pertinent information as part of the listing agreement. The accuracy of the information, however, should be validated by the listing broker.

Business opportunities can involve the transfer of both real and personal property and usually use one escrow.

The business opportunity listing should include all the information necessary for a real property sale. It should also include the:

1. name of business and owner.
2. nature and location of business.
3. price and terms of sale.
4. encumbrances and items that are to be assumed by the buyer.

In addition, if there is a lease, the terms should be stated. The important income information should detail the gross income, expenses, and net income. If there is competition in the area, it should be so stated. The usual business hours each day and the square footage of the building should also be stated. If the current employees are expected to stay, salary and any existing fringe benefits should be explained in detail.

Buyers of businesses differ. They are usually motivated by the thought of becoming their own boss or the need for a steady income, and they usually fall into one of these two categories:

1. The experienced individual with a background in the field or business he or she is buying.
2. The new buyer who is usually young and inexperienced.

The experienced individual will usually need only the basic facts in order to decide whether to purchase or not. The inexperienced buyer needs more help, but is sometimes hesitant to ask questions, so all pertinent facts should be explained in detail to that person. He or she should also be informed of applicable laws that govern that particular business.

## C. BULK SALES (TRANSFER OF BUSINESS INVENTORY)
### (Notice to Creditors Required)

A *BULK TRANSFER is any sale of a substantial part of the 1) inventory, items purchased for resale; 2) other supplies and equipment associated with a business.* Division 6 of the Uniform Commercial Code (UCC) requires the purchaser (transferee) in a bulk transfer to give the seller's (transferor's) creditors fair warning that a sale of all or a major part of the inventory is about to take place.

### 1. Buyer (Transferee) Must Comply with the UCC

If a retail or wholesale merchant transfers a substantial part of his or her materials, supplies, merchandise, or inventory, the transferee involved in the transfer must give notice by:

1. **Twelve business days prior** to transfer, recorded notice with the County Recorder's Office.

2. **Twelve business days prior** to transfer, published notice in a newspaper of general circulation in the county or judicial district.

3. **Twelve business days prior** to transfer, delivered notice (by hand or registered mail) to the County Tax Collector.

### 2. Protection for Creditors

This notice must include:

1. notification that the transfer is going to take place.
2. the name and any business addresses used by the seller.
3. the location and a description of the property.
4. the place and date of the transfer.

If all of the conditions of the bulk transfer notice are not met, any transfer of bulk is fraudulent and void against creditors, but valid between buyer and seller.

## D. CALIFORNIA SALES TAXES (Selling Retail)

*SALES TAXES are taxes imposed on the sale of **tangible personal property** by retailers.* This is important to brokers and salespeople who are in transactions involving the sale of businesses where sales of tangible personal property is involved. A seller's permit from the State Board of Equalization is the permit that allows sellers to buy at wholesale without paying sales tax as long as they collect sales taxes from their customers and forward these taxes to the State Board of Equalization. Before selling a business, escrow should check to see if there are any past due sales taxes.

# IV. Real Estate Law and Regulations

California laws affecting real estate are included in several different acts and codes. The **CALIFORNIA REAL ESTATE LAW** *is the portion of the Business and Professions Code that refers to licensing and subdivisions.* On the other hand, the **COMMISSIONER'S REGULATIONS** *are rules that form part of the California Administrative Code established and enforced by the Commissioner of Real Estate.* All licensees should be familiar with the Real Estate Law, the Commissioner's Regulations, and (as mentioned before) the Subdivided Lands Act administered by the Commissioner.

## A. ENFORCEMENT OF REAL ESTATE LAW

Licensing and regulatory law is effective only to the extent that it is enforced. The Commissioner, as the chief officer of the Department of Real Estate, is duty bound to enforce the provisions of the Real Estate Law. The Commissioner may, by his or her own choice, and must upon a verified complaint in writing, investigate the actions of any person engaged in the real estate business or acting in the capacity of a licensee within this state. He or she has the power to suspend any real estate license or to revoke it permanently. The Commissioner also has the authority to deny a license to an applicant if the applicant does not meet the full requirements of the law. If, through the screening process (including the fingerprint record) of an applicant for license, it is found that he or she has a criminal record or some other record that may adversely reflect on his or her character, an investigation is made by the Commissioner's staff. A formal hearing may be ordered to determine whether or not the applicant meets the requirements of honesty, truthfulness, and good reputation.

## B. HEARINGS FOR LICENSE VIOLATIONS

One function of Real Estate Law is to hold a hearing when there is a question as to the rights of persons to obtain or keep their real estate licenses. The Department of Real Estate and other licensing agencies must conduct hearings with strict regard for the rules set forth in the Administrative Procedure Act. Before denying, suspending, or revoking any license, the licensee is served a statement, and the Commissioner acts as the complainant. The licensee, or respondent as he or she is known in the hearing procedures, may appear with or without counsel. The hearing is conducted according to rules of evidence in civil matters.

A decision is made by the hearing officer based upon his or her findings. The Commissioner may reject or accept the proposed decision or reduce the proposed penalty, and then make his or her official decision. The respondent has the right of appeal to the courts. If the testimony substantiates the charges and they appear to be sufficiently serious, the license of the respondent is suspended or revoked. After a license is revoked, the person affected may not apply for reinstatement until one year has passed.

## C. LICENSES: REVOKE, RESTRICT, SUSPEND

*The Real Estate Commissioner can revoke, restrict, or suspend the license of any real estate agent for misconduct.*

### 1. Child Support Obligations (150-Day License)

*When the Department of Real Estate obtains live-scan fingerprints and performs a background check on a potential licensee, the Department is looking for late child support payments.*

The DRE will not issue or renew a full-term license if the applicant is on a list of persons (obligors) who have not complied with a court order to provide child support payments. The DRE will issue them a 150-day license. The Department of Child Support Services compiles a list of delinquencies of over four months, and active licensees who appear on the list have 150 days to get current or have their licenses suspended. The license will not be issued or suspension revoked until a release is furnished from the district attorneys' office.

**Example:** A real estate salesperson owes the Department of Child Support Services for back child support payments. He may obtain a **temporary license** for 150 days.

# V. Common Real Estate Law Violations

*In order to obtain information about the ethical or unethical conduct of a real estate licensee, one would most likely consult the Business and Professions Code.*

Section 10176 of the Business and Professions Code is the legal guideline for the licensee engaged in the practice and performance of any of the acts within the scope of the Real Estate Law. Section 10177 of the Business and Professions Code applies to situations where the licensee involved was not necessarily acting as an agent or as a licensee.

All agents must adhere to the ethical and legal requirements of Section 10176 and Section 10177 of the Business and Professions Code, which include violations such as misrepresentation and failure to disclose hidden relationships.

## A. SECTION 10176: LICENSEE ACTING IN A LICENSEE CAPACITY

This section of the Real Estate Law is for violations by those licensees who are acting within the scope of their licenses (see **Figure 14-6**).

## B. SECTION 10177: LICENSEE NOT NECESSARILY ACTING AS A LICENSEE

Section 10177 applies to situations where the affected party was not necessarily acting in the capacity of an agent or as a real estate licensee (see **Figure 14-7**). The vast majority of brokers and salespeople are honest and perform their services in a straightforward manner. Occasionally, a section of the Real Estate Law may be violated inadvertently and without intent. In such cases the Commissioner would most likely consider restriction of the real estate license. On the other hand, a flagrant violation would most likely cause a revocation of the license.

*It is "blind advertising" if a broker gives the impression that he or she is the owner of the property for sale. The Real Estate Commissioner does not approve of pocket listings (kept within real estate office)—they are not part of the professional code and guidelines and are unethical.*

**Example:** A broker runs the following ad on his listings: "4 BR, 3 BA home with swimming pool and spa for sale for $300,000. Call 555-1234." This is called a blind ad because there is no name, address, or broker's license number.

## C. REGULATIONS OF THE COMMISSIONER (Found in the Administrative Code)

Real Estate Law empowers the Commissioner to issue regulations to aid in the administration and enforcement of the law. These regulations, which are known formally as the Regulations of the Real Estate Commissioner, have the force and effect of the law itself. Licensees and prospective licensees should be familiar with these regulations. The California Department of Real Estate produces a factual law book entitled *Real Estate Law* (*Real Estate Law and Regulations of the Real Estate Commissioner*), which can be obtained from their office.

## Figure 14-6
# Business & Professions Code 10176
### (Real Estate Licensee <u>Acting</u> As Licensee)
## Grounds for Revocation or Suspension

### Misrepresentation - 10176(a)

The licensee must disclose to his or her principal all material facts that the principal should know. Failure to do so or lying is cause for disciplinary action. A great majority of the complaints received by the Commissioner allege misrepresentation on the part of the broker or his or her salespeople.

### False Promise - 10176(b)

A false promise is a false statement about what the promisor is going to do in the future. Many times a false promise is provided by showing the promise was impossible to perform and that the person making the promise knew it was impossible.

### Continued and Flagrant Misrepresentation by Agents - 10176(c)

This section gives the commissioner the right to discipline a licensee for a continued and flagrant course of misrepresentation or making of false promises through real estate agents or salespeople.

### Divided Agency - 10176(d)

This section requires a licensee to inform all his or her principals if he or she is acting as agent for more than one party in a transaction.

### Commingling - 10176(e)

Commingling takes place when a broker has mixed the funds of his or her principals with his or her own money. A broker should keep all funds separate.

### Definite Termination Date - 10176(f)

A specified termination date, in writing, is required for all exclusive listing transactions.

### Secret Profit - 10176(g)

Secret profit cases usually arise when the broker makes a low offer, usually through a "dummy" purchaser, when he or she already has a higher offer from another buyer. The difference is the secret profit.

### Listing Option - 10176(h)

This section requires a licensee, when he or she has used a form which is both an option and a listing, to obtain the written consent of his or her principal approving the amount of such profit before the licensee may exercise the option. This does not apply where a licensee is using an option only.

### Dishonest Dealing - 10176(i)

Dishonest dealing is a catch-all section used when the acts of the person required a license, but he or she did not have a license.

### Signatures of Prospective Purchasers - 10176(j)

Brokers must obtain a written (business opportunities) authorization to sell from an owner before securing the signature of a prospective purchaser to the agreement. This section strikes at what was once a common practice in some areas in the sale of business opportunities, where the prospective purchaser was forced to deal with the broker who furnished him or her the listing.

**Figure 14-7**

# Business and Professions Code 10177
## (R.E. Licensee <u>Not Necessarily Acting</u> as a Licensee)
## Grounds for Revocation or Suspension

### Obtaining License by Fraud - Section 10177(a)

This section gives the Commissioner the power to take action against a licensee for misstatements of fact in an application for a license and in those instances where licenses have been procured by fraud, misrepresentation, or deceit.

### Convictions - Section 10177(b)

This section permits proceedings against a licensee after a criminal conviction for either a felony or a misdemeanor which involves moral turpitude (anything contrary to justice, honesty, modesty, or good morals).

### False Advertising - Section 10177(c)

This section makes licensees who are parties to false advertising subject to disciplinary action. The ban extends to subdivision sales as well general property sales.

### Violations of Other Sections - Section 10177(d)

This section gives the Department authority to proceed against the licensee for violation of any of the other sections of the Real Estate Law, the regulations of the Commissioner, and the subdivision laws.

### Misuse of Trade Name - Section 10177(e)

Only active members of the national association or local associations of real estate boards are permitted to use the term "REALTOR®." This is a term belonging exclusively to such members, and no licensee may advertise or hold himself or herself out as a "REALTOR®" without proper entitlement.

### Conduct Warranting Denial - Section 10177(f)

This is a general section of the Real Estate Law and almost any act involving crime or dishonesty will fall within it. An essential requirement for the issuance of a license is that the applicant be honest, truthful, and of good reputation.

### Negligence or Incompetence - Section 10177(g)

**Demonstrated negligence or incompetence, while acting as a licensee, is just cause for disciplinary action. The department proceeds in those cases where the licensee is so careless or unqualified that to allow him or her to handle a transaction would endanger the interests of his or her clients or customers.**

### Supervision of Salespersons - Section 10177(h)

A broker is subject to disciplinary action if he or she fails to exercise reasonable supervision over the activities of his or her salespersons.

### Violating Government Trust - Section 10177(i)

Prescribes disciplinary liability for using government employment to violate the confidential nature of records thereby made available.

### Other Dishonest Conduct - Section 10177(j)

Specifies that any other conduct which constitutes fraud or dishonest dealings may subject the ones involved to license suspension or revocation.

### Restricted License Violation - Section 10177(k)

Makes violation of the terms, conditions, restrictions, and limitations contained in any order granting a restricted license grounds for disciplinary action.

### Inducement of Panic Selling (Blockbusting) - Section 10177(l)

It is a cause for disciplinary action to solicit or induce a sale, lease, or the listing for sale or lease, of residential property on the grounds of loss of value because of entry into the neighborhood of a person or persons of another race, color, religion, ancestry, or national origin.

### Violation of Franchise Investment Law - Section 10177(m)

Violates any of the provisions of the Franchise Investment Law or any regulations of the Corporations Commissioner pertaining thereto.

### Violation of Securities Law - Section 10177(n)

Violates any of the provisions of the Corporations Code or any regulations of the Commissioner of Corporations relating to securities as specified.

### Violation of Securities Law - Section 10177(o)

Failure to disclose to buyer the nature and extent of ownership interest licensee has in property in which the licensee is an agent for the buyer. Also, failure to disclose ownership on the part of licensee's relative or special acquaintance in which licensee has ownership interest.

## Importance of Section 10176 and Section 10177
## REGULATIONS OF THE COMMISSIONER

The Real Estate Commissioner is empowered to adopt Regulations for the administration and enforcement of the Real Estate Law and the Subdivided Lands Law. Duly adopted regulations become part of the California Code of Regulations and, in effect, have the force and authority of the law itself. Therefore, all licensees, prospective licensees, and subdividers should be thoroughly familiar with the Real Estate Commissioner's Regulations.

**10176.** The Commissioner may, upon his or her own motion, and shall, upon the verified complaint in writing of any person, investigate the actions of any person engaged in the business or acting in the capacity of a real estate licensee within this state, and he or she may temporarily suspend or permanently revoke a real estate license at any time where the licensee, while a real estate licensee, in performing or attempting to perform any of the acts within the scope of this chapter, has been guilty of any act listed in this Section.

**10177.** The Commissioner may suspend or revoke the license of any real estate licensee or may deny the issuance of a license to an applicant or may suspend or revoke the license of, or deny the issuance of a license to, a corporate applicant if an officer, director, or person owning or controlling 10 percent or more of the corporation's stock has done any of the acts listed in this section.

**www.dre.ca.gov**
**California Department of Real Estate**

# VI. Real Estate General Fund

*All the money collected from license and exam fees goes into the* **REAL ESTATE GENERAL FUND**. Eighty percent of this money is used for the operating expenses of the Department of Real Estate. Twenty percent of the Real Estate General Fund is set aside as follows:

1. Eight percent to the Real Estate Education and Research Fund;
2. Twelve percent to the Recovery Fund.

The **RECOVERY FUND** *was established for the payment of damages and arbitration awards to people who have suffered financial loss due to the wrongful act of a licensee in a real estate transaction.* To qualify for these funds, plaintiffs must first obtain a judgment in civil court (or through arbitration) against a licensee on the grounds of fraud, misrepresentation, deceit, or conversion of trust funds. If after reasonable effort the judgment remains uncollected, a claim may be filed with the Commissioner's office.

*A license is suspended until the fund is reimbursed (plus interest). The maximum award from the Recovery Fund is $250,000 per individual licensee ($50,000 maximum per occurrence).*

California is one of the few states that actively helps protect the public against fraudulent acts by real estate licensees.

# VII. Trade and Professional Associations

A **TRADE OR PROFESSIONAL ASSOCIATION** *is a voluntary, nonprofit organization made up of independent firms in the same industry.* It is formed to promote progress, aid in solving the industry's problems, and enhance its service to the community. We will discuss the role of local boards of REALTORS®, the California Association of REALTORS® (CAR), the National Association of REALTORS® (NAR) and its Code of Ethics, and the term Realtist.

## A. LOCAL REAL ESTATE ASSOCIATIONS

The **LOCAL ASSOCIATION OF REALTORS®** *is a voluntary organization of real estate licensees in a particular community.* A broker is entitled to full membership, a salesperson may be an associate member, and a nonrealtor (who is in a real estate related field) may be an affiliate member. For example, an affiliate member might work for a title insurance company, an escrow company, a lender, or any other business having an interest in local real estate activities.

Local boards usually provide a multiple listing service for their members so that all members can be equally informed. Most local boards provide services such as distribution of educational material, seminars, library services, and other worthwhile services for the local REALTORS®.

**www.bhbr.com**
Beverly Hills, California, Board of REALTORS®

*CAR® subscribes to numerous "Social Networking" sites, including Facebook, Twitter, YouTube, LinkedIn, and other blogs. CAR®'s "Green" website is "green.car.org."*

## B. CALIFORNIA ASSOCIATION OF REALTORS® (CAR)

The *CALIFORNIA ASSOCIATION OF REALTORS® is the state division of the National Association of REALTORS®.* It is a voluntary organization whose membership includes local realty boards throughout the state and individual members who are not affiliated with any particular local board. With the exception of NAR, CAR is the largest REALTOR® organization in the United States, with over 100,000 members in California. The objectives of the California Association of REALTORS® are:

1. To promote high standards and unite its members.
2. To safeguard the property-buying public.
3. To foster legislation for the benefit and protection of the real estate field.
4. To cooperate in the economic growth and development of the state.

CAR has many standing committees that meet at director's meetings, seminars, and annual conventions. These committees specialize in specific areas such as education, ethics, legislation, political affairs, real property taxation, professional standards, and many other areas. There are also many divisions of CAR.

Most of the people who are successful salespeople are also members of the California Association of REALTORS®. We suggest you become a member of this or some other trade association when you are serious about selling real estate.

## C. NATIONAL ASSOCIATION OF REALTORS® (NAR)

The *NATIONAL ASSOCIATION OF REALTORS® is the national trade association for all the state associations and local boards of REALTORS® in the United States.* NAR unifies the real estate industry at the national level. It encourages legislation favorable to the real estate industry and enforces professional conduct standards on behalf of its members across the nation.

### 1. Trade Name

*Misuse of the name "REALTOR" is a violation of the California Real Estate Law.*

Only active members of the National Association of REALTORS® (NAR) or the California Association of REALTORS® (CAR), through their local real estate boards, are permitted to use the term REALTOR®. This is a term belonging exclusively to such members, and no licensee may advertise or present himself or herself to be a REALTOR® if not associated with such a group.

*The NAR website has links to social networking sites, including LinkedIn, Twitter, and Facebook.*

The National Association of REALTORS® has affiliated institutes, societies, and councils that provide a wide-ranging menu of programs and services that assist members in increasing skills, productivity, and knowledge (see **Figure 14-8**).

*If a broker uses the term "Realtor" or "Realtist" and is NOT a member of that group, this is both unethical and unlawful.*

### 2. Code of Ethics

See **Figure 14-9** for the National Association of REALTORS® Code of Ethics. These guidelines show not only how one should act but also how one must act.

The National Association of REALTORS® and its state and local divisions form a composite organization of brokers whose objective is to forward the interests of brokers, encourage education of practitioners and the public, raise the standard of real estate practice and increase the esteem in which brokers are held by their fellow citizens. To this end, a code of ethics has been formulated and adopted. It is the generally accepted code of ethics for real estate people and every REALTOR® swears to abide by it.

## D. REALTIST DEFINED

*"Realtist" is the name for a member of the National Association of Real Estate Brokers (NAREB). They have a social networking presence on Facebook, YouTube, and Twitter, and LinkedIn.*

The National Association of Real Estate Brokers, or "Realtist," is the oldest minority trade association in the United States. *Although composed principally of African Americans and other minority real estate professionals, the **REALTIST** organization is an integrated entity open to all practitioners who are committed to achieving "democracy in housing."*

The organization has local boards in the largest cities in most states. The organization in this state, called the California Association of Real Estate Brokers, has four board affiliations:

1. Associated Real Property Brokers, Oakland
2. Consolidated Real Estate Brokers, Sacramento
3. Consolidated Realty Board, Los Angeles
4. Logan Heights Realty Board, San Diego

A Realtist must be a member of a local board as well as a member of the national organization. Both on the local and national levels, Realtists work for better housing in the communities they serve. In many instances, individuals are both Realtors® and Realtists by virtue of dual membership.

### E. NATIONAL ASSOCIATION OF HISPANIC REAL ESTATE PROFESSIONALS (NAHREP)

The National Association of Hispanic Real Estate Professionals (NAHREP) is a national non-profit trade association made up primarily of Hispanic members. This association was created to establish a venue where members can congregate, exchange ideas, and formulate an agenda beneficial to the collective well-being of the Hispanic segment of the industry. The mission statement of NAHREP is "To increase the Hispanic homeownership rate by empowering the real estate professionals that serve Hispanic consumers."

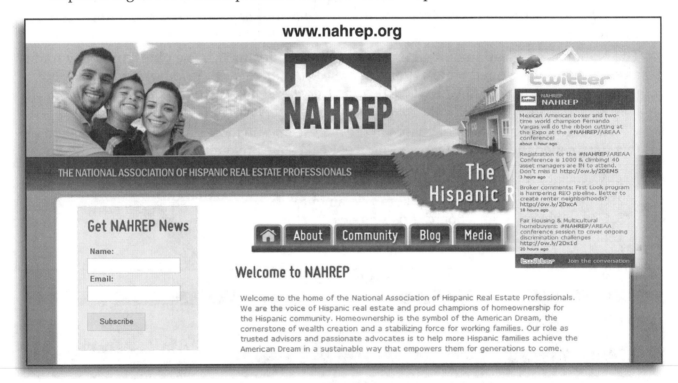

### F. ASIAN REAL ESTATE ASSOCIATION OF AMERICA (AREAA)

The Asian Real Estate Association of America (AREAA) is a national trade association committed to enhancing business opportunities and success of real estate professionals serving the Asian American community. AREAA is dedicated to promoting homeownership opportunities among the many Asian American communities throughout the nation.

**Figure 14-8**

# NAR Affiliates

### 1. American Society of Real Estate Counselors (ASREC)

This division of NAR offers the CRE (Counselor of Real Estate) designation.

### 2. Commercial Investment Real Estate Institute (CIREI)

CIREI enhances the professional development of those engaged in commercial investment real estate. Offers the CCIM (Certified Commercial Investment Member) designation.

www.ccim.com

### 3. Realtors® National Marketing Institute (RNMI)

RNMI promotes professional competence in real estate sales and brokerage, and real estate brokerage management. It has two councils:

### A. Council of Real Estate Brokerage Managers (CRB)

Recognized throughout the industry as the professional peer organization for managers of residential, commercial, industrial, relocation, appraising and property management companies. The CRB designation is available for members who meet experience requirements and complete a series of courses.

www.crb.com

### B. Counselors of Real Estate (CRE)

The Counselors of Real Estate is a professional membership organization established exclusively for leading real property advisors.

www.cre.org

### 4. Certified Residential Specialists (CRS)

This designation is awarded to the top producing agents in the country who complete advanced training in selling and listing.

www.crs.com

▼

## 5. Graduate Realtor® Institute (GRI)

The GRI symbol is recognized nationwide, showing buyers, sellers, and other real estate industry members that you are a true professional, and have a solid grasp of real estate fundamentals. It is the dominant real estate designation in California.

 www.edesignations.com

## 6. Real Estate Buyer's Agent Council (REBAC)

REBAC (Real Estate Buyer's Agent Council) serves Realtors® members who wish to devote all or part of their business to the practice of buyer's agency.

## 7. Society of Industrial and Office Realtors® (SIOR)

An international organization whose members specialize in a variety of commercial real estate activities. They offer the SIOR designation.

 www.sior.com

## 8. Women's Council of Realtors® (WCR)

WCR offers opportunities for developing leadership skills as well as a Referral and Relocation Certification (RRC). This is the only referral and relocation certification offered by NAR.

## 9. Professional Real Estate Executive (PRE)

The PRE designation is available for corporate real estate executives who meet experience and course completion criteria.

 www.realtor.org
NAR - All these affiliates can be accessed here

## 10. Seniors Real Estate Specialist (SRES)

A Seniors Real Estate Specialist® (SRES) is experienced and knowledgeable in meeting the specific needs of clients 45 years or older. SRES has demonstrated requisite knowledge and expertise to counsel senior clients through major financial and lifestyle transitions involved in relocating, refinancing, or selling the family home.

 www.seniorsrealestate.com

## 11. The Institute of Real Estate Management (IREM)

This is an organization, within NAR, of professional property managers. They offer a number of designations including:

**A. Certified Property Manager (CPM)**
**B. Accredited Residential Manager (ARM)**
**C. Accredited Management Organization (AMO)**

 www.irem.org/home.cfm

**Figure 14-9**   NOTE: The Code of Ethics is updated yearly.

## Code of Ethics and Standards of Practice of the National Association of REALTORS® Effective January 1, 2010

Duties to Clients and Customers
Duties to the Public
Duties to REALTORS®

Where the word REALTORS® is used in this Code and Preamble, it shall be deemed to include REALTOR-ASSOCIATE®s.

While the Code of Ethics establishes obligations that may be higher than those mandated by law, in any instance where the Code of Ethics and the law conflict, the obligations of the law must take precedence.

### Preamble

Under all is the land. Upon its wise utilization and widely allocated ownership depend the survival and growth of free institutions and of our civilization. REALTORS® should recognize that the interests of the nation and its citizens require the highest and best use of the land and the widest distribution of land ownership. They require the creation of adequate housing, the building of functioning cities, the development of productive industries and farms, and the preservation of a healthful environment.

Such interests impose obligations beyond those of ordinary commerce. They impose grave social responsibility and a patriotic duty to which REALTORS® should dedicate themselves, and for which they should be diligent in preparing themselves. REALTORS®, therefore, are zealous to maintain and improve the standards of their calling and share with their fellow REALTORS® a common responsibility for its integrity and honor.

In recognition and appreciation of their obligations to clients, customers, the public, and each other, REALTORS® continuously strive to become and remain informed on issues affecting real estate and, as knowledgeable professionals, they willingly share the fruit of their experience and study with others. They identify and take steps, through enforcement of this Code of Ethics and by assisting appropriate regulatory bodies, to eliminate practices which may damage the public or which might discredit or bring dishonor to the real estate profession. REALTORS® having direct personal knowledge of conduct that may violate the Code of Ethics involving misappropriation of client or customer funds or property, willful discrimination, or fraud resulting in substantial economic harm, bring such matters to the attention of the appropriate Board or Association of REALTORS®. (Amended 1/00)

Realizing that cooperation with other real estate professionals promotes the best interests of those who utilize their services, REALTORS® urge exclusive representation of clients; do not attempt to gain any unfair advantage over their competitors; and they refrain from making unsolicited comments about other practitioners. In instances where their opinion is sought, or where REALTORS® believe that comment is necessary, their opinion is offered in an objective, professional manner, uninfluenced by any personal motivation or potential advantage or gain.

The term REALTOR® has come to connote competency, fairness, and high integrity resulting from adherence to a lofty ideal of moral conduct in business relations. No inducement of profit and no instruction from clients ever can justify departure from this ideal.

In the interpretation of this obligation, REALTORS® can take no safer guide than that which has been handed down through the centuries, embodied in the Golden Rule, "Whatsoever ye would that others should do to you, do ye even so to them."

Accepting this standard as their own, REALTORS® pledge to observe its spirit in all of their activities whether conducted personally, through associates or others, or via technological means, and to conduct their business in accordance with the tenets set forth below. (Amended 1/07)

### Duties to Clients and Customers

#### Article 1

When representing a buyer, seller, landlord, tenant, or other client as an agent, REALTORS® pledge themselves to protect and promote the interests of their client. This obligation to the client is primary, but it does not relieve REALTORS® of their obligation to treat all parties honestly. When serving a buyer, seller, landlord, tenant or other party in a non-agency capacity, REALTORS® remain obligated to treat all parties honestly. (Amended 1/01)

#### Standard of Practice 1-1

REALTORS®, when acting as principals in a real estate transaction, remain obligated by the duties imposed by the Code of Ethics. (Amended 1/93)

#### Standard of Practice 1-2

The duties imposed by the Code of Ethics encompass all real estate-related activities and transactions whether conducted in person, electronically, or through any other means.

The duties the Code of Ethics imposes are applicable whether REALTORS® are acting as agents or in legally recognized non-agency capacities except that any duty imposed exclusively on agents by law or regulation shall not be imposed by this Code of Ethics on REALTORS® acting in non-agency capacities.

As used in this Code of Ethics, "client" means the person(s) or entity(ies) with whom a REALTOR® or a REALTOR®'s firm has an agency or legally recognized non-agency relationship; "customer" means a party to a real estate transaction who receives information, services, or benefits but has no contractual relationship with the REALTOR® or the REALTOR®'s firm; "prospect" means a purchaser, seller, tenant, or landlord who is not subject to a representation relationship with the REALTOR® or REALTOR®'s firm; "agent" means a real estate licensee (including brokers and sales associates) acting in an agency relationship as defined by state law or regulation; and "broker" means a real estate licensee (including brokers and sales associates) acting as an agent or in a legally recognized non-agency capacity. (Adopted 1/95, Amended 1/07)

#### Standard of Practice 1-3

REALTORS®, in attempting to secure a listing, shall not deliberately mislead the owner as to market value.

#### Standard of Practice 1-4

REALTORS®, when seeking to become a buyer/tenant representative, shall not mislead buyers or tenants as to savings or other benefits that might be realized through use of the REALTOR®'s services. (Amended 1/93)

#### Standard of Practice 1-5

REALTORS® may represent the seller/landlord and buyer/tenant in the same transaction only after full disclosure to and with informed consent of both parties. (Adopted 1/93)

#### Standard of Practice 1-6

REALTORS® shall submit offers and counter-offers objectively and as quickly as possible. (Adopted 1/93, Amended 1/95)

#### Standard of Practice 1-7

When acting as listing brokers, REALTORS® shall continue to submit to the seller/landlord all offers and counter-offers until closing or execution of a lease unless the seller/landlord has waived this obligation in writing. REALTORS® shall not be obligated to continue to market the property after an offer has been accepted by the seller/landlord. REALTORS® shall recommend that sellers/landlords obtain the advice of legal counsel prior to acceptance of a subsequent offer except where the acceptance is contingent on the termination of the pre-existing purchase contract or lease. (Amended 1/93)

## Standard of Practice 1-8

REALTORS®, acting as agents or brokers of buyers/tenants, shall submit to buyers/tenants all offers and counter-offers until acceptance but have no obligation to continue to show properties to their clients after an offer has been accepted unless otherwise agreed in writing. REALTORS®, acting as agents or brokers of buyers/tenants, shall recommend that buyers/tenants obtain the advice of legal counsel if there is a question as to whether a pre-existing contract has been terminated. (Adopted 1/93, Amended 1/99)

## Standard of Practice 1-9

The obligation of REALTORS® to preserve confidential information (as defined by state law) provided by their clients in the course of any agency relationship or non-agency relationship recognized by law continues after termination of agency relationships or any non-agency relationships recognized by law. REALTORS® shall not knowingly, during or following the termination of professional relationships with their clients: reveal confidential information of clients; or use confidential information of clients to the disadvantage of clients; or use confidential information of clients for the REALTOR®'s advantage or the advantage of third parties unless: clients consent after full disclosure; or REALTORS® are required by court order; or it is the intention of a client to commit a crime and the information is necessary to prevent the crime; or it is necessary to defend a REALTOR® or the REALTOR®'s employees or associates against an accusation of wrongful conduct.

Information concerning latent material defects is not considered confidential information under this Code of Ethics. (Adopted 1/93, Amended 1/01)

## Standard of Practice 1-10

REALTORS® shall, consistent with the terms and conditions of their real estate licensure and their property management agreement, competently manage the property of clients with due regard for the rights, safety and health of tenants and others lawfully on the premises. (Adopted 1/95, Amended 1/00)

## Standard of Practice 1-11

REALTORS® who are employed to maintain or manage a client's property shall exercise due diligence and make reasonable efforts to protect it against reasonably foreseeable contingencies and losses. (Adopted 1/95)

## Standard of Practice 1-12

When entering into listing contracts, REALTORS® must advise sellers/landlords of:

the REALTOR®'s company policies regarding cooperation and the amount(s) of any compensation that will be offered to subagents, buyer/tenant agents, and/or brokers acting in legally recognized non-agency capacities; the fact that buyer/tenant agents or brokers, even if compensated by listing brokers, or by sellers/landlords may represent the interests of buyers/tenants; and any potential for listing brokers to act as disclosed dual agents, e.g. buyer/tenant agents. (Adopted 1/93, Renumbered 1/98, Amended 1/03)

## Standard of Practice 1-13

When entering into buyer/tenant agreements, REALTORS® must advise potential clients of: the REALTOR®'s company policies regarding cooperation; the amount of compensation to be paid by the client; the potential for additional or offsetting compensation from other brokers, from the seller or landlord, or from other parties; any potential for the buyer/tenant representative to act as a disclosed dual agent, e.g. listing broker, subagent, landlord's agent, etc., and the possibility that sellers or sellers' representatives may not treat the existence, terms, or conditions of offers as confidential unless confidentiality is required by law, regulation, or by any confidentiality agreement between the parties. (Adopted 1/93, Renumbered 1/98, Amended 1/06)

## Standard of Practice 1-14

Fees for preparing appraisals or other valuations shall not be contingent upon the amount of the appraisal or valuation. (Adopted 1/02)

## Standard of Practice 1-15

REALTORS®, in response to inquiries from buyers or cooperating brokers shall, with the sellers' approval, disclose the existence of offers on the property. Where disclosure is authorized, REALTORS® shall also disclose, if asked, whether offers were obtained by the listing licensee, another licensee in the listing firm, or by a cooperating broker. (Adopted 1/03, Amended 1/09))

## Article 2

REALTORS® shall avoid exaggeration, misrepresentation, or concealment of pertinent facts relating to the property or the transaction. REALTORS® shall not, however, be obligated to discover latent defects in the property, to advise on matters outside the scope of their real estate license, or to disclose facts which are confidential under the scope of agency or non-agency relationships as defined by state law. (Amended 1/00)

## Standard of Practice 2-1

REALTORS® shall only be obligated to discover and disclose adverse factors reasonably apparent to someone with expertise in those areas required by their real estate licensing authority. Article 2 does not impose upon the REALTOR® the obligation of expertise in other professional or technical disciplines. (Amended 1/96)

## Standard of Practice 2-2

(Renumbered as Standard of Practice 1-12 1/98)

## Standard of Practice 2-3

(Renumbered as Standard of Practice 1-13 1/98)

## Standard of Practice 2-4

REALTORS® shall not be parties to the naming of a false consideration in any document, unless it be the naming of an obviously nominal consideration.

## Standard of Practice 2-5

Factors defined as "non-material" by law or regulation or which are expressly referenced in law or regulation as not being subject to disclosure are considered not "pertinent" for purposes of Article 2. (Adopted 1/93)

## Article 3

REALTORS® shall cooperate with other brokers except when cooperation is not in the client's best interest. The obligation to cooperate does not include the obligation to share commissions, fees, or to otherwise compensate another broker. (Amended 1/95)

## Standard of Practice 3-1

REALTORS®, acting as exclusive agents or brokers of sellers/ landlords, establish the terms and conditions of offers to cooperate. Unless expressly indicated in offers to cooperate, cooperating brokers may not assume that the offer of cooperation includes an offer of compensation. Terms of compensation, if any, shall be ascertained by cooperating brokers before beginning efforts to accept the offer of cooperation. (Amended 1/99)

## Standard of Practice 3-2

To be effective, any change in compensation offered for cooperative services must be communicated to the other REALTOR® prior to the time that REALTOR® submits an offer to purchase/lease the property. (Amended 1/10)

## Standard of Practice 3-3

Standard of Practice 3-2 does not preclude the listing broker and cooperating broker from entering into an agreement to change cooperative compensation. (Adopted 1/94)

## Standard of Practice 3-4

REALTORS®, acting as listing brokers, have an affirmative obligation to disclose the existence of dual or variable rate commission arrangements (i.e., listings where one amount of commission is payable if the listing broker's firm is the procuring cause of sale/lease and a different amount of commission is payable if the sale/lease results through the efforts of the seller/ landlord or a cooperating broker). The listing broker shall, as soon as practical, disclose the existence of such arrangements to potential cooperating brokers and shall, in response to inquiries from cooperating brokers, disclose the differential that would result in a cooperative transaction or in a sale/lease that results through the efforts of the seller/landlord. If the cooperating broker is a buyer/tenant representative, the buyer/tenant representative must disclose such information to their client before the client makes an offer to purchase or lease. (Amended 1/02)

### Standard of Practice 3-5

It is the obligation of subagents to promptly disclose all pertinent facts to the principal's agent prior to as well as after a purchase or lease agreement is executed. (Amended 1/93)

### Standard of Practice 3-6

REALTORS® shall disclose the existence of accepted offers, including offers with unresolved contingencies, to any broker seeking cooperation. (Adopted 5/86, Amended 1/04)

### Standard of Practice 3-7

When seeking information from another REALTOR® concerning property under a management or listing agreement, REALTORS® shall disclose their REALTOR® status and whether their interest is personal or on behalf of a client and, if on behalf of a client, their representational status. (Amended 1/95)

### Standard of Practice 3-8

REALTORS® shall not misrepresent the availability of access to show or inspect a listed property. (Amended 11/87)

### Standard of Practice 3-9

REALTORS® shall not provide access to listed property on terms other than those established by the owner or the listing broker. (Adopted 1/10)

## Article 4

REALTORS® shall not acquire an interest in or buy or present offers from themselves, any member of their immediate families, their firms or any member thereof, or any entities in which they have any ownership interest, any real property without making their true position known to the owner or the owner's agent or broker. In selling property they own, or in which they have any interest, REALTORS® shall reveal their ownership or interest in writing to the purchaser or the purchaser's representative. (Amended 1/00)

### Standard of Practice 4-1

For the protection of all parties, the disclosures required by Article 4 shall be in writing and provided by REALTORS® prior to the signing of any contract. (Adopted 2/86)

## Article 5

REALTORS® shall not undertake to provide professional services concerning a property or its value where they have a present or contemplated interest unless such interest is specifically disclosed to all affected parties.

## Article 6

REALTORS® shall not accept any commission, rebate, or profit on expenditures made for their client, without the client's knowledge and consent.

When recommending real estate products or services (e.g., homeowner's insurance, warranty programs, mortgage financing, title insurance, etc.), REALTORS® shall disclose to the client or customer to whom the recommendation is made any financial benefits or fees, other than real estate referral fees, the REALTOR® or REALTOR®'s firm may receive as a direct result of such recommendation. (Amended 1/99)

### Standard of Practice 6-1

REALTORS® shall not recommend or suggest to a client or a customer the use of services of another organization or business entity in which they have a direct interest without disclosing such interest at the time of the recommendation or suggestion. (Amended 5/88)

## Article 7

In a transaction, REALTORS® shall not accept compensation from more than one party, even if permitted by law, without disclosure to all parties and the informed consent of the REALTOR®'s client or clients. (Amended 1/93)

## Article 8

REALTORS® shall keep in a special account in an appropriate financial institution, separated from their own funds, monies coming into their possession in trust for other persons, such as escrows, trust funds, clients' monies, and other like items.

## Article 9

REALTORS®, for the protection of all parties, shall assure whenever possible that all agreements related to real estate transactions including, but not limited to, listing and representation agreements, purchase contracts, and leases are in writing in clear and understandable language expressing the specific terms, conditions, obligations and commitments of the parties. A copy of each agreement shall be furnished to each party to such agreements upon their signing or initialing. (Amended 1/04)

### Standard of Practice 9-1

For the protection of all parties, REALTORS® shall use reasonable care to ensure that documents pertaining to the purchase, sale, or lease of real estate are kept current through the use of written extensions or amendments. (Amended 1/93)

### Standard of Practice 9-2

When assisting or enabling a client or customer in establishing a contractual relationship (e.g., listing and representation agreements, purchase agreements, leases, etc.) electronically, REALTORS® shall make reasonable efforts to explain the nature and disclose the specific terms of the contractual relationship being established prior to it being agreed to by a contracting party. (Adopted 1/07)

**Duties to the Public**

## Article 10

REALTORS® shall not deny equal professional services to any person for reasons of race, color, religion, sex, handicap, familial status, or national origin. REALTORS® shall not be parties to any plan or agreement to discriminate against a person or persons on the basis of race, color, religion, sex, handicap, familial status, or national origin. (Amended 1/90)

REALTORS®, in their real estate employment practices, shall not discriminate against any person or persons on the basis of race, color, religion, sex, handicap, familial status, or national origin. (Amended 1/00)

### Standard of Practice 10-1

When involved in the sale or lease of a residence, REALTORS® shall not volunteer information regarding the racial, religious or ethnic composition of any neighborhood nor shall they engage in any activity which may result in panic selling, however, REALTORS® may provide other demographic information. (Adopted 1/94, Amended 1/06)

### Standard of Practice 10-2

When not involved in the sale or lease of a residence, REALTORS® may provide demographic information related to a property, transaction or professional assignment to a party if such demographic information is (a) deemed by the REALTOR® to be needed to assist with or complete, in a manner consistent with Article 10, a real estate transaction or professional assignment and (b) is obtained or derived from a recognized, reliable, independent, and impartial source. The source of such information and any additions, deletions, modifications, interpretations, or other changes shall be disclosed in reasonable detail. (Adopted 1/05, Renumbered 1/06)

### Standard of Practice 10-3

REALTORS® shall not print, display or circulate any statement or advertisement with respect to selling or renting of a property that indicates any preference, limitations or discrimination based on race, color, religion, sex, handicap, familial status, or national origin. (Adopted 1/94, Renumbered 1/05 and 1/06)

### Standard of Practice 10-4

As used in Article 10 "real estate employment practices" relates to employees and independent contractors providing real estate-related services and the administrative and clerical staff directly supporting those individuals. (Adopted 1/00, Renumbered 1/05)

### Article 11

The services which REALTORS® provide to their clients and customers shall conform to the standards of practice and competence which are reasonably expected in the specific real estate disciplines in which they engage; specifically, residential real estate brokerage, real property management, commercial and industrial real estate brokerage, land brokerage, real estate appraisal, real estate counseling, real estate syndication, real estate auction, and international real estate.

REALTORS® shall not undertake to provide specialized professional services concerning a type of property or service that is outside their field of competence unless they engage the assistance of one who is competent on such types of property or service, or unless the facts are fully disclosed to the client. Any persons engaged to provide such assistance shall be so identified to the client and their contribution to the assignment should be set forth. (Amended 1/10)

### Standard of Practice 11-1

When REALTORS® prepare opinions of real property value or price, other than in pursuit of a listing or to assist a potential purchaser in formulating a purchase offer, such opinions shall include the following unless the party requesting the opinion requires a specific type of report or different data set: identification of the subject property date prepared defined value or price limiting conditions, including statements of purpose(s) and intended user(s) any present or contemplated interest, including the possibility of representing the seller/landlord or buyers/tenants basis for the opinion, including applicable market data if the opinion is not an appraisal, a statement to that effect (Amended 1/10)

### Standard of Practice 11-2

The obligations of the Code of Ethics in respect of real estate disciplines other than appraisal shall be interpreted and applied in accordance with the standards of competence and practice which clients and the public reasonably require to protect their rights and interests considering the complexity of the transaction, the availability of expert assistance, and, where the REALTOR® is an agent or subagent, the obligations of a fiduciary. (Adopted 1/95)

### Standard of Practice 11-3

When REALTORS® provide consultive services to clients which involve advice or counsel for a fee (not a commission), such advice shall be rendered in an objective manner and the fee shall not be contingent on the substance of the advice or counsel given. If brokerage or transaction services are to be provided in addition to consultive services, a separate compensation may be paid with prior agreement between the client and REALTOR®. (Adopted 1/96)

### Standard of Practice 11-4

The competency required by Article 11 relates to services contracted for between REALTORS® and their clients or customers; the duties expressly imposed by the Code of Ethics; and the duties imposed by law or regulation. (Adopted 1/02)

### Article 12

REALTORS® shall be honest and truthful in their real estate communications and shall present a true picture in their advertising, marketing, and other representations. REALTORS® shall ensure that their status as real estate professionals is readily apparent in their advertising, marketing, and other representations, and that the recipients of all real estate communications are, or have been, notified that those communications are from a real estate professional. (Amended 1/08)

### Standard of Practice 12-1

REALTORS® may use the term "free" and similar terms in their advertising and in other representations provided that all terms governing availability of the offered product or service are clearly disclosed at the same time. (Amended 1/97)

### Standard of Practice 12-2

REALTORS® may represent their services as "free" or without cost even if they expect to receive compensation from a source other than their client provided that the potential for the REALTOR® to obtain a benefit from a third party is clearly disclosed at the same time. (Amended 1/97)

### Standard of Practice 12-3

The offering of premiums, prizes, merchandise discounts or other inducements to list, sell, purchase, or lease is not, in itself, unethical even if receipt of the benefit is contingent on listing, selling, purchasing, or leasing through the REALTOR® making the offer. However, REALTORS® must exercise care and candor in any such advertising or other public or private representations so that any party interested in receiving or otherwise benefiting from the REALTOR®'s offer will have clear, thorough, advance understanding of all the terms and conditions of the offer. The offering of any inducements to do business is subject to the limitations and restrictions of state law and the ethical obligations established by any applicable Standard of Practice. (Amended 1/95)

### Standard of Practice 12-4

REALTORS® shall not offer for sale/lease or advertise property without authority. When acting as listing brokers or as subagents, REALTORS® shall not quote a price different from that agreed upon with the seller/landlord. (Amended 1/93)

### Standard of Practice 12-5

REALTORS® shall not advertise nor permit any person employed by or affiliated with them to advertise real estate services or listed property in any medium (e.g., electronically, print, radio, television, etc.) without disclosing the name of that REALTOR®'s firm in a reasonable and readily apparent manner. (Adopted 11/86, Amended 1/10)

### Standard of Practice 12-6

REALTORS®, when advertising unlisted real property for sale/lease in which they have an ownership interest, shall disclose their status as both owners/landlords and as REALTORS® or real estate licensees. (Amended 1/93)

### Standard of Practice 12-7

Only REALTORS® who participated in the transaction as the listing broker or cooperating broker (selling broker) may claim to have "sold" the property. Prior to closing, a cooperating broker may post a "sold" sign only with the consent of the listing broker. (Amended 1/96)

### Standard of Practice 12-8

The obligation to present a true picture in representations to the public includes information presented, provided, or displayed on REALTORS®' websites. REALTORS® shall use reasonable efforts to ensure that information on their websites is current. When it becomes apparent that information on a REALTOR®'s website is no longer current or accurate, REALTORS® shall promptly take corrective action. (Adopted 1/07)

### Standard of Practice 12-9

REALTOR® firm websites shall disclose the firm's name and state(s) of licensure in a reasonable and readily apparent manner.

Websites of REALTORS® and non-member licensees affiliated with a REALTOR® firm shall disclose the firm's name and that REALTOR®'s or non-member licensee's state(s) of licensure in a reasonable and readily apparent manner. (Adopted 1/07)

## Standard of Practice 12-10

REALTORS®' obligation to present a true picture in their advertising and representations to the public includes the URLs and domain names they use, and prohibits REALTORS® from: engaging in deceptive or unauthorized framing of real estate brokerage websites; manipulating (e.g., presenting content developed by others) listing content in any way that produces a deceptive or misleading result; or deceptively using metatags, keywords or other devices/methods to direct, drive, or divert Internet traffic, or to otherwise mislead consumers. (Adopted 1/07)

## Standard of Practice 12-11

REALTORS® intending to share or sell consumer information gathered via the Internet shall disclose that possibility in a reasonable and readily apparent manner. (Adopted 1/07)

## Standard of Practice 12-12

REALTORS® shall not: use URLs or domain names that present less than a true picture, or register URLs or domain names which, if used, would present less than a true picture. (Adopted 1/08)

## Standard of Practice 12-13

The obligation to present a true picture in advertising, marketing, and representations allows REALTORS® to use and display only professional designations, certifications, and other credentials to which they are legitimately entitled. (Adopted 1/08)

## Article 13

REALTORS® shall not engage in activities that constitute the unauthorized practice of law and shall recommend that legal counsel be obtained when the interest of any party to the transaction requires it.

## Article 14

If charged with unethical practice or asked to present evidence or to cooperate in any other way, in any professional standards proceeding or investigation, REALTORS® shall place all pertinent facts before the proper tribunals of the Member Board or affiliated institute, society, or council in which membership is held and shall take no action to disrupt or obstruct such processes. (Amended 1/99)

## Standard of Practice 14-1

REALTORS® shall not be subject to disciplinary proceedings in more than one Board of REALTORS® or affiliated institute, society or council in which they hold membership with respect to alleged violations of the Code of Ethics relating to the same transaction or event. (Amended 1/95)

## Standard of Practice 14-2

REALTORS® shall not make any unauthorized disclosure or dissemination of the allegations, findings, or decision developed in connection with an ethics hearing or appeal or in connection with an arbitration hearing or procedural review. (Amended 1/92)

## Standard of Practice 14-3

REALTORS® shall not obstruct the Board's investigative or professional standards proceedings by instituting or threatening to institute actions for libel, slander or defamation against any party to a professional standards proceeding or their witnesses based on the filing of an arbitration request, an ethics complaint, or testimony given before any tribunal. (Adopted 11/87, Amended 1/99)

## Standard of Practice 14-4

REALTORS® shall not intentionally impede the Board's investigative or disciplinary proceedings by filing multiple ethics complaints based on the same event or transaction. (Adopted 11/88)

## Duties to REALTORS®

## Article 15

REALTORS® shall not knowingly or recklessly make false or misleading statements about competitors, their businesses, or their business practices. (Amended 1/92)

## Standard of Practice 15-1

REALTORS® shall not knowingly or recklessly file false or unfounded ethics complaints. (Adopted 1/00)

## Standard of Practice 15-2

The obligation to refrain from making false or misleading statements about competitors, competitors' businesses and competitors' business practices includes the duty to not knowingly or recklessly publish, repeat, retransmit, or republish false or misleading statements made by others. This duty applies whether false or misleading statements are repeated in person, in writing, by technological means (e.g., the Internet), or by any other means. (Adopted 1/07, Amended 1/10)

## Standard of Practice 15-3

The obligation to refrain from making false or misleading statements about competitors, competitors' businesses, and competitors' business practices includes the duty to publish a clarification about or to remove statements made by others on electronic media the REALTOR® controls once the REALTOR® knows the statement is false or misleading. (Adopted 1/10)

## Article 16

REALTORS® shall not engage in any practice or take any action inconsistent with exclusive representation or exclusive brokerage relationship agreements that other REALTORS® have with clients. (Amended 1/04)

## Standard of Practice 16-1

Article 16 is not intended to prohibit aggressive or innovative business practices which are otherwise ethical and does not prohibit disagreements with other REALTORS® involving commission, fees, compensation or other forms of payment or expenses. (Adopted 1/93, Amended 1/95)

## Standard of Practice 16-2

Article 16 does not preclude REALTORS® from making general announcements to prospects describing their services and the terms of their availability even though some recipients may have entered into agency agreements or other exclusive relationships with another REALTOR®. A general telephone canvass, general mailing or distribution addressed to all prospects in a given geographical area or in a given profession, business, club, or organization, or other classification or group is deemed "general" for purposes of this standard. (Amended 1/04)

Article 16 is intended to recognize as unethical two basic types of solicitations:

First, telephone or personal solicitations of property owners who have been identified by a real estate sign, multiple listing compilation, or other information service as having exclusively listed their property with another REALTOR®; and

Second, mail or other forms of written solicitations of prospects whose properties are exclusively listed with another REALTOR® when such solicitations are not part of a general mailing but are directed specifically to property owners identified through compilations of current listings, "for sale" or "for rent" signs, or other sources of information required by Article 3 and Multiple Listing Service rules to be made available to other REALTORS® under offers of subagency or cooperation. (Amended 1/04)

## Standard of Practice 16-3

Article 16 does not preclude REALTORS® from contacting the client of another broker for the purpose of offering to provide, or entering into a contract to provide, a different type of real estate service unrelated to the type of service currently being provided (e.g., property management as opposed to brokerage) or from offering the same type of service for property not subject to other brokers' exclusive agreements. However, information received through a Multiple Listing Service or any other offer of cooperation may not be used to target clients of other REALTORS® to whom such offers to provide services may be made. (Amended 1/04)

## Standard of Practice 16-4

REALTORS® shall not solicit a listing which is currently listed exclusively with another broker. However, if the listing broker, when asked by the REALTOR®, refuses to disclose the expiration date and nature of such listing; i.e., an exclusive right to sell, an exclusive agency, open listing, or other form of contractual agreement between the listing broker and the client, the REALTOR® may contact the owner to secure such information and may discuss the terms upon which the REALTOR® might take a future listing or, alternatively, may take a listing to become effective upon expiration of any existing exclusive listing. (Amended 1/94)

## Standard of Practice 16-5

REALTORS® shall not solicit buyer/tenant agreements from buyers/ tenants who are subject to exclusive buyer/tenant agreements. However, if asked by a REALTOR®, the broker refuses to disclose the expiration date of the exclusive buyer/tenant agreement, the REALTOR® may contact the buyer/tenant to secure such information and may discuss the terms upon which the REALTOR® might enter into a future buyer/tenant agreement or, alternatively, may enter into a buyer/tenant agreement to become effective upon the expiration of any existing exclusive buyer/tenant agreement. (Adopted 1/94, Amended 1/98)

## Standard of Practice 16-6

When REALTORS® are contacted by the client of another REALTOR® regarding the creation of an exclusive relationship to provide the same type of service, and REALTORS® have not directly or indirectly initiated such discussions, they may discuss the terms upon which they might enter into a future agreement or, alternatively, may enter into an agreement which becomes effective upon expiration of any existing exclusive agreement. (Amended 1/98)

## Standard of Practice 16-7

The fact that a prospect has retained a REALTOR® as an exclusive representative or exclusive broker in one or more past transactions does not preclude other REALTORS® from seeking such prospect's future business. (Amended 1/04)

## Standard of Practice 16-8

The fact that an exclusive agreement has been entered into with a REALTOR® shall not preclude or inhibit any other REALTOR® from entering into a similar agreement after the expiration of the prior agreement. (Amended 1/98)

## Standard of Practice 16-9

REALTORS®, prior to entering into a representation agreement, have an affirmative obligation to make reasonable efforts to determine whether the prospect is subject to a current, valid exclusive agreement to provide the same type of real estate service. (Amended 1/04)

## Standard of Practice 16-10

REALTORS®, acting as buyer or tenant representatives or brokers, shall disclose that relationship to the seller/landlord's representative or broker at first contact and shall provide written confirmation of that disclosure to the seller/landlord's representative or broker not later than execution of a purchase agreement or lease. (Amended 1/04)

## Standard of Practice 16-11

On unlisted property, REALTORS® acting as buyer/tenant representatives or brokers shall disclose that relationship to the seller/landlord at first contact for that buyer/tenant and shall provide written confirmation of such disclosure to the seller/landlord not later than execution of any purchase or lease agreement. (Amended 1/04)

REALTORS® shall make any request for anticipated compensation from the seller/ landlord at first contact. (Amended 1/98)

## Standard of Practice 16-12

REALTORS®, acting as representatives or brokers of sellers/landlords or as subagents of listing brokers, shall disclose that relationship to buyers/tenants as soon as practicable and shall provide written confirmation of such disclosure to buyers/tenants not later than execution of any purchase or lease agreement. (Amended 1/04)

## Standard of Practice 16-13

All dealings concerning property exclusively listed, or with buyer/tenants who are subject to an exclusive agreement shall be carried on with the client's representative or broker, and not with the client, except with the consent of the client's representative or broker or except where such dealings are initiated by the client.

Before providing substantive services (such as writing a purchase offer or presenting a CMA) to prospects, REALTORS® shall ask prospects whether they are a party to any exclusive representation agreement. REALTORS® shall not knowingly provide substantive services concerning a prospective transaction to prospects who are parties to exclusive representation agreements, except with the consent of the prospects' exclusive representatives or at the direction of prospects. (Adopted 1/93, Amended 1/04)

## Standard of Practice 16-14

REALTORS® are free to enter into contractual relationships or to negotiate with sellers/ landlords, buyers/tenants or others who are not subject to an exclusive agreement but shall not knowingly obligate them to pay more than one commission except with their informed consent. (Amended 1/98)

## Standard of Practice 16-15

In cooperative transactions REALTORS® shall compensate cooperating REALTORS® (principal brokers) and shall not compensate nor offer to compensate, directly or indirectly, any of the sales licensees employed by or affiliated with other REALTORS® without the prior express knowledge and consent of the cooperating broker.

## Standard of Practice 16-16

REALTORS®, acting as subagents or buyer/tenant representatives or brokers, shall not use the terms of an offer to purchase/lease to attempt to modify the listing broker's offer of compensation to subagents or buyer/tenant representatives or brokers nor make the submission of an executed offer to purchase/lease contingent on the listing broker's agreement to modify the offer of compensation. (Amended 1/04)

## Standard of Practice 16-17

REALTORS®, acting as subagents or as buyer/tenant representatives or brokers, shall not attempt to extend a listing broker's offer of cooperation and/or compensation to other brokers without the consent of the listing broker. (Amended 1/04)

## Standard of Practice 16-18

REALTORS® shall not use information obtained from listing brokers through offers to cooperate made through multiple listing services or through other offers of cooperation to refer listing brokers' clients to other brokers or to create buyer/tenant relationships with listing brokers' clients, unless such use is authorized by listing brokers. (Amended 1/02)

## Standard of Practice 16-19

Signs giving notice of property for sale, rent, lease, or exchange shall not be placed on property without consent of the seller/landlord. (Amended 1/93)

## Standard of Practice 16-20

REALTORS®, prior to or after their relationship with their current firm is terminated, shall not induce clients of their current firm to cancel exclusive contractual agreements between the client and that firm. This does not preclude REALTORS® (principals) from establishing agreements with their associated licensees governing assignability of exclusive agreements. (Adopted 1/98, Amended 1/10)

## Article 17

In the event of contractual disputes or specific non-contractual disputes as defined in Standard of Practice 17-4 between REALTORS® (principals) associated with different firms, arising out of their relationship as REALTORS®, the REALTORS® shall submit the dispute to arbitration in accordance with the regulations of their Board or Boards rather than litigate the matter.

In the event clients of REALTORS® wish to arbitrate contractual disputes arising out of real estate transactions, REALTORS® shall arbitrate those disputes in accordance with the regulations of their Board, provided the clients agree to be bound by the decision.

The obligation to participate in arbitration contemplated by this Article includes the obligation of REALTORS® (principals) to cause their firms to arbitrate and be bound by any award. (Amended 1/01)

### Standard of Practice 17-1

The filing of litigation and refusal to withdraw from it by REALTORS® in an arbitrable matter constitutes a refusal to arbitrate. (Adopted 2/86)

### Standard of Practice 17-2

Article 17 does not require REALTORS® to arbitrate in those circumstances when all parties to the dispute advise the Board in writing that they choose not to arbitrate before the Board. (Amended 1/93)

### Standard of Practice 17-3

REALTORS®, when acting solely as principals in a real estate transaction, are not obligated to arbitrate disputes with other REALTORS® absent a specific written agreement to the contrary. (Adopted 1/96)

### Standard of Practice 17-4

Specific non-contractual disputes that are subject to arbitration pursuant to Article 17 are:

Where a listing broker has compensated a cooperating broker and another cooperating broker subsequently claims to be the procuring cause of the sale or lease. In such cases the complainant may name the first cooperating broker as respondent and arbitration may proceed without the listing broker being named as a respondent. When arbitration occurs between two (or more) cooperating brokers and where the listing broker is not a party, the amount in dispute and the amount of any potential resulting award is limited to the amount paid to the respondent by the listing broker and any amount credited or paid to a party to the transaction at the direction of the respondent. Alternatively, if the complaint is brought against the listing broker, the listing broker may name the first cooperating broker as a third-party respondent. In either instance the decision of the hearing panel as to procuring cause shall be conclusive with respect to all current or subsequent claims of the parties for compensation arising out of the underlying cooperative transaction. (Adopted 1/97, Amended 1/07)

Where a buyer or tenant representative is compensated by the seller or landlord, and not by the listing broker, and the listing broker, as a result, reduces the commission owed by the seller or landlord and, subsequent to such actions, another cooperating broker claims to be the procuring cause of sale or lease. In such cases the complainant may name the first cooperating broker as respondent and arbitration may proceed without the listing broker being named as a respondent. When arbitration occurs between two (or more) cooperating brokers and where the listing broker is not a party, the amount in dispute and the amount of any potential resulting award is limited to the amount paid to the respondent by the seller or landlord and any amount credited or paid to a party to the transaction at the direction of the respondent. Alternatively, if the complaint is brought against the listing broker, the listing broker may name the first cooperating broker as a third-party respondent. In either instance the decision of the hearing panel as to procuring cause shall be conclusive with respect to all current or subsequent claims of the parties for compensation arising

out of the underlying cooperative transaction. (Adopted 1/97, Amended 1/07)

Where a buyer or tenant representative is compensated by the buyer or tenant and, as a result, the listing broker reduces the commission owed by the seller or landlord and, subsequent to such actions, another cooperating broker claims to be the procuring cause of sale or lease. In such cases the complainant may name the first cooperating broker as respondent and arbitration may proceed without the listing broker being named as a respondent. Alternatively, if the complaint is brought against the listing broker, the listing broker may name the first cooperating broker as a third-party respondent. In either instance the decision of the hearing panel as to procuring cause shall be conclusive with respect to all current or subsequent claims of the parties for compensation arising out of the underlying cooperative transaction. (Adopted 1/97)

Where two or more listing brokers claim entitlement to compensation pursuant to open listings with a seller or landlord who agrees to participate in arbitration (or who requests arbitration) and who agrees to be bound by the decision. In cases where one of the listing brokers has been compensated by the seller or landlord, the other listing broker, as complainant, may name the first listing broker as respondent and arbitration may proceed between the brokers. (Adopted 1/97)

Where a buyer or tenant representative is compensated by the seller or landlord, and not by the listing broker, and the listing broker, as a result, reduces the commission owed by the seller or landlord and, subsequent to such actions, claims to be the procuring cause of sale or lease. In such cases arbitration shall be between the listing broker and the buyer or tenant representative and the amount in dispute is limited to the amount of the reduction of commission to which the listing broker agreed. (Adopted 1/05)

### Standard of Practice 17-5

The obligation to arbitrate established in Article 17 includes disputes between REALTORS® (principals) in different states in instances where, absent an established inter–association arbitration agreement, the REALTOR® (principal) requesting arbitration agrees to submit to the jurisdiction of, travel to, participate in, and be bound by any resulting award rendered in arbitration conducted by the respondent(s) REALTOR®'s association, in instances where the respondent(s) REALTOR®'s association determines that an arbitrable issue exists. (Adopted 1/07)

The Code of Ethics was adopted in 1913. Amended at the Annual Convention in 1924, 1928, 1950, 1951, 1952, 1955, 1956, 1961, 1962, 1974, 1982, 1986, 1987, 1989, 1990, 1991, 1992, 1993, 1994, 1995, 1996, 1997, 1998, 1999, 2000, 2001, 2002, 2003, 2004, 2005, 2006, 2007, 2008 and 2009.

### Explanatory Notes

The reader should be aware of the following policies which have been approved by the Board of Directors of the National Association:

In filing a charge of an alleged violation of the Code of Ethics by a REALTOR®, the charge must read as an alleged violation of one or more Articles of the Code. Standards of Practice may be cited in support of the charge.

The Standards of Practice serve to clarify the ethical obligations imposed by the various Articles and supplement, and do not substitute for, the Case Interpretations in Interpretations of the Code of Ethics.

Modifications to existing Standards of Practice and additional new Standards of Practice are approved from time to time. Readers are cautioned to ensure that the most recent publications are utilized.

**www.realtor.org**

## G. INDEPENDENT BOARDS

There are also several "independent" boards in California, some of which are large in membership and influential in their communities. Most of these boards are organized for some particular purpose, such as a multiple listing service. Many members of independent boards are also members of boards affiliated with CAR. Examples of independent boards are:

1. Chinese American Real Estate Professionals Association of Southern California
2. Chinese Real Estate Association of America
3. Korean Real Estate Brokers of Southern California
4. Women in Real Estate (WIRE)

## H. OTHER ASSOCIATIONS

In addition to the above-mentioned organizations, there are many trade associations and professional bodies that are related to the real estate business, such as:

1. American Bankers Association
2. American Savings and Loan Institute
3. Building Owners and Managers Association
4. Mortgage Bankers Association
5. National Association of Home Builders
6. National Association of Mutual Savings Banks
7. Prefabricated Home Manufacturers Institute

## I. REAL ESTATE INSTRUCTOR AND LICENSING ASSOCIATIONS

In addition to the above mentioned organizations, there are real estate instructor organizations and other professional bodies that are related to real estate education and licensing (see **Figure 14-10**).

## J. NO AFFILIATION NECESSARY

A real estate licensee need not be a member of any trade or professional association. In this case, he or she is simply referred to as a salesperson or broker. There is no compulsion for any licensee of the Department of Real Estate to join or affiliate with any local or state organization. That decision is strictly individual and personal.

**Figure 14-10** ## Real Estate Teacher's Groups

**California Real Estate Educators Association (CREEA)**

Real estate instructors from throughout the state have come together with the formation of CREEA, the California Real Estate Educators Association. This organization constitutes a chapter of REEA, the Real Estate Educators Association, a private trade association, which is international in scope. REEA has a reputation throughout the world for its comprehensive representation.

California Real Estate
Education Association
P.O. Box 1230
Costa Mesa, CA 92628
714-751-2787 Ext. 204

Real Estate Educators Association (REEA)
Int'l Trust Building, Suite 1
1615 Avenue Q
Lubbock, TX 79401
806-794-5557

www.creea.org (CREEA)
www.reea.org (REEA)
www.ccsf.edu/Resources/Real_Estate_Education_Center/
(California Community Colleges Real Estate Education Center)
www.arello.org (Association of Real Estate License Law Officials - ARELLO)

### CALIFORNIA COMMUNITY COLLEGES
### REAL ESTATE EDUCATION CENTER

The California Community Colleges Real Estate Education Center is a real estate instructors' group sponsored by the California Department of Real Estate. The Center publishes a quarterly newsletter and sponsors educators' conferences three times a year in cooperation with the California Community College Chancellor's office. The newsletter, called *The Informer*, is a useful reference source to keep educators up to date on new laws and real estate practices. The conferences are held in the San Francisco Bay area, the Los Angeles area, and the San Diego area. For information about The Informer and Endowment Fund contact:

Carol Jensen, Director
California Community Colleges
Real Estate Education Center
City College of San Francisco - Downtown Campus
88 Fourth Street
San Francisco, California 94103
415-267-6550
www.reec@ccsf.edu

Association of Real Estate License Law Officials (ARELLO)
2000 Interstate Park, Suite 306
Montgomery, AL 36109
334-260-2928

## VIII. CHAPTER SUMMARY

A person who is actively involved in a real estate transaction at the service of another, in the expectation of receiving a commission must be licensed by the **Department of Real Estate (DRE)**, which is the regulatory agency for real estate in California. The DRE is governed by the **Real Estate Commissioner**, who is appointed by the governor and defended by the state Attorney General. The Commissioner does not settle commission disputes, take the place of a court of law, nor give legal advice, but the rules and regulations he or she issues do have the force and effect of law.

To obtain a **salesperson's license**, a candidate must: be 18 or over, honest and truthful, and complete a Real Estate Principle's course, a Real Estate Practice course, and one other required college-level course real estate course and pass the state exam. The salesperson exam takes 3 hours and 15 minutes, has 150 questions and requires a 70% or better to pass.

Applicants must apply for a license within one year from passing the exam date, at which time he or she will have to submit an electronic **fingerprint scan**.

A **broker's license** is required to operate a real estate office. A broker must be 18 years old, have had two years previous experience or college education, complete the required 8 broker courses, be honest and truthful, and pass the required examination. A four-year degree (B.S. or B.A) = 2 years experience.

The **continuing education requirement of 45 hours every four years** for a license renewal, includes three hours each of **Ethics, Agency, Trust Fund Handling, Fair Housing,** and **Risk Management**. After a second license renewal, these four three-hour courses can be replaced with a **six-hour CE survey course** plus additional courses in Risk Management and Consumer Service and Consumer Protection courses.

In a sale of a business, (**Business Opportunity**) the real property is transferred by deed and the personal property by bill of sale. The three documents in a **personal security transaction** are: 1) a promissory note; 2) a security agreement, and 3) compliance with the UCC-1 financing statement. A **bulk transfer** involves the sale of a substantial part of the 1) inventory, items purchased for resale; 2) other supplies and equipment associated with the business. If tangible personal property is involved, escrow should check to be sure there are no past sales taxes due to the **State Board of Equalization**.

**California Real Estate Law** is the portion of the **Business and Professions Code** that refers to licensing and subdivision. The **Commissioner's Regulations** are rules that form part of the **California Administrative Code** and are enforced by the Real Estate Commissioner. The Commissioner can revoke, restrict, or suspend the license of any real estate agent for misconduct.

All agents must adhere to **Section 10176** (acting in a licensee capacity) and **Section 10177** of the **Business and Professions Code**, which have the force and effect of the law itself.

## IX. TERMINOLOGY

A. Broker's License
B. Business
C. Business Opportunity and Bulk Sales
D. California Association of REALTORS®
E. Commissioner's Code of Ethics (2785)
F. Commissioner's Regulations
G. Continuing Education Requirements
H. Department of Real Estate (DRE)
I. Local Board of REALTORS®
J. NAR Code of Ethics
K. ARELLO
L. National Association of REALTORS® (NAR)
M. Police Power
N. Real Estate Advisory Commission
O. Real Estate Law
P. Realtist
Q. REALTOR®
R. Recovery Fund
S. Trade Association

1.____ A national trade association of real estate professionals who call themselves Realtors®.
2.____ The sale of a business.
3.____ The right of the government to enact laws for the protection of the general public. Laws such as zoning ordinances, building codes, and health and safety requirements are common in real estate.
4.____ Any legitimate activity by which people expect to earn money.
5.____ The division of the state government responsible for the licensing and regulation of persons engaged in the real estate business. Heading the department is the Real Estate Commissioner.
6.____ Composed of ten members, it recommends and makes suggestions to the Commissioner.
7.____ A voluntary, nonprofit organization made up of independent firms in the same industry. CAR and NAR are examples.
8.____ A license that allows a person to represent, for compensation, one or more parties in a real estate transaction.
9.____ Established to compensate people who have suffered financial loss due to the wrongful act of a real estate licensee.
10.____ Rules that form part of the California Administrative Code. Established regulations are enforced by the Commissioner of Real Estate.
11.____ The portion of the Business and Professions Code that refers to licensing and subdivisions.
12.____ A local voluntary organization in a given community, made up of real estate licensees.
13.____ The state division of the National Association of REALTORS®.
14.____ The 45 clock hours of Commissioner-approved courses that must be taken by all real estate licensees during the four-year period preceding license renewal.
15.____ The association made up of real estate license law officials.
16.____ Standards of professional conduct and business practices established by the Commissioner to enhance the professionalism of the California real estate industry.
17.____ A term reserved for active members of the National Association of REALTORS® or the California Association of REALTORS®.
18.____ Members of the National Association of Real Estate Brokers.
19.____ In order to be a realtor, a person must swear to uphold this code.

## X. CHAPTER QUIZ

1. The Real Estate Commissioner will start an action against a licensee with:

    a. an injunction.
    b. a lawsuit.
    c. an accusation.
    d. a lis pendens.

2. The maximum fine the Real Estate Commissioner can levy against a broker who pays an unlicensed person for soliciting borrowers or negotiating loans is:

    a. $2,000.
    b. $5,000.
    c. $20,000.
    d. $30,000.

3. To use a fictitious business name, the broker must:

    a. file a fictitious business name statement in the county where he or she intends to operate.
    b. publish the fictitious business name in a newspaper of general circulation.
    c. obtain approval of the name by the Real Estate Commissioner and be issued a license in the name of the fictitious business name.
    d. all of the above.

4. Which of the following is included as part of the required 45 hours of continuing education?

    a. Agency and Ethics
    b. Trust Fund Handling and Fair Housing
    c. 18 hours of Consumer Protection
    d. All of the above are included in the 45 hours of continuing education

5. When the Department of Real Estate obtains live-scan fingerprints and performs a background check on a potential licensee, the Department is looking for:

    a. late child support payments.
    b. past job history.
    c. credit report.
    d. all of the above.

6. A real estate salesperson owes the Department of Child Support Services for back child support payments. He may:

    a. obtain a temporary license for 150 days.
    b. not obtain a license until the past due funds are paid.
    c. obtain a license after a hearing by the Real Estate Commissioner.
    d. not obtain a license.

7. A broker runs the following ad on his listings: "4 BR, 3 BATH home with swimming pool and spa for sale for $154,000. Call 555-1234." This is called:

  a. misleading.
  b. a false ad.
  c. a blind ad.
  d. a violation of Regulation Z.

8. In order to obtain information about the ethical or unethical conduct of a real estate licensee, one would most likely consult:

  a. the "REALTOR'S® Golden Rule."
  b. the Business and Professions Code.
  c. the California Criminal Code.
  d. generally accepted business practices of highly trained real estate professionals.

9. The maximum recovery from the Recovery Fund is:

  a. unlimited.
  b. $250,000 per individual licensee ($50,000 maximum per occurrence).
  c. $20,000 per individual licensee.
  d. None of the above.

10. Misuse of the name "REALTOR®" is:

  a. a violation of the California Real Estate Law.
  b. a violation of the Business and Professions Code.
  c. a violation of the Civil Code.
  d. a violation of common law.

*ANSWERS: 1. c; 2. c; 3. d; 4. d; 5. a; 6. a; 7. c; 8. b; 9. b; 10. a*

# CHAPTER 15
## *Real Estate Math*

Real Estate, as you have learned, can be an extremely profitable profession. The licensee who is able to compute quickly and accurately the mathematics underlying most transactions will be in a better position to capitalize on opportunities as they arise.

This chapter will illustrate and explain some basic mathematical skills useful to a career in real estate. Familiarity with fundamental arithmetic and a few simple formulas along with plain common sense will provide the necessary background. Such knowledge will not only assist in the practice of real estate, but should also prove advantageous in passing the licensing exam. **Figure 15-1** is a table of common measurements.

It might also prove to your advantage to bring a calculator with you when taking the salesperson's examination. The state permits applicants to use electronic calculators as long as they are battery operated, non-programmable, silent, and without printout capability. Such a device will free you from tedious and time-consuming arithmetic work in order to concentrate on the reasoning behind the problems you will encounter.

# I. Area Measurement

*LAND AREA is the surface space between lot lines measured in square feet.*

## A. AREA OF A RECTANGULAR LOT

A *RECTANGULAR LOT is a four-sided parcel whose opposite sides are equal in length and right angles are formed by the intersection of the sides.* The dimensions of a rectangle are equal on two sides. Most lots encountered will be rectangular in shape.

### 1. How Do We Get "Square" Measurement?

**The area of a rectangular or square lot is determined by multiplying the length by the width.** The result is expressed in square feet, square yards, or some similar expression. The formula is:

$$A = L \ x \ W$$
$$AREA = LENGTH \ x \ WIDTH$$

# CHAPTER 15

## CHAPTER OUTLINE

**EXAMPLE:** How many square feet would there be in a rectangular parcel 100 feet long and 50 feet wide?

A = L x W

AREA = LENGTH x WIDTH

AREA = 100 FEET x 50 FEET

A = 100 x 50

A = 5,000 SQUARE FEET

**ANSWER:** The area of this lot is calculated to be 5,000 square feet.

**Figure 15-1**

# Measurements

## (A Salesperson Should Be Familiar With These)

### LINEAR

**1 foot (ft.)** = 12 inches (in.)
**1 yard (yd.)** = 3 feet (ft.)
**1 rod** = 16.5 ft. = 5.5 yd.
**1 mile** = 5,280 ft. = 1,760 yd. = 320 rods

### SQUARE

**1 sq. ft.** = 144 sq. in. (12 in. x 12 in.)
**1 sq. yd.** = 9 sq. ft. ( 3 ft. x 3 ft.)
**1 acre** = 43,560 sq. ft. = 4,840 sq. yd. = 160 sq. rods
**1 sq. mile** = 5,280 ft. x 5,280 ft.

### CUBIC

**1 cu. ft.** = 1,728 cu. in. (12 in. x 12 in. x 12 in.)
**1 cu. yd.** = 27 cu. ft. (3 ft. x 3 ft. x 3 ft.)

### LAND DESCRIPTION

**1 link** = 7.92 inches
**1 rod** = 25 links
**1 chain** = 100 links = 66 ft. = 4 rods
**1 mile** = 80 chains
**1 acre** = 43,560 sq. ft.
**1 township** = 36 sections = 36 square miles = 23,040 acres
**1 section** = 1 mile square = 640 acres = 1/36 of a township
**1 circle** = 360 degrees (°)
**1 quadrant** = 90 degrees (°)
**1 degree** (°) = 60 minutes (´)
**1 minute** (´) = 60 seconds (´´)

## B. AREA OF A TRIANGULAR LOT

A *TRIANGULAR LOT is a three-sided parcel.*

In order to determine the area of a triangular parcel, we must know the measurements of its base and height.

The *BASE OF A TRIANGULAR LOT is the side that is horizontal.* The *HEIGHT OF A TRIANGULAR LOT is the perpendicular distance from the base to the highest point.*

**The area of a triangular parcel is determined by multiplying the base by the height, and then dividing by two.** This is normally expressed by the formula:

$$A = \frac{B \times H}{2}$$

$$AREA = \frac{BASE \times HEIGHT}{2}$$

Here is a sample exercise for you to try:

**EXAMPLE:** How many square feet would there be in a triangular lot with a 150 foot base and a height of 100 feet?

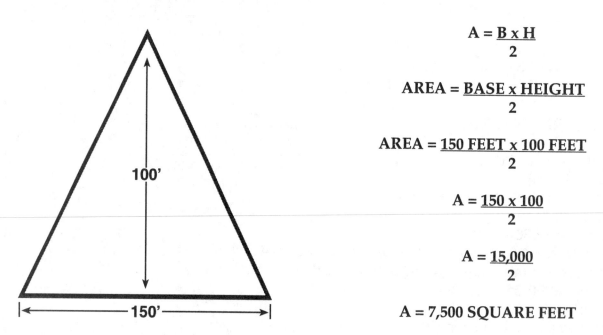

$$A = \frac{B \times H}{2}$$

$$AREA = \frac{BASE \times HEIGHT}{2}$$

$$AREA = \frac{150\ FEET \times 100\ FEET}{2}$$

$$A = \frac{150 \times 100}{2}$$

$$A = \frac{15,000}{2}$$

$$A = 7,500\ SQUARE\ FEET$$

**ANSWER:** The area of this lot is 7,500 square feet.

## C. AREA OF AN IRREGULAR LOT

An *IRREGULAR LOT is a parcel that does not consist of a single known shape.* Often the area of an irregular or circular parcel cannot be measured accurately without the help of a land measurement expert, such as a surveyor. Many times, though, an irregular lot is simply made up of a series of rectangles and triangles, the combined measures of which make up the measure of the whole. In these cases the square footage of the parcel can be determined through the use of techniques already described in this chapter.

*The area of an irregular parcel is determined by breaking the lot up into the various rectangles and triangles which comprise it, and totaling their areas.*

### 1. An Irregular Lot Problem

**EXAMPLE:** What would be the total area of the irregular lot shown below? Use the dimensions given to calculate your answer.

**ANSWER:** The irregular lot is broken up into a square, a rectangle, and a triangle. The area of the parcel is the total of the areas of each of these.

**TOTAL AREA = AREA (S) + AREA (R) + AREA (T)**
**TOTAL AREA = AREA SQUARE + AREA RECTANGLE + AREA TRIANGLE**

**AREA (S) = L x W**

**AREA (S) = LENGTH x WIDTH**

**AREA (S) = 40 FEET x 40 FEET**

**AREA (S) = 40 x 40**

**AREA (S) = 1,600 SQUARE FEET**

The area of the square (S) is 1,600 square feet.

**750 Square Feet (R)**

30'

25'

AREA (R) = L x W

AREA (R) = LENGTH x WIDTH

AREA (R) = 30 FEET x 25 FEET

AREA (R) = 30 x 25

AREA (R) = 750 SQUARE FEET

The area of the rectangle (R) is 750 square feet.

**450 Square Feet (T)**

30'

30'

$$AREA (T) = \frac{B \times H}{2}$$

$$AREA (T) = \frac{BASE \times HEIGHT}{2}$$

$$AREA (T) = \frac{30\ FEET \times 30\ FEET}{2}$$

$$AREA (T) = \frac{30 \times 30}{2}$$

$$AREA (T) = \frac{900}{2}$$

AREA (T) = 450 SQUARE FEET

The area of the triangle (T) is 450 square feet.

### Irregular Problem Solution

AREA (S) = 1,600 SQUARE FEET

AREA (R) = 750 SQUARE FEET

AREA (T) = 450 SQUARE FEET

TOTAL AREA = AREA (S) + AREA (R) + AREA (T)

TOTAL AREA = 1,600 + 750 + 450

TOTAL AREA = 2,800 SQUARE FEET

**ANSWER:** The total area of this irregular lot is 2,800 square feet.

## Conversion: Square Feet to SquareYards

Many questions on area will ask that you present the answer in square yards, rather than square feet. Conversion of square feet to square yards is a simple matter of dividing the answer by nine, because there are nine square feet in a square yard.

**(3 feet x 3 feet = 9 square feet or 1 square yard)**

Square yards, likewise, may be converted into square feet through multiplication by nine.

**SQUARE YARDS = SQUARE FEET**
 **9**
**SQUARE FEET = SQUARE YARDS x 9**

## D. VOLUME OF A STRUCTURE

*STRUCTURAL VOLUME is the square or cubic measure of the space within a structure.* Structural volume measurement is generally used when renting space in a warehouse type structure. Square measure is the area of the floor space, and it is determined through the use of the same techniques that apply to finding the square footage of a lot. *CUBIC MEASURE is the area volume or total air space.* The cubic volume of a structure is determined by multiplying the interior length by the width and the height. This can be expressed by the formula:

$$V = L \times W \times H$$
$$VOLUME = LENGTH \times WIDTH \times HEIGHT$$

**EXAMPLE:** How many cubic feet would there be in a room that is 15 feet long, 10 feet wide, and 10 feet high?

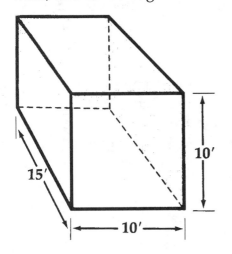

$V = L \times W \times H$
VOLUME = LENGTH x WIDTH x HEIGHT
VOLUME = 15 FEET x 10 FEET x 10 FEET
VOLUME = 15 x 10 x 10
VOLUME = 150 x 10
VOLUME = 1,500 CUBIC FEET

**ANSWER:** The cubic volume of this room would be 1,500 cubic feet.

# II. Percentage Problems

The majority of math problems that you will encounter in real estate involve the use of percent. It is important, therefore, for you to understand certain general rules about percentage problems before dealing with any of the particular types. There are three factors in any percentage problem:

1. The amount *PAID (P) is the amount invested.*
2. The *RATE (%) is the percentage.*
3. The amount *MADE (M) is the amount earned.*

In percentage problems, **one** of the three factors is missing. There are three rules for finding the missing factor:

1. To find the amount **PAID (P)**, divide **MADE (M)** by the **RATE (%)**.
2. To find the amount **MADE (M)**, multiply **PAID (P)** by **RATE (%)**.
3. To find the **RATE (%)**, divide **MADE (M)** by **PAID (P)**.

## A. OTHER FACTOR TERMS

| MADE | PAID | RATE % |
|------|------|--------|
| Return | Investment | Rate of return |
| Profit | Cost | Rate of profit |
| Commission | Price | Rate of commission |
| Net income | Value | Rate of capitalization |
| Interest | Principal | Rate of interest |

Whenever you are working a percent problem, you will be dealing with one of these equations or a modification of one of them. The typical percent problem will supply you with two of the variables. You may easily determine the third through the use of the proper equation.

## B. HUBER'S PYRAMID

If you feel that you might have trouble committing the percent equations to memory, you might want to make use of Huber's pyramid instead. Shown in **Figure 15-2**, this diagram points out what operation is required to find each of the variables.

To use the Huber Pyramid, simply cover the chamber you are trying to find and then perform the required math:

**1. To find M, cover M and multiply P x %**

**2. To find P, cover P and divide M by %**

**3. To find %, cover % and divide M by P**

*When doing a math problem involving three or more variables, first draw the Huber Pyramid and plug in the available figures, then perform the required action.*

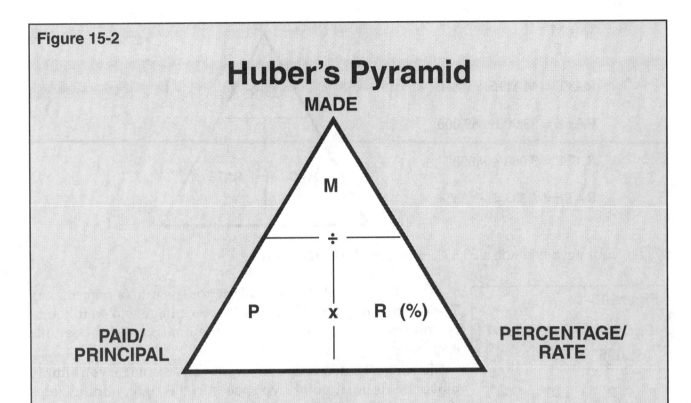

**Figure 15-2**

# Huber's Pyramid

MADE

M

÷

P    x    R (%)

PAID/
PRINCIPAL

PERCENTAGE/
RATE

The Huber Pyramid consists of three sections, or chambers (which can be modified to four chambers for certain problems). The top chamber is the **MADE (M)** chamber. It is separated from the other two chambers by a **division sign**. The bottom left chamber is the **PAID** or **PRINCIPAL (P)** chamber. The bottom right chamber is the **RATE (%)** chamber. It is separated from the PAID chamber by a **multiplication sign**.

Your success in solving percentage problems will depend largely on your ability to spot and identify the three variables as they are presented. In most problems the **PAID** and the **MADE** will both be labeled as money. But the **PAID** (generally the larger amount) will usually be given as a base amount such as a price, investment, or loan balance. The **MADE**, on the other hand (generally the smaller amount), will be a sum made or lost from the **PAID**. Returns, profits, net income, taxes, interest, and commissions are all common labels identifying the **MADE**. The rate is easy to identify because it will always be given as some form of a percentage (%).

Here is a sample percent exercise for you to try:

**EXAMPLE:** Your agency purchases a lot for $9,000. In selling it later, you made a profit of $3,000. What was your percentage of profit?

**ANSWER:** The first step is to identify the variables. The principal (paid) is the purchase price of $9,000. The result (made) is the $3,000 margin of profit that resulted from the transaction. The rate is the percentage that we are asked to determine. To find it we use the rate equation:

$$\% = \frac{M}{P}$$

RATE = MADE ÷ PAID

RATE = \$3,000 ÷ \$9,000

RATE = 3,000 ÷ 9,000

RATE = .3333 = 33.33%

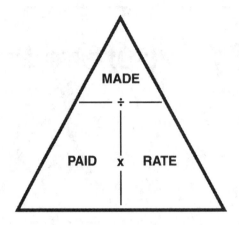

So, your agency made a 33.33% profit on the transaction.

**Figure 15-3**

*DECIMAL TO PERCENT*

.095 = 9.5%

1.2 = 120%

.009 = .9%

The above problem was looking for the rate (a percentage). The decimal number .3333 is not a percentage and so it had to be converted into a percentage in the final step of the sample exercise.

To convert a decimal number into a percentage, you simply move the decimal point two spaces to the right, adding zeros if needed. **Figure 15-3** gives some examples of this type of conversion.

In problems where you are asked to compute the results (paid) and the principal (made) it will be necessary for you to multiply or divide by the rate. In these cases you will have to convert the percentage into a decimal before completing the operation. This is done by reversing the process above: Move the decimal point two spaces to the left, and drop the percent sign. This changes a percent into its equivalent decimal form. **Figure 15-4** demonstrates this process.

Another simple way to remember percents is to relate them to dollars and cents.

**Figure 15-4**

*PERCENT TO DECIMAL*

8.5% = .085

50.% = .5

110% = 1.1

| | | | | |
|---|---|---|---|---|
| 10 cents | = .10 | 10% | = | .10 |
| 50 cents | = .50 | 50% | = | .50 |
| \$1.50 | = 1.50 | 150% | = | 1.50 |

## C. DETERMINING COMMISSIONS AND SELLING PRICE

A *COMMISSION RATE is a percentage of the selling price that is used to calculate the commission.* The *COMMISSION is the dollar amount received by a real estate agent for completing the sale.* A real estate agent wants to know how much he or she will be paid for doing his or her job. Most real estate salespeople are paid on a commission basis. As a licensed real estate agent, one of your most pleasant duties will be determining your commission.

When dealing with math problems in real estate, it is important to translate "words" into "math words" and "math symbols."

| WORD | MATH WORD | MATH SYMBOL |
|------|-----------|-------------|
| OF (Means) | MULTIPLY | x |
| IS (Means) | EQUALS | = |

In commission problems you are supplied with the **PRINCIPAL (PAID)**, which is the property selling price, and the **RATE (%)**, which is the rate of commission, and asked to find the **RESULT (MADE)**, the agent's commission. Such problems use the result equation: **M = P x %**.

**EXAMPLE:** You have completed the sale of a $100,000 home. The rate of commission is 6%. How much money have you made?

M = P x %

MADE = PAID x RATE

MADE = $100,000 x 6% (.06)

MADE = $6,000

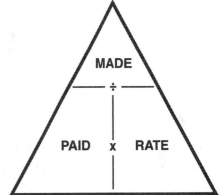

**ANSWER:** Your commission is $6,000.

### 1. Splitting Commissions

Most often when you have completed a sale, your brokerage will not be entitled to the entire commission. If you were representing the seller, for example, you might very likely split your commission with a broker and salesperson for the buyer. You will have earned a percentage of the amount earned by your broker, depending on the percentage both of you have agreed to in advance. The rates here are negotiable and usually vary with your experience and success.

When determining the splits of a commission, you use the result **(MADE)** equation. The total commission represents the principal **(PAID)** and the percentage **(RATE)** is whatever rate of commission was agreed to between the parties. **Figure 15-5** illustrates how a commission might be split.

### D. PROFIT AND LOSS

*When dealing with profit and loss problems, you must establish the value, or cost, before profit (+), or loss (-).*

The terms "value" and "cost" are interchangeable in real estate math problems; **it is what you paid for the property**.

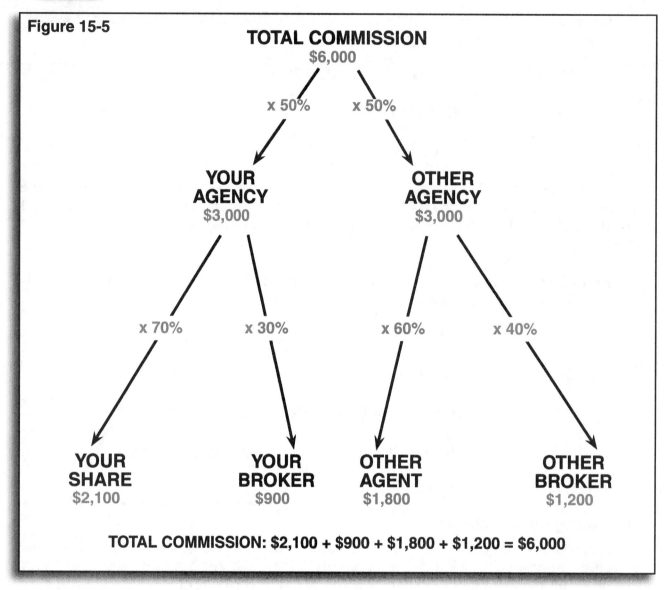

Figure 15-5

TOTAL COMMISSION
$6,000

x 50%     x 50%

YOUR AGENCY
$3,000

OTHER AGENCY
$3,000

x 70%     x 30%     x 60%     x 40%

YOUR SHARE
$2,100

YOUR BROKER
$900

OTHER AGENT
$1,800

OTHER BROKER
$1,200

TOTAL COMMISSION: $2,100 + $900 + $1,800 + $1,200 = $6,000

Key terms when working profit and loss problems:

1. **SELLING PRICE** – the dollar value after the profit or loss has been added or subtracted from the original cost.

2. **COST** – the dollar value before the profit or loss has been added or subtracted. Cost is often stated as purchase price or original price.

3. **1 + % PROFIT** – in a profit problem, the percent used in the formula will always be greater than 100%; in other words, the original cost (100%) plus the percent of profit. If you sold your property for 40% more than you paid for it, your selling price (100% + 40% = 140%) would be the cost x 140 % (1.40). To find the amount of profit (+40%), you would subtract the cost from the selling price.

4. **1 - % LOSS** –  for a loss problem, the percent used will always be less than 100%; in other words, the original cost (100%) minus the percent of loss. If you sold your

property for 25% less than what you paid for it, your selling price (100% - 25% = 75%) would be the cost x 75% (.75). To find the amount of loss (- 25%), you would subtract the selling price from the cost.

*The key to working these types of problems is to determine what percent to use.*

**EXAMPLE:** Ms. Smith sold her home for $250,000, which was 8% more than she paid for the property. How much did Ms. Smith pay for the property?

**SOLUTION:** Remember that profit is **always a % of cost**. If we use the Huber Pyramid, we know the Selling price (MADE) is $250,000 and the rate (%) is 108% (100% + 8%). To find the cost (PAID), we would **divide MADE by %**.

**ANSWER:** (rounded) $250,000 divided by 108% (1.08) = **$231,481**

Ms. Smith paid $231,481 for her property.

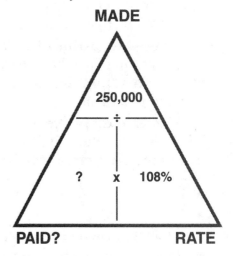

Let's try another problem:

**EXAMPLE:** Mr. Bush bought a new home on January 14 for $280,000. On July 6, he was transferred to a new city and sold his home for $270,000. What was his percent of loss?

**REMEMBER:** the percent of loss is based on what the home cost, not what it sold for.

**SOLUTION:** First we determine the amount of loss: $280,000 - $270,000 = $10,000.

Now we plug in the figures: MADE ($10,000) divided by PAID ($280,000) = percent (%) of loss.

**ANSWER:** Mr. Bush's percent of loss was 4% (.03572, or .04).

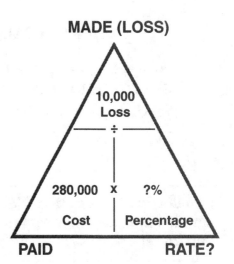

*Remember: In profit problems, percent will always be greater than 100%. In loss problems, percent will always be less than 100%.*

## E. PRINCIPAL AND INTEREST CALCULATIONS

*Use a 30-day month (banker's month) in calculating interest payments; thus 1 year = 360 days (statutory year).*

Great amounts of capital are necessary to complete most real estate transactions. As a licensed real estate agent, financing will often be one of the major concerns of your clients. It will be advantageous, therefore, for you to be able to provide loan counseling as a part of your services. Essential to this service will be your ability to readily calculate principal and interest payments.

*INTEREST is a fee paid for the use of other people's money, stated in dollars and cents.* When one leases an apartment, he or she pays rent to the landlord for the use of the property. Similarly, when one borrows money he or she pays "rent" to the lender for the use of the money. This "rent" is called interest. *SIMPLE INTEREST is the term used to describe interest on the unpaid balance.*

Most interest problems will supply you with the principal (**PAID**), which is the amount borrowed, and the rate (**%**), which is the percentage of rent being charged. You are asked to determine the interest (**MADE**). We learned this formula earlier:

$$M = P \times R \, (\%)$$

**There is an extra variable that is a factor in all interest problems: TIME.** The duration of the loan determines how much interest is owed at the annual rate. One year equals one, one month equals 1/12, and one day equals 1/360. In order to take this factor into consideration, we modify the MADE equation slightly, with **MADE (M)** becoming **INTEREST (I)**:

$$I = P \times R \times T$$

### INTEREST (MADE) = PRINCIPAL (PAID) x RATE (%) x TIME

When doing principal and interest problems, you are trying to find one of four unknowns: **INTEREST (I), PRINCIPAL (P), INTEREST RATE (R),** or **TIME (T).**

We will use this modified Huber Pyramid to work these types of problems:

**Remember: To use the Huber Pyramid, simply cover the chamber you are trying to find and then perform the required math.**

### 1. Interest Problem

Interest is the payment made for using other people's money. The formula for finding interest is:

$$I = P \times R \times T$$

Here is a sample exercise for you to try:

**EXAMPLE:** What would be the interest due on a loan of $10,000, borrowed at 9%, for a period of 2 years?

$I = P \times R \times T$

**INTEREST = PRINCIPAL x RATE x TIME**

**INTEREST = $10,000 x 9% x 2 YEARS**

**INTEREST = $10,000 x .09 x 2**

**INTEREST = $900 x 2**

**INTEREST = $1,800**

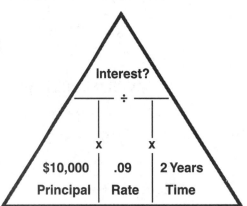

**ANSWER:** The interest would be $1,800 for two years, or $900 a year.

## 2. Principal Problem

As used in real estate finance problems, *PRINCIPAL is the amount borrowed in dollars*. To find the principal (amount borrowed), we would use the following formula:

$$P = \frac{I}{R \times T}$$

**EXAMPLE:** Mr. Johnson has a trust deed loan with annual interest payments of $5,200. If the rate of interest is 10%, how much did he borrow?

**SOLUTION:** We know that the interest (I) is $5,200, the rate (%) is 10% (.10) and the time (T) is 1 year. Using the above formula:

$$P = \frac{\$5,200}{.10 \times 1} = \frac{\$5,200}{.10} = \$52,000$$

**ANSWER:** Mr. Johnson borrowed $52,000.

## 3. Interest Rate Problem

The *INTEREST RATE is the percent of interest charged*. The purpose of principal and interest problems is to determine what we are paying **(INTEREST)** for the use of the amount borrowed **(PRINCIPAL)** and expressing that amount as a percentage **(INTEREST RATE)**. We use the following formula to find the interest rate:

$$R = \frac{I}{P \times T}$$

**EXAMPLE:** Ms. Bishop borrows $150,000 from 1st Bank to purchase a condominium. If, after the first year, she owes the lender $15,000 interest, what is the rate of interest?

**SOLUTION:** We know that the **INTEREST (I)** is $15,000, the **PRINCIPAL (P)** is $150,000 and the **TIME (T)** is one year.

Using the above formula:

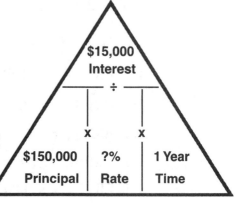

$$R = \frac{\$15,000}{\$150,000 \times 1} = \frac{\$15,000}{\$150,000} = (.10) \text{ or } 10\%$$

**ANSWER:** Ms. Bishop's rate of interest is 10%.

*Unless stated otherwise, the interest rate is assumed to be in annual terms, or the amount paid per year.*

**Figure 15-6** explains some useful terms in calculating interest rate problems.

---

**Figure 15-6**

## In Calculating Interest Rate Problems:

**Annual** = once a year
**Semiannual** = twice a year at 6 month intervals
**Biannual** = twice a year
**Bimonthly** = 6 times a year (every 2 months)
**Monthly** = 12 times a year
**Semimonthly** = twice a month
**Biennial** = once every 2 years
**1 Year** = 12 months = 52 weeks = 360 days
**1 Month** = 30 days

---

### 4. Time Problem

*TIME is used for periods less than or greater than one year.* Time is expressed as a fraction or percent of a year (1/12th or .0833) if a payment is to be made monthly. As stated earlier, **interest rates** are assumed to be annual unless otherwise stated. However the payment of **principal and interest** is usually done on a monthly basis. The previous problems used a one year time period. If the time period is more or less than a year, then **TIME (T)** takes on a different value:

**Monthly payment:** T = 1/12 or .0833
Semiannual payment: T = 1/2 or .5

**EXAMPLE:** Mr. Philips borrows $200,000 at 9.5 % interest. What is the monthly interest payment?

SOLUTION: **PRINCIPAL (P)** is $200,000, **RATE (R)** is 9.5% and **TIME (T)** is 1/12 or .0833.

$$I = P \times R \times T$$

I = $200,000 x .095 x .0833 = $1,583

ANSWER: Mr. Philips makes a monthly interest payment of $1,583.

## F. DISCOUNT POINTS ("Points")

*1 discount point = 1% of the loan amount*

DISCOUNT POINTS *are charges made by a lender to increase the yield on a loan: one point equals 1% of the loan.*

EXAMPLE: Mr. and Mrs. Majors are purchasing a house for $155,000. They will put $30,000 down and borrow the rest, which will include a 4 point charge by the savings bank. How much will the points cost them?

SOLUTION: First we must determine the amount being borrowed:

$155,000 - $30,000 = $125,000

Next we compute the discount rate:

**1 point = 1% of the loan amount  = .01 x $125,000 = $1,250**

Finally, we calculate the amount of discount:

**4 points = 4 x $1,250 = $5,000**

ANSWER: The Majors will pay $5,000 for the discount points from the borrowed $125,000.

# III. Determining Prorations

*Buyer's ownership starts on the day of closing.*

**PRORATION** *is the process of proportionately dividing (prorating) expenses or income to the precise date that escrow closes, or any other date previously agreed upon.* Its purpose is to apportion income and expense items correctly between the parties of a sale. These are divided (or **prorated**) in proportion to the time that each owned or will own the property.

In analyzing proration problems, you will first need to determine **who** will be credited with a dollar amount at closing. It is obvious that a seller has owned the property for the period *before* the day of closing and that the buyer will own the property *after* the day of closing. But who owns the property on the day of the closing itself? The real estate contract will usually answer this question.

# CHAPTER 15

If the contract determines prorations "to the day of closing," the buyer is considered the owner for that day. But if the contract reads "through the day of closing," the seller is considered the owner for that day for the purpose of determining proration calculations.

The contract will also specify the type year to be used for prorations (a calendar-- 365 day year or a banker's statutory year—360 days).

The next thing that you need to consider is **how much** will be credited. Items that are normally prorated include mortgage interest, taxes, homeowners' association dues, rent, and assessments. In some areas, prorations are also known as **adjustments** or **apportionments**.

Proration involves dividing the dollar amount associated with the time an expense or income occurred between two parties (the buyer and seller). Rent and interest are usually paid in one month intervals, while property taxes are paid once or twice a year. An important question that must be answered is who gets credit for an item. The rules are simple.

*On an escrow statement a CREDIT is something that is received and a DEBIT is something that is owed.*

### A. Rents (Income)

In determining the proration of rents, it is important to know what type year is being used (banker's year or calendar year). The calendar year is generally used. The portion of income that is granted to each party can be represented as a fraction. The denominator (bottom number) will be the number of days in the month, while the numerator (top number) will vary depending upon what day in the month escrow closes.

**EXAMPLE:** If the escrow closes on the 20th day of 30-day month, how would you divide a prepaid rent of $1,500 between the seller and the buyer?

**ANSWER:** The seller's share would be 20/30 of the whole, because he holds ownership through the 20th day. The share of the other 10 days (10/30) would go to the buyer.

| SELLER'S SHARE | BUYER'S SHARE |
|---|---|
| $\frac{20}{30}$ x 1,500 = $1,000 | $\frac{10}{30}$ x 1,500 = $500 |

So, the seller would receive $1,000 of the rent money, while the buyer would be prorated $500.

### B. PROPERTY TAXES (EXPENSES) – BUYER'S AND SELLER'S

Property taxes are prorated either from July 1, the beginning of the fiscal year, or January 1, the middle of the fiscal year. Since each of these two installments covers a six-month period, the portion of the expense prorated to each party is represented as a fraction with a denominator of 6. The numerator varies depending upon what month in the six-month period escrow closes.

---

### Buyer's and Seller's Settlement Statements
#### (Also See Chapter 7)

*DOUBLE-ENTRY BOOKKEEPING is the balancing procedure used to complete a settlement statement.* (Accountants will find this the opposite of true accounting.) The statement consists of two parts: a **buyer's statement** and a **seller's statement**. Each of these is divided into a **debit column** and a **credit column**.

A *DEBIT is something that is owed.* A debit entry for a buyer is anything charged against or subtracted from his or her account. The purchase price of the property is an example of something debited to the buyer. A debit entry for a seller means the same thing. Unpaid property taxes are a good example.

A *CREDIT is something that is received.* A credit entry for a buyer is anything received or added to his or her account. The deposit made on the property is a good example of something credited to the buyer. A good example of a credit entry for the seller would be prepaid property taxes.

If an item was **paid** before closing, the buyer's closing statement will be debited and the seller's statement will be credited. If **income** was received before closing, the buyer's statement will be credited and the seller's statement will be debited. Though items on closing statements follow no set order of entry, **the purchase price is usually the first entry and the amount due from/to buyer to close, and the amount due to/from seller to close are the last entries.**

**EXAMPLE:** The second installment of property tax on a home is $500. The seller has paid this tax, which covers a six-month period ending July 1. If he sells this property and escrow closes on April 1, how much of the $500 is his share in the expense? How much would the buyer have to reimburse?

**ANSWER:** The seller's share would be 3/6 of the tax bill (Jan. - Mar.), while the buyer would also be responsible for 3/6 (Apr. - Jun.). This is because both the seller and the buyer owned the property for three months during the six-month period.

| SELLER'S SHARE | BUYER'S SHARE |
|---|---|
| $\frac{3}{6} \times 500 = \$250$ | $\frac{3}{6} \times 500 = \$250$ |

Each would be responsible for $250 of the property tax; the buyer having to reimburse the seller, who already paid the entire property tax bill.

# IV. Depreciation (For Tax Purposes)

*DEPRECIATION (for income taxes) is a diminishing (loss) in the value of buildings and other improvements.* All new depreciation schedules for normal income tax purposes involving real property must be straight-line.

## A. STRAIGHT-LINE DEPRECIATION

*STRAIGHT-LINE DEPRECIATION is a method of computing depreciation on assets other than land for income tax purposes in which the difference between the original cost and salvage value is deducted in installments evenly over the life of the asset.* It is based upon the assumption that depreciation is dependent solely on the passage of time. Depreciation is spread uniformly over the useful life of a property (building).

*When doing depreciation problems, it is important to remember that land does NOT depreciate.*

To find depreciation using the straight-line method use:

**ANNUAL DEPRECIATION (A) = <u>VALUE (COST) OF IMPROVEMENTS (V)</u>**
**ECONOMIC LIFE (E)**

or simplified:

$$A = \frac{V}{E}$$

Let's try a problem using straight-line depreciation:

**EXAMPLE:** Mr. and Mrs. Roberts purchased some income property for $475,000. The land was valued at $200,000. The improvements had an estimated economic life of 27.5 years. What would be the depreciated value of the property after 17 years?

**ANSWER:** We must first determine the value of the depreciable asset (improvements) because land is not depreciated.

**$475,000 (land and improvements)**
**<u>- 200,000</u> (land)**
**$275,000 (COST of improvements)**

**$A = \frac{V}{E} = A = \frac{\$275,000}{27.5} = \$10,000$ depreciation per year**

**$10,000 x 17 years = $170,000 accumulated depreciation**
**$275,000 - $170,000 = $105,000 depreciated value of the improvements only**
**$105,000 + $200,000 (value of land) = $305,000**

$305,000 is the depreciated value of the property after 17 years.

*The IRS allows a minimum of 27.5 years straight-line depreciation on residential properties and 39 years on commercial properties.*

# V. How to Find the Value of a Parcel

**PROBLEM:** The NW¼ of the SW¼ of Section 7 is valued at $800 per acre. The N½ of the NE¼ of Section 4 is valued at $500 per acre. What is the difference in value between the two parcels?

| | | |
|---|---|---|
| **NW**<br><br>160 Acres | | **NE** |
| ■  40<br>Acres | | **SE** |

**SECTION 7**

**SECTION 4**

| | |
|---|---|
| **NW** | ■■■<br>80 Acres |
| **SW** | **SE** |

**SOLUTION:**

1 section = 640 acres
¼ section = 160 acres
¼ of ¼ section = 40 acres     40 acres x $800 per acre = $32,000
½ of ¼ section = 80 acres     80 acres x $500 per acre = $40,000
                                     $40,000 - $32,000 = $8000

**ANSWER: $8,000 is the difference in value between the two parcels**

*I wish you the best of luck in your real estate career, whether it be as a homeowner, investor, or salesperson. The future is yours!* – Walt Huber

*P.S. – Real Estate cycles go up and down. As a professional, it's up to you to turn challenges into opportunities.*

## VI. CHAPTER SUMMARY

This chapter illustrates some of the basic mathematical skills useful for a career in real estate. Familiarity with fundamental arithmetic and a few simple formulas, along with plain common sense, will provide the necessary background. Such knowledge will not only assist in the practice of real estate, but should also prove advantageous in passing the licensing exam. You should know the following common measurements:

### LINEAR

**1 foot (ft.)** = 12 inches (in.)
**1 yard (yd.)** = 3 feet (ft.)
**1 rod** = 16.5 ft. = 5.5 yd.
**1 mile** = 5,280 ft. = 1,760 yd. = 320 rods

### SQUARE

**1 sq. ft.** = 144 sq. in. (12 in. x 12 in.)
**1 sq. yd.** = 9 sq. ft. ( 3 ft. x 3 ft.)
**1 acre** = 43,560 sq. ft. = 4,840 sq. yd. = 160 sq. rods
**1 sq. mile** = 5,280 ft. x 5,280 ft.

### CUBIC

**1 cu. ft.** = 1,728 cu. in. (12 in. x 12 in. x 12 in.)
**1 cu. yd.** = 27 cu. ft. (3 ft. x 3 ft. x 3 ft.)

### LAND DESCRIPTION

**1 link** = 7.92 inches
**1 rod** = 25 links
**1 chain** = 100 links =  66 ft. = 4 rods
**1 mile** = 80 chains
**1 acre** = 43,560 sq. ft.
**1 township** = 36 sections = 36 square miles = 23,040 acres
**1 section** = 1 mile square = 640 acres = 1/36 of a township
**1 circle** = 360 degrees (°)
**1 quadrant** = 90 degrees (°)
**1 degree (°)** = 60 minutes (′)
**1 minute (′)** = 60 seconds (′′)

The agent needs to know measurements. The buyer wants to know how much land and building space he or she is buying. **Area measurements (length times width)** in square feet gives him or her that information.

**Land area** is the surface space between lot lines measured in square feet. **Building area** is the space enclosed by the exterior walls, measured in square feet.

**Rectangular Lot:** 4-sided parcels. Opposite sides are equal in length and right angles are formed by the intersection of the sides. Area equals Length times Width: **A = L x W**.

**Triangular Lot:** 3-sided parcel. Area equals Base (horizontal side) times Height (perpendicular distance from base to highest point) divided by 2: **A = B x H ÷ 2**.

**Irregular Lot:** Parcel that does not consist of a single known shape. Area is determined by breaking lot into rectangles and triangles and totalling the areas: **Total Area = Area (S) + Area (R) + Area (T)**.

**Structural Volume** is the cubic measure of the space within a structure. Structural volume measurement is generally used when renting space in a warehouse type structure. **Cubic Measure** is determined by multiplying the interior length by the width and the height: **V = L x W x H**.

The majority of math problems that you will encounter in real estate involve the use of **percentages**. It is important, therefore, for you to understand certain general rules about percentage problems before dealing with any of the particular types.

**Percentage problems:** Factors are: (1) Amount invested is the amount **Paid (P)**; (2) The rate is the **Percentage (%)**; and (3) The amount **Made (M)** is the amount earned. One of the three factors is usually missing. To compute the missing factor:

**Amount Paid (P)** = **Amount Made (M) ÷ Percentage Rate (%)**
**Amount Made (M)** = **Amount Paid (P) x Percentage (%)**
**Percentage Rate (%)** = **Amount Made (M) ÷ Amount Paid (P)**

The **commission** is the dollar amount received by a real estate agent for completing the sale.

**Determining Commissions and Selling Price:** The **Commission Rate** is a percentage of selling price. The **Commission** is the dollar amount received for completing the sale:

**Commission = Principal Paid x Percentage Rate**

**Profit and Loss: Profit** is the excess of revenues over expenses. **Loss** is the excess of expenses over revenues. **Profits = Revenues minus Expenses**.

Large amounts of capital are necessary to complete most real estate transactions. As a licensed real estate agent, financing will often be one of the major concerns of your clients. It will be advantageous for you to be able to provide loan counseling as a part of your services. Your ability to readily calculate **principal and interest payments** will be essential to this service.

**Principal and Interest Calculations:** Interest is the fee paid for the use of other people's money. **Interest (Amount Made) = Principal (Amount Paid) x Percentage Rate (%) x Time (T).**

**Determining Prorations:** Dividing expenses (property taxes) or income (rents) to a specified date, close of escrow or other agreed upon date, in proportion to time each owned or will own the property is called **proration**. In determining the proration of rents, it is important to remember that all escrow companies use a **30-day base month** (banker's month) and a **360-day statutory year**. The portion of income that is granted to each party can be represented as a fraction. The denominator will be 30, while the numerator will vary depending upon what day in the month escrow closes. **It is important to remember that the buyer's ownership starts on the day of closing.**

**Straight-line depreciation** is the difference between original cost of improvements and salvage value that is deducted in even installments over the life of the asset. When doing depreciation problems, it is important to remember that land does not depreciate, just the cost of improvements depreciate. The IRS allows straight-line depreciation of 27.5 years on residential properties and 39 years on commercial properties.

**Annual Depreciation (A) = Cost of Improvements - salvage value (V) ÷ Economic Life (E)**

## VII. TERMINOLOGY

A. Area
B. Commission
C. Credit
D. Cubic Area
E. Debit
F. Depreciation

G. Discount Points (Points)
H. Interest
I. Interest Rate
J. Irregular Lot
K. Principal (Amount Paid)
L. Proration

M. Rectangular Lot
N. Result (Amount Made)
O. Straight-Line Depreciation
P. Triangular Lot

1. ____ The amount of money borrowed.
2. ____ Money owed as it is shown on the settlement statement.
3. ____ The up-front charge by a lender to obtain and to increase the yield on a loan.
4. ____ The amount paid to a real estate broker usually expressed as a percentage of the sale price.
5. ____ To divide property taxes, insurance premiums, rental income, etc. between buyer and seller proportionately to time of use or the date of closing.
6. ____ Decrease in value to real property improvements by any cause.
7. ____ The rent or charge for the use of money.
8. ____ The surface of land or building. Length (in feet) times width (in feet).
9. ____ The area of this shaped lot is obtained by multiplying base times height and dividing by 2.
10. ____ Money received; it is shown as what on the settlement statement.
11. ____ Principal (paid) times rate (%) equals?
12. ____ The percentage paid for the use of borrowed money. Usually expressed as an annual percentage.
13. ____ Equal amount of depreciation each year. A loss in the value of improvements, used as an accounting (income tax) procedure.
14. ____ A lot with an unusual shape.
15. ____ The result of multiplying length times width times height.
16. ____ Four-sided figure with opposite sides equal in length and intersecting corners forming right angles.

## VIII. CHAPTER QUIZ

1. Ms. Donaldson exchanged her fourplex (fair market value $100,000 with a loan of $52,000) for a larger building (fair market value $150,000 with a loan of $42,000). Using only the above figures, how much money did Donaldson have to pay to complete the exchange?

    a. $48,000
    b. $52,000
    c. $60,000
    d. $108,000

2. Carol borrowed $5,200 and signed a straight note with an interest rate of 7% per annum. If she paid $1,125 in interest during the term of the note, what was the term of the note?

    a. 22 months
    b. 27 months
    c. 32 months
    d. 37 months

3. A woman owns a rental unit that nets her $450 per month. She realizes a 10% return on her investment each year. What is her investment in the property?

    a. $45,000
    b. $48,500
    c. $54,000
    d. None of the above

4. The assessed value of a piece of property is $48,700. The tax is $1.02 per $100 of assessed valuation. The tax is:

    a. $496.74.
    b. $489.60.
    c. $584.40.
    d. $594.14.

5. How much would have to be invested at 7% in order to provide an investor with $640 monthly income?

    a. $9,143
    b. $91,429
    c. $109,714
    d. $53,760

6. The second quarter interest on a $7,600 term loan at 8% interest is:

    a. $76.
    b. $152.
    c. $608.
    d. none of the above.

7. An apartment complex cost $450,000. It brings in a net income of $3,000 per month. The owner is making what percentage of return on her investment?

    a. 7%

    b. 8%

    c. 11%

    d. 12%

8. Broker Jones negotiates a lease for 3,000 square feet of warehouse storage space at a monthly rental of $0.50 per square foot. Jones commission is 8% of the first year's gross. Jones will receive:

    a. $1,180.

    b. $1,340.

    c. $1,440.

    d. none of the above.

9. Frank holds a five-year trust deed and note that was paid off at 7.2% interest per annum. If the total interest he received from the borrower was $4,140, what, approximately, was the original amount of the loan?

    a. $11, 500

    b. $29,700

    c. $33,650

    d. $57,500

10. A builder constructed a home for $350,000 and sold it for a 20% profit. What is the amount of profit?

    a. $17,500

    b. $20,000

    c. $35,000

    d. $70,000

ANSWERS: 1. c; 2. d; 3. c; 4. a; 5. c; 6. b; 7. b; 8. c; 9. a; 10. d

# A

**ALTA Title Policy (American Land Title Association):** A type of title insurance policy issued by title insurance companies that expands the risks normally insured against under the standard type policy to include unrecorded mechanic's liens; unrecorded physical easements; facts a physical survey would show; water and mineral rights; and rights of parties in possession, such as tenants and buyers under unrecorded instruments.

**ALTA Owner's Policy:** An owner's extended coverage policy that provides buyers or owners the same protection the ALTA policy gives to lenders.

**Abatement of Nuisance:** Extinction or termination of a nuisance.

**Absolute Fee Simple Title:** Absolute or fee simple title is one that is absolute and unqualified. It is the most complete title one can have.

**Abstract of Judgment:** A condensation or summary of the essential provisions of a court judgment.

**Abstract of Title:** A summary or digest of the conveyances, transfers, and any other facts relied on as evidence of title, together with any other elements of record which may impair the title.

**Abstraction:** A method of valuing land. The indicated value of the improvement is deducted from the sale price.

**Acceleration Clause:** Clause in trust deed or mortgage giving lender right to call all sums to be immediately due and payable upon the happening of a certain event.

**Acceptance:** When the seller's or agent's principal agrees to the terms of the agreement of sale and approves the negotiation on the part of the agent and acknowledges receipt of the deposit in subscribing to the agreement of sale, that act is termed an acceptance.

**Access Right:** The right of an owner to have ingress and egress to and from his/her property.

**Accession:** Gaining title when property is added to a property by another or a natural action.

**Accretion:** An addition to land from natural causes as, for example, from gradual action of the ocean or river waters.

**Accrued Depreciation:** The difference between the cost of replacement new as of the date of the appraisal and the present appraised value.

**Accrued Items of Expense:** Those incurred expenses that are not yet payable. The seller's accrued expenses are credited to the purchaser in a closing statement.

**Acknowledgment:** A formal declaration before a duly authorized officer by a person who has executed an instrument that such execution is his/her act and deed.

**Acoustical Tile:** Blocks of fiber, mineral or metal, with small holes or rough textured surface to absorb sound, used as covering for interior walls and ceilings.

**Acquisition:** The act or process by which a person procures property.

**Acre:** A measure of land equaling 160 square rods, or 4,840 square yards, or 43,560 square feet, or a tract about 208.71 feet square.

**Adjustments:** A means by which characteristics of a residential property are regulated by dollar amount or percentage to conform to similar characteristics of another residential property.

**Affiant:** A person who has made an affidavit.

**Administrator:** A person appointed by the probate court to administer the estate of a person deceased.

**Ad Valorem:** A Latin phrase meaning, "according to value." Usually used in connection with real estate taxation.

**Advance:** Transfer of funds from a lender to a borrower in advance on a loan.

**Advance Commitment:** The institutional investor's prior agreement to provide long-term financing upon completion of construction.

**Advance Fee:** A fee paid in advance of any services rendered.

**Adverse Possession:** Claiming based on the open and notorious possession and occupancy, usually under an evident claim or right, in denial or opposition to the title of another claimant.

**Affidavit:** A statement or declaration reduced to writing sworn to or affirmed before some officer who has authority to administer an oath or affirmation.

**Affidavit of Title:** A statement in writing, made under oath by seller or grantor, acknowledged before a Notary Public in which the affiant identifies himself/herself and his/her marital status certifying that since the examination of title on the contract date there are no judgments, bankruptcies or divorces, or unrecorded deeds, contracts, unpaid repairs or improvements or defects of title known to him/her and that he/she is in possession of the property.

**Affirm:** To confirm, to aver, to ratify, to verify.

**AFLB:** Accredited Farm and Land Broker.

**Agency:** The relationship between principal and agent which arises out of a contract, either expressed or implied, written or oral, wherein the agent is employed by the principal to do certain acts dealing with a third party.

**Agent:** One who represents another from whom he/she has derived authority.

**Agreement of Sale:** A written agreement or contract between seller and purchaser in which they reach a meeting of minds on the terms and conditions of the sale.

**Air Rights:** The rights in real property to use the air space above the surface of the land.

**Alienation:** The transferring of property to another; the transfer of property and possession of lands, or other things, from one person to another.

**Allodial Tenure:** A real property ownership system where ownership may be complete except for those rights held by government. Allodial is in contrast to feudal tenure.

**Alluvion (Alluvium):** Soil deposited by accretion. Increase of earth on a shore or bank of a river.

**Amenities:** Satisfaction of enjoyable living to be derived from a home; conditions of agreeable living or a beneficial influence arising from the location or improvements.

**AMO:** Accredited Management Organization.

**Amortization:** The liquidation of a financial obligation on an equal installment basis; also, recovery over a period of cost or value.

**Amortized Loan:** A loan that is completely paid off, interest and principal, by a series of regular payments that are equal or nearly equal. Also called a **Level Payments Loan**.

**Annuity:** A series of assured equal or nearly equal payments to be made over a period of time or it may be a lump sum payment to be made in the future.

**Anticipation, Principle of:** Affirms that value is created by anticipated benefits to be derived in the future.

**Appraisal:** An opinion of value as of a certain date; a conclusion resulting from the analysis of facts.

**Appraiser:** One qualified by education, training and experience who is hired to estimate the value of real and personal property based on experience, judgment, facts, and use of formal appraisal processes.

**Appurtenance:** Something annexed to another thing that may be transferred with it. Your real property is burdened with an easement, water rights, or improvements that a person may use.

**Architectural Style:** Generally the appearance and character of a building's design and construction.

**ASA:** American Society of Appraisers.

**Asbestos:** A fibrous insulation and construction material that causes serious lung problems.

**Assessed Valuation:** A valuation placed upon property by a public officer or board, as a basis for taxation.

**Assessed Value:** Value placed on property as a basis for taxation.

**Assessment:** The valuation of property for the purpose of levying a tax or the amount of the tax levied.

**Assessor:** The official who has the responsibility of determining assessed values.

**Assignment:** A transfer or making over to another of the whole of any property, real or personal, in possession or in action, or of any estate or right therein. (The transfer of an entire leasehold estate to a new person.)

**Assignor:** One who assigns or transfers the claim, benefit, or right in property.

**Assigns; Assignees:** Those to whom a lease shall have been transferred or assigned.

**Assumption Agreement:** An undertaking or adoption of a debt or obligation primarily resting upon another person.

**Assumption Fee:** A lender's charge for changing over and processing new records for a new owner who is assuming an existing loan.

**Assumption of Mortgage:** The taking of title to property by a grantee, wherein he/she assumes liability for payment of an existing note secured by a mortgage or deed of trust against the property; becoming a co-guarantor for the payment of a mortgage or deed of trust note.

**Attachment:** Seizure of property by court order, usually done to have it available in event a judgment is obtained in a pending suit.

**Attest:** To affirm to be true or genuine; an official act establishing authenticity.

**Attorney-in-Fact:** One who is authorized to perform certain acts for another under a power of attorney; power of attorney may be limited to a specific act or acts, or be general.

# GLOSSARY

**Avulsion:** The sudden tearing away or removal of land by action of water flowing over or through it.

**Axial Growth:** City growth which occurs along main transportation routes. Usually takes the form of star-shaped extensions outward from the center.

# B

**Backfill:** The replacement of excavated earth into a hole or against a structure.

**Balloon Payment:** Where the final installment payment on a note is greater than the preceding installment payments and it pays the note in full, such final installment is termed a balloon payment.

**Bargain and Sale Deed:** Any deed that recites a consideration and purports to convey the real estate; a bargain and sale deed with a covenant against the grantor's acts is one in which the grantor warrants that the grantor has done nothing to harm or cloud the title.

**Baseboard:** A board placed against the wall around a room next to the floor.

**Base and Meridian:** Imaginary lines used by surveyors to find and describe the location of private or public lands.

**Base Molding:** Molding used at top of baseboard.

**Base Shoe:** Molding used at junction of baseboard and floor. Commonly called a carpet strip.

**Batten:** Narrow strips of wood or metal used to cover joints, interiorly or exteriorly; also used for decorative effect.

**Beam:** A structural member transversely supporting a load.

**Bearing Wall or Partition:** A wall or partition supporting any vertical load in addition to its own weight.

**Bench Marks:** A location indicated on a durable marker by surveyors.

**Beneficiary:** (1) One entitled to the benefit of a trust; (2) One who receives profit from an estate, the title of which is vested in a trustee; (3) The lender on the security of a note and deed of trust.

**Bequeath:** To give or hand down by will; to leave by will.

**Bequest:** That which is given by the terms of a will (applies to personal property).

**Betterment:** An improvement upon property that increases the property value and is considered as a capital asset or distinguished from repairs or replacements where the original character or cost is unchanged.

**Bill of Sale:** A written instrument given to pass title of personal property from vendor to the vendee.

**Binder:** An agreement to consider a down payment for the purchase of real estate as evidence of good faith on the part of the purchaser. Also, a notation of coverage on an insurance policy, issued by an agent, and given to the insured prior to issuing of the policy.

**Blacktop:** Asphalt paving used in streets and driveways.

**Blanket Trust Deed or Encumbrance:** A single mortgage that covers more than one piece of real estate.

**Blighted Area:** A declining area in which real property values are seriously affected by destructive economic forces, such as encroaching inharmonious property usages, infiltration of lower economic inhabitants, and/or rapidly depreciating buildings.

**Board Foot:** A unit of measurement of lumber; one-foot wide, one-foot long, one-inch thick; 144 cubic inches.

**Bona Fide:** In good faith, without fraud.

**Bond:** An obligation under seal. A real estate bond is a written obligation issued on security of a mortgage or trust deed.

**Bracing:** Framing lumber nailed at an angle in order to provide rigidity.

**Breach:** The breaking of a law, or failure of duty, either by omission or commission.

**Breezeway:** A covered porch or passage, open on two sides, connecting house and garage or two parts of the house.

**Bridge Loan (Gap Loan/Swing Loan):** Short-term loan between construction loan and permanent financing.

**Bridging:** Small wood or metal pieces used to brace floor joists.

**Broker:** A person employed by another, to carry on any of the activities listed in the license law definition of a broker, for a fee.

**B.T.U. (British Thermal Unit):** The quantity of heat required to raise the temperature of one pound of water one degree Fahrenheit.

**Building Code:** A systematic regulation of construction of buildings within a municipality established by ordinance or law.

**Building Line:** A line set by law a certain distance from a street line in front of which an owner cannot build on his/her lot. (**Setback Line**)

**Building Paper:** A heavy waterproofed paper used as sheathing in wall or roof construction as a protection against air passage and moisture.

**Built-In:** Cabinets or similar features built as part of the house.

**Bundle of Rights:** Beneficial interests or rights attached to the ownership of real property.

**Buy-Down Loan:** A loan where the seller pays points to a lender so that the lender can offer below market financing.

**Buyer's Agent:** An agent representing the buyer rather than the seller.

# C

**CCIM:** Certified Commercial Investment Member.

**CC&Rs:** Abbreviation for covenants, conditions, and restrictions.

**CPM:** Certified Property Manager, a designation of the Institute of Real Estate Management.

# GLOSSARY

**Capital Assets:** Assets of a permanent nature used in the production of an income, such as: land, buildings, machinery, and equipment, etc. Under income tax law, it is usually distinguishable from "inventory" which comprises assets held for sale to customers in ordinary course of the taxpayers' trade or business.

**Capital Gain:** Income from a sale of an asset rather than from the general business activity. Capital gains are generally taxed at a lower rate than ordinary income.

**Capitalization:** In appraising, determining value of property by considering net income and percentage of reasonable return on the investment. Thus, the value of an income property is determined by dividing annual net income by the capitalization rate (see below).

**Capitalization Rate:** The rate of interest that is considered a reasonable return on the investment, and used in the process of determining value based upon net income. It may also be described as the yield rate that is necessary to attract the money of the average investor to a particular kind of investment. In the case of land improvements which depreciate to this yield rate is added a factor to take into consideration the annual amortization factor necessary to recapture the initial investment in improvements.

**Casement Window:** Frames of wood or metal, which swing outward.

**Cash Flow:** The net income generated by a property before depreciation and other noncash expenses.

**Caveat Emptor:** "Let the buyer beware." The buyer must examine the goods or property and buy at his own risk.

**Certificate of Reasonable Value (CRV):** The federal Veterans Administration appraisal commitment of property value.

**Chain:** A unit of measurement used by surveyors. A chain consists of 100 links equal to 66 feet.

**Chain of Title:** A history of conveyances and encumbrances affecting the title from the time the original patent was granted, or as far back as records are available.

**Change, Principle of:** Holds that it is the future, not the past, which is of prime importance in estimating value.

**Characteristics:** Distinguishing features of a (residential) property.

**Chattel Mortgage:** A claim on personal property (instead of real property) used to secure or guarantee a promissory note. (See definitions of **Security Agreement** and **Security Interest**.)

**Chattel Real:** A personal property interest related to real estate, such as a lease on real property.

**Chattels:** Goods or every species of property movable or immovable that are not real property.

**Circuit Breaker:** An electrical device that automatically interrupts an electric circuit when an overload occurs; may be used instead of a fuse to protect each circuit and can be reset.

**Civil Rights Act of 1866:** The first federal fair housing act (applied to race only).

**Civil Rights Act of 1968:** Federal fair housing act that expanded the Civil Rights Act of 1866.

**Clapboard:** Overlapping boards usually thicker at one edge used for siding.

**Closing Statement:** An accounting of funds made to the buyer and seller separately.

**Cloud on the Title:** Any conditions revealed by a title search that affect the title to property; usually relatively unimportant items, but which cannot be removed without a quitclaim deed or court action.

**Collar Beam:** A beam that connects the pairs of opposite roof rafters above the attic floor.

**Collateral:** This is the property subject to the security interest. (See definition of **Security Interest**.)

**Collateral Security:** A separate obligation attached to contract to guarantee its performance; the transfer of property or of other contracts, or valuables, to insure the performance of a principal agreement.

**Collusion:** An agreement between two or more persons to defraud another of his/her rights by the forms of law, or to obtain an object forbidden by law.

**Color of Title:** That which appears to be good title, but which is not title in fact. Example: title under a forged deed.

**Commercial Acre:** A term applied to the remainder of an acre of newly subdivided land after the area devoted to streets, sidewalks, and curbs, etc., has been deducted from the acre.

**Commercial Paper:** Bills of exchange used in commercial trade.

**Commission:** An agent's compensation for performing the duties of his/her agency; in real estate practice, a percentage of the selling price of property, percentage of rentals, etc.

**Commitment:** A pledge or a promise or firm agreement.

**Common Law:** The body of law that grew from customs and practices developed and used in England. (Based on court decisions, not statutes.)

**Community:** A part of a metropolitan area that has a number of neighborhoods that have a tendency toward common interests and problems.

**Community Property:** Property accumulated during marriage that is owned equally by husband and wife.

**Compaction:** Ability of the soil to support a structure. Compaction tests are important as to filled land.

**Comparable Sales:** Sales that have similar characteristics as the subject property and are used for analysis in the appraisal process.

**Compensator Damages:** Damages to reimburse an injured party for the actual loss suffered.

**Competent:** Legally qualified.

**Component:** One of the features making up the whole property.

**Compound Interest:** Interest paid on original principal and also on the accrued and unpaid interest which has accumulated.

**Conclusion:** The final estimate of value, realized from facts, data, experience and judgment.

**Condemnation:** The act of taking private property for public use. Also a declaration that a structure is unfit for use.

**Condition:** A qualification of an estate granted which can be imposed only in conveyances. They are classified as conditions precedent and conditions subsequent.

# GLOSSARY

**Condition Precedent:** A condition that requires certain action or the happening of a specified event before the estate granted can take effect. **Example:** most installment real estate sale contracts require all payments to be made at the time specified before the buyer may demand transfer of title.

**Condition Subsequent:** When there is a condition subsequent in a deed, the title vests immediately in the grantee, but upon breach of the condition the grantor has the power to terminate the estate if he/she wishes to do so. **Example:** A condition in the deed prohibiting the grantee from using the premises as a liquor store.

**Conditional Commitment:** A commitment of a definite loan amount for some future unknown purchaser of satisfactory credit standing.

**Condominium:** A system of individual fee ownership of units in a multi-family structure, combined with joint ownership of common areas of the structure and the land. (Sometimes referred to as a **Vertical Subdivision**.)

**Conduit:** Usually a metal pipe in which electrical wiring is installed.

**Conduits:** Individuals or firms that purchase loans from originators to resell to investors.

**Confession of Judgment:** An entry of judgment upon the debtor's voluntary admission or confession.

**Confirmation of Sale:** A court approval of the sale of property by an executor, administrator, guardian or conservator.

**Confiscation:** The seizing of property without compensation.

**Conforming Loans:** Loans that meet the purchase requirement of Fannie Mae and Freddie Mac.

**Conformity, Principle of:** Holds that the maximum value is realized when a reasonable degree of homogeneity of improvements is present.

**Conservation:** The process of utilizing resources in such a manner that minimizes their depletion.

**Consideration:** Anything of value given to induce entering into a contract; it may be money, personal services, or anything having value.

**Constant:** The percentage which, when applied directly to the face value of a debt, develops the annual amount of money necessary to pay a specified net rate of interest on the reducing balance and to liquidate the debt in a specified time period. For example, a 6% loan with a 20-year amortization has a constant of approximately 8.5%. Thus, a $10,000 loan amortized over 20 years requires an annual payment of approximately $850.00.

**Contingent Remainder:** A remainder interest that can be defeated by the happening of an event.

**Construction Loans:** Loans made for the construction of homes or commercial buildings. Usually funds are disbursed to the contractor/builder during construction and after periodic inspections. Disbursements are based on an agreement between borrower and lender.

**Constructive Eviction:** Breach of a covenant of warranty or quiet enjoyment, e.g., the inability of a lessee to obtain possession because of a paramount defect in title, or a condition making occupancy hazardous. A lessee can treat it as cause to void a lease.

**Constructive Notice:** Notice given by the public records.

**Consummate Dower:** A widow's dower interest which, after the death of her husband, is complete or may be completed and become an interest in real estate.

**Contour:** The surface configuration of land.

**Contour Lines:** Lines on a map that indicate elevation. When lines are close together, it indicates a steep stoop, but if the lines are far apart, it indicates the land is relatively level.

**Contract:** An agreement, either written or oral, to do or not to do certain things.

**Contribution, Principle of:** Holds that maximum real property values are achieved when the improvements on the site produce the highest (net) return commensurate with the investment.

**Consumer Goods:** These are goods used or bought for use primarily for personal, family or household purposes.

**Conventional Mortgage:** A mortgage securing a loan made by investors without governmental underwriting, i.e., which is not FHA insured or VA guaranteed.

**Conversion:** Change from one character or use to another. Also, the wrongful appropriation of funds of another.

**Conveyance:** This has two meanings. One meaning refers to the process of transferring title to property from one person to another. In this sense it is used as a verb. The other meaning refers to the document used to effect the transfer of title (usually some kind of deed). In this last sense, it is used a noun.

**Cooperative Ownership:** A form of apartment ownership. Ownership of shares in a cooperative venture which entitles the owner to use, rent, or sell a specific apartment unit. The corporation usually reserves the right to approve certain actions such as a sale or improvement.

**Corner Influence Table:** A statistical table that may be used to estimate the added value of a corner lot.

**Corporation:** A group or body of persons established and treated by law as an individual or unit with rights and liabilities or both, distinct and apart from those of the persons composing it. A corporation is a creature of law having certain powers and duties of a natural person. Being created by law it may continue for any length of time the law prescribes.

**Corporeal Rights:** Possessory rights in real property.

**Correction Lines:** A system for compensating inaccuracies in the Government Rectangular Survey System due to the curvature of the earth. Every fourth township line, 24 mile intervals, is used as a correction line on which the intervals between the north and south range lines are remeasured and corrected to a full 6 miles.

**Correlate the Findings:** Interpret the data and value estimates to bring them together to a final conclusion of value.

**Correlation:** To bring the indicated values developed by the three approaches into mutual relationship with each other.

**Correlative User:** Rights of an owner to reasonable use of nonflowing underground water.

**Cost:** A historical record of past expenditures, or an amount that would be given in exchange for other things.

**Cost Approach:** One of three methods in the appraisal process. An analysis in which a value estimate of a property is derived by estimating the replacement cost of the improvements, deducting therefrom the estimated accrued depreciation, then adding the market value of the land.

**Counterflashing:** Sheet metal used around chimneys, at roof line and in roof valleys to prevent moisture entry.

**Covenant:** Agreements written into deeds and other instruments promising performance or nonperformance of certain acts or stipulating certain uses or nonuses of the property.

**CPM:** Certified Property Manager. IREM's highest designation.

**Crawl Space:** Exterior or interior opening permitting access underneath building (**minimum 18″**), as required by building codes.

**CRB:** Certified Residential Broker.

**CRE:** Counselor of Real Estate. Members of American Society of Real Estate Counselors.

**CRS:** Certified Residential Specialist (a NAR designation).

**Cubage:** The number or product resulting by multiplying the width of a thing by its height and by its depth or length.

**Curable Depreciation:** Items of physical deterioration and functional obsolescence that are customarily repaired or replaced by a prudent property owner.

**Curtail Schedule:** A listing of the amounts by which the principal sum of an obligation is to be reduced by partial payments and of the dates when each payment will become payable.

# D

**Damages:** The indemnity (amount) recoverable by a person who has sustained an injury, either in his person, property, or relative rights, through the act or default of another.

**Data Plant:** An appraiser's file of information on real estate.

**Debenture:** Bonds issued without specific security.

**Debtor:** This is the party who "owns" the property that is subject to the security interest.

**Deciduous Trees:** Trees that lose their leaves in the autumn and winter. (Regarded as hardwoods.)

**Deck:** Usually an open area on the roof, or off a ground or higher floor. Similar areas are called porch, patio, lanai, veranda.

**Dedication:** A conveyance of land by its owner for some public use, accepted for such use by authorized public officials on behalf of the public.

**Deed:** Written instrument which, when properly executed and delivered, conveys title.

**Deed in Lieu of Foreclosure:** Mortgagor gives a quit claim deed to mortgagee. There could be a problem as to junior liens.

**Deed Restrictions:** This is a limitation in the deed to a property that dictates certain uses that may or may not be made of the property.

**Default:** Failure to fulfill a duty or promise or to discharge an obligation; omission or failure to perform any act.

**Defeasance Clause:** The clause in a mortgage that gives the mortgagor the right to redeem his/her property upon the payment of his obligations to the mortgagee.

**Defeasible Fee:** Sometimes called a "base fee" or "qualified fee"; a fee simple absolute interest in land that is capable of being terminated upon the happening of a specified event.

**Deferred Maintenance:** Existing but unfulfilled requirements for repairs and rehabilitation.

**Deficiency Judgment:** A judgment given when the foreclosure sale of the security pledge for a loan does not satisfy the debt.

**Depreciation:** Loss of value in real property brought about by age, physical deterioration or functional or economic obsolescence. Broadly, a loss in value from any cause.

**Depth Table:** A statistical table that may be used to estimate the value of the added depth of a lot.

**Desist and Refrain Order:** An order directing a person to desist and refrain (stop) from committing an act in violation of the real estate law.

**Desk Cost:** The cost of operation of a real estate office expressed on a per salesperson basis.

**Deterioration (Physical):** Impairment of condition. One of the causes of depreciation and reflecting the loss in value brought about by wear and tear, disintegration, use in service, and the action of the elements.

**Devisee:** One who receives a bequest made by will.

**Devisor:** One who bequeaths by will.

**Directional Growth:** The location or direction toward which the residential sections of a city are destined or determined to grow.

**Discount:** An amount deducted in advance from the principal before the borrower is given the use of the principal. (See **Points**.)

**Disintermediation:** The relatively sudden withdrawal of substantial sums of money savers have deposited with savings and loan associations, commercial banks, and mutual savings banks. This term can also be considered to include life insurance policy purchasers borrowing against the value of their policies. The essence of this phenomenon is financial intermediaries losing within a short period of time billions of dollars as owners of funds held by those institutional lenders exercise their prerogative of taking them out of the hands of these financial institutions.

**Disposable Income:** The after-tax income a household receives to spend on personal consumption.

**Dispossess:** To deprive one of the use of real estate.

**Documentary Transfer Tax:** A state enabling act allowing a county to adopt a documentary transfer tax to apply on all transfer of real property located in the county. Notice of payment is entered on face of the deed or on a separate paper filed with the deed.

**Dominant Tenement:** Estate benefited by an easement right of use.

**Donee:** A person to whom a gift is made.

**Donor:** A person who makes a gift.

**Dower:** The right that a wife has in her husband's estate at his death.

**Dual Agency:** An agent who has agency duties to both buyer and seller.

# GLOSSARY

TM

**Duress:** Unlawful constraint exercised upon a person whereby he/she is forced to do some act against his/her will.

# E

**Earnest Money:** Down payment made by a purchaser of real estate as evidence of good faith.

**Easement:** Created by grant or agreement for a specific purpose, an easement is the right, privilege or interest which one party has in land of another. **Example:** right of way.

**Easement by Necessity:** Easement granted when lands were formerly under a single owner and there is not other ingress or egress.

**Easement by Prescription:** An easement obtained by open, notorious and hostile use.

**Easement In Gross:** Easement personal to the easement holder where there is no dominant tenement (such as the right of a utility company to run power lines across a property).

**Eaves:** The lower part of a roof projecting over the wall.

**Economic Life:** The period over which a property will yield a return on the investment, over and above the economic or ground rent due to land.

**Economic Obsolescence:** A loss in value due to factors away from the subject property but adversely affecting the value of the subject property.

**Economic Rent:** The reasonable rental expectancy if the property were available for renting at the time of its valuation.

**Effective Age of Improvement:** The number of years of age that is indicated by the condition of the structure, not its actual chronological age.

**Effective Date of Value:** The specific day the conclusion of value applies.

**Effective Interest Rate:** The percentage of interest that is actually being paid by the borrower for the use of the money.

**Electromagnetic Fields:** Possible harmful magnetic fields surrounding high capacity electrical transmission lines.

**Eminent Domain:** The right of the government to acquire property for necessary public or quasi-public use by condemnation; the owner must be fairly compensated. The right of the government to do this and the right of the private citizen to get paid is spelled out in the 5th Amendment to the United States Constitution.

**Encroachment:** The building of a structure or construction of any improvements, partly or wholly on the property of another. A form of trespass.

**Encumbrance:** Anything which affects or limits the fee simple title to property, such as mortgages, easements or restrictions of any kind. Liens are special encumbrances which make the property security for the payment of a debt or obligation, such as mortgages and taxes.

**Environmental Impact Report (EIR):** A report as to the effect of a proposed development on the environment.

**Equity:** The interest or value which an owner has in real estate over and above the liens against it; branch of remedial justice by and through which relief is afforded to suitors in courts of equity.

**Equity of Redemption:** The right to redeem property during or after the foreclosure period, such as a mortgagor's right to redeem within a set period after foreclosure sale (some states).

**Erosion:** The wearing away of land by the action of water, wind or glacial ice.

**Escalation:** The right reserved by the lender to increase the amount of the payments and/or interest upon the happening of a certain event.

**Escalator Clause:** A clause in a contract or lease providing for the upward or downward adjustment of payments.

**Escheat:** The reverting of property to the State when heirs capable of inheriting are lacking.

**Escrow:** The deposit of instruments and funds with instructions to a third neutral party to carry out the provisions of an agreement or contract; when everything is deposited to enable carrying out the instructions, it is called a complete or perfect escrow.

**Estate:** As applied to the real estate practice, the term signifies the quantity of interest, share, right, equity, of which riches or fortune may consist, in real property. The degree, quantity, nature, and extent of interest which a person has in real property.

**Estate of Inheritance:** An estate which may descend to heirs. All freehold estates are estates of inheritance, except estates for life.

**Estate for Life:** A freehold estate, not of inheritance, but which is held by the tenant for his own life or the life or lives of one or more other persons, or for an indefinite period which may endure for the life or lives of persons in being and beyond the period of life.

**Estate from Period-to-Period:** An interest in land where there is no definite termination date but the rental period is fixed at a certain sum per week, month, or year. Also called a **Periodic Tenancy**.

**Estate at Sufferance:** An estate arising when the tenant wrongfully holds over after the expiration of his term. The landlord has the choice of evicting the tenant as a trespasser or accepting such tenant for a similar term and under the conditions of the tenant's previous holding. Also called a **Tenancy at Sufferance**.

**Estate of Will:** The permissive occupation of lands and tenements by a tenant for an indefinite period, without a rental agreement.

**Estate for Years:** An interest in lands by virtue of a contract for the possession of them for a definite and limited period of time. A lease with a definite termination date may be said to be an estate for years.

**Estate Tax:** Inheritance tax.

**Estimate:** To form a preliminary opinion of value.

**Estimated Remaining Life:** The period of time (years) it takes for the improvements to become valueless.

**Estoppel:** A doctrine which bars one from asserting rights which are inconsistent with a previous position or representation.

**Ethics:** That branch of moral science, idealism, justness, and fairness, which sets out the obligations a member of a profession or craft owes to the public, to his clients or patron, and to his professional brethren or members.

**Eviction:** Dispossession by process of law. The act of depriving a person of the possession of lands, in pursuance of the judgment of a court.

**Exclusive Agency Listing:** A written instrument giving one agent the right to sell property for a specified time but reserving the right of the owner to sell the property himself without the payment of a commission.

**Exclusive Right to Sell Listing:** A written agreement between owner and agent giving agent the right to collect a commission if the property is sold by anyone during the term of his agreement.

**Execute:** To complete, to make, to perform, to do, to follow out; to execute a deed, to make a deed, including especially signing, sealing, and delivery; to execute a contract is to perform the contract, to follow out to the end, to complete.

**Executor:** A person named in a will to carry out its provisions as to the disposition of the estate of a person deceased.

**Expansion Joint:** A fiber strip used to separate units of concrete to prevent cracking due to expansion as a result of temperature changes.

**Expenses:** Certain items which may appear on a closing statement in connection with a real estate sale.

# F

**Facade:** Front of a building.

**Facilitator:** A person who acts to bring parties to an agreement but is the agent of neither.

**Fair Market Value:** This is the amount of money that would be paid for a property offered on the open market for a reasonable period of time with both buyer and seller knowing all the uses to which the property could be put and with neither party being under pressure to buy or sell.

**Farm Service Agency (FSA):** An agency of the Department of Agriculture. Primary responsibility is to provide financial assistance for farmers and others living in rural areas where financing is not available on reasonable terms from private sources.

**Federal Deposit Insurance Corporation (FDIC):** Agency of the federal government which insures deposits at commercial banks and savings banks up to $100,000.

**Federal Home Loan Bank (FHLB):** A district bank of the Federal Home Loan Bank system that lends only to member savings and loan associations.

**Federal Home Loan Bank Board (FHLBB):** The administrative agency that charters federal savings and loan associations and exercises regulatory authority over the FHLB system.

**Federal Housing Administration (FHA):** An agency of the federal government that insures mortgage loans.

**Federal National Mortgage Association (FNMA - "Fannie Mae"):** A private corporation whose primary function is to buy and sell FHA and VA mortgages in the secondary market.

**Fee:** An estate of inheritance in real property.

**Fee Simple:** In modern estates, the terms "Fee" and "Fee Simple" are substantially synonymous. The term "Fee" is of Old English derivation. "Fee Simple Absolute" is an estate in real property, by which the owner has the greatest power over the title which it is possible to have, being an absolute estate. In modern use, it expressly establishes the title of real property in the owner, without limitation or end. He may dispose of it by sale, trade, or will, as he chooses.

**Fee Simple Determinable:** An estate that ends automatically when a condition is breached.

**Feudal Tenure:** A real property ownership system where ownership rests with a sovereign who, in turn, may grant lesser interests in return for service or loyalty. In contrast to allodial tenure where ownership is complete.

**Feuds:** Grants of land.

**Fidelity Bond:** A security posted to insure the honesty of a person.

**Fiduciary:** A person in a position of trust and confidence, as between principal and broker; broker as fiduciary owes certain loyalty which cannot be breached under the rules of agency.

**Filtering Down:** The process of housing passing down to successively lower income groups.

**Financial Intermediary:** Financial institutions such as commercial banks, savings and loan associations, mutual savings banks and life insurance companies which receive relatively small sums of money from the public and invest them in the form of large sums. A considerable portion of these funds are loaned on real estate.

**Financing Statement:** This is the instrument which is filed in order to give public notice of the security interest in personal property and thereby protect the interest of the secured parties in the collateral. See definitions of Security Interest and Secured Party.

**Finder's Fee:** A fee for introducing the parties to a transaction.

**Finish Floor:** Finish floor strips are applied over wood joists, and plywood before finish floor is installed; finish floor is the final covering on the floor: wood, linoleum, cork, tile or carpet.

**Fire Stop:** A horizontal board between studs placed to prevent the spread of fire and smoke through such a space.

**First Mortgage:** A legal document pledging collateral for a loan (see "mortgage") that has first priority over all other claims against the property except taxes and bonded indebtedness.

**Fiscal Controls:** Federal tax and expenditure policies used to control the level of economic activity.

**Fixity of Location:** The physical characteristic of real estate that subjects it to the influence of its surroundings.

**Fixtures:** Appurtenances attached to the land or improvements, which usually cannot be removed without agreement as they become real property. **Examples:** plumbing fixtures built into the property.

**Flashing:** Sheet metal or other material used to protect a building from seepage of water.

**Footing:** The base or bottom of a foundation wall, pier, or column.

**Foreclosure:** Legal procedure whereby property pledged as security for a debt is sold to pay the debt in event of default in payments or terms.

**Forfeiture:** Loss of money or anything of value, due to failure to perform.

**Foundation:** The supporting portion of a structure below the first floor construction, or below grade.

**Franchise:** A specified privilege awarded by a government or business firm which awards an exclusive marketing.

**Fraud:** The intentional and successful employment of any cunning, deception, collusion, or artifice, used to circumvent, cheat or deceive another person, whereby that person acts upon it to the loss of his property and to his legal injury.

**Freehold:** An estate of indeterminable duration, e.g., fee simple or life estate.

**Frontage:** Land bordering a street.

**Front Foot:** Property measurement for sale or valuation purposes; the property measures by the front foot on its street line—each front foot extending the depth of the lot.

**Front Money:** The minimum amount of money necessary to initiate a real estate venture.

**Frostline:** The depth of frost penetration in the soil. Varies in different parts of the country. Footings should be placed below this depth to prevent movement.

**Fructus Naturales:** Naturally growing plants and trees.

**Functional Obsolescence:** A loss of value due to adverse factors built into the structure which affect the utility of the structure.

**Funding Fee:** A fee paid to the Department of Veterans Affairs for a VA loan.

**Furring:** Strips of wood or metal applied to a wall or other surface to even it, to form an air space, or to give the wall an appearance of greater thickness.

**Future Benefits:** The anticipated benefits the present owner will receive from his property in the future.

# G

**Gable Roof:** A pitched roof with sloping sides.

**Gambrel Roof:** A curb roof, having a steep lower slope with a flatter upper slope above.

**General Lien:** A lien on all the property of a debtor.

**General Warranty Deed:** The warranty deed where the seller guarantees that the title is marketable.

**Gift Deed:** A deed for which the consideration is love and affection and where there is no material consideration.

**Girder:** A large beam used to support beams, joists and partitions.

**Grade:** Ground level at the foundation.

**Graduated Lease:** Lease which provides for a varying rental rate, often based upon future determination; sometimes rent is based upon result of periodical appraisals; used largely in long-term leases.

**Grant:** A technical term made use of in deeds of conveyance of lands to import a transfer.

**Grant Deed:** A deed in which "grant" is used as the word of conveyance. The grantor impliedly warrants that he has not already conveyed to any other person, and that the estate conveyed is free from encumbrances done, made or suffered by the grantor or any person claiming under him, including taxes, assessments, and other liens.

**Grantee:** The purchaser; a person to whom a grant is made.

**Grantor:** Seller of property; one who signs a deed.

**GRI:** Graduate, Realtors Institute.

**Grid:** A chart used in rating the borrower risk, property, and the neighborhood.

**Gross Income:** Total income from property before any expenses are deducted.

**Gross Domestic Product (GDP):** The total value of all goods and services produced in a economy during a given period of time.

**Gross Rate:** A method of collecting interest by adding total interest to the principal of the loan at the outset of the term.

**Gross Rent Multiplier:** A figure which, times the gross income of a property, produces an estimate of value of the property.

**Ground Lease:** An agreement for the use of the land only, sometimes secured by improvements placed on the land by the user.

**Ground Rent:** Earnings of improved property credited to earnings of the ground itself after allowance is made for earnings of improvements; often termed economic rent.

**Growing Equity Mortgage (GEM):** A mortgage with payments that increase in steps resulting in a rapid payback.

# H - I

**Habendum Clause:** The "to have and to hold" clause in a deed.

**Hard Money Loan:** A cash loan by a noninstitutional lender.

**Header:** The horizontal beam above doors or windows.

**Highest and Best Use:** An appraisal phrase meaning that use which at the time of an appraisal is most likely to produce the greatest net return to the land and/or buildings over a given period of time; that use which will produce the greatest amount of amenities or profit. This is the starting point for appraisal.

**Hip Roof:** A pitched roof with all four sides sloping to the eaves.

**Holder in Due Course:** One who has taken a note, check or bill of exchange in due course:

1. Appears good on its face
2. Before it was overdue;
3. In good faith and for value;
4. Without knowledge that it has been previously dishonored without notice of any defect at the time it was negotiated to him.

**Holdover Tenant:** Tenant who remains in possession of leased property after the expiration of the lease term.

**Homestead:** A home upon which the owner or owners have recorded a Declaration of Homestead. As provided by Statutes in some states, it protects home against judgments up to specified amounts.

**Hundred Percent Location:** A city retail business location which is considered the best available for attracting business.

**Hypothecate:** To give a thing as security without the necessity of giving up possession of it.

**Impounds:** A trust-type account established by lenders for the accumulation of funds to meet taxes and future insurance policy premiums required to protect their security. Impounds are usually collected with the note payment.

**Inchoate Right of Dower:** A wife's interest in the real estate of her husband during his life which upon his death may become a dower interest.

**Income Approach:** One of the three methods in the appraisal process; an analysis in which the estimated net income from the subject residence is used as a basis for estimating value by dividing the net by a capitalization rate.

**Incompetent:** One who is mentally incapable of contracting; judged to be of unsound mind, therefore lacking contractual capacity.

**Incorporeal Rights:** Nonpossessory rights in real estate.

**Increment:** An increase. Most frequently used to refer to the increase of value of land that accompanies population growth and increasing wealth in the community. The term unearned increment is used in this connection since values are supposed to have increased without effort on the part of the owner.

**Indenture:** A formal written instrument made between two or more persons.

**Indorsement:** The act of signing one's name on the back of a check or note, with or without further qualification.

**Injunction:** A writ or order issued under the seal of a court to restrain one or more parties to a suit or proceeding from doing an act which is deemed to be inequitable or unjust in regard to the rights of some other party or parties in the suit or proceeding.

**Input:** Data, information, etc., that is fed into a computer or other system.

**Installment Contract:** Purchase of real estate wherein the purchase price is paid in installments over a long period of time; title is retained by seller; upon default the payments are forfeited. Also known as a land contract.

**Installment Note:** A note which provides that payments of a certain sum or amount be paid on the dates specified in the instrument.

**Installment Reporting:** A method of reporting capital gains by installments for successive tax years to minimize the impact of the totality of the capital gains tax in the year of the sale.

**Instrument:** A written legal document; created to effect the rights of the parties.

**Interest:** The charge in dollars for the use of money for a period of time. In a sense, the "rent" paid for the use of money.

**Interest Rate:** The percentage of a sum of money charged for its use.

**Interim Loan:** A short-term loan until long-term financing is available.

**Intermediate Theory:** That a mortgage is a lien but title transfers to mortgagee automatically upon default.

**Interstate Land Sales Full Disclosure Act:** Disclosure requirements for unimproved land sales made in interstate commerce.

**Intestate:** A person who dies having made no will, or one which is defective in form in which case his estate descends to his heirs at law or next of kin.

**Involuntary Alienation:** Involuntary transfer such as foreclosure for eminent domain.

**Involuntary Lien:** A lien imposed against property without consent of an owner. **Example:** taxes, special assessments, federal income tax liens, etc.

**Inwood Tables:** Concept of using present value of income in a perpetuity table to help appraisers.

**IREM:** Institute of Real Estate Management. Part of NAR.

**Irrevocable:** Incapable of being recalled or revoked; unchangeable.

# J

**Jalousie:** A slatted blind shutter or window, like a venetian blind but used on the exterior to protect against rain as well as to control sunlight.

**Jamb:** The side post or lining of a doorway, window or other opening.

**Joint Note:** A note signed by two or more persons who have equal liability for payment.

**Joint Tenancy:** Joint ownership by two or more persons with right of survivorship; all joint tenants own equal interest and have equal rights in the property and are formed at the same time by the same instrument.

**Joint Venture:** Two or more individuals or firms joining together on a single project as partners.

**Joist:** One of a series of parallel horizontal beams to which the boards of a floor and ceiling laths are nailed, and supported in turn by larger beams, girders, or bearing walls.

**Judgment:** The final determination of a court of competent jurisdiction of a matter presented to it; money judgments provide for the payment of claims presented to the court, or are awarded as damages, etc.

**Judgment Lien:** A legal claim on all of the property of a judgment debtor in the county where recorded, which enables the judgment creditor to have the property sold for payment of the amount of the judgment.

**Junior Mortgage:** A mortgage second in line to a previous mortgage.

**Jurisdiction:** The authority by which judicial officers take cognizance of and decide causes; the power to hear and determine a cause; the right and power which a judicial officer has to enter upon the inquiry.

# L

**Laches:** Delay or negligence in asserting one's legal rights.

**Land Contract:** A contract ordinarily used in connection with the sale of property in cases where the seller does not wish to convey title until all or a certain part of the purchase price is paid by the buyer; often used when property is sold on small down payment.

# GLOSSARY

**Landlord:** One who rents his property to another.

**Lateral Support:** The support which the soil of an adjoining owner gives to his neighbors' land.

**Lath:** A building material of wood, metal, gypsum, or insulating board fastened to the frame of a building to act as a plaster base.

**Lead-Based Paint Disclosure:** Federally mandated disclosure for residential property built prior to 1978.

**Lease:** A contract between owner and tenant, setting forth conditions upon which tenant may occupy and use the property, and the term of the occupancy.

**Leasehold Estate:** A tenant's right to occupy real estate during the term of the lease. This is a personal property interest.

**Legal Description:** A description recognized by law; a description by which property can be definitely located by reference to government surveys metes and bounds or approved recorded maps.

**Lessee:** One who contracts to rent property under a lease contract; a tenant.

**Lessor:** An owner who enters into a lease with a tenant.

**Level Payment Mortgage:** A loan on real estate that is paid off by making a series of equal (or nearly equal) regular payments. Part of the payment is usually interest on the loan and part of it reduces the amount of the unpaid balance of the loan. Also sometimes called an **Amortized Mortgage**.

**Leverage:** Maximizing net by using borrowed funds.

**Lien:** A form of encumbrance which usually makes property security for the payment of a debt or discharge of an obligation. **Example:** judgments, taxes, mortgages, deeds of trust, etc.

**Lien Theory:** A mortgage theory that a mortgage creates only a lien.

**Life Estate:** An estate or interest in real property which is held for the duration of the life of some certain person.

**Limited Partnership:** A partnership composed of some partners whose contribution is financial and liability is limited to their investment.

**Lintel:** A horizontal board that supports the load over an opening such as a door or window.

**Lis Pendens:** Suit pending, usually recorded so as to give constructive notice of pending litigation.

**Liquidated Damages:** A sum agreed upon by the parties to be full damages if an agreement is breached.

**Listing:** An employment contract between principal and agent authorizing the agent to perform services for the principal involving the latter's property; listing contracts are entered into for the purpose of securing persons to buy, lease or rent property. Employment of an agent by a prospective purchaser or lessee to locate property for purchase or lease may be considered a listing.

**Loan Administration:** Also called **Loan Servicing**. Mortgage bankers not only originate loans, but also "service" them from origination to maturity of the loan.

**Loan Application:** The loan application is a source of information on which the lender bases his decision to make the loan, defines the terms of the loan contract; gives the name of the borrower, place of employment, salary, bank accounts, and credit references; and, describes the real estate that is to be mortgaged. It also stipulates the amount of loan being applied for, and repayment terms.

**Loan Closing:** When all conditions have been met, the loan officer authorizes the recording of the trust deed or mortgage. The disbursal procedure of funds is similar to the closing of a real estate sales escrow. The borrower can expect to receive less than the amount of the loan, as title, recording, service, and other fees may be withheld, or he can expect to deposit the cost of these items into the loan escrow. This process is sometimes called "funding" or "settlement."

**Loan Commitment:** Lender's contractual commitment to a loan based on the appraisal and underwriting.

**Loan-To-Value Ratio (LTV):** The percentage of a property's value that a lender can or may loan to a borrower. For example, if the ratio is 80% this means that a lender may loan 80% of the property's appraised value to a borrower.

**Long-Term Gain:** Capital gain on sale of property held over 18 months.

**Louver:** An opening with a series of horizontal slats set at an agle to permit ventilation without admitting rain, sunlight, or vision.

# M

**MAI:** Designates a person who is a member of the Appraisal Institute.

**Margin of Security:** The difference between the amount of the mortgage loan(s) and the appraised value of the property.

**Marginal Land:** Land which barely pays the cost of working or using.

**Market Data Approach:** One of the three methods in the appraisal process. A means of comparing similar type residential properties, which have recently sold, to the subject property.

**Market Price:** The price paid regardless of pressures, motives or intelligence.

**Market Value:** (1) The price at which a willing seller would sell and a willing buyer would buy, neither being under abnormal pressure; (2) as defined by the courts, is the highest price estimated in terms of money which a property will bring if exposed for sale in the open market allowing a reasonable time to find a purchaser with knowledge of property's use and capabilities for use.

**Marketable Title:** Merchantable title; title free and clear of objectionable liens or encumbrances.

**Material Fact:** A fact is material if it is one which the agent should realize would be likely to affect the judgment of the principal in giving his consent to the agent to enter into the particular transaction on the specified terms.

**Mechanic's Lien:** A lien created by statute which exists against real property in favor of persons who have performed work or furnished materials for the improvement of the real estate.

**Meridians:** North-south surveyor lines which intersect base lines to form a starting point for the measurement of land.

**Metes and Bounds:** A term used in describing the boundary lines of land, setting forth all the boundary lines together with their terminal points and angles.

**Mid-Term Gain:** Gain on sale of property held over one year but less than 18 months.

**Mile:** 5,280 feet.

**Mineral, Oil, and Gas Rights:** The right to minerals, oil and gas in the ground and the implied easement to enter to mine or drill.

**Minor:** All persons under 18 years of age who are not emancipated.

**Misplaced Improvement:** Improvements on land which do not conform to the most profitable use of the site.

**Mitigation of Damages:** Duty of lessor to attempt to rent to keep defaulting tenant's damages down.

**Manufactured Home:** A home constructed and then transported on its own chassis.

**Modular:** A building composed of modules constructed on an assembly line in a factory. Usually, the modules are self-contained.

**Moldings:** Usually patterned or curved strips used to provide ornamental variation of outline or contour, such as cornices, bases, window and door jambs.

**Monetary Controls:** Federal Reserve tools for regulating the availability of money and credit to influence the level of economic activity.

**Monument:** A fixed object and point established by surveyors to establish land locations.

**Moratorium:** The temporary suspension, usually by statute, of construction or the enforcement of a debt.

**Mortgage:** An instrument recognized by law by which property is hypothecated to secure the payment of a debt or obligation; procedure for foreclosure in event of default is established by statute.

**Mortgage Guaranty Insurance:** Insurance against financial loss available to mortgage lenders from Mortgage Guaranty Insurance Corporation (MGIC), a private company organized in 1956.

**Mortgage Loan Broker:** A broker who charges borrowers for loans arranged.

**Mortgagee:** One to whom a mortgagor gives a mortgage to secure a loan or performance of an obligation, a lender. (See definition of **Secured Party**.)

**Mortgagor:** One who gives a mortgage on his property to secure a loan or assure performance of an obligation; a borrower. (See definition of **Debtor**.)

**Multiple Listing:** A listing, usually an exclusive right to sell, taken by a member of an organization composed of real estate brokers, with the provisions that all members will have the opportunity to find an interested client; a cooperative listing.

**Mutual Water Company:** A water company organized by or for water users in a given district with the object of securing an ample water supply at a reasonable rate; stock is issued to users.

# N

**Naked Legal Title:** Title held by a trustee until the terms of trust deed and note have been met.

**NAREB:** National Association of Real Estate Brokers.

**NAR:** National Association of REALTORS®.

**Narrative Appraisal:** A summary of all factual materials, techniques and appraisal methods used by the appraiser in setting forth his value conclusion.

**Negative Amortization:** Loan payments that do not cover the interest due so that the loan principal increases.

**Negative Declaration:** A statement that a development will not adversely effect the environment.

**Negotiable:** Capable of being negotiated, assigned, or transferred in the ordinary course of business.

**Net Listing:** A listing which provides that the agent may retain as compensation for his services all sums received over and above a net price to the owner. (Illegal in many states)

**Nominal Interest Rates:** The percentage of interest that is stated in loan documents.

**Notary Public:** An appointed officer with authority to take the acknowledgment of persons executing documents, to sign the certificate, and affix his seal.

**Note:** A signed written instrument acknowledging a debt and promising payment.

**Notice:** Actual knowledge acquired by being or knowing of the occurrence.

**Notice of Nonresponsibility:** A notice provided by law designed to relieve a property owner from responsibility for the cost of work done on the property or materials furnished therefor; when contracted by a tenant or vendee on a land contract notice must be verified, recorded and posted.

**Notice to Quit:** A notice to a tenant to vacate rented property.

**Nuncupative Will:** Oral will. Not generally valid.

*O*

**Obligating Advance:** Required advance on a construction loan as work progresses.

**Obsolescence:** Loss in value due to reduced desirability and usefulness of a structure because its design and construction become obsolete.

**Occupancy Permit:** Required from building inspector prior to occupancy of a new unit.

**Offset Statement:** Statement by owner of property or owner of lien against property, setting forth the present status of liens against said property.

**Open-End Mortgage:** A mortgage containing a clause which permits the mortgagor to borrow additional money without rewriting the mortgage.

**Open Housing Law:** See **Civil Rights Act of 1968**.

**Open Listing:** An authorization given by a property owner to a real estate agent wherein said agent is given the non-exclusive rights to secure a purchaser; open listings may be given to any number of agents without liability to compensate any except the one who first secures a buyer ready, willing and able to meet the terms of the listing, or secures the acceptance by the seller of a satisfactory offer.

**Opinion of Title:** An attorney's evaluation of the condition of the title to a parcel of land after his examination of the abstract of title to the land.

**Option:** A right given for a consideration to purchase or lease a property upon specified terms within a specified time.

**Oral Contract:** A verbal agreement; one which is not reduced to writing.

**Orientation:** Placing a house on its lot with regard to its exposure to the rays of the sun, prevailing winds, privacy from the street and protection from outside noises.

**Overhang:** The part of the roof extending beyond the walls, to shade buildings and cover walks.

**Over Improvement:** An improvement which is not the highest and best use for the site on which it is placed by reason of excess size or cost. An improvement that will not reasonably contribute to income or market value.

# P

**Packaged Mortgage:** A mortgage covering both real and personal property.

**Parquet Floor:** Hardwood flooring laid in squares or patterns.

**Participation:** In addition to base interest on mortgage loans on income properties, a percentage of ownership is given to the lender.

**Partition Action:** Court proceedings by which co-owners seek to sever their joint ownership.

**Partnership:** A contract of two or more persons to unite their property, labor or skill, or some of them, in prosecution of some joint or lawful business, and to share the profits in certain proportions.

**Party Wall:** A wall erected on the line between two adjoining properties, which are under different ownership, for the use of both properties.

**Patent:** Conveyance of title to government land.

**PCPs:** A carcinogenic substance used in insulating fluids in electrical transformers.

**Penalty:** An extra payment or charge required of the borrower for deviating from the terms of the original loan agreement. Usually levied for being late in making regular payment or for paying off the loan before it is due.

**Penny:** The term, as applied to nails, serves as a measure of nail length and is abbreviated by the letter "d."

**Percentage Lease:** Lease on the property, the rental for which is determined by amount of business done by the lessee; usually a percentage of gross receipts from the business with provision for a minimum rental.

**Perimeter Heating:** Baseboard heating, or any system in which the heat registers are located along the outside walls of a room, especially under the windows.

**Personal Property:** Any property which is not real property.

**Physical Deterioration:** Impairment of condition. Loss in value brought about by wear and tear, disintegration, use, and actions of the elements.

**Pier:** A column of masonry, usually rectangular in horizontal cross section, used to support other structural members.

**Pitch:** The incline or rise of a roof.

**Planned Unit Development (PUD):** A land use design with private unit ownership and common areas shared equally with all owners.

**Plate:** A horizontal board placed on a wall or supported on posts or studs to carry the trusses of a roof or rafters directly; a shoe, or base member as of a partition or other frame; a small flat horizontal board placed on or in a wall to support girders, joists, rafters, etc.

**Pledge:** The depositing of personal property by a debtor with a creditor as security for a debt or engagement.

**Pledgee:** One who is given a pledge or a security. (See definition of **Secured Party**.)

**Pledgor:** One who offers a pledge or gives security. (See definition of **Debtor**.)

**Plottage Increment:** The appreciation in unit value created by joining smaller ownerships into one large single ownership.

**Plywood:** Laminated wood made up in panels; several thickness of wood glued together with grain at different angles for strength.

**Point of Beginning (POB):** Beginning point for a metes and bounds description.

**Points:** Each point is one percent of the loan. They are charged by lenders to make the loan more attractive. For buyers they are treated as prepaid interest.

**Police Power:** The right of the State to enact laws and regulations and enforce them for the order, safety, health, morals, and general welfare of the public.

**Power of Attorney:** An instrument authorizing a person to act as the agent of the person granting it, and a general power authorizing the agent to act generally in behalf of the principal. A special power limits the agent to a particular or specific act, as a landowner may grant an agent special power of attorney to convey a single and specific parcel of property. Under the provisions of a general power of attorney, the agent having the power may convey any or all property of the principal granting the general power of attorney.

**Prefabricated House:** A house manufactured, and sometimes partly assembled, before delivery to building site.

**Prepaid Items of Expense:** Prorations of prepaid items of expense which are credited to the seller in the closing statement.

**Prepayment:** Provision made for loan payments to be larger than those specified in the note.

**Prepayment Penalty:** Penalty for the payment of a mortgage or trust deed note before it actually becomes due if the note does not provide for prepayment.

**Present Value:** The lump sum value today of an annuity. A $100 bill to be paid to someone in one year is worth less than if it were a $100 bill to be paid to someone today. This is due to several things, one of which is that the money has time value. How much the $100 bill to be paid in one year is worth today will depend on the interest rate that seems proper for the particular circumstances. For example, if 6% is the appropriate rate, the $100 to be paid one year from now would be worth $94.34 today.

**Presumption:** A rule of law that courts and judges shall draw a particular inference from a particular fact, or from particular evidence, unless and until the truth of such inference is disproved.

**Prima Facie:** Presumptive on its face.

**Principal:** This term is used to mean either the employer of an agent or the amount of money borrowed or the amount of the loan.

**Principal Note:** The promissory note which is secured by the mortgage or trust deed.

**Prior Appropriation:** The superior rights of the first user of flowing water (in some states).

**Private Mortgage Insurance (PMI):** A policy of Private Mortgage Insurance usually required for a conventional loan where the down payment is less than 20 percent.

**Privity:** Mutual relationship to the same rights of property, contractual relationship.

**Procuring Cause:** That cause originating from series of events that, without break in continuity, results in the prime object of an agent's employment producing a final buyer.

**Progression, Principle of:** The worth of a lesser valued residence tends to be enhanced by association with many higher valued residences in the same area.

**Promissory Note:** Following a loan commitment from the lender, the borrower signs a note, promising to repay the loan under stipulated terms. The promissory note establishes liability for its repayment.

**Property:** The rights of ownership. The right to use, possess, enjoy, and dispose of a thing in every legal way and to exclude everyone else from interfering with these rights. Property is generally classified into two groups, personal property and real property.

**Proprietary Lease:** The lease that goes with stock in a cooperative authorizing occupancy of a specific unit.

**Proration:** Adjustments of interest, taxes, and insurance, etc., on a prorate basis as of the closing date. Fire insurance is normally paid for in advance. If a property is sold during this time, the seller wants a refund on that portion of the advance payment that has not been used at the time the title to the property is transferred.

**Proration of Taxes:** To divide or prorate the taxes equally or proportionately to time of use.

**Proximate Cause:** That cause of an event is that which, in a natural and continuous sequence unbroken by any new cause, produced that event, and without which the event would not have happened. Also, the procuring cause.

**Public Trustee:** The county public official whose office has been created by statute, to whom title to real property, in certain states, e.g., Colorado, is conveyed by Trust Deed for the use and benefit of the beneficiary, who usually is the lender.

**Punitive Damages:** Damages in excess of compensatory damages to punish the wrongdoer for an outrageous action.

**Purchase and Installment Sale-Back:** Involves purchase of the property upon completion of construction and immediate sale-back on a long-term installment contract.

**Purchase of Land, Leaseback, and Leasehold Mortgages:** An arrangement whereby land is purchased by the lender and leased back to the developer with a mortgage negotiated on the resulting leasehold of the income property constructed. The lender receives an annual ground rent, plus a percentage of income from the property.

**Purchase and Leaseback:** Involves the purchase of property subject to an existing mortgage and immediate leaseback.

**Purchase Money Mortgage or Trust Deed:** A trust deed or mortgage given as part or all of the purchase consideration for property. In some states the purchase money mortgage or trust deed loan can be made by a seller who extends credit to the buyer of property or by a third party lender (typically a financial institution) that makes a loan to the buyer of real property for a portion of the purchase price to be paid for the property. (In many states there are legal limitations upon mortgagees and trust deed beneficiaries collecting deficiency judgments against the purchase money borrower after the collateral hypothecated under such security instruments has been sold through the foreclosure process. Generally no deficiency judgment is allowed if the collateral property under the mortgage or trust deed is residential property of four units or less with the debtor occupying the property as a place of residence.)

# Q - R

**Quantity Survey:** A highly technical process in arriving at cost estimate of new construction, and sometimes referred to in the building trade as the price takeoff method. It involves a detailed estimate of the quantities of raw material lumber, plaster, brick, cement, etc. used, as well as the current price of the material and installation costs. These factors are all added together to arrive at the cost of a structure. It is usually used by contractors and experienced estimators.

**Quarter Round:** A molding that presents a profile of a quarter circle.

**Quiet Enjoyment:** Right of an owner to the use of the property without interference of possession.

**Quiet Title:** A court action brought to establish title; to remove a cloud on the title.

**Quitclaim Deed:** A deed to relinquish any interest in property which the grantor may have, without claiming to have an interest.

**Radiant Heating:** A method of heating, usually consisting of coils or pipes placed in the floor, wall, or ceiling.

**Radon:** A colorless odorless, naturally occurring hazardous gas. Measured using a **Spectrometer**.

**Rafter:** One of a series of boards of a roof designed to support roof loads. The rafters of a flat roof are sometimes called roof joists.

**Range:** A strip of land six miles wide determined by a government survey, running in a north-south direction.

**Ratification:** The adoption or approval of an act performed on behalf of a person without previous authorization.

**Real Estate Board:** An organization whose members consist primarily of real estate brokers and salespeople.

**Real Estate Settlement Procedures Act (RESPA):** A federal disclosure law effective June 20, 1975 requiring new procedures and forms for settlements (closing costs) involving federally related loans.

**Real Estate Trust:** A special arrangement under Federal and State law whereby investors may pool funds for investments in real estate and mortgages and yet escape corporation taxes.

**Realtist:** A real estate broker holding active membership in a real estate board affiliated with the National Association of Real Estate Brokers (NAREB).

**REALTOR®:** A real estate licensee holding active membership in a real estate board affiliated with the National Association of REALTORS® (NAR).

# GLOSSARY

**Recapture:** The rate of interest necessary to provide for the return of an investment. Not to be confused with interest rate, which is a rate of interest on an investment.

**Reconveyance:** The transfer of the title of land from one person to the immediate preceding owner. This particular instrument of transfer is commonly used when the performance or debt is satisfied under the terms of a deed of trust, when the trustee conveys the title he has held on condition back to the owner.

**Recording:** The process of placing a document on file with a designated public official for everyone to see. This public official is usually a county officer known as the County Recorder. He designates the fact that a document has been given to him by placing his stamp upon it indicating the time of day and the date when it was officially placed on file. Documents filed with the Recorder are considered to be placed on open notice to the general public of that county. Claims against property usually are given a priority on the basis of the time and the date they are recorded with the most preferred claim status going to the earliest one recorded and the next claim going to the next earliest one recorded, and so on. This type of notice is called "constructive notice" or "legal notice."

**Redemption:** Buying back one's property after a judicial sale.

**Refinancing:** The paying-off of an existing obligation and assuming a new obligation in its place.

**Reformation:** An action to correct a mistake in a deed or other document.

**Rehabilitation:** The restoration of a property to satisfactory condition without drastically changing the plan, form, or style of architecture.

**Release Clause:** This is a stipulation that upon the payment of a specific sum of money to the holder of a trust deed or mortgage, the lien of the instrument as to a specific described lot or area shall be removed from the blanket lien on the whole area involved.

**Release Deed:** An instrument executed by the mortgagee or the trustee reconveying to the mortgagor the real estate which secured the mortgage loan after the debt has been paid in full. Upon recording it cancels the mortgage lien created when the mortgage or trust deed was recorded.

**Reliction:** The addition to land by the permanent recession of water.

**Remainder:** An estate which takes effect after the termination of the prior estate, such as a life estate.

**Remainder Depreciation:** The possible loss in value of an improvement which will occur in the future.

**Replacement Cost:** The cost to replace the structure with one having utility equivalent to that being appraised, but constructed with modern materials, and according to current standards, design and layout.

**Reproduction Costs:** The cost of replacing the subject improvement with one that is the exact replica, having the same quality of workmanship, design and layout.

**Request for Notice of Default:** Recorded request so junior lienholder will be notified of foreclosure action.

**Request for Notice of Delinquency:** When filed, mortgagee must notify junior lienholder that mortgagor is delinquent in payments.

**Required Provider:** A lender requiring particular service providers.

**Rescission of Contract:** The abrogation or annulling of contract; the revocation or repealing of contract by mutual consent by parties to the contract, or for cause by either party to the contract.

**Reservation:** A right retained by a grantor in conveying property.

**Restriction:** The term as used relating to real property means the owner of real property is restricted or prohibited from doing certain things relating to the property, or using the property for certain purposes. Property restrictions fall into two general classifications--public and private. Zoning ordinances are examples of the former type. Restrictions may be created by private owners, typically by appropriate clauses in deeds, or in agreements, or in general plans of entire subdivisions. Usually they assume the form of a covenant, or promise to do or not to do a certain thing. They cover a multitude of matters including use for residential or business purposes, e.g. houses in tract must cost more than $150,000 etc.

**Retrospective Value:** The value of the property as of a previous date.

**Reversion:** The right to future possession or enjoyment by the person, or his heirs, creating the preceding estate.

**Reversionary Interest:** The interest which a person has in lands or other property, upon the termination of the preceding estate.

**Ridge:** The horizontal line at the junction of the top edges of two sloping roof surfaces. The rafters at both slopes are nailed to a ridge board at the ridge.

**Ridge Board:** The board placed on edge at the ridge of the roof to support the upper ends of the rafters; also called roof tree, ridge piece, ridge plate or ridgepole.

**Right of First Refusal:** A right to buy or lease only if an owner wishes to sell or lease to another party. (Rights holder must match the offer.)

**Right of Survivorship:** Right to acquire the interests of a deceased joint owner; distinguishing feature of a joint tenancy.

**Right of Way:** A privilege operating as an easement upon land, whereby the owner does by grant, or by agreement, give to another the right to pass over his land, to construct a roadway, or use as a roadway, a specific part of his land, or the right to construct through and over his land, telephone, telegraph, or electric power lines, or the right to place underground water mains, gas mains, sewer mains, etc.

**Riparian Rights:** The right of a landowner to flowing water on, under, or adjacent to his land.

**Riser:** The upright board at the back of each step of a stairway. In heating, a riser is a duct slanted upward to carry hot air from the furnace to the room above.

**Risk Analysis:** A study made, usually by a lender, of the various factors that might affect the repayment of a loan.

**Risk Rating:** A process used by the lender to decide on the soundness of making a loan and to reduce all the various factors affecting the repayment of the loan to a qualified rating of some kind.

# S

**Sales Contract:** A contract by which buyer and seller agree to terms of a sale.

**Sale-Leaseback:** A situation where the owner of a piece of property wishes to sell the property and retain occupancy by leasing it from the buyer.

**Sandwich Lease:** A leasehold interest which lies between the primary lease and the operating lease.

**Sash:** Wood or metal frames containing one or more window panes.

**Satisfaction:** Discharge of mortgage or trust deed lien from the records upon payment of the evidenced debt.

**Satisfaction Piece:** An instrument for recording and acknowledging payment of an indebtedness secured by a mortgage.

**Scribing:** Fitting woodwork to an irregular surface.

**Seal:** An impression made to attest the execution of an instrument in some states, particular documents require seals.

**Secondary Financing:** A loan secured by a second mortgage or trust deed on real property. These can be third, fourth, fifth, sixth—on and on ad infinitum.

**Secured Party:** This is the party having the security interest. Thus the mortgagee, the conditional seller, the beneficiary, etc., are all now referred to as the secured party.

**Security Agreement:** An agreement between the secured party and the debtor which creates the security interest.

**Security Interest:** A term designating the interest of the creditor in the personal property of the debtor in all types of credit transactions. It thus replaces such terms as the following: chattel mortgage; pledge; trust receipt; chattel trust; equipment trust; conditional sale; inventory lien; etc.

**Section:** Section of land is established by government survey and contains 640 acres.

**Seizin:** Possession of real estate by one entitled thereto.

**Separate Property:** Property owned by a husband or wife which is not jointly owned.

**Septic Tank:** An underground tank in which sewage from the house is reduced to liquid by bacterial action and drained off.

**Servicing:** Supervising and administering a loan after it has been made. This involves such things as: collecting the payments, keeping accounting records, computing the interest and principal, foreclosure of defaulted loans, and so on.

**Servient Tenement:** The property that is burdened by an easement. It must "serve" the dominant tenement.

**Setback Ordinance:** An ordinance prohibiting the erection of a building or structure between the curb and the setback line.

**Severalty Ownership:** Owned by one person only. Sole ownership.

**Shopping Center, Regional:** A large shopping center with 250,000 to 1,000,000 or more square feet of store area, serving 200,000 or more people.

**Shake:** A handsplit shingle, usually edge grained.

**Sharing Appreciation Mortgage:** A loan where a lender shares in the value appreciation. It usually requires a sale or appraisal at a future date.

**Sheathing:** Structural covering usually boards, plywood, or wallboards, placed over exterior studding or rafters of a house.

**Sheriff's Deed:** Deed given by court order in connection with sale of property to satisfy a judgment.

**Short-Term Gain:** Gain on sale where property was held for one year or less.

**Sill:** The lowest part of the frame of a house, resting on the foundation and supporting the uprights of the frame (mud sill). The board or metal forming the lower side of an opening, as a door sill, window sill, etc.

**Sinking Fund:** Fund set aside from the income from property which, with accrued interest, will eventually pay for replacement of the improvements.

**SIR:** Society of Industrial Realtors®.

**Soft Money Loan:** Seller financing where cash does not change hands.

**Soil Pipe:** Pipe carrying waste out from the house to the main sewer line.

**Sole or Sole Plate:** A member, usually a 2 by 4, on which wall and partition studs rest.

**Span:** The distance between structural supports such as walls, columns, piers, beams, girders, and trusses.

**Special Assessment:** Legal charge against real estate by a public authority to pay cost of public improvements such as: street lights, sidewalks, street improvements, etc.

**Special Warranty Deed:** A deed in which the grantor warrants or guarantees the title only against defects arising during his ownership of the property and not against defects existing before the time of his ownership.

**Specific Liens:** Liens which attach to only a certain specific parcel of land or piece of property.

**Specific Performance:** An action to compel performance of an agreement, e.g., sale of land.

**Standard-Depth:** Generally the most typical lot depth in the neighborhood.

**Standby Commitment:** The mortgage banker frequently protects a builder by a "standby" agreement, under which he agrees to make mortgage loans at an agreed price for many months in the future. The builder deposits a "standby fee" with the mortgage banker for this service. Frequently, the mortgage banker protects himself by securing a "standby" from a long-term investor for the same period of time, paying a fee for this privilege.

**Starker Exchange:** A delayed tax deferred exchange.

**Statute of Frauds:** State law which provides that certain contracts must be in writing in order to be enforceable at law. **Example:** real property lease for more than one year; agent's authorization to sell real estate.

**Statutory Warranty Deed:** A short form warranty deed which warrants by inference that the seller is the undisputed owner and has the right to convey the property and that he will defend the title if necessary. This type of deed protects the purchaser in that the conveyor covenants to defend all claims against the property. If he fails to do so, the new owner can defend said claims and sue the former owner.

**Straight-Line Depreciation:** A method of depreciation under which improvements are depreciated at a constant rate throughout the estimated life of the improvement.

**Strict Foreclosure:** Foreclosure without a sale if the debt has not been paid after statutory notice. The court transfers title to the mortgagee (a few states).

**String, Stringer:** A timber or other support for cross members. In stairs, the diagonal support on which the stair treads rest.

**Studs or Studding:** Vertical supporting timbers in the walls and partitions spaced 16″ on center.

**Subjacent Support:** The duty of an excavator or miner to support the surface.

**"Subject To" Mortgage:** When a grantee takes a title to real property subject to mortgage, he is not responsible to the holder of the promissory note for the payment of any portion of the amount due. The most that he can lose in the event of a foreclosure is his equity in the property. See also **Assumption of Mortgage**. In neither case is the original maker of the note released from his responsibility.

**Sublease:** A lease, given by a lessee, transferring less than the entire leasehold. Original lessee is primarily liable for the rental agreement.

**Subordinate:** To make subject to, or junior to.

**Subordination Clause:** Clause in a junior or a second lien permitting retention of priority for prior liens. A subordination clause may also be used in a first deed of trust permitting it to be subordinated to subsequent liens as, for example, the liens of construction loans.

**Subpoena:** A process to cause a witness to appear and give testimony.

**Subrogation:** The substitution of another person in place of the creditor, to whose rights he succeeds in relation to the debt. The doctrine is used very often where one person agrees to stand surety for the performance of a contract by another person.

**Substitution, Principle of:** Affirms that the maximum value of a property tends to be set by the cost of acquiring an equally desirable and valuable substitute property, assuming no costly delay is encountered in making the substitution.

**Sum of the Years Digits:** An accelerated depreciation method.

**Supply and Demand, Principle of:** Affirms that price or value varies directly, but not necessarily proportionally with demand, and inversely, but not necessarily proportionately with supply.

**Surety:** One who guarantees the performance of another: Guarantor. A surety bond guarantees contract performance.

**Surplus Productivity, Principle of:** Affirms that the net income that remains after the proper costs of labor, organization and capital have been paid, which surplus is imputable to the land and tends to fix the value thereof.

**Survey:** The process by which a parcel of land is measured and its area is ascertained.

**Syndicate:** A partnership organized for participation in a real estate venture. Partners may be limited or unlimited in their liability.

# T

**Takeout Loan:** The permanent loan arranged by the owner or builder developer for a buyer. The construction loan made for construction of the improvements is usually paid from the proceeds of this loan.

**Tax-Deferred Exchange:** Income property exchanged on for other income property which does not have to pay a capital gain tax at the time.

**Tax Roll:** Total of taxable property assessments in taxing district.

**Tax Sale:** Sale of property by a taxing authority after a period of nonpayment of taxes.

**Tax Shelter:** Use of depreciation to shelter income from taxation.

**Teaser Rate:** An initial rate on an adjustable rate loan less than the index figure plus margin. It is usually only given for a relatively short period of time.

**Tenancy in Common:** Ownership by two or more persons who hold undivided interest, without right of survivorship; interests need not be equal.

**Tenants by the Entireties:** Under certain state laws, ownership of property acquired by a husband and wife during marriage which is jointly owned and cannot be separately transferred. Upon death of one spouse, it becomes the property of the survivor.

**Tentative Map:** The Subdivision Map Act requires subdividers to submit initially a tentative map of their tract to the local planning commission for study. The approval or disapproval of the planning commission is noted on the map. Thereafter a final map of the tract embodying any changes requested by the planning commission is required to be filed with the planning commission.

**Tenure in Land:** The mode or manner by which an estate in lands is held.

**Termites:** Ant-like insects which feed on wood.

**Termite Shield:** A shield, usually of noncorrodible metal, placed on top of the foundation wall or around pipes to prevent passage of termites.

**Testator:** One who leaves a will in force at his death.

**Threshold:** A strip of wood or metal beveled on each edge and used above the finished floor under outside doors.

**Third Party Originator:** A party that prepares loan packages for borrowers for submission to lenders.

**Time is of the Essence:** A requirement that performance be punctual and that any delay will breach the contract.

**Title:** Evidence that owner of land is in lawful possession thereof, an instrument evidencing such ownership.

**Title Insurance:** Insurance written by a title company to protect property owner against loss if title is imperfect.

**Title Report:** A report which discloses condition of the title, made by a title company preliminary to issuance of title insurance (**Preliminary Title Report**).

**Title Theory:** Mortgage arrangement whereby title to mortgaged real property vests in the lender.

**Topography:** Nature of the surface of land; topography may be level, rolling, or mountainous.

**Torrens Title:** System of title records provided by state law (no longer used in California).

**Tort:** A wrongful act; wrong, injury; violation of a legal right.

**Township:** A division by government survey that is six miles long, six miles wide and containing 36 sections, each one mile square.

**Trade Fixtures:** Articles of personal property annexed to real property, but which are necessary to the carrying on of a trade and are removable by the owner of the fixtures.

**Treads:** Horizontal boards of a stairway on which one steps.

**Trim:** The finish materials in a building, such as moldings, applied around openings (window trim, door trim) or at the floor and ceiling (baseboard, cornice, picture molding).

**Trust Account:** An account separate and apart and physically segregated from broker's own funds, in which broker is required by law to deposit all funds collected for clients.

**Trust Deed:** Just as with a mortgage, this is a legal document by which a borrower pledges certain real property or collateral as guarantee for the repayment of a loan. However, it differs from the mortgage in a number of important respects. For example, instead of there being two parties to the transaction, there are three. There is the borrower who gives the trust deed and who is called the trustor. There is the third, neutral party (just as there is with an escrow) who receives the trust deed and who is called the trustee. And, finally, there is the lender who is called the beneficiary since he is the one who benefits from the pledge arrangement in that in the event of a default the trustee can sell the property and transfer the money obtained at the sale to him as payment of the debt.

**Trustee:** One who holds property in trust for another to secure the performance of an obligation.

**Trustor:** One who deeds his property to a trustee to be held as security until he has performed his obligation to a lender under terms of a deed of trust.

# U - V

**Under Improvement:** An improvement which, because of its deficiency in size or cost, is not the highest and best use of the site.

**Underwriting:** The technical analysis by a lender to determine if a borrower should receive a loan.

**Undue Influence:** Taking any fraudulent or unfair advantage of another's weakness of mind, distress, or necessity.

**Unearned Increment:** An increase in value of real estate due to no effort on the part of the owner; often due to increase in population.

**Uniform Commercial Code (UCC):** Establishes a unified and comprehensive scheme for regulation of security transactions in personal property, superseding the existing statutes on chattel mortgages, conditional sales, trust receipts, assignment of accounts receivable and others in this field.

**Unit-In-Place Method:** The cost of erecting a building by estimating the cost of each component part, i.e. foundations, floors, walls, windows, ceilings, roofs, etc. (including labor and overhead).

**Urban Property:** City property; closely settled property.

**Usury:** On a loan, claiming a rate of interest greater than that permitted by law.

**Utilities:** Refers to services rendered by utility companies, such as: water, gas, electricity, and telephone.

**Utility:** The ability to give satisfaction and/or excite desire for possession.

**Valid:** Having force, or binding force; legally sufficient and authorized by law.

**Valley:** The internal angle formed by the junction of two sloping sides of a roof.

**Valuation:** Estimated worth or price. Estimation. The act of valuing by appraisal.

**Vendee:** A purchaser; buyer under a contract of sale (land contract).

**Vendor:** A seller; one who disposes of a thing in consideration of money. Used in a land contract.

**Veneer:** Thin sheets of wood glued to other wood products to form a surface.

**Vent:** A pipe installed to provide a flow of air to or from a drainage system or to provide a circulation of air within such system to protect trap seals from siphonage and back pressure.

**Verification:** Sworn statement before a duly qualified officer to correctness of contents of an instrument.

**Vested:** Bestowed upon someone; secured by someone, such as a title to property.

**Vested Remainder:** A certain remainder interest.

**Void:** To have no force or effect; that which is unenforceable.

**Voidable:** That which is capable of being adjudged void, but is not void unless action is taken to make it so.

**Voluntary Lien:** Any lien placed on property with consent of, or as a result of, the voluntary act of the owner.

# W - Z

**Wainscoting:** The covering of an interior wall with wood (usually panels), tiles, etc., from the floor to a point about half way to the ceiling. The remaining portion is painted, wallpapered or covered with another material different from the lower portion.

**Waive:** To relinquish, or abandon; to forego a right to enforce or require anything.

**Warranty Deed:** A deed used to convey real property which contains warranties of title and quiet possession, and the grantor thus agrees to defend the premises against the lawful claims of third persons. It is commonly used in many states, but in others, the grant deed has supplanted it due to the practice of securing title insurance policies which have reduced the importance of express and implied warranty in deeds.

**Waste:** The destruction, removal, material alteration of, or injury to premises by a tenant for life or years.

**Water Table:** Distance from surface of ground to a depth at which natural groundwater is found.

**Wrap-Around Mortgage:** A second trust deed with a face value of both the new amount it secures and the balance due under the first trust deed. A wrap-around can take the form of a land contract or a deed of trust.

# GLOSSARY

**Yield:** The interest earned by an investor on his investment (or bank on the money it has lent). Also called **Return**.

**Yield Rate:** The yield expressed as a percentage of the total investment. Also called **Rate of Return**.

**Zone:** The area set off by the proper authorities for specific use; subject to certain restrictions or restraints.

**Zoning:** Act of city or county authorities specifying type of use to which property may be put in specific areas.

# INDEX

## Chapter 1

1. P
2. K
3. V
4. I
5. L
6. N
7. E
8. H
9. M
10. F
11. U
12. Q
13. G
14. A
15. R
16. T
17. S
18. C
19. D
20. O
21. J
22. B

## Chapter 2

1. K
2. N
3. P
4. Q
5. O
6. T
7. C
8. V
9. G
10. I
11. DD
12. M
13. J
14. A
15. W
16. H
17. S
18. E
19. BB
20. X
21. D
22. Y
23. AA
24. EE
25. F
26. CC

27. U
28. R
29. Z
30. L
31. B

## Chapter 3

1. J
2. P
3. N
4. U
5. X
6. B
7. Q
8. Y
9. D
10. E
11. H
12. T
13. V
14. A
15. S
16. CC
17. G
18. C
19. W
20. F
21. AA
22. M
23. K
24. I
25. DD
26. Z
27. L
28. R
29. O
30. BB

## Chapter 4

1. C
2. S
3. D
4. U
5. A
6. Y
7. AA
8. H
9. N
10. V
11. E
12. P

13. Z
14. M
15. I
16. J
17. R
18. F
19. W
20. L
21. O
22. Q
23. BB
24. B
25. K
26. G
27. T
28. X

## Chapter 5

1. HH
2. H
3. P
4. BB
5. FF
6. V
7. W
8. D
9. B
10. T
11. L
12. X
13. C
14. J
15. M
16. S
17. E
18. JJ
19. LL
20. AA
21. Z
22. Y
23. A
24. K
25. F
26. GG
27. U
28. EE
29. CC
30. DD
31. Q
32. I
33. N
34. II

35. O
36. KK
37. R
38. G

## Chapter 6

1. T
2. M
3. P
4. C
5. J
6. N
7. O
8. X
9. I
10. E
11. H
12. V
13. U
14. F
15. A
16. G
17. K
18. D
19. S
20. Q
21. B
22. Y
23. W
24. R
25. Z
26. L

## Chapter 7

1. N
2. F
3. B
4. L
5. H
6. G
7. A
8. C
9. D
10. J
11. E
12. M
13. K
14. I
15. O

## Chapter 8

1. AA
2. OO
3. K
4. O
5. J
6. X
7. F
8. Y
9. A
10. L
11. II
12. S
13. GG
14. C
15. V
16. N
17. MM
18. EE
19. LL
20. D
21. NN
22. U
23. T
24. W
25. R
26. I
27. P
28. JJ
29. HH
30. H
31. M
32. G
33. FF
34. E
35. B
36. KK
37. Q
38. CC
39. BB
40. DD
41. Z

## Chapter 9

1. R
2. M
3. S
4. J
5. W
6. C
7. F

8. O
9. N
10. P
11. Z
12. I
13. L
14. K
15. U
16. B
17. E
18. V
19. D
20. Q
21. Y
22. X
23. T
24. H
25. A
26. G

## Chapter 10

1. D
2. L
3. O
4. N
5. K
6. P
7. F
8. A
9. J
10. M
11. B
12. S
13. E
14. U
15. H
16. G
17. I
18. V
19. T
20. C
21. Q
22. R

## Chapter 11

1. X
2. D
3. T
4. N
5. M
6. E

7. J
8. G
9. O
10. W
11. R
12. S
13. U
14. C
15. B
16. H
17. V
18. P
19. K
20. F
21. Q
22. A
23. I
24. L

## Chapter 12

1. N
2. O
3. B
4. S
5. X
6. U
7. R
8. Q
9. I
10. L
11. BB
12. W
13. E
14. D
15. P
16. G
17. A
18. T
19. H
20. M
21. CC
22. Z
23. F
24. Y
25. C
26. K
27. J
28. V
29. AA

## Chapter 13

1. B
2. O
3. A
4. I
5. L
6. H
7. C
8. J
9. Q
10. E
11. D
12. R
13. F
14. S
15. G
16. M
17. P
18. K
19. N
20. T
21. U

## Chapter 14

1. L
2. C
3. M
4. B
5. H
6. N
7. S
8. A
9. R
10. F
11. O
12. I
13. D
14. G
15. K
16. E
17. Q
18. P
19. J

## Chapter 15

1. K
2. E
3. G
4. B
5. L

6. F
7. H
8. A
9. P
10. C
11. N
12. I
13. O
14. J
15. D
16. M

# Textbooks From Educational Textbook Company

www.etctextbooks.com

## Sometimes our textbooks are hard to find!

If your bookstore does not carry our textbooks, please send us a check or money order and we'll mail them to you with our 30-day money back guarantee.

---

### Other Great Books from Educational Textbook Company:*

| | |
|---|---|
| California Real Estate Principles, 13th ed., 2nd Printing, by Huber. | $100.00 ____ |
| California Real Estate Practice, 6th ed., by Huber & Lyons. | $100.00 ____ |
| How To Pass The Real Estate Exam, 7th ed. - e-book (850 Exam Questions), by Huber. | $99.00 ____ |
| California Real Estate Law, 7th ed., by Huber & Tyler. | $100.00 ____ |
| Real Estate Finance, 7th ed., second printing, by Huber & Messick. | $100.00 ____ |
| Real Estate Finance: Appraiser's Edition, 6th ed., by Huber & Messick. | $100.00 ____ |
| Real Estate Economics, 5th ed., by Huber, Messick, & Pivar. | $100.00 ____ |
| Real Estate Appraisal – Principles and Procedures, 3rd ed., by Huber, Messick, & Pivar. | $100.00 ____ |
| Residential Real Estate Appraisal, by Huber & Messick. | $100.00 ____ |
| Mortgage Loan Brokering, 4th ed., by Huber, Pivar, Zozula. | $100.00 ____ |
| Property Management, 5th ed., by Huber, Lyons, & Pivar. | $100.00 ____ |
| Escrow I: An Introduction, 3rd ed., by Huber & Newton. | $100.00 ____ |
| Real Estate Computer Applications, by Grogan & Huber. | $100.00 ____ |
| Homeowner's Association Management, by Huber & Tyler. | $100.00 ____ |
| California Business Law, 2nd ed., by Huber, McGrath, & Tyler. | $100.00 ____ |
| Hubie's Power Prep 700 CD – 700 Questions, by Huber. | $100.00 ____ |

* <u>PRICES EXPIRE 1/1/2013</u>

Subtotal _____

Add shipping and handling @ $10.00 per book _____

Add California sales tax @ 9.75% _____

TOTAL _____

Allow 2-3 weeks for delivery

Name: _____

Address: _____

City, State, Zip: _____

Phone: _____

Check or money order: Educational Textbook Company, P.O. Box 3597, Covina, CA 91722